Lecture Notes in Artificial Intelligence   11357

Subseries of Lecture Notes in Computer Science

More information about this series at http://www.springer.com/series/1244

Shuzhi Sam Ge · John-John Cabibihan
Miguel A. Salichs · Elizabeth Broadbent
Hongsheng He · Alan R. Wagner
Álvaro Castro-González (Eds.)

Social Robotics

10th International Conference, ICSR 2018
Qingdao, China, November 28–30, 2018
Proceedings

 Springer

Editors
Shuzhi Sam Ge (iD)
The National University of Singapore
Singapore, Singapore

John-John Cabibihan (iD)
Qatar University
Doha, Qatar

Miguel A. Salichs
University Carlos III de Madrid
Madrid, Spain

Elizabeth Broadbent (iD)
Canterbury University
Auckland, New Zealand

Hongsheng He (iD)
Wichita State University
Wichita, KS, USA

Alan R. Wagner
The Pennsylvania State University
University Park, PA, USA

Álvaro Castro-González (iD)
Universidad Carlos III de Madrid
Madrid, Spain

ISSN 0302-9743   ISSN 1611-3349   (electronic)
Lecture Notes in Artificial Intelligence
ISBN 978-3-030-05203-4   ISBN 978-3-030-05204-1   (eBook)
https://doi.org/10.1007/978-3-030-05204-1

Library of Congress Control Number: 2018962910

LNCS Sublibrary: SL7 – Artificial Intelligence

This Springer imprint is published by the registered company Springer Nature Switzerland AG
The registered company address is: Gewerbestrasse 11, 6330 Cham, Switzerland

Preface

The 10th International Conference on Social Robotics (ICSR 2018) was held in Qingdao, China, during November 28–30, 2018. This book gathers the proceedings of the conference, comprising 60 refereed papers, reviewed by the international Program Committee, and presented during the technical sessions of the conference.

The International Conference on Social Robotics brings together researchers and practitioners working on the interaction between humans and robots and on the integration of robots into our society. Now on its tenth year, the International Conference on Social Robotics is the leading international forum for researchers in social robotics. The conference gives researchers and practitioners the opportunity to present and engage in dialogs on the latest progress in the field of social robotics.

The theme of the 2018 conference was "Social Robotics and AI." Social robotics and artificial intelligence will help drive economic growth and will be the new normal. ICSR 2018 aimed to foster discussions in the development of AI models and frameworks, robotic embodiments, and behaviors that further encourage invention and innovation. ICSR is the premier forum that looks into the potential of these technologies and provides insights to address the challenges and risks.

In addition to the technical sessions, ICSR 2018 included two workshops: Smart Sensing Systems: Towards Safe Navigation and Social Human–Robot Interaction of Service Robots. ICSR 2018 hosted two distinguished researchers in social robotics as keynote speakers: Professor Hong Qiao, Deputy Director of the State Key Laboratory of Management and Control for Complex Systems, Robotic Theory and Application in the Institute of Automation, Chinese Academy of Science; and Dr. Christoph Bartneck, Associate Professor at the HIT Lab, University of Canterbury, New Zealand.

We would like to express our appreciation to the Organizing Committee for putting together an excellent program, to the international Program Committee for their rigorous review of the papers, and most importantly to the authors and participants who enhanced the quality and effectiveness of the conference through their papers, presentations, and conversations.

We are hopeful that this conference will generate many future collaborations and research endeavors, resulting in enhancing human lives through the utilization of social robots and artificial intelligence.

November 2018

Shuzhi Sam Ge
John-John Cabibihan
Miguel A. Salichs
Elizabeth Broadbent
Hongsheng He
Alan R. Wagner
Álvaro Castro González

Organization

Program Chairs

Emilia Barakova	Eindhoven University of Technology, The Netherlands
Alan R. Wagner	Pennsylvania State University, USA
John-John Cabibihan	Qatar University, Qatar
Adriana Tapus	ENSTA ParisTech, France
Yinlong Zhang	Shenyang Institute of Automation, Chinese Academy of Sciences, China
Ho Seok Ahn	University of Auckland, New Zealand
Xiaolong Liu	University of Tennessee Knoxville, USA
Hongsheng He	Wichita State University, USA
Ali Meghdari	Sharif University of Technology, Iran
Jianbo Su	School of Electronic Information and Electrical Engineering, Shanghai Jiao Tong University, China
Gabriele Trovato	Pontificia Universidad Catolica del Peru, Peru
Kenji Suzuki	Illinois Institute of Technology, USA
Paul Robinette	MIT, USA
Ryad Chellali	Nanjing Forestry University, China
Elizabeth Broadbent	University of Auckland, New Zealand
Silvia Rossi	University of Naples Federico II, Italy
Álvaro Castro-González	Universidad Carlos III de Madrid, Spain
Miguel A. Salichs	Universidad Carlos III de Madrid, Spain

Program Committee

Yan Li	University of Tennessee, USA
Hui Liu	University of Tennessee Knoxville, USA
Xiaodong Yang	Vanderbilt University, USA
John-John Cabibihan	Qatar University, Qatar
Reza YazdanpanahAbdolmalaki	University of Tennessee Knoxville, USA
Mariacarla Staffa	University of Naples Federico II, Italy
Ning Li	Mechanical, Aerospace and Biomedical Engineering, The University of Tennessee, Knoxville
Yanan Li	University of Sussex, UK

Contents

Online Learning of Human Navigational Intentions

Mahmoud Hamandi[1] and Pooyan Fazli[2(✉)]

[1] Electrical Engineering and Computer Science Department,
Cleveland State University, Cleveland, OH 44115, USA
m.hamandi@csuohio.edu
[2] Department of Computer Science, San Francisco State University,
San Francisco, CA 94132, USA
pooyan@sfsu.edu

Abstract. We present a novel approach for online learning of human intentions in the context of navigation and show its advantage in human tracking. The proposed approach assumes humans to be motivated to navigate with a set of imaginary social forces and continuously learns the preferences of each human to follow these forces. We conduct experiments both in simulation and real-world environments to demonstrate the feasibility of the approach and the benefit of employing it to track humans. The results show the correlation between the learned intentions and the actions taken by a human subject in controlled environments in the context of human-robot interaction.

Keywords: Navigational intentions · Human tracking
Human-robot interaction

1 Introduction

With recent developments in artificial intelligence and robotics, robots are increasingly being assigned tasks where they have to navigate in crowded areas [1–4]. While humans learn over the years to understand each other's intentions and plan their paths accordingly, robots still have difficulty understanding human intentions, forcing them to navigate in an over conservative way in human-populated environments.

Previous work on robot navigation within crowds mostly rely on the Social Force Model (SFM) [5] to understand humans, where each is assumed to navigate with a set of known imaginary social forces. Luber *et al.* [6] assumed fixed weights for the social forces based on average human weight and dimensions and track humans with the corresponding motion model. This approach might fail in the real world where humans have different characteristics and might change their intentions over time.

Ferrer *et al.* [7] proposed to control a robot with the Social Force Model to navigate similar to humans by learning a fixed weight for each force from a

© Springer Nature Switzerland AG 2018
S. S. Ge et al. (Eds.): ICSR 2018, LNAI 11357, pp. 1–10, 2018.
https://doi.org/10.1007/978-3-030-05204-1_1

dataset on human navigation. Although learning a fixed weight for each force works for controlling a robot to navigate similar to humans, it might fail to track multiple humans in the real world where each has different preferences for these forces.

On the other hand, Vasquez *et al.* [8] used the social forces and other human features to learn to navigate around humans using an Inverse Reinforcement Learning framework [9] without the need to track humans.

Recently, Alahi *et al.* [10] suggested to use an LSTM-based neural network to track humans with the network learning the connection between one human's position and another. While this approach is very promising, it is not obvious how to extract human intentions from the end-to-end neural network.

In this work, we present Human Intention Tracking (HIT). HIT learns the intentions of each human in the scene to reach a fixed target point or to interact with a robot directly from the Social Force Model. The assumption made here is that intentions are valid for the current time span and change over time. In addition, we assume that instantaneous navigational intentions can be fully understood from observing the human navigation. We do acknowledge that the incorporation of other cues such as gaze or incorporating more information about the environment, such as a semantic map, can allow a better understanding of human intentions. However, we assume this information is not available for the robot, which relies solemnly on the humans' positions in an occupancy grid map to learn their intentions. The proposed approach integrates a Kalman Filter with a motion model based on SFM to track humans and learns their intentions in the environment. While reducing the difference between the predicted and observed human positions, we learn SFM weights specific to each human. Our experiments show the advantage of this method in tracking humans as well as the direct connection between the learned intentions and the actual human motions in the environment.

2   Human Tracking and Intention Learning

We rely on the Social Force Model [5] to track humans and learn their intentions. For a human moving to a fixed target with robots and other humans in the environment as shown in Fig. 1, the resultant social force can be expressed as:

$$\mathbf{F} = \alpha_3 F_{robot} + \alpha_2 F_{human} + \alpha_1 F_{obstacle} + \alpha_0 F_{target}, \tag{1}$$

where $\mathbf{F}$ is the resulting force driving the human, F_{robot} is the force pushing the human toward or away from the robot, F_{human} is the force pushing the human toward or away from other humans, $F_{obstacle}$ is the force driving the human away from obstacles, and F_{target} is the force pushing the human to the target.

Each of the forces is exponentially related to the distance between the two objects enforcing it, with the exception of the last force which is linearly related to the human speed. α_0, α_1, α_2, and α_3 represent the weight of each force, and it can be considered as the intention of the human to consider the corresponding force while navigating. For example, if the human ignores the robot's existence

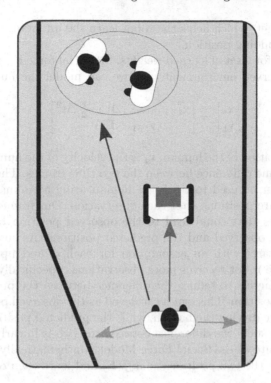

Fig. 1. Example social forces in the environment, showing interaction force to a robot, interaction force to other humans, and interaction force to obstacles. (Color figure online)

completely, the corresponding α should be zero. If the human interacts with the robot, the corresponding α should be positive, while if he runs away from the robot, the corresponding α should be negative. Mathematically, the forces are represented as follows:

$$F_o = A_o \times e^{(\delta_o - \|\mathbf{d_o}\|)/B_o} \times \frac{\mathbf{d_o}}{\|\mathbf{d_o}\|}, \tag{2}$$

where o is a member of the set $O = \{robot, human, obstacle\}$, A_o, δ_o, and B_o are fixed parameters specific to each member of the set, $\mathbf{d_o}$ is the distance vector between the human and the corresponding object in O, and $\|\mathbf{d_o}\|$ is its norm. Ferrer *et al.* [7] show how to learn A_o, δ_o, and B_o from a human dataset and provide typical values for each. On the other hand, we model the force to a fixed target as:

$$F_{target} = \kappa \frac{\mathbf{v}}{\|\mathbf{v}\|}(1 - cos\theta), \tag{3}$$

where κ is a fixed parameter, θ is the angle between the human trajectory and the target direction, and $\|\mathbf{v}\|$ is the norm of the human velocity $\mathbf{v}$. This equation emphasizes the difference in direction between the actual trajectory and the one leading to the target, which helps the robot learn the intention of the human to reach the corresponding position.

Consequently, for a set of learned weights, the social force $\mathbf{F}$ can be calculated based on the observed environment, and we can model the human motion as presented in [6]:

$$\begin{bmatrix} \mathbf{x_t} \\ \mathbf{v_t} \end{bmatrix} = \begin{bmatrix} \mathbf{x}_{t-1} + \mathbf{v}_{t-1}\Delta t + \frac{\mathbf{F}}{2}\Delta t^2 \\ \mathbf{v}_{t-1} + \mathbf{F}\Delta t \end{bmatrix}, \tag{4}$$

where $\mathbf{x_t}$ is the position of the human, $\mathbf{v_t}$ is the velocity of the human at time step t, and Δt is the time difference between the two time frames. The motion model of each human can be used to track the human using a Kalman Filter, which predicts their future positions after each observation. Our framework learns the underlying weights that could lead to the observed position by reducing the error between the observed and the predicted positions. As such, the tracking of each human starts with an assumption for each α and updates them for each human as the robot receives more observations. Specifically, the algorithm updates the parameters to reduce the difference between the predicted and the observed human position. This can be achieved as the observed position presents the real social force driving the human, while the predicted position presents the estimated one. As such, the difference between the two is linearly related to the error in the estimate of the Social Force Model. Mathematically, we denote the difference between the two positions as $diff(\mathbf{F})$ and learn each α as:

$$\alpha_{i,t} = \alpha_{i,t-1} + diff(\mathbf{F}) \times F_i \times \gamma, \tag{5}$$

where F_i is the interaction force corresponding to α_i as presented in Eq. 1, and γ is the learning rate.

In this work, we are mainly concerned with the two interaction forces that show the intention of the human to interact with the robot and the intention to reach a fixed target point in the environment.

3   Experiments and Results

We have proposed a method to learn human intentions while observing their navigation paths. Due to the complexity of human intentions, it is difficult to define a single test that can prove the viability of the proposed algorithm. Instead, we split our experiments into three parts:

1. First, we investigate the tracking ability of our algorithm on the ETH walking pedestrians dataset [11]. The dataset provides annotated trajectories of 650 humans recorded over 25 min of time on two different maps referred to as *ETH-Univ* and *ETH-Hotel*.
2. Second, we choose scenes from the dataset with an obvious change in the human direction and study the change in the weight of reaching the human's final goal. This test shows the ability of the algorithm to learn the intention of the human to reach a fixed target.

3. Finally, we test the system on a real robot with humans in the scene. As the humans navigate around the robot, we study their intentions to interact with it.

Table 1. Comparison of average displacement error (m)

	ETH-Univ	ETH-Hotel
HIT	0.11	0.036
Target [6]	0.16	0.085
Social-LSTM [10]	0.008	0.15

3.1 Human Tracking

To assess the tracking ability, we compare the average displacement error between the predicted and the observed human position of our algorithm against the one achieved by the methods in [6,10] based on a one-step look-ahead analysis.

Luber et al. [6] presented *Target*, a tracking algorithm that combines the Social Force Model with a Kalman filter to predict humans' future positions. Their approach assumes fixed intentions for each human and learns their targets online. While this method allows the tracker to adapt to the target location, it does not adapt to the changes or preferences in intentions toward other humans and obstacles.

On the other hand, Alahi et al. [10] presented *Social-LSTM*, a deep learning algorithm for human tracking. Their approach employs an LSTM based network to predict future positions based on previous ones. In addition, they introduce the social pooling layer where the network predicting a human's position shares a hidden layer with other humans' networks. This approach allows the network to learn the interaction among humans in a scene and predict the future positions accordingly.

Our results presented in Table 1 show that our algorithm outperforms *Target* in both datasets and outperforms *Social-LSTM* on the *ETH-Hotel* dataset. While *Social-LSTM* outperforms our algorithm on the *ETH-Univ* dataset, its performance drops drastically on the *ETH-Hotel* dataset, where obstacles are closer than the former and human crowds are denser. This can be related to the network not being able to generalize to a dataset with settings different than the social aspects it was trained on. However, the increased human proximity improved the performance of our algorithm and *Target*'s due to the importance of social forces in such scenes.

3.2 Intention Learning

We mapped the ETH dataset into a 2-dimensional simulator as explained in our previous work [12]. In this simulator, we searched manually for scenarios where the human intends to reach a final goal that is changing over time, represented by a sudden or gradual change of motion direction and plotted the learned intention to reach that goal.

We show two samples of these scenarios in Fig. 2. In Fig. 2(a), we can see the human is traversing in a direction that might not lead to the target for the first few frames and then changing his direction toward the target. It can be observed in Fig. 2(b) that the change in direction is directly related to the stabilization of α_0, namely the intention weight for reaching the target, after decreasing for the first few frames. Figure 2(c) shows an opposite scenario where the human moves toward a target in the first few frames, after which he changes his direction away from the target. Consequently, it can be observed in Fig. 2(d) that the intention weight decreases substantially after the change in the direction.

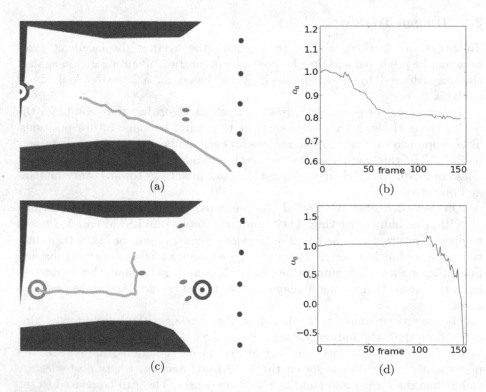

Fig. 2. Two sample trajectories from the dataset mapped into the simulator. The environments in (a) and (c) show static obstacles in dark gray and humans as blue ellipses. The start point is shown in green and the target region is shown in red. The start point in (a) is in the lower-right corner outside the view frame. The orange line depicts the human's trajectory. (b) shows the intention to reach the target for the trajectory in (a), and (d) shows the intention to reach the target for the trajectory in (c). (Color figure online)

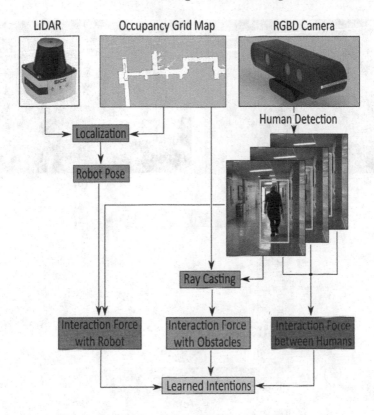

Fig. 3. System implementation on the real robot.

These two scenarios show that our algorithm is able to learn the intention of the human to reach the target and update its belief about the intentions as they change.

3.3 Robot Experiments

Our system implementation on the robot is outlined in Fig. 3. The experiments were conducted on a Segway RMP110 based robot [13] equipped with a SICK TiM LiDAR scanner for localization and an Orbbec Astra Pro RGBD camera for human detection and tracking. To detect humans, we rely on the human detection open-source code presented by the Spencer project [14], which provides a variety of algorithms to detect humans using an RGBD camera.

The robot continuously localizes itself in an occupancy grid map with the aid of the LiDAR. At the same time, its position and velocity as well as the human's are employed to calculate the interaction force between the two entities. To calculate the interaction forces between the human and nearby obstacles, we apply Eq. 2 between his location and the closest obstacle to that location in the occupancy grid map. Finally, the relative positions of the detected humans allow the calculation of the interaction forces between them.

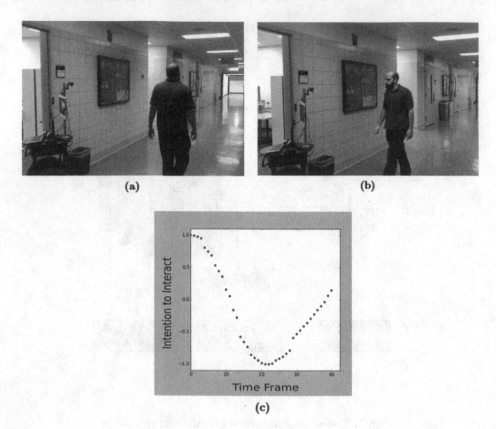

Fig. 4. (a) Human walking away from the robot. (b) Human approaching the robot to interact with it after he was walking away from it in the previous frame. (c) Plot of the learned intention to interact decreasing when the human was not reaching for the robot and then increasing gradually to the value corresponding to the scene in (b).

During the experiments, the robot was either static or navigating in the environment. In both cases, the robot continuously detected humans around it and learned their intentions. When the robot is navigating, it stops just before the human when it detects an intention to interact. For the sake of clarity and brevity, we only show the intention analysis of the human when the robot is static in the environment, as this analysis is not affected by the robot's movement.

Figure 4 shows an example scenario where the human started its path by moving away from the static robot to come back later and interact with it. The learned intention to interact shows a decrease while the human was moving away from the robot and then increases while the human moves toward the robot. This shows the algorithm was able to adapt to the change in intentions and correct its parameters as soon as the human changed their intentions.

These experiments show the viability of the algorithm when applied on a real robot, where the robot was able to learn the human intentions to interact despite the short range of the camera.

4 Conclusion and Future Work

We presented HIT, a novel approach to track humans while learning their navigational intentions. The proposed method was tested in simulation and real-world scenarios, where in the former we observed the change in the learned intentions as the human changed their direction of motion, and in the latter, we observed the learned intentions of a human to interact with the robot in controlled test scenarios. These experiments proved the ability of the algorithm to learn human navigational intentions and adapt to changes quickly. In addition, we tested the effect of the learned intentions on human tracking and showed its advantage over other tracking algorithms from the literature.

In the future, our approach can be implemented into a hierarchical system where the locally learned intentions can be modeled to infer global human intentions. In such a system, the local intentions can be treated as the observations of a Hidden Markov Model used to learn the latent global intentions similar to [15]. We would expect the implementation of such a system to be around a semantic map representing the function of each object and location in the environment and the connections among them. We also intend to use the proposed approach to improve the legibility and social navigation of service robots in human-populated environments.

References

1. Veloso, M., et al.: CoBots: collaborative robots servicing multi-floor buildings. In: Proceedings of the IEEE/RSJ International Conference on Intelligent Robots and Systems, IROS, pp. 5446–5447 (2012)
2. Hawes, N., et al.: The STRANDS project: long-term autonomy in everyday environments. IEEE Robot. Autom. Mag. 24(3), 146–156 (2017)
3. Chen, X., Ji, J., Jiang, J., Jin, G., Wang, F., Xie, J.: Developing high-level cognitive functions for service robots. In: Proceedings of the 9th International Conference on Autonomous Agents and Multiagent Systems, AAMAS, pp. 989–996 (2010)
4. Patel, U., Hatay, E., D'Arcy, M., Zand, G., Fazli, P.: Beam: a collaborative autonomous mobile service robot. In: Proceedings of the AAAI Fall Symposium Series, pp. 126–128 (2017)
5. Helbing, D., Molnar, P.: Social force model for pedestrian dynamics. Phys. Rev. E 51(5), 4282–4286 (1995)
6. Luber, M., Stork, J.A., Tipaldi, G.D., Arras, K.O.: People tracking with human motion predictions from social forces. In: Proceedings of the IEEE International Conference on Robotics and Automation, ICRA, pp. 464–469 (2010)
7. Ferrer, G., Zulueta, A.G., Cotarelo, F.H., Sanfeliu, A.: Robot social-aware navigation framework to accompany people walking side-by-side. Auton. Robot. 41(4), 775–793 (2017)

8. Vasquez, D., Okal, B., Arras, K.O.: Inverse reinforcement learning algorithms and features for robot navigation in crowds: an experimental comparison. In: Proceedings of the IEEE/RSJ International Conference on Intelligent Robots and Systems, IROS, pp. 1341–1346 (2014)

9. Ziebart, B.D., Maas, A.L., Bagnell, J.A., Dey, A.K.: Maximum entropy inverse reinforcement learning. In: Proceedings of the AAAI Conference on Artificial Intelligence, AAAI, pp. 1433–1438 (2008)

10. Alahi, A., Goel, K., Ramanathan, V., Robicquet, A., Fei-Fei, L., Savarese, S.: Social LSTM: human trajectory prediction in crowded spaces. In: Proceedings of the IEEE Conference on Computer Vision and Pattern Recognition, CVPR, pp. 961–971 (2016)

11. Pellegrini, S., Ess, A., Schindler, K., Van Gool, L.: You'll never walk alone: Modeling social behavior for multi-target tracking. In: Proceedings of the 12th IEEE International Conference on Computer Vision, ICCV, pp. 261–268 (2009)

12. Hamandi, M., D'Arcy, M., Fazli, P.: DeepMoTIon: learning to navigate like humans. arXiv preprint arXiv:1803.03719 (2018)

13. Khandelwal, P., et al.: BWIBots: a platform for bridging the gap between AI and human-robot interaction research. Int. J. Robot. Res. **36**(5–7), 635–659 (2017)

14. Linder, T., Arras, K.O.: Multi-model hypothesis tracking of groups of people in RGB-D data. In: Proceedings of the International Conference on Information Fusion, FUSION, pp. 1–7 (2014)

15. Kelley, R., Tavakkoli, A., King, C., Nicolescu, M., Nicolescu, M., Bebis, G.: Understanding human intentions via hidden markov models in autonomous mobile robots. In: Proceedings of the ACM/IEEE International Conference on Human Robot Interaction, HRI, pp. 367–374 (2008)

Autonomous Assistance Control Based on Inattention of the Driver When Driving a Truck Tract

Elvis Bunces$^{(\boxtimes)}$ and Danilo Zambrano$^{(\boxtimes)}$

Universidad de las Fuerzas Armadas ESPE, Sangolquí, Ecuador
{eabunces, vdzambrano}@espe.edu.ec

Abstract. This article proposes the autonomous assistance of a Truck based on a user's inattention analysis. The level of user inattention is associated with a standalone controller of driving of assistance and path correction. The assistance algorithm is based on the kinematic model of the Truck and the level of user inattention In addition, a 3D simulator is developed in a virtual environment that allows to emulate the behavior of the vehicle and user in different weather conditions and paths. The experimental results using the virtual simulator, show the correct performance of the algorithm of assistance proposed.

Keywords: Driver's inattention · Truck · Drivers of assistance Car-like

1 Introduction

The transit accidents attribute grave problems in today's society interfering directly with the global economy. This particularly affects countries low economic income, where 65% of injuries in the population are attributed to these accidents [1, 2], registering that the last two decades the current social transformation, migration and industrialization, they locate the developing countries as the most in having high rates of car accident and it is estimated that each year die 1.25 million people around world [3]. However, the mortality rate among users of rural roads highly developed countries is lower in comparison to the countries en paths developing [4] this is how transit accidents are a priority problem in public health for the World Health Organization (WHO) in terms of high mortality rates and economic costs that have been generated in recent years [5]. Previous studies have identified some main factors that are directly related to this phenomenon, as are: negligence, noncompliance with traffic laws and lack of attention when driving, showing that the latter is the leading cause of accidents of transit on road [6, 7].

The driving of vehicles entails to perform specific tasks and in some cases with a degree of complexity at different levels and unlimited time scales the attention, coordination and concentration play an important role in skills of driving to prevent road accidents. However, the driver must not only do this work but also carry out secondary tasks how to observe the GPS, talk on a cell phone, etc. Regardless of any activity that might attract your attention, this causes stress in the driver, that can disturb your

© Springer Nature Switzerland AG 2018
S. S. Ge et al. (Eds.): ICSR 2018, LNAI 11357, pp. 11–24, 2018.
https://doi.org/10.1007/978-3-030-05204-1_2

attention, and generate affectations not only personal but in other cases to third persons [8]. For this reason, different accident prevention techniques have been put into practice with the aim of tackling the problematic presented, among them are have artificial or intelligent vision systems, these techniques are denominates ITS (Intelligent Transportation Systems), the new generation of safety systems is made up mainly of innovative technologies commensurate to the performance of the vehicles of in the actuality [9]. These systems detect driver fatigue and can easily react in real time with an audible signal. [10], which not only fit into two seater or family vehicles but are also implemented in public transport vehicles, mining and heavy transport, obtaining from the latter the longest time a driver is behind the wheel at extended times with an estimated up to 15 h of continuous driving according to the NHTSA (National Highway Traffic Safety Administration) resulting in a high level of fatigue and drowsiness, [11, 12].

The ITS systems and auditory alerts, if well propose a preventive in car accidents, they have been generated drawbacks with the type of alert they issue, the loud noise and location of the emitter, are some causes that have caused an instinctive reaction of the motor reflex at the moment of driving that are reflected in potential accidents [13, 14]. One of the tools currently available to deal with these problems is the use of driving simulators, which are indistinctly designed with scenarios to evaluate a driver's characteristics in the face of unexpected events that also occur in real driving. On the other hand, researchers have shown that drivers modify their behavior according to the risk they perceive, thus defining an analysis of a driver's inattention and reaction to a visual alert [15].

Taking into account the analysis and problems presented above, this document is defined with the purpose of analyzing the inattention of a user by means of the realization of a driving simulator of a vehicle type Truck in virtual reality. Coupling to this an autonomous path correction control; the simulator is designed in such a way that it generates an immersion to the user identical to the driving on the road and feedback of vibratory and axial forces emitted by the haptic device. In addition, the haptic control devices of the vehicle, they fulfill the same function as the devices controls of a real vehicle, and allows an evaluation of the user's performance when performing driving maneuvers.

2   Virtual Environment with Driving Simulator

Figure 1 shows how the software and hardware components are linked. The inattention control program, uses information about the movement of the user's head, provided by the virtual device Óculus Rift.

The stage of simulation of the scene in Unity 3D contains all the programming of virtual reality, where the 3D model of the Truck and the haptic input devices are linked with the physical and kinematic properties of vehicle movement; The stage of SCRIPTS, manages communication with haptic devices and 3D Model of the vehicle, providing the virtual environment with the required functionality.

In addition, position, velocity and orientation variables are shared bidirectional with Matlab through a shared memory. The output phase provides the user surround audio, a virtual environment sensitive to the movement of scenes, haptic response with feedback

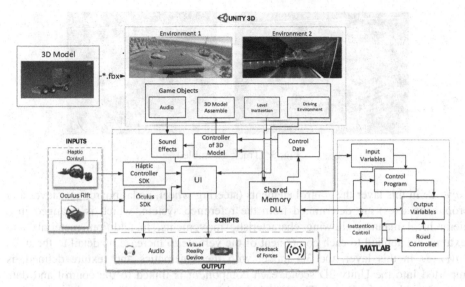

Fig. 1. Operative scheme

of vibratory forces and axial forces generated by the path control. The design of the 3D model of the Truck starts in a CAD software, which is a tool that generates on detail solids 3D. In Fig. 2, the multilayer scheme for the development of applications in virtual environments is shown with the aim of providing greater immersion to users in driving tasks (Fig. 3).

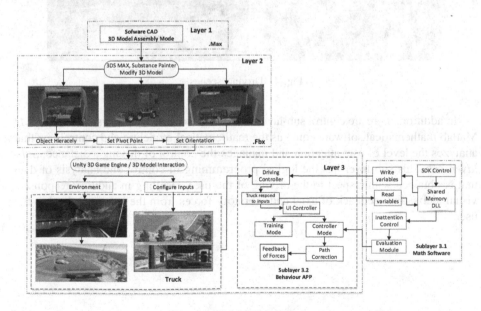

Fig. 2. Multi-layer diagram

Fig. 3. Truck assembled

Layer 2: in this layer the control elements (steering wheel, pedal board, gear lever and propulsion axes) are determined from the reference system, which is arranged in a hierarchical manner, allowing characteristic movements. In addition, materials and textures are applied to each component of the vehicle to increase its detail to the user; *Layer 3:* In this layer, the 3D model with the kinematics and texture defined, is imported into the Unity 3D scene, each component is linked to the control and data entry algorithms. In Fig. 4. The vehicle is shown in two virtual scenarios created to perform driving maneuvers.

Fig. 4. Driving scenes

In addition, there are control sub-layers that are described as follows; *Sub-layer 3.1:* Matlab mathematical software contains the mathematical modeling and control law that analyzes the level of user attention and manages the control of driving assistance; *Sub-layer 3.2*: This sub-layer has the logical programming of control and analysis of data that is obtained with respect to the driving of the user, resulting in auditory responses, visual alerts, and feedback of axial and vibratory forces from the steering wheel to the user.

3 Controller Design

The control of paths tracking, although it is a subject very used in the case of the robots type car-like, in this section, an autonomous assistance algorithm is proposed based on: visual inattention of the user; mathematical model of the Truck; and in the paths tracking problem.

(a) Kinematic Modeling

The kinematic model of the Truck, consider the point of interest $h_T = (x_T, y_T)$ at a distance a of the rear axle wheels propulsion, to the center of the vehicle, as shown in Fig. 5.

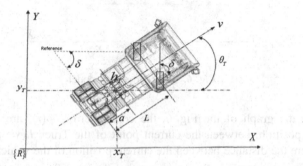

Fig. 5. Kinematic model of the car-like truck

From Fig. 5 the kinematic model of the Truck is defined

$$\begin{cases} \dot{x}_T = \mu \cos(\theta_T) - a\omega \sin(\theta_T) \\ \dot{y}_T = \mu \sin(\theta_T) + a\omega \cos(\theta_T) \\ \dot{\theta}_T = \omega = \frac{v}{L}\tan(\delta) \end{cases} \tag{1}$$

The cinematic model (1), It can be expressed in a compact form as:

$$\begin{aligned} \dot{\mathbf{h}}_T(t) &= \mathbf{J}(\theta_T)\mathbf{v}(t) \\ \dot{\theta}_T(t) &= \tfrac{\mu}{L}(\theta_T)\mathbf{v}(t) \end{aligned} \tag{2}$$

where $\mathbf{J}(\theta_T)$, is the Jacobiana matrix, that defines a rectilinear mapping between the velocity vector $\mathbf{v}(t)$ of the Truck, and $\dot{\mathbf{h}}_T(t)$ it is the final vector of the control speeds, with respect to the reference system $\{R\}$.

(b) Path Specification

In Fig. 6, the path correction problem is shown, represented by $P(s)$ where, $P(s) = \big(x_p(s), y_p(s)\big)$; $h_d(s) = \big(x_p(s_d), y_p(s_d)\big)$ is the current desired point of the Truck, which is considered as the closest distance to $P(s)$; the profile of errors, in the orientation X, is given by $\tilde{x} = x_p(s_d) - x$; and in the orientation Y is given by $\tilde{y} = y_p(s_d) - y$.

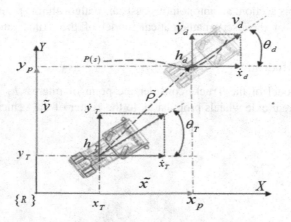

Fig. 6. Path correction model

Based on the graph of the Fig. 6, the control errors $\rho(t)$, are deducted by the difference in position, between the current point of the Truck $h(x, y)$ and the desired point h_d, where the distance between the current position of the vehicle $h(x, y)$ and the reference point, it's zero $\tilde{\rho} = 0 - \rho = -\rho$; $\tilde{\theta} = \theta_p(s_d) - \theta_T$, where $\theta_p(s_d)$ is the orientation of the unitary vector that is tangent to the path h_d in relation to the reference system $\{R\}$.

(c) **Definition of the Desired Velocity**

For consideration of Truck velocity, the manipulation of the desired speed is proposed, depending on different quantifications, *i.e.*, driving errors; curvature of the path; inattention index.

$$v_d(t) = \frac{v_{\max}}{1 + k_1\|\tilde{\rho}\| + k_2\|\Upsilon\|} \tag{3}$$

where, $v_{\max}$ is the maximum speed desired on the chosen path; k_1; k_2 represent constants that ponder the error and the radius of curvature Υ of the desired path. When considering a path P as an aggregate of points, the curvature value is defined as:

$$\Upsilon(k) = \frac{\left|\dot{\mathbf{P}}(k) \times \ddot{\mathbf{P}}(k)\right|}{\left|\dot{\mathbf{P}}(k)\right|^3} \tag{4}$$

The values of the radius curvature in each time interval of (4), can only be found if you have the analytical expression of the path. This limits to a large extent the use of this type of considerations, since for real applications the route to follow is not always available in the form of derivable mathematical equations. To solve the limitation of not having the analytical expression, it is proposed to use the following point $\mathbf{P}(k+1)$ and the previous point $\mathbf{P}(k-1)$ of the sampling cycle, in this way, $\dot{\mathbf{P}}(k)$ is determined in this case as: $\dot{\mathbf{P}}(k) = \frac{\mathbf{P}(k-1)-\mathbf{P}(k+1)}{2T_s}$ and the $\ddot{\mathbf{P}}(k)$ value is calculated by: $\ddot{\mathbf{P}}(k) = \frac{\mathbf{P}(k+1)-2\mathbf{P}(k)+\mathbf{P}(k-1)}{T_s^2}$.

(d) Definition of the Inattention Index

The inattention index is based on the driver's vision area, with respect to the visible area of the path and the angle of movement of the head inside the cabin of the Truck.

$$i_p(t) = 1 - \frac{A_{path_i}(t)}{A_{path_{max}}(t)} \tag{5}$$

where: $A_{path_i}(t)$; is the user's vision intersection area, within the visible section of the path in the direction of vehicle movement and it depends on the driver's angle of vision, shown in Fig. 7; $A_{path_{max}}(t)$; is the maximum area of intersection that exists between the visible area of the driver and the path in real time *i.e.*

$$A_{path_{max}}(t) = \max\left(A_{path_i}\right); ang_i \in \left[-\frac{\pi}{2}, \frac{\pi}{2}\right]$$

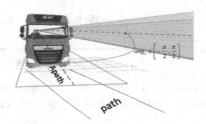

Fig. 7. Area of vision

(e) Assistance Control Design

The proposed kinematic controller design, they are based on numerical methods tools. Particularly for the solution of systems of equations, these systems can be constituted in matrix form, for which theorems and axioms of linear algebra are applied.

Considering the first order differential equation

$$\dot{\mathbf{h}}(t) = f(\mathbf{h}, \mathbf{v}, \Gamma) \text{ with } \mathbf{h}(0) = \mathbf{h}_0 \tag{6}$$

where, $\mathbf{h}$ represents the output of the controller system; $\dot{\mathbf{h}}$ it is the first derivative with respect to time; $\mathbf{v}$ is the control action; and Γ represents different driving criteria. The values of $h(t)$ in time discrete $t = kT_0$ they are called $h(k)$, where T_0 represents the sampling time and $k \in \{1, 2, 3, 4, 5...\}$ in addition, the use of numerical methods for calculating system progression, is based on the possibility of bringing the system closer to a state of time k, if the state, and the control action are known at the moment of time $k - 1$, this approach is called Euler's method. Hence, the design of the kinematic controller is based on the kinematic model of vehicle. In order to design the kinematic controller, the model of the Truck (2) can be approximated as:

$$\frac{\mathbf{h}_T(k) - \mathbf{h}_T(k-1)}{T_0} = \mathbf{J}(\theta_T(k))\mathbf{v}(k) \tag{7}$$

Taking into account that the path correction which consists of locating the vehicle within a predefined path without parameterization in time. Therefore the control objective is to position the desired point, at the closest point of the path $P(s)$ at a desired velocity v_d. To have a scope of the exposed objective the following expression is considered:

$$\frac{\mathbf{h}_T(k) - \mathbf{h}_T(k-1)}{T_0} = v_d(k) + \mathbf{W}\left(\frac{\mathbf{h_d}(k-1) - \mathbf{h}_T(k-1)}{T_0}\right) \tag{8}$$

where, $\mathbf{h_d}$ is the desired path, $\mathbf{W}\big(\tilde{\mathbf{h}}_T(k-1)\big)$ is a diagonal matrix that control error weights, defined as: $\mathbf{W}\big(\tilde{h}_{Tm}(k-1)\big) = \frac{w_m}{1+|\tilde{h}_{Tm}(k-1)|}$ where m represents the operational coordinates of the vehicle. Now, to generate the system equations consider (7) and (8), the system can be rewritten as $\mathbf{Au} = \mathbf{b}$

$$\underbrace{\mathbf{J}(\theta_T(k))}_{\mathbf{A}}\underbrace{\mathbf{v}(k)}_{\mathbf{u}} = \underbrace{i_p(k)\mathbf{v_d}(k) + \frac{\mathbf{W}(\mathbf{h_d}(k-1) - \mathbf{h}_T(k-1))}{T_0}}_{\mathbf{b}} \tag{9}$$

Whereas the Jacobiana matrix $\mathbf{J} \in R^{m \times n}$ has the same number of unknowns as equations $(m = n)$ with rank $r = n$ for each $\mathbf{b} \in R^m$, then (9) represents a linear system with general solution.

$$\mathbf{v}_{ref} = \underbrace{\mathbf{J}(\theta_T(k))^{-1}\left(i_p(k)\mathbf{v_d}(k) + \frac{\mathbf{W}(\mathbf{h_d}(k-1) - \mathbf{h}_T(k-1))}{T_0}\right)}_{\mathbf{v_1}} + \underbrace{g_i(k)\mathbf{v_h}(k)}_{\mathbf{v_2}} \tag{10}$$

where, $g_i \in [0, 1]$ is defined as $g_i(k) = 1 - i_p(k)$; and $\mathbf{v_h}(k) = [u_h(k) \ \omega_h(k)]^T$ is the vehicle's maneuverability vector, generated by man. The proposed control law consists of two main terms $\mathbf{v}_{ref} = \mathbf{v_1} + \mathbf{v_2}$, where, $\mathbf{v_2}$ represents the driver's maneuverability to the vehicle in relation to the inattention rate i_p, i.e., The greater the inattention of the driver, the lower the incidence of the maneuverability signals generated by the user through the haptic devices; while $\mathbf{v_1}$ is the term in charge of correcting the control errors produced when the vehicle does not follow the desired path i.e., when there is user inattention the desired velocity of movement of the vehicle is weighted in relation to i_p. In conclusion when the index of inattention i_p increase $\mathbf{v_2}$ decreases and $\mathbf{v_1}$ it increases, which ensures that the vehicle does not get out of the path desired what could cause an accident.

(f) Feedback of Forces

To generate the feedback of forces in the steering wheel the equation is used (11), that describes the relationship between lateral forces $F_{x,y}$, that are generated on the wheels of direction when taking a curve, in relation to the torque applied on the steering wheel to correct the orientation of the Truck.

$$M_v = \frac{M_r}{rd(\eta)} \tag{11}$$

Where M_v is the moment on the steering wheel, M_r defines the torque that exists in the wheels of steering, rd the transmission ratio with regard to the steering angle of the steering wheel $vs.$, the angle of rotation of the wheels and η, is the performance of the direction of the Truck. According to the Eq. (11) it defines: $M_r = F_{x,y}(r_w)$ with $F_{x,y} = \frac{m_T(v_{ref})}{\Upsilon}$ whereby r_w, is the radius of the wheels; m_T It is the mass of the Truck; Υ, represents the radius of curvature of the path and the Eq. (10), v_{ref} you get the current operating velocity of the Truck. $i.e.$, M_v it's the torque that is exercised in the steering wheel, according to each curve that present in the driving.

(g) Stability Analysis

For the stability analysis, the most critical case is considered, $i.e.$, when the user's inattention level is the maximum $i_p = 1$, therefore (10) depends solely on v_1 It is also considered perfect velocity tracking $v_{ref}(t) = v(t)$, (7) so it can be replaced in the kinematic model (7) on (10), obtaining the following closed loop equation:

$$\frac{\mathbf{h}_T(k) - \mathbf{h}_T(k-1)}{T_0} = \underbrace{i_p(k)\mathbf{v_d}(k) + \frac{\mathbf{W}(\mathbf{h_d}(k-1) - \mathbf{h}_T(k-1))}{T_0}}_{b} \tag{12}$$

It is considered that $i_p(k)\mathbf{v_d}(k) = \mathbf{v_d}(k) + \dot{\boldsymbol{\eta}}(k)$, In addition, the signal is defined $\dot{\gamma}$ as the difference between $\mathbf{h_d}$ and $\mathbf{v_d}$, $i.e.$

$$\mathbf{v_d}(k) = \dot{\mathbf{h}}_\mathbf{d}(k) + \dot{\gamma}(k)$$

$$\mathbf{h}_T(k) - \mathbf{h}_T(k-1) = T_0\left(\left(\dot{\mathbf{h}}_\mathbf{d}(k) - \dot{\gamma}(k) + \dot{\boldsymbol{\eta}}(k)\right) + \frac{\mathbf{W}(\mathbf{h_d}(k-1) - \mathbf{h}_T(k-1))}{T_0}\right)$$

$$\mathbf{h}_T(k) - \mathbf{h}_T(k-1) = T_0\left(\frac{\mathbf{h_d}(k) - \mathbf{h_d}(k-1)}{T_0} + \frac{\Delta\boldsymbol{\eta}}{T_0} + \frac{\Delta\gamma}{T_0} + \frac{\mathbf{W}(\mathbf{h_d}(k-1) - \mathbf{h}_T(k-1))}{T_0}\right)$$

The control error is defined as: $e(k-1) = \mathbf{h_d}(k-1) - \mathbf{h}(k-1)$, thus

$$e(k-1) = e(k) + \mathbf{W}(e(k-1)) - \Delta\gamma - \Delta\boldsymbol{\eta}$$

if $\Delta\xi = \Delta\gamma + \Delta\boldsymbol{\eta}$, so:

$$\Delta\xi = e(k) - e(k-1) + \mathbf{W}(e(k-1))$$
$$\Delta\xi = e(k) + e(k-1)(\mathbf{W} - 1)$$

For this case, the transformed of z applies:

$$(1 - z^{-1})\xi(z) = e(z) + e(z)z^{-1}(\mathbf{W} - 1)$$
$$(1 - z^{-1})\xi(z) = e(z)(1 + z^{-1}(\mathbf{W} - 1))$$

$$e(z) = \frac{1 - z^{-1}}{1 + z^{-1}(\mathbf{W} - 1)}\xi(z) \tag{13}$$

the poles of the system (13) are;

$$1 + z^{-1}(\mathbf{W} - 1) = 0$$

So that the poles of the system (12) are within the unit radius then, it is necessary that the profit matrix $0 < \mathbf{W}(\tilde{h}_T(k-1)) < 1$ Thus, in this way it is concluded that control errors $\tilde{\mathbf{h}}(k) = 0$ when $k \to \infty$, has asymptotic stability, that is to say, the vehicle follows the desired path when there is a level of inattention of the user when driving.

4 Experimental Results

In this stage, conduction tests for the purpose of evaluate the performance of the control of assistance based on the user's inattention while driving Truck in virtual reality. In Fig. 8 the experiments performed are shown, for this, an HP laptop is used (AMD Dual-Core, 3 GB RAM, 500 GB HDD), Óculus Rift, Headphones, Logitech steering wheel (G920 Force Feedback Racing), pedals and gear lever.

Fig. 8. Driving test

In Fig. 9, a menu is displayed in which the user can select two types of driving stage, the first stage is generated with a night driving environment, vs., to the second scenario that has a driving in the day.

Fig. 9. Select scene

Figure 10 shows the relationship between the desired path *vs.*, the path executed by the user, where (a) shows the path executed with the autonomous driving assistant deactivated and in (b) the driving assistant is activated and permanently monitors every action of the driver for correction the orientation and velocity of the Truck.

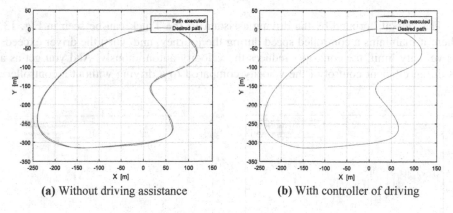

(a) Without driving assistance   (b) With controller of driving

Fig. 10. Path executed

The inattention index presented by the driver during the driving test phases is measured permanently in a continuous numerical range: $(0, 0.1, 0.2, 0.3 \ldots \ldots 1)$, where, 0, represents an efficient level of care, until 1, which represents a higher level of inattention. As shown in Fig. 11.

To perform the ideal path correction, from the driver's steering wheel, by feedback of axial forces, a ratio adjustment is used, between the steering angle of the steering wheel and the angle of rotation of the wheels, *i.e.,* for a Truck the total turn angle of the direction γ_w, is 900°, and the blocking angle λ_b, of the wheels is 30°, where the following formula is applied $\lambda_b \frac{\gamma_w}{2}$ obtaining as a result a ratio of $rd = 15 : 1$, that for every 15° of turn of steering wheel, the wheels will turn 1°. The trajectory control results are shown in Fig. 12, in which a conduction is carried out with absence of the driving controller and another with the driving assistant activated, and it is observed that the axial force feedback, controls the rotation of the steering wheel continuously along the desired trajectory.

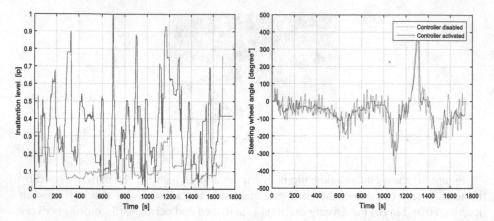

Fig. 11. Inattention level   **Fig. 12.** Steering wheel angle

The velocity printed by the driving assistant to the Truck can be seen in Fig. 13, where it maintains a controlled speed during the journey, and when the driver exceeds the velocity limit, the controller reduces the velocity autonomously. And you get as a result, an efficient control of the velocity compared to a driving without a controller.

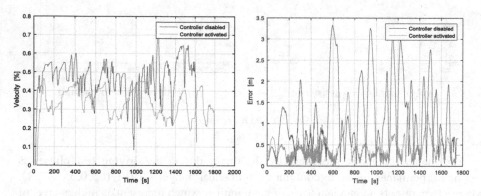

Fig. 13. Controller of velocity   **Fig. 14.** Path error

Figure 14, shows the error that was obtained with the driving assistant activated, during the performance of driving maneuvers with a Truck in virtual reality, *vs.* a driving with the driving assistant turned off, therefore the loss of trajectory was greater.

When the user turns his head out of the area of the visible section of the path, the inattention detection system, sends a visual warning signal to the driver as shown in Fig. 15.

Fig. 15. Inattention warning sign

5 Conclusions

This document presented a design that analyzes the inattention index that a driver has when performing driving maneuvers, and the design of a driving assistant, based on control of tracing of paths car-like, that helps the user to obtain better driving habits. The high degree of detail added in the 3D model, increases driving immersion to the user. The advantage of this, is the ability to perform driving maneuvers similar to driving on the road, with the uniqueness of being a Truck. So, focusing on the application, from the point of view of driver training, in this type of vehicle of heavy transport, it becomes a tool for students who are learning to drive a vehicle following the conventional educational process. The use of virtual reality has benefits from a secure environment, where the driving tests are also monitored by the driving assistant, which records the ability to maneuver this vehicle, even in situations of risk, allowing to know the level of concentration that the driver can have, when facing this type of situations, that are part of a daily driving on the road.

Acknowledgements. The author would like to thanks to the Corporacion Ecuatoriana para el Desarrollo de la Investigación y Academia-CEDIA for the financing given to research, development, and innovation, though the CEPRA projects, especially the project CEPRA-XI-2017-06; Control Coordinado Multi-operador aplicado a un robot Manipulador Aéreo; also to Univeridad de las Fuerzas Armadas ESPE, Universidad Técnica de Ambato, Escuela Superior Politécnica de Chimborazo, Universidad Nacional de Chimborazo, and Grupo de Invesigación en Automatización, Robótica y Sistemas Inteligentes, GI-ARSI, for the support to develop this paper.

References

1. Shruthi, P., Venkatesh, V.T., Viswakanth, B., Ramesh, C., Sujatha, P.L., Domonic, I.R.: Analysis of fatal road traffic accidents in a metropolitan city of South India. J. Indian Acad. Forensic Med. **35**(4), 317–320 (2013)
2. Farooqui, J.M., et al.: Pattern of injury in fatal road traffic accidents in a rural area of western Maharashtra. India. Australas. Med. J. **6**, 476–482 (2013)
3. Davoudi-Kiakalayeh, A., Mohammadi, R., Yousefzade-Chabok, S., Saadat, S.: Road traffic crashes in rural setting: an experience of a middle-income country. Chin. J. Traumatol. **17**, 327–330 (2014)

4. Moafian, G., Aghabeigi, M.R., Hoseinzadeh, A., Lankarani, K.B., Sarikhani, Y.: An epidemiologic survey of road traffic accidents in Iran: analysis of driver-related factors. Chin. J. Traumatol. **16**, 140–144 (2013)
5. Montes, S.A., Introzzi, I.M., Ledesma, R.D., López, S.S.: Selective attention and error proneness while driving: research using a conjunctive visual search task. Av. Psicol. Lat. **34**, 195–203 (2016)
6. Chavez, G.D., Slawinski, E., Mut, V.: Modeling the inattention of a human driving a car. In: 11th IFAC/IFIP/IFORS/IEA Symposium on Analysis, Design, and Evaluation of Human-Machine Systems, vol. 43, pp. 7–12 (2010)
7. Lansdown, T.C., Stephens, A.N., Walker, G.H.: Multiple driver distractions: a systemic transport problem. Accid. Anal. Prev. Mag. **74**, 360–367 (2015)
8. Young, K.L., Salmon, P.M.: Sharing the responsibility for driver distraction across road transport systems: a systems approach to the management of distracted driving. Accid. Anal. Prev. Mag. **74**, 350–359 (2015)
9. Bengler, K., Dietmayer, K., Farber, B., Maurer, M., Stiller, C., Winner, H.: Three decades of driver assistance systems. IEEE Intell. Transp. Syst. Mag. **6**, 6–22 (2014)
10. Casner, S.M., Hutchins, E.L., Norman, D.: The challenges of partially automated driving. Mag. Commun. ACM **59**, 70–77 (2016)
11. Caird, J.K., Johnston, K.A., et al.: The use of meta-analysis or research synthesis to combine driving simulation or naturalistic study results on driver distraction. J. Saf. Res. Mag. **49**, 91–96 (2014)
12. Stavrinos, D., Jones, J.L., et al.: Impact of distracted driving on safety and traffic flow. Accid. Anal. Prev. Mag. **61**, 63–70 (2013)
13. Overton, T.L., Rives, T.E., et al.: Distracted driving: prevalence, problems, and prevention. Int. J. Injury Control Saf. Promot. **22**, 187–192 (2015)
14. Llaneras, R.E., Salinger, J., Green, C.A.: Human factors issues associated with limited ability autonomous driving systems: drivers' allocation of visual attention to the forward roadway. In: Proceedings of the Seventh International Driving Symposium on Human Factors in Driver Assessment, Training and Vehicle Design, pp. 92–98 (2013)
15. Park, M., Lee, S., Han, W.: Development of steering control system for autonomous vehicle using geometry-based path tracking algorithm. ETRI J. **37**(3), 617–625 (2015)

The Robotic Archetype: Character Animation and Social Robotics

Cherie Lacey[1](✉) ⓘ and Catherine Barbara Caudwell[2] ⓘ

[1] School of English, Film, Theatre, and Media Studies,
Victoria University of Wellington, Wellington, New Zealand
cherie.lacey@vuw.ac.nz
[2] School of Design, Victoria University of Wellington, Wellington,
New Zealand

Abstract. This paper delves into the surprisingly under-considered convergence between Hollywood animation and 'Big Tech' in the field of social robotics, exploring the implications of character animation for human-robot interaction, and highlighting the emergence of a robotic character archetype. We explore the significance and possible effects of a Hollywood-based approach to character design for human-robot sociality, and, at a wider level, consider the possible impact of this for human relationality and the concept of 'companionship' itself. We conclude by arguing for greater consideration of the socio-political and ethical consequences of importing and perpetuating relational templates that are drawn from powerful media conglomerates like Disney. In addition to facing a possible degradation of social relations, we may also be facing a possible *delimitation* of social relationality, based on the values, affects, and ideologies circulating in popular Hollywood animation.

Keywords: Social robots · Character animation · Social relations
Interaction templates · Hollywood ideology · Companionship

1 'Artificially Intelligent, Authentically Charming'

Much-anticipated and long-promised social robots are slowly becoming available on the commercial market. The first wave of companion robots such as Jibo, Kuri [1], and Cozmo, are already available to consumers in some countries. Meanwhile, firms like Amazon, Huawei, and Alphabet are reportedly working on "secret robot products", due to be released to the consumer market over the next two years [2]. Intended primarily as companionate "members of the family" [3], home robots are marketed as being capable of fulfilling complex, real-world social roles across a range of social-relational interactions [4], with potentially positive applications in healthcare and elderly care, for example. More than technologically advanced, then, social robots promise to be *socially* significant, fundamentally changing the way we interact with technology [3].

The development of robotic *character*—to be distinguished from robotic *personality*—is increasingly seen as important to the social competency of companion robots. Consumers are enticed to purchase a social robot not purely as an assistive technology, but also as an appealing character. Jibo, for example, whose character was developed

© Springer Nature Switzerland AG 2018
S. S. Ge et al. (Eds.): ICSR 2018, LNAI 11357, pp. 25–34, 2018.
https://doi.org/10.1007/978-3-030-05204-1_3

by a team of ex-Disney animators, is marketed as "artificially intelligent, *authentically charming*" [5]. "Jibo is a character", the website insists. "His design team has used tried and true principles of animation to make Jibo believable as a family member and companion" [6]. The blog section of the company's website chronicles the design decisions that went into the robot, and differentiates Jibo from other social technologies. For example, in 'Jibo, The World's First Living Character Property' [7], Jibo is cast as "a someone, not a something". The article comments further that, while digital assistants are referred to as 'tools', Jibo "genuinely wants to and can be a meaningful, helpful member of your family" [8].

Jibo is just one example of an increasing focus on character applied to consumer technology. From his inception, Anki's Cozmo robot has similarly been considered a "living character" [9]. According to Anki's CEO, the company was founded on the belief that the "ultimate expression of robotics would be a physical character coming to life", comparing the experience of interacting with Cozmo to having "a favourite cartoon character in your living room" [10]. Drawing inspiration from Hollywood animation, Cozmo comes with a backstory that is linked to his design iterations, and which goes some way to explain his "inherent instincts" [11], or even what one might call his 'neuroses'—including a pathological fear of heights and desire not to be constrained. In respect of both Jibo and Cozmo, agency and the impression of consciousness are presented as authentic attributes, and contribute to the impression of a "believable" [3] and "credible" [12] character—suggestive of a life beyond the human user's interaction with it [13].

Other commercial social robot companies are likewise turning to animators from Hollywood studios to develop characters for their products. Doug Dooley from Pixar was hired by Mayfield Robotics to create Kuri's character, and Alonso Martinez, also from Pixar, is the animator behind the character of Mira robot. Both Dooley and Alonso argue that character animators from Hollywood studios are ideally placed to bring robots to life using the "tricks" of animation [14]. As Alonso puts it: "animation experts have got emotion down to a 'T'. They are able to draw on a huge toolbox… to appeal to the viewer. These codes can also be applied to robotics" [15]. Despite a significant amount of research in human-robot interaction (HRI) drawing from the field of psychology to design and implement robotic personality, it is, arguably, the field of Hollywood animation that is having just as much impact on the field of social robotics.

If social robots are "inheriting certain traits from the animation industry" [16] for the development of robotic character, then more attention needs to be paid to how this might affect human-robot sociality. This paper delves into the surprisingly under-considered convergence between Hollywood animation and 'Big Tech' in the field of social robotics, exploring the implications of character animation for human-robot interaction, and identifying the emergence of a robotic character archetype. We explore the possible effects of a Hollywood-based approach to character design for human-robot sociality, and, at a wider level, consider the possible impact of this for human relationality and the concept of 'companionship' itself. Ultimately, we argue for a greater need to consider the socio-political and ethical consequences of importing, and perpetuating, relational templates that are fundamentally related to powerful media conglomerates like Disney. In addition to facing a possible degradation of social relations [17], we may also be facing a possible *delimitation* of social relations based on the values, affects, and ideologies circulating in popular Hollywood animation.

2 Designing Robots with Personality

Before examining what popular animation offers social robotics, it is worthwhile briefly outlining current research in robot persona—in part, to provide a more fine-grained understanding of how robotic character might be distinguished from robotic persona. In the field of HRI, persona tends to be understood as "perceived or evident personalities" [18] based on identifiable and expressible traits—for example, habitual patterns of thought, displays of emotion, and behaviour [19]. This research has largely drawn on leading trait theories developed in the study of human personality [20, 21], which identifies five core human traits: openness, conscientiousness, extraversion, agreeableness, and neuroticism [22]. Personality trait theory has often been applied to understand both the user and the robot in order to develop a robot personality that best 'fits' a user [19]. To many HRI researchers, personality in robots can serve to establish and maintain social relationships [23], and provide clear models of behaviour [24] and decision-making processes for the consumer [25, 26]. The design of robot persona is generally considered to advance a user-centric approach to interaction with robots, providing consumers with clear mental models to help make sense of, and anticipate, the robot's behaviour.

For the purposes of this paper, we are interested in drawing out two aspects of persona research in HRI. The first is the emphasis on that which can be measured, modelled and evaluated using scientifically recognised methods—specifically, personality traits, behaviours, and habitual patterns of thought. The second is the tendency of HRI to import interaction templates and relational models based on human-human sociality [27]. What this scientifically informed method does not adequately account for are the intangible aspects of social-relationality that have been perfected by Hollywood modes of storytelling, and which social robot developers are increasingly drawing upon —aspects that are fundamentally tied up with the development and communication of *character* within a story-world context.

Since Aristotle, it has been known that character is a quality that appears to both precede and exceed identifiable and measurable personality traits, giving the impression that, when we are not interacting with them, their lives continue outside us. Character concerns the "enduring traits" [28], or "permanent states" [29], of a social agent, subsuming personality into a greater schema across the (real or projected) course of a lifetime. "Character", argues Sherman, "gives a special sort of accountability and pattern to action" by explaining "not merely why someone acted this way now, but why someone can be counted on to act in certain ways in the future" [30]. Therefore, although personality may be considered the identifiable manifestations of character at particular moments in time, character is the underlying logic that binds these things together over a lifetime.

The enduring quality of character comes largely from its inseparability from its context or story-world. Eagleton argues that character can never be "ripped rudely out of context" [29]. The realism of a character, he argues, is derived almost entirely from her or his ability to be interwoven into a complex story-world, formed by social and historical forces greater than her- or himself [29]. The context-dependent nature of character provides an interesting challenge for the animators hired to 'bring to life' social robots. As the Character Lead at Anki put it, social robots are effectively interacting in a story setting that is, to skewer the common expression in film, "off the rails" [31]. That is to say, social robots are commonly understood to be co-creators in a *spontaneous* and unique household story; this 'personality growth model', as we have argued elsewhere [32], is one of the key selling points for social robots, which are marketed as being able to "grow alongside you and your family" [3]. However, we question whether character-animated robots are truly operating 'off the rails', even when operating in a domestic setting. We propose that the social robots that are inheriting character traits from popular animation remain, to some extent, embedded within the Hollywood-approved story contexts.

3 Fictional Interaction with Robots

The character-driven approach to social robotics could be seen to provide what Seibt calls an "interaction template" for the human-robot relationship [33]. In the examples described above, the user is encouraged to interact with the robot *as if* it were an "adored" [34] or "beloved" [35] character from a popular animation fiction. Although it is tempting to consider comparisons between social robots and cartoon characters merely as useful analogies to make sense of a new category of relata [17], we argue that such comparisons may, in fact, represent a potentially concerning evolution of practices of human sociality and companionship alongside social robots. If, as Turkle argues, we may be entering a techno-social era in which the "performance of connection is connection enough" [36], then it is also pertinent to consider the ways in which that connection is being shaped by the technology itself.

Seibt's work explores simulated models of interaction with social robots [33]. She questions whether interactions with social robots could qualify as 'real' instances of social interaction [37], even with the acknowledgement that the concepts like 'sociality' are not fixed and immutable [38]. Identifying two types of simulated social interaction, (1) make-believe, and (2) fictional interactions, Seibt argues that interactions with social robots fall under the category of 'fictional interaction'. Make-believe scenarios are typified by a one-sided analogical projection, where only the human agent involved executes the action [33]. Fictional interactions, on the other hand, involve both agents interacting in ways that resemble the actions and reactions prescribed by an interaction template [39]. "Importantly", Seibt writes, "a fictional interaction can take place even if one of the agents is not aware of any convention of fictionality being in place, or is not even an agent proper at all" [40].

Certain elements need to be present before a fictional interaction between a social robot and a human can occur, however. The social robot requires the "relevant resemblances" [41], including an approximation of familiar modes of interaction [42]. Importantly, this approximation comes not from the aesthetic qualities of the social robot [43], but from acting in ways that makes sense to the user. Following Seibt's argument, it is possible to see that the character-driven animation of social robotics represents an important shift from the realm of make-believe (i.e. watching a film), to a two-way 'fictional interaction' with the social robot in a domestic setting. Comparisons between social robots and animated cartoon characters (i.e. a robot is *like* a cartoon character in your living room) need to be taken seriously for what this might mean for unfolding practices of human-robot sociality.

An important further step in Seibt's argument is the fine-tuning of the processes at work within the space of fictional interaction itself. Interacting with another social agent 'as if' they were a real social agent, she argues, is effectively the same as interacting with them *as* a social agent. Fictional interaction qualifies as a "real social interaction... It is *factual by its undertaking*" [44]. In fictional interaction, there is a point at which the fictionality of the interaction begins to disappear—at which there ceases to be a "fictionality gap" at all [45]. The dissolution of the fictional quality of human-robot relations finds a point of comparison with theories of popular ideology [46], which caution us to be most conscious at the point at which a process becomes invisible. The staggering success of Disneyland, as well as the entire range of Disney merchandising, reveals the agglutinative force of the Disney culture to "interactive texts" such as these; and if the Disney 'way of life' [47] adheres to objects so firmly, we suggest that robots that are based on the Disney principles might also be doing the ideological work of the Disney conglomerate.

4 Animation and Robotics

Cartoon animation is strongly associated, or even synonymous, with the work of Walt Disney Studios [48], whose style of animation has been defined by the quest for hyperrealism, "a mode of animation which, despite the medium's obvious artifice, strives for 'realism'" [49]. Meaning 'to give life', animation's ultimate goal is to bestow a character with the impression of consciousness, or sense of 'inner life'—even as the character might appear aesthetically unreal [50]. As Jackson (Disney's biographer) said, "Walt wanted his drawings that were animated to seem to be real things that had feelings and emotions and thoughts, and the main thing was that the audience would believe them and that they *would care what happened to them*" [51].

Commonly referred to as the 'animation bible', Thomas and Johnston's *The Illusion of Life: Disney Animation* sets out the 12 principles of animation that define Disney's iconic 'realist' representational style. The 12 principles of squash and stretch, anticipation, staging, straight ahead action and pose to pose, follow through and overlapping action, slow in and slow out, arcs, secondary action, timing, exaggeration, solid drawing, and appeal [52] work together to creating the 'illusion of life'. For animation in the Disney tradition, "it is the change of shape that shows the character is thinking. It is the thinking that gives the illusion of life. It is the life that gives meaning to the expression" [53].

These animation principles have been applied to robots in the pursuit of creating life-like characters by a number of HRI researchers [54–57], for whom the 'illusion of (robotic) life' is thought to manifest primarily through movement and gesture. Bates [58], for example, wrote about the Disney principles of animation as a strategy to create an *emotional believability* in AI and interactive agents. Meanwhile, Van Breeman [59],

Takayama et al. [60], and Saldien et al. [61] have applied the Disney animation principles to robots to make the robot's behaviour legible to the user. Ribeiro and Paiva [54] saw value in using animation techniques to improve the robot's integration in, and reaction to, its surrounding environment.

For those researchers, then, the Disney principles provide a familiar corporeal and affective language for the robot, which in turn enhances human-robot communication. As Takayama et al. put it, "the animation techniques... help create robot behaviours that are human-readable" [62]. Van Breeman articulates this notion even more directly when he writes that the animation principles bestow the robot with a *life*-like, as opposed to *machine*-like quality. The acceptance of social robots as socially significant companions in the domestic space is considered to be extraordinarily reliant on the ability of the user to make sense of the robot's behaviours, including thought patterns, reactions, and future actions, along a familiar, even *comforting*, pattern—precisely that which is 'known and long familiar' [63] through the long history of Disney character animation.

5   The Question of Home

Utilising the 12 Disney principles in robot design intrinsically connects them to the characters, affects, ideologies, and story-worlds that (Disney) animation prescribes. First and foremost, the animated medium deals in emotion. Wells [64] argues that animation "invites a greater degree of *highly charged emotive or abstract interpretation*". Whitely [65] says that Disney films in particular, are associated, above anything else, with the realm of feeling [66]. This technique is something that Whitely refers to as "engagement through sentiment" [67], a process that, arguably, has the effect of stultifying critical thought and long-term decision making processes, allowing for a relatively unobstructed transfer of Disney ideology to occur.

Furthermore, Disney's stock-in-trade is the powerfully affective domain of childhood, involving an admixture of nostalgia, comfort, and familiarity alongside traditional, conservative family values. All Disney stories, Whitely argues, return to the same foundational question: *what makes a home?* [68]. This question is also what is at stake in the introduction of companion robots, whose success fundamentally depends on the consumer's capacity to reshape their concept of 'home'. If the legacy of Hollywood animation is visible in current designs of social robot characters, then the companies behind these robots are already well on the way towards achieving some degree of popular consumer acceptance.

Finally, the convergence of Hollywood animation and 'Big Tech' appears to be leading to the emergence of a particular kind of character archetype for social robots. The first wave of consumer social robots all possess remarkably consistent character traits: they are "naive yet curious" [69], cheeky, inquisitive, and fun-loving. They look at the world with the freshness and excitement of a child, and are what old Hollywood would call 'plucky'. These character traits are familiar to us through a long history of Disney characters whose genealogy we can trace back to Mickey Mouse or, even further, to Charlie Chaplin. Disney's famous mouse has been described as "[a] peppy, cheerful, never-say-die guy" [70] and "a caricature of the optimistic adventurer that mankind has had to be to survive through the centuries" [71]. Wills defines these traits as fundamental to Disney Culture itself: "Early Mickey Mouse cartoons reveal the evolution of a Disney way: a way of tackling the world based around clever animation, prankishness, and naive sentimentality" [72]. The current wave of companion robots like Jibo and Cozmo possess character traits that are remarkably similar to those described above, suggesting they have inherited certain core sensibilities from their animated predecessors. Cozmo is an innocent yet adventurous robot; Jibo is a cheeky, charming and lovable assistant who, upon visiting the Jibo Inc. website, greets the consumer with a knock-knock joke. Indeed Jibo, perhaps more than any other social robot, embodies the character archetype of Charlie Chaplin/Mickey Mouse through his use of humour. Like Mickey Mouse, Jibo deploys to great effect the 'autonomous gag'. "The autonomous gag", as Wells argues, "may be understood as the comic motif of investing objects and materials with an upredictable life of their own" [73]. Jibo's playful and somewhat cheeky gag-based humour communicates an 'illusion of life' and impression of autonomy, suggesting that he, too, has an unpredictable life of his own.

6 Conclusion

The relationship between social robots and Disney character animation create powerful associations. While Disney's representational style may be the "dominant discourse of animation" [74], Wills goes as far as to argue that "Disney Culture intrinsically shapes our world" [75]. To Wills, Disney Culture "includes all Disney products, corporate and work practices, education, slogans, media, and advertising. Disney Culture incorporates such popular terms as the 'Disney way' and the 'Disney smile'... Disney Culture promotes a distinctive way of viewing the world [76]. Following Wills, the 12 principles of animation are elements of Disney Culture, inseparable from ideologies and story-worlds of the Disney worldview [77]. The range of values and narratives possible through this lens has an impact on what interactions can occur with social robots. Crucially, as Wills notes, "Disney asks the audience to leave their real world behind for uniform childlike fantasies and simulations" [78]. If applied to social robots, we might well ask: are we interacting with robot *as if* it were a child, or as though *we* are children?

If companionship with robots is delineated by a fictional interaction based on an imported interaction template, the possibilities for that relationship are distinctly limited. Perhaps at stake is not just the degradation of the social relation (in which the social relation becomes increasingly 'functionalised'), as well as concepts like 'friend' or 'companion', but a *delimitation* of the social relation and notions of companionship prescribed by the Hollywood-Big Tech complex. Further, as 'members of the family', social robots are well-placed to collect a wealth of intimate data, which makes them more powerful than their 'characters' may convey. As argued earlier in this paper, HRI studies of human-robot companionship favour scientific methods of evaluation, often focusing on personality and behavioural traits. Seibt states a need "to conceptually clarify the phenomenon of human-robot interactions in all its diversity in order to make progress in the professional and public ethical debates about social robots" [79]. To do so, we argue for the need to develop a methodological approach that considers the cultural factors that inform not just our relationships with social robots, but how that relationship might be shaped.

References

1. Mayfield Robotics has announced that Kuri Robot will be discontinued
2. Gurman, M.: Big tech is throwing money and talent at home robots. Bloomberg, 24 July 2018. https://www.bloomberg.com/news/articles/2018-07-24/big-tech-is-throwing-money-and-talent-at-home-robots. Accessed 01 Aug 2018
3. Jibo Inc. https://www.jibo.com/. Accessed 01 Aug 2018
4. Ruckert, J.: Unity in multiplicity: searching for complexity of persona in HRI. In: HRI 2011, no. 11, pp. 237–238 (2011)
5. Ibid
6. Ibid
7. Ibid
8. Ibid
9. Jibo Inc., Personal communication
10. Heater, B.: Anki aims to bring a Pixar character to life with its plucky little robot'. Techcrunch, 26 June 2016. https://techcrunch.com/2016/06/27/cozmo/. Accessed 01 Aug 2018
11. Jibo Inc., Personal communication
12. Jibo Inc., Personal communication
13. Eagleton, T.: 'Character' in How to Read Literature. Yale UP, New Haven (2013)
14. Dooley, D.: Robot Appeal. http://www.ezmicro.com/robot/index.html. Accessed 01 Aug 2018
15. Martinez, A.: Disney remains an inspiration for designing robot-assistants. https://atelier.bnpparibas/en/prospective/article/disney-remains-inspiration-designing-robot-assistants. Accessed 01 Aug 2018
16. Dooley and Martinez, Personal communication
17. Turkle, S.: Alone Together. Basic Books, New York (2011)
18. Fong, T., Nourbaksh, I., Dautenhahn, K.: A survey of socially interactive robots. Robot. Auton. Syst. **42**, 143–166 (2003)
19. Ruckert, J. (2011)
20. Fong, T., et al. (2003)
21. Meerbeek, B., Saerbeck, M., Bartneck, C.: Iterative design processes for robots with personality. In: Proceedings of the AISB2009 Symposium on New Frontiers in Human-Robot Interaction, Edinburg, pp. 94–101 (2009)
22. Woods, S., et al.: Is this robot like me? Links between human and robot personality traits. In: Proceedings of IEEES-RAS International Conference on Humanoid Robots, Tsukuba, pp. 375–380 (2005)
23. Walters, M., et al.: The influence of subjects' personality traits on personal spatial; zones in a human-robot interaction experiment. In: Proceedings of 14th IEEE International Workshop on Robot and Human Interactive Communication, pp. 347–352 (2005)
24. Kiesler, S., Goetz, J.: Mental models of robotic assistants. In: Proceedings of CHI EA02 Extended Abstracts on Human Factors in Computing Systems, pp. 576–577 (2002)
25. Embgen, S., et al.: Robot-specific social cues in emotional body language. In: Proceedings of IEEE RO-MAN: the 21st IEEE International Symposium on Robot and Human Interactive Communication, pp. 1019–1025 (2012)

26. Williams, M.-A.: Decision-theoretic human-robot interaction: designing reasonable and rational robot behavior. In: Agah, A., Cabibihan, J.-J., Howard, Ayanna M., Salichs, Miguel A., He, H. (eds.) ICSR 2016. LNCS (LNAI), vol. 9979, pp. 72–82. Springer, Cham (2016). https://doi.org/10.1007/978-3-319-47437-3_8
27. Seibt, J.: Towards an ontology of simulated social interaction: varieties of the "As If" for robots and humans. In: Hakli, R., Seibt, J. (eds.) Sociality and Normativity for Robots. SPS, pp. 11–39. Springer, Cham (2017). https://doi.org/10.1007/978-3-319-53133-5_2
28. Sherman, N.: The Fabric of Character. Oxford UP, New York (1989)
29. Eagleton, T. (2013)
30. Sherman, N. (1989)
31. Eagleton, Personal communication
32. Caudwell, C., Lacey, C.: What Do Home Robots Want? The Ambivalent Power of Cuteness in Human-Robotic Relationships. Convergence (2018, forthcoming)
33. Seibt, J.: pp. 11–39 (2017)
34. Brazier, G., Gwynn, S.: Meet Cozmo, the AI robot-pet influenced by Wall-E and R2-D2. Campaign, December 2017. https://www.campaignlive.co.uk/article/meet-cozmo-ai-robot-pet-influenced-wall-e-r2-d2/1452555. Accessed 01 Aug 2018
35. Seibt, Personal communication
36. Ibid, p. 9
37. Seibt, J.: Varieties of the 'As-If': five ways to simulate an action. In: Seibt, J., Hakli, R., Norskov, M. (eds.) Sociable Robots and the Future of Social Relations: Proceedings of Robo-Philosophy, pp. 97–104. IOS Press, Amsterdam (2014)
38. Hakli, R.: Social Robots and social interactions. In: Seibt, J., Hakli, R., Norskov, M. (eds.) Sociable Robots and the Future of Social Relations: Proceedings of Robo-philosophy, pp. 105–114. IOS Press, Amsterdam (2014)
39. Ibid
40. Ibid, p. 20
41. Seibt, J.: pp. 97–104 (2014)
42. Ibid
43. Mori, M.: The uncanny valley. IEEE Robot. Autom. 19(2), 98–100 (2012)
44. Seibt, J.: pp. 100 (2014). Emphasis added
45. Seibt, J.: p. 20 (2017)
46. Althusser, L.: Ideology and ideological state apparatuses. In: Lenin and Philosophy, pp. 127–186. Monthly Review Press, New York (1971)
47. Wasko, J.: Corporate disney in action. In: Guins, R., Cruz, O.Z. (eds.) Popular Culture Reader, pp. 184–196. Sage, London (2015)
48. Wells, P.: Understanding Animation. Routledge, New York (1998)
49. Pallant, C.: Demystifying Disney: A History of Disney Feature Animation, p. 40. Bloomsbury, New York (2011)
50. Wells, P. (1998)
51. Thomas, F., Johnston, O.: p. 35 (1981). Emphasis added
52. Ibid, p. 47
53. Ibid, p. 47
54. Ribeiro, T.G., Paiva, A.: Creating interactive robotic characters. In: Proceedings of the Tenth Annual ACM/IEEE International Conference on Human-Robot Interaction Extended Abstracts (HRI 2015 Extended Abstracts), pp. 215–216. ACM, New York (2015)
55. Saldien, J., et al.: A motion system for social and animated robots. Int. J. Adv. Robot. Syst. 11(5), 72 (2014)

56. Takayama, L., et al.: Expressing thought: improving robot readability with animation principles. In: Proceedings of the 6th International Conference on Human-Robot Interaction, pp. 69–76. ACM, New York (2011)
57. Van Breemen, A.J.N.: Bringing robots to life: applying principles of animation to robots. In: Proceedings of Shaping Human-Robot Interaction Workshop Held at CHI, Italy (2004)
58. Bates, J.: The role of emotion in believable agents. Commun. ACM 37(7), 122–125 (2004)
59. Van Breemen, A.J.N. (2004)
60. Takayama, L., et al. (2011)
61. Saldien, J., et al. (2014)
62. Takayama, L., et al.: p. 69 (2011)
63. Freud, S.: The Uncanny (1909)
64. Wells, P.: The Animated Bestiary: Animals, Cartoons, and Culture, p. 5. Rutgers University Press, New Jersey (2009). Emphasis added
65. Whiteley, D.: The Idea of Nature in Disney Animation. Ashgate, Surrey (2012)
66. Ibid, p. 2
67. Ibid, p. 2
68. Ibid
69. Wills, Personal communication
70. Quindlen, A.: Modern Museum Celebrates Mickey. In: Apgar, G. (ed.) A Mickey Mouse Reader, pp. 173–175. University Press of Missipippi, Jackson (2014). p. 173
71. Culhane, J.: A mouse for all seasons. In: Apgar, G. (ed.) A Mickey Mouse Reader, pp. 169–172. University Press of Missipippi, Jackson (2014)
72. Wills, J.: Disney Culture, p. 4. Rutgers University Press, New Jersey (2017)
73. Wells, P.: Understanding Animation, p. 162. Routledge, New York (1998)
74. Ibid. p. 35
75. Wills, J.: Disney Culture, p. 5. Rutgers University Press, New Jersey (2017)
76. Ibid, pp. 3–4
77. Ibid, p. 4
78. Ibid, p. 44
79. Seibt, J.: p. 13 (2017)

A Proposed Wizard of OZ Architecture for a Human-Robot Collaborative Drawing Task

David Hinwood[1]($\boxtimes$)(iD), James Ireland[1](iD), Elizabeth Ann Jochum[2](iD), and Damith Herath[1](iD)

[1] University of Canberra, Canberra, ACT 2617, Australia
David.Hinwood@canberra.edu.au
[2] University of Aalborg, 9220 Aalborg, Denmark
https://www.canberra.edu.au/about-uc/faculties/SciTech,
https://www.en.aau.dk/

Abstract. Researching human-robot interaction "in the wild" can sometimes require insight from different fields. Experiments that involve collaborative tasks are valuable opportunities for studying HRI and developing new tools. The following describes a framework for an "in the wild" experiment situated in a public museum that involved a Wizard of OZ (WOZ) controlled robot. The UR10 is a non-humanoid collaborative robot arm and was programmed to engage in a collaborative drawing task. The purpose of this study was to evaluate how movement by a non-humanoid robot could affect participant experience. While the current framework is designed for this particular task, the control architecture could be built upon to provide a base for various collaborative studies.

Keywords: Control architecture · Wizard of OZ · ROS
Non-anthropomorphic robot · Human robot interaction
Artistic collaboration

1 Introduction

Human Robot Interaction (HRI) involves the study of how humans perceive, react and engage with robots in a variety of environments. Within the field of HRI is the study of how humans and machines can collaborate on shared tasks, commonly referred to as Human Robot Collaboration (HRC) [3]. Robotic interaction/collaboration can be beneficial in many fields including healthcare [11,12], education [4,25], construction [1,23] and the arts [9,10]. As both HRI and HRC are multidisciplinary fields, they often require a collection of individuals with different skill sets [8,10].

The following is a proposed software framework that enables researchers to run a HRC study with minimal development time. In this particular application, the software is implemented in a HRC study [5] with the deliverable being an

© Springer Nature Switzerland AG 2018
S. S. Ge et al. (Eds.): ICSR 2018, LNAI 11357, pp. 35–44, 2018.
https://doi.org/10.1007/978-3-030-05204-1_4

art work. This architecture is based around the Wizard of OZ (WOZ) experimental design methodology [21], allowing an operator to control the robot's behaviour in real time. The project results in a framework that provides non-technical individuals a means to conduct HRC research with minimal software development.

The wizard of OZ control method is a widely accepted technique for experiments evaluating human response to robotic behaviour, especially when the robot is required to demonstrate a certain level of intelligence. Consistent behaviour is crucial to maintaining uniformity in experience across all participants. An example of a WOZ system includes the work done by Lu and Smart [13] in which a GUI was built to control a robot and receive feedback from its current activity.

A similar system created by Villano et al. [24] had the capability to assist therapists while conducting sessions with children afflicted by ASD (Autism Spectrum Disorder). Much like Kim et al. [11] whom also used WOZ to control a robot that acted as a partner for a therapist. Additionally WOZ systems are useful when examining a new unit or agent which was the direction taken by studies such as Maulsby et al. [15], Green et al. [7] or Shiomi et al. [20] where data could be collected and provide feedback from real world experiments. However, it is important to recall that the operator's decisions were generally based on some predetermined algorithm before deployment and this could potentially impact the collected data.

Other facets of this research experiment involve anthropomorphic movement and the physical motion of drawing. Previous works such as Tresset and Leymarie [22] along with Munoz et al. [16] describe robots that are able to create artwork from real images. There are issues with noise and slight accuracy deficiencies when it comes to the translation of image coordinates to endpoints of robotic units. In our case, we emphasized easy recognition of basic objects and images that participants could readily contribute to regardless of drawing ability.

Anthropomorphic movements have been a significant focus of robotic studies for several applications, including psychology and social sciences [2,19]. The majority of this research focuses on the likeability and human reaction to a robot based on gestures and other behaviours. Behind many of these projects such as Barntneck et al. [2] or Salem et al. [19], anthropomorphism was analysed through a WOZ implementation. While there have been multiple instances of robotic drawing experiments and social collaborative robots controlled via WOZ, there has been little overlap between these two topics. As this architecture was designed for an experiment involving anthropomorphic behaviour, it was decided that a WOZ approach best gave the non-technical team members sufficient control over the UR10.

The experiment described below was designed for an "in the wild" HRC investigation developed in collaboration with humanities researchers. The location for this study was the Questacon - National Science and Technology Centre in Canberra, Australia. The public was invited to interact with the UR10 in a collaborative drawing task in which an individual would sit at the table in a position that would enable both participants (human and robot) to physically interact.

Fig. 1. Experiment setup, participant left, WOZ operator right

The UR10, under direction of the WOZ operator, would lead the interaction by prompting a participant to complete various actions through non-verbal cues. The UR10 would first greet the participant upon meeting and wait for them to take a seat. The robot would then begin to render a drawing, pausing momentarily to observe its progress. The UR10 under the direction of the WOZ operator would prompt the user to pick up a pen to contribute to the unfinished artwork. After several rounds of turn-taking, the robot drew a line in the lower right corner of the canvas to "autograph" the drawing to signal completion of the task. Once signed by both parties, the UR10 would indicate the participant was free to take the drawing home.

2 Architecture Overview

The applied experiment [5] required the UR10 to give the appearance of an autonomous social entity while having the capability to both draw and react to external stimuli. This section describes the software and hardware platforms utilised in this implementation including the Robot Operating System (ROS) module descriptions, the UR10 control method and the motion planning details.

2.1 Robot Operating System

Robot Operating System (ROS) is a popular open source middle-ware for the development of robotic applications [18]. Benefits of ROS include integrated communication between independent software modules (referred in ROS as 'nodes'), a diverse series of dynamic libraries and open source tools to assist development. The following implementation runs on a Linux platform and is compatible with both the Kinetic Kame and Indigo Igloo distributions of ROS. ROS is the primary source of communication between different software and hardware modules. The nodes communicate via pairs of publishers and subscribers sharing a specific topic, represented as one-way arrows in Fig. 2. There are three ROS nodes running simultaneously that make up the framework's core. They are the *interrupt*, *social_command* and *robot_interface* nodes. The *social_command* node contains two publishers with subscribers in the *robot_interface* node. The *WOZ_command* publisher sent the majority of commands across including all social actions, drawing routines and parameter calibrations, while the *override_command* was used to disable any running actions if needed. The *robot_interface* node returned values to the *social_command* node indicating what state the robot was operating in via the *robot_feedback* publisher. Any messages received from the *robot_feedback* publisher were displayed back to the user.

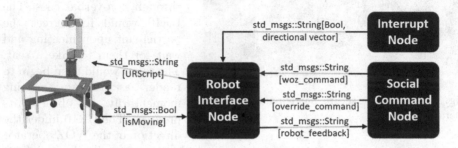

Fig. 2. Topic overview for ROS communication

The *interrupt* node was created as a safety feature that allowed the WOZ operator to send a signal that caused the robot to withdraw to a safe distance in the event of a potential collision with a participant. Currently, this is manually triggered by the WOZ operator; however the same signal can be sent by a computer vision node that automatically triggers the robot to withdraw if the participant comes within a given distance. Following a withdraw motion; the UR10 would attempt to execute the last task, be it drawing or gesturing to the participant.

2.2   The UR10

The UR10 is an industrial robot arm with 7 degrees of freedom and a 1.3 m maximum reach. To achieve communication between the proposed framework and the UR10, the python-urx [14] library was implemented to send commands through a TCP connection via a remote call procedure (RCP). This meant that content needed to contain executable code written in URScript, a language specifically designed to interface with the UR3, UR5 and UR10 robots.

The motions of the UR10 can be executed as a single linear trajectory or a movement between a series of points creating a smooth, fluid motion. Both motions are based around the end-effectors position relative to the world coordinate, where the rotational values of the arm are calculated via the UR10's inverse kinematics system. There are several constraints when it comes to movement of the UR10. Within a single motion the robot arm requires a certain minimum distance to accelerate and then decelerate. The increase while accelerating is constant until either a defined maximum velocity is reached or the UR10 needs to begin decelerating so the arm can arrive at its intended target endpoint. This constraint could cause a program malfunction when the robot's speed was too fast to accurately move between two points, or the start and target endpoints were too close together. This limitation presented an issue when planning the drawing actions. As sketching is a dexterous task, being able to accurately draw detailed lines was a priority. To overcome this constraint, contours that were being drawn were separated into a series of points an acceptable distance apart. This solution is expanded upon in the drawing subsection below.

Animating

The animations were made to exhibit anthropomorphic behaviour in order to establish non-verbal communication with a participant. The animations were designed using a simple interface that allowed the recording and play back of each individual animation. To streamline the animation process, the robot was set to free drive mode in which the researcher could freely and securely manipulate the UR10 into a desired position. Once in position, the researcher would record the end-effectors coordinates. The various coordinates/positions were saved to a CSV (comma separated value) file along with animation titles and required delays between movements. The primary use of the animations was to prompt the participant to complete a desired action, such as picking up a pen. This and other animations are initiated by the WOZ operator from the command-line terminal. Animation speeds differ significantly from the drawing motions. Depending on how fast the robot was needed to move, a maximum velocity of $50\,\text{cm/s}$ was acceptable. The acceleration was usually within the range of $10\,\text{cm/s}^2$ and $20\,\text{cm/s}^2$. These speed parameters were determined to be the optimal solution based on early testing phases and initial feedback with test-groups. While performing an animated movement, the robot did not account for accidental collision between its two aluminium tubes and the steel base. The priority was to ensure that all combinations of animated motions did not result in a collision.

Drawing

The motivation for using a collaborative drawing task was to initiate a collaboration between robot and participant in an open-ended task that was mutual, involved turn-taking, and was enjoyable for the participants. It was also important that the interaction fit within a limited time frame. Simple line drawings proved the most effective for this purpose, as the images were readily recognisable to the participants and did not require advanced artistic skills. The focus was on the interaction, rather than aesthetic criteria. When called upon, the contour extraction method would first apply a binary threshold converting the image to grayscale. This grayscale image would then be the primary parameter into the 'findContours' function which output a series of points for each contour in the original image. To reduce the amount of time needed to render the image, the number of points on each contour was reduced by implementing the Ramer-Douglas-Peucker [6] algorithm. Both the 'findContours' method and the Ramer-Douglas-Peucker algorithm were implemented through use of the OpenCV library [17]. Once extracted each point on a contour was iterated through to check that the distance between points met the hardware requirements discussed above. In the case where a point was found to be closer than this threshold, it was ignored and the next point on the contour was verified. Once all of the contours were extracted, this method would pass them along to be translated, scaled and physically rendered.

Each point provided by the contour extraction method was mapped in turn onto a three-dimensional plane defined by four coordinates set in the calibration stage. These coordinates were described within the implementation as *bottom left, bottom right, top left* and *top right* areas of the canvas as it relates to the observational position of the robot. Participants were seated opposite, facing the robot, thus the image coordinates where mapped to be drawn from their perspective, see Fig. 1. We presumed that participants would be better able to collaborate on a drawing when the image was easily recognised and drawn from their perspective. Once translated, the image coordinates needed scaling in relation to the canvas size chosen. First, the image was evaluated based on its ratio of height to width, leading to the creation of a drawing space being an area within the canvas, sharing the same aforementioned ratio. Unlike the animation speed parameters, the speed of motion while drawing had to be limited. While acceleration settings remained consistent with the animation motions, the velocity was limited to a maximum of 30 cm/s to allow for more accurate movements.

3   WOZ Commands

The command system of this implementation was a crucial component for establishing the interface between the WOZ operator and the robot. By placing the WOZ operator away from direct view, participants more readily interacted with the robot as a social actor. With the operator out of direct view, the illusion of social intelligence was achieved. To support the interaction, the operator would use a series of commands to puppeteer the robot's behaviour depending on the situation. If asked, the WOZ operator would inform the participant after the interaction that the robot was manually controlled.

The drawing routine was comprised of a series of actions preformed sequentially. The robot would start by greeting the participant, begin drawing, pause to "evaluate" its efforts (using a predetermined animation), complete the drawing and return to an idle state. These actions began when a participant initiated an interaction with the robot. This was controlled by the WOZ operator who would control the timing, execution and sequence of events. Afterwards, the series of aforementioned commands could be executed to complete the desired interaction.

The commands were separated into the three categories: *maintenance, states* and *actions*. Apart from the maintenance category, all commands generally applied to social actions. Each command was sent via a command-line interface developed in ROS with Python. Sending instructions via the UR10 application programming interface (API) from the python-urx [14] library.

The maintenance directives set parameters for the experiment. These instructions handled settings such as velocity, acceleration, animations and calibrations.

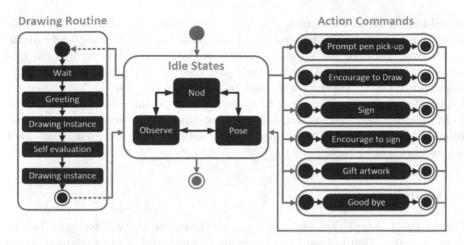

Fig. 3. WOZ command structure

The maintenance commands also were able to run individual actions of the experiment for testing purposes. These test instructions were built on overloaded functions that were embedded within the social routine code structure. The UR10 has two motion-based parameters that were adjustable within the python-urx library, velocity and acceleration.

The calibration routine could be called on start up or user request. This command would place the robot in free-drive mode, allowing the robot to be moved by external force. While calibrating, a WOZ operator would move the robot to each corner of the canvas recording positions in three-dimensional space relative to the robot base. From here the lowest corner, along with its neighbours, make up a three dimensional plane representing the canvas.

The state commands instruct the robot how to behave in a continuous waiting manner. The WOZ operator could choose between three predetermined states with either a "nodding" motion, an "observing" animation or a "withdrawn" pose. These three options of idle states allowed the participant to contribute within the interaction between the robot and themselves. These states also assisted the WOZ operator with control of the exhibit as specific actions could only be executed from this idle state. The nodding command would give the robot the appearance of looking at a participant and nodding with random time intervals. The observe command would give an illusion of the robot evaluating both the canvas and participant via a series of linear endpoint transitions. Finally, the withdrawn state caused the robot to pull away from the human to a safe position and remain motionless.

The action commands were the series of motions to communicate non-verbally and interact with the participant. Action commands were called when the robot was in a continuous state of idle motion. These commands are listed in the right column of Fig. 3. The 'prompt pen pick-up' command could be issued in multiple scenarios where a participant was required to pick up or place a pen (held in the cup on the table). The purpose of the 'encourage to draw' command was to signal the participant to collaborate on the drawing and initiate turn-taking. Through the 'sign' instruction the UR10 would autograph the artwork. If necessary, the WOZ operator could re-send the 'prompt pen pick-up' command to encourage the participant to take back the pen. To focus the participant's attention on to the empty space adjacent to the robots signature, the WOZ operator calls the 'encourage to sign' command. The conjunction of these commands were intended to prompt participants to write their signature next to the robot's autograph.

4   Conclusion

Human robot interaction and collaborative research can involve very labour intensive integration between the hardware (robot) and study variables, which can be a constraint for members from different disciplinary backgrounds. The proposed architecture was designed such that researchers without any programming experience could still facilitate a collaborative experiment with minimal technical assistance. The framework in question currently centres around an interaction in which a participant and a UR10 contribute to a shared artwork. However this can be adapted to test a multitude of social and physical variables. Here, we have summarised the control architecture for the WOZ setup. The results of the experiments with participants, including analysis and discussion, are summarised in [5]. A complete analysis of the experimental data is forthcoming.

5   Future Direction

The current framework is hard coded to a fixed set of commands and one collaborative task. Future development will investigate how to make this architecture more flexible and allow for different collaborative tasks to be integrated. One contribution of control architecture is that in enables researchers with little technical knowledge to add, remove and execute animations with greater control. At the present, the WOZ commands are terminal-based therefore certain tasks become more convoluted. For this reason, a graphical user interface (GUI) will be added to give the WOZ application a more intuitive user interface and streamlined functionality. Other features could include forms of data logging and recording to make the experiment evaluations easier to monitor.

Acknowledgements. The study was conducted with ethical approval by the Human Research Ethics Committee of the University of Canberra (HREC 20180158). In collaboration with the University of Aalborg, namely Jonas Elbler Pedersen and Kristoffer Wulff Christensen whom we thank. This work would not have been possible without the Innovation Vouchers Program jointly funded by the ACT Australia Government, University of Canberra and Robological PTY LTD.

References

1. Andersen, R.S., Bøgh, S., Moeslund, T.B., Madsen, O.: Task space HRI for cooperative mobile robots in fit-out operations inside ship superstructures. In: 2016 25th IEEE International Symposium on Robot and Human Interactive Communication, RO-MAN, pp. 880–887 (2016)
2. Bartneck, C., Kulić, D., Croft, E., Zoghbi, S.: Measurement instruments for the anthropomorphism, animacy, likeability, perceived intelligence, and perceived safety of robots. Int. J. Soc. Robot. 1(1), 71–81 (2009)
3. Bauer, A., Wollherr, D., Buss, M.: Human–robot collaboration: a survey. Int. J. Humanoid Robot. 5(01), 47–66 (2008)
4. Baxter, P., Ashurst, E., Read, R., Kennedy, J., Belpaeme, T.: Robot education peers in a situated primary school study: personalisation promotes child learning. PloS One 12(5), e0178126 (2017)
5. Christensen, K.W., Pedersen, J.E., Jochum, E.A., Herath, D.: The truth is out there: capturing the complexities of human robot-interactions. In: Workshop on Critical Robotics - Exploring a New Paradigm, NordiCHI 2018, Nordic Conference on Human-Computer Interaction, Oslo, Norway (2018)
6. Douglas, D.H., Peucker, T.K.: Algorithms for the reduction of the number of points required to represent a digitized line or its caricature. Cartographica: Int. J. Geograph. Inf. Geovis. 10(2), 112–122 (1973)
7. Green, A., Huttenrauch, H., Eklundh, K.S.: Applying the Wizard-of-OZ framework to cooperative service discovery and configuration. In: 13th IEEE International Workshop on Robot and Human Interactive Communication, ROMAN 2004, pp. 575–580. IEEE (2004)
8. Herath, D., Jochum, E., Vlachos, E.: An experimental study of embodied interaction and human perception of social presence for interactive robots in public settings. IEEE Trans. Cogn. Dev. Syst. 1–11 (2017)
9. Herath, D.C., Kroos, C., Stevens, C.J., Cavedon, L., Premaratne, P.: Thinking head: towards human centred robotics. In: 2010 11th International Conference on Control Automation Robotics & Vision, pp. 2042–2047 (2010)
10. Herath, D., Kroos, C., Stelarc: Robots and Art: Exploring an Unlikely Symbiosis. Cognitive Science and Technology. Springer, Singapore (2016). https://doi.org/10.1007/978-981-10-0321-9
11. Kim, E.S., et al.: Social robots as embedded reinforcers of social behavior in children with autism. J. Autism Dev. Disord. 43(5), 1038–1049 (2013)
12. Koceski, S., Koceska, N.: Evaluation of an assistive telepresence robot for elderly healthcare. J. Med. Syst. 40(5), 121 (2016)
13. Lu, D.V., Smart, W.D.: Polonius: a Wizard of OZ interface for HRI experiments. In: Proceedings of the 6th International Conference on Human-Robot Interaction, pp. 197–198. ACM (2011)
14. Sintef Raufoss Manufacturing: GitHub - sintefraufossmanufacturing/python-urx: Python library to control a robot from 'universal robots', July 2018. https://github.com/SintefRaufossManufacturing/python-urx
15. Maulsby, D., Greenberg, S., Mander, R.: Prototyping an intelligent agent through Wizard of OZ. In: Proceedings of the INTERACT 1993 and CHI 1993 Conference on Human Factors in Computing Systems, pp. 277–284. ACM (1993)
16. Munoz, J.-M., Avalos, J., Ramos, O.E.: Image-driven drawing system by a NAO robot. In: Electronic Congress, E-CON UNI, pp. 1–4. IEEE (2017)

17. OpenCV: Structural analysis and shape descriptors - OpenCV 2.4.13.7 documentation, July 2018. https://docs.opencv.org/2.4/modules/imgproc/doc/structural_analysis_and_shape_descriptors.html
18. Quigley, M., et al.: ROS: an open-source Robot Operating System. In: ICRA Workshop on Open Source Software, Kobe, Japan, vol. 3, p. 5 (2009)
19. Salem, M., Eyssel, F., Rohlfing, K., Kopp, S., Joublin, F.: To err is human (-like): effects of robot gesture on perceived anthropomorphism and likability. Int. J. Soc. Robot. **5**(3), 313–323 (2013)
20. Shiomi, M., Kanda, T., Koizumi, S., Ishiguro, H., Hagita, N.: Group attention control for communication robots with Wizard of OZ approach. In: Proceedings of the ACM/IEEE International Conference on Human-Robot Interaction, pp. 121–128. ACM (2007)
21. Torres, R.J., Heck, M.P., Rudd, J.R., Kelley, J.F.: Usability engineering: a consultant's view of best practices and proven results. Ergon. Des. **16**(2), 18–23 (2008)
22. Tresset, P., Leymarie, F.F.: Portrait drawing by Paul the robot. Comput. Graph. **37**(5), 348–363 (2013)
23. Vasey, L., et al.: Human and robot collaboration enabling the fabrication and assembly of a filament-wound structure. In: ACADIA 2016: Posthuman Frontiers: Data, Designers, and Cognitive Machines, Proceedings of the 36th Annual Conference of the Association for Computer Aided Design in Architecture, pp. 184–195 (2016)
24. Villano, M., et al.: DOMER: a Wizard of OZ interface for using interactive robots to scaffold social skills for children with autism spectrum disorders. In: Proceedings of the 6th International Conference on Human-Robot Interaction, pp. 279–280. ACM (2011)
25. Zia-ul-Haque, Q.S.M., Wang, Z., Li, C., Wang, J., Yujun: A robot that learns and teaches English language to native Chinese children, pp. 1087–1092. IEEE (2007)

Factors and Development of Cognitive and Affective Trust on Social Robots

Takayuki Gompei and Hiroyuki Umemuro[✉] [iD]

Tokyo Institute of Technology, Tokyo 152-8552, Japan
umemuro.h.aa@m.titech.ac.jp
http://www.affectivelaboratory.org

Abstract. The purpose of this study is to investigate the factors that contribute to cognitive and affective trust of social robots. Also investigated were the changes within two different types of trust over time and variables that influence trust. Elements of trust extracted from literature were used to evaluate people's trust of social robot in an experiment. As a result of a factor analysis, ten factors that construct trust were extracted. These factors were further analyzed in relations with both cognitive and affective trust. Factors such as Security, Teammate, and Performance were found to relate with cognitive trust, while factors such as Teammate, Performance, Autonomy, and Friendliness appeared to relate with affective trust. Furthermore, changes in cognitive and affective trust over the time phases of the interaction were investigated. Affective trust appeared to develop in the earlier phase, while cognitive trust appeared to develop over the whole period of the interaction. Conversation topics had influence on affective trust, while robot's mistakes had influence on the cognitive trust. On the other hand, prior experiences with social robots did now show any significant relations with neither cognitive nor affective trust. Finally, Familiarity attitude appeared to relate with both cognitive and affective trust, while other sub-dimensions of robot attitudes such as Interest, Negative attitude, and Utility appeared to relate with affective trust.

Keywords: Affective trust · Cognitive trust · Conversation · Attitude

1 Introduction

Trust is an essential factor in relations between human and robots. Billings, Schaefer, Chen, and Hancock [1] discussed that human trust on robots is essential because it influences the results of human-robot interaction.

There have been past studies focusing on the two aspects of trust: cognitive trust and affective trust. Schaefer [2] proposed four categories of trust on robots: propensity of trust, affect-based trust, cognition-based trust, and trustworthiness. Schaefer discussed that affect-based and cognition-based trust as emergent or dynamic states that may change along the interactions, while propensity of trust is a stable trait and trustworthiness is attributed to characteristics of

© Springer Nature Switzerland AG 2018
S. S. Ge et al. (Eds.): ICSR 2018, LNAI 11357, pp. 45–54, 2018.
https://doi.org/10.1007/978-3-030-05204-1_5

robots, thus rather stable over time. The constructs, or what factors contribute to these dynamic process of developing cognitive and affective trust, and the time phases they affect, have not been fully studied.

Existing studies on the constructs of trust are mostly focusing on cognitive aspects [3–5]. For example, Hancock et al. [3] extracted factors on human-robot trust by meta analysis of literature. Most of the extracted factors were those that related to robots and environments, while factors related to human were rather limited, such as demographics, abilities, attitudes and traits. Factors studied within these previous studies were mostly related to rational aspects contributing to cognitive trust or trustworthiness. On the other hand, identifying what factors contribute to the development of affective trust and in which particular time phases have rarely been studied.

Factors contributing to affective trust have been studied in social psychology for interpersonal trust. Lewis and Weigert [6] pointed out the existence of cognitive and affective aspects in interpersonal trust. Rempel et al. [7] discussed the difference between cognitive and affective trust; cognitive trust is self-efficacy to rely on capabilities and reliabilities of a specific party, while affective trust is self-efficacy on the party based on human affective responses to the behavior of the party. McAllister [8] emphasized the importance of measuring the two dimensions of interpersonal trust and discussed that cognitive trust contributes to the development of affective trust. Johnson and Grayson [9] investigated factors influencing cognitive trust and affective trust in the context of the service industry. They discussed that cognitive trust is a willingness to rely on a service provider based on specific instances of reliable conduct, and is a trust based on knowledge. On the other hand, affective trust is based on affects experienced through interactions with the service provider. As social robots are aimed to interact with human users, they may be designed to have a nature of anthropomorphism. Thus it is assumed that these insights into interpersonal trust might imply for affective trust that human users might have on social robots.

Both cognitive and affective trust are considered to be developed over periods of time while the users are interacting with the robot. Considering the difference in the nature of information necessary for cognitive and affective trust, the time phase of interactions where these factors have a major contribution might be different, across factors and between both cognitive and affective trust.

The purpose of this study was to investigate the factors that contribute to people's cognitive and affective trust on social robots. Furthermore, contributions of such factors to the development of these two types of trust were investigated by time phases, i.e. early and late phases, of a human-robot interaction.

2   Elements for Cognitive and Affective Trust

This study adopted potential elements of both cognitive trust and affective trust from previous studies. Trust elements were adopted from previous human-robot interaction studies as well as interpersonal trust studies in social psychology. These elements were used within the experiment described below on subjects to evaluate their own trust on the robot during different time phases.

In order to reflect on previous results in the human-robot interaction field, elements of trust were adopted from the items developed by Schaefer [2]. Schaefer proposed 40 items covering various aspects of human-robot trust.

To incorporate the insights from interpersonal trust, items proposed by Johnson and Grayson [9] were also adopted. Johnson and Grayson proposed elements for both cognitive and affective interpersonal trust, with seven items for each.

3 Hypotheses

McAllister [8] discussed that affinity activities would increase affective trust. When social robots spontaneously speak to a human user, this might be recognized by the user as affinity activity and may increase affective trust. On the other hand, Johnson and Grayson [9] discussed that the demonstration of high performance of the party may result in a higher cognitive trust of people. Thus we derived the following hypotheses about the spontaneous speech of the robots, depending on the topic of the speech.

H1-1 Robots who spontaneously speak personal or casual topics to human user increase the user's affective trust.
H1-2 Robots who spontaneously speak to a human user with topics related to utility information increase the user's cognitive trust.

As Johnson and Grayson [9] discussed, performance of the party would influence on people's cognitive trust. When robots make mistakes, it may influence negatively on people's cognitive trust. On the other hand, if the robot could correct its own mistakes, it may contribute to the improvement of cognitive trust. Thus we derived the following hypotheses.

H2-1 Robots who make mistakes result in a lower cognitive trust of users than those who do not.
H2-2 Robots who correct their own mistakes result in users higher cognitive trust than robots who make mistakes but do not correct themselves.

Previous studies discussed that repetition of expectation–satisfaction cycles are essential to develop cognitive trust, while affective trust may develop from the first impression. It implies that the time phases where these two types of trust may differ. Thus we derived the following hypotheses.

H3-1 Affective trust develops more in earlier phases of human-robot interaction than cognitive trust.
H3-2 Cognitive trust develops more in later phases of human-robot interaction than affective trust.

Johnson and Grayson [9] discussed that satisfaction on prior experiences would have a positive influence on cognitive trust. Even in the context of human-robot interaction, people's experiences with robots in the past may contribute to cognitive trust. Thus we derived the following hypothesis.

H4 The satisfaction of past experiences with robots would positively correlate with cognitive trust on robots.

Schaefer [2] discussed that people with positive attitudes towards robots would have a higher affective trust. Thus we derived the following hypothesis.

H5 People with more positive attitudes toward robots have a higher affective trust on robots.

4   Method

4.1   Experiment Design

In order to pursue the purpose and validate the hypotheses, an experiment with human-robot interaction tasks was conducted. The experiment had two factors. Topics of conversation (three levels: casual topic, information topic, and reply-only) and mistakes (three levels: mistakes, mistakes-and-correction, and no-mistake) were between-subject factors.

4.2   Subjects

The subjects were fifty-six undergraduate and graduate students of an engineering school aged between 18 and 26 years old ($M = 23.1$, $SD = 1.5$). Forty-seven subjects were males and nine subjects were female. Subjects were randomly assigned to one of nine groups according to the nine (3×3) combinations of the two between-subjects conditions: topics of conversation and mistakes of robots. Within each group contained five or six males and one female subjects.

4.3   Apparatus

NAO [10] was adopted as the social robot to interact with all subjects. NAO was settled in a quiet laboratory room where at each interaction session only one subject along with an experimenter were seated at a time. NAO was programmed with Choregraphe [11] to implement the conversation scenarios described below.

4.4   Procedure

When subjects first entered the experiment room, the subjects were explained the outline of the experiment and asked to sign the consent form. Then subjects were asked to fill out the first questionnaire that assessed their prior experiences, satisfaction and attitudes toward robots, as well as demographic information.

After the completion of the first questionnaire, NAO was placed in front of the subject. Subjects were explained the flow of the following sessions; having a conversation with the robot, and then experience further functions of the robot. Subjects were also told that they will complete questionnaires to assess their trust on the robot three times: before conversation, after conversation, and at the end after they experiences the robots functions. Then subjects completed the questionnaire that assessed their trust on robots for the first time.

In the conversation session, subjects were instructed to have conversation with the robot. In the "casual topic" condition, the robot was programmed to try to ask subjects for their personal information and interest such as names or hobbies. In the "information topic" condition, the robot was programmed to provide with useful information spontaneously. Finally, in the "reply-only" condition, the robot was programmed to respond to subject's questions only when asked, and unable to speak anything spontaneously. The period of the conversation was designed to be around five minutes based on a previous study [12]. After completing the conversation session, subjects were asked to complete the questionnaire for their trust on the robot for the second time.

In the session for experiencing functions, subjects were instructed to experience five different functions of the robot: weather report, search for nearby events, news search, sending messages, and reminder. With two of the five functions, namely search for nearby events and sending messages, the robot was programmed to make a mistake in either "mistakes" and "mistakes-and-correction" conditions. In the "mistakes-and-correction" condition, the robot made a correction immediately after the mistake. On the other hand, in the "no-mistake" condition, the robot simply completed the task correctly. After completing the function experience session, subjects were asked to complete the questionnaire to assess their trust on the robot for the third time and dismissed from experiment.

The total time of experiment for one subject was approximately 50 min.

4.5 Measurement

To assess subjects' trust on the robot, the scale developed by Schaefer [2] was adopted, with the scale consisting of 40 items. Subjects rated their trust on the robot in the range of 0% to 100% according to each item.

In addition, to assess affective and cognitive trust, the trust scale used in the study by Johnson and Grayson [9] was adopted. The scale was modified so the descriptions originally referring to a person were modified to refer to a robot. This scale consists of ten items, five for cognitive and five for affective trust. Subjects evaluated their feeling of trust with seven-point Likert scales. Averages of responses for five items each yielded scores for cognitive and affective trust.

Subjects' satisfaction with social robots were assessed with the satisfaction scale developed by Johnson and Grayson [9]. This scale assessed the satisfaction of interaction experiences in the past with four items on a seven-point semantic differential scale. The average of responses for four items yields the satisfaction score.

Finally, the subjects' attitudes towards robots were assessed with the Multidimensional Robot Attitude Scale [13]. This scale consists of 49 items that yield twelve sub-dimensions: Familiarity, Interest, Negative attitude, Self-efficacy, Appearance, Utility, Cost, Variety, Control, Social support, Operation, and Environmental fit. Subjects were asked to evaluate to what extent each of the items matched their feelings and perceptions of domestics robots using a seven-point

Likert scale. The averages of the responses for corresponding items per sub-dimension yielded the score for each sub-dimension.

5   Results

5.1   Factors of Robot Trust and Relations with Cognitive and Affective Trust

A factor analysis was conducted on all subjects' ratings of trust on robots. The method of the maximum likelihood with promax rotation revealed a ten-factor structure. The ten factors' cumulative contribution was 68.5%. These ten factors were considered to represent the dimensions of people's trust on robots.

Variables that had high loadings on the first factor included responses to items such as "Warn people of potential risks in the environment", "Keep classified information secure", "Perform many functions at one time", and "Protect people". This factor was considered to represent people's expectation that robots would avoid risks and work properly and was thus labeled as "Security".

Variables that had high loadings on the second factor included "Considered part of the team", "A good teammate", and "Act as a part of team". This factor was considered to represent people's expectations for robots to work in collaboration with people and was thus labeled as "Teammate".

Variables that had high loadings on the third factor included "Dependable", "Incompetent (reversed)", "Supportive", and "Perform a task better than a novice human user". This factor was considered to represent people's expectation for good performance of robots and was thus labeled as "Performance".

Variables that had high loadings on the fourth factor included "Have errors (reversed)", "Malfunction (reversed)", and "Require frequent maintenance (reversed)". This factor was considered to represent people's expectation that robots should work free of troubles and was thus labeled as "Trouble-free".

Variables that had high loadings on the fifth factor included "Clearly communicate", "Openly communicate", and "Provide feedback". This factor related to people's expectations that robots should provide information appropriately. Thus this factor was labeled as "Communication".

Variables that had high loadings on the sixth factor included "Conscious", "Predictable", "Autonomous", and "Possess adequate decision-making capability". This factor was considered to represent people's perceptions that robots should be able to perform by themselves and was thus labeled as "Autonomy".

Variables that had high loadings on the seventh factor included "Friendly" and "Pleasant". This factor was considered to represent people's expectation for intimacy robots would have with human users and was thus labeled as "Friendliness".

Variables that had high loadings on the eighth factor included "Perform exactly as instructed" and "Follow directions". This factor represents people's expectations for robots to obey orders and was thus labeled as "Obedience".

Variables that had high loadings on the ninth factor included "Meet the needs of the mission", "Responsible", and "Provide feedback". This factor was considered to represent people's expectation for the responsibility of robots to accomplish own tasks and was thus labeled as "Accomplishment".

Variables that had high loadings on the tenth factor included "Work in close proximity with people". This factor was considered to represent people's expectations for robots to work closely to people and was thus labeled as "Companion".

Table 1 summarizes Pearson's correlation coefficients between factor scores of the extracted ten factors and scores of cognitive and affective trust.

Table 1. Pearson's correlation coefficients between trust factor scores and cognitive and affective trust scores by the measurement phases.

Factors	Cognitive trust			Affective trust		
	Initial	After conversation	After experience	Initial	After conversation	After experience
Security	.504**	.405**	.500**	.241	.522**	.563**
Teammate	.420**	.659**	.661**	.432**	.442**	.434**
Performance	.505**	.630**	.784**	.278*	.567**	.555**
Trouble-free	.156	.371**	.268*	.193	−.136	.108
Communication	.198	.289*	.296*	.387**	.242	.209
Autonomy	.257	.363**	.444**	.459**	.391**	.383**
Friendliness	.191	.211	.384**	.640**	.667**	.755**
Obedience	.088	.457**	.405**	.236	.194	.175
Accomplishment	−.033	.223	.310*	.030	−.114	−.075
Companion	.374**	.101	.167	.121	.308*	.228
n	56	55	56	56	55	56

** $p < .01$. * $p < .05$.

Scores of factors such as Security, Teammate, and Performance consistently relate with cognitive trust for all phases of the interactions. On the other hand, factors such as Trouble-free, Communication, Autonomy, Obedience showed a significant correlations with cognitive trust only after some conversation, and Friendliness and Accomplishment relate only in the final phase.

Scores of factors such as Teammate, Performance, Autonomy, Friendliness showed significant correlations with affective trust for all phases. Security factor showed correlations only after some conversation. On the other hand, Communication factor related only in the initial phase.

Finally, Pearson's correlations between cognitive trust and affective trust scores were 0.128 ($p = 0.348$), 0.340 ($p = 0.010$), and 0.455 ($p < .001$), for initial, after conversation, and after experience measurements, respectively. While these two trust did not show significant correlations in the beginning, they correlated significantly in the latter phase of the interaction.

5.2   Changes in Cognitive and Affective Trust over Time

In order to assess the differences in the cognitive and affective trust scores across the three phases of measurement and across the conditions, analyses of variances

(ANOVAs) were conducted with cognitive and affective trust scores as characteristic variables, measurement phase (three levels: initial, after conversation, and after experience) as within-subject factor, and conversation topic (three levels: casual topic, information topic, and reply-only) and mistake (mistakes, mistakes-and-correction, no-mistake), and gender as between-subject factors.

There were significant effects of the measurement phases for both cognitive trust score ($F(2, 148) = 17.4, p < .001$) and affective trust score ($F(2, 148) = 18.4, p < .001$). Post hoc analyses revealed that cognitive trust score after conversation ($M = 20.2, SD = 4.9$) was significantly higher than the initial phase ($M = 17.0, SD = 4.0, p < .01$), while the score for the after experience phase ($M = 22.4, SD = 5.8$) was significantly higher than initial phase ($p < .01$) and after conversation phase ($p < .05$), respectively. On the other hand, affective trust scores after conversation ($M = 22.9, SD = 4.7$) and after experience phase ($M = 23.6, SD = 5.4$) were significantly higher than that of initial phase ($M = 18.7, SD = 4.0, p < .01$) respectively, although the scores after conversation and after experience were not significantly different. These results suggested that affective trust has developed in earlier phase of conversation, but did not change much in the latter experience phase, while cognitive trust has developed for whole of the interaction period. Thus these results supported H3-1 and H3-2.

5.3   Influence of Conversation and Mistake on Cognitive and Affective Trust

There was a significant main effect of the conversation topic on affective trust score ($F(2, 148) = 4.26, p < .05$), while the main effect was not significant on cognitive trust score. Post hoc analysis revealed that affective trust score in casual topic condition ($M = 22.6, SD = 5.8$) was significantly higher than the score in reply-only condition ($M = 20.3, SD = 4.7, p < .05$). The affective trust score in information topic condition ($M = 22.4, SD = 4.7$) was moderately higher than the score in reply-only condition ($p < .10$). There was no significant difference between casual topic and information topic conditions. These results partially supported H1-1, while H1-2 was rejected.

There was a significant main effect of the mistake condition on cognitive trust score ($F(2, 148) = 3.87, p < .05$), while the effect was not signifiant on affective trust. Post hoc analysis revealed that cognitive trust score in the no-mistake condition ($M = 21.1, SD = 5.6$) was significantly higher than the mistakes condition ($M = 18.6, SD = 5.4$), but there were no significant differences between mistakes-and-correction condition ($M = 20.0, SD = 5.0$) and the other two conditions. These results supported H2-1, while H2-2 was not supported.

5.4   Prior Experiences and Cognitive and Affective Trust

Subjects were divided into two groups, one with prior experiences with social robots ($n = 24$) and the other group with no experiences ($n = 32$). A series of t-tests showed there were no significant differences in the cognitive trust scores nor on the affective trust scores between these two groups.

The group with prior experiences were further divided into two groups with high satisfaction score and low satisfaction score, based on the standardized score of the reported satisfaction. There were no significant differences in the scores of both cognitive and affective trust between the two groups. Thus H4 was rejected.

5.5   Attitudes and Cognitive and Affective Trust

For each of twelve sub-dimension scores of the Multi-dimensional Robot Attitude Scale, subjects were divided into two groups, namely a group with higher scores and another group with lower scores, based on the standardized sub-dimension score. The cognitive trust score and affective trust score were compared between the two groups for each of the twelve sub-dimensions.

Cognitive trust score were significantly higher for the subjects with higher scores in the Familiarity attitude sub-dimension ($p < .05$). On the other hand, affective trust score were significantly higher for the groups with higher scores in Familiarity ($p < .05$), Interest ($p < .001$), Negative attitude ($p < .01$), and Utility ($p < .01$) sub-dimensions of the robot attitudes. These results imply that attitudes are more related with affective trust than cognitive trust, and therefore partially supported H5.

6   Conclusion

This study investigated the factors of trust that contribute to cognitive and affective trust on social robots. Furthermore, the changes in the two types of trust over time and influencing variables were also investigated.

Elements of trust extracted from literature were used to evaluate people's trust on a social robot during an experiment. As a result of factor analysis, ten factors that construct trust were extracted. These factors were further analyzed in relations with cognitive and affective trust. Factors such as Security, Teammate, and Performance were found to relate with cognitive trust, while factors such as Teammate, Performance, Autonomy, and Friendliness appeared to relate with affective trust.

Changes in cognitive and affective trust over the time phases of the interaction were investigated. Affective trust appeared to develop in the earlier phase, while cognitive trust appeared to develop along the whole interaction period.

The influences of some variables on the development of cognitive or affective trust were also investigated. The topics of the conversation had an influence on the affective trust, while the robot's mistakes had an influence on the cognitive trust. Prior experiences with social robots did not show any significant relations with neither cognitive nor affective trust. Finally, Familiarity attitude appeared to relate with both cognitive and affective trust, while some other sub-dimensions of the robot attitudes such as Interest, Negative attitude, and Utility appeared to relate with affective trust.

The subjects of this study were limited to university students. In the near future, broader ranges of the population are supposed to interact with social robots. In order to further generalize the findings of this study, subjects with broader ranges of generations, backgrounds, and cultures should be involved.

As this study was an experiment in laboratory setting, only one kind of robot was used and the variations of the interactions were rather limited. Wider variations of social robots with various different kinds of interactions should be examined for further generalizations of the studies results.

Finally, the development period of the two types of trust observed in this experiment was over a short time. In practice, trust on robots should be developed over longer period of time such as weeks or even years. Longitudinal studies on long term development of trust should be conducted.

References

1. Billings, D.R., Schaefer, K.E., Chen, J.Y., Hancock, P.A. : Human-robot interaction: developing trust in robots. In: Proceedings of the 7th Annual ACM/IEEE International Conference on Human-Robot Interaction, pp. 109–110. ACM, Boston (2012)
2. Schaefer, K.E.: The Perception and Measurement of Human-Robot Trust. Doctoral Dissertation. University of Central Florida, Orlando (2013)
3. Hancock, P.A., Billings, D.R., Schaefer, K.E., Chen, J.Y.C., de Visser, E.J., Parasuraman, R.: A meta-analysis of factors affecting trust in human-robot interaction. Hum. Factors **53**(5), 517–527 (2011)
4. Freedy, A., DeVisser, E., Weltman, G., Coeyman, N.: Measurement of trust in human-robot collaboration. In: Proceedings of the 2007 International Symposium on Collaborative Technologies and Systems, pp. 106–114. IEEE, Orlando (2007)
5. Schaefer, K.E., Sanders, T.L., Yordon, R.E., Billings, D.R., Hancock, P.A.: Classification of robot form: factors predicting perceived trustworthiness. In: Proceedings of the 56th Human Factors and Ergonomics Society Annual Meeting, pp. 1548–1552. Sage, Boston (2012)
6. Lewis, J.D., Weigert, A.: Trust as a social reality. Soc. Forces **63**(4), 967–985 (1985)
7. Rempel, J.K., Holmes, J.G., Zanna, M.P.: Trust in close relationships. J. Pers. Soc. Psychol. **49**(1), 95 (1985)
8. McAllister, D.J.: Affect- and cognition-based trust as foundations for interpersonal cooperation in organizations. Acad. Manage. J. **38**(1), 24–59 (1995)
9. Johnson, D., Grayson, K.: Cognitive and affective trust in service relationships. J. Bus. Res. **58**(4), 500–507 (2005)
10. Softbank Robotics. http://www.softbankrobotics.com/emea/en/robots/nao. Accessed 29 July 2018
11. Aldebaran Documentation Webpage. http://doc.aldebaran.com/2-4/dev/community_software.html. Accessed 29 July 2018
12. Dougherty, E.G., Scharfe, H.: Initial formation of trust: designing an interaction with Geminoid-DK to promote a positive attitude for cooperation. In: Mutlu, B., Bartneck, C., Ham, J., Evers, V., Kanda, T. (eds.) ICSR 2011. LNCS (LNAI), vol. 7072, pp. 95–103. Springer, Heidelberg (2011). https://doi.org/10.1007/978-3-642-25504-5_10
13. Ninomiya, T., Fujita, A., Suzuki, D., Umemuro, H.: Development of the multidimensional robot attitude scale: constructs of people's attitudes towards domestic robots. In: Tapus, A., André, E., Martin, J.C., Ferland, F., Ammi, M. (eds.) Social Robotics. LNCS (LNAI), vol. 9388, pp. 482–491. Springer, Cham (2015). https://doi.org/10.1007/978-3-319-25554-5_48

Smiles of Children with ASD May Facilitate Helping Behaviors to the Robot

SunKyoung Kim[1], Masakazu Hirokawa[1], Soichiro Matsuda[1],
Atsushi Funahashi[2], and Kenji Suzuki[1(✉)]

[1] Artificial Intelligence Laboratory, University of Tsukuba,
1-1-1 Tennodai, Tsukuba, Ibaraki 305-8573, Japan
{kim,matsuda}@ai.iit.tsukuba.ac.jp, {hirokawa_m,kenji}@ieee.org
[2] Nippon Sport Science University,
1221-1 Kamoshida, Aoba, Yokohama, Kanagawa 227-0033, Japan
funahashi@nittai.ac.jp

Abstract. Helping behaviors are one of the important prosocial behaviors in order to develop social communication skills based on empathy. In this study, we examined the potentials of using a robot as a recipient of help, and helping behaviors to a robot. Also, we explored the relationships between helping behaviors and smiles that is an indicator of a positive mood. The results of this study showed that there might be a positive correlation between the amount of helping behaviors and the number of smiles. It implies that smiles may facilitate helping behaviors to the robot. This preliminary research indicates the potentials of robot-assisted interventions to facilitate and increase helping behaviors of children with Autism Spectrum Disorder (ASD).

Keywords: Smile · Helping behavior · Autism Spectrum Disorder
Robot-assisted intervention · NAO

1 Introduction

Robots can perform various roles in a social context [1]. The potentials of using robots for psychological and clinical interventions have been reported [2,3]. An application of robots is for children who have difficulties in communicating with other people [4,5]. Deficits in social communication skills are one of the diagnostic criteria for Autism Spectrum Disorder (ASD), which is a neurodevelopmental disorder [6]. It is difficult for children with ASD to use verbal and nonverbal communication appropriate to diverse social situations. The effects of interventions using robots for children with ASD have been investigated to facilitate social communication behaviors, such as joint attention, imitation, and verbal responsiveness [7–9].

Helping behaviors are one type of prosocial behaviors, which involve verbal and nonverbal communication. Prosocial behaviors occur in a social situation where at least two persons can interact with each other as a helper and a recipient of help. A helper can give emotional, informative, material, or action-based

© Springer Nature Switzerland AG 2018
S. S. Ge et al. (Eds.): ICSR 2018, LNAI 11357, pp. 55–64, 2018.
https://doi.org/10.1007/978-3-030-05204-1_6

support to a recipient [10,11]. Helping behaviors are an act of help to achieve the others' goals. When a person drops a pen, a helper can provide help by picking it up and giving it to the person. This instrumental behavior can be manifested from around two years of age before showing prosocial behaviors based on empathy. Research findings imply that instrumental helping behaviors are the starting point to develop prosocial behaviors [12,13].

Helping behaviors can be increased by positive moods [14]. Various environmental factors, such as music, fragrance, and weather, have been used to find a relationship between moods and helping behaviors [15,16]. Research results show that a changed mood can influence helping behaviors. Social communication behaviors can also affect moods and helping behaviors. When a recipient of help smiled or used expressive voice, the probability of receiving help was increased [17,18]. It can be explained by the feel-good, do-good phenomenon, which indicates people tend to be helpful when in a positive mood [19].

It is considered that smiles can be an indicator as well as an inducer of positive mood. The frequency and intensity of smiles have been used to measure happiness or enjoyment [20,21]. In particular, contractions of specific facial muscles, which are zygomaticus major and orbicularis oculi, were observed when people are in a good mood. These facial expressions accompanies changes around the eyes and lips [22]. A correlation among smile, mood, and helping behavior was found in previous research. The results show that positive moods induced by smiles increased the willingness to help, and smiles of recipients elicited smiles of helpers [17,23].

The development of rudimentary helping behaviors is important for all children in that it can be the basis of the higher level of empathic prosocial behaviors. Previous research results, which show moods can influence empathy, indicate that there might be positive correlations between moods and overall prosocial behaviors [24]. Recent research investigating relationships between positive moods and helping behaviors of children, particularly children with ASD, focused on interactions with an animal. The research results suggest that dogs can increase smiles and positive social behaviors including helping behaviors of children with ASD [25–27].

However, there are few research that examined the effects of interventions using robots on smiles and helping behaviors. In this study, we propose that robot-assisted interventions can facilitate the helping behaviors of children with ASD, when considering that robots can be applied in various social contexts. Robot-assisted therapy is using robots to assist the process of an intervention. Robots' capable interventions and roles between a therapist and a child have been discussed by researchers and professionals. Robots might be applied for various therapy objectives, such as increasing social skills, self-care skills, or motor skills. Robots might be a peer as well as a trainer of children with ASD [2,3,5].

In this research, we focused on the robot's role as a recipient of help in a social situation where helping behaviors can occur. This social situation is created by a therapist for interventions. We used a robot control method by combining a robot teleoperation method and a wearable device to detect affective cues [28].

This allows the operator to improvise the robot's behavior in real-time and in a flexible manner. Through this study, we explore the potentials of using a robot to facilitate helping behaviors of children with ASD, and explore the relationships between smiles and helping behaviors.

2   Exploratory Study

The purpose of this preliminary study is to investigate the potentials of robot-assisted interventions to facilitate helping behaviors. We designed an experiment using specific behaviors of a robot in four session stages. Particularly, stage 2 (play) and stage 3 (helping behavior) were designed to explore the relationships between smiles and helping behaviors. In this study, we considered smiles as an indicator of positive moods before helping behaviors to a robot were shown, and investigated the number of smiles and the duration of helping behaviors.

2.1   Participants

We recruited 17 children with ASD and 14 typically developing (TD) children. The data from 4 children with ASD and 2 typically developing children (around 10-years-old six boys) for this exploratory study were used. A father or a mother accompanied his or her child with ASD during the whole interventions. Although the children with ASD showed a lack of facial expressions compared to TD children, they were able to show smiles during interactions with a robot. We obtained informed consents from all parents of the children, and approval by the Ethical Committee based on the ethical rules established by the Institute of Developmental Research, Aichi Human Service Center.

2.2   Robot

NAO was adopted for this study. NAO is a humanoid robot designed by Aldebaran Robotics. NAO has been used for research on education, rehabilitation, and therapy. These research fields require interactions with humans. The robot's joints, which include head, hip, ankle, shoulder, elbow, wrist, knee, and finger joints, can express various motions, such as walking, grasping small objects, and playing games using hands. These characteristics of NAO can enable it to interact with humans by expressing nonverbal communication behaviors.

The appearance and behaviors of NAO can make the friendly atmosphere for children. The doll-like size (58 cm in height), round eyes, and a small mouth look like a child. Also, the robot can communicate with children by making various movements, and at the same time, joints and flat feet are not flexible and agile, which can make children feel the robot as a younger sister or brother. In this regard, NAO has a potential to facilitate helping behaviors of children. NAO can be applied in a helping situation as a recipient of help from children. In particular, simple and less sophisticated behaviors of NAO can help children with ASD feel familiar and understand a social situation.

Another advantage of using NAO for interventions is that it has cameras and sensors, such as touch, gyro, 3D sensors, on head, chest, hands, and legs. NAO can capture behaviors of children by using these cameras and sensors, which can help therapists analyze each session and plan the next interventions.

2.3 Procedure

At least two sessions consisting of the planned session stages were carried out for each child every two to three weeks. Each session lasted for 20–30 min. Children were allowed to move around, talk to a therapist, their mother, or father, and interact with NAO unconstrainedly during all sessions. The process of a session is as follows (Table 1).

Table 1. Session stage and behaviors of NAO in each stage

Session stage	Behaviors of NAO
Stage 1: Greetings	standing up, turning head, moving arms
Stage 2: Play	rock-paper-scissors game, playing with small bean bags
Stage 3: Helping behavior	standing up, reaching out arms, turning head, walking
Stage 4: Farewell	turning head, waving a hand

In a session, first, each child was introduced to a room for interventions. Before starting interactions with a child, NAO remained still with a slight stoop. When a child was near, NAO greeted by standing up, turning head (looking around), and moving arms.

In stage 2, children played with NAO while playing rock-paper-scissors games or playing with small beanbags.

In stage 3, the therapist created a social situation where NAO can receive help to walk, and facilitated children to do helping behaviors. When NAO showed help-seeking behaviors, which include standing up, reaching out arms, and turning head (looking around), the therapist said: "Let's go for a walk." "You can walk, robot," "Now, the robot can walk well," "Thank you." A father or a mother of each child with ASD watched his or her child's interactions with NAO and played a role as a model of behaviors when the child had difficulties showing helping behaviors (see Fig. 1).

In stage 4, NAO turned its head (nodding) and waved farewell to a child before finishing the session.

The behaviors of NAO were controlled by the Wizard of OZ method. A human operator observed interactions between each child and NAO and made more interactive behaviors, which can increase positive moods, depending on a child's responses.

All sessions were video-recorded using four ceiling cameras and an RGB camera on NAO's forehead.

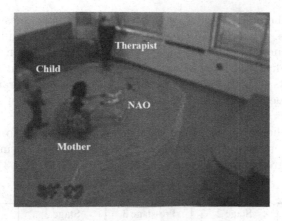

Fig. 1. An activity and participants in a session for a child with ASD

2.4   Behavior Analysis

We analyzed two video files for each session. One is a video taken from a camera on NAO's head. Another video file was taken from the cameras installed on the ceiling of the intervention room (Fig. 2). Video-recorded behaviors of each child during two sessions were examined.

Fig. 2. Two types of video used for analysis (Left figure shows images from cameras installed on the ceiling, and right figure shows an image from a camera on NAO's head)

To analyze behaviors related to helping behaviors and smiles, we identified the starting points and ending points of help-seeking behaviors (standing up to walk, reaching out arms, turning head) from NAO and helping behaviors of each child. Standing up to help NAO, holding NAO's hands, and making NAO stand up were counted as helping behaviors. Making NAO stand up was observed when NAO swayed or fell down, which are uncontrolled by the operator of NAO. When a child showed a helping behavior, we identified the time as the starting point of helping behaviors. When a child released his hold on NAO's hands, we identified the time as the ending point of helping behaviors. The duration of help-seeking behaviors was calculated by the sum of the difference between starting points and ending points of help-seeking behaviors. Likewise, the duration of helping behaviors was calculated by the sum of the difference between starting points and ending points of helping behaviors.

Smiles were checked by counting changes of lips or eyes. To investigate the effects of positive moods on helping behaviors, the number of smiles was examined in stage 1 (greetings, 60 s) and the pre-stage 3 (60 s) (Fig. 3).

Stage 1	Stage 2	Pre-stage 3	Stage 3	Stage 4
Analyzed smiles (60 sec)		Analyzed smiles (60 sec)	Analyzed helping behaviors (~ 653 sec)	

Fig. 3. Analyzed stages

3   Results

In the first session (session 1 of both children with ASD and TD children), the number of smiles of children with ASD was lower than that of TD children ($M = 4.75$, $SD = 4.27$; $M = 17.50$, $SD = 4.95$). The proportion (%) of helping behaviors while NAO needs the help of children with ASD was lower than that of TD children ($M = 26.32$, $SD = 23.23$; $M = 98.92$, $SD = 0.01$).

In the second session (session 3 of children with ASD, and session 2 of TD children), the number of smiles of children with ASD was lower than that of TD children ($M = 4.25$, $SD = 3.40$; $M = 21.5$, $SD = 7.78$). The proportion (%) of helping behaviors while NAO needs the help of children with ASD was lower than that of a TD children ($M = 22.25$, $SD = 17.73$; $M = 99.02$, $SD = 0.01$).

When compared to the first session, TD children showed an increase in the number of smiles and an increase in the duration of helping behaviors. Although the number of smiles and the duration of helping behaviors of children with ASD decreased on average, each child showed different changes. Two children with ASD (ASD-p2 and ASD-p3) showed a higher number of smiles during the second session than during the first session ($M = 6.50$, $SD = 4.24$; $M = 3.00$, $SD = 3.54$). The children with ASD also showed a higher proportion of helping behaviors ($M = 27.25$, $SD = 0.06$; $M = 9.21$, $SD = 0.08$). Other two children with ASD (ASD-p1 and ASD-p4) showed a lower number of smiles during the second session than during the first session ($M = 2.00$, $SD = 1.41$; $M = 6.50$, $SD = 4.95$).

The two children with ASD also showed a lower proportion of helping behaviors ($M = 9.68$, $SD = 0.13$; $M = 43.43$, $SD = 0.19$). Figure 4 shows the number of smiles against the proportion (%) of helping behaviors for each participant. Empty symbols denote the first session and filled symbols denote the second session. ASD-p* denote children with ASD. TD-p* denote typically developing children. These results imply the possibility of a positive correlation between smiles and helping behaviors.

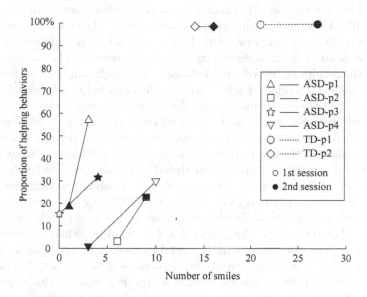

Fig. 4. An X-Y graph showing the number of smiles against the proportion of helping behaviors for each participant

4   Discussion

We performed an exploratory study to investigate the potentials of robot-assisted interventions for children with ASD in a situation where there are opportunities for showing helping behaviors. We focused on facilitating helping behaviors of the participants, when the robot needs help to walk. In stage 3 of the sessions for facilitating helping behaviors, the therapist created a social context with NAO by setting the robot as a younger brother who asks for help to walk, and a mother or a father played a role as a model of helping behaviors. Identified helping behaviors in this study were standing up to help the robot, holding the robot's hands, and making the robot stand up. Two TD children responded immediately to the robot's help-seeking behaviors, and continued to show helping behaviors during the stage 3 of a session. Four children with ASD, on the other hand, took more time to start the helping behaviors, and frequently released their hold on the robot's hands. Children with ASD also showed fewer helping behaviors than TD children. However, all participants showed helping behaviors to the robot in the social setting. It implies that the robot can be used as a recipient of help.

We also explored the relationships between smiles and helping behaviors. Previous research results suggest the possibility that facial expressions and helping behaviors, which are nonverbal communication behaviors, can be found in sequence. To explore if this chain of behaviors can be found from both children with ASD and TD children, we counted the number of smiles in stage 1 and the pre-stage 3 in each session. TD children showed a higher number of smiles than children with ASD, and in the second session, they showed increased smiles and increased helping behaviors. On the other hand, two children with ASD showed decreased smiles and decreased helping behaviors in the second session. Although their helping behaviors decreased, this result implies the possibility that there might be a relationship between smiles and helping behaviors. When looking into the behavioral changes and the number of smiles, two children with ASD showed increased smiles and increased helping behaviors, and two other children with ASD showed decreased smiles and decreased helping behaviors in the second session. It indicates that smiles may facilitate helping behaviors.

In this preliminary research, we analyzed the video-recorded behaviors of the participants. Videos from ceiling cameras were analyzed to examine helping behaviors, and videos from an RGB camera on NAO were analyzed to examine smiles. There is a disadvantage that cameras cannot completely capture the participants' behaviors depending on angles. For example, when the robot turns head, the robot camera cannot capture a child's face. A behavior analysis using technologies will be necessary to obtain a more accurate result. We obtained electromyography (EMG) data by using a wearable device in this experiment. Further studies will include using an EMG-based face detection system and a movement detection system, thus helping behaviors can be analyzed more accurately [29].

This research has the significance of investigating a possible chain of behaviors, and the potentials of using the robot to facilitate helping behaviors of children with ASD. Helping behaviors are the starting point of empathic prosocial behaviors. In this respect, it is important to facilitate helping behaviors of all children. The results of this research imply that it might be possible to facilitate helping behaviors of children with ASD by increasing smiles using a robot.

5   Conclusion and Future Work

In this research, we proposed the potentials of robot-assisted interventions to facilitate helping behaviors of children with ASD. Both children with ASD and TD children showed helping behaviors to the robot. This result indicates that robots can be applied to facilitate helping behaviors of children with ASD. We can increase their opportunities to help others by setting a social situation with robots.

Also, we investigated the relationships among these helping behaviors and increase/decrease of smiles. Depending on the number of smiles before doing helping behaviors, the duration of helping behaviors was changed. When smiles are increased by the interactions with a robot, helping behaviors might be facilitated. This tendency implies the possibility of a chain of behaviors, which are smiles and helping behaviors. If we can increase the chain of behaviors by using robots, it can be of help for children with ASD to develop the foundation of a higher level of prosocial behaviors based on empathy.

In future research, we plan to analyze more data including EMG and videos over several sessions with children. Robots could be used for robot-assisted interventions in various helping situations as a helper or a recipient of help. We plan to investigate the relationships between smiles and helping behaviors in various directions.

References

1. Broadbent, E.: Interactions with robots: the truths we reveal about ourselves. Annu. Rev. Psychol. **68**(1), 627–652 (2017)
2. Huijnen, C.A.G.J., Lexis, M.A.S., Jansens, R., de Witte, L.: How to implement robots in interventions for children with autism? A co-creation study involving people with autism, parents and professionals. J. Autism Dev. Disord. **47**(10), 3079–3096 (2017)
3. Diehl, J.J., Schmitt, L.M., Villano, M., Crowell, C.R.: The clinical use of robots for individuals with Autism Spectrum Disorders: a critical review. Res. Autism Spectrum Disord. **6**(1), 249–262 (2012)
4. Ismail, L.I., Shamsudin, S., Yussof, H., Akhtar, F., Hanapiah, F.A., Zaharid, N.I.: Robot-based intervention program for autistic children with humanoid robot NAO: initial response in stereotyped behavior. Procedia Eng. **41**, 1441–1447 (2012)
5. Bharatharaj, J., Huang, L., Mohan, R.E., Al-Jumaily, A., Krägeloh, C.: Robot-assisted therapy for learning and social interaction of children with Autism Spectrum Disorder. Robotics **6**(1), 1–11 (2017)
6. American Psychiatric Association: Diagnostic and Statistical Manual of Mental Disorders (DSM-5), 5th edn. American Psychiatric Publishing, Arlington (2013)
7. Warren, Z.E., et al.: Can robotic interaction improve joint attention skills? J. Autism Dev. Disord. **45**(11), 3726–3734 (2015)
8. Zheng, Z., Young, E.M., Swanson, A.R., Weitlauf, A.S., Warren, Z.E., Sarkar, N.: Robot-mediated imitation skill training for children with autism. IEEE Trans. Neural Syst. Rehabil. Eng. **24**(6), 682–691 (2015)
9. Srinivasan, S.M., Eigst, I.-M., Gifford, T., Bhat, A.N.: The effects of embodied rhythm and robotic interventions on the spontaneous and responsive verbal communication skills of children with Autism Spectrum Disorder (ASD): a further outcome of a pilot randomized controlled trial. Res. Autism Spectrum Disord. **27**, 54–72 (2016)
10. Warneken, F., Tomasello, M.: The roots of human altruism. Br. J. Psychol. **100**(3), 455–471 (2009)
11. Bierhoff, H.W.: Altruism and patterns of social interaction. In: Staub, E., Bar-Tal, D., Karylowski, J., Reykowski, J. (eds.) Development and Maintenance of Prosocial Behavior, Critical Issues in Social Justice, vol. 31, pp. 309–321. Springer, Boston (1984). https://doi.org/10.1007/978-1-4613-2645-8_18
12. Svetlova, M., Nichols, S.R., Brownell, C.A.: Toddlers' prosocial behavior: from instrumental to empathic to altruistic helping. Child Dev. **81**(6), 1814–1827 (2010)

13. Warneken, F., Tomasello, M.: Varieties of altruism in children and chimpanzees. Trends Cogn. Sci. **13**(9), 397–402 (2009)
14. Carlson, M., Charlin, V., Miller, N.: Positive mood and helping behavior: a test of six hypotheses. J. Pers. Soc. Psychol. **55**(2), 211–229 (1988)
15. Baron, R.: The sweet smell of... helping: effects of pleasant ambient fragrance on prosocial behavior in shopping malls. Pers. Soc. Psychol. Bull. **23**(5), 498–503 (1997)
16. Cunningham, M.: Weather, mood, and helping behavior: quasi experiments with the sunshine samaritan. J. Pers. Soc. Psychol. **37**(11), 1947–1956 (1979)
17. Guéguen, N., de Gail, M.: The effect of smiling on helping behavior: smiling and good Samaritan behavior. Commun. Rep. **16**(2), 133–140 (2003)
18. Goldman, M., Fordyce, J.: Prosocial behavior as affected by eye contact, touch, and voice expression. J. Soc. Psychol. **121**(1), 125–129 (1983)
19. Salovey, P., Mayer, J.D.: Emotional intelligence. Imagination, Cogn. Pers. **9**, 185–211 (1990)
20. Messinger, D.S., Cassel, T.D., Acosta, S.I.: Infant smiling dynamics and perceived positive emotion. J. Nonverbal Behav. **32**(3), 133–155 (2008)
21. Frank, M.G., Ekman, P., Friesen, W.V.: Behavioral markers and the recognizability of the smile of enjoyment. J. Pers. Soc. Psychol. **64**(1), 83–93 (1993)
22. Ekman, P., Davidson, R.J., Friesen, W.V.: The Duchenne smile: emotional expression and brain physiology II. J. Pers. Soc. Psychol. **58**(2), 342–353 (1990)
23. Vrugt, A., Vet, C.: Effects of a smile on mood and helping behavior. Soc. Behav. Pers.: Int. J. **37**(9), 1251–1258 (2009)
24. Li, X., Meng, X., Li, H., Yang, J., Yuan, J.: The impact of mood on empathy for pain: evidence from an EEG study. Psychophysiology **54**(9), 1311–1322 (2017)
25. Funahashi, A., Gruebler, A., Aoki, T., Kadone, H., Suzuki, K.: Brief report: the smiles of a child with Autism Spectrum Disorder during an animal-assisted activity may facilitate social positive behaviors - quantitative analysis with smile-detecting interface. J. Autism Dev. Disord. **44**(3), 685–693 (2014)
26. O'Haire, M.E., McKenzie, S.J., Beck, A.M., Slaughter, V.: Social behaviors increase in children with autism in the presence of animals compared to toys. PLoS ONE **8**(2), e57010 (2013)
27. Grandgeorge, M., Tordjman, S., Lazartigues, A., Lemonnier, E., Deleau, M., Hausberger, M.: Does pet arrival trigger prosocial behaviors in individuals with autism? PLoS ONE **7**(8), e41739 (2012)
28. Hirokawa, M., Funahashi, A., Itoh, Y., Suzuki, K.: Adaptive behavior acquisition of a robot based on affective feedback and improvised teleoperation. IEEE Trans. Cogn. Dev. Syst. **54**(9) (in press)
29. Gruebler, A., Suzuki, K.: Design of a wearable device for reading positive expressions from facial EMG signals. IEEE Trans. Affect. Comput. **5**(3), 227–237 (2014)

If Drones Could See: Investigating Evaluations of a Drone with Eyes

Peter A. M. Ruijten[✉] and Raymond H. Cuijpers

Eindhoven University of Technology, Eindhoven, The Netherlands
{p.a.m.ruijten,r.h.cuijpers}@tue.nl

Abstract. Drones are often used in a context where they interact with human users. They, however, lack the social cues that their robotic counterparts have. If drones would possess such cues, would people respond to them more positively? This paper investigates people's evaluations of a drone with eyes versus one without. Results show mainly positive effects, i.e. a drone with eyes is seen as more social and human-like than a drone without eyes, and that people are more willing to interact with it. These findings imply that adding eyes to a drone that is designed to interact with humans may make this interaction more natural, and as such enable a successful introduction of social drones.

Keywords: Social drones · Attitudes · Godspeed · RoSAS

1 Introduction

Most of the work in social robotics investigates interactions between robots and humans in a large variety of contexts, showing that robots need to be designed such that their appearance matches their behavioural capabilities [5,14]. For a social robot this entails that certain social cues or elements should be included in their design to make them perceived as more or less human-like. Ultimately this could contribute to a future in which humans and robots have frequent encounters.

Social robots are not widely introduced on the commercial market yet, although their availability increases rapidly. For example, robots like Pepper™, Buddy™ and Jibo™show increasing sales numbers. What these robots have in common is that they are equipped with elements that represent human form or behaviour. In other words, most social robots have humanoid forms and can move by walking or driving.

Fairly recently, a different type of robot was introduced to the market: drones. A drone is defined as "an unmanned aircraft or ship guided by remote control or onboard computers" [18]. It does not have human shape or form, nor is it (deliberately) equipped with social cues. Drones are used in a wide variety of applications like site inspection, surveillance tasks and package delivery. Since drones are cheap and versatile, the number of applications is growing including

© Springer Nature Switzerland AG 2018
S. S. Ge et al. (Eds.): ICSR 2018, LNAI 11357, pp. 65–74, 2018.
https://doi.org/10.1007/978-3-030-05204-1_7

applications that involve close interactions with people. As drones will be frequently used in a context where they need to interact with people, it is important to understand how their design influences people's evaluations of and responses to them.

It would seem natural to transfer knowledge of the use of social cues from (humanoid) social robots to drones. However, several key differences exist between the appearance and behaviour of drones versus that of social robots. Whereas social robots are bound to the ground plane, drones can fly in three dimensions. Additionally, social robots usually have human-like elements in their design such as arms, legs, or heads (sometimes even with faces). Due to this human-like resemblance, social robots tend to be reasonably well accepted for having social interactions with humans [10,12,13]. Drones on the other hand have more resemblance to insects, due to the noise from the propellers and their hoovering behaviour. If drones were to have more social interactions with humans, their design also may need to change.

1.1 Design of Social Drones

The design of social robots is often inspired by human-like appearance and behaviour, because resemblance with humans is found to improve human-robot interaction [13,14]. We assume that the same holds for interactions with drones, which is why it is important to look at the key aspects of human interactions. We classify these key aspects as speech and turn-taking, gestures and other physical non-verbal behaviours, and eye contact.

Speech is argued to be the most prevalent cue of human-ness [19]. Indeed, verbal interactions are a crucial aspect of human life, and coordination of turns regulates who speaks when [23]. Recent work on turn-taking behavior in humans shows that people are able to predict both the content and timing of the coming turn, and thereby can do this faster than automatic language encoders [17]. In human-robot interaction, this ability is lacking, and thus a properly timed special cue is needed to improve people's performance in a turn-taking conversation [22]. Since most drones do not have a speech module on board, we will not focus on speech.

Gestures are a key aspect of human communication [16], which is likely one of the reasons why they are an important element of social learning in robots [4]. Hand and arm gestures have been shown to improve the efficiency of human-robot communication [24]. These results are in line with [20] who argued that a minimal social cue can already evoke social responses. While the behaviour of social robots is often designed to imitate human motion, this is hard to achieve with drones. However, earlier work in this domain does show that the flying behavior of drones can make people perceive different emotions [7] or navigational intentions [8].

Eye contact plays a role in human-human interactions, because gaze and eye contact enable humans to provide information and regulate interactions [15]. In addition, gaze direction is related to the emotion that is experienced, with people showing direct gaze when they are seeking friendship and averted gaze as a sign of anxiety [15]. When applied to social robots, this means that people easily attribute emotional states to robots when they are equipped with eyes [12]. This would suggest that adding eyes to a social drone would lead to changes in people's attitudes towards the drone.

1.2   Research Aims

The aim of the current study was to investigate how adding eyes to a drone changes people's attitudes towards drones. We expected the addition of eyes to have a positive effect on these evaluations. This was tested by letting people evaluate a drone with or without eyes in an online survey, using two scales to assess people's attitude towards robots [2,6]. Since movement may be an important factor, we presented the drone both as an image and as a video.

2   Method

2.1   Participants and Design

One hundred and twenty two participants, 60 males and 62 females ($M_{age} = 22.6$, $SD_{age} = 3.1$, Range $-$ 18 to 33), participated in this study with a 2(type of drone: with vs. without eyes) $\times$ 2(type of stimulus: image vs. video) mixed design. Type of drone was manipulated between-subjects, with participants watching either a drone with eyes ($n = 64$) or without eyes ($n = 58$). Type of stimulus was manipulated within-subjects, with all participants watching both an image and a video of the drone. Most participants had seen or used a drone before, and 6 of them owned a drone.

2.2   Materials and Procedure

Participants performed the study online. On the welcome page, they were provided information about the procedure of the study and gave informed consent. Next, several questions were asked about their previous experiences with and expectations of social robots and drones.

Depending on the experimental condition they were in, participants were shown an image of the drone without or with eyes (see Fig. 1). Participants then completed a questionnaire about their attitudes towards the drone, consisting of the Godspeed scale [2], the Robotic Social Attributes Scale [6] and their Willingness to interact with the drone.

The Godspeed scale consisted of five sub-scales that measured Animacy (5 items, $\alpha = 0.88$), Aanthropomorphism (5 items, $\alpha = 0.87$), Likeability (5 items, $\alpha = 0.94$), Perceived Intelligence (5 items, $\alpha = 0.91$), and Perceived Safety (3 items, $\alpha = 0.28$). All items were measured on 5-point semantic differentials. Due to its unreliable Cronbach's alpha, Perceived Safety was not included in any further analyses.

The Robotic Social Attributes Scale (RoSAS) consisted of three sub-scales that measured Competence (6 items, $\alpha = 0.88$), Warmth (6 items, $\alpha = 0.93$),

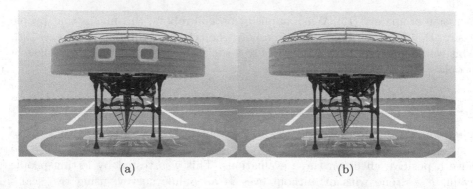

Fig. 1. Pictures used in the study of the drone (a) with and (b) without eyes.

and Discomfort (6 items, $\alpha = 0.88$). All items were measured on 9-point scales ranging from 'not applicable' to 'applicable'. Because of its negative direction, averages on the Discomfort sub-scale are reversed to make comparisons between the sub-scales easier.

Willingness to interact was measured by asking participants to what extent they would like the drone to give them a drink, to have a conversation with the drone, to play a game with the drone, to see the drone more often, and whether they would be annoyed by the drone if it were in their house ($\alpha = 0.79$). Items were measured on a 7-point scale ranging from 'do not agree' to 'totally agree'.

After completing the scales, participants were shown a video of the drone bringing a cup to a table, and completed the same scales again. Consistent with the notion that social robots can be perceived as having different roles [11], participants were asked to what extent they thought a drone could be of practical help or a social buddy (both on 0–100 scales). Finally, participants indicated their previous experience with drones, and they finished with answering demographic questions. The study took approximately 10–15 min to complete. A lottery was performed in which one out of ten participants was selected to receive a €30 reward.

3   Results

In this section, average scores on people's attitudes towards the drone are presented, and the effects of adding eyes to a drone on these attitudes are tested. Table 1 shows the means and standard deviations on all sub-scales for all groups. When these averages are visualized in Fig. 2, it becomes clear that the drone with eyes scored higher than the one without eyes on almost all sub-scales, and the video of the drone scored higher than the image of the drone on almost all sub-scales. The evaluations of the image and the video of the drone with eyes seem to be very similar, whereas evaluations of the drone without eyes seem to differ between the image and the video. That is, the video of the drone without eyes

Table 1. Mean values and standard deviations for all sub-scales per type of drone and type of stimulus.

Sub-scale	No eyes		Eyes	
	Image	Video	Image	Video
	M (SD)	M (SD)	M (SD)	M (SD)
Animacy	2.43 (0.81)	2.72 (0.97)	2.98 (0.75)	3.09 (0.75)
Anthropomorphism	2.13 (0.84)	2.48 (0.94)	2.63 (0.81)	2.86 (0.85)
Likeability	2.99 (0.88)	3.49 (0.90)	3.72 (0.70)	3.83 (0.72)
Perceived Intelligence	3.35 (0.75)	3.40 (0.87)	3.58 (0.75)	3.58 (0.79)
Competence	5.55 (1.20)	5.67 (1.42)	5.96 (1.26)	6.06 (1.30)
Warmth	2.85 (1.47)	3.68 (1.78)	4.77 (1.54)	4.77 (1.45)
Discomfort	4.87 (1.52)	5.57 (1.17)	5.07 (1.64)	5.66 (1.27)
Willingness	4.36 (1.20)	4.56 (1.31)	4.88 (1.07)	5.02 (1.13)

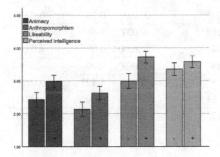

(a) Godspeed: image of the drone

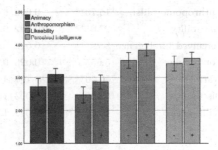

(b) Godspeed: video of the drone

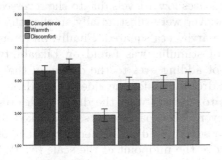

(c) RoSAS: image of the drone

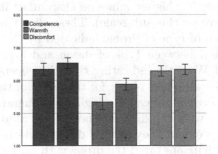

(d) RoSAS: video of the drone

Fig. 2. Average evaluations on the Godspeed and RoSAS measures for the image and the video of the drone with (+) and the one without (-) eyes. Error bars represent 95% confidence intervals.

appears to be evaluated higher on Animacy, Anthropomorphism, and Likeability compared to the image of that same drone.

In order to test these effects, data on all sub-scales were submitted to a multivariate ANOVA with the type of drone and the type of stimulus as independent variables. Table 2 shows an overview of the results. As can be seen in this table, the type of drone significantly influences scores on all sub-scales except Discomfort. The strongest effects were found on the concepts Animacy, Anthropomorphism, Likeability, Warmth, and Willingness to interact. The biggest effects of type of drone were found on Warmth and Likeability, two sub-scales that seem to consist mainly of social and affective traits.

Table 2. Effects and effect sizes per type of drone, type of stimulus, and interaction between type of drone and type of stimulus. Stars indicate the significance level, with * for <0.05, ** for <0.01, and *** for <0.001.

Concept	$F_{\text{type of drone}}$	η_p^2	$F_{\text{type of stimulus}}$	η_p^2	$F_{\text{interaction}}$	η_p^2
Animacy	19.25***	0.075	3.49	0.014	0.81	0.003
Anthropomorphism	15.70***	0.062	6.89**	0.028	0.26	0.001
Likeability	27.01***	0.102	9.10**	0.037	3.58*	0.015
Perceived Intelligence	3.79*	0.016	0.07	<0.001	0.07	<0.001
Competence	5.65*	0.023	0.44	0.002	0.00	<0.001
Warmth	56.56***	0.191	4.28*	0.018	4.42*	0.018
Discomfort	0.65	0.003	12.71***	0.050	0.09	<0.001
Willingness	10.50***	0.042	1.27	0.005	0.05	<0.001

Interestingly, the type of stimulus appeared to have an effect on Anthropomorphism, Likeability, Warmth, and Discomfort, indicating that the drone in the video was evaluated as more human-like, likeable, emotional and comfortable (note that higher values on Discomfort indicates lower levels due to the reversed scores on this sub-scale). These effects however were substantially smaller than those of type of drone, indicated by their partial eta squared. Finally, an interaction between type of drone and type of stimulus was found on Likeability and Warmth, indicating that the effects of adding eyes to the drone on these sub-scales were bigger for the image of the drone than for the video of the drone.

People indicated a higher Willingness to interact with the drone with eyes than with the drone without eyes. Moreover, when participants were asked to what extent they think a drone could be a social buddy, a higher percentage of participants rated the drone with eyes above the midpoint of the scale (57.1%) than the drone without eyes (45.6%). Interestingly, the distribution of the extent to which people rated the drone to be a social buddy seemed to show two separate groups. As can be seen in Fig. 3a, about half of the participants rated the drone below the midpoint of the 'social-buddy' scale, and the other half rated the drone above this midpoint. A Kolmogorov-Smirnov test was used to test for normality (with $D(122) = 0.11$, p <0.001), indicating a significant deviation from normality. This deviation from normality is most likely caused by the dip in the middle of the scale, clearly indicating a difference between two groups.

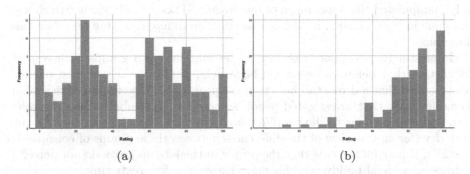

(a)   (b)

Fig. 3. Participants' ratings of the extent to which a drone can be (a) 'a social buddy', and (b) 'of practical help'.

No difference was found on the extent to which a drone was evaluated to be of practical help between the drone with ($M = 81.5$, $SD = 16.4$) and without eyes ($M = 79.8$, $SD = 18.0$), t <1, p >0.5. As can be seen in Fig. 3b, it appears that the number of people with a specific rating increases with higher ratings. As such, no clear division between groups can be made on the extent to which people rate the drone as being of practical help.

4 Discussion

The current study investigated people's evaluations of a drone with or without eyes. Adding eyes to the drone was expected to positively influence their attitudes towards that drone. Results show that the drone with eyes was indeed evaluated more positively on most sub-scales. Additionally, the type of stimulus (image versus video) appeared to have an effect on the socio-emotional sub-scales, although these effects were smaller than those of adding eyes to the drone.

Eyes are an obvious human-like element, so it makes sense that the drone with eyes was perceived as more human-like. The fact that the drone with eyes was perceived as more animated, likeable, and warm, shows that the increased perceived human-likeness relates to other socio-emotional dimensions. It is interesting to note that the design of the eyes was very basic. There was no pupil, the drone was not able to 'see' anything, and still the effects occurred. This strengthens the argument that a simple human-like cue can be sufficient to make people respond to technology as if it were another human being [20], although people's behavioural responses do not necessarily have to match their attitudes [1].

The smallest effects were found on the dimensions Perceived Intelligence, Competence, and Discomfort. Intelligence and Competence measure similar concepts (with items like 'competent' and 'knowledgeable' on both the Godspeed and the RoSAS scale), and the increased human-likeness of the drone apparently does not contribute to having better intellectual skills. Discomfort is more related to the *behaviour* of social robots than their *form* [9,10,12]. Since we only manipulated the appearance of the drone and not its behaviour (which was the same in both videos), it makes sense that no differences were found on this dimension.

Interestingly, participants seemed to be split into two groups with respect to whether they believe a drone can be a social 'buddy', whereas most participants agreed that a drone can be a technological tool. These findings are similar to earlier work that investigated people's perceptions of robots and their roles [11], and it also seems to show a difference between early adopters and the late majority (for an overview of the differences between these groups of consumers, see [21]). It may be the case that the people in the late majority do not perceive a drone as a social buddy yet, this may change in a few years time.

4.1 Limitations and Future Work

This study investigated people's responses to images and short videos of a drone with or without eyes. Based on evaluations of a picture, it is hard to assess to what extent people would really accept such a drone in their immediate surroundings. Even though some work has been done in this domain [7,8], much is still unknown about how people evaluate various social cues of an object that is flying around them. Despite this limitation, this study is to our knowledge one of the first in showing the strength of adding a human-like cue to a drone in terms of people's attributions of human traits.

One of the traits that was measured was Perceived Safety, but this scale showed a surprisingly low internal reliability. One reason for this could be the way in which the question was formulated. For all Godspeed dimensions, participants were asked to rate their impression of the drone on the presented scale, whereas the original version of the scale as presented in [2] asks people to rate *their* emotional state on the Perceived Safety items. Attributing the dimensions of this sub-scale to the drone versus oneself may be of great influence for the results, so care needs to be put into the phrasing of these questions in further studies.

Finally, many participants were familiar with or had been using drones before. This may have also affected their evaluations of the drone, since more experience with a specific type of technology is shown to be related to people's perceptions of that technology [3]. Nevertheless, our results show, despite of this familiarity, that people show a more positive attitude towards a drone that is equipped with eyes than towards the same drone without eyes. Future studies can be designed to investigate effects of combinations of social cues in the appearance and behaviour of drones on people's responses to those drones.

4.2 Conclusion

The current study investigated the extent to which a drone with eyes would be evaluated differently than one without. Results show mainly positive effects, meaning that adding eyes to a drone (especially when it is designed to fulfil a social role) makes people attribute more social traits to it, and at the same time more willing to interact with it. As one of the first studies investigating responses to social drones, we hope this paper contributes to the design of such drones and social robots in general, ultimately leading to a future in which humans and drones interact naturally with one another.

References

1. Ajzen, I., Fishbein, M.: The influence of attitudes on behavior. Handb. Attitudes **173**(221), 31 (2005)
2. Bartneck, C., Kulić, D., Croft, E., Zoghbi, S.: Measurement instruments for the anthropomorphism, animacy, likeability, perceived intelligence, and perceived safety of robots. Int. J. Soc. Robot. **1**(1), 71–81 (2009)
3. Bhattacherjee, A., Premkumar, G.: Understanding changes in belief and attitude toward information technology usage: a theoretical model and longitudinal test. MIS Q. **28**(2), 229–254 (2004)
4. Breazeal, C., Scassellati, B.: Robots that imitate humans. Trends Cogn. Sci. **6**(11), 481–487 (2002)
5. Broadbent, E.: Interactions with robots: the truths we reveal about ourselves. Annu. Rev. Psychol. **68**, 627–652 (2017)
6. Carpinella, C.M., Wyman, A.B., Perez, M.A., Stroessner, S.J.: The robotic social attributes scale (rosas): development and validation. In: Proceedings of the 2017 ACM/IEEE International Conference on Human-Robot Interaction, pp. 254–262. ACM (2017)
7. Cauchard, J.R., Zhai, K.Y., Spadafora, M., Landay, J.A.: Emotion encoding in human-drone interaction. In: 2016 11th ACM/IEEE International Conference on Human-Robot Interaction (HRI), pp. 263–270. IEEE (2016)
8. Colley, A., Virtanen, L., Knierim, P., Häkkilä, J.: Investigating drone motion as pedestrian guidance. In: Proceedings of the 16th International Conference on Mobile and Ubiquitous Multimedia, pp. 143–150. ACM (2017)
9. Cuijpers, R.H., Knops, M.A.M.H.: Motions of robots matter! the social effects of idle and meaningful motions. Social Robotics. LNCS (LNAI), vol. 9388, pp. 174–183. Springer, Cham (2015). https://doi.org/10.1007/978-3-319-25554-5_18
10. Dautenhahn, K.: Socially intelligent robots: dimensions of human-robot interaction. Philos. Trans. Royal Soc. B: Biol. Sci. **362**(1480), 679–704 (2007)
11. Dautenhahn, K., Woods, S., Kaouri, C., Walters, M.L., Koay, K.L., Werry, I.: 2005 IEEE/RSJ International Conference on What is a robot companion-friend, assistant or butler? In: Intelligent Robots and Systems, IROS 2005, pp. 1192–1197. IEEE (2005)
12. Duffy, B.R.: Anthropomorphism and the social robot. Robot. Auton. Syst. **42**(3), 177–190 (2003)
13. Eyssel, F., De Ruiter, L., Kuchenbrandt, D., Bobinger, S., Hegel, F.: 'If you sound like me, you must be more human': on the interplay of robot and user features on human-robot acceptance and anthropomorphism. In: 2012 7th ACM/IEEE International Conference on Human-Robot Interaction (HRI), pp. 125–126. IEEE (2012)
14. Fink, J.: Anthropomorphism and human likeness in the design of robots and human-robot interaction. In: Ge, S.S., Khatib, O., Cabibihan, J.-J., Simmons, R., Williams, M.-A. (eds.) ICSR 2012. LNCS (LNAI), vol. 7621, pp. 199–208. Springer, Heidelberg (2012). https://doi.org/10.1007/978-3-642-34103-8_20

15. Kleinke, C.L.: Gaze and eye contact: a research review. Psychol. Bull. **100**(1), 78–100 (1986)
16. Knapp, M.L., Hall, J.A., Horgan, T.G.: Nonverbal Communication in Human Interaction. Cengage Learning, Boston (2013)
17. Levinson, S.C.: Turn-taking in human communication-origins and implications for language processing. Trends Cogn. Sci. **20**(1), 6–14 (2016)
18. Merriam-Webster Online: Merriam-Webster Online Dictionary (2018). http://www.merriam-webster.com
19. Nass, C., Brave, S.: Wired for Speech: How Voice Activates and Advances the Human-Computer Relationship. MIT Press, Cambridge (2005)
20. Reeves, B., Nass, C.: How People Treat Computers, Television, and New Media Like Real People and Places. CSLI Publications and Cambridge University Press, Stanford and Cambridge (1996)
21. Rogers, E.M.: Diffusion of Innovations. Simon and Schuster, New York (2010)
22. van Schendel, J.A., Cuijpers, R.H.: Turn-yielding cues in robot-human conversation. New Front. Human-Robot Interact. **85** (2015)
23. Stivers, T., et al.: Universals and cultural variation in turn-taking in conversation. Proceed. Nat. Acad. Sci., 10587–10592 (2009)
24. Torta, E., van Heumen, J., Cuijpers, R.H., Juola, J.F.: How can a robot attract the attention of its human partner? a comparative study over different modalities for attracting attention. In: Ge, S.S., Khatib, O., Cabibihan, J.-J., Simmons, R., Williams, M.-A. (eds.) ICSR 2012. LNCS (LNAI), vol. 7621, pp. 288–297. Springer, Heidelberg (2012). https://doi.org/10.1007/978-3-642-34103-8_29

Validation of the Design of a Robot to Study the Thermo-Emotional Expression

Denis Peña$^{(\boxtimes)}$ ⓘ and Fumihide Tanaka$^{(\boxtimes)}$ ⓘ

University of Tsukuba, Tsukuba 305-8573, Japan
penia@ftl.iit.tsukuba.ac.jp,
fumihide.tanaka@gmail.com

Abstract. The thermal sensation can be used by humans to interpret emotions. Hence, a series of questions arise as to whether the robot can express its emotional state through the temperature of its body. Therefore, in this study, we carry out the design process of a robot and its validation as a platform to study the thermo-emotional expression. The designed robot can vary the temperature of its skin between 10–55 °C. In this range, it is possible to perform thermal stimuli already studied that have an emotional interpretation, and also to study new ones where the pain receptors are activated. The robot's shape is designed to look like the body of a creature that is neither human nor animal. In addition, it was designed in such a way that the physical interaction occurs mainly in its head. This is because it was decided to locate the robot's thermal system there. The results of an experiment with a free interaction showed that the main regions to be caressed were the superior, lateral and upper diagonal faces of the cranium. These regions coincide with the location of the robot's thermal system. Therefore, the robot can transmit different thermal stimuli to the human when a physical interaction occurs. Consequently, the designed robot will be appropriate to study the body temperature of the robot as a medium to express its emotional state.

Keywords: Thermal emotional expression · Robot skin temperature · Physical HRI

1 Introduction

Emotional expressions are important for social robots to improve their interaction with humans. Its implementation is inspired by human emotional expression. The emotional expressions conventionally used by robots are facial expressions, body movements, and tone of voice. These three modalities are perceived by the human sense of sight or hearing. However, there are almost no modalities that stimulate the other human senses like the sense of touch. Moreover, taking into account that humans express their emotions through various modalities [1], we believe that a robot with more variety of emotional expressions may improve the naturalness of its interaction. Therefore, we attempt to investigate an unconventional robotic emotional expression: the temperature.

The thermal stimulus is selected for three main reasons. Firstly, it is measured constantly. The human being is sensing all the time thermal stimulus about the

© Springer Nature Switzerland AG 2018
S. S. Ge et al. (Eds.): ICSR 2018, LNAI 11357, pp. 75–85, 2018.
https://doi.org/10.1007/978-3-030-05204-1_8

temperature of his environment, the objects he is touching and even the temperature of his own body. Secondly, the human's body temperature reacts naturally and involuntarily to emotions. For instance, an embarrassed person will feel his emotion reflected in the involuntary increase of the temperature of his face. Even though this change in temperature could be minimal in other emotional states, Nummenmma et al. [2] revealed the human perception about the body sensation associated with different emotions through maps. In each of these maps, it is possible to visualize the activity of body regions that increase or decrease according to an emotional stimulus. Thirdly, humans can give emotional interpretations to thermal sensations [3, 4]. Wilson et al. [3] mapped various thermal stimuli in the circumflex model of emotion. The results provide information on how thermal stimuli can convey to emotions. Thus, humans can use thermal sensation as a medium not only to get information but also to interpret emotions [5].

There are few studies on the effect of temperature during an interaction between a human and a social robot [6, 7]. For instance, Nie et al. [6] suggest that a warmth temperature in a robot's hand increase the human perception of friendship toward a robot; while Park and Lee [7] exposed that different levels of the robot's skin temperature affect the human perception of the robot as a companion. However, as far as previous research is concerned, there is no investigation of how a social robot can use its body temperature to express its emotional state.

As mentioned previously, humans express their emotion states through various modalities. While the change of temperature in the body is an involuntary reaction, facial expressions and body movements can be voluntaries expression [8]. Thus, pseudo-emotions might be expressed by them. That is the case when people control, for instance, their facial expression in order to hide their real feeling. Bearing this in mind, the ultimate aims of this project are: (1) Analyze the change of the robot's body temperature by itself as a medium to express the robot's emotions. Then, with the thermal stimuli that have a strong emotional interpretation, we plant to (2) Analyze the effects of combining thermal stimulus, an unconventional and involuntary emotional expression, with facial expression, traditional and voluntary expression. The combination will be made in two conditions: (a) Both expressing the same emotion; and (b) both expressing different emotions. In the first case, we expect to have a stronger multimodal emotional interpretation. In the second case, we expect to generate a confusing emotional interpretation. For instance, have the feeling that the robot is actually sad, based on the emotional interpretation of its body temperature, even though it has a happy face.

To address these research questions, the main features of a suitable robot should be the capability of varying the temperature of its skin above or below the ambient temperature, as well as the ability to perform facial expressions. Because there is no robot platform that can fulfill these features, the objective of this work is to validate the design process of a robot to adequately investigate the thermo-emotional expression.

2   Anatomical Background

The human body is characterized by a thermoregulation process. This consist of maintaining an almost constant core internal temperature around 37 °C. In addition, human beings can detect "gradations of cold and heat, from freezing cold to cold to cool to indifferent to warm to hot to burning hot" [9] (Fig. 1). The body obtains this information through thermoreceptors. There are at least three types, those receptors for pain, those for warm stimuli, and those for cold stimuli. Each of them generate different sensation. The activation temperature range of each thermoreceptor is presented in the Fig. 1.

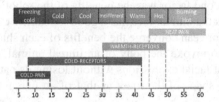

Fig. 1. Temperature range of activation for each thermoreceptor. Graphic based on [9]

3   Features of Thermal Stimuli as Robotic Emotional Medium

3.1   Universal

Human being can perceive thermal stimuli through thermoreceptors. Moreover, the sensation among humans is similar, regardless of gender, age or any other social status.

3.2   Unaltered Shape

To provide temperature to the skin of the robot, it is not required to modify its shape. Therefore, a robot can communicate thermal sensation without changing its shape.

3.3   Privacy

Feature pointed out by Lee [5]. A thermal stimulus can be perceived only by the person who interacts with the robot without anybody else knowing.

3.4   Non Disturbing

It does not disturb any person who does not physically interact with the robot.

4 General Design Decision for the Robot

4.1 Shape of the Robot

Two main factors were considered to decide the shape of the robot. First, the benefits of the robot's shape for a physical interaction with its body. This is desirable because the change of the robot's body temperature will be felt through a physical contact. When analyzing the physical interaction in the human-human case, we believe that this depends to a large extent on the type of relationship that exists between them. Even then, this is usually reduced to the greeting process. In contrast, we think that the physical interaction with a pet (caresses and touching) can extend in duration and frequency. Thus, a pet shape could be more suitable than a human shape for our research interest. The second factor was the benefits of the robot's shape to make facial expressions. In this aspect, a human face has a good versatility compared to the face of a pet. A shape of a creature can converge the benefits of each shape. This is because its shape can be designed to invoke the body of an unreal animal and, at the same time, can make several evident facial expressions without losing its naturalness. Therefore, it is decided to design the shape of the robot as that of an unreal creature.

4.2 Thermal System

It is desired that the robot can vary its skin temperature in such a way that it can convey emotions. However, there is no defined temperature range as the most appropriate to express emotions. Previous works have explored different temperatures within the range of 17.9–39.5 °C [3, 4]. In this range, only the cold and warm receptors are activated, but not the pain receptors. However, based on Fig. 1, the temperature range between 10–55 °C covers the stimulation of all human thermoreceptors. This range includes the temperatures already studied and, at the same time, also allows the study of thermal stimuli where the pain receptors are activated. Thus, this range was selected as a requirement for the skin of the robot.

R1: The skin of the robot must reach temperatures from 10 °C to 55 °C.

Among the thermal systems, the thermoelectric module (TE) can generate both heat and cold. This is achieved by controlling the polarity of the DC power applied along with an adequate heat dissipation system. In addition, the TE has no movable parts, is compact and economical. Based on its benefits, the TE is selected as the robot's thermal system. However, it is not flexible and its shape is usually a flat rectangle. Therefore, the surfaces of the robot where the TE will be placed will be limited to flat surfaces.

4.3 Location of the Thermal System

Since the use of TE will restrict the design of the robot's external surfaces to flat surfaces, it is desirable to locate the thermal system only in the area of the robot most likely to be caressed. As mentioned previously, the selected shape of the robot is of a creature. For this shape, we speculate that its head could react to caresses better than other parts of its body. Therefore, we seek to design the robot in such a way that the main area to caress it is its head. Additionally, to reduce the possibility that other parts of the robot could be caressed, the upper and lower extremities are removed.

H1: The head will be the area of the robot most likely to be caressed or touched.

5 Structure of the Robot's Body

The structure of the robot's body is divided into three main sections: head, neck, and body base (see Fig. 2b).

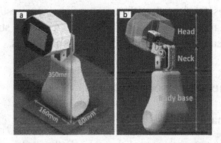

Fig. 2. (a) Isometric view and (b) sections of the robot's body and the 3 DoF on the neck [10]

5.1 Head

Two sub-sections are distinguished: the face and the cranium. In the case of the robot's face, it consists of a screen and a cover. The screen is part of a smartphone and it is used to visualize different facial expressions; while the cover is used to prevent the human from associating the robot's face with a mere smartphone's screen. On the other hand, the cranium stands out for being the only area of the robot that has the ability to modify the temperature of its skin, although limited to the 5 surfaces indicated by a red color in Fig. 3c. This is because the thermal system is located here. It is integrated by a set of thermoelectric units (TEUs) and heatsinks. There is a total of 12 TEUs distributed in two rows of 6 units. They are placed on the superior, upper diagonal and lateral faces of the cranium (Fig. 3c). The heat generated by the TEUs is dissipated by a piece of heatsink under each TEU. These pieces are obtained by cutting a heatsink LAM4 by Fisher Electronik. The heatsink originally is a square bar.

5.2 Neck

This section stands out for allowing the mechanical movement of the head in different orientations during interaction with a human. The neck's mechanism has in total 3 DoF, where each join has a Dynamixel AX-12+ servo (see Fig. 2b).

Fig. 3. (a) The heat sink LAM4 by Fisher Electronik are cut into pieces. Then, (b) these pieces are assembled to form the head structure. Finally, (c) the TEUs and the screen are added. [10] (Color figure online)

5.3 Body Base

It is composed of pieces fabricated with a 3D printer. Its aesthetical function is to provide the robot with a morphology of a creature, whereas its structural functions are to support the robot's head and contain electronic components.

6 Validation of the Designed Robot

6.1 About the Thermal System

It was evaluated the temperature range of the robot's thermal system. Thus, a test was performed to (1) determine the minimum achievable temperature, and (2) determine if the thermal system can achieve 55 °C. It is not calculated the maximum reachable temperature because, taking into account **R1**, it is more relevant to verify that the thermal system can reach 55 °C. The current system has not incorporated its own temperature sensor; therefore, it uses an open-loop temperature control. The test was done in an ambient temperature of 22 °C. It was applied 9V to an individual TEU 5 times. The average of the temperature measured on the side of the TEU that has no contact with the heatsink is shown in Table 1. Based on these results, it is verified that the thermal system can achieve the temperature range of 10–55 °C in an ambient temperature of 22 °C. Thus, the robot satisfies the requirement **R1**.

Table 1. Average temperature range of a TEU placed on the robot's thermal system

	Voltage (V)	Current (A)	Temperature (°C)	Time (s)
(1) Min. temperature	9	1.6	>68	3.3
(2) Reach 55 °C	9	2.2	8.9	5.5

6.2 About the Location of the Thermal System

An experiment was carried out to identify by regions the degree of intention to caress the robot's body. This experiment was approved by the ethical committee of the University of Tsukuba (IRB number: 2017R166-1). We expect that the location of the thermal system is contained or coincides in the regions with the greatest intention of caressing. Night right-handed participants without a physical disability were recruited (age: M = 25.89, SD = 6.05; 66.7% male).

Before the experiment, a preparation session was carried out. In this, the participant was instructed to interact freely with the robot. In other words, the participant could talk, ask, touch, caress, or do any other activity with the robot. It was also explained that the robot will react according to its capabilities, although no details were given about which they are. The experiment had no time limit and ended once the participant indicated it. After the explanation, the participant was taken to sit on the sofa in front of the robot to begin the experiment (Fig. 4a).

Fig. 4. (a) Experimental setup. The participant is sitting on a sofa facing the robot. (b) The face of the robot. The movement of the iris is controllable.

During the experiment, the robot was capable of activating the mechanical system located in its neck in order to move its head. In addition, on the robot's face, two eyes were displayed with an iris capable of moving around the sclera (see Fig. 4b). The movement of the neck and the iris were controlled using the Wizard of Oz (WoZ) technique. Although the robot had the TEUs installed in its cranium, the thermal system was not utilized in the experiment. In addition, the robot did not express any sound.

At the end of the experiment, a survey composed of a questionnaire and two colorable maps was carried out. In the questionnaire, the participant was asked about the appearance of the robot; which areas he touched or caressed and which ones did not. Six areas were established: cranium; face; neck; upper, middle and lower part of the body. The experimenter inquired about the reasons behind each answer. As for the colorable maps (see Fig. 5a), they were used to know more precisely where the participant will touch the robot. Thus, the body of the robot was divided into 33 zones (See Fig. 5b). Each map is colored according to a 10-steps linear color bar. In the first colorable map, the participant was explicitly asked to indicate the degree of intention to touch or caress the robot, whereas in the second map the intention of no-touch or no-caress the robot.

The results of the questionnaire showed that all participant tend to consider the shape of the robot like not a real animal, but a living creature. Each of them touched the robot at least 4 times. In addition, 100% answered that they will touch or caress the cranium, 44.4% the face, 0% the neck, 66.7% the upper part of the body, 77.8% the middle part of the body, 66.7% the lower part of the body. Moreover, when they were asked for the main part of the robot they will caress or touch, 100% said the cranium. The noted reasons were that they felt a logic reaction of the robot as well as it was

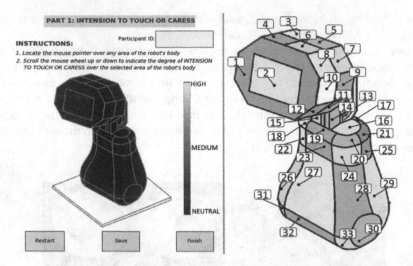

Fig. 5. (a) Colorable map for the degree of intention to touch or caress. There was a similar map for the degree of intention to no-touch. (b) Enumeration of the 33 zones in which the body of the robot is divided. (Color figure online)

natural for them to touch the head like in the case of a pet. About the main part of the robot they will no-touch or no-caress, 77.8% said the neck because it seems unsafe to touch it, whereas 22.2% indicate the lower part of the body because it was unaffordable or the area was associated with an intimate private zone of the robot.

On the other hand, the average result of the colorable maps for intention to touch or caress is shown in Fig. 6a, whereas the one for intention to no-touch is in Fig. 6b. Because each map shows half of the total scale of intention to touch/no-touch, they are combined into a single map (See Fig. 6c). In this map, if a zone has a negative value of intention to be touched, it does not mean that the zone is not touched by the human, but it means that in average the zone tends to be no-touch. Thus, it is possible to visualize that the most touchable zones are located in the head. In the case of the most no-touchable zones, there are on the neck. Moreover, a further analysis by zones was made (See Fig. 6d). The objective was to group neighboring zones with the similar intention to touch into regions. Thereby, it is possible to identify 3 regions in the head: A, B C. Region A alludes to the robot's face and has an almost neutral intention to touch. In this, although the cover has a slightly positive intention value, the robot's screen has a slightly negative value. In the case of region B, this is the one with the greatest intention to be touched (on average 7.52 points out of 10). It comprises the superior, upper diagonal and lateral faces of the cranium. Then, region C refer to the lower lateral face of the cranium and it has a low intention to no-touch. Probably, in this regions the lower face of the cranium is also included; however, this is not possible to verify with the robot view shown on the maps. On the other hand, the neck is composed only by the region D. This clearly has the greatest intention of no-touch. Finally, the base body of the robot can be divided into 7 regions. Among them, the region H is the only one that is composed of zones with a positive value to intention to touch. Taking this result into account, this region could be considered a potential area to locate also a thermal system, nevertheless, its degree is considerably lower compared to that of region B. In the next place, region G, although it has a large area, has an almost neutral value. Then, region F, the second nearest neighbor D, and I, the only concave region, have a low degree of intention to no-touch. Finally, region E, the nearest neighbor to region D in the neck, and J, the lowest area of the robot, have the greatest intention of no-touch.

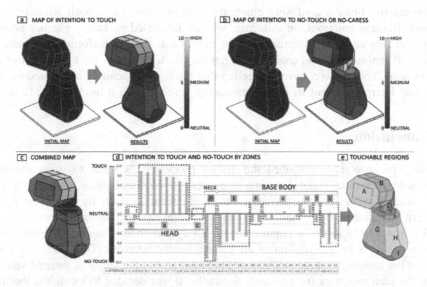

Fig. 6. (a) Results of the map of intention of "touch" or "cares" and (b) the map of the intention of "no-touch" or "no-caress" (c) are combined on a single map. (d) Through an analysis by zones, (e) the body of the robot can be divided into regions according to the intention to touch. (Color figure online)

Based on the results, region B (superior, upper diagonal and lateral faces of the cranium) had the greatest intention to be touched was. This region coincides with the location of the thermal system proposed in Sect. 4.2. Therefore, these results support our hypothesis **H1**. Even more important, considering that there is no other region with high intention to be touched, it is concluded that it is possible to dispense with locating the thermal system in other areas.

7 Limitation and Future Work

At the present moment, the robot cannot perform facial expressions related to emotions, which is a desirable feature for future works. Regarding the thermal system, it has currently an open loop temperature control. Therefore, setting an accurate temperature is limited. To improve this feature, a closed loop temperate control can be implemented by adding a temperature sensor over the side of the TEU that is not in contact with the heatsink. Solving these limitations, the robot will be optimal for studies on the use of the robot body temperature as a medium to express its emotional state. Then, as mentioned in Sect. 1, we aim to study the robot's body temperature as a robotic emotional expression. For that, we plan to use a basic trapezoidal model to express the thermal stimuli. We expect to find some of them with a strong emotional interpretation. Then, we plan to combine thermal stimulus with facial expression in two conditions. Firstly, both expressing the same emotion. As a consequence, we expect that the emotional interpretation will be stronger. Secondly, both expressing different emotions. We expect to obtain a confusing emotional interpretation since each stimulus will transmit different emotions. In this case, we are interested to know whether people could find this confusing interpretation as if the robot were performing a pseudo-emotion. If that is that case, analyze whether people will tend to trust more in one of this stimulus. For instance, have the feeling that the robot is actually sad, based on the emotional interpretation of its body temperature, even though it has a happy face.

8   Conclusion

In this paper, we have described the design process of a robot to study thermo-emotional expression. This robot aims to express its emotional state by changing the temperature of its body. An experiment was conducted to evaluate its design. Firstly, it was verified that the robot's thermal system can achieve temperatures between 10–55 ° C. This range was set as a requirement to study the thermo-emotional expression because it covers the stimulation of all human thermoreceptors. This range not only includes the temperatures already studied, but also allows the study of thermal stimuli where the pain receptors are activated. Secondly, it was decided to locate the thermal system only in the most potential area of the robot to be touched or caressed. Having set the shape of the robot as that of a creature, the robot was designed in such a way that the people tend to caress mainly the robot's head. Through a questionnaire and colorable maps, it was showed that the mainly regions to be caressed were the superior, lateral and upper diagonal faces of the cranium. These regions are coincident with the location of the thermal system of the robot. Moreover, it was concluded that it is possible to dispense with locating the thermal system in other areas because the other regions of the robot's body have low intention to be caress. In summary, the robot presented in this study is suitable to investigate the robot body temperature as a medium to express its emotional state. This is because, when a physical interaction occurs, the robot can transmit a thermal stimulus to the human.

Acknowledgment. This work is supported by KAKENHI 17K19993. A special thanks to Kosmech workshop of the University of Tsukuba for the support in the manufacture of the robot.

References

1. Darwin, C.: The Expression of the Emotions in Man and Animals, vol. 526. University of Chicago Press, Chicago (1965)
2. Nummenmaa, L., Glerean, E., Hari, R., Hietanen, J.K.: Bodily maps of emotions. Proc. Natl. Acad. Sci. **111**(2), 646–651 (2014)
3. Wilson, G., Dobrev, D., Brewster, S.A.: Hot under the collar: mapping thermal feedback to dimensional models of emotion. In: CHI Conference on Human Factors in Computing Systems, pp. 4838–4849. ACM, New York (2016)
4. Salminen, K., et al.: Cold or Hot? How thermal stimuli are related to human emotional system? In: Oakley, I., Brewster, S. (eds.) HAID 2013. LNCS, vol. 7989, pp. 20–29. Springer, Heidelberg (2013). https://doi.org/10.1007/978-3-642-41068-0_3
5. Lee, W., Lim, Y.-K.: Explorative research on the heat as an expression medium: focused on interpersonal communication. Pers. Ubiquit. Comput. **16**(8), 1039–1049 (2012)
6. Nie, J., Park, M., Marin, A.L., Sundar, S.S.: Can you hold my hand? Physical warmth in human-robot interaction. In: 7th ACM/IEEE International Conference on Human-Robot Interaction, pp. 201–202 (2012)
7. Park, E., Lee, J.: I am a warm robot: the effects of temperature in physical human–robot interaction. Robotica **32**(1), 133–142 (2014)
8. Vargas, M.F.: Louder than Words: An Introduction to Nonverbal Communication. Iowa State University Press, Iowa City (1986)
9. Guyton, A.C., Hall, J.E.: Textbook of Medical Physiology, 13th edn. Elsevier Saunders, Philadelphia (2011)
10. Peña, D., Tanaka, F.: Touch to feel me: designing a robot for thermo-emotional communication. In: 13th ACM/IEEE International Conference on Human-Robot Interaction (HRI 2018), pp. 207–208. ACM, New York (2018)

Training Autistic Children on Joint Attention Skills with a Robot

Kelsey Carlson[1,2](✉), Alvin Hong Yee Wong[1], Tran Anh Dung[1],
Anthony Chern Yuen Wong[1], Yeow Kee Tan[1],
and Agnieszka Wykowska[3]

[1] A*STAR, 1 Fusionopolis Way, #20-10 Connexis North Tower,
Singapore 138632, Singapore
kelsey.leigh.carlson@gmail.com, {hyawong, tanhdung,
cywong}@i2r.a-star.edu.sg, tanyeowkee@gmail.com
[2] Department of Psychology, Ludwig Maximilian University,
Leopoldstr. 13, 80802 Munich, Germany
[3] Istituto Italiano Di Tecnologia, Via Morego, 30, 16163 Genoa, Italy
agnieszka.wykowska@iit.it

Abstract. Children with Autism Spectrum Disorder have issues with the development of social skills and communication. One such skills is that of joint attention (JA). JA is the sharing of attention between two people in regards to an object. There are two mechanism of JA, initiating joint attention (IJA) and responding to joint attention (RJA). This article details an experiment wherein a social robot was used to train children with ASD on their JA skills. This experiment contained a robot training group and a control group. Both groups' JA skills were tested before and after training with the robot (or a waiting period for the control group). The groups did not significantly differ on their pre-tests scores for RJA or IJA. The training group had significant improvements in both their IJA and RJA scores, while the control group did not have significant improvements. However, the groups did not significantly differ on their post-test scores for either RJA or IJA.

Keywords: Autism spectrum disorder · Social robotics · Joint attention
Skills training

1 Introduction

The DSM-5 describes autism spectrum disorder (ASD) as a range of disorders characterized by social deficits and communication difficulties, stereotyped or repetitive behaviors and interests, sensory issues, and in some cases, delayed cognitive development [1]. While there is no cure for ASD, when therapy is provided early on, symptoms can greatly be reduced and abilities can be increased. Prior research has focused on therapy geared towards language, communication, and social skills [2–4]. In this article the skill of joint attention (JA) will be investigated.

Joint attention is defined as the sharing of attention between a person (child), another person, and an object or event [5, 6]. There are two mechanisms for joint attention, one

© Springer Nature Switzerland AG 2018
S. S. Ge et al. (Eds.): ICSR 2018, LNAI 11357, pp. 86–92, 2018.
https://doi.org/10.1007/978-3-030-05204-1_9

for initiation (IJA) and one for responding (RJA). IJA is a bid to direct someone's attention toward an object, an example is a child showing a toy to a parent [7]. RJA refers to a child responding to a bid for their attention, an example is a child turning their head and looking where their parent is pointing or looking [7]. Neurotypical children develop the skill of joint attention between the ages of 6 to 12 months [5, 8].

Research has suggested that joint attention is necessary for language development [2]. It is suggested that children develop language by attending to their parent as their parent says the name of an object and point to it, this pairing of the name with an object results in language acquisition. Since children with ASD are less likely than their peers to follow the gaze or pointing of their parents, these children may not develop language skills [2]. These issues along with a propensity to make less eye contact and initiatie less showing or pointing gestures can result in a lack of both communication and social skills [2, 5, 9]. However, it has been shown that early intervention can improve non-verbal communication skills which can lead to increases in language skills and social development [2, 3, 5]. In recent years social robots have become a novel therapy for children with ASD [10–12]. It has been suggested that children with ASD respond better to robots than human therapists due to the fact that robots have stable and predictable behavior, facial expressions, and voice.

The current experiment used a robot named "CuDDler" (A*Star) to improve the joint attention skills of children with ASD, this work was an expansion of prior work [13]. The current study consisted of testing a new larger group of children, additional sessions of training, and a control group (no robot training group). The current study was a pre-post test design, wherein the children's joint attention skills were measured via the abridged Early Social Communications Scale, ESCS [14] before and after robot training (or a waiting period for the control group). Based on the prior study [13], it was hypothesized that the robot training group would show improvements in RJA skills, but not IJA skills [13]. It was also hypothesized that the robot training group would show improvements in RJA skills, but that the control group would not.

2 Materials and Methods

2.1 Participants

Participants were recruited via the early intervention center THK EIPIC Centre (Singapore). Each group (training and control) contained 10 children, for a total of 20 children (Mean age 5.3, SD = 0.7). All of the children were male, and between the ages of 4 and 6. None of the children took medication and all of them were diagnosed with ASD. Furthermore, all of them were of Singaporean descent and spoke English. The THK EIPIC Centre also provided the AEPS scores of the children. These scores were provided for fine motor, gross motor, cognitive, adaptive, social communication, and social. The researcher did not collect these scores or intend to change them, they were merely a piece of information that the Centre provided. Although the researcher did compare the training and control group on these scores to see if either of the groups had significantly different abilities. This comparison showed that the groups were not significantly different.

2.2 Stimuli and Apparatus

An embodied robot (CuDDler, A*Star) was controlled by the experimenter via a computer interface (operating system: Windows 7) which interacted with a smartphone (Google Nexus 4) inside of the robot. The control system for CuDDler was programmed using android java and C++. Stimuli were presented with two BePhones (resolution: 640×480 and screen size: 136.6×70.6 mm) using android java. The screens were placed left and right of the robot with at a distance of 40 cm ($11°$ of visual angle of participants). The screens were tilted approximately $45°$ relative to the robot, making it seem as if the robot was viewing the images.

There were ten stimuli which were colorful line drawings of various objects (star, apple, ball, candle, flower, hat, heart, ice cream, plane, sweet). These stimuli were presented in four different colors (red, blue, green or yellow). Each session consisted of 20 trials with all objects in all colors appearing once. In each trial the same object (e.g., heart) was presented on both phones, but the objects were of different color (e.g., left heart blue and right heart yellow).

The stimuli were fit to the center of the phone screens (136.6×70.6 mm) and covered $2°$ in height and approximately $3.5°$ in width of visual angle of participants. On each trial the robot randomly moved its head approximately $2.3°$ in visual angle of participants either left or right from the midline with equal probability. The participants were seated 200 cm from the robot.

A trial ran as such, 1. the robot looked straight ahead, 2. it turned its head and said, "Look a [object type]!", this could be any of the ten object types, 3. two similar objects appeared on the phone screens (only varying by color), 4. the robot asked, "What color is this?", 5. the child named the color verbally (e.g., yellow), 6. the robot moved its arms and head around while saying "good job", and finally, 7. the robot returned to its starting position.

2.3 Procedure

There were three phases in the experiment. During Phase 1, the pre-test, the children's' joint attention skills were measured via the Object Spectacle Task (1 x), the Gaze Following Task (2 x) and the Book Presentation Task (2 x) sections of the abridged Early Social Communications Scale, ESCS [14], this test lasted about ten minutes. During Phase 2 the children either did or did not receive robot training based on the group they were in. During Phase 3, the post-test, the children were assessed with the ESCS again.

The training group, who received joint attention training via the robot, first took part in a training session where they learned the task. Then over the next four weeks they attended two training sessions per week, this resulted in a total of eight sessions (each of which were ten minutes long). The control group, who did not received training via the robot, attended the same number of sessions (all ten minutes long), however, these children played with a teddy bear or other toys and never saw the robot.

3 Analysis

Scores for IJA and RJA were analyzed based on the guidelines of the ESCS by two separate researchers [9]. One of the researchers had conducted the study and the other researcher was naive and blind to the study. No participants were excluded from data analysis. Intraclass Correlation Coefficients were used to compare the researchers' scores on the IJA and RJA measures. The results are presented in the following format: average measures intraclass correlation (lower bound, upper bound). Pre-test IJA scores: 0.884 (0.706, 0.954), pre-test RJA scores: 0.853 (0.370, 0.952), post-test IJA scores: 0.862 (0.636, 0.946), and post-test RJA scores: 0.723 (0.305, 0.890). Before being submitted to the statistical tests the scores of the two researchers were averaged.

The IJA and the RJA scales were analyzed separately. The following tests were conducted: 1. an independent samples t-test was conducted on the pre-test scores for both the IJA and RJA, to see if the two groups differed before the experiment began; 2. a paired samples t-test comparing the pre-test and post-tests scores was conducted for the robot group and for the control group; and 3. an independent samples t-test was conducted comparing the post-test scores of the robot and the control groups on both scales (IJA and RJA).

4 Results

The groups did not significantly differ on their pre-test scores for either IJA or RJA. For the IJA the training group significantly differed from pretest to post-test, $t(9) = -3.11$, $p = 0.013$, pre-test (M = 5.75, SD = 3.56) and post-test (M = 11.15, SD = 4.96), see Fig. 1. For the RJA the training group significantly differed from pretest to post-test, t (9) = -2.75, p = 0.023, pre-test (M = 159.17, SD = 49.14) and post-test (M = 197.92, SD = 6.59) see Fig. 2. While the control group did not significantly improve for either IJA or RJA from pre-test to post-test. There were no group differences on the post-tests for either the IJA or RJA.

5 Discussion

The current study used a social robot "CuDDler" (A*Star) to train children with ASD on their joint attention skills. This study was an expansion of prior work done by [13]. This expansion consisted of testing a new larger group of children, additional sessions of training, and a control group (no robot training group). Based on the prior work by [13], it was hypothesized that the training group would have improvements in their RJA (responding to joint attention) skills, however it was not expected that the training group would improve on their IJA (initiating joint attention) skills.

The two groups (training and control) did not significantly differ on their pre-tests scores for either the RJA or the IJA. However, the training group had significant improvements in both their RJA and IJA scores from pre-test to post-test. Whereas, the control group did not have significant improvements in either their RJA or their IJA scores from pre-test to post-test. However, the two groups were not significantly

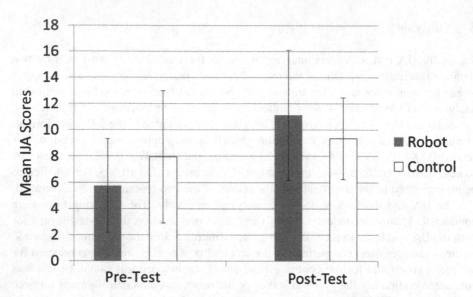

Fig. 1. Mean IJA scores with standard deviation bars for the robot training group (gray bars) and the control group (white bars). Pre-test scores on the left, post-test scores on the right.

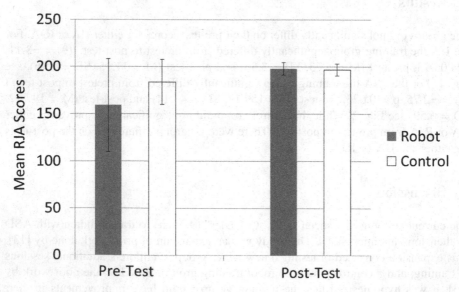

Fig. 2. Mean RJA scores with standard deviation bars for the robot training group (gray bars) and the control group (white bars). Pre-test scores on the left, post-test scores on the right.

different on the post-test scores for the RJA or the IJA. These results are contrary to [13] who only found improvements in RJA skills. However, it is suspected that the current study not only found improvements in RJA scores, but also IJA scores due to the increased sample size. Interestingly, although the groups did not have significantly different pre-test scores, and the training group showed significant improvements from pre-test to post-test on both RJA and IJA, the training and control group were not significantly different on their post-tests scores for either RJA or IJA. It is suspected that these results may be due to individual variances and the small sample size. However, it is important to note that two of the children who had great variation in their data, but showed improvement from the pre-test to the post-test had mild-to-moderate and moderate-to-severe ASD. Therefore, it may be that this type of therapy is more beneficial for those children who are in these functionality ranges.

In conclusion, while this study did show that a social robot can be used to improve the joint attention skills (both RJA and IJA) of children with ASD, the training groups scores did not surpass those of the control group. Therefore, one may wonder if this therapy is actually beneficial, however, the authors would argue that there is proof of improvement. Furthermore, it seems that this type of therapy might be the most beneficial for children with mild-to-moderate and moderate-to-severe ASD. It may be beneficial to repeat this study with only children who suffer from mild-to-moderate and moderate-to-severe ASD. Furthermore, it would be beneficial to increase the sample size of the study.

Acknowledgements. This study was funded by Singapore-MIT Alliance for Research and Technology (SMART) Ignition Grant (grant number: ING149087-ICT). The authors declare that they have no conflict of interest.

References

1. American Psychiatric Association: Diagnostic and Statistical Manual of Mental Disorders, 5th edn. Author, Washington, DC (2013)
2. Meindl, J., Cannella-Malone, H.: Initiating and responding to joint attention bids in children with autism: a review of the literature. Res. Dev. Disabil. **32**(5), 1441–1454 (2011). https://doi.org/10.1016/j.ridd.2011.02.013
3. Mundy, P., Sigman, M., Kasari, C.: A longitudinal study of joint attention and language development in autistic children. J. Autism Dev. Disord. **20**(1), 115–128 (1990)
4. Whalen, C., Schreibman, L.: Joint attention training for children with autism using behavior modification procedures. J. Child Psychol. Psychiatry **44**(3), 456–468 (2003). https://doi.org/10.1111/1469-7610.00135
5. Charman, T.: Why is joint attention a pivotal skill in autism? Philos. Trans. R. Soc. London. Ser. Biol. Sci. **358**(1430), 315–324 (2003). https://doi.org/10.1098/rstb.2002.1199
6. Leekam, S.R., López, B., Moore, C.: Attention and joint attention in preschool children with autism. Dev. Psychol. **36**(2), 261–273 (2000). https://doi.org/10.1037/0012-1649.36.2.261
7. Mundy, P., Crowson, M.: Joint attention and early social communication; implications for research on intervention with autism. J. Autism Dev. Disord. **27**(6), 653–676 (1997)
8. Moore, C., Dunham, P.J.: Joint Attention: Its Origins and Role in Development. Psychology Press, New York (2014)
9. Taylor, B.A., Hoch, H.: Teaching children with autism to respond to and initiate bids for joint attention. J. Appl. Behav. Anal. **41**(3), 377–391 (2008). https://doi.org/10.1901/jaba.2008.41-377

10. Cabibihan, J.J., Javed, H., Ang Jr., M., Aljunied, S.: Why robots? A survey on the roles and benefits of social robots in the therapy of children with autism. Int. J. Soc. Robot. **5**(4), 593–618 (2013). https://doi.org/10.1007/s12369-013-0202-2
11. Dautenhahn, K.: Roles and functions of robots in human society: implications from research in autism therapy. Robotica **21**(04), 443–452 (2003). https://doi.org/10.1017/S0263574703004922
12. Scassellati, B., Admoni, H., Matarić, M.: Robots for use in autism research. Annu. Rev. Biomed. Eng. **14**(1), 275–294 (2012). https://doi.org/10.1146/annurev-bioeng-071811-150036
13. Kajopoulos, J., Wong A.H.Y., Zuen, A.W.C., Dung, T.A., Tan, Y.K., Wykowska, A.: Robot-assisted training of joint attention skills in children diagnosed with autism. Accepted for presentation at ICSR 2015, to be published in LNAI 2015 (2105)
14. Mundy, P., Delgado, C., Block, J., Venezia, M., Hogan, A., Seibert, J.: A manual for the abridged early social communication scale (ESCS) (2003)

Robotic Understanding of Scene Contents and Spatial Constraints

Dustin Wilson[1], Fujian Yan[2], Kaushik Sinha[2], and Hongsheng He[2(✉)]

[1] Kansas State University, Manhattan, KS 66506, USA
[2] Wichita State University, Wichita, KS 67260, USA
hongsheng.he@wichita.edu

Abstract. The aim of this paper is to create a model which is able to be used to accurately identify objects as well as spacial relationships in a dynamic environment. This paper proposed methods to train a deep learning model which recognizes unique objects and positions of key items in an environment. The model requires a low amount of images compared to others and also can recognize multiple objects in the same frame due to the utilization of region proposal networks. Methods are also discussed to find the position of recognized objects which can be used for picking up recognized items with a robotic arm. The system utilizes logic operations to be able to deduct how different objects relate to each other in regard to their placement from one another based off of the localization technique. The paper discusses how to create spacial relationships specifically.

Keywords: Robot spatial constraints reasoning
Spatial logic understanding · Object detection
Convolutional neural networks · Robotic grasping · Faster R-CNN

1 Introduction

Many robots today are programmed to move to certain positions at set periods of time and do a task without really knowing what it is doing. This works well in an extremely controlled environment where it's surroundings remain constant, but when things are even slightly off, the robot cannot correct itself and often fails to complete the task. Robots will not be able to only follow a set of commands, but will need to continually be processing their environment and making decisions based off of it's surroundings and the given task.

The overarching goal is to develop a program which follows natural-language instructions to move objects in a given work area to specified positions. This can be as simple as, "Move the rightmost object to the left of the leftmost object," or it can be as complex as detailed plans to build a tower. Figure 1 shows an example of a plan which could be given to the robot. The image in Fig. 1 would be ran through the model which recognizes objects and then it would begin to reason all the relationships which would exist after the building is complete. This

© Springer Nature Switzerland AG 2018
S. S. Ge et al. (Eds.): ICSR 2018, LNAI 11357, pp. 93–102, 2018.
https://doi.org/10.1007/978-3-030-05204-1_10

reasoning would be what drives the building process. Once the object has been located and the position has been set for it to move to, the robot determines what is the best way to grip the object based on information which can be given to it as descriptors, found with the molecular senor, or what it has been trained to recognized with machine learning.

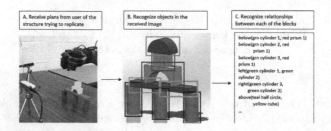

Fig. 1. Representation of how the robot may operate. The figure on the left depicts an example of an image which could be given to the robot. The goal is for the robot to understand the relationships among each of the blocks well enough to re-create the structure on its own.

Machine learning is a process which allows a machine to not only be engineered to do a certain task, but allows the robot to "understand" its environment [7]. This means not blindly moving to an arbitrary point in space, and once it gets there moving different servos to a hand position. Instead, the robot would be able to understand what and where the object it needs to pick up is, and then, move to that point and manipulate it's servos to positions which would be most effective to grasp it.

With machine learning, many challenges exist such as how to gather the large amounts of information needed for the model [1]. For applications that do not have pre-made data sheets however, the information needs to be gathered manually. An additional challenge to increase the flexibility of robotics would be that many objects are designed to be picked up by humans. Besides that, many robotics hands today, however, utilize a simpler griper [2,4], but their versatility is limited. A humanoid hand adds a more natural usage of the robot and allows robots to interact with devices made for humans with no modifications needed. According to [3], the traditional method for spatial approach is based on the distance between pixels.

The goal of this research is also to observe how robots understand the spatial relationships between different objects through usages of reasoning. People have been trained their whole lives to be able to recognize simple relationships like "right of" or "on top of." These same relationships can be difficult to keep track of for a robot. Teaching robots logic such as "if A comes before B and B comes before C, A must also come before C," is a stepping stone for robots also understand more complex reasoning problems. This relationship was not explicitly described although it is true. This can be used by the robot because it is often difficult to describe an object and easier just to describe what is around it. This type of description is also more natural for humans as it has be ingrained into our everyday lives.

2 Developing Object Recognition

2.1 Basic Deep Learning Model

A convolutional neural network was used for the model training. To create the testing data, around 10,000 pictures were obtained of each object and annotated with the object's tagging letter which were ranging in the letters from A to F.

Both Keras and TensorFlow as used to train the model. One hot method was used to annotate the date. Images for training were augmented because of the small size of the data set to prevent over fitting [5]. Methods used were shearing, zooming, and flipping horizontally as well as converting all images to gray scale. A dropout rate of 50% was also used to prevent over fitting. The model, having four layers and one fully-connected, was trained for 100 epochs on the images with 20% of the data set aside for testing.

2.2 Bounding Objects Inside Images

A second model was created using the method described for a Faster R-CNN model [6] to address the problem of not being able to identify multiple. An additional step from the original model was also taken by labeling the location of the objects in the training images. This would allow a faster method to find the location of various objects in pictures and allow pictures to contain multiple objects. This was done for all six of the objects and about 600 images from each category. The images used were randomly selected from the 10,000 gathered during the CNN step to hopefully allow the greatest amount of variety.

Two dataset are made for organizing each object. The first one uses the type of block as the key and is then followed by the coordinates of it's bounds $\{\chi_1 : [\chi_{1,x}, \chi_{1,y}, \chi_{1,w}, \chi_{1,h}], \cdots, \chi_n : [\chi_{n,x}, \chi_{n,y}, \chi_{n,w}, \chi_{n,h}],\}$ where χ stands for the shape of the particular object. χ represents the bounds of the box. The bounds are labeled as follows: χ_x is the x coordinate of the bottom left corner of the box, χ_y is the y coordinate of that same point, χ_w is the width of the box, and χ_h is the height of the box. If there are multiple blocks of the same shape they will all be contained inside the same χ. The boundaries are then converted into the center location of the box. The center of the box is represented by

$$[C_x, C_y] = \left[\frac{\chi_w + \chi_x}{2}, \frac{\chi_h + \chi_y}{2} \right] \tag{1}$$

C_x represents the x coordinate of the center of the box and the y coordinate is contained under the expression C_y. Those values are found by determining the average of both the x and the y values given with the width standing for the second x value and height being equivalent to the second y value.

The center is used to create a new dataset which will contain the shape also as the key, the center coordinates as an index $\{\chi_1 : [C_{1,x}, C_{1,y}], \cdots, \chi_n[C_{n,x}, C_{n,y}]\}$.

A sorting algorithm is used next to order the bounds from closest to the y-axis to the farthest based off of the center of the bounds and a list is created. The algorithm first compares the first x value against the second x value in the list to determine which is the greatest. It kepdf which ever value is greater and continues comparing until it has found the highest x value of the list and places it in the last position. It repeats the same process to find the second largest which it places in the second to last position. This method is continued until all of the values are in order which is one less than the length of the list $[C_{1,x}, \cdots, C_{n,x}]$ where $C_{1,x}$ stands for the smallest value of the array and $C_{n,x}$ represents the largest.

Color was also labeled by detecting the RGB values for the center point. A method is used to retrieve return the color intensity list which is containing the intensity of each color is returned in the format $[\beta_r, \beta_g, \beta_b]$ with β standing for the experiment image. The returned list is then compared against the RGB values of common colors $[\alpha_r, \alpha_g, \alpha_b]$ and distance from the color for each list is determined

$$\omega = |\beta_r - \alpha_r| + |\beta_g - \alpha_g| + |\beta_b - \alpha_b| \qquad (2)$$

ω substitutes for the color. The lowest value of ω is the color and added to the index $\{C_1 : [C_{1,x}, C_{1,y}, \omega_1], \cdots, C_n : [C_{n,x}, C_{n,y}, \omega_n]\}$.

The key of the dataset is then added after the color and the process is repeated for the length of 2. This returns a list represented in the following $[\theta_1\epsilon_1, \cdots, \theta_n\epsilon_n]$ where the object is represented by θ and the type of block given by ϵ.

3 Determining Spacial Constraints from Recognition Stage

A reasoning application was implemented after the positions of each of the objects were identified and the list in the final stage of the recognition was created. The spacial relations can be implemented not only for left-right, but also for other spacial relations. Both input objects and coordinations of input objects.

Based on these coordination information, all spacial relations can be reasoned. The left-right relation is shown in this paper. Immediateleft relationships are based on observation from the list $L^-[(\theta, \epsilon_1), \cdots (\theta_n, \epsilon_n)]$ where L^- denotes the immediateleft function, θ denotes the object, and ϵ denotes the type of block. For inference left relation,

$$L^+(A, C) := L^-(A, B) + L^-(B, C) \qquad (3)$$

where L^+ denotes the left function. A, B, and C are three objects.

Right relationships are also established by a process of reversing any left relationships that are created $R^+(B, A) := \neg L^+(A, B)$, where R^+ denotes the right function.

Another approach for inference is based on natural language. The spacial relationships for current situations are needed. Logic is then implemented to begin to see how the objects must be ordered, based off of the rules, by first using a dataset. The dataset is implemented by placing the objects inside based off of their relationship between each other. The program first checks if the object already exists in the dataset. If it does not it uses the object on the left and creates a new key with it. The object on the left is then used as the first index $L^+(A, B)$. If at least one of the objects exist and it is a key, it knows that it must be one the right side of whatever object because otherwise it would not exist as a key and be a new immediate relationship. It must then check if the second object in the relationship exists as an index under a different key. If it does, the key which is apart of the relationship and all the items under it are placed under the other object $R^+(C, B)$, if the second object does not exist as an index, the object is made to be a new key and all the contents under the original key are translated over $L^+(A, B)$, going back to the beginning, if the either of the objects do not exist as a key but rather an item, the second object is added as another index under the same key the first exist under $R^+(C, B)$, once the entire text document has been read by the program, all of the items will be under one key. The dictionary will be used to create list keeping the order of all the items. The list is then used by the portion first mentioned in this section to find all of the relationships between each of the objects. Once the relationships among the given objects are established, the program allows users to add other objects the robot may not have been able to recognize. This option was added because there may be times where an object is in the workplace that the robot may not have been trained to recognize. This may be because it is an item which has a unique job and will not be present in enough environments to make it worth the time training the model to recognize it. This is also because the neural network may have not recognized an object which it should have. It is not desirable to have to adjust the environment so that it may be picked up in a future test, but rather is easier and more efficient to allow the user to add it manually. Users only specify a block that it shares an immediate relationship with and which side it is on based on the specified block. The logic of the program then adds all the new relationships the other blocks have with this new block. This is beneficial to the program because there are many cases where a block may not be fully visible or it is just not something the robot has been trained to recognize and has already recognized relationships for.

4   Experimental Results

4.1   Experiment Setup

In this experiment, A Sawyer robotic arm is used. It has seven degree of freedom. An AR-10 humanoid hand is used. The degree of freedom of the hand is ten degree of freedom. An Intel-RealSence R435 has been used for image acquisition. ROS system for robot controlling is run on a machine with Intel Core i7-5930 processors. With TITAN X GPU. Toy building blocks which are teal cylinder, teal rectangular, prism-thin, yellow half circle, teal rectangular prism-thin, and red rectangular prism-wide.

4.2 Experiment on Prediction

To determine the accuracy of the block recognition model and the reasoning, 100 pictures were taken: 20 with each 2, 3, 4, 5, and 6 resulting in a total of 400 blocks in the images altogether. These image must have each of the blocks in full view of the camera and not be placed farther than 30 in. away. The program was able to bound 295 blocks which means that it recognized that the object was significant and drew bounds around it. This label did not have to be correct however. The model correctly labeled 190 objects out of the 400. To be counted for this, the model needed to accurately recognize it's significance and label it with the correct box shape.

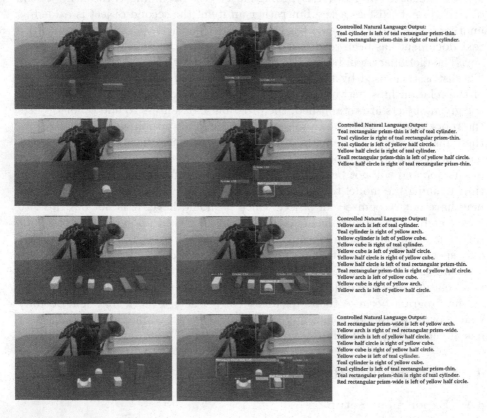

Fig. 2. Sample results from the testing demonstrating the process used in the model. The figure is setup to demonstrate the same method described in the introduction and how that method actually works throughout the entire process (Color figure online).

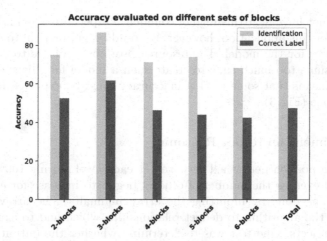

Fig. 3. Accuracy of the model to recognize objects of importance and correctly label them.

Though the accuracy is not as high as some other models, it performs well considering the difficulty of it's task. The blocks being used are very similar to each other. Many of the image sets that already exist are identify objects which are distinctly different from each other like a kite and a car. These data sheets also use millions of pictures to train from. In this particular problem, however, from some angles it is even difficult for humans to distinguish the different objects from each other.

There were two pairs that a majority of the labeling mistakes came from: the cube and the half circle, the cylinder and the rectangular prism-thin. The cube and the half circle are the two smallest objects and are both yellow. The model had a tendency to label them both as half circles though on a couple of occasions the half circle was labeled as a cube. The arch was also confused with the half circle because they are both yellow and the half circle is a cut out from arch. Cylinder and rectangular prism-thin were the other pair commonly confused. These were both teal and had a tall shape. This pair was labeled correct more often then the yellow pair was. Cylinder was used more often than the other label. Sometimes, the prism would be labeled as both a cylinder and a rectangular prism as is shown in the first example in Fig. 2.

In Fig. 2, the robotic arm is also identified as a Rectangular Prism-Wide. This is a result of it's rectangular shape as well as it's red color. This error was not considered into the number of bounded objects because it would have increased the accuracy making it appear more accurate than it actually is because it is failing to bound the objects it is supposed to be focusing on.

Despite the blocks similarity, this difficulty in distinguishing could have been lessened with the use of more pictures like many of the other data sheets have. There is most likely over fitting in the model because many of the guesses have a high accuracy which is shown in Fig. 2. Due to how similar each of the objects are it should not have near this high of confidence especially when it is guessing incorrectly. For this application, however, it would be impractical to gather millions of pictures for the model. The resources are not available to do that and it would consume too much time to create such a model for this specialized as a task. This means that some level of inaccuracy must be expected for a model such as this one (Fig. 3).

4.3 Experiment on Robot Reasoning

The reasoning portion performed very well at each level scoring 100% accuracy at every level even as the number of objects began to increase for each frame. The testing was done by inputting the array manually. The array was then processed by the algorithm to deduct relationships which had to exist between each of the objects. One test was to determine whether the output contained the correct number of relationships. This was done by using the following $\frac{\vartheta!}{(\vartheta-\tau)!}$, where ϑ represents the number of objects which the program must distinguish relationships between that are present in a particular frame. In the denominator, this value is subtracted from τ which is the number of objects that can exist in a single relationship which would always be two. This is a probability equation which is used to determine the number of possible outcomes without repeats and where order is important. The equation is used to know how many different relationships exist between left and right. The equation is used only as a means of determining this number and serves as a representation of how the reasoning works.

In addition to this test, the relationships were also analyzed to make sure each one was unique from the others. The algorithm was successful at not producing any repeat relationships. The output was also analyzed to ensure that all the reasoning was valid which it was for each scenario as well.

The reason lists for the reasoning portion of the testing was inputted by hand was because the mistakes of the recognition portion should not be counted against the reasoning. This reasoning model could be used with any model as long as it could display it's results in the form of an ordered list for the reasoning portion. Therefore if the model was more accurate at recognizing relationship, it would be outputting the correct list anyways. The reasoning then must be tested individually to ensure that it's reasoning is correct in many different situations. A sample of the results from the testing are also shown in Fig. 4. Only a sample is shown because for six objects 30 different relationships are identified which is found.

Figure 4 shows why the use of reasoning is vital to robotic applications. By adjusting the positions of just one of the object, many of the relationships between the other objects have to also adjust. In an environment which is constantly changing, robots need to recognize these changes so it can create a plan which is appropriate for the current condition. Figure 4 tests the effectiveness of the reasoning described throughout this paper to observe if it meets this need. It proves it is able to by adjusting relationships as it changes. A task which moved

['Yellow Arch','Red Rectangular Prism-Wide','Yellow Cube', 'Teal Rectangular Prism-Thin']

Yellow arch is left of red rectangular prism-wide.
Red rectangular prism-wide is right of yellow arch.
Red rectangular prism-wide is left of yellow cube.
Yellow cube is right of red rectangular prism-wide.
Yellow cube is left of teal rectangular prism-thin.
Teal rectangular prism-thin is right of yellow cube.
Yellow arch is left of yellow cube.
Yellow cube is right of yellow arch.
Yellow arch is left of teal rectangular prism-thin.
Teal rectangular prism-thin is right of yellow arch.
Red rectangular prism-wide is left of teal rectangular prism-thin.
Teal rectanular prism-thin is right of red rectangular prism-wide.

['Teal Rectangular Prism-Thin', 'Yellow Arch', "red Rectangular Prism-Wide",'Yellow Cube"]

Teal rectangular prism-thin is left of yellow arch.
Yellow arch is right of teal rectangular prism-thin.
Yellow arch is left of red rectangular prism-wide.
Red rectangular prism-wide is right of yellow arch.
Red rectangular prism-wide is left of yellow cube.
Yellow cube is right of red rectangular prism-wide.
Teal rectangular prism-thin is left of red rectangular prism-wide.
Red rectangular prism-wide is right of teal rectangular prism-thin.
Teal rectangular prism-thin is left of yellow cube.
Yellow cube is right of teal rectangular prism-thin.
Yellow arch is left of yellow cube.
Yewllo cube is right of yellow arch.

Fig. 4. Demonstrates how the relationships among the objects is dynamic. By moving one of the blocks, many of the relationships also must adjust to represent this change (Color figure online).

the farthest right object to the farthest left position would now have a different result after the move then it would have before the move.

5   Conclusion

In this paper, robotic understanding of scene contents and spatial constraints is discussed. The deep learning model with reasoning implemented is proposed in this paper. This reasoning can be used with the grasping in two ways. The first is understanding instruction. If the robot is given an image like Fig. 1, it needs to understand what the final relationships need to be. It can also be used in the instruction stage when the robot receives natural language instruction to move on object to a different position. The second time this is useful is for analyzing the work environment and the objects in an area when the robot prepares to start working. This paper also looked at different techniques for deep learning models. Convolutional Neural Networks were compared against the Faster R-CNN method to show their similarities, but also the advantage of the Region Proposal Network in faster identification and to recognize multiple objects in the same image.

References

1. Deng, J., Dong, W., Socher, R., Li, L.J., Li, K., Fei-Fei, L.: ImageNet: a large-scale hierarchical image database. In: 2009 IEEE Conference on Computer Vision and Pattern Recognition, pp. 248–255, June 2009. https://doi.org/10.1109/CVPR.2009.5206848
2. Feng, C., Xiao, Y., Willette, A., McGee, W., Kamat, V.: Towards autonomous robotic in-situ assembly on unstructured construction sites using monocular vision. In: Proceedings of the 31st International Symposium on Automation and Robotics in Construction, pp. 163–170 (2014)
3. Hossain, M.A., Mukit, M.: A real-time face to camera distance measurement algorithm using object classification. In: 2015 International Conference on Computer and Information Engineering (ICCIE), pp. 107–110, November 2015. https://doi.org/10.1109/CCIE.2015.7399293
4. Kennedy, M., Queen, K., Thakur, D., Daniilidis, K., Kumar, V.: Precise dispensing of liquids using visual feedback. In: 2017 IEEE/RSJ International Conference on Intelligent Robots and Systems (IROS), pp. 1260–1266, September 2017. https://doi.org/10.1109/IROS.2017.8202301
5. Krizhevsky, A., Sutskever, I., Hinton, G.E.: Imagenet classification with deep convolutional neural networks. In: Advances in Neural Information Processing Systems, pp. 1097–1105 (2012)
6. Ren, S., He, K., Girshick, R., Sun, J.: Faster R-CNN: towards real-time object detection with region proposal networks. In: Advances in Neural Information Processing Systems, pp. 91–99 (2015)
7. Stratigopoulos, H.G.: Machine learning applications in IC testing. In: 2018 IEEE 23rd European Test Symposium (ETS), pp. 1–10, May 2018. https://doi.org/10.1109/ETS.2018.8400701

Social Robots and Wearable Sensors for Mitigating Meltdowns in Autism - A Pilot Test

John-John Cabibihan[1(✉)], Ryad Chellali[2], Catherine Wing Chee So[3],
Mohammad Aldosari[4], Olcay Connor[5], Ahmad Yaser Alhaddad[1,7],
and Hifza Javed[6]

[1] Mechanical and Industrial Engineering Department, Qatar University, Doha, Qatar
john.cabibihan@qu.edu.qa
[2] College of Electrical Engineering and Control Science, Nanjing Tech University,
Nanjing, China
[3] Department of Educational Psychology, Chinese University of Hong Kong,
Shatin, Hong Kong
[4] Center for Pediatric Neurology, Cleveland Clinic, Cleveland, OH, USA
[5] Step by Step Special Needs Center, Doha, Qatar
[6] Biomedical Engineering Department, George Washington University,
Washington DC, USA
[7] Department of Electronics, Information and Bioengineering, Politecnico di Milano,
Milano, Italy

Abstract. Young individuals with ASD may exhibit challenging behaviors. Among these, self-injurious behavior (SIB) is the most devastating for a person's physical health and inclusion within the community. SIB refers to a class of behaviors that an individual inflicts upon himself or herself, which may potentially result in physical injury (e.g. hitting one's own head with the hand or the wrist, banging one's head on the wall, biting oneself and pulling out one's own hair). We evaluate the feasibility of a wrist-wearable sensor in detecting challenging behaviors in a child with autism prior to any visible signs through the monitoring of the child's heart rate, electrodermal activity, and movements. Furthermore, we evaluate the feasibility of such sensor to be used on an ankle instead of the wrist to reduce harm due to hitting oneself by hands and to improve wearable tolerance. Thus, we conducted two pilot tests. The first test involved a wearable sensor on the wrist of a child with autism. In a second test, we investigated wearable sensors on the wrist and on the ankle of a neurotypical child. Both pilot test results showed that the readings from the wearable sensors correlated with the children's behaviors that were obtained from the videos taken during the tests. Wearable sensors could provide additional information that can be passed to social robots or to the caregivers for mitigating SIBs.

Keywords: Social robots · Wearable sensors · Autism · Meltdown
Challenging behaviors

© Springer Nature Switzerland AG 2018
S. S. Ge et al. (Eds.): ICSR 2018, LNAI 11357, pp. 103–114, 2018.
https://doi.org/10.1007/978-3-030-05204-1_11

1   Introduction

Autism Spectrum Disorder (ASD) is a complex developmental disability that causes problems with social interaction and communication. Symptoms usually start before the age of three [2] and can cause delays or problems in many different skills, which develop from infancy to adulthood. The manifestations of ASD usually appear in different forms, including the inability to relate to other people, little use of eye contact, difficulty in understanding gestures and facial expressions, difficulties with verbal and non-verbal communication, and difficulty in understanding others' intentions, feelings, and mental states [13,35,42].

Although not included in the official diagnostic criteria, there are certain maladaptive responses that are found to co-vary with ASD at a high rate. These are termed "challenging behaviors", which is one of the most distressing and difficult behaviors that parents, caregivers, family members, and individuals with autism themselves may be faced with. They have been defined as culturally abnormal behaviors of such intensity, frequency or duration that the physical safety of the person or others is likely to be placed in serious jeopardy, or behavior which is likely to seriously limit use of, or result in the person being denied access to, ordinary community facilities [15]. These can take several forms, ranging from physical aggression, verbal aggression, property destruction, tantrums and self-injurious behaviors (SIBs). Of these, SIBs have been studied in more detail. SIBs commonly manifest as head-banging, self-scratching, self-biting, hair pulling, self-cutting, and self-pinching.

A recent study suggests that 60% of young individuals with ASD exhibit challenging behaviors [30]. Studies from the UK and the US report that 10–15% of people with intellectual disabilities show such behaviors [20]. Among these practices, SIB is the most devastating for a person's physical health and inclusion within the community. Researchers studying the lifetime prevalence in those with ASD report that at least 50% engage in some form of SIB [15,30]. At the heart of such behavior is the inability to communicate feelings and needs, which cause frustration and stress that eventually manifest as challenging behaviors. Other than the immediate negative physical impact, such behaviors also have the dire consequences of social exclusion, limited educational and vocational opportunities, inability to learn new skills, as well as diminishing the effectiveness of other therapies. The fact that such behaviors aggravate with age emphasizes the need for early intervention.

Among early intervention techniques, antecedent interventions create the most opportunity for impact. These techniques aim to alter the environment of the child ahead of the challenging behavior so as to reduce the likelihood of the behavior occurring in the future. Once such a behavior is underway, it cannot be stopped and has to be allowed to run its course. Figure 1a depicts a scenario when a child experiences a negative stimulus (e.g. noise, unwanted object) and an unwanted behaviour occurs. The parent or therapist sees this behavior and intervenes. If the intervention is not effective, the unwanted behavior continues until the intervention is successful. Through wearable sensors and social robots, we investigate whether signals can be used to detect challenging behaviors and then be sent to the therapist (Fig. 1b) or to a social robot (Fig. 1c) to make an early intervention. Once the child experiences a negative stimulus, the sensors worn by the child will report a high anxiety signal to the human or to the robot who will intervene in removing the stimulus. In partnership with the therapist, the social robot could be used as a mediator or as a co-therapist to help in calming the child once the stress signals are received from the wearable sensors.

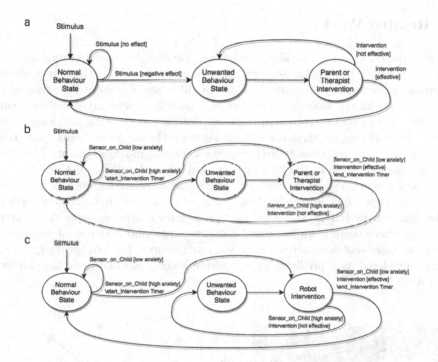

Fig. 1. Framework for antecedent intervention with wearable sensors. (a) For the typical intervention without wearable sensors, an unwanted behavior occurs when a child experiences a negative stimulus (e.g. noise, unwanted object). The parent or therapist sees this behavior and intervenes. If the intervention is not effective, the unwanted behavior continues until the intervention is successful. (b) Intervention by the therapist. (c) Intervention by the child's preferred social robot companion. Once the child experiences a negative stimulus, the sensors worn by the child will report a high anxiety signal to the human and to the robot who will intervene in removing the stimulus.

For this framework to be successfully implemented, it would be necessary to investigate the physiological signals that will be sent to the therapist or to the social robot before the intervention can be made. In this paper, we aim to investigate the physiological signals from a child with autism when the child interacts with a robot. Some children might exhibit hypersensitivity or annoyance toward wrist wearables and thus, they will refuse to wear them. Furthermore, having devices on the wrist could increase harm during the manifestation of SIBs. For these reasons, we investigate the possibility on whether the signals from a sensor worn at the wrist would be similar to a wearable sensor worn at the ankle.

In the next section, we present the related works on the potential of wearable sensors and social robots for mitigating meltdowns. In Sect. 3, we describe the materials and methods used in the study. In Sect. 4, we present the results. Section 5 concludes the paper.

2   Related Works

Human physiological data, like heart rate, sweat rate, and movements, can be detected using wearable sensors. In an earlier work [7], the physiological responses of university students ($n = 30$; 18–30 years old) were investigated as they watched an emotionally-laden movie. Figure 2 shows that when the heart rate data are increasing, the skin response data are decreasing and vice versa. There was a strong negative correlation between the subjects' heart rate (HR) and galvanic skin response (GSR) responses for the movie segment. The data crossed the zero slope at the 20 to 24 s period when the death of a child in the movie was impending. This result was consistent to other results where movies that show impending injury or death cause an increase in GSR activity and a deceleration in HR [8,43]. This pattern follows a stimulus-specific aversive response where there is an increased sensory intake and attentional processing as well as more sustained attention [3,38]. Furthermore, physiological signals are being considered as a predictor of aggression among minimally-verbal children with ASD [17].

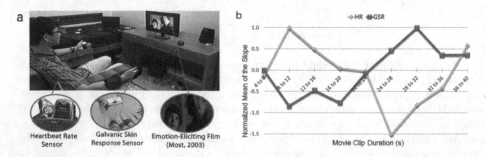

Fig. 2. Physiological responses to induced emotional stimuli. (a) Normalized slope of the heart rates and sweat rates of subjects were collected as they watched a movie wherein a child died. (b) Inverse relationship between heart rate and sweat rate [7].

A movement detection method was described for assessing problem behaviors of children with ASD (i.e., aggression, disruption, and self-injury) [8,38]. Using accelerometers on the wrist and machine learning techniques, severe behavioral episodes were detected with a precision greater than 95%. Accuracy close to 80%

was achieved for specific differentiation among aggression, disruption, self-injury, and unrelated movements. Because any devices worn on the wrist might be used by the children with autism to hurt themselves during episodes of problem behaviors, other locations aside from the wrist is worth investigating. Moreover, it would be ideal to investigate technologies (e.g. social robots) that can prevent unwanted behaviors to escalate rather than allowing the behavior to occur.

According to the social motivation theory of autism, individuals with ASD show deficits in orienting toward social stimuli, engaging with humans, and maintaining social relations [12,19,23]. Empirical evidence has shown that individuals with ASD tend to have low interest in other humans and have a weaker understanding of the interpersonal world than of the object-related world [25,26]. In addition, they find it challenging to pay attention to multiple cues during social interactions with humans [27,28]. Thus, they are not sensitive to other people's behaviors [32]. Furthermore, some studies have shown that individuals with ASD may find it difficult to learn social skills from human therapists. For example, Dewey and colleagues [13] showed that five to 18 year old individuals with ASD (with a wide range of IQs) were less likely to imitate isolated gestures, which were demonstrated by a human experimenter, and produce gestures on command than children with other developmental disorders.

In contrast to therapists, social robots may be more suitable for individuals with ASD. Based on the empathizing-systemizing theory [4], robots are operated on predictable and lawful systems, thereby providing children with ASD with a highly structured learning environment and helping them to focus on the relevant stimuli [6,14]. Additionally, children with ASD do not need to consider socioemotional expectations when interacting with robots [41], thus reducing their social anxiety [35]. Social robots have been widely used in therapy for individuals with ASD over the past decade [9,16,33]. Children with ASD treat their talking robot as a social agent, which attracts their attention [29,36]. Social robots are also found to arouse interest in children, thereby eliciting positive and productive responses from them [39], which in turn helps them to develop interpersonal distance, joint attention behaviors, self-initiated interactions, non-verbal communication skills, and an ability to make eye contact [10,11,18,21,22,49].

Several studies have been conducted to evaluate whether individuals with ASD respond to social robots more favorably than to human beings. Previous studies have shown that children with ASD respond faster [5,37], manifest eye contact more frequently [44], and need fewer prompts [46] when interacting with a robot than when interacting with a human. Shamsuddin et al. [40] even reported that children with ASD produced fewer stereotyped behaviors (e.g., avoiding eye contact, turning in circles, rocking back and forth) during the interaction session with a robot than in the regular classroom setting in which a human teacher was involved. Michaud et al. [34] also reported similar findings. Additionally, they found that children with ASD who interacted with a robot were more likely to show shared attention and to imitate facial expressions than those who interacted with a human mediator. A study by Kim et al. [24] showed that children with ASD spoke more when interacting with a social robot than when interacting with an adult during a computer game. Lee and Obinata [31] further used the robot to provide feedback to children with ASD in a task and found that these children accomplished more than their peers who received feedback from a caregiver and a laptop. On the other hand, Wainer et al. [47] found that children with ASD who played with an autonomous robot in the first session were more engaged in the video game with a human partner in the second session, whereas those who played with a human in the first session did not show any increase in engagement in the second session. This result was replicated in their later study [48]. These results suggest that children with ASD might have gained some social skills when interacting with the autonomous robots and they transferred those skills to human-to-human interactions.

3   Materials and Methods

3.1   Participants

A 10 year old boy participated in the first pilot test. He was diagnosed with mild autism and attended the Step By Step Center for Special Needs in Doha, Qatar. For the second pilot test, a 6 year old neurotypical boy participated in the experiment. The consent from the parents were secured. The children were accompanied by either a teacher or a parent. Both participants were close in age and their physiological signals are believed to be comparable (cf. [17]). The procedures for this work did not include invasive or potentially hazardous methods and were in accordance with the Code of Ethics of the World Medical Association (Declaration of Helsinki).

3.2   Sensors and Stimuli

The wearable sensor E4 wristband (Empatica, S.r.l., Milano, Italy) was used in the experiments. The wristband has multiple sensors. The electrodermal activity (EDA) sensor detects changes in the sweat rates, a photoplethysmograph (PPG) sensor for the heart rate, a 3-axis accelerometer for movements, and an optical infrared thermometer for detecting the skin temperature. There were two sets of stimuli that were used to help interact with the child with autism. The first set were toys that produced bubbles: a multi-colored toy train and a toy bubble gun. The other set was a robotic seal (PARO Robots USA, Inc., IL, USA). The movements of the robot seal were autonomous and were limited to the built-in functions.

3.3   Experimental Design

For the first test, an unstructured play scenario was implemented to investigate the child's reactions to the stimuli and for us to see the sensors' response. The sensor was worn on the wrist. The child with ASD that exhibited anxiety and aggressive reactions was one of the children that participated in an earlier study

[1]. In that study, different stimuli were presented to ten children with ASD and videos were taken. All videos were annotated to record their reactions. More details about the experimental setup, protocol, analysis, and stimuli used can be found in the aforementioned study [1].

For the second test, the child was asked to stand still, rotate ten times, and stand still again for us to investigate whether the sensor that is worn on the wrist has similar responses to the sensor that is worn on the ankle. This was done to evaluate the possibility of implementing an ankle-worn sensor to prevent a child to hit himself/herself with a sensor on the wrist.

The children's interactions were monitored with a network camera (MyDlink DCS- 931L, D-Link, Taipei, Taiwan), which was placed in front of the child. Care was taken in the setup of the equipment to ensure that it remained unobtrusive throughout the length of the experiment. The timestamps of the raw data of the wearable sensor were then matched with the timing of the annotated videos that were then used in the analysis.

4   Results

4.1   Wearable Sensors on a Child with ASD

The child wore sensors that can detect heart rate, sweat rate, and acceleration. In Fig. 3a, the child's electrodermal activity (EDA) showed low values when he interacted with bubbles. His hands were moving as he was catching the bubbles, hence, there is an increase in movement (acceleration). In Fig. 3b, the bubble-producing toys are slowly being removed. The EDA increased by 93.17% and the clustering in the blood volume pulse (BVP) increased. In Fig. 3c, the bubbles were totally removed and a new toy was presented. The high EDA was sustained and there was increased acceleration due to the movement of the hands as the child covered his right ear. In Fig. 3d, the robotic seal was presented in front of the child. The high EDA was sustained. There was clustering of the BVP and there was sustained increase in hand movements because the child covered both his left and right ears.

4.2   Sensors When Worn on the Wrist and on the Ankle

Some of the children that we tested in earlier experiments did not like the contact of the sensors at their wrists [1]. It is also conceivable that children could use the wrist-based device to hurt themselves during an episode of a challenging behavior. Figure 4a shows our results for a sensor on the ankle that has a 3-axis accelerometer. In this pilot test, we made a neurotypical child simulate a spinning behavior of a child with autism. In Fig. 4b and d, the child was instructed to stand still. We can observe that the acceleration on the wrist and on the ankle was a near-horizontal line, implying a non-movement of the child. In Fig. 3c, the child was instructed to turn around 10 times. We can find that the sensors on the wrist and on the ankle showed patterns of correlated activity in the acceleration

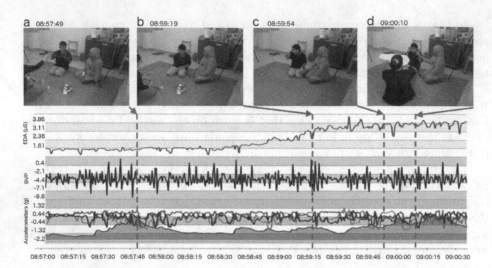

Fig. 3. Results showing a timestamped video and physiological sensors on a child with autism (a) The boy played with bubbles. The increase in hand movement showed high values in acceleration readings; (b) The bubble toy was removed. Blood volume pulse (BVP) increased; (c) Toys completely removed and the boy heard the sound of the robot seal. He covered his right ear and showed increase values in the accelerometer readings. Electrodermal Activity (EDA) was at high level; (d) The robot seal was shown to the boy. He covered both ears. EDA was at a high level.

and blood volume pulse (BVP). This confirms that there is a potential to transfer sensors from the wrist to the feet and get useful measures when machine learning algorithms are implemented.

5   Discussion and Conclusions

Meltdowns can occur when a child with autism experiences sensory overload [45]. This paper offered insights into answering a longer-term question: Can we bypass a child's meltdown using some form of technology? (cf. Fig. 1). Once a child experiences a stimulus, it is desired that a wearable sensor will detect whether a certain stimulus can cause high anxiety to the child or not. If the sensor reports high anxiety signals (i.e. increases in heart rate, sweat rate and/or unnecessary movements), intervention will be done by a social robot or by a parent. The goal is to remove or minimize the negative stimulus. However, this aim could not be achieved if we do not have an idea on whether the wearable sensors work.

In this paper, we ran two pilot tests to see what signals are recorded by the sensors. In the first pilot test, we saw that the child's EDA increased close to 100% when the child's preferred toys were removed from him (cf. Fig. 3). Likewise, the BVP showed 3 successive peak values when the toys were removed (cf. Fig. 3b). In a second pilot test, we aimed to evaluate whether a sensor on the wrist can have a similar output when the sensor is placed on the ankle. As

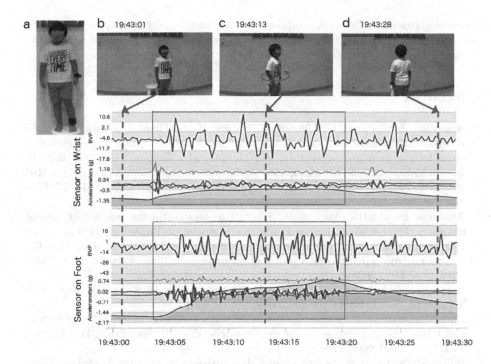

Fig. 4. Results showing the sensors when worn by a neurotypical child doing 10 rotations. (a) Sensors mounted on the left wrist and on the ankle. (b) Child standing, accelerometer readings on the wrist and on the ankle show static response. (b) Child rotating, accelerometers showing movements. Blood volume pulse (BVP) showing higher values compared to standing position. (c) Child standing, accelerometers show static response.

designers, we need to anticipate that a stiff object like a wearable device can be used by the child to hurt himself or herself. We found that a child's standing behavior correlated with static responses from the sensor while a rotational behavior correlated with dynamic responses in both sensors, which were worn on the wrist and on the ankle. In summary, wearable sensing is a promising approach to correlate physiological measures to changes in the environment and the movements of a child. This is significant because some of the children with ASD may be non-verbal and they could not express their needs and wants.

For future work, we will be able to calculate the total time of intervention from the start of the high anxiety signal until the child returns to the normal behavior state after the intervention. We will also be able to compare the advantages and disadvantages between interventions from a parent or a social robot considering that the anxiety levels from a child can now be detected by wearable sensors.

Acknowledgments. The work is supported by a research grant from Qatar University under the grant QUST-1-CENG-2018-7. The statements made herein are solely the responsibility of the authors.

References

1. Alhaddad, A.Y., Javed, H., Connor, O., Banire, B., Al Thani, D., Cabibihan, J.J.: Robotic trains as an educational and therapeutic tool for autism spectrum disorder intervention. In: Lepuschitz, W., Merdan, M., Koppensteiner, G., Balogh, R., Obdržálek, D. (eds.) International Conference on Robotics and Education RiE 2017, vol. 829, pp. 249–262. Springer, Cham (2018). https://doi.org/10.1007/978-3-319-97085-1_25
2. American Psychiatric Association: Diagnostic and statistical manual of mental disorders (DSM-5®). American Psychiatric Association Publishing (2013)
3. Baldaro, B., Mazzetti, M., Codispoti, M., Tuozzi, G., Bolzani, R., Trombini, G.: Autonomic reactivity during viewing of an unpleasant film. Percept. Mot. Skills **93**(3), 797–805 (2001)
4. Baron-Cohen, S.: Autism: the empathizing-systemizing (E-S) theory. Ann. New York Acad. Sci. **1156**(1), 68–80 (2009)
5. Bird, G., Leighton, J., Press, C., Heyes, C.: Intact automatic imitation of human and robot actions in autism spectrum disorders. Proc. R. Soc. Lond. B: Biol. Sci. **274**(1628), 3027–3031 (2007)
6. Bölte, S.: Evidenzbasierte intervention. In: Autismus. Spektrum, Ursachen, Diagnostik, Intervention, Perspektiven, pp. 221–228(2009)
7. Cabibihan, J.J., Chauhan, S.S.: Physiological responses to affective tele-touch during induced emotional stimuli. IEEE Trans. Affect. Comput. **8**(1), 108–118 (2017)
8. Cabibihan, J.J., Javed, H., Aldosari, M., Frazier, T.W., Elbashir, H.: Sensing technologies for autism spectrum disorder screening and intervention. Sensors **17**(1), 46 (2016)
9. Cabibihan, J.J., Javed, H., Ang, M., Aljunied, S.M.: Why robots? A survey on the roles and benefits of social robots in the therapy of children with autism. Int. J. Soc. Robot. **5**(4), 593–618 (2013)
10. Cabibihan, J.-J., So, W.C., Nazar, M., Ge, S.S.: Pointing gestures for a robot mediated communication interface. In: Xie, M., Xiong, Y., Xiong, C., Liu, H., Hu, Z. (eds.) ICIRA 2009. LNCS (LNAI), vol. 5928, pp. 67–77. Springer, Heidelberg (2009). https://doi.org/10.1007/978-3-642-10817-4_7
11. Cabibihan, J.J., So, W.C., Pramanik, S.: Human-recognizable robotic gestures. IEEE Trans. Auton. Ment. Dev. **4**(4), 305–314 (2012)
12. Chevallier, C., Kohls, G., Troiani, V., Brodkin, E.S., Schultz, R.T.: The social motivation theory of autism. Trends Cogn. Sci. **16**(4), 231–239 (2012)
13. Dewey, D., Cantell, M., Crawford, S.G.: Motor and gestural performance in children with autism spectrum disorders, developmental coordination disorder, and/or attention deficit hyperactivity disorder. J. Int. Neuropsychol. Soc. **13**(2), 246–256 (2007)
14. Duquette, A., Michaud, F., Mercier, H.: Exploring the use of a mobile robot as an imitation agent with children with low-functioning autism. Auton. Robots **24**(2), 147–157 (2008)
15. Emerson, E.: Challenging Behaviour: Analysis and Intervention in People with Learning Disabilities. Cambridge University Press, Cambridge (1995)

16. Fong, T., Nourbakhsh, I., Dautenhahn, K.: A survey of socially interactive robots. Robot. Auton. Syst. **42**(3–4), 143–166 (2003)
17. Goodwin, M.S., et al.: Predicting imminent aggression onset in minimally-verbal youth with autism spectrum disorder using preceding physiological signals. In: Proceedings of the 12th EAI International Conference on Pervasive Computing Technologies for Healthcare, pp. 201–207. ACM (2018)
18. Ham, J., van Esch, M., Limpens, Y., de Pee, J., Cabibihan, J.-J., Ge, S.S.: The automaticity of social behavior towards robots: the influence of cognitive load on interpersonal distance to approachable versus less approachable robots. In: Ge, S.S., Khatib, O., Cabibihan, J.-J., Simmons, R., Williams, M.-A. (eds.) ICSR 2012. LNCS (LNAI), vol. 7621, pp. 15–25. Springer, Heidelberg (2012). https://doi.org/10.1007/978-3-642-34103-8_2
19. Hoa, T.D., Cabibihan, J.J.: Cute and soft: baby steps in designing robots for children with autism. In: Proceedings of the Workshop at SIGGRAPH Asia, pp. 77–79. ACM (2012)
20. Holden, B., Gitlesen, J.P.: A total population study of challenging behaviour in the county of Hedmark, Norway: prevalence, and risk markers. Res. Dev. Disabil. **27**(4), 456–465 (2006)
21. Javed, H., Cabibihan, J.J., Al-Attiyah, A.A.: Autism in the Gulf States: why social robotics is the way forward. In: ICTA, pp. 1–3 (2015)
22. Javed, H., Cabibihan, J.-J., Aldosari, M., Al-Attiyah, A.: Culture as a driver for the design of social robots for autism spectrum disorder interventions in the middle east. In: Agah, A., Cabibihan, J.-J., Howard, A.M., Salichs, M.A., He, H. (eds.) ICSR 2016. LNCS (LNAI), vol. 9979, pp. 591–599. Springer, Cham (2016). https://doi.org/10.1007/978-3-319-47437-3_58
23. Javed, H., Connor, O.B., Cabibihan, J.J.: Thomas and friends: implications for the design of social robots and their role as social story telling agents for children with autism. In: 2015 IEEE International Conference on Robotics and Biomimetics (ROBIO), pp. 1145–1150. IEEE (2015)
24. Kim, E.S., et al.: Social robots as embedded reinforcers of social behavior in children with autism. J. Autism Dev. Disord. **43**(5), 1038–1049 (2013)
25. Klin, A., Jones, W.: Attributing social and physical meaning to ambiguous visual displays in individuals with higher-functioning autism spectrum disorders. Brain Cogn. **61**(1), 40–53 (2006)
26. Klin, A., Lin, D.J., Gorrindo, P., Ramsay, G., Jones, W.: Two-year-olds with autism orient to non-social contingencies rather than biological motion. Nature **459**(7244), 257 (2009)
27. Koegel, L.K., Koegel, R.L., Harrower, J.K., Carter, C.M.: Pivotal response intervention I: overview of approach. J. Assoc. Pers. Sev. Handicaps **24**(3), 174–185 (1999)
28. Koegel, L.K., Koegel, R.L., Shoshan, Y., McNerney, E.: Pivotal response intervention II: preliminary long-term outcome data. J. Assoc. Pers. Sev. Handicaps **24**(3), 186–198 (1999)
29. Kozima, H., Michalowski, M.P., Nakagawa, C.: Keepon. Int. J. Soc. Robot. **1**(1), 3–18 (2009)
30. Lecavalier, L., Leone, S., Wiltz, J.: The impact of behaviour problems on caregiver stress in young people with autism spectrum disorders. J. Intellect. Disabil. Res. **50**(3), 172–183 (2006)
31. Lee, J., Obinata, G.: Interactive educational material for children with ASD. In: 2015 International Symposium on Micro-NanoMechatronics and Human Science (MHS), pp. 1–6. IEEE (2015)

32. Lee, J., Takehashi, H., Nagai, C., Obinata, G., Stefanov, D.: Which robot features can stimulate better responses from children with autism in robot-assisted therapy? Int. J. Adv. Robot. Syst. **9**(3), 72 (2012)
33. Li, H., Cabibihan, J.J., Tan, Y.K.: Towards an effective design of social robots. Int. J. Soc. Robot. **3**(4), 333–335 (2011)
34. Michaud, F., et al.: Assistive technologies and child-robot interaction. In: AAAI Spring Symposium on Multidisciplinary Collaboration for Socially Assistive Robotics (2007)
35. Mitchell, P., Parsons, S., Leonard, A.: Using virtual environments for teaching social understanding to 6 adolescents with autistic spectrum disorders. J. Autism Dev. Disord. **37**(3), 589–600 (2007)
36. Miyamoto, E., Lee, M., Fujii, H., Okada, M.: How can robots facilitate social interaction of children with autism?: Possible implications for educational environments (2005)
37. Pierno, A.C., Mari, M., Lusher, D., Castiello, U.: Robotic movement elicits visuomotor priming in children with autism. Neuropsychologia **46**(2), 448–454 (2008)
38. Plötz, T., Hammerla, N.Y., Rozga, A., Reavis, A., Call, N., Abowd, G.D.: Automatic assessment of problem behavior in individuals with developmental disabilities. In: Proceedings of the 2012 ACM Conference on Ubiquitous Computing, pp. 391–400. ACM (2012)
39. Scassellati, B., Admoni, H., Matarić, M.: Robots for use in autism research. Annu. Rev. Biomed. Eng. **14**, 275–294 (2012)
40. Shamsuddin, S., Yussof, H., Miskam, M.A., Hamid, A.C., Malik, N.A., Hashim, H.: Humanoid robot NAO as HRI mediator to teach emotions using game-centered approach for children with autism. In: HRI 2013 Workshop on Applications for Emotional Robots (2013)
41. Silver, M., Oakes, P.: Evaluation of a new computer intervention to teach people with autism or asperger syndrome to recognize and predict emotions in others. Autism **5**(3), 299–316 (2001)
42. So, W.C., Wong, M.Y., Cabibihan, J.J., Lam, C.Y., Chan, R.Y., Qian, H.H.: Using robot animation to promote gestural skills in children with autism spectrum disorders. J. Comput. Assist. Learn. **32**(6), 632–646 (2016)
43. Steptoe, A., Wardle, J.: Emotional fainting and the psychophysiologic response to blood and injury: autonomic mechanisms and coping strategies. Psychosom. Med. **50**(4), 402–417 (1988)
44. Tapus, A., et al.: Children with autism social engagement in interaction with nao, an imitative robot: a series of single case experiments. Interact. Stud. **13**(3), 315–347 (2012)
45. Teo, H.T., Cabibihan, J.J.: Toward soft, robust robots for children with autism spectrum disorder. In: FinE-R@ IROS, pp. 15–19 (2015)
46. Vanderborght, B., et al.: Using the social robot probo as a social story telling agent for children with ASD. Interac. Stud. **13**(3), 348–372 (2012)
47. Wainer, J., Dautenhahn, K., Robins, B., Amirabdollahian, F.: A pilot study with a novel setup for collaborative play of the humanoid robot KASPAR with children with autism. Int. J. Soc. Robot. **6**(1), 45–65 (2014)
48. Wainer, J., Robins, B., Amirabdollahian, F., Dautenhahn, K.: Using the humanoid robot kaspar to autonomously play triadic games and facilitate collaborative play among children with autism. IEEE Trans. Auton. Ment. Dev. **6**(3), 183–199 (2014)
49. Wykowska, A., Kajopoulos, J., Obando-Leiton, M., Chauhan, S.S., Cabibihan, J.J., Cheng, G.: Humans are well tuned to detecting agents among non-agents: examining the sensitivity of human perception to behavioral characteristics of intentional systems. Int. J. Soc. Robot. **7**(5), 767–781 (2015)

Autonomous Control Through the Level of Fatigue Applied to the Control of Autonomous Vehicles

Oscar A. Mayorga[✉] and Víctor H. Andaluz[✉]

Universidad de las Fuerzas Armadas ESPE, Sangolquí, Ecuador
{oamayorga,vhandaluz1}@espe.edu.ec

Abstract. In this article we present the detection of fatigue level of a vehicle driver and according to this level the autonomous driving assistance is implemented, the detection of fatigue level is based on facial recognition using deep learning (Deep Learning) developed in the Matlab software, applying neural networks previously trained and designed, this detection sends us a metric that comprises four levels, according to the metric the position and velocity control of a simulated Car-Like vehicle in the Unity3D software is performed which presents a user friendly environment with the use of haptic devices, the development of the control algorithm is based on path correction which calculates the shortest distance to reenter the desired path.

Keywords: Face recognition · Deep learning · Path tracking

1 Introduction

Traffic accidents are unforeseen events that cause harm to a person or thing, suddenly caused by an involuntary external agent [1, 2]. Over the years, the continuous increase in paths, and the number of vehicles in most countries, the velocity, lack of concentration, failure to respect regulatory traffic signals, driving under the influence of alcohol, driving in a state of drowsiness, they have produced an increase in the mortality rate and disability in people [2–6]. Some studies show that from 25% to 30% of traffic accidents are related to fatigue [7], so the way to reduce this type of accident is a major problem that must be resolved to reduce the threat of life, health and property of people.

Some researchers have developed some methods to improve driving safety based on: sensors and parking cameras [8, 9], cognitive information processing [10], threat assessment during semiautonomous driving [11]. If the driver's fatigue state can be detected, it will be possible to prevent drivers from driving in a sleepy state [12]. Some physiological characteristics, such as brain wave, blinking frequency, heart rate and blood pressure are aspects that identify fatigue in drivers [13–15].

.The level of fatigue is detected through the recognition of characteristics defined in the human face and the positions it presents. For the detection of faces, the following aspects are considered: shape of the face, alignment of the face and face representation [16]. The main methods of face recognition can be classified into methods based on

© Springer Nature Switzerland AG 2018
S. S. Ge et al. (Eds.): ICSR 2018, LNAI 11357, pp. 115–126, 2018.
https://doi.org/10.1007/978-3-030-05204-1_12

geometric characteristics, sub-spatial analysis methods, model-based methods, local methods based on characteristics, techniques based on machine learning [17], among others. However, since a few years ago, the methods based on deep learning combine massive data training, this manages to recognize faces quickly and effectively [18].

Deep learning is a set of machine learning algorithms that attempts to model high-level abstractions in data using architectures composed of multiple non-linear transformations [19]. Several deep learning architectures, such as deep neural networks, deep convolutional neural networks, and deep belief networks, have been applied to fields such as computer vision, automatic speech recognition, and recognition of audio and music signals, this has generated results state of the art in various tasks [20].

For what has been described, the present work shows an alternative to this problem, considering levels of fatigue in the driver identified by means of deep learning, and with the assistance of a driver decreases the velocity of the vehicle to avoid traffic accidents. The driver's fatigue level detection is based on the gestures and facial positions that the driver makes when he shows a certain degree of drowsiness or fatigue. The present work presents three main stages: *(i) Fatigue detection* is the one that is responsible for determining the driver's level of tiredness that is based on the gestures and positions.

For the detection of fatigue level, a detection algorithm will be implemented through deep learning that classifies the images obtained by means of a webcam processed by the Matlab software, the algorithm contains a neural network trained by means of a database in which they are located images of the levels of fatigue. *(ii) Driving assistance,* in this stage is proposed a control algorithm that uses the variables of velocity, position and orientation that are received from the haptic devices, to perform the correction of these variables with respect to a pattern and according to the level of fatigue presented by the driver; *(iii) Simulation environment,* this contains user-friendly driving simulation software which obtains velocity, position and direction data once a control algorithm has been made according to the levels of fatigue to move the vehicle and feedback the value of the variables that are in that moment towards the control algorithm.

2 Fatigue Level Detection

The recognition of the level of fatigue presented by a driver is based on the detection of the facial features, the levels have been divided into four: (i) level zero, the driver does not present any change of facial features that he usually has; (ii) level one, there are constant yawns, (iii) level two, the eyes of the driver have been partially closed with the upper eyelid in half, (iv) level three, the driver has completely closed the eyes and then makes a tilt mild face that indicates total drowsiness.

To identify the aforementioned levels, object detection and recognition techniques are used; because they are similar techniques which vary when performing their execution, the processing based on Deep Learning takes it with a subset of characteristics where the level of fatigue that is presented at that moment is identified.

The deep learning approach is based on the transfer which involves a previously trained neural network with thousands of categories, the Deep Learning algorithm consist of 4 stages in which the structure of the neural network is included: (i) import of the convolutional neuronal network previously trains, (ii) modification of the layers final, (iii) new training of the network, (iv) prediction and evaluation of the accuracy of the network; between layer three and four there is a retro feed for the improvement of the network.

The first stage uses the Alexnet network [21], which has been trained with a database with more than 15 million tagged images corresponding to 22000 categories, the structure of this network consists of 13 layers of learning and 3 fully-connected layers for classification. The learning layers have three sublayers: (i) convolution, (ii) grouping, (iii) Rectified Rectilinear Unit (ReLU). Each of the layers takes the data from the previous layer, transforms them according to the parameters it needs to learn and finally transfers them to the next layer, *i.e,* each layer learns different properties of the image, activates with the characteristics of the image such as colors, shapes, contours, gray scale among others.

In the second stage corresponds to the reconfiguration of the last three layers of the Alexnet network [21], which must contain the necessary information to combine the characteristics that the network extracts in the classification and label probabilities; the modification of the antepenultimate layer corresponds to the fully connected layer that obtains the new weights of each of the previous layers to perform deep learning, the penultimate layer corresponds to the Softmax layer that contains the probabilities of the new trained objects and the last layer corresponds to the output layer where the classification of the input image is made.

The network training stage uses the new images corresponding to fatigue levels, grouped into four categories: (i) normal, (ii) yawning, (iii) medium and (iv) drowsiness, all of them contained in a database with 100 images in each one of the categories, Fig. 1, that contain the characteristics of the facial features that each person presents in both men and women. The greatest difference in traits can be identified in the category of yawning because the opening of the mouth of people is different, the likelihood that they close their eyes when yawning is high and the formation of other physical features such as expression lines changes from person to person. For network training a stochastic gradient descent is used with a lot size of 5 examples, an impulse of 0.9 and a weight decrease of 0.0005, this small amount of weight reduction is not a simple regulator, but that reduces the training error of the model.

To perform the training, the database contains images of size 227×227 pixels, the parameters that are defined in the training options, the database is divided into 70% of the images for the training and 30% for validation, the initial learning rate, frequency and validation estimation are defined. The final stage corresponds to the evaluation of

(a) Yawn   (b) Medium   (c) Normal   (d) Somnolence

Fig. 1. Level of fatigue categories

the new trained network, where the percentage of operation of the new data is seen, for this the matrix of confusion of dimension is obtained *kxk*, *k* is the number of categories trained, the matrix contains the new trained categories. Each of the positions in the matrix indicates how many images have confusion in the same category as in the other categories; if the matrix diagonal contains the total number of images trained per layer, this indicates that the network had no errors when performing the training and has a 0% error. Figure 2 shows the confusion matrix of the facial features training where the diagonal contains 70% of the total network training, and in each of the positions of the matrix corresponds the number of images that is confused by identifying the four levels of fatigue that a driver represents.

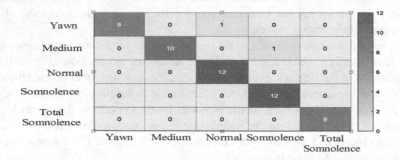

Fig. 2. Matrix of confusion of the training of the network for the detection of fatigue.

In the classification of images, the prediction is made according to the probabilities and the network continues training until the error decreases to 0% in the prediction of each of the images that are entered for the classification. To have a good workout the Accuracy must be greater than 65% and the error must be close to zero.

3 Control System Implemented

The proposed control algorithm is implemented in the Matlab software, which allows the programming of the control algorithms in an efficient way. The structure of the control is in closed loop with a force feedback that indicates the behavior of the terrestrial vehicle within the virtual environment that is developed in the Unity 3D graphics engine, with this behavior the controller sends the corresponding control actions to correct the error. In Fig. 3 we propose the control structure that is carried out depending on the level of fatigue that is detected in the driver, to execute the appropriate control in Matlab for path correction.

The control stage consists of three parts: *(i) Fatigue index*, which is given by the algorithm of Deep Learning according to the level of fatigue, which presents the driver of the vehicle as indicated in (1), levels of fatigue they have discrete values between 0 and 1, thus: normal is 0, yawn is 0.25, medium is 0.5, drowsiness and total drowsiness is 1 because they are levels that occur immediately in the driver.

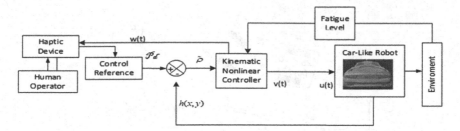

Fig. 3. Control scheme for driver assistant

$$I_s = 1 - L \tag{1}$$

(ii) Input devices, consisting of the Human Operator, the haptic devices, and the desired path that represents the control reference, the force fed back by the Logitech G29 haptic devices has a maximum force of 2.1 [N], this haptic device consists of two servomotors with position encoders that make possible an insertion of haptic experience.

(iii) Kinematic control, the movement of the vehicle is based on the kinematic model of the mobile robot type Car-Like with point of interest in $h(t) = f(x, y)$, which is represented by (2); where x, y are the coordinates of the center of the two rear wheels; θ indicates the direction of the mobile robot type Car-Like with respect to the axis X; $\emptyset$ is the steering angle of the front wheels and is the distance from the center of the robot to the control point of interest as indicated in Fig. 4.

$$h(t) = J(\theta)v(t) \tag{2}$$

with:

$$\begin{bmatrix} \dot{h}_x \\ \dot{h}_y \end{bmatrix} = \begin{bmatrix} \cos\theta & -a\sin\theta \\ \sin\theta & a\cos\theta \end{bmatrix} \begin{bmatrix} u \\ \omega \end{bmatrix}$$

$$\omega = \frac{u}{p}\tan\emptyset$$

where, ρ represents the distance between the front and rear wheels; u is the linear velocity of the vehicle; and ω represents the angular velocity.

The kinematic controller calculates the position errors in each sampling period, in order to be used to determine the linear velocity and angular velocity of reference, which will allow an assistance of automatic handling in the vehicle in order to reduce errors and with this avoid traffic accidents In Fig. 4 the denoted path tracking problem is indicated $P(s)$, where $P(s) = (x_p(s), y_p(s))$; P_d represents the current desired point of the Car-Like type robot which is considered as the closest point to $P(s)$ he traced path, this is defined as $P_d = (x_p(s_D), y_p(s_D))$, where s_D is the defined curvilinear abscissa of the point P_d; $\tilde{x} = x_p(s_D) - x$ represents the position error in the address X; and $\tilde{y} = y_p(s_D) - y$ it is the positional error in the address Y.

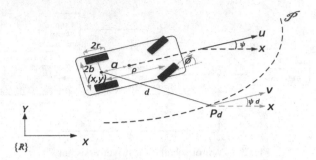

Fig. 4. Problem of the Car-Like for path tracking.

In this regard, the control errors for the human-car operator system are $\rho(t)$ that it represents the distance between the Car-Like vehicle position $h(x, y)$ and the desired point, P_d, where the position error in the direction ρ is $\tilde{\rho} = 0 - \rho$, i.e., the distance between the position of the vehicle $h(x, y)$ and the desired point P_d is zero; is the orientation error of the vehicle that is defined as $\tilde{\psi} = \psi_d - \psi$, where ψ_d is the orientation of the unitary vector tangent to the trajectory of the point P_d with respect to the reference system.

The reference velocity is defined by the control errors and the angular velocity of the vehicle that it has as indicated in (3):

$$v_r = \frac{v_{dmax}}{1 + K_r\|\rho\| + K_f\|\omega\|} \tag{3}$$

where; v_d is the maximum desired velocity, K_r defines the positive constant that weighs the control error; K_f is the positive constant that weighs the change of angular velocity of vehicle type Car-Like.

As described above, the following control law is proposed as autonomous management assistance according to the fatigue levels presented:

$$\begin{bmatrix} u_c \\ \omega_c \end{bmatrix} = \underbrace{\mathbf{J}^{-1}\left(K_s\begin{bmatrix} \dot{x}_p \\ \dot{y}_p \end{bmatrix} + K_c\begin{bmatrix} \tanh(\tilde{x}) \\ \tanh(\tilde{y}) \end{bmatrix}\right)}_{V_1} + \underbrace{I_s\mathbf{v_m}}_{V_2} \tag{4}$$

where, $\dot{x}_p = |v_r|\cos(\psi_d)$ and $\dot{y}_p = |v_r|\sin(\psi_d)$ being u_c y ω_c the output velocities of the kinematic controller; $|v_r|$ represents the module of the input reference velocity for the vehicle controller; $\dot{x}_p$ is the projection of the vector v_r in the direction X, $\dot{y}_p$ is the projection of the vector v_r in the direction Y; $\mathbf{J}^{-1}$ represents the matrix of inverse kinematics of the robot described in (4), in addition $\tilde{x}$ and $\tilde{y}$ are the errors of position in the directions x, y respectively, with respect to the reference system, in order to saturate the vehicle velocities the function has been included $\tanh(.)$.

Remark 1: The control law described in (4) is comprised of two main terms: V_1 it represents the kinematic control that is responsible for correcting the control errors produced when the fatigue index is 1, with K_s which it is a gain with values $[0-1]$, that allows applying the desired velocity, V_2 represents the maneuverability of the driver according to the level of fatigue with linear and angular velocity entered from the haptic devices, *i.e*, when the fatigue index I_s indicated in (1) is greater, the incidence of the signals of the haptic devices on the vehicle is smaller because V_1, it begins to increase.

According to the velocities obtained from the proposed algorithm, this is used to generate feedback from the wheel through the relationship of lateral forces $F_{x,y}$, these forces are generated in the wheels when taking the curve, to generate a torque that is indicated in (5), applied to the steering wheel with which the orientation of the vehicle is corrected:

$$M_v = \frac{M_r}{rd(K_z)} \tag{5}$$

where M_v is the moment in the steering wheel, M_r defines the torque that exists in the steering wheels, rd he ratio of reduction in terms of the angle of rotation of the steering wheel and the angle of rotation of the wheels $\varnothing$ and K_z is the performance of the steering. According to Eq. (5) is defined: $M_r = F_{x,y}(r_w)$ with $F_{x,y} = \frac{m_T(v_{ref})}{\Upsilon}$, where r_w is the radius of the steering wheels; m_T it is the mass of the vehicle; Υ, represents the radius of curvature of the vehicle.

For the analysis of stability is considered (4), when the fatigue index is zero because the level of fatigue is one thus canceling the velocities of haptic devices and starts by the relationship:

$$\tilde{x} = -\tilde{\rho}\,\sin(\psi_d)\text{ and }\tilde{y} = \tilde{\rho}\,\cos(\psi_d) \tag{6}$$

in addition to:

$$\dot{\rho} = -\tilde{x}\sin(\psi_d) + \tilde{y}\cos(\psi_d) \tag{7}$$

Now it is considered that $\tilde{\rho} = -\rho$, from which the derivative is obtained as a function of the time obtained,

$$\dot{\tilde{\rho}} = -\dot{\rho} \tag{8}$$

If (7) are replaced in (8) it is obtained:

$$\dot{\tilde{\rho}} = \dot{x}\sin(\psi_d) - \dot{y}\cos(\psi_d) \tag{9}$$

Now if it enter $\dot{x}_p$, $\dot{y}_p$ and (4) in (9), result:

$$\dot{\tilde{\rho}} = (\tanh(\tilde{x})\sin(\psi_d) - \tanh(\tilde{y})\cos(\psi_d)) \tag{10}$$

To know the behavior of $\tilde{\rho}$ in the closed loop system of the vehicle, substitute (6) in (9) and obtain:

$$\dot{\tilde{\rho}} = (\tanh(-\tilde{\rho}\sin(\psi_d))\sin(\psi_d) - \tanh(\tilde{\rho}\cos(\psi_d))\cos(\psi_d)) \tag{11}$$

It is observed that from (11) it is concluded that the system has only one equilibrium point, *i.e.* $\tilde{\rho} = 0$. To analyze the stability of the car-like vehicle system, the candidate function to Lyapunov is proposed, $V(\tilde{\rho}) = \frac{1}{2}\tilde{\rho}^2 > 0$. While the derivative of the trajectory versus time is defined as $\dot{V}(\tilde{\rho}) = \tilde{\rho}\dot{\tilde{\rho}}$, a sufficient condition for the equilibrium stability of the closed loop system is that $\dot{V}(\tilde{\rho})$ it be defined as negative. In this regard, the closed loop system of (11) is introduced in $\dot{V}(\tilde{\rho})$, obtaining:

$$\dot{V}(\tilde{\rho}) = \tilde{\rho}\tanh(-\tilde{\rho}\sin(\psi_d))\sin(\psi_d) - \tilde{\rho}\tanh(\tilde{\rho}\cos(\psi_d))\cos(\psi_d) \tag{12}$$

that is $\dot{V}(\tilde{\rho}) < 0$, the stability of the closed loop system is guaranteed if the controller's profit constants that weigh the control error are: $K_s > 0$ and $K_c > 0$.

In context, from (12) it can be concluded that $\lim_{t\to\infty}\tilde{\rho}(t) \to 0$, *i.e.*, $\tilde{x}(t) \to 0$ and $\tilde{y}(t) \to 0$ with $t \to \infty$ asymptotically. Therefore, from (4) it is concluded that the final velocity of the point of interest when the driver is in a state of somnolence or total somnolence $V = |\mathbf{v}_p(s_D, h)|\cos\psi_d$, will therefore be $\tilde{\psi}(t) \to 0$ asymptotically.

4   Experimental Results

This section presents the performance of the proposed handling assistance control based on the level of fatigue of the vehicle driver. The experimental tests were implemented in a 3D virtual environment that interacts in real time with the Matlab software. Figure 5 shows the system operation which is implemented in an Intel Core i5 PC, with 8 GB of RAM, N-VIDIA GTX960 graphics card and Logitech G29 handwheel, for the detection of fatigue level by means of Deep Learning, which indicates the probability of each detected level and classifies it according to the percentage found.

Fig. 5. Interaction between haptic devices and simulation software

To indicate the performance of the proposed controller, two experimental tests were carried out: *(i) Fatigue level detection without assistance,* in this test the Deep Learning algorithm has detected the level of fatigue and the driver for path assistance it is inactive, thus obtaining the desired path and the one made in Fig. 6(a). While the error that causes the level of fatigue is observed in Fig. 6(b), which is not greater than 2.5 [m] in virtue that protective barriers were incorporated in the simulation environment.

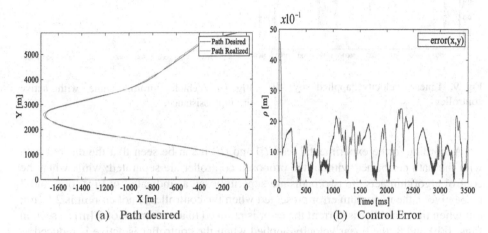

(a)   Path desired   (b)   Control Error

Fig. 6. Driving without assistance.

(ii) Detection of the fatigue level of the driver with driving assistance, for this test the algorithm of Deep Learning and the active control algorithm were applied for all levels of fatigue recognized, thus obtaining the desired path and the path performed in Fig. 7, the path error presented by the vehicle is in Fig. 8, while the linear velocity applied by the controller is indicated in Fig. 9, the angle of rotation of the vehicle applied by the controller is indicated in Fig. 10.

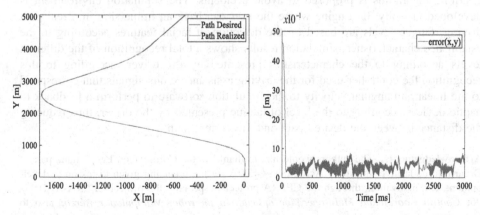

Fig. 7. Desired path and path realized by the proposed controller

Fig. 8. Path error with active control algorithm

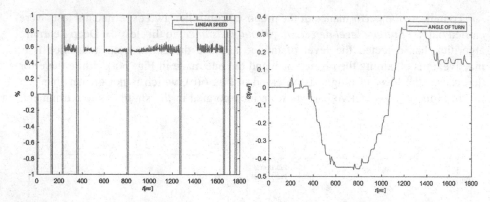

Fig. 9. Linear velocity applied by the controller

Fig. 10. Vehicle turning angle with active driving assistance.

According to the experimental tests *(i)* and *(ii)* it can be seen that the desired path with the path performed without the proposed controller are separated; while when the control algorithm acts the two paths are superimposed as indicated in Figs. 6(a) and 7 respectively, the maximum error presented when the controller is not current is 2.5 [m], but when the controller is current the error is reduced to a maximum of 1 [m] as seen in Figs. 6(b) and 8, the linear velocity applied when the controller is active is reduced to an average from 0.83 as shown in Fig. 9, according to the fatigue index, and finally the angle of rotation of the vehicle which has a linear variation when the driver is activated. according to the desired path as indicated in Fig. 10.

5 Conclusions

In this article, a fatigue level detection system of a terrestrial vehicle driver using Deep Learning algorithms is proposed to avoid accidents. The simulation environment is developed in Unity 3D Engine where the user can have an immersion in a real path driving, fatigue levels are based on the detection of facial features according to the established characteristics, simulation results shows a total recognition of the different levels according to the characteristics presented by the driver, according to this recognition the controller used for the driving assistance emits signals that correspond to the linear and angular velocity to the simulation software to perform a feedback to haptic devices according to the level of fatigue presented by the driver, thus reducing the distance between the desired path and the current path.

Acknowledgements. The authors would like to thanks to the Corporación Ecuatoriana para el Desarrollo de la Investigación y Academia –CEDIA for the financing given to research, development, and innovation, through the CEPRA projects, especially the project CEPRA-XI-2017-06; *Control Coordinado Multi-operador aplicado a un robot Manipulador Aéreo;* also to

Universidad de las Fuerzas Armadas ESPE, Universidad Técnica de Ambato, Escuela Superior Politécnica de Chimborazo, and Universidad Nacional de Chimborazo, and Grupo de Investigación en Automatización, Robótica y Sistemas Inteligentes, GI-ARSI, for the support to develop this work.

References

1. Wei, W., Hanbo, F.: Traffic accident automatic detection and remote alarm device. In: 2011 International Conference on Electric Information and Control Engineering, Wuhan, pp. 910–913 (2011)
2. Lia, C.: Intelligent traffic accident detection system based on mobile edge computing. In: 2017 3rd IEEE International Conference on Computer and Communications, China, pp. 2110–2115 (2017)
3. World Health Organization: Global status report on road safety 2015. World Health Organization (2015)
4. Agencia Nacional de Transito del Ecuador. Estadísticas de Siniestros. https://ant.gob.ec
5. Agencia Nacional de Transito del Ecuador. Estadísticas de mortalidad. https://ant.gob.ec
6. Traffic Incident Management: Federal Highway Administration. http://ops.fhwa.dot.gov/aboutus/one_pagers/tim.htm. Accessed 15 Oct 2013
7. The Royal Society for the Prevention of Accidents: Driver fatigue and road accidents: a literature review and position paper, Birmingham, U.K. (2001)
8. Eriksson, M., Papanikotopoulos, N.P.: Eye-tracking for detection of driver fatigue. In: 1997 IEEE Conference on Intelligent Transportation System. LTSC 1997. IEEE (1997)
9. Shu-ming, S., et al.: Driver mouth monitoring method based on machine vision. J. Jilin Univ. Technol. (Nat. Sci. Ed.) 2, 014 (2004)
10. Tomlin, R., Villa, V.: Attention in Cognitive Science and Second Language Acquisition. Stud. Sec. Lang. Acquis. 16, 183–203 (2008)
11. Shia, V., et al.: Semiautonomus vehicular control using driver modeling. IEEE Trans. Intell. Transp. Syst. 15(6), 2696–2709 (2014)
12. Tomas-Gabarron, J.B., Lopez, E., García, J.: Vehicular trajectory optimization for cooperative collision avoidance at high speeds. IEEE Trans. Intell. Transp. Syst. 14(4), 1930–1941 (2013)
13. Lin, C.-T., et al.: EEG-based drowsiness estimation for safety driving using independent component analysis. IEEE Trans. Circ. Syst. I: Regul. Pap. 52(12), 2726–2738 (2005)
14. Swarnkar, V., Abeyratne, U., Hukins, C.: Objective measure of sleepiness and sleep latency via bispectrum analysis of EEG. Med. Biol. Eng. Comput. 48(12), 1203–1213 (2010)
15. Roy, R.N., Charbonnier, S., Bonnet, S.: Eye blink characterization from frontal EEG electrodes using source separation and pattern recognition algorithms. Biomed. Signal Process. Control 14, 256–264 (2014)
16. Tan, X., Triggs, B.: Enhanced local texture feature sets for face recognition under difficult lighting conditions. IEEE Trans. Image Process. 19, 1635–1650 (2010)
17. Zeng, J.: Deep learning based forensic face verification in videos. In: IEEE Conference on Computer Vision and Pattern Recognition, pp. 77–80 (2017)
18. Parkhi, O.M., Vedaldi, A., Zisserman, A.: Deep face recognition. In: Proceedings of the British Machine Vision Conference, pp. 41.1–41.12 (2015)
19. Taigman, Y., Yang, M., Ranzato, M., Wolf, L.: DeepFace: closing the gap to human-level performance in face verification. In: IEEE Conference on Computer Vision and Pattern Recognition, pp. 1701–1708 (2014)

20. Schroff, F., Kalenichenko, D., Philbin, J.: FaceNet: a unified embedding for face recognition and clustering. In: IEEE Conference on Computer Vision and Pattern Recognition, pp. 815–823 (2015)
21. Krizhevsky, A., Sutskever, I., Hinton, G.: ImageNet classification with deep convolutional neural networks. In: NIPs Proceedings of Neural Information Processing Systems Conference (2012)

Dialogue Models for Socially Intelligent Robots

Kristiina Jokinen[✉]

AIRC AIST Tokyo Waterfront, Tokyo, Japan
kristiina.jokinen@aist.co.jp

Abstract. Dialogue capability is an important functionality of robot agents: interactive social robots must not only help humans in their everyday tasks, they also need to explicate their own actions, instruct human partners about practical tasks, provide requested information, and maintain interesting chat about a wide range of topics. This paper discusses the type of architecture required for such dialogue capability, emphasizing the need for robot communication to afford natural interaction and provide complementarity to standard cognitive architectures.

Keywords: Multimodal dialogue · Social robots
Knowledge-based architecture

1 Introduction

Dialogue management is already a mature technology (see an overview in [12]) enabling the development of interactive systems for both text and speech interfaces, with functionalities ranging from elaborated question-answering to chat-bots. Dialogue models are typically based on manually designed rules or statistical correlations, and recently intensive research and development has focussed on end-to-end dialogue systems using big data and neural models (e.g. [21, 30, 31, 33]). Intelligent speakers like IBM Watson, Alexa, Siri, Cortana, and Google Home exhibit high-level question-answering skills combining search strategies, big data, reinforcement learning, and deep learning techniques.

On the robotics side, however, communicating robot systems are primarily research platforms rather than technology-ready applications. Although such commercially available robots as Nao and Pepper (Softbank), iCub (IIT), and Sota (NTT DATA) are sophisticated platforms which offer possibilities to develop speech-based applications, robot agents that would assist human agents in their everyday tasks and exhibit social capabilities of natural language communication with the user, are still mostly experimental setups. Despite the success of spoken dialogue systems and robot agents in their respective research fields, integration of the two is still rare.

Research on communicating robots has mainly focussed on societal and individual acceptance of social robotics, as well as on experimenting with different dialogue phenomena in robot context. For instance, Herme [8] was built to study how users perceive non-verbal channels that deliver cognitive information, while ROBISUKE [6]

© Springer Nature Switzerland AG 2018
S. S. Ge et al. (Eds.): ICSR 2018, LNAI 11357, pp. 127–138, 2018.
https://doi.org/10.1007/978-3-030-05204-1_13

concerned feedback in human-robot interaction, and SCHEMA [23] showed how a robot can participate in multiparty conversations. Learning linguistic concepts and their grounding in communication was studied in [20], and recently robot gestures and co-speech gesturing has been explored in second language learning [2, 39].

One of the first open-domain spoken dialogue systems with a robot is WikiTalk [18, 37] which, together with related applications MoroTalk and SamiTalk, is implemented on the Nao robot. These applications access Wikipedia and digital newspapers and provide the user with information on the topics which the individual user finds interesting. The Disco-RT [28] is a conversational agent architecture for both virtual and robotic embodiments which aims at social support for isolated older adults, and the android robots like ERICA [7, 10, 25] are sophisticated research platforms to study the effect of human likeness on users with regard to the robot's appearance and behavior.

This paper concerns dialogue modelling that enables interactions between users and robot agents in natural language. The starting point is Constructive Dialogue Modelling [11] applied to care service dialogues in order to develop robot agents which can function as friendly companions and enable users to have access to digital services, e.g. to get instructions of how to perform particular tasks. The paper discusses human-robot interaction and requirements for the dialogue model in Sect. 2, presents a dialogue architecture for the robot agent in Sect. 3, and concludes in Sect. 4. The theoretical approach is complemented by sketching a real application, and demonstration.

2 Human-Robot Dialogue Interaction

Dialogue interactions with social robots are "situated": they take place in a dynamically changing world and cannot be totally specified in advance; reasoning processes and the exact information that is exchanged in the interaction depend on the situation in the real world. Social robot interfaces are qualitatively different from the typical computer interfaces like laptops and mobile phones: the robot tends to be regarded as an agent instead of a tool for manipulation. As argued in [11], spoken dialogue systems are often seen as intelligent agents rather than tools, since speech creates expectations about the system's ability to conduct natural language communication (cf. anthropomorphization of computers as discussed in [29]). Humanoid robots reinforce such expectations with their human-like appearance, e.g. they can be perceived as having stereotypical roles and gender [34]. However, robot dialogues differ from traditional speech interfaces because of the robot's autonomous nature: the robot can independently move and perceive its environment without explicit human presence (cf. rescue robots), and the robot's knowledge of the context can thus differ from that of the human's. The robot's independent moving and exploration of its physical environment also distinguishes robots from virtual humans which are implemented on 2-dimensional screens.

The robot is also a computer device with an elaborated hardware and software. Its operation and overt behaviour may not be represented by explicit rules, but be automatically learnt from large input data, and thus explicating or validating the resulting actions may no longer be possible by referring to simple rules only: the robot's behaviour extends to automated decision-making process. Information received through the robot's sensors and audio-visual perception process imposes further challenges for dialogue management as the robot needs to learn to interpret its perceptions correctly (to ground visual and vocal information in the physical and dialogue context), and to make sure that the human partner shares the same information (mutual context).

The robot thus has a dual character: on one hand, it is an agent acting in a physical and dynamic world, on the other hand, it is a computer with access to large, dynamic data sources (web, digital databases, sensor devices, etc.). Consequently, pertinent questions for dialogue modelling are related to the robot's functioning and acceptability as an agent as well as its accurate and fast performance as a computer. Table 1 summarizes a social robot's characteristics: items [a–b] relate to the robot's communicative capability, items [c–d] concern its autonomy, and item [e] captures the basis for its knowledge. The main difference to autonomous agents (industrial robots, robot cars) lies in features [a–b] whereas features [c–d] distinguish social robots from virtual agents.

Table 1. Social robot's characteristic features.

a	Use of multimodal signals (speech, gaze, gesture, body) to communicate with the human
b	Observations of human multimodal behaviour (speech, gaze, gesture, body) to learn human intentions and to react appropriately
c	Autonomous decisions of actions
d	Independent moving in a 3-dimensional world
e	Receiving and sharing information via internet and IoT (Internet of Things)

Figure 1 depicts two types of environments which determine the context for the robot's agent's actions and interaction. The micro environment is the immediate context in which normal face-to-face dialogues among the agents takes place. The macro environment deals with IoT communications that extend the context to ubiquitous environment. IoT is a dynamic global network infrastructure which allows various smart objects to communicate with each other: the physical and virtual "things" have identities, physical attributes, and virtual personalities, so they are uniquely addressable, allowing communication and data transfer over internet and network protocols [32]. Our work does not focus on IoT protocols, but rather on the ubiquitous presence of smart objects that surround human interlocutors. Smart objects can interactively provide important information about humans and their environments, so it can be assumed that they function like third partners in human conversations. Interaction among the various types of communicating agents (humans, robots, intelligent devices) thus resembles a multi-party conversation. However, what kind of consequences dynamic IoT networks have on the shared context in human and robot interactions, and how smart objects and their activities affect multi-agent interactions in ambient environments, is yet an open question.

Fig. 1. Context for social robots.

Table 2 summarizes some basic functionalities for natural interaction between humans and social robots. They stem from natural interaction as perceived and experienced by the human user, and the underlying assumption is that in order to support greater operational efficiency in service fields, the interface should take spoken dialogues into account and develop concepts that allow users to talk about their activities and experiences in a natural manner, while supporting the system to explicate its actions and show understanding of human intentions. Communication is necessary for collaboration, and the varied dialogue possibilities among humans, robots, and smart objects presuppose that the interface should *afford* intuitive and natural interaction [11] (cf. affordances in robot control [22, 27]). Such functionalities do not concern communication protocols between agent systems as defined for autonomous agent communities, but rather, conversational features geared towards natural language interaction and extensively studied in HCI and spoken dialogue research (see an overview in [12]).

Table 2. Some basic functionalities for social robot agents described from the view-point of human and robot dialogue capabilities.

Human should be able to	The robot should be able to
Change topics	Provide relevant information
Point to objects	Perceive actions
Use gaze	Recognize face and gazing
Collaborate on tasks	Engage with the human

3 Dialogue Management Model

3.1 Constructive Dialogue Management

The starting point for designing the architecture of a dialogue management model has been two-fold. First, the architecture aims at empowering the robot by communicative behavior that takes into account the functional requirements described in Table 2, by reflecting a theoretical model of human-human communication. Second, the architecture should be modular and re-configurable to allow for building usable, integrated dialogue systems for various applications and activities.

The selected theoretical approach is the Constructive Dialogue Model (CDM) [11] which has already been used e.g. in [17, 18]. It is chosen over Cognitive Robotics architectures (ACT-R, Soar, Standard Model [19]) because of its focus on natural language dialogues. Cognitive architectures do not explicitly concern communication, and the CDM architecture is thus a complementary model which can be implemented on top of the perception-action modules as a component which is responsible for higher-level reasoning dealing with verbal and multimodal communication.

Along with other approaches [4, 28, 35], it regards conversational interactions as cooperative activities through which the interlocutors build common ground. Agents can assume a variety of different roles in these activities, e.g. a robot may act as an instructor which tells the user how to perform a certain task, or as an information provider which searches for suitable and accurate answers. However, to enable communication, the agents must adopt the same co-operation goal and be willing to communicate with the partner. This creates social pressure for the agents to exchange new information with the partner on their intentions. Since the agents do not possess the same knowledge about the situation or the task, nor life experience in general, they need to keep track of the introduced topics and mutually understood information, to be able to provide relevant and coherent contributions in the given dialogue context.

The participants are regarded as rational agents, engaged in cooperative activity whereby they try to achieve their communicative goals by means of dialogue acts which carry information about their intentions and task-related topics. The agents exchange new information on the relevant topics in order to construct mutual understanding and coordinate their actions. Rationality refers to the agent's ability to make decision and deliberate on situationally appropriate actions (in AI, such agents have been called BDI agents), and it also considers the agent's affective state which influences the agent's reasoning. Emotions are not explicitly represented in the architecture, since they are assumed to be manifestations of the agent's internal state: the levels of arousal and valence of the agent's affects are inherent to the agent's general activity rather than computed by a particular emotion component. In fact, emotional activity can be regarded as one of the connection points to cognitive architectures under the assumption that the processing of input signals results in an internal state which determines the emotional quality of the agent's response.

Conversation progresses in a cyclic manner where various enablements for communication [1] are checked to maintain interaction. For instance, the agents must be in *contact* and *aware* of the partner's attempt to communicate, by paying attention to (multimodal) signals that indicate their willingness to interact. The agents must also *perceive* the emitted vocal and visual signals as communicative signals, i.e. recognize them having been produced with an intention to convey some meaning. The agents must also intend to engage themselves in the communication, which consists of making an effort to *understand* the partner's message and intentions, and to produce one's own *reaction*. Reaction encodes new information about the agent's current view-point in verbal or physical actions. It changes the current state of the world and enforces the agents to re-start their reasoning. The cycle then continues until the conversation is finished by the agents mutually agreeing to stop, or for other reason.

3.2 System Architecture

Figure 2 shows how the four communication enablements are included in the processing architecture on top of a cognitive architecture [14, 18, 19]. The initial Contact is managed by signal detection modules including audio and visual signal detection which can determine the direction of a voice signal or detect a human face in the vision field. The first interpretations of the input signals are made in Perception modules such as the speech recognizer (ASR), gaze tracker, or gesture recognizer. The Reaction modules for text-to-speech synthesis (TTS) and motor control take care of executing the robot's behavior, i.e. speaking utterances and actuating co-speech gesturing and movements.

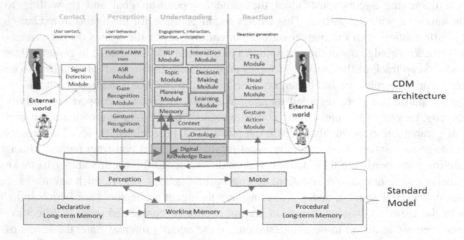

Fig. 2. CDM-based dialogue architecture [14] on top of the cognitive Standard Model [19].

The Perception and Reaction modules make up the robot's user interface, while the main dialogue processing takes place in the Understanding modules. Natural Language Processing (NLP) module translates the ASR output into a natural language utterance from which the dialogue topic is determined and further relevant processing initiated to produce the robot's response in Interaction and Decision modules. They are also important in recognizing the other agents' intentions and affective states. Context is a data structure dynamically updated with the current dialogue state and it stores short-term information such as Topic and Proposal (what has been talked about and what tasks have been completed so far). Digital Knowledge Base contains the robot's long-term knowledge, and it can be Wikipedia or Internet as in [18, 37] or a special purpose digital database as in the present demo. Ontology mediates between natural language representations and task concepts, and thus connects the knowledge to dialogue processes.

The Planning, Learning and Memory modules concern the robot's cognitive processes related to deliberation of actions and learning of new skills. They are not implemented in the current demo system. Planning requires ontological knowledge of the objects, events, and their relations in the world, as well as reasoning rules about beliefs, desires, and intentions (BDI) of the agents. Learning and Memory modules are related to acquisition of new knowledge and they take care of the robot's *grounding* of its knowledge in the physical world [9]. These modules also incorporate issues discussed in Theory of Mind [38]: the agent needs to distinguish its own view-point from that of the partner, and construct partitioned knowledge that includes private and mutual beliefs and those beliefs that the agent assumes the partner holds. Such issues have been extensively studied in the cooperative dialogue modelling approaches mentioned above.

Figure 2 also shows how the CDM architecture complements cognitive architectures like ACT-R, Soar, and the Standard Model [19], with an explicit dialogue model. The CDM model is a separate yet interconnected structure on top of the cognitive architectures, which tend to focus on cognitive functions in the "brain" of a single agent rather than inter-agent communication. It is possible to consider the Standard Model being connected to CDM via points in Contact and Perception, in Memory, Context, and Digital Knowledge Base, and in Reaction Modules. Future work will study these points further.

3.3   Dialogue Coherence and Topic Modelling

Dialogues move fluently from one topic to another, and the Topic module takes care of managing such smooth topic shifts. Earlier work with open-domain information access systems [17, 18] shows that unstructured user searches through digital repositories makes open-domain interactions depend on the user's own interest. Since it is impossible to know in advance what the user is interested in and what topics she wishes to discuss, it is not feasible to try to provide interaction scripts or frames with necessary pieces of information to be conveyed to the user [11]. Instead, the robot should be aware of potentially interesting topics and of the user's attention, interest and understanding through multimodal signals. In CDM, this is done via Contact and Perception modules which monitor the user's state and output an engagement measure through MM Fusion. Interaction and Decision-Making modules take the engagement measure into account when deciding on the suitable next action. Dialogue content is managed by topic tracking and anticipating possible continuations, calculated by coherence measures using semantic distance between possible topics. In our application [14], the robot instructs care-giving staff and trainees how to perform basic care-giving tasks according to the task-hierarchy, and dialogue coherence is determined by the task structure.

3.4   Multimodal Interaction

Non-verbal signals such as pauses, intonation, nods, smiles, frowns, eye-gaze, hand gestures, body posture etc. are effectively used to signal the speaker's understanding and affective state [5]. The robot agent can learn interaction patterns by observing the partner's reaction; for instance, it can learn a user's interest and preferences for a particular topic by interpreting the user's multimodal signals, or it can use eye-gaze information to successful anticipate turn-taking, or tailor its presentation according to the user needs (see [3, 6, 8, 13, 16, 18, 40]). The CDM modules Contact and Perception take care of the user signals by recognizing visual and vocal signals in the context, and covering cross-modal alignment (relations among different modalities) and multimodal fusion (joining information from the different modalities).

3.5   Interaction and Knowledge Learning

A challenge for dialogue agents is to manage the rich knowledge of the participants and the context in which the dialogues take place. In fact, one of the main challenges for deep learning models is the integration of knowledge and reasoning in the algorithms, since these aspects are not directly countable in observable items, but their representations need to be learnt and their distributions manipulated and shared in the network.

Traditionally human knowledge is structured into ontologies, systematic collections of facts, events, objects, and their relations. In dialogue systems, ontologies describe the knowledge structure of the task which the application is intended to talk about. Although ontology building and reasoning tools (RDF, OWL, Protégé) are available, genuine ontology-based dialogue systems are uncommon: [26] shows how a dialogue system can exploit information about hyponyms or hypernyms of the expected terms, while [36] describes how to generate system responses from RDF information. The DARPA programme Communicating with Computers is exceptional in that it aims to create a common representational framework that supports semantic reasoning in dialogue systems, by developing ECI-pedia [24], a repository of concepts and their inferential consequences, incorporating and adapting existing ontological and lexical resources. In robotics, a notable exception is [20] with OpenRobots common-sense ontology used for learning and grounding objects. [14] discusses types of knowledge in dialogue systems.

The CDM architecture follows the current trends by adopting an ontology as a light layer on top of a digital database which allows the agent to generalize over certain types of topics (e.g. type of restaurant, type of care task). In our case, the knowledge includes various care-giving tasks [14, 15], presented in JSON format. Purpose-built ontologies in JSON format offer lightly-structured knowledge where the ontology bridges database concepts to more general processing classes. However, such ontologies cannot do simple reasoning to distinguish referents for ambiguous words (*mouse*, *bank*). In the future, a richer and more complex inferencing is needed by adopting a knowledge base representation and an interface that integrates a reasoning component over the digital database, or via an open-domain dialogue chat-system.

3.6   Application and Interaction Models

Figure 3 depicts how the application model and the dialogue model can be integrated into a complete system. The application model refers to care-giving knowledge and its co-creation via the community-sourcing method. Figure 3 shows various stages of building a database, from manual collection by interviewing care-giving experts, to online data collection with the help of a mobile service. The robot interaction can further extend the traditional and mobile QA-systems, and thus the learning support for care-givers can be based on structured knowledge of the care-giving domain and interactive instruction via a robot assistant, ultimately leading to cooperation through which the robot can also learn via human interaction. The current version uses the Nao robot platform from Softbank [14, 15]. Examples of the first simple instruction scenarios are below.

English version:

https://drive.google.com/file/d/1yq_YtjCwP42xTl-Cvsc7l46vtWmuys2E/view?usp=sharing

Japanese version:

https://drive.google.com/file/d/1x8lD9Bba-2WjQee_8MgcADqSNB6NtjKE/view?usp=sharing

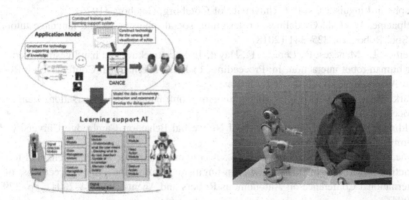

Fig. 3. Dialogue model and application model in a service context for learning care-giving support, and a screenshot of an interactive situation.

4 Conclusion

This paper has focused on the basic requirements for spoken dialogue models to enable interactions between social robots and human users. The double nature of the robot as an agent and as a computer system sets requirements for the dialogue model. As an agent, the robot can be perceived as a communicating partner with expectations of possible dialogues varying from task-based instructions to free chatting. As a computer system, the robot has access to vast digital information which it can also share with other agents through its connection via Internet. The paper outlines the basic functionality for social robots and presents the CDM architecture which has been implemented on the Nao robot. The architecture emphasizes the need for the robot interfaces to afford natural and intuitive interaction, and it is regarded as complementary to the Standard Model of cognitive architectures due to its explicit modelling of communication.

Future research concerns theoretical and practical work. CDM architecture will be further elaborated with respect to the Standard Architecture to investigate integration of dialogue modelling in cognitive architectures. Deep learning techniques will be studied in the context of gaze and gesturing, to learn suitable representations for multi-modal information processing and to explore neural models in interaction. On practical social robotics side, knowledge-base and reasoning capabilities will be enhanced so as to develop dialogue modelling for care-giving services, and to assess usability, acceptability, and ethical issues concerning communicating social robots in real contexts.

Acknowledgements. The author wishes to thank the team members for useful discussions on ontologies and dialogue modelling, and the NEDO project for the support of the work.

References

1. Allwood, J.: Linguistic Communication as Action and Cooperation. Gothenburg Monographs in Linguistics, vol. 2. University of Göteborg, Göteborg (1976)
2. Belpaeme, T., et al.: Guidelines for designing social robots as second language tutors. Int. J. Soc. Robot. **10**, 325–341 (2018)
3. Brethes, L., Menezes, P., Lerasle, F., Hayet, J.: Face tracking and hand gesture recognition for human-robot interaction. In: Proceedings of IEEE International Conference on Robotics and Automation, pp. 1901–1906 (2004)
4. Clark, H.H., Schaefer, E.F.: Collaborating on contributions to conversation. Lang. Cogn. Process. **2**, 19–41 (1987)
5. Feldman, R., Rim, B.: Fundamentals of Nonverbal Behavior. Cambridge University Press, Cambridge (1991)
6. Fujie, S., Fukushima, K., Kobayashi, T.: A conversation robot with back-channel feedback function based on linguistic and non-linguistic information. In: Proceedings of 2nd International Conference on Autonomous Robots and Agents (ICARA-2004), pp. 379–384 (2004)
7. Hagita, N., Ishiguro, H., Miyashita, T., Kanda, T., Shiomi, M., Kuwabara, K.: Symbiosis of human and communication robots. In: Cetto, J.A., Ferrier, J.L., Costa dias Pereira, J., Filipe, J. (eds.) Informatics in Control Automation and Robotics, vol. 15. Springer, Heidelberg (2008). https://doi.org/10.1007/978-3-540-79142-3_2
8. Han, J.G., et al.: Collecting multi-modal data of human-robot interaction. In: Proceedings of the 2nd International Conference on Cognitive Infocommunications (CogInfoCom), pp. 1–4 (2011)
9. Harnad, S.: The symbol grounding problem. Physica D **42**, 335–346 (1990)
10. Inoue, K., Milhorat, P., Lala, D., Zhao, T., Kawahara, T.: Talking with ERICA, an autonomous android. In: Proceedings of the SIGDIAL 2016 Conference, Los Angeles, USA, pp. 212–215 (2016)
11. Jokinen, K.: Constructive Dialogue Modelling – Speech Interaction with Rational Agents. Wiley, Chichester (2009)
12. Jokinen, K., McTear, M.: Spoken Dialogue Systems. Morgan and Claypool, San Rafael (2009)
13. Jokinen, K., Furukawa, H., Nishida, M., Yamamoto, S.: Modelling eye-gaze behaviour for intraction management. In: ACM TiiS (2012)
14. Jokinen, K., Nishimura, S., Watanabe, K., Nishimura, T.: Human-robot dialogues for explaining activities. In: Proceedings of IWSDS 2018, Singapore (2018)
15. Jokinen, K., Nishimura, S., Fukuda, K., Nishimura, T.: Dialogues with IoT companions - enabling human interaction with intelligent service items. In: Proceedings of the 2nd International Conference on Companion Technology (ICCT 2017), pp. 1–3. IEEE (2017)

16. Jokinen, K., Trong, T.N., Wilcock, G.: Body movements and laughter recognition: experiments in first encounter dialogues. In: Proceedings of the ICMI Workshop MA3HMI 2016 (2016)
17. Jokinen, K., Wilcock, G.: Constructive interaction for talking about interesting topics. In: Proceedings of the 8th LREC 2012, Istanbul (2012)
18. Jokinen, K., Wilcock, G.: Multimodal open-domain conversations with the Nao robot. In: Mariani, J., Rosset, S., Garnier-Rizet, M., Devillers, L. (eds.) Natural Interaction with Robots, Knowbots and Smartphones, pp. 213–224. Springer, New York (2014). https://doi.org/10.1007/978-1-4614-8280-2_19
19. Laird, J.E., Lebiere, C., Rosenbloom, P.S.: A standard model of the mind: toward a common computational framework across artificial intelligence, cognitive science, neuroscience, and robotics. AI Mag. 38(4), 13–26 (2017)
20. Lemaignan, S., Ros, R., Sisbot, E.A., Alami, R., Beetz, M.: Grounding the interaction: anchoring situated discourse in everyday human-robot interaction. Int. J. Soc. Robot. 4, 181–199 (2012)
21. Li, J., Monroe, W., Ritter, A., Galley, M., Gao, J., Jurafsky, D.: Deep reinforcement learning for dialogue generation (2016)
22. Marin-Urias, L.F., Sisbot, E.A., Pandey, A.K., Tadakuma, R., Alami, R.: Towards shared attention through geometric reasoning for human robot interaction. In: The 9th IEEE-RAS International Conference on Humanoid Robots, Humanoids 2009, pp. 331–336 (2009)
23. Matsuyama, Y., Taniyama, H., Fujie, S., Kobayashi, T.: Framework of communication activation robot participating in multiparty conversation. In: AAAI Fall Symposium Dialog with Robots (2010)
24. McDonald, D., Burstein, M., Pustejovsky, J.: Assembling the ECIpedia: refining concepts in context. ACS Poster Collection, pp. 1–19 (2018)
25. Milhorat, P., et al.: A conversational dialogue manager for the humanoid robot ERICA. In: Proceedings of the International Workshop Spoken Dialogue Systems (IWSDS) (2017)
26. Milward, D., Beveridge, M.: Ontology-based dialogue systems. In: IJCAI Workshop on Knowledge and Reasoning in Practical Dialogue Systems (2003)
27. Moratz, R., Tenbrink, T.: Affordance-based human-robot interaction. In: Rome, E., Hertzberg, J., Dorffner, G. (eds.) Towards Affordance-Based Robot Control. LNCS (LNAI), vol. 4760, pp. 63–76. Springer, Heidelberg (2008). https://doi.org/10.1007/978-3-540-77915-5_5
28. Nooraei, B., Rich C., Sidner, C.: A real-time architecture for embodied conversational agents: beyond turn-taking. In: The 7th International Conference on Advances in Computer-Human Interactions (2014)
29. Reeves, N., Nass, C.: The Media Equation: How People Treat Computers, Television, and New Media Like Real People and Places. Cambridge University Press, New York (1996)
30. Serban, I.V., Sordoni, A., Bengio, Y., Courville, A., Pineau, J.: Building end-to-end dialogue systems using generative hierarchical neural network models. In: Proceedings of AAAI (2016)
31. Serban, I.V., et al.: A hierarchical latent variable encoder-decoder model for generating dialogues. arXiv:1605.06069 (2016)
32. Smith, I.G. (ed.): The Internet of Things 2012: New Horizons. IERC-Internet of Things European Research Cluster, Halifax (2012)
33. Sordoni, A., et al.: A neural network approach to context-sensitive generation of conversational responses. In: Proceedings of the Conference of the NAACL-HLT 2015 (2015)
34. Tay, B., Jung, Y., Park, T.: When stereotypes meet robots: the double-edge sword of robot gender and personality in human–robot interaction. Comput. Hum. Behav. 38, 75–84 (2014)

35. Traum, D.R., Allen, J.F.: Discourse obligations in dialogue processing. In: Proceedings of the 32nd Annual Meeting of ACL, Morristown, NJ, USA, pp. 1–8 (1994)
36. Wilcock, G., Jokinen, K.: Generating responses and explanations from RDF/XML and DAML + OIL. In: Proceedings of the IJCAI-03 Workshop on Practical Dialogue Systems, Mexico (2003)
37. Wilcock, G., Jokinen, K.: Multilingual WikiTalk: Wikipedia-based talking robots that switch languages. In: Proceedings of the SIGDIAL 2015 Conference, pp. 162–164 (2015)
38. Wimmer, H., Perner, J.: Beliefs about beliefs: representation and constraining function of wrong beliefs in young children's understanding of deception. Cognition **13**, 103–128 (1983)
39. de Wit, J., et al.: Exploring the effect of gestures and adaptive tutoring on children's comprehension of L2 vocabularies. In: Proceedings of HRI 2017 Workshop on Robots for Learning (2017)
40. Yoshida, Y., Nishimura, T., Jokinen, K.: Biomechanics for understanding movements in daily activities. In: Proceedings of the LREC Workshop on Language and Body in Real Life (2018)

Composable Multimodal Dialogues Based on Communicative Acts

Enrique Fernández-Rodicio(✉), Álvaro Castro-González, Jose C. Castillo,
Fernando Alonso-Martin, and Miguel A. Salichs

Robotics Lab, Universidad Carlos III de Madrid, Av. de la Universidad 30,
28911 Leganés, Madrid, Spain
{enrifern,acgonzal,jocastil,famartin,salichs}@ing.uc3m.es

Abstract. In Social Robotics, being able to interact with users in a
natural way is a key feature. To achieve this, we need to model dialogues
that allow the robot to complete its tasks and to adapt to unforeseen
changes in the conversation. We present an approach where these dialogues are modelled as a combination of basic interaction units, called
Communicative Acts or CAs. With this, our system aims to provide all
the necessary tools so each of the robot's applications can tailor their own
dialogues in a simpler way. These applications make the decisions that
need task-related information and request the activation of the CAs in
order to create complex dialogues. The CAs handle decisions that require
communication-related information (e.g. giving the user some information, or asking a question). They also manage some of the problems that
can appear in any interaction, like not being able to understand the other
peer, or not getting an answer to a question. A case study associated to
a cognitive stimulation exercise is presented in this paper to validate our
system.

Keywords: Dialog management · Human-Robot Interaction
Social Robotics · Multimodal interaction

1 Introduction

In recent years, robotics have experienced a big expansion and robots are starting
to be present in many aspects of our daily lives. One of the reasons for this interest is that robots can serve as 24/7 companions to help people in need of assistance. Under these circumstances, it is desired that robots behave autonomously
[5] and interact with the users in a natural way, to make them feel like they are
bonding with another living being.

These situations pose different challenges for Human-Robot Interaction (HRI
from now on) research. One of them is that, during the interaction, the robot
should be able to manage information of different types, such as voice or touch.
This is referred as multimodal interaction and implies both understanding and
expressing messages that use different types of information. Time also plays an

© Springer Nature Switzerland AG 2018
S. S. Ge et al. (Eds.): ICSR 2018, LNAI 11357, pp. 139–148, 2018.
https://doi.org/10.1007/978-3-030-05204-1_14

important role in the conversation and the robot has to comply with the rhythm of human communication. For example, the robot has to answer questions with in a certain window of time. Also, the flow of a dialogue depends on the context and the task that the robot is performing at each moment, so the robot needs to adapt the dialogue to these circumstances. Another potential problem is that, during the interaction, the other peer may suddenly change the subject of the conversation, or simply ask a question that has nothing to do with the current dialogue. In these situations, the robot has to handle those changes of topic while keeping a coherent dialogue.

In order to overcome these problems, robots should integrate a system that controls the interaction process, manages the information provided by the users and the environment, and reacts accordingly. This type of systems is known as Dialogue System (DS). The different modules of a DS handle the inputs and outputs, and control the flow of the interaction, along with other secondary tasks, such as managing errors in communication. Applied to robotics, a DS processes the information perceived from the environment, particularly the one given by users, and decides the appropriate response. While many applications, such as booking assistants, have been developed using only one channel of information (typically text-based or speech-based), DSs for robotics need to manage multimodal information in order to provide a natural experience for the user.

Although the structure of a DS is different for each implementation, many have a module called Dialogue Manager (DM) at its core [6,12]. This module is in charge of making all the decisions needed to complete the dialogue and controlling the progress of the conversation. Its inputs are the information extracted from the environment (for example, the result of an automatic speech recognition module), and its outputs are the expressions the robot has to perform (e.g. the robot waves its arm to greet someone).

This work presents our approach to dialogue modelling and management. At the core of our system we can find basic interaction units called Communicative Acts, or CAs. The applications of the robot combine these CAs in order to create dialogues that suit their needs and control how these dialogues advance based on task-related information. Our DM executes the CAs requested by the applications and governs how the interaction is conducted. Finally, the CAs make low-level decisions, such as finding how to output questions, analysing whether the answer given by a user is coherent with the question, or managing communication problems, among others. Opposed to some robots, where the DS is the central module of the robot and all robot functions organise around it, in our case, the DM and the CAs are tools at the disposal of the rest of the robot's architecture. We aim to simplify the process of developing new dialogues by providing those functionalities that will be required in every interaction, so the developers can focus on designing the flow of the dialogue.

The rest of this manuscript is structured as follows. Section 2 analyses the related works in the field of dialogue management applied to robotics. In Sect. 3 we present the Communicative Acts, the basic interaction units our applications will use to create their dialogues. Section 4 shows how our solution has been implemented and integrated alongside the rest of the robot's architecture. In Sect. 5 we discuss a case of use, where all the capabilities of our system are demonstrated. Finally, Sect. 6 contains the conclusions extracted from this work.

2   Related Work

In dialogue management, is important to design systems that allow for flexibility and that simplify the design of new dialogues. Spiliotopoulos et al. [12] presented a state-based dialogue manager for the Hygeiorobot robot focused on spoken dialogues, modelled as state machines, where the user takes the initiative. Asoh et al. [3] proposed a system for managing spoken dialogues that allows for bi-directional communication, and maintains three different representations for the current state of the dialogue: a state machine, a set of frames (groups of information slots that are needed in order to execute a task) and a list of salient entities (people, places, objects...) that appeared in previous utterances and that can be needed to solve ambiguities that arise later in the conversation. Souvignier et al. [11] presented a frame-based approach for spoken communication that allows for bi-directional dialogues, and that analyses application-specific information to develop a hypothesis about what will be the next utterance provided by the user. In their work, dialogues are represented as a series of information slots that have to be filled in order to advance in the dialogue. Niklasson [9] developed a dialogue manager for web assistants that represents dialogues as a set of frames (group of information slots related to the same topic). This system maintains three different types of slots: primary, secondary and auxiliary. Each possible topic that can be managed is represented as a frame. The manager starts the topics based on their priority, but can switch among them if the user requires it, even if the previous frame is missing information. Fodor [6] presented a speech-based mixed-initiative dialogue manager based on decision trees, which represents a dialogue as a set of dialogue acts (information slots filling) ordered chronologically. The DM uses a set of dialogues collected by human operators beforehand to learn and build the decision tree. Lemon et al. [7] proposed a dialogue system for controlling the WITAS robot helicopter. The dialogue manager, which is multimodal and mixed-initiative, maintains an Information State, which represents the context of the dialogue. The DM keeps a stack of issues that need to be raised in the conversation, and once an issue is raised, it is moved to the Issue Raised stack. This operation is called Dialogue Move. A series of rules interpret inputs and outputs as Dialogue Moves related to the Information State. Bohus et al. [4] presented RavenClaw, a framework for designing plan-based DMs. It provides a series of basic skills needed in most managers, such as error-handling or turn-taking, while the developers focus only on creating the control logic for the dialogue itself. RavenClaw uses two data structures: (i) a task tree, which is a plan for performing certain tasks; (ii) and the agenda, an ordered list of what the system expects to receive at that moment. Inputs are matched against this agenda in order to see if any node of the task tree is expecting them. The developers are the ones that have to create the task tree. Alonso-Martin et al. [1,2] proposed a multimodal HRI architecture based on VoiceXML, a document standard for developing voice dialogues based on the Extended Markup Language (XML). This architecture also allows for mixed initiative in the communication. Dialogues in this system are represented as a combination of information slots that have to be filled. Nguyen et al. [8] presented an approach that enables multimodal interaction for controlling a series of office applications. The manager agent maintains a number of plans, grouped in four types (Conversational Agents, Intention Identification, Task Processing and Response Generation), each of them in charge of a different aspect of the dialogue. The manager will send information requests to the agents managing system devices in order to get the information needed for completing the dialogue.

Instead of focusing on developing ad-hoc dialogues, in this work, we try to identify common structures that might appear in any dialogue, and build our interactions as a combination of those basic atomic units.

3   Modelling Human-Robot Dialogues

Human communication is a complex process that involves many different variables and levels of knowledge. Trying to simplify the process of developing new dialogues, we have decided to look for the common fundamental elements present in any conversation that, adequately combined, will allow to represent the possible dialogues that our robot might need. These pieces are called Communicative Acts.

A Communicative Act, or CA, is the basic unit of interaction between two parties. In our case, we have only considered one-to-one interactions, as our robot is designed with this type of interactions in mind. CAs are considered as atomic entities, i.e. they cannot be decomposed, that are able to work either alone or in conjunction with others. In our approach, complex dialogues are modelled as a combination of multiple CAs that may be customized according to a communicative objective.

When facing the task of reducing a dialogue to its basic components, we decided to consider two dimensions of the communication: initiative and intention. *Initiative* states which speaker starts the conversation and, in general, is in charge of controlling the flow of the interaction to fulfil a goal. In our case, we have two possibilities: either the robot takes the initiative (e.g. the robot greets a bystander trying to start an interaction), or the user initiates the interaction (e.g. a person asks a robot for information about the location of a shop). In the case of *intention*, we refer to the direction of information relevant to an application. Here we consider also two cases: the speaker wants to give some information, or he/she wants to obtain some information. Combining these two concepts, we came up with four CAs: *Robot Gives Information, Robot Asks for Information, User Gives Information,* and *User Asks for Information.* The CAs related to asking for information could be modelled as a combination of the CAs Robot Gives information and User Gives information, or vice-versa. However, considering that asking for information is very common in daily dialogues and in the interest of easiness when creating dialogues, we have decided to consider them as two proper CAs. Table 1 describes the main features of the CAs.

Table 1. Communicative acts based on the initiative (rows) and the intention (columns)

		Intention	
		Providing inf.	Obtaining inf.
Initiative	Robot	*Robot Gives Information:* it communicates a particular message to the other party using the different robot's modes of interaction	*Robot Asks for Information:* it asks the user about a particular information and waits for the answer. The answer could be an open response, where any answer is accepted, or a specific response, checking whether it is right or not. The answer could come through one or more interaction channels simultaneously
	User	*User Gives Information:* this CA manages the interaction initiated by the user to communicate a message to the robot. When this CA receives the information from the user, it verifies whether or not this information is relevant for any of the ongoing applications and, if so, sends this information to the corresponding application	*User Asks For Information:* this CA controls an user petition when he/she expects an answer. After the user's request, it waits for the corresponding application to provide the response and communicates it to the user

4   Using CAs in Our Robots

In our robots, the main control decides among several applications which to execute, based on the interaction with the users. The main control and the different applications model all the dialogues they need as a combination of CAs, and then rely on the DM to handle the interaction with the user through them. The overview of this system can be seen in Fig. 1.

The applications model the dialogues they need using the four CA previously presented and task-related knowledge. When these CAs need to be executed, the application requests their activation to the DM, sends the parameters needed to customize them, and waits for the result. The DM is in charge of activating/deactivating those CAs and configuring them adequately. When the result is received, the application decides the next step in the conversation. Since several applications may be running on the robot concurrently, our DM is able to activate and manage multiple CAs at the same time. The CAs use interaction-related information to perform their goals (e.g. if the CA asks a question, this information can include the number of tries or the right answer). When using CAs, developers focus on how to combine them to meet the requirements of the particular application they are creating. Most of the low-level tasks that appear in every dialogue (for instance, error handling, mixed-initiative management, or

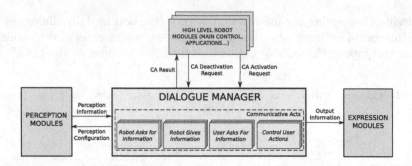

Fig. 1. Modules involved in dialogue management. The applications of the robot request the activation/deactivation of CAs to the Dialogue Manager, while the perception and expression modules manage the inputs and outputs of the robot.

analysing the information given by the user) are handled by the CAs and thus developers do not care about these issues.

The process starts when the DM receives a request for activating a CA. This request contains all the parameters needed to configure and adapt it to the specific needs of the dialogue we are currently running: (i) a unique *id* that is used to create the communication channels between that specific CA and the DM, through which the perception information is sent; (ii) the *type* indicates the DM which of the CAs has to start; (iii) the *mode* allows configuring each CA as one of the following: *ending* or *continuous*. Ending CAs are executed only once and, after the execution is completed, the application receives the result and the CA is deactivated. Continuous CAs are active until a deactivation request is received. All CAs can be configured both ways, although usually the ones for managing the robot's initiative are configured as ending CAs, and the ones used when the user takes the initiative are configured as continuous CAs; and (iv) regarding the *configuration of the input channels*, the DM configures the convenient perception modules depending on the parameters included in the activation request. For example, if the CA needs to use a grammar-based Automatic Speech Recognition module (ASR), the activation request will contain the grammar that has to be loaded. Besides, the input data sent to a CA can be limited by where they are coming from; this means that, in the activation request, the application can specify the sources of data that will allowed. Thus, every time a user communicates with the robot, the DM receives the perception information, which contains the communicative channel it came through and sends it to all the active CAs that are expecting inputs through the same channel.

In addition, our CAs have to be able to manage different uncertainties that are present in any communication. If the modules in charge of perceiving inputs given by the user or taken from the environment fail when retrieving the requested information, the CA asks the user to repeat what he/she has said or done (this is mostly used in spoken dialogues). If the CA seeks to obtain an answer, but the user gives a wrong one, then the CA gives him/her a certain number of retries. Finally, if the CA is expecting an answer, but the user does nothing, the CA may try to encourage him/her to answer, or decide that no answer is going to be obtained if this situation happens several times. All of these features can be configured when the CA is activated.

5   Case Study

In order to show the capabilities of our CAs, we present a case study where the robot Mini [10] uses our DM to handle the interaction. Among the variety of applications this robot offers, in this case of study, we will focus on two applications. The first one is a cognitive stimulation exercise, inspired by the quiz games, where the robot asks the user several questions ($App_{exercise}$). In the second application, the robot replies a variety of questions that the user asks frequently at any time. Note that people suffering cognitive impairment tend to constantly ask the time or where they are, for example. Next, we describe a fragment of the interaction of a user while conducting an exercise. Figure 2 shows a time line with the different CAs and the modules that requested them.

Initially, the robot was alone so it was waiting and there were not active CAs. When the robot perceived that a user approached, simultaneously, the main control asked the user what she wanted to do, using a *Robot Asks for Information* CA, and activated the $App_{frequent\_questions}$, which requested the activation of a *Robot Asks for Information* CA to handle the user's requests (remember that the user can ask these questions at any moment). Verbally, the user answered "I want to do an exercise" and the perception module (using the ASR software) sent this information to the main control, which launched the stimulation exercise. The $App_{exercise}$ activated a *User Gives Information* CA to manage all user commands that might come during the session (in this particular case, the only command that the user can use is *stop*, to exit the exercise without finishing it). This CA was configured as continuous so it will be active untill a deactivation request arrives (in this case this happens at the end of the exercise). At the same time, $App_{exercise}$ sends a *Robot Gives Information* CA to explain how the first exercise worked (the type of questions that were going to be asked and how the user has to answer). This exercise started requesting the activation of a *Robot Asks for Information* CA which asked the user: "Which season are we in?". In this particular case, the activation request included the input mode (voice), the right answer, the grammar that has to be loaded in the ASR module, the number of tries, and the maximum answering time. This example was set on July 24th, so the correct answer in this case was "Summer". On the first try, the user didn't gave an understandable answer, so the DM told the user: "Sorry, I can't understand you", and then notified the problem to the application. In this case, the app is designed to repeat the question, but this time the answer is expected to be received through a menu in a tablet. The user then gave the right answer, the DM informed $App_{exercise}$ of the success and the application moved to the next question. If the user had failed, e.g. saying "Spring", then the CA would have encouraged the user to try again until he/she reached the maximum number of tries. In that case, the CA would have sent the result "fail" to the

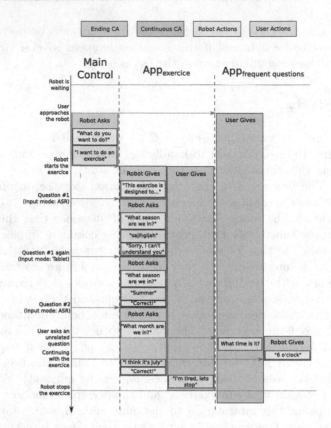

Fig. 2. Flow diagram that shows how the CAs are activated by different modules. Events affecting the CAs are highlighted

$App_{exercise}$, which would move to the next question. It is important to mention that this process is entirely controlled by the CA according to its configuration.

The exercise then moved on to the next question: "What month are we in?". In this case, the user, instead of answering, asked the robot "What time is it?". The robot processed the request through the *User Gives Information* CA previously activated by the $App_{frequent\_questions}$. The DM knows which CA is expecting the user's input by checking which grammar the ASR used to identify that input. This CA sent the question to the $App_{frequent\_questions}$, which read the time and communicated it to the user through a *Robot Gives Information* CA. Once all this process ended, the user continued with the exercise and answered: "July", which was the right answer, so the robot congratulated the user and the exercise moved on.

Finally, the user decided to stop the session by taking the initiative, and asking the robot: "I'm tired, lets stop". The ASR found in this utterance the semantic value "stop" and the *User Gives Information* requested by the $App_{exercise}$

sent this command to the application. The application then cancelled any active CA related to the exercise, finishing this process.

6   Conclusions

In this work, we have presented an approach that aims at providing tools to develop complex dialogues as a combination of basic building blocks present in every dialogue called CAs. The different modules of the robot that need to manage HRI can combine these interaction units according to its particular needs. This allows to simplify the design of new dialogues for our robot's applications. Although currently the dialogues are fixed, they could be created dynamically, using these building blocks. The CAs can be used to provide information to the user or request information from him/her, and also face certain challenges, present in any dialogue, as seen in the case study. These situations a showed in this case of study allow us to show the different problems that usually arise when interacting with users, and how our system manages them. These challenges include communication problems, wrong answers from the user, or actions where the user has the initiative, both related and unrelated to the topic of the dialogue. In order to test our system, we present a study case where two applications are active at the same time. This system has been used in a series of experiments with users designed to evaluate a cognitive stimulation session, showing promising results about its robustness and its ability to handle uncertainties related to communication problems.

Acknowledgment. The research leading to these results has received funding from the projects: Development of social robots to help seniors with cognitive impairment (ROBSEN), funded by the Ministerio de Economia y Competitividad; and RoboCity2030-III-CM, funded by Comunidad de Madrid and cofunded by Structural Funds of the EU.

References

1. Alonso-Martin, F., Castro-González, Á., Gorostiza, J.F., Salichs, M.A.: Multidomain voice activity detection during human-robot interaction. In: Herrmann, G., Pearson, M.J., Lenz, A., Bremner, P., Spiers, A., Leonards, U. (eds.) ICSR 2013. LNCS, vol. 8239, pp. 64–73. Springer, Cham (2013). https://doi.org/10.1007/978-3-319-02675-6_7
2. Alonso Martín, F., Castro-González, A., Fernandez de Gorostiza Luengo, F.J., Salichs, M.A.: Augmented robotics dialog system for enhancing human-robot interaction. Sensors (Basel, Switzerland) **15**, 15799–15829 (2015)
3. Asoh, H., Matsui, T., Fry, J., Asano, F., Hayamizu, S.: A spoken dialog system for a mobile office robot. In: Proceedings of Eurospeech, Budapest, pp. 1139–1142 (1999)
4. Bohus, D., Rudnicky, A.I.: The RavenClaw dialog management framework: architecture and systems. Comput. Speech Lang. **23**(3), 332–361 (2009)

5. Castro-González, Á., Malfaz, M., Salichs, M.A.: Learning the selection of actions for an autonomous social robot by reinforcement learning based on motivations. Int. J. Soc. Robot. **3**(4), 427–441 (2011). https://doi.org/10.1007/s12369-011-0113-z
6. Fodor, P.: Dialog management for decision processes. In: Proceedings of the 3rd Language and Technology Conference: Human Language Technologies as a Challenge for Computer Science and Linguistics, Poznan, Poland, pp. 1–4 (2007)
7. Lemon, O., Bracy, A., Gruenstein, A., Peters, S.: The WITAS multi-modal dialogue system I. In: Proceedings of INTERSPEECH, pp. 1559–1562 (2001)
8. Nguyen, A., Wobcke, W.: An agent-based approach to dialogue management in personal assistants. In: Proceedings of International Conference on Intelligent User Interfaces (IUI) (2005)
9. Niklasson, A.: Dialogue systems using web-based language tools. Master's thesis in Computing Science, Umea University, Sweden (2017)
10. Salichs, E., Castro-González, Á., Malfaz, M., Salichs, M.A.: Mini: a social assistive robot for people with mild cognitive impairment. New Friends, 31–32 (2016). ISBN 978-84-945603-9-2
11. Souvignier, B., Kellner, A., Rueber, B., Schramm, H., Seide, F.: The thoughtful elephant: strategies for spoken dialog systems. IEEE Trans. Speech Audio Process. **8**(1), 51–62 (2000)
12. Spiliotopoulos, D., Androutsopoulos, I., Spyropoulos, D.C.: Human-robot interaction based on spoken natural language dialogue. In: Proceedings of European Workshop on Service and Humanoid Robots, Santorini (2001)

How Should a Robot Interrupt a Conversation Between Multiple Humans

Oskar Palinko$^{(\boxtimes)}$, Kohei Ogawa, Yuichiro Yoshikawa,
and Hiroshi Ishiguro

Osaka University, Osaka 560-8531, Japan
palinko@irl.sys.es.osaka-u.ac.jp

Abstract. This paper addresses the question of how and when a robot should interrupt a meeting-style conversation between humans. First, we observed one-to-one human-human conversations. We then employed raters to estimate how easy it was to interrupt each participant in the video. At the same time, we gathered behavioral information about the collocutors (presence of speech, head pose and gaze direction). After establishing that the raters' ratings were similar, we trained a neural network with the behavioral data as input and the interruptibility measure as output of the system. Once we validated the similarity between the output of our estimator and the actual interruptiblitiy ratings, we proceeded to implement this system on our desktop social robot, CommU. We then used CommU in a human-robot interaction environment, to investigate how the robot should barge-in into a conversation between multiple humans. We compared different approaches to interruption and found that users liked the interruptibility estimation system better than a baseline system which doesn't pay attention to the state of the speakers. They also preferred the robot to give advance non-verbal notifications of its intention to speak.

Keywords: Human robot interaction · Conversational turn-taking
Social robotics

1 Introduction

Humans are very able communicators. We can partake in conversations while effortlessly managing many variables: roles, pauses, interruptions, etc. Having conversations with multiple people is a very essential human ability. For this reason, we think it would be very important for a robot to be able to participate in such interactions too, see Fig. 1(a). This involvement should be very efficient and courteous. To achieve this, the robots should be able to estimate what is a good time to barge-in when it has something to say. Not only the timing is important but also how this interruption would occur. Addressing these issues could lead to a wider acceptance of robots in conversational environments. Neglecting these issues could lead to robots being ignored or even excluded from human conversations. By studying this topic, we could not only design better robots but also advance the understanding of human behavior.

S. S. Ge et al. (Eds.): ICSR 2018, LNAI 11357, pp. 149–159, 2018.
https://doi.org/10.1007/978-3-030-05204-1_15

Fig. 1. (a) Multi-party conversation with a robot. (b) CommU, desktop robot.

2 Background

Turn-taking is an essential approach to understanding many human activities, including multi-party conversations. Sacks et al. defined a widely used model for conversational turn-taking [1]. Gaze also plays a critical role in selecting the next speaker in such a scenario [2]. Very often the next in turn corresponds to whomever the previous speaker was looking at last.

According to [3, 4] a period of silence in conversational turn-taking signals the relinquishment of the turn by the previous speaker. This means that anyone who wishes to barge-in is welcome to take over the conversation.

Spoken dialog systems are very good examples of turn-taking [5]. Barge-ins are common events in such systems [6]. This is when a user interrupts an automatic voice system to reduce the waiting time. In our research the barger-in would not be the person, but rather the robot. None the less, there are lessons to be learned from the human experience of barging-in.

Typically, human-robot conversation studies involve one robot and one human. For example, Snider et al. explored what influences engagement in human-robot conversations [7]. They found that gestures are important for creating a more engaging environment. Other specific HRI research setups might involve two or more robots. Hayashi et al. looked at how two robots talking to each other might influence a human listener. They found that robots can be effective passive social agents [8]. Iio et al. investigated how multiple robots can improve conversation initiation with a human [9]. They found that attracting people's attention works better with two robots than with one. On the other hand, not many studies looked at a robot interacting with multiple humans in conversations. Mutlu et al. researched how eye gaze can influence the interaction between a robot and two people [10]. Even though the conversation was kept almost the same, gaze could effectively influence people's attitude towards the robot. Matsusaka et al. designed a robot system which could interrupt a conversation between two people when it had corrective information to provide [11, 12]. It used multi-modal sensing (voice, face, speech, etc.) to determine when to barge-in. The authors did not validate or test their system in an experimental study in these papers.

Interruptions are essential parts of human-computer interaction. Coordinating these is a non-trivial task, which warrants in-depth study [13]. Interruptions arriving at wrong times can lead to decrease in human performance [14]. Therefore, it would be important to know the level of interruptibility of people in conversations and other tasks. Stern et al. define interruptibility as "the current state of a user regarding her receptiveness to receive messages" [15]. In other words, high levels of this measure indicate a person who is very able to receive interruptions, while low levels mean that the person is very involved with another task and should not be bothered. This measure is also very important in human-robot interaction [16–19] for robots to understand when they should talk to humans. Banerjee and Chernova designed a discreet value estimator of interruptibility for a mobile robot [20]. It was able to tell how interruptible people were in its environment. They did not focus on conversations between people and robots. Their work included validation of the estimator but not an experimental study of the designed system.

3 Approach – Interruptibility Estimator

Instead of coming up with our own rules on when interruptions should occur we decided to take the learning approach: learn from humans when it is good to interject a conversation. In this sense we adopted the concept of interruptibility: the higher the value, the easier it is to interrupt the person. We decided to use a regression-type artificial neural network (ANN) for learning this measure, a multilayer perceptron. The inputs to the network would be signals which can be observed by our senses during a conversation, e.g. speech, head pose and eye gaze, while the output would be the level or interruptibility. By speech, we mean the presence or absence of a speech signal (on/off) which could be determined using a microphone with a given threshold. Of course, there is more information embedded in speech itself in terms of linguistic analysis which could help to determine how interruptible someone is, but here we chose to focus on simple signals, as presence of speech. The reason for this simplified approach is that today's state-of-the-art speech recognition systems include a considerable amount of delay, which could undermine the ability of a robot to interrupt a conversation quickly. Also, only speech recognition would not be enough. Rules should be devised based on language models which would allow a conversation to be interrupted. This would add even more complexity and delay.

The output signal of the ANN was the level of interruptibility. It is a subjective measure, thus we collected ground truth data from several raters and checked for their agreement, similarly as in [20]. We decided to use one hidden layer of 15 neurons with hyperbolic tangent activation function so that the system could account for non-linearities which might occur.

4 Learning and Validation Experiment

We asked 6 pairs of students from our lab to have one-to-one conversations about topics of common interest. They were seated in a quiet room facing each other. Separate videos of each of the subjects were recorded with sound coming from directional headset microphones. Each interaction lasted for about 2 min and 15 s. Other than talking, we asked the participants to spend around 15 s in silence while writing something down on a piece of paper in front of them. We also asked them to look up something on their smartphones for another 15 s. These additional tasks were added to create a varied input signal for the ANN. Once the videos were recorded the experimenter annotated the conversations to determine when there was speech. We also ran a face pose [21] and eye gaze [22] detection algorithm and recorded the data. These three groups of signals (audio, head pose, gaze) were then used as the input for our estimation system. As we used a supervised learning approach, we needed to obtain the output signal ground truth. For this, we divided the video recordings of the conversations into one second long clips. The step was 0.5 s, so two subsequent clips had 50% overlap. The first author and two hired raters watched the clips of all subjects, giving an interruptibility rating at every 0.5 s. They were asked to rate the interruptibility at the end point of each clip. The ratings were integer numbers from 1 to 7. The value '1' meant: Only interrupt with an emergency message like 'the house is on fire'. The value '7' meant: easily interruptible with any message. All the other values were evenly spaced between the two extremes. The two raters' ratings were used to check for inter-rater reliability of the first author's values. Once the ratings were obtained we calculated Cronbach's alpha, which resulted in $\alpha = 0.826$. This means good inter-rater reliability, so we continued with using the experimenter's interruptibility ratings for training the ANN, similarly as [20].

The input signal of the ANN consisted of audio presence and its past 9 values, head pose (roll, pitch, yaw angles) and gaze (roll, pitch, yaw angles). The output layer used linear activation. We tried including past values of head pose and gaze too, but they did not make a difference in results.

Once the estimator was trained, we proceeded to evaluate the quality of estimation. To do so we used the leave-one-out approach: we trained the system with the data of 11 subjects and then tested on the 12th person. We repeated this 12 times once to test on each subject's data. We recorded the output of the estimator in each case. Then we compared the similarity of the estimator's output to the original interruptibility rating of the experimenter, again using Cronbach's alpha. We compared using only audio data as input to using additional signals as head pose and eye gaze in addition to the audio data. The results can be found in Table 1. For both situations Cronbach's alpha indicated a good agreement between the original and estimated values. It should be noted that adding head pose and eye gaze improved the output of the estimator, proving that these additional signals can be used for enhancing interruptibility estimation.

Table 1. Validation results between ground-truth and ANN output.

	Cronbach's alpha
Audio only	0.804
Audio, head pose, gaze	0.815

5 Exploratory Human-Robot Interaction Study

Once we successfully verified our interruptibility estimator, we proceeded to test it in an actual human-robot interaction study. The purpose of the study was to explore in what exact ways a robot could interrupt a conversation between humans with minimal negative effects.

5.1 CommU, the Desktop Social Robot

The robot in question was CommU, a 30 cm tall desktop humanoid robot, see Fig. 1 (b). It is a commercially available robot with a fixed platform and quite sophisticated movements (for its size) in its torso, arms, head, eyes, mouth and eyelids. Its strong points are its oversized eyes which are capable of both gradual and fast movements, thus emulating smooth pursuit and saccades of the human eye. It has a built-in speaker and its mouth emulates human mouth movements while it speaks using a text-to-speech engine.

5.2 Experimental Setup

Our experimental setup included a round table (d = 105 cm) with CommU on top of it, two webcams, three chairs and three subjects with headset microphones. Figure 2(a) shows the layout.

Fig. 2. (a) Experimental setup. (b) Face, gaze and interruptibility tracking.

The cameras were set up to track the faces of the three participants. We used two Logitech C920 webcams to cover a 180-degree field around the robot. We used the CLM algorithm to track faces [21] and the approach in [22] to track gaze direction, see Fig. 2(b). This information was directly fed into the interruptibility estimator algorithm. The audio signal of each participant was captured using a directional headset microphone. After thresholding, the microphone signal was also connected to the input of the estimator system. The robot was shifting its gaze from face to face in a random order, but when somebody started speaking, the robot looked at the speaker. If more than one person was speaking, the gaze was shifted towards the loudest one.

As there were three subjects at a time we created one estimator for each of them. The condition was to have the interruptibility level for all three persons above the middle value of 4, for the robot to start speaking or raise its hand.

5.3   Experimental Conditions

The only independent variable of the experiment was the strategy used by the robot to interact with people. The following were the three levels of the variable:

(1) *direct speech* – the robot starts speaking immediately after receiving a command
(2) *wait to speak* – the robot passively waits until the interruptibility levels for all participants rise above the middle value of 4 then speaks,
(3) *hand up* – the robot waits for interruptibility to rise as in the previous condition but does not do so passively. Rather, it raises its hand right away after receiving the command to signal that it has something to say, see Fig. 1(b). After this, it waits for the levels to rise. If that doesn't happen, after 5 s it says, "Excuse me" and waits again. If the levels do not become satisfactory again, after 10 s it says, "Can I say something?" After this, it continues waiting for interruptibility to reach appropriate values, passively. These three conditions were selected to test a wide range of robot behaviors.

5.4   Experimental Procedure

We recruited 18 participants through university advertising (11 male and 7 female). Their average age was 24.3 years. As we needed 3 people for the conversation, we invited them three by three. Most of the subjects within a group were familiar with each other. All groups were exposed to all three conditions. The order of the 3 conditions was counter-balanced between groups. Each of them received a participation reward equivalent of about 18USD. All participants were naïve towards the purpose of the experiment and have not interacted with CommU before.

After the subjects arrived they were given a description of the experiment and asked to sign consent forms. An initial questionnaire gauged their affinity towards robots ("How open are you towards robots in general?", "How open are you towards robots participating in conversations?") and asked for their basic data (name, age, etc.) They were asked to have a natural conversation between each other and let the robot join in as much as possible. Other than this we didn't tell them anything else about what kind of behavior they could expect from the robot and how to interact with it. We ensured they stay naïve towards the goal of our study. They were assured that the robot will not make any unexpected actions and that it cannot harm them. In each experiment the subjects were asked to have a conversation about these topics: (1) food you would suggest visitors to try in Japan, (2) places to visit in Japan, (3) how to learn to speak Japanese. The topics always followed this order (food first, travel second, language third), while the interaction conditions were counter-balanced in order. Each session lasted for about 15 min with a short break after each.

After the experiment ended, participants were asked to fill out a post-experiment questionnaire, checking if their affinity for robots changed and asking them to give their opinion about four statements. The statements were: (1) the robot could participate in the conversation, (2) I was satisfied with the robot's behavior, (3) the robot was very polite in this session, (4) I would like to have a robot with this behavior in a meeting/conversation. The offered answers to these questions were similar as for interruptibility rating: evenly spaced integers from 1 to 7.

During the sessions the experimenter provided robot utterances (unbeknownst to the subjects) from a predefined set of sentences, similarly as in [10]. About half of these were non-topic-specific ("I completely agree", "I'm afraid I disagree with that.", "Interesting! Could we get anyone else's opinion?"), while the other half were topic-specific for each session (Session A: "I like sushi. How about you?", "Have you tried soba noodles?", etc. Session B: "Have you been to Hokkaido?", "I hear the ocean is really beautiful in Okinawa. What do you think?", etc. Session C: "What book would you suggest for a beginner?", "Does the university offer free Japanese classes?", etc.) The robot utterances were dispatched by the experimenter only at times when people were actively engaged in conversation. This was done because we wanted to study how conversation interruptions could be managed by the robot and how people would react to them. If we would have generated utterances during times without conversations, those would be wasted, because they do not need any strategy to deliver: they could be said right away in all conditions because the interruptiblity would be high.

For the first two groups of subjects the *hand up* condition consisted of the robot raising its hand without saying anything and waiting for the interruptibility level to rise for all participants before uttering the sentence. But both groups of subjects failed to recognize this signal as a sign of the robot wanting to speak, thus we realized that the signal needs to be emphasized for it to be successfully interpreted. This is why we changed it for the subsequent four groups as follows: hand is raised and interruptibility rise is expected. If that doesn't happen, after 5 s the robot says, "Excuse me" and waits again. If the levels do not become satisfactory again, after another 5 s it says, "Can I say something?" After this, it continues waiting for the levels to reach appropriate values, passively. This sequence of actions was much better recognized by participants as a request to speak (100% recognition rate). In the following section we report on the results generated by the last four groups of subjects (12 people in total) who performed the *hand up* condition in the same enhanced way.

6 Experimental Results

An important measure of how efficiently the system performed is the delay between when a command was sent to the robot and the time when the robot uttered the sentence. For the *direct* condition this time was by definition equal to zero, because the robot was programmed to say the received utterance without delay. In the *wait* and *hand up* conditions CommU waited until interruptibility rose before speaking. Figure 3 (a), shows how the delay compares for the two conditions.

The difference between these two delays was found to be statistically significant using a paired t-test with $t = 3.47$ and $p < 0.05$. In the *wait* condition, the delay times were quite long because the robot did not give any signal to the humans that it wanted to speak. On the other hand, in the *hand up* condition the robot clearly signaled its intention to speak by first raising its arm and then politely uttering if needed. Clearly the *hand up* option performed much more efficiently, saving a lot of time.

In the *hand up* condition 53% of the time the robot had only to raise its hand and was allowed to talk. Another 35% of the times the robot had to add "Excuse me" and only

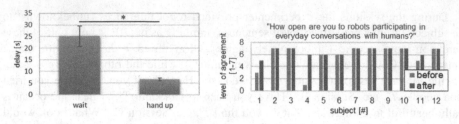

Fig. 3. (a) Time delay to utterance ± 1 std. error. (b) Before/after question.

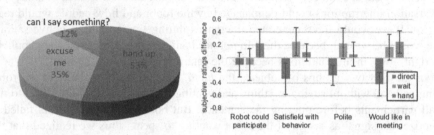

Fig. 4. (a) Robot action types. (b) Subjective opinions ± 1 std. error.

12% of the time it had to say the second sentence too "Can I say something?", see Fig. 4 (a). This meant that people realized quite easily that the robot is asking for attention.

We gauged the participants' opinion of robots in general and robots in conversations by asking them the same two questions before and after the experiment. The results can be seen in Fig. 3(b). It can be noticed that one quarter of the participants experienced an increase in their opinion of robots during our experiment. Three quarters maintained their opinions, while no one thought worse of robots after interacting with CommU. The majority of those who maintained their opinions already had a top mark at the beginning of the experiment, so they could not increase it at the end.

Finally, we report on the results of the experiment questionnaire. Even though none of the differences were found to be statistically significant, we still decided to include them to show the trends of opinions as this was an exploratory HRI study.

To be able to easily compare opinions, we subtracted the means of the three conditions for each subject and each question before averaging them together. This operation is warranted as we are interested in the relative differences between the three conditions and not their absolute values.

When asked the question if "The robot could participate in the conversation well", the *hand up* condition tended to score higher compared to the other two, Fig. 4(b). When asked if they were satisfied with the robot's behavior, participants were dismissive towards the *direct* condition and liked more the other two. In the same figure, we can notice that they rated the *wait* option as most polite, *direct* as least polite while *hand up* was in between. When asked the question "Would you like to have this system in a meeting?" subjects disliked the *direct* method while rating the *hand up* condition as best.

7 Discussion

Looking at the time delay data, Fig. 3(a), we can see that the *wait* condition caused long delays. This was because subjects were not informed about the robot's intention. There was also a lot of variation in this condition because the robot had no control over people's behavior. In the *hand up* condition, the delays were much shorter and less varied, because people received a signal that the robot wants to speak. At first, some of the subjects could have been confused what the robot wants with the raised hand (as in the first two groups which were excluded from the analysis), but if they didn't start paying attention to CommU, it would say "Excuse me" and "Can I say something?" These were very explicit requests for letting the robot take its turn in the conversation. This behavior turned out to be much more efficient in terms of delay, but it could also be interpreted as somewhat intrusive, as the robot could raise its hand at any time, with no regard to the state of the conversation. The addition of this behavior very significantly reduced the waiting time in the conversation compared to the *wait* condition.

Analyzing subjective measures, we have seen in Fig. 4(b) that people's opinion of robots either increased or stayed the same as before the experiment. Even though this measure might be biased by the participants' potential kindness towards the experiment, it is still noteworthy that nobody reported a decrease in satisfaction.

As mentioned before, subjective results were not found to be statistically significant, but we still think reporting on the trends of opinions might be beneficial, because of the exploratory nature of our experiment. As the *direct* method received the worst ratings from participants compared to the other two reactive approaches we think it justifies the need to detect and try to adapt to people's level of interruptibility.

8 Conclusion and Future Work

In this study, we set out to explore how and when robots should interrupt the conversation of multiple people in a meeting-style environment. At first, we employed a learning approach to model participants' interruptibility (the measure of how easy it is to interrupt them). As common sense would dictate, we have found that when people were silent, they were deemed to be more interruptible by raters than when they talked. But we also expanded this by signals which improved the estimation, namely head pose and eye gaze. The ANN estimator we created for this purpose was validated to be good at recognizing interruptibility. Once the modeling was done, we set out to explore how a robot equipped with this system would perform in an experimental scenario where three people would have a conversation with it. We found that the robot could barge-in into a conversation more efficiently when it first gave non-verbal signals that it wants to speak (*hand up* vs. *wait*). At the same time, the robot was deemed to be more polite and more appropriate for a conversation environment if it did give non-verbal signals as opposed to just barging-in without any notification (*hand up* vs. *direct*).

We do recognize that even though we were able to design an efficient and polite system, its performance could be improved if the robot would be equipped with a real-time speech recognition system that would allow linguistic modeling of the conversation. We are considering including this kind of improvement in future versions of the system. We also note that participants of the learning phase of this study had a direct influence on the robot's behavior. Therefore, in the future, we could influence the robot's communication style by selecting participants with desired behavior.

Acknowledgements. This research was partially supported by ERATO ISHIGURO Symbiotic Human-Robot Interaction Project and Itoki Corporation. The authors would like to thank Yutaka Nakamura for his help with learning algorithms.

References

1. Sacks, H., Schegloff, E.A., Jefferson, G.: A simplest systematics for the organization of turn-taking for conversation. Language (Baltim) **50**(4), 696 (1974)
2. Argyle, M., Cook, M.: Gaze and Mutual Gaze. Cambridge University Press, Cambridge (1976)
3. Schiffrin, D.: Discourse Markers, vol. 107. Cambridge University Press, Cambridge (1987)
4. Nagao, K., Takeuchi, A.: Social interaction: multimodal social interaction: conversation with social agents, vol. 94. In: AAAI (1994)
5. Heins, R., Franzke, M., Durian, M., Bayya, A.: Turn-taking as a design principle for barge-in in spoken language systems. Int. J. Speech Technol. **2**(2), 155–164 (1997)
6. Ström, N., Seneff, S.: Intelligent barge-in in conversational systems. In: International Conference on Spoken Language Processing, pp. 1–4 (2000)
7. Sidner, C.L., Lee, C., Kidd, C.D., Lesh, N., Rich, C.: Explorations in engagement for humans and robots. Artif. Intell. **166**(1–2), 140–164 (2005)
8. Hayashi, K., Kanda, T., Miyashita, T., Ishiguro, H., Hagita, N.: Robot Manzai - robots' conversation as a passive social medium. In: Proceedings of 2005 5th IEEE-RAS International Conference on Humanoid Robots, vol. 2005, pp. 456–462 (2005)
9. Iio, T., Yoshikawa, Y., Ishiguro, H.: Starting a conversation by multi-robot cooperative behavior. In: Kheddar, A., et al. (eds.) Social Robotics, vol. 10652. Springer, Cham (2017)
10. Mutlu, B., Shiwa, T., Kanda, T., Ishiguro, H., Hagita, N.: Footing in human-robot conversations: how robots might shape participant roles using gaze cues. Hum. Factors **2**(1), 61–68 (2009)
11. Matsusaka, Y., Fujie, S., Kobayashi, T.: Modeling of conversational strategy for the robot participating in the group conversation. In: Proceedings of the 7th European Conference on Speech Communication and Technology, pp. 2173–2176 (2001)
12. Matsusaka, Y., Tojo, T., Kubota, S.: Multi-person conversation via multi-modal interface - a robot who communicate with multi-user. In: Eurospeech, pp. 1723–1726 (1999)
13. Sasse, A., Johnson, C., et al.: Coordinating the interruption of people in human-computer interaction. In: Human-computer interaction, INTERACT, vol. 99, p. 295 (1999)
14. Gillie, T., Broadbent, D.: What makes interruptions disruptive? A study of length, similarity, and complexity. Psychol. Res. **50**(4), 243–250 (1989)
15. Stern, H., Pammer, V., Lindstaedt, S.N.: A preliminary study on interruptibility detection based on location and calendar information. In: Proceedings of CoSDEO, vol. 11 (2011)
16. Mutlu, B., Forlizzi, J.: Robots in organizations: the role of workflow, social, and environmental factors in human-robot interaction. In: 3rd International Conference on Human-Robot Interaction (HRI) (2008)
17. Rosenthal, S., Veloso, M.: Is someone in this office available to help me? J. Intell. Robot. Syst. **66**, 205–221 (2011)

18. Shi, C., Shiomi, M., Kanda, T., Ishiguro, H., Hagita, N.: Measuring communication participation to initiate conversation in human–robot interaction. Int. J. Soc. Robot. **7**(5), 889–910 (2015)
19. Satake, S., Kanda, T., Glas, D.F., Imai, M., Ishiguro, H., Hagita, N.: How to approach humans?: strategies for social robots to initiate interaction. J. Robot. Soc. Japan **28**(3), 109–116 (2010)
20. Banerjee, S., Chernova, S.: Temporal models for robot classification of human interruptibility. In: Proceedings of the 16th Conference on Autonomous Agents and Multiagent Systems (2017)
21. Baltrusaitis, T., Robinson, P., Morency, L.P.: 3D constrained local model for rigid and non-rigid facial tracking. In: Proceedings of the IEEE Computer Society Conference on Computer Vision and Pattern Recognition, pp. 2610–2617 (2012)
22. Palinko, O., Rea, F., Sandini, G., Sciutti, A.: A robot reading human gaze: why eye tracking is better than head tracking for human-robot collaboration. In: Proceedings of 2016 IEEE/RSJ International Conference on Intelligent Robots and Systems (IROS)

Grasping Novel Objects with Real-Time Obstacle Avoidance

Jiahao Zhang[1], Chenguang Yang[1(✉)], Miao Li[2(✉)], and Ying Feng[1]

[1] Key Laboratory of Autonomous Systems and Networked Control,
College of Automation Science and Engineering,
South China University of Technology, Guangzhou, China
cyang@ieee.org
[2] The Institute of Technological Sciences, Wuhan University, Wuhan, China
miao.li@whu.edu.cn

Abstract. This paper proposes a new approach to grasp novel objects while avoiding real-time obstacles. The general idea is to perform grasping of novel objects and do collision avoidance at the same time. There are two main contributions. Firstly, a fast and robust method of real-time grasp detection is presented based on morphological image processing and machine learning. Secondly, we integrate our robotic grasping algorithms with some existing collision prediction strategies. It is really helpful to grasp objects on the condition that a robot is surrounded by obstacles. Additionally, it is very practical, runs in real-time and can be easily adaptable with respect to different robots and working conditions. We demonstrate our approaches using the Kinect sensor and the Baxter robot with a series of experiments.

Keywords: Grasp novel objects · Avoid real-time obstacles
Morphological image processing · Machine learning

1 Introduction

Robotic grasping in unknown environments is a complex task involving object detection, motion planning and robot control. Many current approaches focus on detection, one common approach is trying to detect objects' special feature relying on their shapes, such as handle-like objects and symmetric objects (Abhijit et al. 2018). However, accurate grasping of novel objects is one of the necessary things for robots. So using machine learning methods like convolutional neural networks is state-of-the-art methods which can effectively grasp novel objects. The most common machine learning method to detect grasps is using a sliding windows [4,5]. This approach applies a classifier to make sure whether or not sub-components of a image are good for grasping an object. Apparently, the cost of time will be much more expensive by applying sliding windows into numerous spaces when a potential grasp is detected. An improvement for this method is using deep learning methods [1,11] which can quickly predict graspable locations. We develop a different approach which predicts potential grasps quickly

S. S. Ge et al. (Eds.): ICSR 2018, LNAI 11357, pp. 160–169, 2018.
https://doi.org/10.1007/978-3-030-05204-1_16

by morphological image processing. Then, we use a support vector machine to determine which one is the best potential grasp.

After good grasps have been located, motion planning is very important for a robot to operate in complex scenarios where obstacles may exist. But most of research overlook surrounding environments. Our work distinguishes from current grasp detection approaches which can grasp objects and avoid obstacles simultaneously.

In summary, the contribution of this paper are:

- We present a quickly image processing algorithm for detect potential robotic grasps.
- In order to get the best grasp, we apply the Radial Basis Function (RBF) kernel SVM for classifying and scoring the grasps.
- By applying existing obstacle avoidance algorithms, we achieve grasping in condition of no collision.
- We implement our algorithms on Baxter robot and Kinect sensor. It demonstrates how to apply our approach to real scenes.

2   Related Work

3-D simulations (like GraspIt!) are used by a considerable amount of researchers to detect feasible grasp points [8,9,16]. Their works are extremely robust to grasp an object but their algorithms rely on full 3D model of objects. However, it is very difficult for a robot to get the full knowledge of objects in a real-world.

With RGB-D sensors like Kinect being used increasingly, Some researchers try to detect grasp poses with insufficient information of objects, their algorithms are powerful to grasp a heap of objects [3,7,10,13]. It is not so practical, because general purpose robots may be asked to grasp novel feature objects rather than only handle-like or symmetric objects.

Current researches find grasps solely relying on RGB-D data [12]. Most of them implement machine learning methods to detect features of forming a good grasp. Lenz et al. successfully classifies grasps into good and bad by using convolutional nerual networks in a sliding window detection pipeline [5]. Our methods are different from Lenz's, We use a image processing algorithm which can find grasp more quickly. Also, we consider obstacle avoidance, it makes our algorithm to operate in a more complex situation.

3   Grasp Detection with Obstacle Avoidance

3.1   Grasp Detection

We want to find out a location which can grasp an object stably through a given RGB-D data of an object. Like the method proposed by Lenz et al. [5], we implement the five-dimensional representation for grasps. This representation can be sued to determine the position and orientation for a parallel plate gripper.

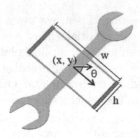

Fig. 1. A five-dimensional rectangle which represents ground truth grasp. The red line remarks the width that a parallel gripper opens when executing a grasp. The blue line shows the position and orientation that a gripper plate should be. (Color figure online)

As we can see Fig. 1, a ground truth grasp is represented by a rectangle where (x, y) is the center of r, θ is the orientation of r and (h, w) represents the height and width.

$$r = \{x, y, \theta, h, w\}$$

By using rectangle to stand for grasp, we execute our overall algorithm by the following steps (see Algorithm 1). We take a background RGB image as input, it can be quickly use locate where objects are. But our algorithm is not rely on I_b, we can also locate table quickly by setting region of interest in our image.

Definition 1. *A grasp rectangle, $r \in R_{potential}$, is the best rectangle which get high scores from our SVM classifier. $I_{potential}$, $D_{potential}$ is corresponding to the part which $R_{potential}$ is located at I and D.*

Algorithm 1. Grasp Detection
___
Input:
    a RGB image, I, and a aligned depth map, D, and a background RGB image, I_b
Output:
    a grasp rectangle, r
1: $R_{potential} = MorphologicalProcessing(I, D, I_b)$
2: $I_{potential}, D_{potential} = DataPreprocessing(R_{potential})$
3: $r = SVMClassifier(I_{potential}, D_{potential}, R_{potential})$

3.1.1   Morphological Image Processing

When we use RGB-D sensor to obtain data, it is important to use local information. By processing image through morphology, we can quickly get the region of interest in a image and avoid time-consuming. Our algorithm has the following steps (see Algorithm 2). The most important thing is to do blob detection (Step 1 and 2), it can help us figure out how many objects we need to deal with and get the minimal bounding box to include objects. Then, we use filter to denoise.

We find out the area near the objects can be the right place for gripper plate to locate (Step 4). Finally, we calculate the centers of the potential areas and form grasp rectangle (Step 5 and 6), the reason to do this is that after choosing two different centers to form grasping rectangle, our rectangle can be form closed. The processing result of our algorithm can be seen from Fig. 2.

Algorithm 2. Morphological Processing

Input:
  a RGB image, I, and a aligned depth map, D, and a background RGB image, I_b
Output:
  potential rectangular $R_{potential}$
1: Get region of interest of an Image, I_{roi}
2: Figure out the number of objects, N
3: **for** i = 1 **to** N **do**
4:    Estimate the potential areas where grasps may happen
5:    Calculate centers($C_{potential}$) of the potential areas
6:    Iteratively choose two different centers from $C_{potential}$, then form potential grasp
      rectangle, $R_{potential}$
7: **end for**

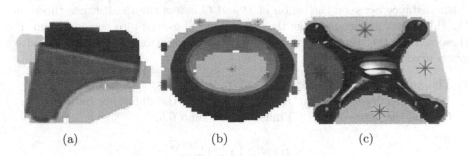

(a)   (b)   (c)

Fig. 2. (a) Potential grasps area of a triangular object, (b) potential grasps area of a tape; and (c) potential grasps area of a object looking like quadrotor. The plot symbol, * in the image represents the center of potential grasps area.

3.1.2 Data Preprocessing

We evaluate our method on a famous grasping dataset [4]. Inspired by the processing method which Lenz et al. have proposed, firstly, we extract the rectangles (both positive and negative) contained in the dataset. Secondly, because the size of each rectangle is different, and the dimension of the input layer of this algorithm is invariable, we scale all the captured grasping rectangles to the same size (24 * 24). At the same time, we extract RGB data, depth map and corresponding surface normal vectors from the resized grasping rectangles. As shown in Fig. 3, we convert the RGB color space to YUV, because YUV represents the concentration and color of the image separately and apparently RGB is not so useful to recognize an object.

Fig. 3. Conversion between RGB space and YUV space (Color figure online)

3.1.3   Grasp Detection Metrics

Definition 2. *We use P and G to represent the predicted rectangle and the ground truth rectangle respectively. The angle bias, A is equal to the orientation error between P and G.*

Two different metrics have been used for evaluating grasps on the Cornell dataset. Due to the point metric identifies grasp rectangle as a positive one only if the distance between the center of P and G is less than a distance threshold. We think that it does not take the orientation of grasps into consideration. For these reason, We use the rectangle metric for evaluation. Therefore, a positive grasp need to satisfy:

1. The angle bias, $A \in \{-15°, +15°\}$
2. We use the Jaccard index, $J(P, G)$ to evaluate the difference between P and G. And the value of $J(P, G)$ must be less than 0.5.

$$J(P, G) = \left(1 - \left|\frac{P \cap G}{P \cup G}\right|\right)$$

3.1.4   Train Classifier

Before training our network, we use seven channels' information including YUV, depth and surface normal which is a three-dimensional vector to constitute input features. Now the number of our input features x_i is $24 \times 24 \times 7 = 4032$. And our output is $y_i \in \{0, 1\}$ which represent negative and positive grasp.

We random split the Cornell Dataset to a train set and a test set with a ratio of 7:3. Out train set is $T = \{(x_1, y_1), (x_2, y_2), \cdots, (x_n, y_n)\}$, and we train our network by a RBF kernel SVM [2]. Our network is showed in Fig. 4. After training, we get an accuracy of 94.7% on the test dataset. The result of our classification can be seen from Fig. 5.

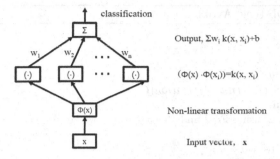

Fig. 4. Our network architecture in classification.

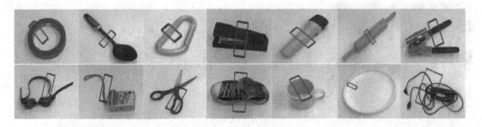

Fig. 5. Some examples on test sets. Positive grasp is shown on top while the bottom represents negative grasps

3.2 Obstacle Avoidance

Dynamic obstacle avoidance plays a key role in robot operation where collision maybe happen. In such case, in order to make our grasp algorithm behave well, it is important to employ a method which can avoid collision stably and effectively. Our perception pipeline is shown in Algorithm 3.

Definition 3. c_r, c_o and c_s are denoted as points on robot, obstacle and other scenes respectively. d is the distance that robot is away from obstacle, d_o and d_c is the distance to start to avoid and avoid at full speed (denoted as v_{max}).

3.2.1 Obstacle Recognition

In step 3 (See Algorithm 3), we implement Wangs' algorithm [14] which can perform self-identification and recognize obstacle fast and accurately. The identification result is shown in Fig. 6.

3.2.2 Robot Control Strategy

According to [6], the general solution for redundant manipulator is given by Eq. 1, where $\dot{\theta}$ is the joint velocities, $\dot{x}$ is the end-effector velocity, the pseudo-inverse of J denoted as $J^{\dagger}$ is equal to $J^T(JJ^T)^{-1}$ and z is an arbitrary vector.

$$\dot{\theta} = J^{\dagger}\dot{x} + (I - J^{\dagger}J)z \tag{1}$$

Algorithm 3. Obstacle Avoidance

Input:
    a point cloud c
Output:
    joint velocities $\dot{\theta}$
1: $(c_r, c_o, c_s) = Self - Indentification(C)$
2: **if** $d < d_o$ **then**
3:     Calculating $\dot{x}_o$ using Eq.2 and through Eq.1, we get $\dot{\theta}$
4: **else**
5:     **print** No Obstacles
6: **end if**

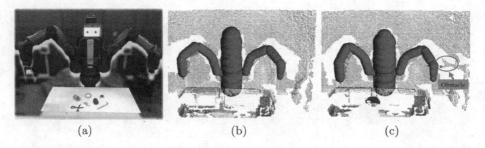

(a)   (b)   (c)

Fig. 6. (a) Our scenario, (b) the self-identification model (c) the identification result when obstacles occur.

Definition 4. *Collision points on the robot and on the obstacle is p_{cr} and p_{co}. $\dot{x}_o$ is the desired velocity to move away from the approaching obstacle.*

Referring to the method mentioned in [15], our control strategy is shown in Eqs. 2 and 3. When the obstacle is coming closer and closer, our avoid velocity increases under the restriction of v_{max}.

$$\dot{x}_o = k \bullet sign(\frac{p_{cr} - p_{cr}}{d}) \bullet v_{max} \tag{2}$$

$$k = \min\{\frac{d_o - d}{d_o - d_c}, 1\} \tag{3}$$

4 Experiments

We set up experiments on the right arm of the Baxter robot and Kinect sensor. And our algorithm is implemented on a computer with an Intel i5 2.70 GHz system with 8 GB memory. The experimental scene is shown in Fig. 6(a). Our goal is to clean the table and avoid unexpected obstacles.

    In order to test our algorithm's performance, we set up ten groups of experiments for every object in each sub image in Fig. 7. Rectangles in Fig. 7 represent

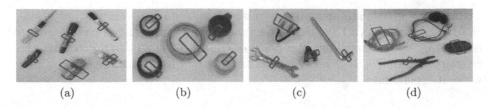

(a)   (b)   (c)   (d)

Fig. 7. Our grasp recognition results on different objects: (a) cylinder objects; (b) annular objects (the green one is a little bowl); (c) and (d) are some mechanical tools and office supplies. (Color figure online)

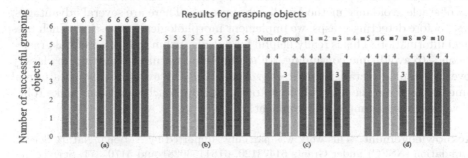

Fig. 8. Results for ten grasp trials on objects in our experiments (a), (b), (c) and (d) are corresponding to objects in the sub images of Fig. 7 respectively.

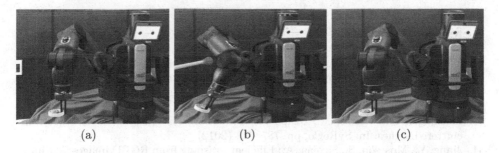

(a)   (b)   (c)

Fig. 9. (a) Grasp an object without obstacle. (b) Grasp an object with an obstacle (to keep grasping, the position of end effector has no change though an obstacle occurs). (c) After obstacles moving away, the origin pose of end effector is recovered.

the recognize results for robotic grasps. We convert the rectangles to a set of grasp poses, then execute grasp.

Our grasping results is shown in Fig. 8. In Fig. 7, for objects in sub image (a), We can see it failed once because the orange bottle is easy to slip away from Baxter's finger, and for sub image (c) and (d) scenarios, we fail in grasping the hook-shaped object and clamp. It is reasonable for us because our algorithm neglect objects' center of gravity.

To verify we can still execute our grasp when obstacles occur, we put obstacles in the trajectory of the right arm randomly. Figure 9 shows the right arm is avoiding obstacle without the position change of our end-effector and the recovery system [15]. It is really helpful for the right arm to continue its motion without replanning.

5   Conclusions

We propose a novel approach to detect robotic grasps from RGB-D image using morphological image processing and machine learning. And we integrate an existing obstacle avoidance method with our approach. There are several advantages, first, before detecting grasps, we implement morphological processing which uses local information. This is really helpful for our algorithm to find potential grasps. Second, to avoid time consuming, we use machine learning algorithm to classify several grasping rectangles indirectly. And finally, by avoiding obstacles in real time, we increase the adaptability of our grasp approach which can make robot to work in more complex environment.

Acknowledgement. This work was partially supported by National Nature Science Foundation (NSFC) under Grants 61473120, 61811530281 and 51705371, Science and Technology Planning Project of Guangzhou 201607010006, State Key Laboratory of Robotics and System (HIT) Grant SKLRS-2017-KF-13, and the Fundamental Research Funds for the Central Universities 2017ZD057.

References

1. Chu, F.J., Vela, P.A.: Deep grasp: detection and localization of grasps with deep neural networks. arXiv preprint arXiv:1802.00520 (2018)
2. Cortes, C., Vapnik, V.: Support-vector networks. Mach. Learn. **20**(3), 273–297 (1995)
3. Fischinger, D., Vincze, M.: Shape based learning for grasping novel objects in cluttered scenes. In: SyRoCo, pp. 787–792 (2012)
4. Jiang, Y., Moseson, S., Saxena, A.: Efficient grasping from RGBD images: learning using a new rectangle representation. In: 2011 IEEE International Conference on Robotics and Automation (ICRA), pp. 3304–3311. IEEE (2011)
5. Lenz, I., Lee, H., Saxena, A.: Deep learning for detecting robotic grasps. Int. J. Robot. Res. **34**(4–5), 705–724 (2015)
6. Maciejewski, A.A., Klein, C.A.: Obstacle avoidance for kinematically redundant manipulators in dynamically varying environments. Int. J. Robot. Res. **4**(3), 109–117 (1985)
7. Makhal, A., Thomas, F., Gracia, A.P.: Grasping unknown objects in clutter by superquadric representation. In: 2018 Second IEEE International Conference on Robotic Computing (IRC), pp. 292–299. IEEE (2018)
8. Miller, A.T., Allen, P.K.: Graspit! A versatile simulator for robotic grasping. IEEE Robot. Autom. Mag. **11**(4), 110–122 (2004)
9. Miller, A.T., Knoop, S., Christensen, H.I., Allen, P.K.: Automatic grasp planning using shape primitives. In: 2003 Proceedings of the IEEE International Conference on Robotics and Automation, ICRA 2003, vol. 2, pp. 1824–1829. IEEE (2003)

10. ten Pas, A., Platt, R.: Using geometry to detect grasp poses in 3D point clouds. In: Bicchi, A., Burgard, W. (eds.) Robotics Research. SPAR, vol. 2, pp. 307–324. Springer, Cham (2018). https://doi.org/10.1007/978-3-319-51532-8_19
11. Redmon, J., Angelova, A.: Real-time grasp detection using convolutional neural networks. In: 2015 IEEE International Conference on Robotics and Automation (ICRA), pp. 1316–1322. IEEE (2015)
12. Saxena, A., Driemeyer, J., Ng, A.Y.: Robotic grasping of novel objects using vision. Int. J. Robot. Res. **27**(2), 157–173 (2008)
13. ten Pas, A., Platt, R.: Localizing handle-like grasp affordances in 3D point clouds. In: Hsieh, M.A., Khatib, O., Kumar, V. (eds.) Experimental Robotics. STAR, vol. 109, pp. 623–638. Springer, Cham (2016). https://doi.org/10.1007/978-3-319-23778-7_41
14. Wang, X., Yang, C., Ju, Z., Ma, H., Fu, M.: Robot manipulator self-identification for surrounding obstacle detection. Multimedia Tools Appl. **76**(5), 6495–6520 (2017)
15. Wang, X., Yang, C., Ma, H., Cheng, L.: Shared control for teleoperation enhanced by autonomous obstacle avoidance of robot manipulator. In: 2015 IEEE/RSJ International Conference on Intelligent Robots and Systems (IROS), pp. 4575–4580. IEEE (2015)
16. Weisz, J., Allen, P.K.: Pose error robust grasping from contact wrench space metrics. In: 2012 IEEE International Conference on Robotics and Automation (ICRA), pp. 557–562. IEEE (2012)

Augmenting Robot Knowledge Consultants with Distributed Short Term Memory

Tom Williams[1(✉)], Ravenna Thielstrom[2], Evan Krause[2], Bradley Oosterveld[2], and Matthias Scheutz[2]

[1] Colorado School of Mines MIRRORLab, Golden, CO, USA
`twilliams@mines.edu`
[2] Tufts University Human-Robot Interaction Lab, Medford, MA, USA
{`ravenna.thielstrom,evan.krause,`
`bradley.oosterveld,matthias.scheutz`}`@tufts.edu`
`http://hrilab.tufts.edu/`, `http://mirrorlab.mines.edu/`

Abstract. Human-robot communication in situated environments involves a complex interplay between knowledge representations across a wide variety of modalities. Crucially, linguistic information must be associated with representations of objects, locations, people, and goals, which may be represented in very different ways. In previous work, we developed a Consultant Framework that facilitates modality-agnostic access to information distributed across a set of heterogeneously represented knowledge sources. In this work, we draw inspiration from cognitive science to augment these distributed knowledge sources with Short Term Memory Buffers to create an STM-augmented algorithm for referring expression generation. We then discuss the potential performance benefits of this approach and insights from cognitive science that may inform future refinements in the design of our approach.

Keywords: Natural language generation · Working memory
Cognitive architectures

1 Introduction

Social robots engaging in natural task-based dialogues with human teammates must understand and generate natural language expressions that refer to entities such as people, locations, and objects [18,23]. These tasks, known as *reference resolution* and *referring expression generation (REG)*, are particularly challenging in realistic robotics applications due to the realities of how knowledge is represented and distributed in modern robotic architectures.

We previously presented a *Consultant Framework* [35] that allows a robot to use its distributed sources of knowledge during reference resolution [39] and REG [40], without requiring the language processing system to understand how

© Springer Nature Switzerland AG 2018
S. S. Ge et al. (Eds.): ICSR 2018, LNAI 11357, pp. 170–180, 2018.
https://doi.org/10.1007/978-3-030-05204-1_17

that knowledge is represented and accessed. We've used this framework in previous work to enable a modern take on the classic Incremental Algorithm (IA) [9] for REG, relaxing several assumptions: that knowledge is certain, that knowledge is centrally stored, and that a list of all properties known to hold for each known entity is centrally available during REG. Our Consultant Framework allows these assumptions to be relaxed, producing a REG algorithm tailored to the realities of robotic architectures. Domain independence, however, comes at a computational cost, especially for language generation.

The IA requires, for each property that could be included, consideration of whether it holds for the to-be-described target and not for at least one distractor. Under the assumptions of the IA, this can be performed via set-membership checks on centrally available property sets. When the assumption of such property sets is relaxed, however, as is the case in the modified algorithm designed to leverage our Consultant Framework, these considerations must instead be made through queries to the Consultants responsible for the target and distractors. The computational complexity of REG combined with the computational cost of these queries results in a significant computational burden.

To address this computational burden, we propose (see also [38]) an augmented Consultant Framework that includes Consultant-Specific Short Term Memory (STM) Buffers that cache a small number of properties recently determined to hold for various entities. We will begin by defining this augmented framework, and by describing how it reduces the complexity of REG. We will then discuss different possible assumptions that can be made in the design of these STM Buffers, and discuss how these different choices impact both efficiency and cognitive plausibility. Next, we will discuss insights that can be gleaned from psychological models of memory decay and forgetting and computational caching strategies, and how these insights apply to the design of these STM Buffers. Finally, we will discuss how these Buffers can be exploited by processes beyond REG, and their potential relation to other cognitive models maintained throughout the architecture.

2   Augmented Framework

Our previously presented Consultant Framework [40] allows information about entities to be assessed when knowledge is uncertain, heterogeneous, and distributed, facilitating IA-inspired approaches to REG. Specifically, each Consultant c facilitates access to one KB k, and must be capable of four functions:

1. providing a set c_{domain} of atomic entities from k,
2. advertising a list $c_{constraints}$ of constraints that can be assessed with respect to entities from c_{domain}, *and that is ordered by descending preference.*
3. assessing constraints from $c_{constraints}$ with respect to entities from c_{domain}, and
4. adding, removing, or imposing constraints from $c_{constraints}$ on entities from c_{domain}.

In this section, we define an *(STM)-Augmented Consultant Framework* that adds an additional requirement:

5. providing a list c_{STM} of properties that hold for some entity from c_{domain}.

Crucially, the properties returned through this capability do not need to be all of the properties that hold for the target entity. A Consultant may have a large number of properties that it could assess for a given entity if need be, some of which might be very expensive to compute. As such, the purpose of this capability is not to request evaluation of all possible properties for the specified entity, but rather to request the contents of a small cache of properties recently determined to hold for the specified entity.

Models of Working Memory suggest that humans maintain cached knowledge of a small number of activated entities. While early models of working memory suggested that the size of working memory is bounded to a limited *number of chunks* (as in Miller's famous "magical number" of seven, plus or minus two [19]), more recent models instead suggest that the size of working memory is affected by the complexity of those chunks [17]. For example, needing to maintain multiple *features* of a single entity may detract from the total number of maintainable entities, and accordingly, the number of features maintainable for other entities [1,20,31]. Moreover, recent research has suggested that humans may have different resource limits for different *types* of representations (e.g., visual vs. auditory [11], or different types of visual features [34]) either due to the existence of separate domain-specific cognitive resources [2,15] or do to decreased interference between disparate representations [22].

Drawing on these insights, the new capability required in the *STM-Augmented Consultant Framework* requires each Consultant to maintain its own set of *features* currently remembered for the set of entities for which it is responsible. This serves to allow fast access to a set of entity properties likely to be relevant, in order to avoid the expensive long-term memory queries that make processes such as referring expression generation so expensive in the current Consultant framework. In the next section we describe how our newly proposed framework can be used during the course of REG.

3   Algorithmic Approach

We now present *SD-PIA*, the STM-Augmented variant of the Distributed, Probabilistic IA [40]. We will describe the main differences between *DIST-PIA* and *SD-PIA*, the key difference being our use of the properties stored in STM before performing LTM-Query intensive operations. While DIST-PIA crafted sub-descriptions through the use of a single algorithm (DIST-PIA-H), *SD-PIA* begins by crafting an initially (possibly partial) sub-description using the *SD-PIA-STM-H* algorithm, which utilizes only the properties found in STM Buffers. If the sub-descriptions returned through this algorithm are not fully discriminating, the partial sub-description is augmented by passing the set of still-to-be-eliminated distractors to *SD-PIA-H*, which operates much the same as the original *DIST-PIA-H* algorithm.

The other main difference between *DIST-PIA* and *SD-PIA* is in the design of the *SD-PIA-STM-H* function. Instead of considering all properties advertised in the target's domain, *SD-PIA-STM-H* considers only the properties returned by querying that Consultant's STM buffer, requiring a single query rather than $O(c_m^\Lambda)$ queries. For each of these already-known-to-hold and already-bound queries, *SD-PIA-STM-H* iteratively rebinds the query to refer to each distractor x rather than the target entity. For each re-bound query, *SD-PIA-STM-H* calls a function *stm-apply*, which checks whether that property holds for that distractor (x), by first checking whether the property exists in the STM Buffer maintained by Consultant c_x for x, or, if and only if this is not the case, by checking whether the property is known to hold by Consultant c_x using its' *apply* method, as usual.

Notation

C A set of *Consultants* $\{c_0, \ldots, c_n\}$
c_m^Λ The set of formulae $\{\lambda_0, \ldots, \lambda_n\}$ advertised by Consultant c responsible for m.
$c_m^{\Lambda STM}$ The STM buffer of formulae maintained by Consultant c responsible for m.
M A robot's *world model* of entities $\{m_0 \ldots m_n\}$ found in the domains provided by C.
D The incrementally built up description, comprised of mappings from entities M to sets of pairs (λ, Γ) of formulae and bindings for those formulae.
D^M The set of entities $m \in M$ for which sub-descriptions have been created.
d^M The set of entities $m \in M$ involved in sub-description d.
P The set of candidate (λ, Γ) pairs under consideration for inclusion.
Q The queue of referents which must be described.
X The incrementally pruned set of distractors

Algorithm 1. *SD-PIA*(m, C)

1: $D = $ new Map() // *The Description*
2: $Q = $ new Queue(m) // *The Referent Queue*
3: **while** $Q \neq \emptyset$ **do**
4:     // *Consider the next referent*
5:     $m\prime = $ pop(Q)
6:     // *Craft a description d for it*
7:     $(d, X) = $ *SD-PIA-STM-H*$(m\prime, C)$
8:     $d = $ *SD-PIA-H*$(m\prime, C, X, d)$
9:     $D = D \cup \{m \to d\}$
10:     // *Find all entities used in d*
11:     **for all** $m\prime\prime \in d^M \setminus keys(D)$ **do**
12:         // *And add undescribed entities to the queue*
13:         push($Q, m\prime\prime$)
14:     **end for**
15: **end while**
16: **return** D

---

4   Demonstration

We will now present a proof-of-concept demonstration of our proposed algorithm, implemented in the ADE [27] implementation of the DIARC architecture [25, 29]. The ADE (Agent Development Environment) middleware provides a well-validated infrastructure for enabling agent architectures through parallel distributed processing. The Distributed Integrated Affect Reflection Cognition

Algorithm 2. $SD\text{-}PIA\text{-}STM\text{-}H(m, C)$

```
 1: d = ∅ // The Sub-Description
 2: X = M \ m // The Distractors
 3: P = order([∀λ ∈ c_m^{Λ STM} : (λ, ∅)], c_m^Λ)
 4: while X ≠ ∅ and P ≠ ∅ do
 5:     (λ, Γ) = pop(P)
 6:     X̄ = [x ∈ X | stm_apply(c_x, λ, rebind(Γ, m → x)) < τ_{dph}]
 7:     if X̄ ≠ ∅ then
 8:         d = d ∪ (λ, Γ)
 9:         X = X \ X̄
10:     end if
11: end while
12: return  (d, X)
```

Algorithm 3. $SD\text{-}PIA\text{-}H(m, C, X, d)$

```
 1: // Initialize a set of properties to consider: those advertised by the Consultant c responsible
    for m and not already part of the sub-description
 2: P = [∀λ ∈ c_m^Λ : (λ, ∅)] \ d
 3: // While there are distractors to eliminate or properties to consider
 4: while X ≠ ∅ and P ≠ ∅ do
 5:     (λ, Γ) = pop(P)
 6:     // Find all unbound variables in the next property
 7:     V = find_unbound(λ, Γ)
 8:     if |V| > 1 then
 9:         // If there's more than one, create copies under all possible variable bindings that leave
            one variable of the same type as the target unbound
10:         for all Γ' ∈ cross_bindings(λ, Γ, C) do
11:             // And push them onto the property list
12:             push(P, (λ, Γ'))
13:         end for
14:         // Otherwise, if sufficiently probable that the property applies to the target...
15:     else if apply(c_m, λ, Γ ∪ (v_0 → m)) > τ_{dph} then
16:         // And sufficiently probable that it does not apply to at least one distractor...
17:         X̄ = [x ∈ X | apply(c_x, λ, Γ ∪ (v_0 → x)) < τ_{dph}]
18:         // Then bind its free variable to the target, and add it to the sub-description...
19:         if X̄ ≠ ∅ then
20:             // And remove any eliminated distractors
21:             d = d ∪ (λ, Γ ∪ (v_0 → m))
22:             X = X \ X̄
23:         end if
24:     end if
25: end while
26: return  d
```

(DIARC) Architecture is a component-based architecture that has been under development for over 15 years, with a focus on robust spoken language understanding and generation. For our demonstration scenario, the following architectural components were used: Speech Recognition (using the Sphinx4 Speech Recognizer [33]), Parsing (which uses the most recent iteration [28] of the TLDL Parser [10]), the Dialogue and Pragmatics Components [6], the NLG Component (in which the $SD\text{-}PIA$ algorithm was implemented), the Goal Manager [26], the Belief Component (which provides a Prolog Knowledge Base [8]), the Resolver Component [39], the GROWLER HyperResolver Component [37], and a simulated Vision Component [14] (which serves as a Consultant).

For this demonstration walkthrough, we use a simple scenario involving a single "objects Consultant" (the aforementioned simulated Vision Component), which advertises a variety of constraints, e.g., related to object type and object color, with type constraints having higher preference than color constraints and ordered according to specificity. The scene in front of the robot contains a red teabox (known to the objects Consultant as $object_1$) and a green teabox (known to the objects Consultant as $object_2$) sitting on a table (known to the objects Consultant as $object_3$).

For this walkthrough, we begin by instructing the simulated robot "Look at the box". The TLDL Parser [10, 28] parses this into an utterance of type *Instruction*, with primary semantics $lookat(self, X)$ and supplemental semantics $\{box(X)\}$. The GROWLER reference resolution algorithm described in our recent work [37] (see also [36, 42]), then identifies the two teaboxes ($object_1, object_2$), as candidate referents satisfying the given description. During the reference resolution process, when the property $box(X)$ is determined to hold for each entity, it is placed into that entity's STM Buffer within the simulated Vision Component. Because the expression is ambiguous, a clarification request is automatically generated [41] to determine whether $object_1$ or $object_2$ is the target referent. For each of these entities, *SD-PIA* is recruited to generate referring expressions. In this section, we will describe the process followed in the selection of properties for $object_1$ alone (hereafter o_1), as the process for $object_2$ is identical in structure.

SD-PIA begins by creating empty description $D = \emptyset$ and referent queue $Q = \{o_1\}$ (Algorithm 1, Lines 1–2). Because there are still referents to describe (Line 5), *SD-PIA* calls helper function *SD-PIA-STM-H* (*STM-H* hereafter) to craft a sub-description for o_1, which is popped off of Q (Line 7).

STM-H begins by asking the Consultant responsible for o_1 for a set of distractors X (e.g., $\{o_2, o_3\}$) and the set of properties P stored in its STM Buffer for o_1, sorted by that Consultant's preference ordering c_m^A. (Algorithm 2 Lines 2–3), in this case $box(X)$. Next, *STM-H* constructs the reduced set of distractors $\bar{X}$ for which the property does *not* appear in STM (i.e., o_3). Because this is nonempty, o_3 is removed from the set of distractors, and $box(o_1)$ is added to sub-description d (Algorithm 2 Lines 8–9). Because there are no more properties to examine in P, sub-description d and the set of remaining distractors $\{o_2\}$ is returned.

The second helper function, *SD-PIA-H* (Algorithm 3, hereafter simply *HELPER*), is then used to complete the referring expression. *HELPER* begins by asking the Consultant responsible for o_1 for the set of properties P it can use in descriptions, sorted according to its predetermined preference ordering, and ignoring properties already contained in sub-description d, e.g., teabox(X), table(X), red(X), green(X), on(X,Y) (Algorithm 3 Line 2).

From this list, *HELPER* pops the first unconsidered property (i.e., $teabox(X)$) and its (empty) set of bindings. $teabox(X)$ has exactly one unbound variable, so *HELPER* will use Consultant o's *apply* method (as per Capability 3) to ask how probable it is that $teabox(X)$ applies to o_1 (Algorithm 3

Line 15). Because it is sufficiently probable that this property applies to this entity, *HELPER* uses the same method to determine whether it also applies to the single remaining distractor (o_2). Because it does, the property will be ignored.

HELPER will then repeat this process with other properties. Suppose it is insufficiently probable that $table(X)$ holds: it will be ignored. Suppose it *is* sufficiently probable that $red(X)$ holds but not for the lone remaining distractor (o_2), allowing o_2 to be ruled out. Thus, $\{o_2\}$ will be removed from X, and $red(o_1)$ will be added to d. Since X is now empty, the sub-description $\{(box(o_1), red(o_1)\}$ will be returned to *SD-PIA* (Line 26) and added to full description D. Since this sub-description does not refer to any entities that have yet to be described and Q is empty, *SD-PIA* will return description D (Algorithm 1, Line 16). This process is then repeated for object o_2. It will be the responsibility of the next component of the natural language pipeline to translate this into an RE, e.g. "Do you mean the red box or the green box?" [41].

5   Discussion

Potential Benefits: The primary motivation behind our approach is performance: the number of queries needed when determining what properties to use may be much lower when those properties are sufficiently discriminating. Similarly, determining whether properties rule out distractors may be possible using set-membership checks rather than costly long term memory queries. Moreover, we believe these buffers may facilitate *lexical entrainment* [4,5], where conversational partners converge on common choices of labels and properties over the course of a conversation, resulting in more comprehensible referring expressions [32]. If a robot's STM Buffers are populated with properties used by itself and its interlocutors, and if the properties contained in those buffers are considered before others, this may directly lead to such entrainment.

Potential Limitations: On the other hand, because the robot arbitrarily restricts itself to a subset of the properties it *could* otherwise choose to use, it may force the robot into local maxima in the landscape of referring expressions. Moreover, the robot runs the risk of using a property that does not actually hold if it does not appropriately handle contextual dynamics. For example, an object previously described as "on the left" may no longer be "on the left" if the object, robot, or interlocutor has moved since the object was last discussed.

Design Decisions: Buffer Size Limitations: Many insights from psychology could be leveraged to prevent such mistakes. A context-sensitive decay-based model of working memory might prevent this by having different properties "decay" out of cache, with time or probability of decay proportional to how likely it is to change over time [3,30]. A resource-based model might prevent this by having a limited total buffer size, and have property dynamics factor into the decision of what to bump from memory when new things need to be inserted into an already-full buffer [13,16]. Finally, an interference-based model might prevent this by having properties added to a buffer "overwrite" the most similar property currently in the buffer [21,24]. These are loose characterizations of the respective theories from cognitive psychology; a comprehensive discussion of these theories and the relative evidence for them from a psychological perspective can be found in [20]. Of course, the approach taken need not be cognitively plausible. The robot could, for example, statistically model the dynamics of different properties, and use them to periodically re-sample the properties held in its buffers.

The question of cognitive plausibility also raises a different question: how extensive should the robot's memory caches be? Should the robot keep property caches for all entities, for only those that are relevant in the current context, or for an even smaller set? And for each entity, should the robot track all relevant knowledge for so long as that entity is tracked, or should it track only a fixed, small number of properties? And should such limits be local, or global limits shared between tracked entities? These are once again questions for which candidate answers can be gleaned from the psychological literature [20]. Here, interesting tradeoffs can be made. On the one hand, robots can be made to remember much more than humans can. On the other hand, expanded memory may come at a computational cost; and moreover, choosing to remember more means increased risk of incorrect behavior due to mishandling of property dynamics. Further evidence from neuroimaging studies suggests that the contents of working memory in humans is biased by humans' current goals, with only task-relevant features being maintained in visual working memory [43]. For robots, task-relevance may be similarly useful for optimally selecting what to maintain in Consultants' STM Buffers.

Design Decisions: Buffer Population: Similar tradeoffs arise when deciding when to add properties used in natural language to a robot's STM Buffers. In this work, properties are added to buffers as soon as they are determined to hold for a referent, rather than waiting until the end of the reference resolution process. This means that lexical entrainment effects may be seen for entities other than intended referents. For example, consider "the tall red box". Assuming properties are processed in the order $tall(X)$, $red(x)$, $box(X)$, all tall objects in the scene will have $tall(X)$ added to their STM Buffers, all tall red objects will also have $red(X)$ added to their STM Buffers, and tall red boxes will have all three properties added to their STM Buffers. Accordingly, the robot will prefer to use height and potentially color and shape to refer to other objects even if they have not been referred to. This is not dissimilar from psycholinguistic observations of syntactic and semantic carry-over from previous object references to references to previously unmentioned entities [7,12]. This could be particularly effective in the case of the Vision Consultant, as additional caching reduces the risk of needing to conduct future (potentially expensive) visual searches. If this particular memory-performance tradeoff is not optimal for Consultants associated with non-visual modalities, the decision to add properties to STM Buffers may need to be made on a per-Consultant basis.

6   Conclusions

We have presented a caching strategy augmenting a robot's set of distributed knowledge sources with cognitively inspired STM Buffers so as to increase computational efficiency. We have explained how these buffers may facilitate linguistic phenomena such as lexical entrainment, and identified insights from cognitive science that may inform future refinements of these Buffers. Two tasks will be crucial for future research building off this work. First, the presented approach must be evaluated both in terms of computational performance and with respect to objective and subjective measures such as those used in our previously presented evaluative approach [40]. Second, insights from cognitive science must be leveraged to enable alternate design decisions that may be explored both from the perspectives of artificial intelligence for human-robot interaction, cognitive modeling, and cognitive architecture.

Acknowledgments. This work was in part supported by ONR grant N00014-16-1-0278.

References

1. Alvarez, G.A., Cavanagh, P.: The capacity of visual short-term memory is set both by visual information load and by number of objects. Psychol. Sci. **15**, 106–111 (2004)
2. Baddeley, A.: Working memory. Science **255**(5044), 556–559 (1992)
3. Baddeley, A.D., Thomson, N., Buchanan, M.: Word length and the structure of short-term memory. J. Verbal Learn. Verbal Behav. **14**, 575–589 (1975)
4. Brennan, S.E.: Lexical entrainment in spontaneous dialog. ISSD **96**, 41–44 (1996)
5. Brennan, S.E., Clark, H.H.: Conceptual pacts and lexical choice in conversation. J. Exp. Psychol.: Learn. Mem. Cogn. **22**, 1482 (1996)
6. Briggs, G., Scheutz, M.: A hybrid architectural approach to understanding and appropriately generating indirect speech acts. In: Proceedings of AAAI (2013)
7. Carbary, K., Tanenhaus, M.: Conceptual pacts, syntactic priming, and referential form. In: Proceedings of CogSci Workshop on Production of Referring Expressions (2011)
8. Clocksin, W., Mellish, C.S.: Programming in PROLOG. Springer, Heidelberg (2003). https://doi.org/10.1007/978-3-642-55481-0
9. Dale, R., Reiter, E.: Computational interpretations of the gricean maxims in the generation of referring expressions. Cognit. Sci. **19**(2), 233–263 (1995)
10. Dzifcak, J., Scheutz, M., Baral, C., Schermerhorn, P.: What to do and how to do it: translating natural language directives into temporal and dynamic logic representation for goal management and action execution. In: Proceedings of ICRA (2009)
11. Fougnie, D., Zughni, S., Godwin, D., Marois, R.: Working memory storage is intrinsically domain specific. J. Exp. Psychol.: Gen. **144**, 30 (2015)

12. Goudbeek, M., Krahmer, E.: Alignment in interactive reference production: content planning, modifier ordering, and referential overspecification. TiCS **4**, 269–289 (2012)
13. Just, M.A., Carpenter, P.A.: A capacity theory of comprehension: individual differences in working memory. Psychol. Rev. **99**(1), 122 (1992)
14. Krause, E., Zillich, M., Williams, T., Scheutz, M.: Learning to recognize novel objects in one shot through human-robot interactions in natural language dialogues. In: Proceedings of the Twenty-Eighth AAAI Conference on Artificial Intelligence (2014)
15. Logie, R.H.: Visuo-Spatial Working Memory. Psychology Press, London (2014)
16. Ma, W.J., Husain, M., Bays, P.M.: Changing concepts of working memory. Nat. Neurosci. **17**(3), 347 (2014)
17. Mathy, F., Feldman, J.: What's magic about magic numbers? chunking and data compression in short-term memory. Cognition **122**(3), 346–362 (2012)
18. Mavridis, N.: A review of verbal and non-verbal human-robot interactive communication. Robot. Auton. Syst. **63**, 22–35 (2015)
19. Miller, G.A.: The magical number seven, plus or minus two: some limits on our capacity for processing information. Psychol. Rev. **63**, 81 (1956)
20. Oberauer, K., Farrell, S., Jarrold, C., Lewandowsky, S.: What limits working memory capacity? Psychol. Bull. **142**, 758 (2016)
21. Oberauer, K., Kliegl, R.: A formal model of capacity limits in working memory. J. Mem. Lang. **55**(4), 601–626 (2006)
22. Oberauer, K., Lewandowsky, S., Farrell, S., Jarrold, C., Greaves, M.: Modeling working memory: an interference model of complex span. Psychon. Bull. Rev. **19**, 779–819 (2012)
23. Popescu-Belis, A., Robba, I., Sabah, G.: Reference resolution beyond coreference: a conceptual frame and its application. In: Proceedings of COLING (1998)
24. Saito, S., Miyake, A.: On the nature of forgetting and the processing-storage relationship in reading span performance. J. Mem. Lang. **50**, 425–443 (2004)
25. Schermerhorn, P.W., Kramer, J.F., Middendorff, C., Scheutz, M.: DIARC: a testbed for natural human-robot interaction. In: Proceedings of AAAI (2006)
26. Schermerhorn, P.W., Scheutz, M.: The utility of affect in the selection of actions and goals under real-world constraints. In: IC-AI, pp. 948–853 (2009)
27. Scheutz, M.: Ade: steps toward a distributed development and runtime environment for complex robotic agent architectures. Appl. Artif. Intell. **20**, 275–304 (2006)
28. Scheutz, M., Krause, E., Oosterveld, B., Frasca, T., Platt, R.: Spoken instruction-based one-shot object and action learning in a cognitive robotic architecture. In: 16th Conference on Autonomous Agents and Multiagent Systems (AAMAS) (2017)
29. Scheutz, M., Williams, T., Krause, E., Oosterveld, B., Sarathy, V., Frasca, T.: An overview of the distributed integrated cognition affect and reflection DIARC architecture. In: Cognitive Architectures (2018, in press)
30. Schweickert, R., Boruff, B.: Short-term memory capacity: magic number or magic spell? J. Exp. Psychol.: Learn. Mem. Cogn. **12**, 419 (1986)
31. Taylor, R., Thomson, H., Sutton, D., Donkin, C.: Does working memory have a single capacity limit? J. Mem. Lang. **93**, 67–81 (2017)
32. Tolins, J., Zeamer, C., Fox Tree, J.E.: Overhearing dialogues and monologues: how does entrainment lead to more comprehensible referring expressions? Discourse Process. **55**, 1–21 (2017)
33. Walker, W., Lamere, P., Kwok, P., et al.: Sphinx-4: a flexible open source framework for speech recognition. Technical report (2004)

34. Wang, B., Cao, X., Theeuwes, J., Olivers, C.N., Wang, Z.: Separate capacities for storing different features in visual working memory. J. Exp. Psychol.: Learn. Mem. Cogn. **43**, 26 (2017)
35. Williams, T.: A consultant framework for natural language processing in integrated robot architectures. IEEE Intell. Inform. Bull. (2017)
36. Williams, T., Acharya, S., Schreitter, S., Scheutz, M.: Situated open world reference resolution for human-robot dialogue. In: Proceedings of HRI (2016)
37. Williams, T., Krause, E., Oosterveld, B., Scheutz, M.: Towards givenness and relevance-theoretic open world reference resolution. In: RSS Workshop on Models and Representations for Natural Human-Robot Communication (2018)
38. Williams, T., Krause, E., Oosterveld, B., Thielstrom, R., Scheutz, M.: Towards robot knowledge consultants augmented with distributed short term memory. In: RSS Workshop on Models and Representations for Natural Human-Robot Communication (2018)
39. Williams, T., Scheutz, M.: A framework for resolving open-world referential expressions in distributed heterogeneous knowledge bases. In: Proceedings of AAAI (2016)
40. Williams, T., Scheutz, M.: Referring expression generation under uncertainty: algorithm and evaluation framework. In: Proceedings of the 10th International Conference on Natural Language Generation (INLG) (2017)
41. Williams, T., Scheutz, M.: Resolution of referential ambiguity in human-robot dialogue using dempster-Shafer theoretic pragmatics. In: Proceedings of RSS (2017)
42. Williams, T., Scheutz, M.: Reference in robotics: a givenness hierarchy theoretic approach. In: The Oxford Handbook of Reference (2018, in press)
43. Yu, Q., Shim, W.: Occipital, parietal, and frontal cortices selectively maintain task-relevant features of multi-feature objects in visual working memory (2017)

3D Virtual Path Planning for People with Amyotrophic Lateral Sclerosis Through Standing Wheelchair

Jessica S. Ortiz[1,2(✉)], Guillermo Palacios-Navarro[1(✉)],
Christian P. Carvajal[2(✉)], and Víctor H. Andaluz[2(✉)]

[1] Department of Electronic Engineering and Communications, University of
Zaragoza, Zaragoza, Spain
guillermo.palacios@unizar.es
[2] Universidad de Las Fuerzas Armadas ESPE, Sangolquí, Ecuador
{jsortiz4, vhandaluz1}@espe.edu.ec,
chriss2592@hotmail.com

Abstract. This article presents the development of an autonomous control system of an electric standing wheelchair for people with amyotrophic lateral sclerosis. The proposed control scheme is based on the autonomous maneuverability of the standing wheelchair, for which a path planner is implemented to which the desired 3D position is defined through the eye-tracking sensor. The eye-tracking is implemented in a virtual reality environment which allows selecting the desired position of the standing wheelchair. The wheelchair has a standing system that allows the user to position himself on the Z axis according to his needs independently of the displacement in the X-Y plane with respect to the inertial reference system $<R>$. To verify the performance of the proposed control scheme, several experimental tests are carried out.

Keywords: Virtual reality · Unity 3D · Standing wheelchair
Amyotrophic lateral sclerosis

1 Introduction

Currently there is an increase in people with motor disabilities, due to aging, longevity and injuries that are usually the result of traffic accidents, this leads to the need to use mechanisms to facilitate the mobility of people. The integration of robotic issues into the medical field has become of great interest in recent years. Service, assistance, rehabilitation and surgery are the more benefited human health-care areas by the recent advances in robotics. Specifically, autonomous and safe navigation of wheelchairs inside known and unknown environments is one of the important goals in assistance robotics [1–9]. The technological advance in the area of robotics has allowed the development of wheelchair prototypes, there are two types of wheelchair (*i*) *standard wheelchair* which requires a person to move to the chair and (*ii*) *electric wheelchair* with some degree of autonomy designed for people who can not perform actions of movements of their extremities; these wheelchairs allow improving the lives of people with disabilities, perform daily tasks and see the world with other possibilities [1, 2].

© Springer Nature Switzerland AG 2018
S. S. Ge et al. (Eds.): ICSR 2018, LNAI 11357, pp. 181–191, 2018.
https://doi.org/10.1007/978-3-030-05204-1_18

There are research works associated with mobility in wheelchairs, *e.g.*, in [4] the automatic control is carried out that allows to position a wheelchair. In [5] it presents a cascade controller in which it mentions a kinematic controller that saturates the speeds of the wheelchair and a dynamic controller that compensates the dynamics of the system; while in [8] the automation for the inclination of assisted wheelchairs is presented. Within the field of assistance the excessive use of wheelchairs leads to several problems in the patient due to the position that is adopted in a wheelchair is not what the human body should be subjected to. The most common problems due to the lack of an upright posture are: affections in the intestinal functions, decreased blood circulation to the lower extremities, increased pressure in the hip area, etc. To prevent this type of anomalies, standing wheelchair has been designed which has the ability to walk on two lower extremities, facilitating the use of the two upper extremities for the development of daily activities and in humans can be determined as a natural posture [4, 10].

A robotic standing wheelchair is useful for handicapped people who are not able to drive a standing wheelchair. Using a human-machine interface based on brain signals, voice or eye movement the disabled person can select a desired target. Then, a path will be automatically generated and a path tracking control will guide the standing wheelchair to the desired target. Hence, a path will be automatically generated and a path tracking control will guide the standing wheelchair to the desired target. As indicated, the fundamental problems of the path following has been well studied and many solutions have been proposed and applied in a wide range of applications. Let $\mathcal{P}_d(s) \in \Re^2$ be a desired geometric path parameterized by the curvilinear abscissa $s \in \Re$. In the literature is common to find different control algorithms for path following where is consider $s(t)$ as an additional control input [11–21].

Este trabajo propone un sistema de mobilidad autónomo para personas con amyotrophic lateral sclerosis a través de eye-tracking sensor. The amyotrophic lateral sclerosis is a degenerative disease that affects the motor neurons of the brain, brainstem and spinal cord, which are the cells that control the voluntary muscular activity of acts as essential as speaking, walking, eating or breathing. The degeneration of these neurons causes the ability of the brain to perform muscle movement is lost and, consequently, those affected have progressive muscle atrophy and causes a general progressive paralysis. The capacity for voluntary movement is lost, but not the basic senses or the intellectual capacity. In such context, this work considers that the user can mobilize to a desired position through positioning in virtual reality environments, that is, the user locates the desired position in a virtual environment and the system defines the path that must be followed autonomously by the standing wheelchair. The path following problem is addressed in this subsystem. It is worth noting that the proposed controller does not consider $s(t)$ as an additional control input as it is frequent in literature. In addition, both stability and robustness properties to parametric uncertainties in the dynamic model are proven through Lyapunov's method. To validate the proposed control algorithm, experimental results are included and discussed.

2 Structure System

For the development of the application and its functionalities, 4 stages are defined as shown in Fig. 1.

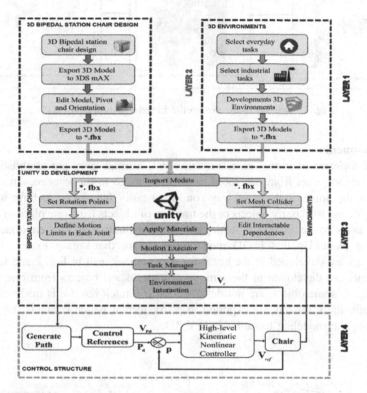

Fig. 1. Multilayers diagram of system 3D design for path planning.

2.1 3D Bipedal Station Chair Design

The mechanical design of an object or robot is done in CAD software, in this case Solid Works is used, which allows creating solids to be later assembled, allowing to obtain complete 3D models. In Fig. 2 you can see the methodology to create the 3D model of the chair and this model is used to interact in virtual environments.

The design of the chair recomposes by the coupling of two wheels that allow the movement from one place to another, to lift a certain distance to the person in the chair develops a system that rises together with the person safely and without sudden movements, each part that makes up the chair is developed in Solid Works, parts are assembled according to the real model obtaining as a result an assembly file *.sldasm. Finally, the design becomes a model compatible with the UNITY 3D platform, using the 3ds MAX software that allows exporting the Solid Works file to an extension file *. fbx, this file format is fully compatible with the UNITY platform.

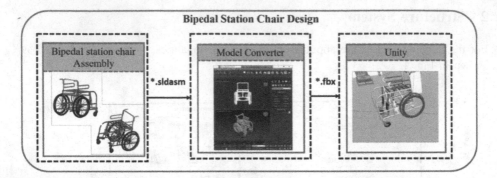

Fig. 2. Scheme of the design the bipedal station chair 3D.

3D Environments

In the development of virtual environments, first, normal tasks are established by a person, either to refuel from one room to another, to go to the kitchen, among other tasks within the home, in the same way you select tasks that can be perform within an industrial process to classify objects or the transfer of objects from one place to another. Once the tasks to be done are stable, the implementation of the environments is outlined, in SketchUp that is 3D modeling software that's easy to use. Habitual environments are developed in the home for a person as seen in Fig. 3 and industrial environments are developed in the same way to transport objects from one place to another Fig. 4, some objects are not designed from scratch but use is made of objects already built, these models are exported in *.fbx format which contains the textures given during the modeling towards UNITY 3D.

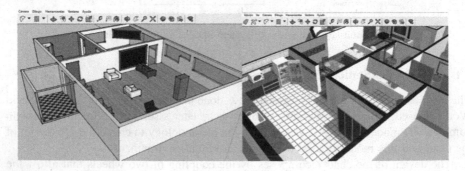

Fig. 3. 3D scenarios for tasks at home.

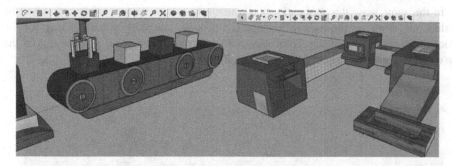

Fig. 4. 3D scenarios for tasks in industries.

Unity 3D Development

For development the 3D environments of the different tasks proposed for the Unity application, you import the 3D models that will be part of the application. In the case of the chair, the corresponding rotation points are assigned to each degree of freedom that makes up Fig. 5. For the creation of the scenario, the developed 3D models are imported, adding physical properties to be able to move and have the effect of collision with objects during the displacement Fig. 6.

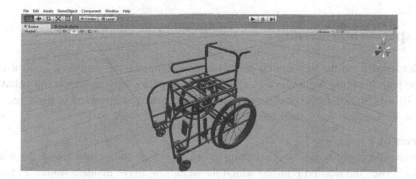

Fig. 5. Import model of the bipedal station chair to unity 3D.

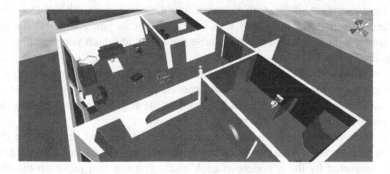

Fig. 6. Import of the environment models to unity 3D.

In the same way, the application has a menu to select the type of task that will be carried out, allowing the user to manage the process that will be carried out, for the selection is made use of the Tobii sensor that through the visual positioning of the person is in the chair choose the 3D environment Fig. 7.

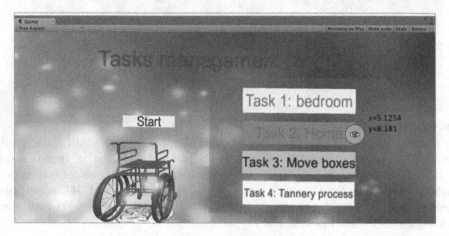

Fig. 7. Task management menu

3   Experimental Results

In order to perform the application performance validation, the proposed control law, and the path planning method, two experiments are performed, in which the behavior of the Bipeda Station Chair is observed in physical form and observed in time. real the location of it within the virtual environment.

Experiment 1
The first experiment consists of selecting a task in which the person using the visual sensor chooses the desired point to which he wishes to arrive inside a home, allowing to obtain information of the desired point $\mathbf{P_d} = [x_d \quad y_d \quad z_d]$. Once the user selects this desired point to get this information, it is sent to the Matlab software to correctly manage the generation of the path to arrive avoiding collisions with objects that are within the user's path, in the Fig. 8 it is indicated first as you can select the desired position to reach, in the same way you choose the height at which you want the chair to reach the final point.

To continue with the execution of the system, the mathematical software is expected to process this environment and generate the appropriate path for the person to move autonomously to the desired position, in the Fig. 9 it is indicated as Matlab through the algorithm of path planning.

In the same way in the virtual environment Fig. 10 you can see how the chair is moving in real time by placing it in the position that should be according to the odometry measured by the encoders in each of the engines that make up the chair.

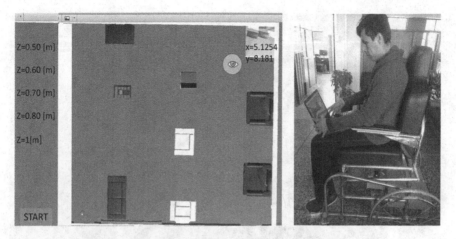

Fig. 8. Selection of the desired point through the view.

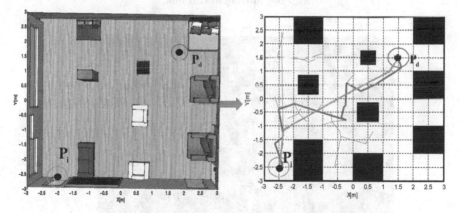

Fig. 9. Post-processing the path in Matlab.

Experiment 2

The second experiment consists of selecting an another task, its task is about an industrial process, consist translate a box to desired point $\mathbf{P_d} = \begin{bmatrix} x_d & y_d & z_d \end{bmatrix}$. The process to generate the path is similar to the first experiment, in the Fig. 11 it is indicated first as you can select the desired position to reach, in the same way you choose the height at which you want the chair to reach the final point.

The information is processed in Matlab for to generate the path, using the path planning method implemented in this article, The Fig. 12. show the process information for to create the path.

With the path generated in Matlab to reach the desired point, the control algorithm enters execution, thus leading from the initial point of the chair to the desired point that the user selected by sight, in Fig. 13 show the stroboscopic movement by the bipedal station chair.

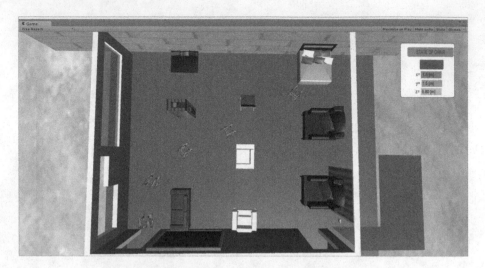

Fig. 10. Moving in real time

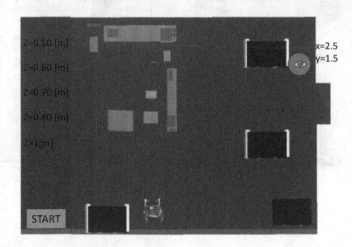

Fig. 11. Selection of the desired point through the view.

Finally, in the Fig. 14 you can see the movie made by the chair in the virtual environment develops, you can see how it moves without colliding and reaching the desired point.

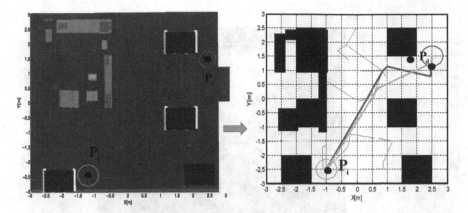

Fig. 12. Post-processing the path in Matlab.

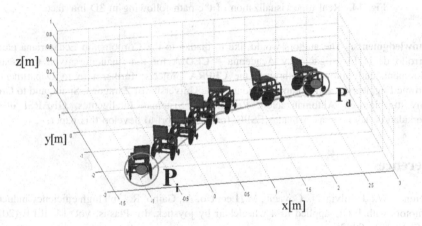

Fig. 13. Stroboscopic movement of the chair.

4 Conclusions

In this work, the design and implementation of a system of autonomous mobility of a bipedestación wheelchair was carried out. The system consists of defining the desired position in a virtual environment through an eye-tracking sensor. The wheelchair has a standing system that allows the user to position himself on the Z axis according to his needs independently of the displacement in the X-Y plane with respect to the inertial reference system $<R>$. To verify the performance of the proposed control scheme, several experimental tests are carried out.

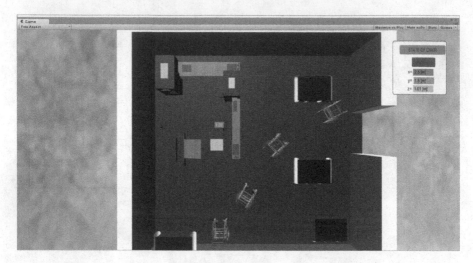

Fig. 14. Real-time visualization of the path following in 3D interface.

Acknowledgments. The authors would like to thanks to the Corporación Ecuatoriana para el Desarrollo de la Investigación y Academia – CEDIA for the financing given to research, development, and innovation, through the CEPRA projects; furthermore to Department of Electronic Engineering and Communications of the University of Zaragoza, Spain, and to Grupo de Investigación en Automatización, Robótica y Sistemas Inteligentes, GI-ARSI of the Universidad de las Fuerzas Armadas ESPE, for the support to develop this paper.

References

1. Nunes, W., da Silvia, N., Covacic, M., Leoncio, A., Gaino, R.: 3ph high efficiency induction motors with IFOC applied to a wheelchair by joystick. In: Plastis, vol. 14. IEEE (2016). ISSN: 1548-0992
2. Velazquez., R., Gutierrez, C.A.: Modeling and control techniques for electric powered wheelchairs: an overview. IEEE (2015)
3. Andaluz, V.H., et al.: Modeling and control of a wheelchair considering center of mass lateral displacements. In: Liu, H., Kubota, N., Zhu, X., Dillmann, R., Zhou, D. (eds.) ICIRA 2015. LNCS (LNAI), vol. 9246, pp. 254–270. Springer, Cham (2015). https://doi.org/10.1007/978-3-319-22873-0_23
4. Trenoras, L., Gregory, U., Monacelli, E., Hugel, V.: Mechatronic design of the gyrolift verticalization wheelchair, pp. 1308–1333. IEEE (2014)
5. Achkar, R., Haidar, G., Dourgham, A., Semaan, D., Araji, H.: Mobile controlled wheelchair, pp. 429–434. IEEE (2015)
6. Leela, R.J., et al.: Android based automated wheelchair control, pp. 349–353. IEEE (2017)
7. Young, G.O.: Synthetic structure of industrial plastics (Book style with paper title and editor). In: Peters, J. (ed.) Plastics, vol. 3, 2nd edn, pp. 15–64. McGraw-Hill, New York (1964)
8. Goher, K.: Modelling and simulation of a reconfigurable wheelchair with a sit-to stand facility for a disabled child. In: Methods & Models in Automation & Robotics (MMAR), pp. 430–434 (2013)

9. Gharooni, S., Awada, B.: Modeling and control of upright lifting wheelchair. IEEE Trans. Rehabil. Eng. 343–353 (2006)

10. Kayani, S., Malik, M.: Modeling and simulation of biped kinematics using bond-graphs. In: 2da International Conference on Emerging Technologies, Peshawar, Pakistan (2006)

11. Kuno, Y., Shimada, N.: A robotic wheelchair based on the integration. IEEE Robot. Autom. Mag. **10**, 26–34 (2003)

12. Nejati, M., Argall, B.D.: Automated incline detection for assistive powered wheelchairs, pp. 1007–1012. IEEE (2016)

13. Huang, C.K., Wang, Z.W., Chen, G.W., Yang, C.Y.: Development of a smart wheelchair with dual functions: real-time control and automated guide, pp. 73–76. IEEE (2017)

14. Puanhvuan, D., Khemmachotikun, S., Wechakam, P., Wijam, B., Wongsawat, Y.: Automated navigation system for eye-based wheelchair controls, pp. 1–4. IEEE (2014)

15. Bae, J., Moon, I.: Design of seat mechanism for multi-posture-controllable wheelchair, pp. 1994–1997. IEEE (2014)

16. Auger, C., et al.: Development and feasibility of an automated call monitoring intervention for older wheelchair users: the MOvIT project. BMC Health Serv. Res. **15**(1), 1–2 (2015)

17. Velázquez, R., Gutiérrez, A., et al.: Modeling and control techniques for electric powered wheelchairs: an overview, pp. 397–408. IEEE (2014)

18. Ortiz, J.S., Andaluz, V.H., Rivas, D., Sánchez, J.S., Espinosa, E.G.: Human-wheelchair system controlled by through brain signals. In: Kubota, N., Kiguchi, K., Liu, H., Obo, T. (eds.) ICIRA 2016. LNCS (LNAI), vol. 9835, pp. 211–222. Springer, Cham (2016). https://doi.org/10.1007/978-3-319-43518-3_21

19. Jeseong, R., et al.: Optimal seat and footrest positions of manual standing wheelchair. Int. J. Precis. Eng. Manuf. **18**, 879–885 (2017)

20. Salmiah, A., Nazmul, H., Osman, T.: A modular fuzzy control approach for two-wheeled wheelchair. J. Intell. Robot. Syst. **64**, 401–426 (2014)

21. Gharooni, S.C., Awada, B., Tokhi, M.O.: Modeling and control of upright lifting wheelchair. In: Tokhi, M.O., Virk, G.S., Hossain, M.A. (eds.) Climbing and Walking Robots, pp. 969–979. Springer, Heidelberg (2006). https://doi.org/10.1007/3-540-26415-9_116

Physiological Differences Depending on Task Performed in a 5-Day Interaction Scenario Designed for the Elderly: A Pilot Study

Roxana Agrigoroaie[✉] and Adriana Tapus

Autonomous Systems and Robotics Laboratory, U2IS, ENSTA-ParisTech,
Université Paris-Saclay, Palaiseau, France
{roxana.agrigoroaie,adriana.tapus}@ensta-paristech.fr

Abstract. This paper investigates the relationship between different physiological parameters and three tasks performed by an elderly individual in a 5-days interaction scenario. The physiological parameters investigated are: the galvanic skin response, the facial temperature variation, the heart rate, and the respiration rate. The three tasks were the same during all interactions. More specifically, the participant started with a relaxation period of 3 min, continued with 5 cognitive games, and finished with a news reading task. Each day consisted of two sessions: morning session (at around 11am), and afternoon session (at around 3pm). Our hypotheses were validated, meaning that we can differentiate between the three tasks by looking only at the physiological parameters, and we can differentiate between two difficulty levels of the cognitive games. A discussion of these results is also provided.

1 Introduction

As the worldwide population is growing older [8], viable solutions have to be found in order to enable the elderly to stay independent for longer and to improve their quality of life. Moreover, it is desired to enable them to stay in their own home environments. Research has shown that one solution for providing personalized care is to use socially assistive robots (RAS) [5]. Multiple such robots have been developed in the recent years [15,19]. Some of their applications found in the literature include: stimulation of cognitive functions [6,21], alert family and caregivers in care of emergencies [7].

HOBBIT project [15] had as aim the development of an assistive robot that is capable to visually observe and interpret the actions of the elderly so as to provide appropriate assistive services. RAMCIP project [19] focused on how a robot can monitor the behaviour of an elderly individual with mild cognitive impairment (MCI) in order to provide assistance in case of need.

ENRICHME project[1] focused on developing a personal socially assistive robot for the elderly with MCI. The ENRICHME system used a mixture of

---

[1] www.enrichme.eu.

© Springer Nature Switzerland AG 2018
S. S. Ge et al. (Eds.): ICSR 2018, LNAI 11357, pp. 192–201, 2018.
https://doi.org/10.1007/978-3-030-05204-1_19

RGB-D, thermal, and ambiental data to detect and recognize the individual it interacts with [3]. Moreover, it adapted its behavior based on the profile of that individual. The selection criteria for the testing users of this research project includes: at least 65 years old, to have received the diagnosis of MCI from a neuropsychologist or to be identified with mild dementia on the MMSE score. The aim of the robot and of the developed applications is to improve the everyday life of the elderly with MCI.

The purpose of the current study is to investigate how a robot can use physiological parameters to determine what task an elderly individual is performing, the current difficulty level of a cognitive game played, and to find the correlations between the game performance and the variation of the physiological state. To the best of our knowledge, this is one of the first studies to investigate both GSR and thermal data in an in the wild scenario with the elderly.

Research shows that different physiological parameters can be used to measure the reactions of individuals in different situations. The physiological parameters mostly used are: heart rate (HR), respiration rate (RR), galvanic skin response (GSR), facial temperature variation. The emotional state of an individual can be determined by how the temperature varies across certain regions of interest (ROI) on the face [11]. Stress, for example, is characterized by a decrease of the temperature in the nose region. In [10], the authors show which facial regions provide valuable information regarding the internal state of an individual. Their literature review identified six main ROIs: nose, chin, cheeks, periorbital region, the forehead, and the maxillary area. GSR has received much attention for many years in the research field of psychophysiology. A literature review shows that it was used to differentiate between different levels of cognitive load [13], to differentiate between stress and cognitive load [17]. The main physiological parameters used are: accumulative GSR (summation of GSR values over task time [13]), the number of peaks [13], the event based features: latency time, amplitude, and recovery time [17]. While performing certain physical and cognitive activities the HR and RR are important parameters to be monitored. They can be measured by using contact sensors (e.g., respiration belt [12]), or by using a RGB camera [16].

The current study investigates the relationship between different physiological parameters (i.e., GSR, facial temperature, HR, RR) and the task performed during a 5-days interaction scenario with an elderly individual. The paper is structured as follows: Sect. 2 presents the experimental setup. The methodology is presented in Sect. 3. The results are summarized in Sect. 4. A discussion of the results is provided in Sect. 5. While the conclusions and a perspective on future works are part of Sect. 6.

2   Experimental Setup

2.1   Robotic Platform and Sensors

The robotic platform used for this experiment is TIAGo [14] (see Fig. 1a), which was developed by PAL Robotics[2]. The robot is equipped with a touch-screen mounted on its torso. An environmental sensor was placed on the robot in order to measure the environmental temperature and luminosity level. The robot's head incorporates an Orbbec RGB-D camera and a speaker. A thermal camera (Optris PI450) was placed on the head of the robot. A Grove GSR[3] sensor was used to measure electrodermal activity. The data from the three sensors (i.e., RGB-D, thermal, and GSR) was recorded in order to extract the physiological parameters.

2.2   Scenario

For the purpose of this experiment, two elderly participants were recruited from an elderly housing facility in the UK. Both participants tested the ENRICHME system for a duration of 10 weeks. The experiment took place in their own houses, which are part of the housing facility. For the experimental procedure a 3 days interaction was planned with each participant. However, due to the degradation of the visual capabilities of one of the participants, the experiment could be carried out with only one participant. In the end, there were 5 days of interaction with only one participant. Each day of interaction consisted of two sessions: one in the morning (around 11 am) and one in the afternoon (around 3 pm). The tasks performed during each session were the same. Each interaction took place in the living room of the participant (see Fig. 1a).

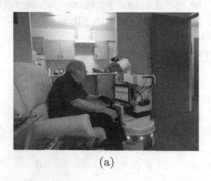   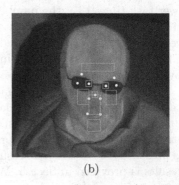

(a)   (b)

Fig. 1. (a) Experimental setup; (b) Facial feature points and ROIs

As the participant was not familiarized with neither the experimenter, nor the experimental tasks, the data recorded on the first day of interaction was not used

---

[2] www.pal-robotics.com.

[3] http://wiki.seeedstudio.com/Grove-GSR_Sensor/.

for the analysis. We wanted to eliminate all influences of different novelty factors (e.g., the presence of the experimenter). Therefore, the data was recorded only during 8 interaction sessions. Each interaction session consisted of three main phases: Relaxation, Cognitive Games, and News Reading.

Relaxation: each interaction session started with a relaxation period of three minutes. On the first day, the participant was asked to choose one song that he would like to listen to that had a relaxing effect. For the following sessions the same song was played by the robot. The purpose of this phase was to relax the participant before the following tasks.

Cognitive Games: three cognitive games were chosen for this experiment. They were used to exercise attention, speed, and mental arithmetic. For two of the games, two difficulty levels were implemented. Therefore, there were five cognitive games that the participant had to play during each interaction. Each game had to be played only once in an order chosen by the participant. The three games were: Digit Cancellation, Integer Matrix Task, and Stroop Game. During all games the participant was very careful not to make any mistakes.

Digit Cancellation: during the game the participant was shown a list of shuffled digits. The length of the list determined the difficulty level of the game (easy level - 20 items; difficult level (Fig. 2a) - 40 items). In a given amount of time (i.e., 50 s) the participant had to find all occurrences of a randomly chosen digit. The game ended either when the time was up, or when the participant found all occurrences. The performance was assessed by three parameters: average time to find an occurrence, game time, and the correct answers.

(a)   (b)

Fig. 2. Difficult level of: (a) Digit cancellation; (b) Integer Matrix Task

Integer Matrix Task: during this game the participant had to solve as many matrices as he could in a given amount of time (i.e., 5 min). A matrix was considered solved when the 2 digits whose sum equals 10 were found. The difficulty level of this game was determined by the size of the matrix (easy level - 2×2; difficult level (Fig. 2b) - 4×4). The performance parameters recorded are: the number of matrices solved, and the time needed to solve a matrix.

Stroop Game: for this game, a variation of the word-color Stroop test [20] was developed. The participant had to press on the button corresponding to the color of the text written on the screen. There were a total of 50 trials, half of them congruent (i.e., the color of the text was the same as the color written on the screen), and half incongruent (i.e., the color of the text was not the same as the color written on the screen). The order of the trials was randomized.

News Reading: a news reading application was also tested. The robot used either only visual (condition C1) or a combination of auditory and visual stimuli (condition C2) in order to present the news to the participant. The news were presented at two interaction distances (i.e., 70 cm, and 100 cm). For each condition and each interaction distance there were two news presented. The conditions and interaction distances were chosen in a random order. Each interaction session consisted of a total of eight news.

2.3   Participant Description

The participant is a 69 years old male. He is currently retired, but was a self employed decorator. He used to live alone, but due to some injuries (broken hip, injured shoulder) he had to move into an elderly housing facility. Due to the injured shoulder, the participant could not use his dominant hand for the interaction with the touch-screen. As a result, the GSR sensor was positioned on the dominant hand, while the non-dominant hand was used for the interaction. He did not interact with a robot before. However, he has some general knowledge about robotics from the news he sees on the television. He likes to drink at least two cups of coffee each day, and he has been smoking (between 5 and 10 cigarettes each day) for at least 40 years. He does not drink any alcohol. Due to his hip injury he is not very active physically. He uses a frame in order to move around the housing facility. He wears glasses all the time. As he is one of the testing participants of the ENRICHME project, he was previously diagnosed with MCI.

In order to profile the participant, we used different psychological questionnaires. We wanted to find out his personality and his morningness-eveningness (ME) type. He is an extraverted individual (score of 12 out of 12 by using the Eysenck Personality Questionnaire [4]). For measuring the ME level, we used the ME Questionnaire [9]. With a score of 56, he is an intermediate type.

2.4   Hypotheses

Based on the information presented in Sects. 1 and 3 we developed the following hypotheses:
H1. The variation of the physiological parameters is dependent on the task performed.
H2. The difficult levels of the games are characterized by higher values of the GSR parameters.

3   Methodology: Data Extraction and Analysis

As seen in Sect. 1 the physiological parameters that are good indicators of an individual's internal state are: facial temperature variation, GSR, HR, and RR, among others. For this research, we are going to extract the facial temperature variation from the thermal data, the accumulative GSR (AccGSR) and the number of peaks from the GSR data, and the HR and the RR from the RGB data. The data extraction and analysis algorithms are presented next.

3.1 Facial Temperature Variation

We have previously developed a thermal face detector and facial feature point predictor [2]. The predictor locates 11 feature points on the face. Based on these feature points the following ROIs are defined: the forehead, the left, and right periorbital region, the left, and right cheek, the chin, the nose, and the perinasal region. The facial feature points and the regions are shown in Fig. 1b. The sizes of the ROIs are dependent on the distance between the inner corners of the eyes. For each of these ROIs the average temperature is extracted and used for the analysis. As for the entire duration of the experiment the participant wore glasses, the data from the periorbital regions was not used for the analysis.

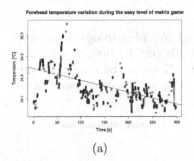
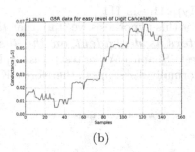

(a)   (b)

Fig. 3. (a) Filtered temperature data for the forehead region during the easy level of the Integer Matrix Task on Day 4 morning session. The linear model was fitted with $r^2 = 0.4, p < 2.2e-16$; (b) GSR data during the easy level of Digit cancellation on Day 2 morning session

The analysis procedure is based on the algorithm presented by the authors of [18]. The data can include false measurements, which are mostly due to the movement of the participant. To eliminate these false measurements, the data was filtered with a moving average filter with a window of 40 samples (2 s). Next, the difference between immediate samples was computed. Any sample that presented an absolute difference of more than 0.1 °C per second was discarded. Finally, a linear model was fitted with a least-square regression on the data. Figure 3a shows a typical filtered data from the experiment with the result of the linear regression.

3.2 GSR

For the GSR data, two parameters present interest: AccGSR [13], and the total number of peaks. A typical recorded GSR signal can be seen in Fig. 3b.

As the output of the GSR sensor that was used is the resistence of the skin, first the data had to be converted to conductance. Next, the algorithm presented in [13] was applied to extract the AccGSR for each task. For the peaks, only the peaks that were at least 5% of the total range of values were extracted.

3.3   Heart Rate and Respiration Rate

The HR and RR were extracted from the RGB data. For this purpose the algorithm presented in [16] was used. First, the face of the participant is detected, together with 68 facial feature points. The forehead region is defined and the mean value of the green channel is extracted. The HR and RR can be extracted due to the periodicity of the data. For the analysis, we extracted the average HR (AvgHR) and average RR (AvgRR) for each of the tasks executed.

4   Experimental Results

Hypothesis H1
For this hypothesis we state that *the variation of the physiological parameters is dependent on the task performed.* To test it, first, a normality test (Shapiro Wilks test) was applied on the data. None of the parameters are normally distributed, therefore a Kruskal Wallis analysis of variance was applied.

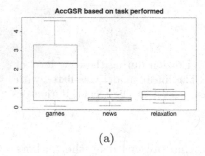
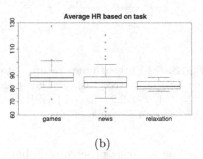

(a)   (b)

Fig. 4. H1 results: (a) Boxplot for AccGSR; (b) Boxplot for AvgHR

Significant differences were found for the number of GSR peaks ($\chi^2 = 15.97$, $p < .001$). A pairwise Wilcoxon rank sum test with a Bonferroni correction revealed significant differences between the games and relaxation ($p = .01$), and news activity and relaxation ($p < .001$). Another significant result was found for the AccGSR ($\chi^2 = 16.25, p < .001$) (see Fig. 4a). A pairwise Wilcoxon rank sum test with a Bonferroni correction revealed significant differences between the news activity and games ($p < .001$).

A significant result was found for the AvgHR ($\chi^2 = 10.66, p = .004$). A pairwise Wilcoxon rank sum test with a Bonferroni correction revealed significant differences between the news activity and games ($p = .019$), and games and relaxation ($p = .023$). A boxplot of the results is shown in Fig. 4b. In [22] the authors have found that the HR increases in a mental arithmetic task compared to a baseline level. Our results are thus in accordance with the literature, with higher HR levels during the cognitive games compared to the relaxation phase.

Considering these results, we can state that **hypothesis H1 is confirmed**. By looking at the GSR parameters and the AvgHR we can differentiate between the tasks performed.

Hypothesis H2

For this hypothesis we state that *the difficult levels of the games are characterized by higher values of the GSR parameters*. In order to test this hypothesis, we have to first select only the games that have multiple difficulty levels (i.e., Digit Cancellation and Integer Matrix Task).

For Digit Cancellation, we found significant differences for the AccGSR with higher AccGSR during the difficult level than the easy level ($F_{1,14} = 11.22$, $p = .004$). For the Integer Matrix Task, we found significant results both for the AccGSR ($F_{1,14} = 35.5, p < .001$) and for the number of peaks ($F_{1,14} = 9.47$, $p = .008$). Both parameters show higher values during the difficult level (Fig. 5).

Based on these results, we can state that during the difficult levels of the games, significantly higher values of the GSR parameters were found. Therefore **hypothesis 2 is confirmed**.

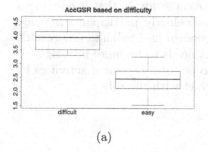

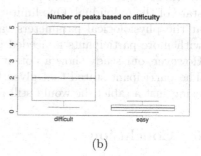

(a)   (b)

Fig. 5. Integer Matrix Game: (a) Boxplot for AccGSR; (b) Boxplot for peaks

Other Results

We are also interested in investigating the correlation that exists between the games performance and the variation of the physiological parameters.

During the difficult level of Digit Cancellation, two positive correlations were found between the temperature variation in the nose region and the average time to find an occurrence ($p = 0.03, r(3) = 0.89$), and the total game time ($p = 0.01, r(3) = 0.93$). For the difficult level of the Integer Matrix Task the following significant results were found. A negative correlation was found between the number of peaks and the average time needed to solve a matrix ($p = 0.03, r(6) = -0.73$). In contrast, a positive correlation was found between the temperature variation in the forehead region and the average time needed to solve a matrix ($p = 0.01, r(6) = 0.8$). For the total number of matrices solved, there is a positive correlation with the number of peaks ($p = 0.02, r(6) = .78$), and a negative one with the temperature variation in the forehead region ($p = 0.01, r(6) = -0.83$).

5   Discussion

As seen in the Results section, all our hypotheses are confirmed. The variation of some physiological parameters depend on the task being performed (AccGSR, peaks, AvgHR). The GSR parameters (i.e., AccGSR and number of peaks) can be used to differentiate between two difficulty levels of the games used in this study (i.e., Digit Cancellation and Integer Matrix Task).

An in depth analysis of the performance during the cognitive games was already performed [1]. The correlation between the physiological parameters and the cognitive games performance parameters was also analyzed. The results show that there is a correlation between the two. Significant correlations between the performance and the variation of the physiological parameters were found only for the difficult levels. We can conclude that the difficult levels of the games were more cognitively arousing for our participant than the easy levels.

Our results show that in a human-robot interaction scenario it is important to also look at the physiological parameters of the individual that the robot interacts with. They could provide valuable information regarding the internal state of the individual. One limitation of the current study, is that it only looks at the physiological parameters variation for one elderly participant. A study with more participants is needed in order to confirm and validate our results. However, our study show a potential trend that needs to be more investigated. The participant stated that given the option to perform the same activities by using just a tablet, he would still prefer to interact with the robot.

6   Conclusion

In conclusion, this research paper presents the results of a 5-day interaction scenario between an elderly user and a humanoid robot. The interaction took place in the house of the participant, and was composed of two interaction sessions each day (i.e., one session at around 11 am, and one at around 3 pm). The activities performed were the same during all 10 sessions. More specifically, they start with a relaxation period of three minutes. Next, the participant selected in a random order 5 cognitive games to be performed only once per session. The interaction ended with a news reading activity in which the robot used either only visual or a combination of visual and auditory stimuli. Our results show that physiological parameters can be used to differentiate between the tasks performed by an individual. Moreover, we can differentiate between two difficulty levels of some cognitive games. Some of our future work include to perform the same experiment with multiple participants, from different age groups.

Acknowledgement. This work was funded and done in the context of the EU Horizon2020 ENRICHME project, Grant Agreement No: 643691

References

1. Agrigoroaie, R., Tapus, A.: The outcome of a week of intensive cognitive stimulation in an elderly care setup: a pilot test. In: Accepted in RO-MAN (2018)
2. Agrigoroaie, R., Tapus, A.: Physiological parameters variation based on the sensory stimuli used by a robot in a news reading task. In: Accepted in RO-MAN (2018)
3. Bellotto, N., et al.: Enrichme integration of ambient intelligence and robotics for AAL. In: AAAI Spring Symposium Series (2017)
4. Eysenck, S., et al.: A revised version of the psychoticism scale. Pers. Individ. Differ. **6**, 21–29 (1985)
5. Feil-Seifer, D., Mataric, M.J.: Defining socially assistive robotics. In: 9th International Conference on Rehabilitation Robotics (2005)
6. Femandes, F.E., et al.: Cognitive orientation assessment for older adults using social robots. In: International Conference on Robotics and Biomimetics (2017)
7. Graf, B., et al.: Robotic home assistant care-o-bot 3-product vision and innovation platform. In: IEEE Workshop on Advanced Robotics and its Social Impacts (2009)
8. He, W., et al.: An aging world: 2015. International Population Reports (2016)
9. Horne, J., et al.: A self-assessment questionnaire to determine me in human circadian rhythms. Int. J. Chronobiol. **4**, 97–110 (1976)
10. Ioannou, S., et al.: Proximity and gaze influences facial temperature: a thermal infrared imaging study. Front. Psychol. **5**, 845 (2014)
11. Ioannou, S., et al.: Thermal infrared imaging in psychophysiology: potentialities and limits. Phychophysiology **51**, 951–963 (2014)
12. Merritt, C.R., et al.: Textile-based capacitive sensors for respiration monitoring. IEEE Sens. J. **9**, 71–78 (2009)
13. Nourbakhsh, N., et al.: Detecting users cognitive load by galvanic skin response with affective interference. Trans. Interact. Intell. Syst. **7**, 12 (2017)
14. Pages, J., Marchionni, L., Ferro, F.: Tiago: the modular robot that adapts to different research needs. In: International Workshop on Robot Modularity, IROS (2016)
15. Papoutsakis, K., et al.: Developing visual competencies for socially assistive robots: the hobbit approach. In: PETRA (2013)
16. Rahman, H., et al.: Real time heart rate monitoring from facial RGB color video using webcam. In: SAIS (2016)
17. Setz, C., et al.: Discriminating stress from cognitive load using a wearable EDA device. IEEE Trans. Inf. Technol. Biomed. **14**, 410–417 (2010)
18. Sorostinean, M., et al.: Reliable stress measurement using face temperature variation with a thermal camera in human-robot interaction. In: Humanoids (2015)
19. Stavropoulos, G., et al.: Automatic action recognition for assistive robots to support MCI patients at home. In: Proceedings of PETRA (2017)
20. Stroop, J.: Studies of interference in serial verbal reactions. J. Explor. Psychol. **18**, 643 (1935)
21. Tapus, A., et al.: Music therapist robot for individuals with cognitive impairments. In: Proceedings of ACM/IEEE International Conference on HRI (2009)
22. Turner, J.R., Carroll, D.: Heart rate and oxygen consumption during mental arithmetic, a video game, and graded exercise. Psychophysiology **22**, 261–267 (1985)

Character Design and Validation on Aerial Robotic Platforms Using Laban Movement Analysis

Alexandra Bacula[✉] and Amy LaViers

Mechanical Science and Engineering Department,
University of Illinois Urbana-Champaign, Urbana, IL 61801, USA
{bacula2,alaviers}@illinois.edu

Abstract. Exploring the application of aerial robots in human-robot interaction is a currently active area of research. One step toward achieving more natural human-robot interactions is developing a method in which an aerial robot successfully portrays a character or exhibits character traits that a human can recognize. Recognizable character types are conveyed through movement in many performing arts, including ballet. However, past work has not leveraged the movement expertise of ballet dancers to create a method and portray complex characters on low-degree-of-freedom aerial robots. This paper explores the recognition and differentiation of archetypal characters used in classical ballet using Laban Movement Analysis (LMA) and applies the results from tracking the movements to an aerial robotic platform. Movement sequences were created on a Bebop Drone to emulate these character types. This process was subsequently validated by a user study, highlighting the successful application of state recognition through movement on aerial robots. Such work can be used to create robots with recognizable movement signatures for quick identification by human counterparts in social settings.

Keywords: Human robot interaction · Robot characters
Mobile robots · Laban Movement Analysis · Aerial robots

1 Introduction

Aerial mobile robots are desirable for consumer applications as they have become robust, affordable platforms. If such a robot is assisting someone or sharing a living space with a person, the person is more likely to be accepting and comfortable with the robot if it moves in a manner that varies according to context and task and can be understood by a human viewer. One way this could be accomplished is by tapping into archetypal characters that are familiar to human viewers. For example, we recognize the movement signatures of close friends. We also communicate information by taking on characteristic movement profiles of character archetypes, e.g., in telling a story or making a joke. For example, in the fairy tale *Little Red Riding Hood*, one would associate different movements with

© Springer Nature Switzerland AG 2018
S. S. Ge et al. (Eds.): ICSR 2018, LNAI 11357, pp. 202–212, 2018.
https://doi.org/10.1007/978-3-030-05204-1_20

the sneaky, conniving Wolf (perhaps slow, intricate, and encircling movements) than they would with innocent, open Little Red Riding Hood (perhaps light, expansive, and arching movements).

In a ballet performance, a set of distinct characters mimicking traits and emotions is used to convey the story to the audience [24]. While costumes, sets, and lighting also provide some information to the viewer, the movement is a key feature that differentiates one character from another [2]. Ballet dancers are experts at expressing characters through their refined movement vocabulary, and analyzing how they do this can provide insight into using movement on robotic platforms to create a character. Ballet has also been used in robotics applications as a formalized movement system that can provide insight to how stylized motion can be generated in [15,16].

One method of analyzing human movement is Laban Movement Analysis (LMA), as used in [4,14]. LMA has been previously used in robotics to generate movement sequences on robotic platforms, such as in [17,18] where the Effort system was used as an inroad to defining motion quality. The use of LMA in humanoid robotics for motion specification has also been studied [1]. Specifically, it has been used for human-robot interaction in [22], where an anticipatory interface that worked to characterize human responses was developed and in [9], where LMA Efforts were used to make a robot's head motions more legible to humans.

Additionally, work with simple mobile robots for recreating Effort, the component of LMA dealing with motion intent [11], was presented on ground robots in [19] and on aerial robots in [23]. Then, the work in [7] used the concept of Effort in order to generate distinct motions on mobile robots based on the movement of human actors; the same researchers applied Effort to existing motions in [8].

Expressing character traits on robots is thought to be important for human-robot interactions [26]. Using characters with mobile robots in a human-robot interaction setting has been explored in [20,21] where user studies were done to see how users react to interacting with different robotic characters and how it changed their perception of the robot. The effect of a mobile robot's motion on human response was similarly studied in [6,10].

This paper will build on prior work, incorporating a design process, first described for a humanoid platform in [3], that begins with expert observation and then translates high-level movement features to specific platforms, in this case an aerial robot. Section 2 will detail the Laban Movement Analysis concepts used and the observation process and results. Section 3 will explain the implementation of the Laban Movement Analysis concepts on the aerial robot. Section 4 will outline the user study and present the results. Concluding remarks are given in Sect. 5.

2   Observing Archetypal Characters in Ballet

Ballet is a domain that has been developing characters and expressing them through movement for centuries [5]. This has led to the creation of common character archetypes that new ballets are able to immediately tap into for quick recognition and effective storytelling. We use this arena, therefore, as a rich source of expertise and cultural priors. By linking to existing conventions and techniques in ballet, the characters we design for robotic platforms may be easily identifiable.

2.1 Laban Movement Analysis

In order to view characters with a detailed, descriptive lens, we will leverage the taxonomy established in the Laban/Bartenieff Movement System [12,13,25]. This taxonomy is an established set of concepts for detailed movement analysis divided into four main categories: Body, Effort, Shape, and Space. Key terms from this system, as used in this work, are described here.

Body: Initiation and Sequencing. Body Initiation refers to the area of the body in which a movement begins. There are four categories of Body Initiation: Core, Proximal, Mid-limb, and Distal. Core Initiation is the closest to the center of the body, for example initiating a movement in the spine. Proximal Initiation is initiation in the areas next to the core, such as initiating a movement in the shoulder or hip. For the upper body, Mid-limb Initiation refers to initiating movement in the elbows. Distal initiation occurs in the extremities farthest away from the core, for example the hands and fingertips.

Body Sequencing refers to the timing and order of the core, proximal, mid-limb, and distal body parts relative to each other. The body sequence of a movement can be Simultaneous, Successive, or Sequential. Simultaneous Body Sequencing is when all the body parts move at the same time, beginning the movement and ending a movement together. Successive Body Sequencing is moving the body parts one at a time. Either the most proximal body part begins a movement and the most distal body part finishes it, or vice versa. An example of a successive movement in the upper body is the ripple that a break dancer might pass from one hand through their shoulder girdle and out, finishing in the other hand. Sequential Body Sequencing is when the body parts do not begin or end the movement at the same time, and they do not go in any particular order, unlike Successive Body Sequencing.

Effort: Effort Factors. The Effort system describes the mover's intent, which often manifests as varying motion quality for a given action. It is described by four Effort Factors: Weight, Time, Space, and Flow[1]. Each of these categories has two opposing Effort qualities. This is visualized in the Effort graph shown Fig. 1. The Weight axis describes "intention" and "sensing" and includes Light and Strong Effort, where light movement is "delicate" and strong is "forceful" [25]. Time describes the timing of the movement, in which Sustained is slow

---

[1] We will capitalize these terms to indicate they do not align exactly with colloquial notions of each of these words.

and prolonged and Sudden is quick (note this may be affined with duration of movement, but is not the same idea). The Flow axis represents "progression" and "feeling" in the movement with Free and Bound, describing "released ongoingness" and "controlled ongoingness" respectively [25]. Space describes the outward focus of the movement, where Indirect has an "expansive" outer focus and Direct has a "channeled" outer focus [25].

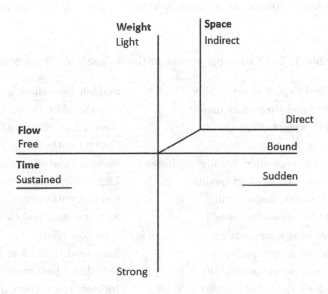

Fig. 1. The Laban Effort graph shows the 4 Effort Factors, which he proposed as the basic components of motion quality [11].

Shape: Shape Quality. Shape Quality has six categories: Rising and Sinking, Advancing and Retreating, and Spreading and Enclosing. Sinking is when the movement, particularly of the body's core area around the spine, proceeds from a higher level to a lower level; Rising is the opposite. Retreating is when it flows in the posterior direction in the sagittal plane; Advancing when the movement flows in the anterior direction. Enclosing is when the distal body parts come towards the core; Spreading is when they move away.

Space: Pathway. Pathways describe the movement between two points within the Kinesphere (the sphere describing the space a mover can reach without translating in space). Central Pathway is a movement which passes through or starts at the center of the body. Peripheral Pathway is a movement on the outer edges of the Kinesphere. Transverse pathway is in between Central and Peripheral Pathways, involving complex accommodation of the body.

2.2   Laban Movement Analysis Observations

The observation process involved watching different examples of each character type and annotating on an observation guide which LMA concepts were present in that character, as seen in previous work [3]. In Table 1, four of the most prevalent LMA concepts were chosen for application to robotic platforms. These concepts were chosen for both their prevalence and their ability to be applied to not only humanoid robots, as we have previously done, but to aerial robots as well.

Table 1. LMA concepts present in the six analyzed characters

Bird	Indirect space effort quality	Doll	Sudden time effort quality
	Sustained time effort quality		Sequential body sequencing
	Light weight effort quality		Bound flow effort quality
	Rising shape quality		Central pathways
Villain	Direct space effort quality	Jester	Sudden time effort quality
	Strong weight effort quality		Light weight effort quality
	Advancing shape quality		Central pathways
	Sudden time effort quality		Simultaneous body sequencing
Dying	Enclosing shape quality	Magician	Free flow effort
	Sinking shape quality		Sustained time effort quality
	Retreating shape quality		Peripheral pathways
	Sudden time effort quality		Indirect space effort quality

3   Implementing Characters on Bebop Drone

The aerial robot chosen for this work is the Bebop 2 drone made by Parrot, which is a small, lightweight quadcopter. Since the Bebop is a rigid body, Body Sequencing is ignored in this work. Shape Quality, Effort Quality, and Pathway were the main focus in character generation on the Bebop. The Bebop has only one shape, so Shape Quality was applied to the shape of the trajectory as opposed to the shape of the Bebop. Pathway is traditionally applied to the space the mover can reach without moving, however the Bebop is a rigid body so Pathway was applied to the Bebop within the space of the room.

To generate characters, first an analysis of the kinetic properties of the Bebop was performed to determine which LMA concepts would be useful in generating the movement of the Bebop and what types of trajectories could be pieced together to create a sequence highlighting the LMA concepts present in the character types. Some of the basic movements were used in combination to create the characters. For example the Villain character flew quickly towards the audience, then stopped suddenly to show Advancing Shape Quality (moving forward towards the viewer), Direct Space Effort (not wavering from the path), and Strong Weight Effort (moving from high to low).

The simplest way to control the Bebop was to give it a single velocity command until some condition (either position or time) was satisfied. Each velocity command was comprised of x, y, z linear velocities and roll, pitch, yaw angular velocities. This was done using python scripts in Robotic Operating System (ROS) with the Vicon motion capture system to track the Bebop position. The motion in the python scripts was based on

4   User Study

A user study was conducted to understand whether this process created characters that could be recognized by lay human viewers. A training process was used to ensure that people without prior expertise in ballet knew something about each designed character. The results are presented here.

4.1   Layout of User Study

This user study was an extension of the user study in [3] and follows the same general layout, instead applying to the Bebop drone characters. These studies were done alongside humanoid platform, the NAO, characters as well. This paper presents only the aerial platform.

First, the study trained the user with one of the videos analyzed for each character type. The user is told which dancer is portraying the character in the video and which character type they are portraying. The user is then tested on their recognition using another one of the videos of the ballet dancers analyzed for each character type. They are shown six videos and asked to match the character type to the video, with each character only being used once. If the user is unable to correctly match the human characters, they were considered "untrained" by the priming and are returned to the beginning of the training to repeat it. The user is then shown the videos again individually, told which character type is in the video, and asked how well they think the video portrays that character type. This rating process is a simple cognitive task that causes the user to study the character example before answering, which prepares them for the next part of the survey.

After the testing of recognition on the ballet dancers, they were shown the Bebop videos and asked questions to understand whether the characters were recognizable on this distinct platform. First they were shown all six videos and asked to match them to the character type. Then they were shown the same videos individually, told the character type, and asked to rate how well the movement in the video represents that character type along with the reasoning for their rating. The evaluation of the characters is an important step in the user study because the matching could be done by process of elimination if the user was unsure which character was which. These final ratings will be used to determine the success of the sequences in demonstrating the character types. Since the user is primed with the human characters before evaluating the Bebop characters, it is possible that the results also reflect the user's learning ability, not just the character representation on the Bebop.

A background survey was then used to understand aspects of culture and prior movement training of the participant pool. The participants were asked about prior ballet training, LMA training, and how many ballet performances they have seen. Prior ballet training, or significant experience watching ballet would give the user an advantage since they have seen the characters and possibly the choreography prior to taking the survey. Training in LMA would also give the user an advantage because they are able to look at movement through the same lens in which the videos were analyzed and created. However, the majority of users had no training in dance and none had extensive training in LMA.

Participants were recruited on Amazon Mechanical Turk (mTurk). The surveys took approximately 60 min to complete. Participants were compensated with the standard mTurk rate of $0.10 per minute, which for this study was estimated to be $6 for successfully completing the survey. A total of 50 participants successfully completed the survey.

4.2   Results and Analysis for Bebop Drone

In the matching section, 33 participants correctly identified at least half of the character types correctly. 22 participants identified all six characters correctly. These results can be seen in Fig. 2. This result is encouraging, however, the main purpose of this task was for users to see the features of all three videos at one time and become accustomed to the robot's motion before advancing to the rating questions.

In Fig. 3, the average ratings for the human characters and the Bebop characters are compared. The ratings were on a scale from 1 to 7, where 1 means the video did not represent the character at all and 7 means it represented the character very well. All of the characters were rated above a neutral rating of 4 for the Bebop drone. In Table 2, it can be seen that for all characters over half the users rated the Bebop as a "good" representation of that character. It is also notable that for the Bebop Dying Character, 26% of users rated it as a perfect representation (7).

It is important to note that even the human characters are not rated perfect, receiving an average rating below 7, despite being trained professionals and nearly perfect examples of these characters in ballet, suggesting some deficiencies in the training process, lack of expertise, or startlingly high standards in the human viewers. The bird character got an unexpectedly low rating compared to the other characters. This may be because the Bebop quadcoptor is an aerial robot, and the bird character is the only character that evokes flying. This may have resulted in higher expectations of the bird character on the aerial robot than the expectations of other characters, resulting in a lower rating.

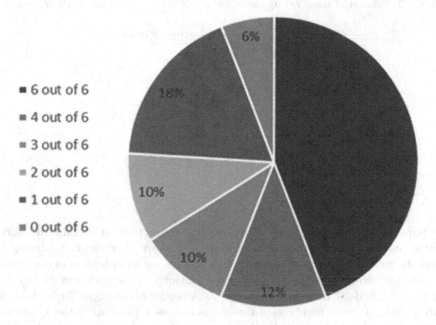

Fig. 2. Percentage of users matching X out of 6 Characters correctly in matching exercise for Bebop drone.

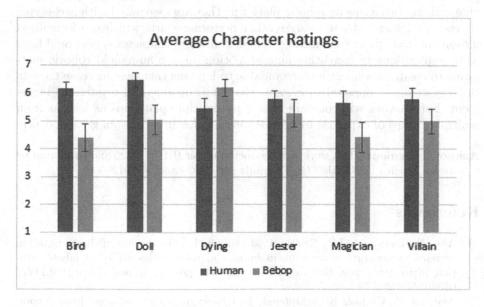

Fig. 3. Average ratings with 95% confidence interval for all characters on human and Bebop drone.

Table 2. Percent of users rating character as "good" representation (5 or above)

Character	Percent of user ratings 5 or above
Bird	54%
Doll	74%
Dying	96%
Jester	72%
Magician	62%
Villain	70%

5   Conclusions

The paper reviewed prior work in expressing characters on mobile and aerial robotic platforms and expert observation in Laban Movement Analysis. An observational guide was used to generate a feature set from human expert ballet dancers that should be applied to an aerial platform. This work was undertaken and then verified by a large user study on Amazon Mechanical Turk. Approximately 70% of users highly rate the sequences as representing the character, showing this method is viable for expressing archetypal characters used in classical ballet on low degree of freedom mobile robots.

The results of this work, particularly paired with prior work on a humanoid platform [3], indicate that this method is robust way of establishing recognizable stylistic variations on robotic platforms that are associated with archetypal characters. Using LMA to analyze other performing arts which use formalized movements to express recognizable human traits and character types could have wide implications in recreating human motion on non-humanoid robotic platforms to create movement understandable to humans that may increase trust in these systems, as opposed to systems that have opaque and mysterious movement. Future work will compare results on multiple platforms as well as from multiple groups of expertise to understand this design process in greater depth.

Acknowledgement. This work was conducted under IRB #16225 and supported by a National Science Foundation (NSF) grants #1528036 and #1701295.

References

1. Abe, N., Laumond, J.P., Salaris, P., Levillain, F.: On the use of dance notation systems to generate movements in humanoid robots: the utility of laban notation in robotics. Soc. Sci. Inf. **56**(2), 328–344 (2017). https://doi.org/10.1177/0539018417694773
2. Alaoui, S.F., Carlson, K., Schiphorst, T.: Choreography as mediated through compositional tools for movement: Constructing a historical perspective. In: Proceedings of the 2014 International Workshop on Movement and Computing, p. 1. ACM (2014)

3. Bacula, A., LaViers, A.: Character recognition on a humanoid robotic platform via a Laban movement analysis. In: Proceedings of the 2018 International Workshop on Movement and Computing, p. 17. ACM (2018)
4. Groff, E.: Laban movement analysis: charting the ineffable domain of human movement. J. Phys. Educ. Recreat. Danc. **66**(2), 27–30 (1995)
5. Homans, J.: Apollo's Angels: A History of Ballet. Penguin Random House, New York City (2010)
6. Knight, H., Lee, T., Hallawell, B., Ju, W.: I get it already! the influence of chairbot motion gestures on bystander response. In: 2017 26th IEEE International Symposium on Robot and Human Interactive Communication (RO-MAN). IEEE (2017)
7. Knight, H., Simmons, R.: Expressive motion with x, y and theta: Laban effort features for mobile robots. In: The 23rd IEEE International Symposium on Robot and Human Interactive Communication, pp. 267–273. IEEE (2014)
8. Knight, H., Simmons, R.: Layering Laban effort features on robot task motions. In: Proceedings of the Tenth Annual ACM/IEEE International Conference on Human-Robot Interaction Extended Abstracts, pp. 135–136. ACM (2015)
9. Knight, H., Simmons, R.: Laban head-motions convey robot state: a call for robot body language. In: 2016 IEEE International Conference on Robotics and Automation (ICRA), pp. 2881–2888. IEEE (2016)
10. Knight, H., Veloso, M., Simmons, R.: Taking candy from a robot: speed features and candy accessibility predict human response. In: 2015 24th IEEE International Symposium on Robot and Human Interactive Communication (RO-MAN), pp. 355–362. IEEE (2015)
11. Laban, R., Lawrence, F.C.: Effort. Macdonald & Evans, London (1947)
12. Laban, R., Ullmann, L.: Choreutics. Dance Books, Alton (2011)
13. Laban, R., Ullmann, L.: The Mastery of Movement, 4th edn. Dance Books, Alton (2011)
14. Larboulette, C., Gibet, S.: A review of computable expressive descriptors of human motion. In: Proceedings of the 2nd International Workshop on Movement and Computing, pp. 21–28. ACM (2015)
15. LaViers, A., Chen, Y., Belta, C., Egerstedt, M.: Automatic sequencing of ballet poses. Robot. Autom. Mag. **18**(3), 87–95 (2011)
16. LaViers, A., Egerstedt, M.: The ballet automaton: a formal model for human motion. In: Proceedings of the 2011 American Control Conference (2011)
17. LaViers, A., Egerstedt, M.: Style-based robotic motion. In: Proceedings of the 2012 American Control Conference (2012)
18. LaViers, A., Egerstedt, M.: Style-based abstractions for human motion classification. In: 2014 ACM/IEEE International Conference on Cyber-Physical Systems (ICCPS), pp. 84–91. IEEE (2014)
19. Nakata, T., Mori, T., Sato, T.: Analysis of impression of robot bodily expression. J. Robot. Mechatron **14**(1), 27–36 (2002)
20. Pakrasi, I., Chakraborty, N., Cuan, C., Berl, E., Rizvi, W., LaViers, A.: Dancing droids: an expressive layer for mobile robots developed and validated through dance performance (in progress)
21. Pakrasi, I., LaViers, A., Chakraborty, N.: A design methodology for abstracting character archetypes onto robotic systems. In: Proceedings of the 2018 International Workshop on Movement and Computing, pp. 28–30. ACM (2018)
22. Rett, J., Dias, J.: Human-robot interface with anticipatory characteristics based on Laban movement analysis and Bayesian models. In: 2007 IEEE 10th International Conference on Rehabilitation Robotics (2007). https://doi.org/10.1109/icorr.2007.4428436

23. Sharma, M., Hildebrandt, D., Newman, G., Young, J.E., Eskicioglu, R.: Communicating affect via flight path: exploring use of the Laban effort system for designing affective locomotion paths. In: Proceedings of the 8th ACM/IEEE International Conference on Human-Robot Interaction, pp. 293–300. IEEE Press (2013)
24. Smith, M.E.: Ballet and Opera in the Age of Giselle, vol. 13. Princeton University Press, Princeton (2000)
25. Studd, K., Cox, L.L.: Everybody is a Body. Dog Ear Publishing, Indianapolis (2013)
26. Tapus, A., Mataric, M.J.: Socially assistive robots: the link between personality, empathy, physiological signals, and task performance. In: AAAI Spring Symposium: Emotion, Personality, and Social Behavior, pp. 133–140 (2008)

Social Robots in Public Spaces:
A Meta-review

Omar Mubin[1(✉)], Muneeb Imtiaz Ahmad[2], Simranjit Kaur[1], Wen Shi[1],
and Aila Khan[3]

[1] SCEM, Western Sydney University, Penrith, Australia
o.mubin@uws.edu.au
[2] The MARCS Institute, Western Sydney University, Penrith, Australia
[3] School of Business, Western Sydney University, Penrith, Australia

Abstract. Social robots can prove to be an effective medium of instruction and communication to users in a public setting. However their range of interaction in current research is not known. In this paper, we overview a range of research works that utilized NAO and Pepper robot in the public settings. Our results show that Education scenarios are one of the more popular and most interaction is centered around providing information. In conclusion, we present key design implications that researchers can employ whilst designing social robot interactions in the public space.

Keywords: Human-Robot Interaction · Pepper robot · NAO robot
Public spaces

1 Introduction

A privately or publicly owned well-designed inside or outside place, where people have accessibility and opportunity to socialize while interacting with each other is known as a public space [6]. A few examples of public spaces are shopping malls, parks, hotels, restaurants and hospitals etc. In all such places, customer service plays a major role in driving customer satisfaction. Commonly, the popular use of Kiosk technology in retail industry saves customers time in completing transactions, in the meanwhile, it helps the retail shops or restaurants increase customer flow.

Interactive technology researchers are currently designing novel technologies to assist people in numerous ways at these public spaces using artificial intelligence or machine learning. In particular, social robots are being designed and their utilization has been evaluated in different public settings [2]. We witness a great amount of development of different social robots such as Pepper, NAO, Robovie in the recent past and similarly many studies have been conducted with these robots at Hotels as a receptionist for assisting guests [20], at Museums as tour guide [7], at Health care centre for motivating patients and entertaining them and providing medication [18] and lastly also within the educational context, such as schools [3].

© Springer Nature Switzerland AG 2018
S. S. Ge et al. (Eds.): ICSR 2018, LNAI 11357, pp. 213–220, 2018.
https://doi.org/10.1007/978-3-030-05204-1_21

We understand that operating robots in these public spaces is a great challenge. It is a complex job to implement communicating skills of humans on a robot. A number of factors such as user mood, situation, personality, age and gender [8] are needed to be considered for a successful Human-Robot Interaction (HRI) in public spaces. Additionally, it is a known challenge to adapt to different users in the HRI field [2]. We therefore believe that it is pertinent to review the existing studies before implementing new robotic interaction for social robots in public spaces. Another motivation for reviewing the previous studies that employ social robots in public spaces lies in providing the HRI community with guidelines to generate a safe environment during HRI in public spaces [5].

In order to complete our overview and to reduce the scope from several humanoid robots to a more manageable number we decided to focus on the robots from the Softbank Robotics. In particular, we focused on the NAO humanoid robot initially. The NAO robot from (previously owned by Aldebaran Robotics) is clearly one of the more popular off the shelf social robotic platforms [15]. Several thousand editions have been sold to various research and commercial institutions. A quick search on Google scholar with the keywords "NAO social robot" brings up more than 5000 hits with several papers having more than 100 citations. On a social note, one of the most popular YouTube videos of the NAO robot has more than 5 million views. A video of the NAO robot dancing to Gangnam Style has generated more than 1 million views. The official twitter channel of the NAO robot has more than 15 thousand followers. Subsequently, we later also looked at the applications of the Pepper robot in public spaces. The utilization of the Pepper robot in public spaces is also growing in various countries including Japan and America [10].

Despite the extensive popularity and penetration of the NAO and Pepper robots in the social robotics research community, we do not find a meta overview signifying how the robots are being used in public spaces in the area of HRI. We now discuss our methodology of searching articles and the main trends and results observed.

2   Usage Trends of NAO in Public Spaces

We conducted an in-depth literature review on the use of social robots (specifically NAO) in public spaces. Firstly, we searched for the following keywords combinations such as "robots public spaces", "HRI in public spaces", "Pepper public space" and "NAO public space" in Google Scholar. The articles were selected such that the testing target was the NAO robot. To extract the content from each paper, a coding scheme was implemented. The criteria of filtering out the target articles was based on whether the robot employed was the NAO robot and the site of research was public spaces. We considered public spaces as research conducted in the wild outside of the laboratory in a real environment.

2.1   Coding Scheme

In order to study HRI with the NAO robot in public spaces, the coding scheme is made by extracting meta data associated with the paper as well as the details of the interaction in the public space with the NAO robot. The summary of the coding scheme was as follows:

1. Year of Publication
2. Country where the research was conducted
3. Venue or Site of the research (includes various possible categories such as hospitals, museums, schools, hotels, etc)
4. Type of participants (children, elderly or adults) as mentioned in the research
5. Physical movement and gestures of NAO
6. Type of Dialogue and interaction from NAO

2.2   Results

A total number of 30 articles were retrieved from our search. Figure 1 shows the timeline of the literature published from the year 2010 to the year 2017, among them, the papers published in 2015 and 2017 were more than 2/3 of the whole data set. With the NAO launched around 2008, the starting point of the data set is understandable. In terms of the country where the research was conducted, United Kingdom, United States, Malaysia and China were the most popular (with 5, 4, 4 and 3 papers respectively). It was observed that the countries using NAO to study human robot interaction are mainly concentrated in Europe, Asia Pacific and North America. Japan was not as popular as one would expect (only a single paper was found).

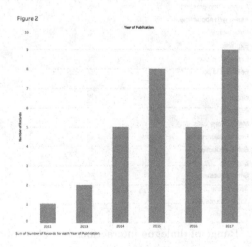

Fig. 1. Frequency of papers across years

A number of public sites were utilized for situated and contextualized research studies with the NAO robot. Schools (or Educational domain) were the most popular with 7 papers followed by Health with 6. We also checked for the type of users involved in the research with the NAO in public spaces. 60.61% of participants were adults, 30.30% of total participants were children and Elderly were 9.09%.

We also analyzed the behaviour of the NAO robot. It can be summarised that NAO robots are used to interact with a human by the design of two main categories which are non-verbal interaction and verbal interaction. More than 70% (22) of the papers in our sample utilized the physical gestures of the NAO robot. Similarly 21 papers in our sample incorporated verbal interaction from the NAO robot. Range of movements included head movement, waving, hi-five, pointing, etc. The research described in 6 papers also relied on gaze based interaction.

Figure 2 indicates the types of dialogue and assistance provided by the NAO in the public space setting. The size shows the sum of number of records broken down by types of dialogue. The view is filtered on types of dialogue. It can be concluded as three types - "Greeting", "Information Providing" and "Concern Expressing". The NAO robot was tested in a dialogue method usually by starting a conversation with "Greeting". There were two cases that NAO robots introduced themselves after the greeting. Another type of dialogue was summarized as "Information Providing", such dialogue cases were mainly designed in public places where provide services such as in retailing and hotel. The last type of dialogue was defined as "Concern Expressing", where it occurred in health-care and educational scenarios.

Figure 7   Types of Dialogues

Types of Dialogue

A single Nao greeting	■
Assist with appointment	■
Easy words	■
Explanation	■
Express the concren	■
Formal and polite	■
Greeting	■
Guide	■
Indicating	■
Make phone calls	■
Provide information	■
Self-introduction	■
Shouting	■
Simple questions	■
Story-telling	■
Tell game results	■

Fig. 2. Range of dialogue interactions by NAO robot

3   Usage Trends of Pepper in Public Spaces

As a secondary step in our analysis, we also scanned the usage of Pepper; Soft-bank Robotics other popular social robot in public spaces. Pepper is a humanoid robot supplemented with the presence of a tablet in its chest for user interaction. In addition, Pepper has sonar detection and emotional intelligence. Similar to our usage exploration with NAO, we searched for relevant academic articles in Google Scholar. Since the number of papers retrieved were not as high in number as for the case of NAO, we followed a more case study style of reporting usage trends of Pepper in public spaces. We found examples of Pepper being used in a shopping mall [1]. In this particular study, short sentences were found to be more engaging and easy to understand. Eye gaze was also integral to the inter-action. One limitation found in this study was that Pepper could only interact with one person at a time, which increased the waiting time for other people to interact with the robot. Another study showcased the ability of Pepper to assist the elderly in aged care homes so that they can remember their medication and overcome their loneliness [19]. An example of the application of Pepper in the educational domain was also interesting; where Pepper and the children learned together [17]. In this study, yet again the main results showed that gestures like hi-five and expressions like "ah" with facial expressions like smile or surprised were preferred and also proved that a number of one line simple sentences, led to long term communication between children and Pepper. Lastly, we found another study showcasing the use of Pepper in a public space, this time conducted at Hotel, where Pepper played the role of a Receptionist. The study showed that participants perceived the interaction with the robot similar to human-human interactions [16].

4   Discussion

Based on the study of the 30 articles on NAO robots, as well as a brief overview of Pepper in public spaces, we can see that the way such social robots interact with humans is similar to the way that humans communicate with each other by using both non-verbal gestures and verbal language. Both mediums of interaction are integral to situated and public interactions. A number of papers were also found that discuss about different strategies [13], behavioural constraints [9] and evaluation formulas [14] of a social robot in a public spaces. For instance the behaviour constraints apart from verbal and non-verbal cues such as switching from one user to another while communicating include handling conversation with more than one person at a time. A study has been conducted to evaluate the response of robot while interacting between 2 persons simultaneously, where robot is acting as a tour guide in a museum. The intelligent strategy is multi-modal that helps in focusing attention between 2 persons one by one [4]. The tablet on the chest of Pepper provides leverage to the user to interact with the robot whereas verbal interaction in isolation can result in ambiguity. We observed that NAO was less popular in Japan as compared to Pepper which had several studies based in Japan [11]. This can perhaps be explained by the numerous unique features of Pepper, whereas the NAO is easily replacable by other similar social robots. Education was a popular domain area for research in public spaces with both NAO and Pepper. NAO in particular is thought to be cute and hence an attractive proposition for children to interact with. We noted that the NAO was utilized to provide information, guidance or as a greeting mechanism in public interactions with users. We can speculate that the NAO robot is limited in its performance due to the absence of a display screen; a disadvantage over kiosks or other social robots with a display screen such as Pepper.

Based on our review of research studies that employed the use of NAO and Pepper in public spaces, we can enlist some design guidelines that can be considered prior to the involvement of social robots in public spaces:

1. Proactive Approach: It is important to have proactive approach for a robot to start the interaction with customers, especially in public spaces where people may have reluctance towards robots [13]. Therefore, we need to train robots to initiate the interaction rather than waiting for the people to start the interaction, particularly by greeting or welcoming them or by providing them relevant information.
2. Short Communication: Furthermore, initiating the conversation for the robot with unknown users was also discussed as an interesting challenge. Researchers have argued for the robot to start the conversation by a simple one word (such as "Hello"), rather than wait for the user to make the first move [13].
3. Sensing People Behaviour and Position: In order to initiate the conversation, it is important to sense the location of human. As, in public spaces the people can be walking, standing or just passing by the robot. So, it is important for the robots to decide the appropriate people for conversation. Robots should sense the person to whom the conversation will be engaged with and direct the face towards that person. Robots like Pepper have sonar detection, which help in recognizing the communicator [12].
4. Effectiveness and Safety: Robots should be designed to showcase human friendly interaction. We need to build controlled, reactive and planned algorithms while implementing scenarios which require robot arm or head movements [5].

5   Conclusion

As researchers in social robots we must slowly and gradually encourage the penetration of such agents in the public setting and real world. Laboratory studies are mainstream in HRI research and the challenge of conducting research in the real world is well acknowledged. As such, the incorporation of social robots in public settings requires both technical and interaction based advancements. In this paper, we have presented some of the ongoing works in public spaces using two popular social robots. The importance of engaging users and providing the right information at the right time is imperative. Safety and privacy remain two key considerations and seemingly under-represented whilst most robotics research in this domain remains work in progress. We have also discussed how communication should be brief and relevant whilst attracting the attention of the user. Our guidelines are not by any means comprehensive and future work must consider further the suitability of various social robots in the public domain.

References

1. Aaltonen, I., Arvola, A., Heikkilä, P., Lammi, H.: Hello pepper, may i tickle you?: Children's and adults' responses to an entertainment robot at a shopping mall. In: Proceedings of the Companion of the 2017 ACM/IEEE International Conference on Human-Robot Interaction, pp. 53–54. ACM (2017)
2. Ahmad, M., Mubin, O., Orlando, J.: A systematic review of adaptivity in human-robot interaction. Multimodal Technol. Interact. 1(3), 14 (2017)
3. Ahmad, M.I., Mubin, O., Orlando, J.: Adaptive social robot for sustaining social engagement during long-term children-robot interaction. Int. J. Hum.-Comput. Interact. 33(12), 943–962 (2017)
4. Bennewitz, M., Faber, F., Joho, D., Schreiber, M., Behnke, S.: Towards a humanoid museum guide robot that interacts with multiple persons. In: 2005 5th IEEE-RAS International Conference on Humanoid Robots, pp. 418–423. IEEE (2005)
5. Campa, R.: The rise of social robots: a review of the recent literature. J. Evol. Technol. 26(1), 106–113 (2016)
6. Ewick, P., Silbey, S.S.: The Common Place of Law: Stories from Everyday Life. University of Chicago Press, Chicago (1998)
7. Faber, F., et al.: The humanoid museum tour guide robotinho. In: The 18th IEEE International Symposium on Robot and Human Interactive Communication, 2009, RO-MAN 2009, pp. 891–896. IEEE (2009)
8. Fong, T., Nourbakhsh, I., Dautenhahn, K.: A survey of socially interactive robots. Robot. Auton. Syst. 42(3–4), 143–166 (2003)
9. Ludewig, Y., Döring, N., Exner, N.: Design and evaluation of the personality trait extraversion of a shopping robot. In: 2012 IEEE RO-MAN, pp. 372–379. IEEE (2012)
10. Middlehurst, C.: 'Human' robot pepper proves popular again and sells out in less than a minute in japan. Telegr. 2 (2015)
11. Mubin, O., Khan, A., Obaid, M.: #naorobot: exploring Nao discourse on Twitter. In: Proceedings of the 28th Australian Conference on Computer-Human Interaction, pp. 155–159. ACM (2016)
12. Orji, R.: Design for behaviour change: a model-driven approach for tailoring persuasive technologies. Ph.D. thesis, University of Saskatchewan (2014)
13. Satake, S., Kanda, T., Glas, D.F., Imai, M., Ishiguro, H., Hagita, N.: How to approach humans?: strategies for social robots to initiate interaction. In: Proceedings of the 4th ACM/IEEE International Conference on Human Robot Interaction, pp. 109–116. ACM (2009)
14. Scholtz, J.: Theory and evaluation of human robot interactions. In: Proceedings of the 36th Annual Hawaii International Conference on System Sciences, 2003, pp. 10–pp. IEEE (2003)
15. Softbank Robotics (2017). https://www.ald.softbankrobotics.com/en/robots/nao

16. Stock, R.M., Merkle, M.: Can humanoid service robots perform better than service employees? A comparison of innovative behavior cues (2018)
17. Tanaka, F., Isshiki, K., Takahashi, F., Uekusa, M., Sei, R., Hayashi, K.: Pepper learns together with children: development of an educational application. In: 2015 IEEE-RAS 15th International Conference on Humanoid Robots (Humanoids), pp. 270–275. IEEE (2015)
18. Wada, K., Shibata, T.: Robot therapy in a care house-its sociopsychological and physiological effects on the residents. In: Proceedings 2006 IEEE International Conference on Robotics and Automation, 2006, ICRA 2006, pp. 3966–3971. IEEE (2006)
19. Yang, C.Y., Lu, M.J., Tseng, S.H., Fu, L.C.: A companion robot for daily care of elders based on homeostasis. In: 2017 56th Annual Conference of the Society of Instrument and Control Engineers of Japan (SICE), pp. 1401–1406. IEEE (2017)
20. Zalama, E., et al.: Sacarino, a service robot in a hotel environment. In: Armada, M.A., Sanfeliu, A., Ferre, M. (eds.) ROBOT2013: First Iberian Robotics Conference. AISC, vol. 253, pp. 3–14. Springer, Cham (2014). https://doi.org/10.1007/978-3-319-03653-3_1

On the Design of a Full-Actuated Robot Hand with Target Sensing Self-adaption and Slider Crank Mechanism

Chao Luo and Wenzeng Zhang$^{(\boxtimes)}$

Department of Mechanical Engineering, Tsinghua University,
Beijing 100084, China
wenzeng@tsinghua.edu.cn

Abstract. The robot hand is one of the most important subsystems of an industrial system, it can interact with the environment directly and are often required to deal with objects with different positions, sizes, and shapes. To meet these requirements, many self-adaptive hands have been developed. However, the traditional finger cannot perform a linear translation of its distal phalanx. The linear translation of the distal phalanx is useful in grasping thin objects on a flat surface without additional motion of manipulators. This paper designs a novel linear-parallel and sensing self-adaptive robot hand (LPSS hand) and its corresponding control system, the hand combines the self-adaptive grasping mode and linear-parallel pinching mode, and it can switch among different grasping modes according to signals provided by the sensors. The hand consists of 3 fingers, 6 sensors, and one palm. Each finger includes 2 actuators, 2 phalanxes, and 2 DOF (degree of freedom). The hand was designed based on a novel straight-line mechanism, kinematics and force analysis of the hand are conducted to give more detail properties of the design and provide some method for optimization. The hand has much application potential in the industrial field.

Keywords: Robot hand · Kinematic analysis · Self-adaption
Linear-parallel grasp · Straight-line mechanism

1 Introduction

The robot hand is one of the most useful end effectors in the industrial sector, the robot hands are often required to deal with objects with different positions, sizes, and shapes. Depending on the application situations, the robot hand mainly have three kinds of functions, preparation of a contact, establishing a contact, and depositing of gripping objects.

The existing robot hands can be divided into 4 categories, which includes industrial gripper, underactuated hand, dexterous hand, and special gripper [1, 2]. These hands have their unique features and are often required to deal with objects with different positions, sizes, and shapes. In practice, the robot hand is chosen by specific requirements, to meet these requirements and enlarge the application filed of robot hand, many researchers have developed many self-adaptive hands, and the examples are: Utah/MIT hand [3], SARAH hand [4], Gifu hand II [5], PASA-GB hand [6], and MPJ hand [7]. As

© Springer Nature Switzerland AG 2018
S. S. Ge et al. (Eds.): ICSR 2018, LNAI 11357, pp. 221–229, 2018.
https://doi.org/10.1007/978-3-030-05204-1_22

for these hands, to achieve parallel pinching, the trajectory of their distal phalanges is circular. These hands can accomplish most grasping tasks but still low in gripping accuracy, especially for thick objects on the flat surface, because they cannot perform a linear translation of its distal phalanx, which is useful in grasping typical objects put on a table without motion of manipulators. The straight-line motion is one of the most commonly used properties in the industrial field [8]. The straight-line mechanism is often used to produce a straight-line motion. A robot hand with straight-line output has many advantages over others, especially in the case of precision-grasping and dealing with small objects. A straight-line output motion means no backlash and does not require the complex control system to achieve the aimed path [9]. Such structure often converts rotary motion to straight-line motion. To make the trajectory of the distal phalange becomes linear, and to solve the above-mentioned problem, the concept of the hands with linear-parallel grasping mode was proposed in recent years, the examples are LIPSA hand [10], LPSA hand [11], and the CLIS hand [12]. These hands combine the advantages of self-adaption and linear-parallel pinching, but there is no sensing device to meet the requirements of gripping force control and monitoring and quality control.

In this paper, a novel straight-line mechanism is introduced and based on the mechanism, a novel linear-parallel and sensing self-adaptive robot hand (called LPSS hand) is proposed. The hand consists of 3 fingers, one palm, 6 sensors, and 8 degrees of freedom. The grasping forces and quality are decided by the signals from the multiple sensors. The hand can execute linear-parallel pinching via the straight-line mechanism, and perform self-adaptive grasping modes with the help of sensors. It has wide application potential in the industrial sector.

The paper has been structured as follows: the second part introduces the working principle, movement properties, and grasping mode of the proposed hand, the third part shows both the mechanical and control system design of the hand and discusses how to switch among different grasping modes. The fourth gives the kinematic and force analysis of the hand, the last part gives the conclusion and research direction for future work.

2   Working Principle and Grasping Mode of the Hand

Grasping objects on a flat surface is useful for robot hand, in order to perform a linear translation of its distal phalanx, a novel straight-line mechanism is proposed and the robot hand was designed based on the mechanism. Figure 1 shows the working principle of the mechanism.

As shown the in Fig. 1, when point D and E are arranged along a vertical line, the point F will move along a horizontal line, and the length relationship among all linkages are:

$$|DG| : |EG| : |FG| = 2 : 3 : 5 \tag{1}$$

According to structure of the mechanism, one can obtain,

$$\overrightarrow{DG} + \overrightarrow{GE} = \overrightarrow{DE} \tag{2}$$

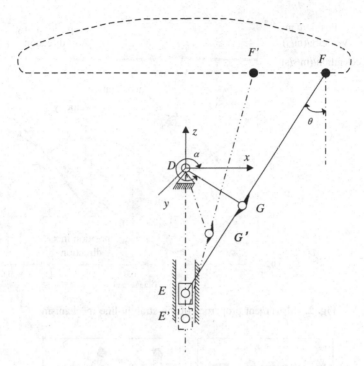

Fig. 1. Working principle of the proposed straight-line mechanism

$$\overrightarrow{DG} + \overrightarrow{GF} = \overrightarrow{DF} \tag{3}$$

Due to the position relationship between point D and E, it can be concluded that,

$$|DE| \cos \alpha - |EG| \cos \theta = 0 \tag{4}$$

A local Cartesian coordinate is fixed on point D, and the position of the point F should be,

$$\overrightarrow{DF} = (|DE| \cos \alpha + |GF| \cos \theta, |DE| \sin \alpha + |DE| \sin \theta) \tag{5}$$

$$\begin{bmatrix} x_F \\ y_F \end{bmatrix} = \begin{bmatrix} \cos \alpha & \cos \theta \\ \sin \alpha & \sin \theta \end{bmatrix} \begin{bmatrix} |DG| \\ |GF| \end{bmatrix} \tag{6}$$

According to Eq. (6), the expression of point F and the movement properties of the mechanism can be obtained.

By simulations the movement curves of point F can be obtained, as shown in Fig. 2. According to the figure, one can obtain that point F moves along a straight line, which verify the working principle of the mechanism, and indicates that the mechanism is suitable for grasping thick objects on the flat surface. Besides, the range of acceleration if small, it can help avoid big peak force when the robot interacts with the environment.

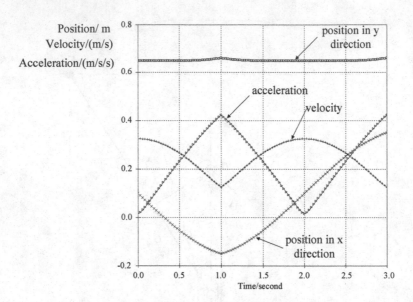

Fig. 2. Movement properties of the straight-line mechanism.

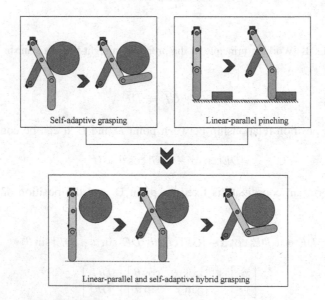

Fig. 3. Hybrid grasping mode of the proposed hand.

Based on the proposed mechanism, a robot hand was designed, which combines the self-adaptive grasping mode and the linear-parallel pinching grasping mode. When sensors receive different signals, the hand will shift among the grasping modes. Figure 3 shows the grasping mode of the proposed finger. In reality, the hand consists of at least 2 fingers, and in this way, the hand can grape objects stably due to the multiple contact points.

3 Mechanical and Control System Design of the Hand

As shown in Fig. 4, the robot hand consists of 3 fingers and one palm. Each finger includes 2 motors, a straight-line mechanism, one bar and 2 phalanxes. There is one contact sensor on each phalanx when the phalanx reaches objects, signals will be received by the control system. The finger can work in several grasping modes, in the linear-parallel pinching grasping mode, the base, first phalanx, distal phalanx, the bar form a parallelogram, due to the straight-line mechanism, the distal phalanx moves along a straight line, which is suitable for grasping thick objects on the desktop. When the first phalanx reaches the object firstly, the finger will work under the self-adaptive grasping mode. When the first phalanx reaches the object, it cannot rotate anymore, another motor continues driving the bar, which breaks the parallelogram, and the distal phalanx will rotate to reach the objects until all the phalanx in the finger contact with the object.

The control system design for the robot hand is shown in Fig. 5. By using the control system, the hand can switch among different grasping modes according to signals provided by the sensors.

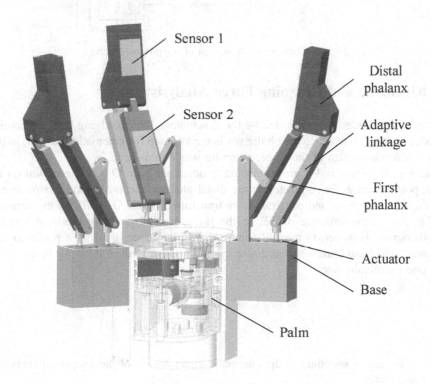

Fig. 4. The mechanical structure of the proposed hand.

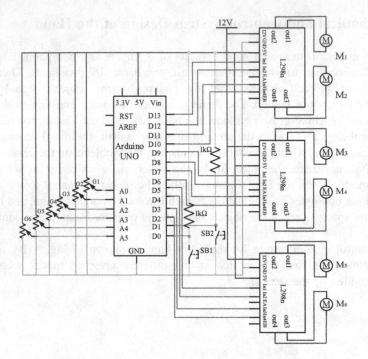

Fig. 5. Control system design of the proposed hand

4 Kinematic and Grasping Force Analysis

The grasping modes are controlled by the 2 actuators, thus, studying how the motion transfer from the actuator to the phalanxes is the key step for kinematic analysis, in this part, a kinematic chain of the finger structure was established.

In Fig. 6, joint E and A are connected to actuators; joint D is a fixed point on the base; point B and F are connected to the distal phalanx. According to the structure of the finger, the motions and constraints are transformed from AE to BF by the structure $ABFE$. As for the structure $ABFE$, in the linear-parallel pinching mode, it forms a parallelogram, however, in the self-adaptive grasping mode, it is not a parallelogram anymore. The local Cartesian coordinate system was established as shown in the figure and one can obtain that:

$$\$_E = [1 \quad 0 \quad 0 \quad 0 \quad 0 \quad 0]^T \tag{6}$$

$$\$_A = [1 \quad 0 \quad 0 \quad 0 \quad l_{EA} \quad 0]^T \tag{7}$$

The terminal constraints of the kinematic chain consist of the reciprocal screws of kinematic chain:

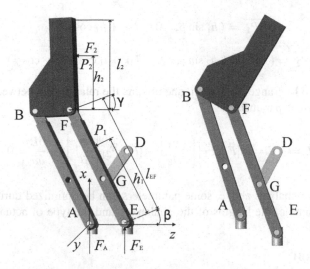

Fig. 6. Hybrid kinematic chains of the proposed finger when under different grasping modes.

$$\$_{EA} = \begin{bmatrix} \$_1^r & \$_2^r & \$_3^r & \$_4^r \end{bmatrix} \tag{8}$$

In Eq. (8), $\$_1^r$, $\$_3^r$ and $\$_4^r$ form the planar constraints, and $\$_2^r$ restricts the relative motion of the line EA. The specific expression of the four elements should be
$\$_1^r = \begin{bmatrix} 1 & 0 & 0 & 0 & 0 & 0 \end{bmatrix}^T$, $\$_2^r = \begin{bmatrix} 1 & 0 & 0 & 0 & 0 & 0 \end{bmatrix}^T$,
$\$_3^r = \begin{bmatrix} 1 & 0 & 0 & 0 & 0 & 0 \end{bmatrix}^T$, $\$_4^r = \begin{bmatrix} 1 & 0 & 0 & 0 & 0 & 0 \end{bmatrix}^T$.

Besides, one can obtain the free mobility space of the link BF (the distal phalanx),

$$S_F = \{T_{y1}\}, T_{y1} = \begin{bmatrix} 0 & 0 & 0 & 0 & 1 & 0 \end{bmatrix}^T \tag{9}$$

Combine the analysis above with the working principle of the straight-line mechanism, one can get the twist of the structure determined by ABFE,

$$T_{y1} = \begin{bmatrix} 0 & 0 & 0 & \left|\overrightarrow{AE}\right| & 0 & \overrightarrow{EF} \cdot (1 \ 0 \ 0) \end{bmatrix}^T \tag{10}$$

Similarly, the contact force during the grasping process can be obtained. As shown in Fig. 6, F_A and F_E are the forces provided by the two actuators.

$$\overrightarrow{F_A} = (F_A, \ 0, \ 0) \tag{11}$$

$$\overrightarrow{F_E} = (F_E, \ 0, \ 0) \tag{12}$$

P_1 and P_2 are the two contact points, other symbols and their corresponding physical meaning are also shown in the figure.

$$\overrightarrow{P_1} = (\, h_1 \sin\beta, \quad 0, \quad l_{AE} + h_1 \cos\beta \,) \tag{13}$$

$$\overrightarrow{P_2} = (\, l_1 \sin\beta + h_2 \sin\gamma, \quad 0, \quad l_{AE} + l_1 \cos\beta + h_2 \cos\gamma \,) \tag{14}$$

According to Lagrange's equation, one obtains the relationship between the contact forces and different parameters.

$$L = -V = -[\vec{F}_A, \vec{F}_E]\begin{bmatrix} \Delta y_A \\ \Delta y_E \end{bmatrix} + [\vec{F}_1, \vec{F}_2]\begin{bmatrix} \overrightarrow{P}_1^t \\ \overrightarrow{P}_2^t \end{bmatrix}, -\frac{\delta L}{\delta q} = \vec{0} \tag{15}$$

Based on the analysis above, some parameters can be optimized during the design process, for example, the lengths of the phalanxes and the type of actuators.

5 Conclusion

This paper designs a novel straight-line mechanism, and based on the mechanism, a novel linear-parallel and sensing self-adaptive robot hand (called LPSS hand) is proposed. The hand consists of 3 fingers, one palm, 6 sensors, and 8 degrees of freedom. The grasping forces and quality are decided by the signals from the multiple sensors. The hand can execute linear-parallel pinching via the straight-line mechanism, and perform self-adaptive grasping modes with the help of sensors. Both the mechanical and control system designs of the hand are discussed. Motion analysis indicates that the mechanism has good kinematic properties and is suitable for robot hand design. Besides, kinematic and forces analysis were conducted to give more details about the design, based on the analysis, the structure of the hand can be optimized further. The hand has wide application potential in the industrial sector. Moreover, as studied by some researchers that EMG control, artificial skins, and social touching can be applied to the proposed design to humanizing this robot hand [13–15].

Acknowledgment. This Research was supported by National Natural Science Foundation of China (No. 51575302) and Beijing Natural Science Foundation (No. J170005).

References

1. Yang, S., Song, J., Li, G., et al.: Development of the CA robot finger with a novel coupled and active grasping mode. Int. J. Humanoid Robot. **13**(03), 1650012 (2016)
2. Yang, S., Li, G., Zhang, W.: SCHU hand: a novel self-adaptive robot hand with single-column hybrid underactuated grasp. In: IEEE International Conference on Robotics and Biomimetics, pp. 1337–1342. IEEE (2015)
3. Jacobsen, S.C., Iversen, E.K., Knutti, D.F., et al.: Design of the Utah/MIT dextrous hand. In: Proceedings of IEEE International Conference on Robotics and Automation, pp. 1520–1532 (1986)
4. Thierry, L., Gosselin, C.M.: Simulation and design of underactuated mechanical hands. Mech. Mach. Theory **33**(1–2), 39–57 (1998)

5. Kawasaki, H., Komatsu, T., Uchiyama, K., et al.: Dexterous anthropomorphic robot hand with distributed tactile sensor: Gifu hand II. In: IEEE International Conference on Systems, Man, and Cybernetics (SMC), pp. 782–787 (1999)
6. Liang, D., Zhang, W.: PASA-GB hand: a novel parallel and self-adaptive robot hand with gear-belt mechanisms. J. Intell. Robot. Syst. **3**, 1–15 (2017)
7. Luo, C., Yang, S., Zhang, W., et al.: MPJ hand: a self-adaptive underactuated hand with flexible fingers of multiple passive joints. In: International Conference on Advanced Robotics and Mechatronics, pp. 184–189. IEEE (2016)
8. Hricko, J.: Straight-line mechanisms as one building element of small precise robotic devices. In: Applied Mechanics & Materials, vol. 613, no. 1, pp. 96–101 (2014)
9. Luo, C., Zhang, W.: Development of a novel linear-parallel robot hand. In: Chen, Z., Mendes, A., Yan, Y., Chen, S. (eds.) ICIRA 2018. LNCS (LNAI), vol. 10985, pp. 16–26. Springer, Cham (2018). https://doi.org/10.1007/978-3-319-97589-4_2
10. Yang, Y., Zhang, W., Xu, X., Hand, L.I.P.S.A., et al.: A novel underactuated hand with linearly parallel and self-adaptive grasp. In: Zhang, X., Wang, N., Huang, Y. (eds.) Mechanism and Machine Science. Lecture Notes in Electrical Engineering, vol. 408. Springer, Heidelberg (2017). https://doi.org/10.1007/978-981-10-2875-5_10
11. Luo, C., Zhang, W.: MPJ hand: a linear-parallel and self-adaptive underactuated hand with parallel pulleys. In: International Conference on Advanced Robotics and Mechatronics, pp. 324–329. IEEE (2018)
12. Xu, J., Liang, W., Cai, J., et al.: LPSA underactuated mode of linearly parallel and self-adaptive grasping in the CLIS robot hand with Chebyshev linkage and idle stroke. In: International Conference on Advanced Robotics and Mechatronics, Hefei, pp. 322–327. IEEE (2017)
13. Kim, S., Kim, M., Lee, J., Park, J.: Robot hand synergy mapping using multi-factor model and EMG signal. In: Hsieh, M.A., Khatib, O., Kumar, V. (eds.) Experimental Robotics. STAR, vol. 109, pp. 671–683. Springer, Cham (2016). https://doi.org/10.1007/978-3-319-23778-7_44
14. Yousef, H., Nikolovski, J.P., Martincic, E.: Flexible 3D force tactile sensor for artificial skin for anthropomorphic robotic hand. Procedia Eng. **25**(35), 128–131 (2011)
15. Yohanan, S.: The role of affective touch in human-robot interaction: human intent and expectations in touching the haptic creature. Int. J. Soc. Robot. **4**(2), 163–180 (2012)

Towards Dialogue-Based Navigation with Multivariate Adaptation Driven by Intention and Politeness for Social Robots

Chandrakant Bothe[1]([✉]), Fernando Garcia[2], Arturo Cruz Maya[2],
Amit Kumar Pandey[2], and Stefan Wermter[1]

[1] Knowledge Technology, Department of Informatics, University of Hamburg,
Hamburg, Germany
{bothe,wermter}@informatik.uni-hamburg.de
[2] SoftBank Robotics Europe, Paris, France
{ferran.garcia,arturo.cruzmaya,akpandey}@softbankrobotics.com

Abstract. Service robots need to show appropriate social behaviour in order to be deployed in social environments such as healthcare, education, retail, etc. Some of the main capabilities that robots should have are navigation and conversational skills. If the person is impatient, the person might want a robot to navigate faster and vice versa. Linguistic features that indicate politeness can provide social cues about a person's patient and impatient behaviour. The novelty presented in this paper is to dynamically incorporate politeness in robotic dialogue systems for navigation. Understanding the politeness in users' speech can be used to modulate the robot behaviour and responses. Therefore, we developed a dialogue system to navigate in an indoor environment, which produces different robot behaviours and responses based on users' intention and degree of politeness. We deploy and test our system with the Pepper robot that adapts to the changes in user's politeness.

Keywords: Social Robots · Dialogue System · Effect of Politeness
Natural Language Understanding · Human-Robot Interaction

1 Introduction

The perception of politeness of a user can be a reflection of their patience during interaction. In addition to other factors such as the robot appearance, robot behaviour is a crucial aspect for their acceptance. Hence, politeness cues are intimately related to the dynamics of behavior and interaction [4,7,12,23]. It is useful for adapting to the dynamic tension [20] that occurs as a user tries to maintain a sufficient degree of politeness while interacting with the robot. For example, sentence-initial *you* or an action directive verb can be impolite

© Springer Nature Switzerland AG 2018
S. S. Ge et al. (Eds.): ICSR 2018, LNAI 11357, pp. 230–240, 2018.
https://doi.org/10.1007/978-3-030-05204-1_23

"You need to show..." or *"Show me the..."*, whereas sentence-medial *you* or sentence-initial *could* or *would* often indicates the politeness like in these sentences *"Could you show me..."* or *"Would you take me to..."*.

Multivariate adaptive and affective dialogue systems based on linguistic features have been subject to previous research [1,8,22]. The effect of politeness on the conversation is prominent and it has been researched in the sociolinguist community [7,12,20]. The effect of such a feature on human-robot interaction (HRI) has been a subject of study with various aspects: an impolite vs. a polite robot playing a game [5], in determining social robot acceptance with multi-cultural background people [21], making robots sociable and to achieve safe HRI [8]. Hence, a robot that can recognize the intention of the user during interaction should also adapt to the human's linguistic behavioural changes. For example, different sociolinguistic features such as politeness, emotion, sentiment, etc. represent the user's behavioural dynamics. If the user's utterance is impolite, then he/she might be in a hurry and vice versa. In such cases, the robot might need to change its behaviour or even alter some actions or speed up or down the movements. We develop a modular dialogue system (DS) that can process such features and make a robot to adapt accordingly. The natural language understanding part of the DS uses recurrent neural networks (RNNs) [25,26] and the Snips library [6] for extracting the structured information from the user input. The politeness detection is learned from the human-annotated corpus and fine-tuned for the scenario-specific data. The navigation of the Pepper robot is achieved by using the NAOqi framework. The robot behaviour and responses are driven by dialogue flow module using the intention and politeness. The main contributions of the present work towards bridging the gap between sociolinguistic research and HRI community are:

- developing a dialogue-based navigation for incorporating politeness, and
- incorporating sociolinguistic features for robotic behavioural modelling.

To the best of our knowledge, our system is the first dialogue-based navigation that incorporates politeness as an important social cue to drive the robot behaviour and responses.

2 Approach

We propose a dialogue system which takes into account the degree of politeness as a factor that affects the conversation flow and the robot behaviour. The dialogue system takes the intention and other information, for example, slot-value pairs (see details in Sect. 3.1) into account to understand the input utterance [25]. However, in the proposed model, the dialogue system processes sociolinguistic features to make inferences regarding the input utterance. The overall architecture is shown in Fig. 1. The proposed system is customizable to any extent as the robot is controlled using a client-server architecture. The state and motion managers are wrapped into an application programming interface (API) as a server [10] and communicated via the dialogue flow module. The dialogue system can be accessed also if the robot is not connected to the server.

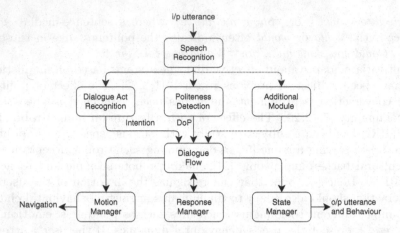

Fig. 1. The overall architecture of the dialogue system. DoP: degree of politeness.

3   Dialogue System

3.1   Natural Language Understanding

The input speech from a user is converted into text using the speech recognition module (from NAOqi). The language understanding module takes the converted input utterance forms a symbolic representation and provides the degree of politeness. The dialogue act recognition module is used to extract the symbolic representation and politeness detection module to detect the degree of politeness of that input utterance.

Dialogue Act Recognition Module. The dialogue act (DA) recognition is a crucial process in the dialogue system. The task is to decode the input utterance and form the symbolic representation, such as dialogue acts and slot-value pairs. For example, the utterance *"could you please show me the retail department"* can be decoded as $\{da : TakeToPlace, room : retail\}$ where *da* represents the dialogue act or intention, *room* is a slot and *retail* its value. We created a dataset for the given scenario to be able to drive the conversation (some examples are given in Table 1). The following methods are used in conjunction for robustness by validating one another based on heuristics of their confidence values:

(1) **Dialogue act recognition using RNNs:** The architecture is shown in Fig. 2, where RNNs are used in a hierarchical fashion to learn the dialogue acts and slot-value pairs [3, 14, 26]. The RNNs are better at encoding the contextual and sequential information in the utterance [14]. The dialogue acts are classified with the first layer of the RNN, preserving the utterance representation *utt_rep1*. *utt_rep1* is then used to recognize slots on the next layer of the RNN, producing a new utterance representation *utt_rep2*. The values of slots are learned with next layer of the RNN using *utt_rep2* and the detected slot as a switch ($\in$) for

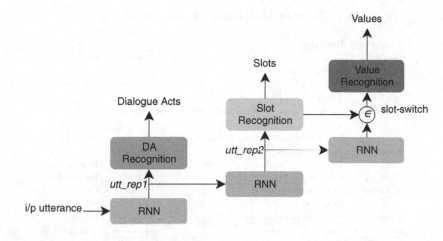

Fig. 2. Dialogue acts and slot-value pairs recognition using RNNs.

the belonging values learned in this layer (see the output in Fig. 5 for better understanding). We fit the model to the data and use the trained model for inference [3].

(2) Snips Natural Language Understanding (NLU) Engine: Snips NLU Engine[1] is an open source Python library that uses two approaches: (a) a deterministic parser and (b) a probabilistic parser [6]. The deterministic parser is basically a pattern matching mechanism which uses regular expressions to parse the input utterance. The probabilistic parser uses logistic regression for intent classification and conditional random fields (CRFs) for slot filling. For the given input utterance, the engine provides the intention and slot-value pairs.

Politeness Detection Module. The politeness detection module takes the input utterance as an input and computes its degree of politeness. An RNN is used to learn the degree of politeness from Stanford Politeness Corpus[2] [7]. We fine-tune the trained model for the dataset (mentioned in the previous section) that is created for the particular scenario to minimize uncertainty in prediction. The degree of politeness (DoP) varies from 1 to −1 (very polite to very impolite). For the sake of conceptual and computational simplicity, we discretized them into categories: polite (1), neutral (0) and impolite (−1); see the examples below:

```
DoP    Class      Utterance
1      polite     Could you please show me the education department?
0      neutral    Can you show me the education department?
-1     impolite   Show me the education department.
```

---

[1] https://snips-nlu.readthedocs.io.
[2] https://www.cs.cornell.edu/~cristian/Politeness.html.

Table 1. Examples of dialogue act and slot-value pairs

Dialogue acts	Examples	Slots	Values
Greeting	*Hello* *Hi, how are you?*	no_slot	no_value
Thanking	*Thank you* *Thank you very much*	no_slot	no_value
TakeToPlace	*Could you show me the education department?* *Take me to the retail section* *Can you take me to tourism department?*	Room	retail education tourism
MoveRobot	*Please go ahead* *Could you move ahead?* *Go back please*	Direction	 forward backward
TurnRobot	*Can you turn right?* *Could you turn left*		right left
Accept	*Yes, I would like to visit*	no_slot	no_value
AbortRobot	*Stop, wait, be careful...*	no_slot	no_value

Additional Module. This module is open to adding additional sociolinguistic features such as sentiment, emotion, etc. Adding more features can increase the complexity of the dialogue system. However, it could be useful in some cases to incorporate multiple features and modalities to produce the required behaviour.

3.2   Dialogue Flow

The dialogue flow is a central engine of the system which communicates with most of the modules. It is implemented as a main function to drive the DS. A rule-based and probabilistic belief tracking or dialogue state tracking model could be used to maintain the dialogue flow [25]. We used a rule-based model where the dialogue flow module keeps track of the input dialogue acts and DoP and send them to the response manager to fetch responses. The complete state loop has a queue to store the context information of the preceding utterances. It is helpful to trigger new dialogue acts based on the context information. For example, if the last dialogue act is *TakeToPlace*, it triggers a new dialogue act called *FinishedOne* to inform the system that the last action was finished and asks the user if he/she wishes to visit the next place. Another loop keeps track of whether the user accepts or rejects the proposal using *Accept* and *Reject* dialogue acts. If one of the dialogue acts appears, the robot takes the user to the next location until either the list of locations is finished or the user rejects to visit the next place.

3.3   Response Manager

The response manager is responsible for picking up the right response for the given intention and degree of politeness. Pre-defined response templates are stored in a data file that is accessed continuously during the interaction.

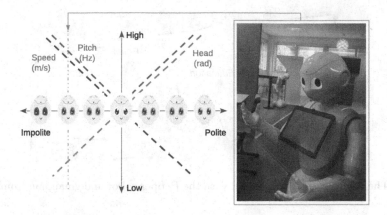

Fig. 3. The behavioural model used to create the verbal and non-verbal responses based on the cumulative sum of the DoP. The Pepper robot shown in the right is in the position of the vertical orange line in the plot during the interaction.

4   Robot Control and Navigation

4.1   Robot Platform

Pepper is a 1.2 m tall omnidirectional wheeled humanoid robot platform capable of exhibiting body language, perceiving and interacting with its surroundings, and move autonomously. Due to its 17 joints and 20 degrees of freedom (DoF) kinematic configuration and edgeless design, the system is suitable for safe HRI [18]. The platform is equipped with a large variety of sensors and actuators that ensure safe navigation and a high degree of expressiveness: LED's are distributed across the head (eyes and ears) and torso (shoulders) to support non-verbal communication by modifying colour and intensity. The microphones and speakers allow verbal interaction as well as environmental awareness. Sensing components include three laser sensors, two sonars and two infrared sensors located in the robot's base, as well as two cameras and a three-dimensional camera located in the head. Finally, the platform is powered by an Atom processor with a 1.91 GHz quad-core unit that allows the NAOqi SDK to orchestrate the different hardware elements as well as their access from other APIs.

4.2   State Manager

In order to produce the physical and verbal responses in accordance with the degree of politeness exhibited during the interaction, a behavioural model inspired by the valence and arousal model [2] has been designed. The model is given the discrete DoP computed from the last utterance being [1, 0, −1] and maps the cumulative sum of the politeness of the previous and current utterances to different actuators. In this way, a variability is provided to every single social cue that can vary in order to fit the interaction needs.

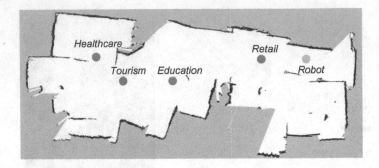

Fig. 4. The environment map created with the Pepper robot and gmapping from ROS.

The actuators used to externalize the robot's change of state are the LED's color [17], head pitch orientation [15], voice pitch [13] and navigation speed, and are mapped following the intuition (shown in Fig. 3). For example, a user repetitively polite during the whole interaction will experience a decrement in the navigation speed of the robot, a head position oriented towards the user, green coloured eyes and a slightly higher voice pitch.

4.3 Motion Manager

The motion manager is responsible for navigation and can be operated in the following modes:

Tele-Operation. In this mode, the Pepper robot could be teleoperated with the help of the NAOqi framework using the *moveToward* function from ALMotion service and the keys on the keyboard are used for moving or stopping the robot.

Scripted Navigation. The scripted navigation is achieved by commanding a robot to move to the specific positions/places with the known distances in the environment. This is also achieved with NAOqi framework using *moveTo* command from ALMotion service. We specify how far the robot has to move (in meters) and the orientations (in radians) it has to take during motion.

Navigation: Mapping and Planning. This module requires the use of the Robot Operating System (ROS), an open source middle-ware framework. To fit our need for navigation, we have adopted the following approach for generating and post-processing the map. The current readings of the Pepper's depth image are converted into virtual laser data, using the package *depthimage_to_laserscan* [19,24]. An offline map (shown in Fig. 4, and post-processed for testing purposes) can be acquired using *gmapping* (laser-based SLAM) [11]. Then, the localization is performed using Adaptive Monte Carlo Localization (*acml*) [9]. Finally, the

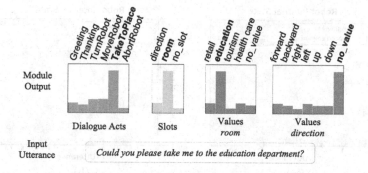

Fig. 5. Output of the DA recognition module.

navigation uses a global planner with a map with inflated obstacles (costmap) and a local costmap with observations from the virtual laser data. The Dialog Flow requests a location from the API server (on the robot using a virtual machine) using an ID and this one sends the coordinates to the ROS navigation stack to execute the path.

5   Experiments and Results: A Real-World Scenario

The task is to navigate in the given environment to show a user the different departments. Our tour scenario in the lab consists of four departments: retail, education, tourism and healthcare as shown in the map in Fig. 4. The robot is a guide which takes the user to the particular department using verbal interaction as mentioned in Sect. 3.2. When the user asks the robot, the input utterance gets processed by the DA recognition module which produces the result as shown in Fig. 5. The politeness detection module provides the DoP of that utterance. The dialogue flow communicates this information with all the managers. The robot adapts its behaviour such as speeding up or down while navigating to the locations and changing the pitch of speech, changing the pitch angle of the head.

We tested our system on the Pepper robot with different users, expressing different levels of politeness. The behavioural changes and adaptation to speed change based on a change in DoP are shown in Fig. 6. The robot behavioural adapts to the human being polite; the robot slows down and spends more time with the user. When the user is impolite, the robot speeds up and executes motion faster. The proposed behaviour of the robot for different situations shown in the figure is mainly to demonstrate the developed system and the efficacy of the proposed framework. The results indicate that the system is able to consider the linguistic features to modulate the navigation behaviour of the robot in a coherent theoretical and functional framework. As aforementioned, to the best of our knowledge such a framework and implementation in a practical situation is one of the first attempts of its kind. However, it is important to mention that the validation of the hypotheses about the most appropriate behaviours of the robot is not within the scope of this paper and it will require further investigation and

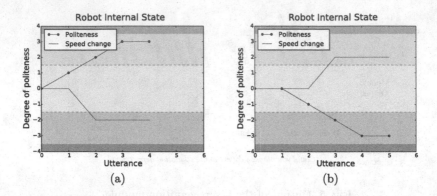

Fig. 6. Robot internal state for polite (a) and impolite (b) interactions.

user studies. As mentioned in the conclusion such studies are one of the next steps to utilize the framework for different situations. The demonstration video and dialogue logs of the generated graphs in Fig. 6 are available at the SECURE EU Project website: https://secure-robots.eu/fellows/bothe/secondment-project/

6   Conclusions and Future Work

We developed a dialogue-based navigation system for integrating intention and politeness features for multivariate adaptation of the robot. We successfully deployed and tested our system on the robot with different levels of politeness. Currently, our work does not elicit the causal explanation for the behaviour and the multivariate adaptation of the robot. However, our experimental framework opens up a new challenge for the study of the effect of politeness in human-robot social interaction. We strongly believe that our work will be helpful in bridging the gap between sociolinguistic research and the HRI community. This research shall also be helpful in targeting the deployment of social-service robots with adaptation to sociolinguistic features such as politeness. In this work, the behaviours are based on previous research [8,16,21,23]. The validation of the system is crucial and it will be addressed in future work through user studies.

Acknowledgements. This project has received funding from the European Union's Horizon 2020 framework programme for research and innovation under the Marie Sklodowska-Curie Grant Agreement No. 642667 (SECURE), the Industrial Leadership Agreement (ICT) No. 779942 (CROWDBOT), and No. 688147 (MuMMER).

References

1. Adam, C., Johal, W., Pellier, D., Fiorino, H., Pesty, S.: Social human-robot inter-action: a new cognitive and affective interaction-oriented architecture. In: Agah, A., Cabibihan, J.-J., Howard, A.M., Salichs, M.A., He, H. (eds.) ICSR 2016. LNCS (LNAI), vol. 9979, pp. 253–263. Springer, Cham (2016). https://doi.org/10.1007/978-3-319-47437-3_25

2. Beck, A., Cañamero, L., Bard, K.A.: Towards an affect space for robots to display emotional body language. In: 19th International Symposium in Robot and Human Interactive Communication, pp. 464–469 (2010)
3. Bothe, C., Magg, S., Weber, C., Wermter, S.: Discourse-wizard: discovering deep discourse structure in your conversation with RNNs. arXiv:1806.11420 (2018)
4. Brown, P., Levinson, S.C.: Politeness: Some Universals in Language Usage, vol. 4. Cambridge University Press, Cambridge (1987)
5. Castro-González, Á., Castillo, J.C., Alonso-Martín, F., Olortegui-Ortega, O.V., González-Pacheco, V., Malfaz, M., Salichs, M.A.: The effects of an impolite vs. a polite robot playing rock-paper-scissors. In: Agah, A., Cabibihan, J.-J., Howard, A.M., Salichs, M.A., He, H. (eds.) ICSR 2016. LNCS (LNAI), vol. 9979, pp. 306–316. Springer, Cham (2016). https://doi.org/10.1007/978-3-319-47437-3_30
6. Coucke, A., Saade, A., Ball, A., Bluche, T., Caulier, A., Leroy, D., Doumouro, C., Gisselbrecht, T., Caltagirone, F., Lavril, T., et al.: Snips voice platform: an embedded spoken language understanding system for private-by-design voice interfaces. arXiv preprint arXiv:1805.10190
7. Danescu-Niculescu-Mizil, C., Sudhof, M., Jurafsky, D., Leskovec, J., Potts, C.: A computational approach to politeness with application to social factors. In: Proceedings of ACL 2013 (Volume 1: Long Papers), pp. 250–259 (2013)
8. Fong, T., Nourbakhsh, I., Dautenhahn, K.: A survey of socially interactive robots. Robot. Auton. Syst. **42**(3–4), 143–166 (2003)
9. Fox, D.: Adapting the Sample Size in Particle Filters Through KLD-Sampling. Int. J. Robot. Res. **22**(12), 985–1003 (2003)
10. Grinberg, M.: Flask Web Development: Developing Web Applications with Python. O'Reilly Media, Inc., Sebastopol (2018)
11. Grisettiyz, G., Stachniss, C., Burgard, W.: Improving grid-based SLAM with rao-blackwellized particle filters by adaptive proposals and selective resampling. In: International Conference on Robotics and Automation, pp. 2432–2437 (2005)
12. Holmes, J., Stubbe, M.: Power and Politeness in the Workplace: A Sociolinguistic Analysis of Talk at Work. Routledge, Abingdon (2015)
13. Hubbard, D.J., Faso, D.J., Assmann, P.F., Sasson, N.J.: Production and perception of emotional prosody by adults with autism spectrum disorder. Autism Res. **10**(12), 1991–2001 (2017)
14. Kumar, H., Agarwal, A., Dasgupta, R., Joshi, S., Kumar, A.: Dialogue act sequence labeling using hierarchical encoder with CRF. In: AAAI Conference on Artificial Intelligence, pp. 3440–3447 (2018)
15. Lemaignan, S., Garcia, F., Jacq, A., Dillenbourg, P.: From real-time attention assessment to "with-me-ness" in human-robot interaction. In: International Conference on Human Robot Interaction, pp. 157–164 (2016)
16. Manav, B.: Color-emotion associations and color preferences: a case study for residences. Color Res. Appl. **32**(2), 144–150 (2007)
17. Nijdam, N.A.: Mapping emotion to color. Citeseer (2009)
18. Pandey, A., Gelin, R.: A mass-produced sociable humanoid robot: pepper: the first machine of its kind. IEEE Robot. Autom. Mag. **25**(3), 40–48 (2018). https://ieeexplore.ieee.org/document/8409927
19. Perera, V., Pereira, T., Connell, J., Veloso, M.: Setting up pepper for autonomous navigation and personalized interaction with users. arXiv:1704.04797 (2017)
20. Rogers, P.S., Lee-Wong, S.M.: Reconceptualizing politeness to accommodate dynamic tensions in subordinate-to-superior reporting. J. Bus. Tech. Commun. **17**(4), 379–412 (2003)

21. Salem, M., Ziadee, M., Sakr, M.: Marhaba, how may I help you?: effects of politeness and culture on robot acceptance and anthropomorphization. In: International Conference on Human-robot Interaction, pp. 74–81 (2014)
22. Shi, W., Yu, Z.: Sentiment adaptive end-to-end dialog systems. In: Proceedings of ACL 2018, pp. 1509–1519 (2018)
23. Srinivasan, V., Takayama, L.: Help me please: robot politeness strategies for soliciting help from people. In: Proceedings of the Conference on Human Factors in Computing Systems, pp. 4945–4955. ACM (2016)
24. Suddrey, G., Jacobson, A., Ward, B.: Enabling a pepper robot to provide automated and interactive tours of a robotics laboratory. arXiv:1804.03288 (2018)
25. Ultes, S., Rojas Barahona, L.M., Su, P.H., Vandyke, D., Kim, D., Casanueva, I., Budzianowski, P., Mrkšić, N., Wen, T.H., Gasic, M., Young, S.: PyDial: a multidomain statistical dialogue system toolkit. In: Proceedings of ACL 2017, System Demonstrations, pp. 73–78 (2017)
26. Yang, X., Chen, Y.N., Hakkani-Tür, D., Crook, P., Li, X., Gao, J., Deng, L.: End-to-end joint learning of natural language understanding and dialogue manager. In: Proceedings of IEEE ICASSP 2017, pp. 5690–5694 (2017)

Design and Implementation of Shoulder Exoskeleton Robot

Wang Boheng[1]([✉]) [iD], Chen Sheng[1,2], Zhu Bo[1], Liang Zhiwei[1],
and Gao Xiang[1]

[1] Nanjing University of Posts and Telecommunications, Nanjing 210023, China
{1216053228, chensheng}@njupt.edu.cn
[2] Key Laboratory of Measurement and Control of Complex Systems
of Engineering, Ministry of Education,
Southeast University, Nanjing 210096, China

Abstract. An exoskeleton robot for shoulder rehabilitation training is designed for patients with hemiplegia due to stroke. In respect of the human upper limb physiology, a series of mechanical structures are integrated: the retractable link meets the upper arm size of different people; the adjustable module relieves the discomfort caused by the scapulohumeral rhythm; and the gravity compensation module ensures patient safety. Then estimate the joint torque and power of the robot to determine the hardware and materials and make the robot prototype. Finally, the robot and PC form a CAN bus communication network and design the robot's control software based on the ROS (Robot Operating System) platform to realize the basic rehabilitation training of the patient's shoulder flexion/extension, abduction/adduction and internal/external rotation. Finally, the comfort of the exoskeleton robot is evaluated through the actual experience of healthy people and in the form of a questionnaire. The test results verify the rationality and comfort of the exoskeleton robot to some extent.

Keywords: Hemiplegia · Shoulder rehabilitation robot · Exoskeletons
ROS

1 Introduction

Millions of people worldwide are affected by Cerebrovascular accidents (CVA) or stroke each year, resulting in arm movement dysfunction. Restoring arm function is essential for restoring activities in daily life [1]. The research and popularization of rehabilitation robots are expected to effectively alleviate this phenomenon, improve the quality of life of disabled patients and the elderly, and promote the development of related industries, increase employment, and promote social harmony. Therefore, it has important social significance. But at the same time, there are many problems with rehabilitation robots [2, 3]:

- The joints of the end-effector-based rehabilitation robot and the joints of the human body are not directly suited matched [4], and the traction force applied to the joints of the human body cannot be precisely controlled, which is easy to cause damage to the affected arm.

© Springer Nature Switzerland AG 2018
S. S. Ge et al. (Eds.): ICSR 2018, LNAI 11357, pp. 241–252, 2018.
https://doi.org/10.1007/978-3-030-05204-1_24

- The actual use of upper limb rehabilitation robots is generally unfriendly, and the cost of learning for ordinary people is too high.
- The current structure of most upper limb rehabilitation robots cannot be adjusted for different patient types, which may cause patients to feel uncomfortable or even cause injury during rehabilitation training.
- Rehabilitation systems are mostly lack of versatility.

A shoulder exoskeleton rehabilitation robot system is implemented to improve the above problems through a series of structural and software designs. The main features of the robot include:

- It can help and partly replace the rehabilitation doctor for long-term repetitive and complex shoulder rehabilitation training for patients.
- Reasonable structural design makes the robot more compact, lighter and comfortable to wear.
- The rehabilitation robot system has a convenient human-computer interaction program [5], which measures the robot motion parameters in real time, visualizes the robot motion state and processes the feedback information.

The rest of this paper is organized as follows. Section 2 introduces the mechanical structure design of the various components of the shoulder rehabilitation robot. Section 3 describes the kinematics analysis. The production of the rehabilitation robot prototype and the realization of rehabilitation training are in Sect. 4. The final section is the conclusion and outlook.

2 Mechanism Design

2.1 The Overall Structure of the Rehabilitation Robot

In general, the human shoulder joint consists mainly of three DOF, including flexion/extension, abduction/adduction and internal/external rotation [6]. The overall structure of the robot is determined for the characteristics of the shoulder joint movement and different body sizes. Figure 1(left) shows the overall design of the exoskeleton shoulder rehabilitation robot. The distribution of DOF (see Fig. 1(right)), and the range of robot motion shown in Table 1 satisfies the range of human motion [7]. In order to meet the sitting height of different people, the robot is designed to be fixed on the lifting platform.

Table 1. Shoulder motion reference amplitude

Degrees of freedom	Movement range of human	Movement range of robot
Flexion/extension	0°–180°/0°–60°	0°–45°/0°–135°
Abduction/adduction	0°–60°/0°–180°	0°–45°/0°–135°
Internal/external rotation	0°–90°/0°–90°	0°–90°/0°–90°

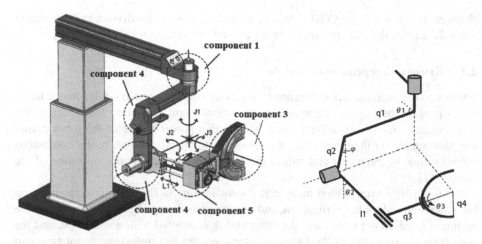

Fig. 1. CAD model of the exoskeleton shoulder rehabilitation robot (left); Degree of freedom distribution and motion diagram (right)

2.2 Passive Adjustment Module

When the structure of the exoskeleton rehabilitation robot is being designed, it is necessary to make the movement of the robot match the movement of the shoulder joint of the human body as much as possible. According to the studies by Tobias Nef, Robert Riener etc. [8, 9], when the human shoulder joint is doing abduction/adduction exercise, the height of the center of glenohumeral (CGH) will change on the vertical plane; this phenomenon is caused by the scapulohumeral rhythm (see Fig. 2(left)).

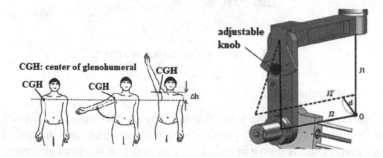

Fig. 2. Scapulohumeral rhythm (left); J2 rotation axis adjustment diagram (right)

Therefore, if the above situation is neglected, the person who wears the rehabilitation robot may feel uncomfortable during exercises. In order to alleviate this negative experience as much as possible, an adjustment mechanism is added to the rehabilitation robot (see Fig. 2(right)). The structure is consisted of a passive joint that adjusts the angle θ by adjusting the knob and is fixed by screwing. By adjusting the angle θ, the position of the J2 rotation axis changes, so that the rotation center O of the robot changes. It is possible for CGH trajectory to match the scapular rhythm to some extent when J2 carries the patient's shoulder for abduction/adduction movement [10].

2.3 Gravity Compensation Module

There are two main reasons for designing a gravity compensation module: on one hand, it can prevent the secondary damage to the patient's arm caused by the falling of the robot vertical movement module due to the sudden power failure of the robot during the movement. On the other hand, it is possible to effectively reduce the continuous output torque of the motor and reduce the burden on the continuous operation of the motor [11].

The gravity compensation module is shown in Fig. 3. The module is mounted on the inner side wall of the vertical link and compensated by spring force. One end of the spring is fixed on the baffle, and the other end is connected with a wire rope, and the wire rope is connected to the fastening screw on the flexing/extension rotating part through the pulley block.

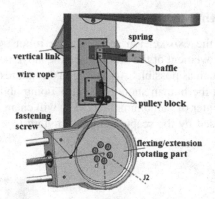

Fig. 3. Gravity compensation module

2.4 Structural Optimization

In the exoskeleton structure, the joint that implements the internal/external rotation motion of the arm is made by 3D printing with resin material, and the semi-circular exoskeleton part is used as shown in Fig. 4(a). This structure is more convenient for the patient to wear than the conventional closed toroidal structure. For this structure, an open synchronous belt is used to achieve movement transmission. Synchronous belt drive can realize high-speed rotation transmission, compact structure, high transmission efficiency and wide power adaptation range [12]. The drive component is placed in a gearbox with a main synchronous pulley and an auxiliary pulley block.

A sliding block component with pulleys mounted between the gearbox and the semi-circular exoskeleton structure is adopted with respect to the modular idea, compact structure and convenient installation, which is shown in Fig. 4(b). The slider slides in the semi-circular chute through the surrounding pulleys, which makes the structure stronger in all directions and makes the semi-circular components more stable during movement.

Since different patients have different height and length of arms, in order to satisfy different users, a link with adjustable length is designed as shown in Fig. 4(c). On the basis of the original fixed link, it can be adjusted according to the length of the patient's arm. The two steel cylinders and the lead screw connect the vertical link of the robot to the gear box, and the inside of the gear box is equipped with a linear bearing for auxiliary movement.

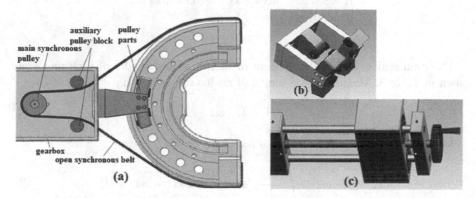

Fig. 4. (a) Schematic diagram of internal/external rotation joint structure (b) pulley parts (c) retractable link

2.5 Robot Joint Torque and Power Estimation

The structure that the robot is subjected to a large force is made of aluminum alloy machining, and the structure subjected to less force is made by a 3D printing SLA photosensitive resin one-shot forming technique [13]. Then estimate the required torque and power of each joint in combination with the robot structure diagram (see Fig. 5).

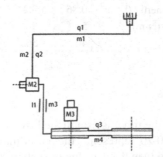

Fig. 5. Robot structure diagram

The density of the aluminum alloy material used was 2710 kg/m3, the density of the resin material used was 1100 kg/m3, and the quality of the links was evenly distributed. The attribute parameters of each component are shown in Table 2.

Table 2. Length and quality of each link

Link length	Link quality	Motor quality
q1 = 308 mm	m1 = 1.68 kg	M2 = 1.2 kg
q2 = 232 mm	m2 = 1.6 kg	
l1 = 330 mm	m3 = 1 kg	M3 = 1 kg
q3 = 308 mm	m4 = 2.5 kg	

The estimated values of the moment of inertia at the spindle of each motor are shown in Table 3. Maximum load torque of no-load of motor 1:

$$T1 = J1 \cdot \omega1 \tag{1}$$

Maximum load torque of no-load of motor 2:

$$T2 = J2 \cdot \omega2 + \int_0^{l1} \frac{m3}{l1} gldl + M3 \cdot g \cdot l1 + m4 \cdot g \cdot l1 \tag{2}$$

Maximum load torque of no-load of motor 3:

$$T3 = J3 \cdot \omega3 + m4 \cdot q3 \tag{3}$$

The maximum torque and power required for each joint motor of the exoskeleton robot are shown in Table 3.

Table 3. Motor spindle moment of inertia estimation and maximum torque and power required for each joint motor

	Motor 1	Motor 2	Motor 3
Moment of inertia (kg·m²)	0.86	0.24	0.5
Load torque (N·m)	5	8	3
power (W)	40	36.8	30

3 Kinematics Analysis

A joint coordinate system of the robot is established by the Denavit-Hartenberg (D-H) method (see Fig. 6). The x0-z0 represents the coordinate system (base coordinate system) of the robot base, and then the coordinate system of the joint 1 to the joint 3 is sequentially settled [14]. The D-H parameter table of the rehabilitation robot is shown in Table 4.

The kinematic equation is constructed as follows:

$$^0_1T = \begin{pmatrix} \cos\theta_1 & -\sin\theta_1 & 0 & 0 \\ \sin\theta_1 & \cos\theta_1 & 0 & 0 \\ 0 & 0 & 1 & 0 \\ 0 & 0 & 0 & 1 \end{pmatrix} \quad ^1_2T = \begin{pmatrix} \cos\theta_2 & -\sin\theta_2 & 0 & 0 \\ 0 & 0 & -1 & -L_1 \\ \sin\theta_2 & \cos\theta_2 & 0 & 0 \\ 0 & 0 & 0 & 1 \end{pmatrix}$$

$$^2_3T = \begin{pmatrix} \cos\theta_3 & -\sin\theta_3 & 0 & 0 \\ 0 & 0 & -1 & -L_2 \\ \sin\theta_3 & \cos\theta_3 & 0 & 0 \\ 0 & 0 & 0 & 1 \end{pmatrix}$$

$$^0_3T = {^0_1T}\,{^1_2T}\,{^2_3T} = \begin{pmatrix} n_x & o_x & a_x & p_x \\ n_y & o_y & a_y & p_y \\ n_z & o_z & a_z & p_z \\ 0 & 0 & 0 & 1 \end{pmatrix} \tag{4}$$

Table 4. The Denavit-Hartenberg parameters and values

Link	θ_i	α_i	a_i	d_i
1	θ_1	0	0	0
2	θ_2	90°	0	L_1
3	θ_3	90°	0	L_1

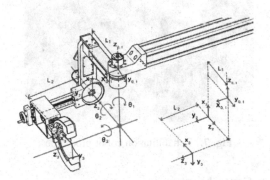

Fig. 6. Joint coordinate system of the robot

Algebraic methods are used to solve each joint variables.

$$\theta_1 = \arctan\frac{a_y}{a_x} \tag{5}$$

$$\theta_2 = \arcsin\left(\frac{p_x - L_1 \sin\theta_1}{L_2 cos_{\theta_1}}\right) \tag{6}$$

$$\theta_3 = \arcsin\left(\frac{n_z \sin\theta_1 - o_x \sin\theta_2}{\cos\theta_1 \cos\theta_1 \sin\theta_2}\right) \tag{7}$$

4   Prototype Production and Rehabilitation Training Experiment

4.1   Prototype Production

The physical prototype of the rehabilitation robot obtained after the finished components are assembled is shown in Fig. 7. Among them, the patient's arm is fixed by the binding strap on the component 3. The load of joint 1 and joint 2 should be the largest, then the motor power corresponding to joint 1 and joint 2 is 180 W, and joint 3 is 100 W. The driver of the motor is used as a slave node and a PC as a master node to form a can communication network [15]. The pc adds an usb-to-can expansion card to increase the ability of can communication.

Fig. 7. Rehabilitation robot prototype

4.2   Rehabilitation Control System

Rehabilitation robot system realizes passive rehabilitation training through software control. The main body of the software consists of ubuntu14.04 and Robot Operating System (ROS-indigo) [16, 17] built on the PC.

The entire software control system is divided into three layers: GUI, controller and driver (see Fig. 8). The GUI layer implements the control panel and 3D model of robot as a graphical user interface (see Fig. 9). Flexion/extension, abduction/adduction and internal/external are the basic movements of the shoulder joint and the important

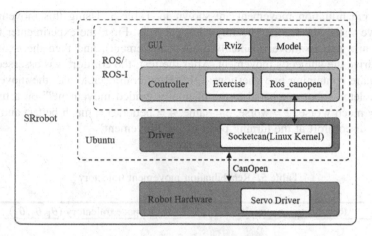

Fig. 8. Rehabilitation robot prototype

movements in the rehabilitation training. It is realized by exercise node and ros_-canopen node controlling the movement trajectory of the robot in the controller layer. Driver layer is mainly the driver of usb-to-can expansion card. In order to be more convenient and friendly than the traditional rehabilitation robot, we designed the Graphical User Interface at the GUI level to enable non-rehabilitation physicians to control the robot to perform rehabilitation on the patient as shown in Fig. 9.

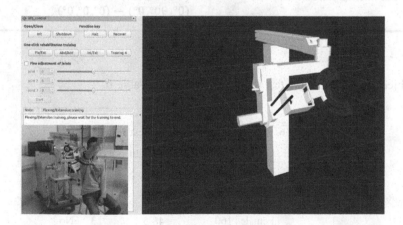

Fig. 9. Graphical user interface

4.3 Rehabilitation Training Experiment

The rehabilitation robot takes the initial pose as shown in Fig. 1. The direction of the axis of the joints J1, J2, and J3 points to the intersection point, and they comply with the right hand rule. The joint space trajectory and pictures of the robot leading the subject's rehabilitation movement are shown in Table 5. Using this movement trajectory, we tested six different healthy adult subjects. First, the experimenter took the subject's arm and to move (manually guided movement), and then the exoskeleton robot to drive the subject's movement. After the test, the comfort was assessed with a questionnaire containing two questions: Q1: "How comfortable was the movement in the exoskeleton robot compared to the manually guided movement?" on a five-point scale (1 = much worse, 2 = worse, 3 = same, 4 = better, 5 = much better) and Q2: "Is there any discomfort at the turning point of the movement".

Table 5. Rehabilitation movement trajectory

Rehabilitation exercise		Joint space trajectory $(\theta_1, \theta_2, \theta_3)$
flexion/extension		$(0°, 0°, 0°) \rightarrow (0°, -40°, 0°) \rightarrow$ $(0°, 90°, 0°) \rightarrow (0°, 0°, 0°)$
abduction/adduction		$(0°, 0°, 0°) \rightarrow (90°, 0°, 0°) \rightarrow$ $(90°, -40°, 0°) \rightarrow (90°, 90°, 0°) \rightarrow$ $(90°, 0°, 0°) \rightarrow (0°, 0°, 0°)$
internal/external rotation		$(0°, 0°, 0°) \rightarrow (0°, 90°, 0°) \rightarrow$ $(0°, 90°, 45°) \rightarrow (0°, 90°, -45°) \rightarrow$ $(0°, 90°, 0°) \rightarrow (0°, 0°, 0°)$

Subject information and test results are shown in Table 6.

Table 6. Subject information and test results

Subject number	Gender	Height (cm)	Weight (kg)	Q1	Q2
1	Male	170	66.3	3	No
2	Male	178	70.7	4	No
3	Male	185	75.1	3	No
4	Female	160	48.5	3	No
5	Female	164	49.1	3	No
6	Female	170	53.6	3	No

5 Conclusion and Outlook

This paper describes the design and implementation of an exoskeleton robot system for shoulder rehabilitation, in order to achieve a comfortable and friendly shoulder rehabilitation training. Based on the test results, we can see that to some extent, the exoskeleton robot is comfortable. This can also be used as a reference for further research later. However, the exoskeleton structure has not covered the entire upper limb, and the sample of the subject is not enough. Therefore, after that, we will further realize the entire upper limb exoskeleton structure, increase the sample of the subject, and add the active rehabilitation training mode [18, 19] for better rehabilitation.

Acknowledgments. This paper is supported by the Primary Research & Development Program of Jiangsu Province (Grant No. BE2015701), the Natural Science Foundation of Jiangsu Province, China (Grant No. BK20170898, BK20140878), the Opening Project of Southeast University Key Laboratory of Complex Engineering System of Measurement and Control of the Ministry of Education (Grant No. MCCSE2016A06), the Natural Science Foundation of Higher Education Institutions of Jiangsu Province, China (Grant No. 16KJB460017 and No. 17KJD535001), National Natural Science Foundation of China (61603195) and the NUPTSF (Grant No. NY215050 and No. NY218027).

References

1. Marichal, S., Malaisé, A., Modugno, V., Dermy, O., Charpillet, F., Ivaldi, S.: One-shot evaluation of the control interface of a robotic arm by non-experts. In: Agah, A., Cabibihan, J.-J., Howard, A.M., Salichs, M.A., He, H. (eds.) ICSR 2016. LNCS (LNAI), vol. 9979, pp. 458–468. Springer, Cham (2016). https://doi.org/10.1007/978-3-319-47437-3_45
2. Niyetkaliyev, A.S., Hussain, S., Ghayesh, M.H., Alici, G.: Review on design and control aspects of robotic shoulder rehabilitation orthoses. IEEE Trans. Hum.-Mach. Syst. **47**, 1134–1145 (2017)
3. Hu, W., et al.: A review of upper and lower limb rehabilitation training robot. In: Huang, Y., Wu, H., Liu, H., Yin, Z. (eds.) ICIRA 2017. LNCS (LNAI), vol. 10462, pp. 570–580. Springer, Cham (2017). https://doi.org/10.1007/978-3-319-65289-4_54
4. Krebs, H., et al.: Robot-aided neurorehabilitation: a robot for wrist rehabilitation. IEEE Trans. Neural Syst. Rehabil. Eng. **15**, 327–335 (2007)
5. Babaiasl, M., Mahdioun, S.H., Jaryani, P., Yazdani, M.: A review of technological and clinical aspects of robot-aided rehabilitation of upper-extremity after stroke. Disabil. Rehabil.: Assist. Technol. **11**(4), 263–280 (2016). https://doi.org/10.3109/17483107.2014
6. Okada, M., Nakamura, Y.: Development of a cybernetic shoulder-a 3-DOF mechanism that imitates biological shoulder motion. IEEE Trans. Robot. **21**, 438–444 (2005)
7. Chen, Y., Li, G., Zhu, Y., Zhao, J., Cai, H.: Design of a 6-DOF upper limb rehabilitation exoskeleton with parallel actuated joints. Bio-Med. Mater. Eng. **24**(6), 2527–2535 (2014)
8. Nef, T., Riener, R., Müri, R., Mosimann, U.P.: Comfort of two shoulder actuation mechanisms for arm therapy exoskeletons: a comparative study in healthy subjects. Med. Biol. Eng. Comput. **51**, 781–789 (2013)
9. Nef, T., Riener, R.: Shoulder actuation mechanisms for arm rehabilitation exoskeletons. In: 2008 2nd IEEE RAS & EMBS International Conference on Biomedical Robotics and Biomechatronics (2008)

10. Koo, D., Chang, P.H., Sohn, M.K., Shin, J.-H.: Shoulder mechanism design of an exoskeleton robot for stroke patient rehabilitation. In: 2011 IEEE International Conference on Rehabilitation Robotics (2011)
11. Nef, T., Guidali, M., Riener, R.: ARMin III – arm therapy exoskeleton with an ergonomic shoulder actuation. Appl. Bionics Biomech. **6**, 127–142 (2009)
12. Guo, Y., Ding, G.L., Li, Z.Q.: Development and application of a synchronous belt drive design system. Adv. Mater. Res. **971–973**, 450–453 (2014)
13. Ceccarelli, M., Carbone, G., Cafolla, D., Wang, M.: How to use 3D printing for feasibility check of mechanism design. In: Borangiu, T. (ed.) Advances in Robot Design and Intelligent Control. AISC, vol. 371, pp. 307–315. Springer, Cham (2016). https://doi.org/10.1007/978-3-319-21290-6_31
14. Xiao, F., Gao, Y., Wang, Y., Zhu, Y., Zhao, J.: Design and evaluation of a 7-DOF cable-driven upper limb exoskeleton. J. Mech. Sci. Technol. **32**, 855–864 (2018)
15. Zhang, Y.X., Zeng, X.Q., Wang, X.J.: Control system design based on CANopen network for multi-legged robot with hand-fused foot. In: Zhao, B., Zhang, Y.D., Wang, G.L., Zhang, H., Zhang, J.B., Jiao, F. (eds.) History of Mechanical Technology and Mechanical Design, vol. 42. Applied Mechanics and Materials, pp. 307–312 (2011)
16. Hernandez-Mendez, S., et al.: Design and implementation of a robotic arm using ROS and MoveIt! In: 2017 IEEE International Autumn Meeting on Power, Electronics and Computing (ROPEC) (2017)
17. ROS.org. http://wiki.ros.org/
18. Xu, G., Song, A., Li, H.: Control system design for an upper-limb rehabilitation robot. Adv. Robot. **25**, 229–251 (2011)
19. Kwakkel, G., Kollen, B.J., Krebs, H.I.: Effects of robot-assisted therapy on upper limb recovery after stroke: A systematic review. Neurorehabil. Neural Repair **22**(2), 111–121 (2008). https://doi.org/10.1177/1545968307305457

Cooperative Control of Sliding Mode
for Mobile Manipulators

Jorge Mora-Aguilar[(⊠)], Christian P. Carvajal[(⊠)],
Jorge S. Sánchez[(⊠)], and Víctor H. Andaluz[(⊠)]

Universidad de las Fuerzas Armadas ESPE, Sangolquí, Ecuador
{jlmora2, jssanchez, vhandaluz1}@espe.edu.ec,
chriss2592@hotmail.com

Abstract. This article describes the design and implementation of a centralized cooperative control algorithm of mobile manipulators (mobile differential platform manipulator and an omnidirectional platform manipulator) for the execution of diverse tasks in which the participation of two or more robots is necessary, e.g., the handling or transport of objects of a high weight, keeping a platform level at a fixed height, among others. For this, a sliding mode control technique is used that is applied to a fixed operating point located in a virtual line that is generated between the end effectors of the manipulator arms. For the validation of the proposed controller, the stability criterion of Lyapunov will be used and the simulation will be performed to validate the performance and performance of the proposed controller between two heterogeneous manipulators.

Keywords: Cooperative control · Mobile manipulators · Centralized control
Sliding mode control

1 Introduction

The human being throughout history, has specialized in developing multiple ways to manufacture machines or devices that manage to facilitate their daily life. The industry being one of the first areas in the automation of machinery and processes giving way to industrial robotics. However, the automation of processes is not only necessary for the development of the market, this new trend generated different investigations in the implementation of autonomous robots in everyday environments for the human, this generated the concept of service robotics that has been important for multiple applications in different areas and environments [1–5]. In this way, the development of terrestrial robots occurred due to their different physical configurations [6–8], and it has given way to the use of their advantages of locomotion for the development of more complex systems for the exponential increase of their applications, thus generating the concept of mobile manipulator.

The amount of research that has been done about mobile manipulators has been focused mainly on the control algorithms that can be implemented in this type of systems, thus producing applications in the area of education, mining, construction and multiple facilities in the industry. [9] There are several control techniques for mobile

© Springer Nature Switzerland AG 2018
S. S. Ge et al. (Eds.): ICSR 2018, LNAI 11357, pp. 253–264, 2018.
https://doi.org/10.1007/978-3-030-05204-1_25

manipulators that can be classified into two broad categories. The first one is the decoupled control scheme that is mainly based on separating both systems, *i.e.*, a controller for the mobile platform and a controller for the manipulator arm is generated. The second category is the coordinated control scheme; it proposes a combined control taking both robot parts as a single general system. One of the main challenges in the handling of these robots is the redundancy, both the kinematic redundancy that exists due to the surplus amount of degrees of freedom in the different actuators before the variables of the workspace, as well as the dynamic redundancy due to the quantity of forces and controlled pairs to perform a specific task. There are experiments based on a decentralized control scheme focused on a primary algorithm that controls the dynamic interactions of the final effector with the environment, and a secondary controller of null space to control internal reconfigurations and that the system does not conflict [10]. On the other hand, the main problem that exists when performing control of a mobile manipulator is coordination, due to the dynamic characteristics of the two systems, *i.e.*, the mobile platform has a slower dynamic response than the manipulator and if the mobile platform is non-holonomic, it generates restrictions, while the robotic arm normally has no restrictions on its movement [11]. In the named work, a coordinated control scheme based on the dynamics of the entire mobile manipulator is proposed; it has two internal controllers, a kinematic controller for speed saturation and a second controller that performs a dynamic compensation of the speeds calculated by the first controller [12]. Similarly, in the scientific community, one of the main challenges that exists at the level of control is the participation of two or more mobile manipulators to execute a task, thus generating the concept of cooperative control.

Like people, there are various actions that cannot be executed individually; this inevitably leads to the need for another or more individuals participate to carry out a task. In the case of mobile manipulators, it is necessary to coordinate them so that they fulfill a specific function, such as transporting a large or heavy object, lifting a platform at the same level, among others [13]. For this, appropriate information and the restrictions of each of the mobile manipulators must be efficiently shared in real time, in order to generate a robust closing force, without damaging the object to be transported. There are several control techniques for the cooperative control of mobile manipulators that can be classified into two broad categories: *(i) Decentralized Control*, this control scheme raises the objective of control each mobile manipulator independently, communicating with each other by sensors such as force sensors, infrared lasers and artificial vision, there are various control techniques for this type of decentralized scheme, *e.g.*, as the implementation of an algorithm for the control of multiple manipulators based on force sensors to be able to follow a specific trajectory, applying a diffuse control that adapts to various parameters as well as restrictions and disturbances [14]. *(ii) Centralized Control*, this is a control scheme that proposes the implementation of a controller for the system in general, *i.e.*, all mobile manipulators will work as a single system, there are different types of controllers developed as for centralized control, *e.g.*, an adaptive dynamic compensation controller based on a set of three manipulators formed a prism between the end effectors of the mobile manipulators in which the operating point is the centroid of the prism [15]. In the same way with regard to coordinated control systems, there is a controller based on numerical methods for two manipulator arms in which a virtual line is generated between both manipulators and a system is created based on an operating point that is located throughout of this virtual line [16].

This document proposes to perform the coordinated cooperative control of two heterogeneous mobile manipulators, *i.e.*, each manipulator will have a mobile base of different physical configuration than the other, based on a kinematic transformation focused on the form and position of an operation point. inside the object to be transported; this will be done through the implementation of a nonlinear control in a sliding way to perform the transfer of an object autonomously along a path defined by the user, demonstrating that this control algorithm has several advantages over others, since being a coordinated control, a single controller is required for both mobile manipulators.

2 Problem Structure

The control applied to the formation of robots is studied and applied by several researchers, who have seen remarkable advantages in implementing controllers in a group of robots so that they can manipulate or move an object from one place to another.

In the Fig. 1, the reference generator is in charge of configuring the initial input data (desired trajectory, the initial positions of the robots among others), depending on the application or task that is required to comply, *e.g.*; manipulate or carry an object from one place to another between two or more mobile manipulators, in environments dangerous to the human, regardless of the physical characteristics or configurations of the mobile manipulators.

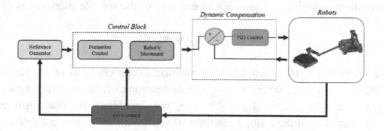

Fig. 1. Block diagram of the problem

The control block has been subdivided into two: *(i) Formation control:* in which the new references are configured, in such a way that the formation of the mobile manipulators reacts to the environment, *e.g.*; modify the trajectory to avoid obstacles detected by the different sensors. This controller will generate the desired reference signals from each of the operative ends of the mobile manipulators in order to fulfill the collaborative tasks. *(ii) Robot's Movement:* this control is responsible for coordinating the movements of mobile manipulators, considering the different control objectives, this control is the kinematics that is interested in the analytical description of the robot's spatial movement as a function of time, and in particular by the relations between the position and orientation of the operative end of the manipulator and the values taken by its joint coordinates.

In the dynamic compensation block, the different types of platforms that can be considered are: car like, omnidirectional and unicycle; as well as the degrees of freedom that the robotic arm has, in such a way that the dynamics of these can be compensated by means of the internal PID of each of the actuators that make up the mobile manipulator. The dynamics deals with the relationship between the forces that act on a body and the movement that originates in it as a result of them.

In the environment block, all the objects that surround the mobile manipulators are considered, including other mobile manipulators with their respective instrumentation system and sensors that provide feedback to the controllers in order to achieve their objective or task to be fulfilled.

3 Kinematic Transformation

The coordinated and cooperative control method consists of two mobile platforms each with robotic arms. The direct kinematic model of a manipulator arm $i - th$ of n_a degrees of freedom is given by:

$$\dot{\mathbf{h}}_{ai} = \mathbf{J}_a(q_{1i}, q_{2i}, \ldots, q_{ni})\dot{\mathbf{q}}_{ai} \tag{1}$$

In which the matrix $\dot{\mathbf{h}}_{ai} \in R^{m_a}$ represents the coordinates of the end effector to the system of reference coordinates $<G>$, m_a represents the dimensions of the workspace where the system acts; $\mathbf{J}_a \in R^{m_a \times n_a}$ is the Jacobian matrix in function of the $\dot{q}_{ni}$ actuators; n_a are the degrees of freedom of the robotic arm; and finally $\dot{\mathbf{q}}_i \in R^{n_a}$ are the actuators of the manipulator. The direct kinematics of the mobile platform is given by:

$$\dot{\mathbf{h}}_{pi} = \mathbf{J}_{pi}(\psi)\mathbf{v}_{pi} \tag{2}$$

where the vector $\dot{\mathbf{h}}_{pi} \in R^{m_p}$ represents the position of the centroid of the mobile platform in the $X - Y$ plane, where m_p are the dimensions of the working space of the mobile platform. The matrix $\mathbf{J}_{pi} \in R^{m_p \times n_p}$ is the Jacobian one that represents the internal configuration of the mobile platform; ψ represents the rotation angle respect to axis Z of $<G>$; n_p are the degrees of freedom of the system and $\mathbf{V}_{pi} \in R^{n_p}$ are the velocities applied to each of the actuators of the mobile platform.

Given the kinematic model of each of the components of the system, the mobile manipulator can be generalized as:

$$\begin{bmatrix} \dot{h}_{yi} \\ \dot{h}_{yi} \\ \dot{h}_{zi} \end{bmatrix} = \mathbf{J}_{Ti}(\psi, q)\begin{bmatrix} \mathbf{v}_{mi} \\ \dot{\mathbf{q}}_{ai} \end{bmatrix} \tag{3}$$

in which $\mathbf{J_{Ti}} \in R^{m \times n}$ is the Jacobian matrix of the behavior of the mobile manipulator, $m = m_a + m_p$ is the working space of the mobile manipulator and $n = n_a + n_p$ are the DOF of it.

The control technique consists of generating a virtual connection between the end-effectors of the mobile manipulators and locating an operation point along this virtual line, as is shown in Fig. 2. This operating point has a position in the plane given by the vector $\mathbf{P_F}$ that represents the coordinates in the axes X, Y, Z of a R^3 reference system, $<G>$. In the same way, the virtual line that joins the two final end-effectors of the manipulators has a vector of form given by $\mathbf{S_F} = [D_F \quad \beta_F \quad \alpha_F]^T$, D_F is the distance between the end-effectors; α_F is the angle of rotation of the line with respect to the axis Z of the workspace, $<G>$; and β_F is the angle of elevation or depression that the virtual line has.

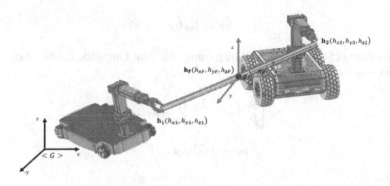

Fig. 2. Manipulators mobile's configuration.

The location of the operation point will be made in the centroid of the virtual line that joins both end effectors, taking into account the following parameters:

$$
\mathbf{S_F} = \begin{bmatrix} D_F = \sqrt{(h_{x2} - h_{x1})^2 + (h_{y2} - h_{y1})^2 + (h_{z2} - h_{z1})^2} \\ \alpha_F = \tan^{-1}\left(\frac{h_{zF}}{h_{xF}}\right) \\ \beta_F = \tan^{-1}\left(\frac{h_{yF}}{h_{xF}}\right) \end{bmatrix} ; \mathbf{P_F}
$$

$$
= \begin{bmatrix} h_{xF} = \dfrac{h_{x1} + h_{x2}}{2} \\ h_{yF} = \dfrac{h_{y1} + h_{y2}}{2} \\ h_{zF} = \dfrac{h_{z1} + h_{z2}}{2} \end{bmatrix} (4)
$$

The general modeling of the plant is given by the following equation:

$$\dot{\mathbf{h}}_T = \begin{bmatrix} \mathbf{J}_{T1} & 0 \\ 0 & \mathbf{J}_{T2} \end{bmatrix} \boldsymbol{\mu}_T = \mathbf{J}_{TS}\boldsymbol{\mu}_T \tag{5}$$

in which the vector $\dot{\mathbf{h}}_T \in R^{2m}$ is the vector of the positions of the final effectors of each of the mobile manipulators with respect to $<G>$; $\mathbf{J}_{TS} \in R^{2m \times 2n}$ is the total Jacobian of the system constituted by the Jacobian of each one of the mobile manipulators; and $\boldsymbol{\mu}_T \in R^{2n}$ represents the velocities of DOFs to be controlled of the system.

By deriving the matrix of position $\mathbf{P}_F$ and the matrix of form $\mathbf{S}_F$ from the point of operation to be able to obtain their respective kinematic models with respect to $\dot{\mathbf{h}}_T$.

$$\dot{\mathbf{P}}_F = \mathbf{J}_{PF}\dot{\mathbf{h}}_T \tag{6}$$

$$\dot{\mathbf{S}}_F = \mathbf{J}_{SF}\dot{\mathbf{h}}_T \tag{7}$$

By replacing (5) in (6) and (7) thus forming the final kinematic model of the system of two mobile manipulators.

$$\begin{bmatrix} \dot{\mathbf{S}}_F \\ \dot{\mathbf{P}}_F \end{bmatrix} = \begin{bmatrix} \mathbf{J}_{SF}\mathbf{J}_{TS} \\ \mathbf{J}_{PF}\mathbf{J}_{TS} \end{bmatrix} \boldsymbol{\mu}_T(t)$$

$$\dot{\boldsymbol{\rho}}_T = \mathbf{J}_{SP}\mathbf{J}_{TS}\boldsymbol{\mu}_T(t) \tag{8}$$

4   Controller Design

It is proposed a control by variable structure, same that by its robustness is applied in multiple applications for nonlinear systems and variants in time, the controller configuration is given by:

$$\boldsymbol{\mu}_C(t) = \boldsymbol{\upsilon}_C(t) + \boldsymbol{\upsilon}_D(t) \tag{9}$$

Where, $\boldsymbol{\upsilon}_C(t)$ is the continuous part, which allows the system to remain on the sliding surface and $\boldsymbol{\upsilon}_D(t)$ represents the discontinuous part of the controller, this one allows the system to look for the sliding surface. Considering the kinematic model of the system (8):

$$\dot{\boldsymbol{\rho}}_T = \mathbf{J}_{SP}\mathbf{J}_{TS}\boldsymbol{\mu}(t) \tag{10}$$

Where is the vector that contains the velocities of the operating coordinates of the training-posture system, $\boldsymbol{\mu}(t) = \begin{bmatrix} \boldsymbol{\upsilon}_{R1} & \boldsymbol{\upsilon}_{R2} \end{bmatrix}$ represents the vector of all maneuverability velocities of each robot that is part of the system.

Case I: for the unicycle type manipulator $\boldsymbol{\upsilon}_R = \begin{bmatrix} u & \omega & \dot{q}_1 & \dot{q}_2 & \dot{q}_3 \dots \dot{q}_n \end{bmatrix}$ where $\boldsymbol{\upsilon}_{R1} \in \Re^m$.

Case II: for the omnidirectional type manipulator $\upsilon_R = \begin{bmatrix} u_l & u_m & \omega & \dot{q}_1 & \dot{q}_2 \end{bmatrix}$ $\dot{q}_3 \ldots \dot{q}_n]$ where $\upsilon_R \in \Re^m$.

A sliding surface of the form is proposed:

$$s = \widetilde{\rho}_T + \lambda \int \widetilde{\rho}_T dt \tag{11}$$

where $\widetilde{\rho}_T$ is the vector of training errors and system position, the partial derivative to (11) is applied, and the following equation is presented:

$$\dot{s} = \dot{\widetilde{\rho}}_T + \lambda \widetilde{\rho}_T \tag{12}$$

it is known that the error of training and posture is obtained as $\widetilde{\rho}_T = \rho_d - \rho_T$, in the same way deriving it is obtained:

$$\dot{\widetilde{\rho}}_T = \dot{\rho}_d - \dot{\rho}_T \tag{13}$$

For the continuous part υ_C we have $\dot{s} = 0$, since it is considered that the system is on the sliding surface, substituting (13) in (12) is presented:

$$0 = \dot{\rho}_d - \dot{\rho}_T + \lambda \dot{\rho}_T \tag{14}$$

although, replacing (10) in (14) and $\mu = \upsilon_C$ is obtained $0 = \dot{\rho}_d - J_{SP} J_{TS} \upsilon_C + \lambda \dot{\rho}_T$, then υ_C is defined as:

$$\upsilon_C = J_{TS}^+ J_{SP}^+ (\dot{\rho}_d + \lambda \dot{\rho}_T) \tag{15}$$

where, $J_{TS}^+ J_{SP}^+$ are the pseudo-inverse matrices. For the discontinuous part υ_D is analyzed by means of the Lyapunov's stability where:

$$V = ss^T \tag{16}$$

by deriving (16) is defined as $\dot{V} = s^T \dot{s}$, replacing (12) and applying that $\dot{\widetilde{\rho}}_T = \dot{\rho}_d - \dot{\rho}_T$ it is obtained:

$$\dot{V} = s^T (\dot{\rho}_d - \dot{\rho}_T + \lambda \widetilde{\rho}_T) \tag{17}$$

replacing (10) in (16) and $\mu = \upsilon_C$, is obtained:

$$\dot{V} = s^T (\dot{\rho}_d - J_{SP} J_{TS} \upsilon_C + \lambda \widetilde{\rho}_T) \tag{18}$$

If in (15) is defined υ_C and the sliding control is composed by $\mu_C = \upsilon_C + \upsilon_D$, supplying $\mu_C = J_{SP}^+ J_{TS}^+ (\dot{\rho}_d + \lambda \dot{\rho}_T) + \upsilon_D$ thus:

$$\dot{V} = s^T \left(\dot{\boldsymbol{\rho}}_d - \mathbf{J}_{SP}\mathbf{J}_{TS} \left(\mathbf{J}_{SP}^+ \mathbf{J}_{TS}^+ (\dot{\boldsymbol{\rho}}_d + \lambda \dot{\boldsymbol{\rho}}_T) + \upsilon_D \right) + \lambda \widetilde{\boldsymbol{\rho}}_T \right) \tag{19}$$

then:

$$\dot{V} = s^T \left(\dot{\boldsymbol{\rho}}_d - \mathbf{J}_{SP}\mathbf{J}_{TS}\mathbf{J}_{TS}^+ \mathbf{J}_{SP}(\dot{\boldsymbol{\rho}}_d + \lambda \dot{\boldsymbol{\rho}}_T) - \mathbf{J}_{SP}\mathbf{J}_{TS}\upsilon_D + \lambda \widetilde{\boldsymbol{\rho}}_T \right) \tag{20}$$

as $\mathbf{J}_{SP}\left(\mathbf{J}_{TS}\mathbf{J}_{TS}^+\right)\mathbf{J}_{SP}^+ = \mathbf{J}_{SP}(\mathbf{I})\mathbf{J}_{SP}^+$ and $\mathbf{J}_{SP}(\mathbf{I})\mathbf{J}_{SP}^+ = \mathbf{I}$ then (20) is reduced to:

$$\dot{V} = s^T \left(\dot{\boldsymbol{\rho}}_d - \dot{\boldsymbol{\rho}}_d - \lambda \dot{\boldsymbol{\rho}}_T - \mathbf{J}_{SP}\mathbf{J}_{TS}\upsilon_D + \lambda \widetilde{\boldsymbol{\rho}}_T \right)$$

$$\dot{V} = s^T \left(-\mathbf{J}_{SP}\mathbf{J}_{TS}\upsilon_D \right) \tag{21}$$

If $V < 0$, by Lyapunov's stability is defined as:

$$\upsilon_D = \mathbf{J}_{TS}^+ \mathbf{J}_{SP}^+ \mathbf{K}_1 sgn(s) \tag{22}$$

by substituting (22) in (21):

$$\dot{V} = -s^T \mathbf{J}_{SP}\mathbf{J}_{TS}\mathbf{J}_{TS}^+ \mathbf{J}_{SP}^+ \mathbf{K}_1 sgn(s) \tag{23}$$

as $\mathbf{J}_{SP}\mathbf{J}_{TS}\mathbf{J}_{TS}^+ \mathbf{J}_{SP}^+ = \mathbf{I}$ (23) is expressed as:

$$\dot{V} = -s^T \mathbf{K}_1 sgn(s) \tag{24}$$

As $\mathbf{K}_1$ is a vector with positive gains, then $\dot{V} < 0$ and thus the Lyapunov's stability is verified. If $\lambda > 0$ of υ_C, i.e., $s \to 0$, therefore the system manage to reach the sliding surface and the training and posture errors $\widetilde{\boldsymbol{\rho}}_T \to 0$ tends to 0. To reduce the oscillations in the compensation asymptotically of the value $s(t) = 0$, it is replaced $sgn(s)$ with the sigmoid function.

$$\upsilon_D = \mathbf{J}_{TS}^+ \mathbf{J}_{SP}^+ \mathbf{K}_1 \frac{s}{|s| + \delta} \tag{25}$$

Where $\delta > 0$, then the sliding mode controller is defined replacing (25) y (15) in (9):

$$\boldsymbol{\mu}_C = \mathbf{J}_{TS}^+ \mathbf{J}_{SP}^+ \left(\dot{\boldsymbol{\rho}}_d + \lambda \dot{\boldsymbol{\rho}}_T + \mathbf{K}_1 \frac{s}{|s| + \delta} \right) \tag{26}$$

5 Results

For the validation of the controller for formation and position, two mobile devices are used, one of them has a mobile platform unicycle type and the other for an omnidirectional platform, both have a built-in device. They have six and seven DOF, respectively, as shown in Fig. 3.

Fig. 3. Mobile manipulators: omnidirectional and unicycle platforms

The following task is proposed in which two heterogeneous mobile manipulators move an object autonomously in a desired path is given by: $x_d = \frac{3}{5}t + 1$, $y_d = \sin\left(\frac{1}{5}t\right) + \frac{3}{100}t$ and $z_d = \frac{1}{10}\sin\left(\frac{1}{5}t\right) + \frac{1}{2}$ which throughout its journey will maintain a form given by: $D_F = 1.5$ [m], $\alpha_F = 0$ [rad], finally during the time interval of execution of 30 to 60 [s], the formation will have a rotation of $\beta_F = \arctan\left(\frac{\dot{y}_d}{\dot{x}_d}\right) + \frac{\pi}{2}$; it is the angle perpendicular to the desired trajectory.

Figure 4 shows the Stroboscopic movement of the robots transporting the object, it can be seen that the proposed task is executed correctly.

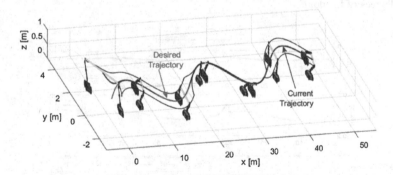

Fig. 4. Stroboscopic movement of the mobile manipulators.

In the Fig. 5 observe the control errors both for system formation and posture respectively, and tend to zero asymptotically keeping the system stable.

The maneuverability velocities of each mobile manipulator applied generated by the controller are shown in Figs. 6 and 7.

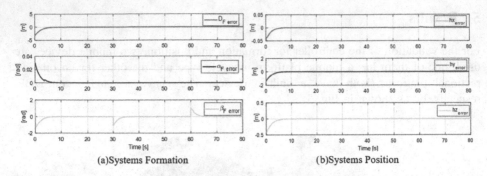

(a)Systems Formation   (b)Systems Position

Fig. 5. Control errors

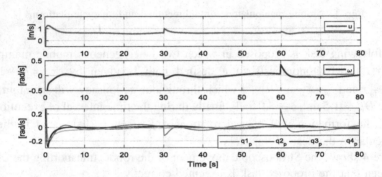

Fig. 6. Maniobrability velocity of mobile manipulator of platform differential with robotic arm of four degrees of freedom.

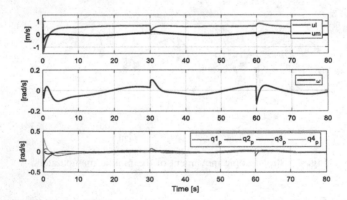

Fig. 7. Maniobrability velocity of mobile manipulator of omnidirectional platform with robotic arm of four degrees of freedom.

Acknowledgements. The authors would like to thanks to the Corporación Ecuatoriana para el Desarrollo de la Investigación y Academia –CEDIA for the financing given to research, development, and innovation, through the CEPRA projects, especially the project CEPRA-XI-2017- 06;

Control Coordinado Multi-operador aplicado a un robot Manipulador Aéreo; also to Universidad de las Fuerzas Armadas ESPE, Universidad Técnica de Ambato, Escuela Superior Politécnica de Chimborazo, and Universidad Nacional de Chimborazo, and Grupo de Investigación en Automatización, Robótica y Sistemas Inteligentes, GI-ARSI, for the support to develop this work.

References

1. Ollero, A., Merino, L.: Control and perception techniques for aerial robotics. Ann. Rev. Control **28**(2), 167–178 (2004)
2. Andaluz, V.H., et al.: Nonlinear controller of quadcopters for agricultural monitoring. In: Bebis, G., et al. (eds.) ISVC 2015. LNCS, vol. 9474, pp. 476–487. Springer, Cham (2015). https://doi.org/10.1007/978-3-319-27857-5_43
3. Williams, S.B., Pizarro, O., Mahon, I., Johnson-Roberson, M.: Simultaneous localisation and mapping and dense stereoscopic seafloor reconstruction using an AUV. In: Khatib, O., Kumar, V., Pappas, G.J. (eds.) Experimental Robotics. Springer Tracts in Advanced Robotics, vol. 54. Springer, Heidelberg (2009). https://doi.org/10.1007/978-3-642-00196-3_47
4. Kuwata, Y., Wolf, M.T., Zarzhitsky, D., Huntsberger, T.L.: Safe maritime autonomous navigation with COLREGS, using velocity obstacles. IEEE J. Ocean. Eng. **39**(1), 110–119 (2014)
5. Tsai, C.C., Huang, H.C., Lin, S.C.: FPGA-based parallel DNA algorithm for optimal configurations of an omnidirectional mobile service robot performing fire extinguishment. IEEE Trans. Ind. Electron. **58**(3), 1016–1026 (2011)
6. Haddad, M., Khalil, W., Lehtihet, H.E.: Trajectory planning of unicycle mobile robots with a trapezoidal-velocity constraint. IEEE Trans. Robot. **26**(5), 954–962 (2010)
7. Li, T.H.S., Chang, S.J.: Autonomous fuzzy parking control of a car-like mobile robot. IEEE Trans. Syst. Man Cybern. Part A Syst. Hum. **33**(4), 451–465 (2003)
8. Kanjanawanishkul, K., Zell, A.: Path following for an omnidirectional mobile robot based on model predictive control. In: IEEE International Conference on Robotics and Automation 2009, ICRA 2009, pp. 3341–3346 (2009)
9. Bischoff, R., Huggenberger, U., Prassler, E.: KUKA youBot - a mobile manipulator for research and education. In: Proceedings of IEEE International Conference on Robotics and Automation, pp. 3–6 (2011)
10. White, G.D., Bhatt, R.M., Tang, C.P., Krovi, V.N.: Experimental evaluation of dynamic redundancy resolution in a nonholonomic wheeled mobile manipulator. IEEE/ASME Trans. Mechatron. **14**(3), 349–357 (2009)
11. Zhong, G., Kobayashi, Y., Hoshino, Y., Emaru, T.: System modeling and tracking control of mobile manipulator subjected to dynamic interaction and uncertainty. Nonlinear Dyn. **73**(1–2), 167–182 (2013)
12. Andaluz, V., Roberti, F., Toibero, J.M., Carelli, R.: Adaptive unified motion control of mobile manipulators. Control Eng. Pract. **20**(12), 1337–1352 (2012)
13. Erhart, S., Sieber, D., Hirche, S.: An impedance-based control architecture for multi-robot cooperative dual-arm mobile manipulation. In: IEEE International Conference on Intelligent Robots and Systems, pp. 315–322 (2013)
14. Li, Z., Yang, C., Su, C.Y., Deng, S., Sun, F., Zhang, W.: Decentralized fuzzy control of multiple cooperating robotic manipulators with impedance interaction. IEEE Trans. Fuzzy Syst. **23**(4), 1044–1056 (2015)

15. Andaluz, V.H., Ortiz, J.S., Pérez, M., Roberti, F., Carelli, R.: Adaptive cooperative control of multi-mobile manipulators. In: IECON Proceedings of Industrial Electronic Conference, pp. 2669–2675 (2014)
16. Andaluz, V.H., Molina, M.F., Erazo, Y.P., Ortiz, J.S.: Numerical methods for cooperative control of double mobile manipulators. In: Huang, Y., Wu, H., Liu, H., Yin, Z. (eds.) ICIRA 2017. LNCS (LNAI), vol. 10463, pp. 889–898. Springer, Cham (2017). https://doi.org/10.1007/978-3-319-65292-4_77

When Should a Robot Apologize?
Understanding How Timing Affects Human-Robot Trust Repair

Mollik Nayyar[(✉)] and Alan R. Wagner

The Pennsylvania State University, University Park, PA 16802, USA
{mxn244, alan. r. wagner}@psu. edu

Abstract. If robots are to occupy a space in the human social sphere, then the importance of trust naturally extends to human-robot interactions. Past research has examined human-robot interaction from a number of perspectives, ranging from overtrust in human robot interactions to trust repair. Studies by [15] have suggested a relationship between the success of a trust repair method and the time at which it is employed. Additionally, studies have shown a potentially dangerous tendency in humans to trust robotic systems beyond their operational capacity. It therefore becomes essential to explore the factors that affect trust in greater depth. The study presented in this paper is aimed at building upon previous work to gain insight into the reasons behind the success of trust repair methods and their relation to timing. Our results show that the delayed trust repair is more effective than the early case, which is consistent with the previous results. In the absence of an emergency, the participant's decision were similar to those of a random selection. Additionally, there seem to be a strong influence of attention on the participants' decision to follow the robot.

Keywords: Social robotics · HRI · Trust · Trust repair

1 Introduction

Trust in human interpersonal interactions is an integral component of human social behavior. It facilitates a number of fundamental interactions that are essential for our economic and social systems. Robots will play an increasingly important role in the human social sphere in the near future. It is therefore valuable to examine the concept of trust for human-robot interactions.

A variety of applications are currently being explored for robots to assist human beings in everyday life. One such application is robot assisted emergency evacuation [18, 19]. Robot assisted emergency evacuation may save lives by being constantly vigilant and providing valuable situation awareness to first responders. However, since the reliability of robots cannot be guaranteed, trusting these systems can potentially put evacuees and first responders at risk. Since robots will be used in multiple domains such as transportation, healthcare, and the military, developing an understanding of human-robot trust is crucial for safe introduction of robotic applications.

© Springer Nature Switzerland AG 2018
S. S. Ge et al. (Eds.): ICSR 2018, LNAI 11357, pp. 265–274, 2018.
https://doi.org/10.1007/978-3-030-05204-1_26

Past research in this domain has highlighted various aspects of human robot trust. In particular, [14] show that during emergencies, even in cases where the robot exhibits poor prior performance, people nevertheless tend to rely on it rather than their own instincts. In cases where trust is violated due to poor performance, it has been shown that a robot can repair trust by promising to do better or apologizing for mistakes if the robot promises or apologies at the right time [15]. The study in this paper is aimed at building upon this previous work to tease apart why the timing of trust repair statements impact a person's trust in an autonomous system. We hope to identify factors that affect trust repair. Any insight gained here will help us develop better models of trust from a human-robot perspective and will aid in our understanding of trust in general.

The following sections first present a small portion of the human-robot trust literature, focusing primarily on research related to trust repair. Next we present insights related to the how timing may impact trust repair. We then introduce our experimental setup and the different experimental cases are discussed. We conclude with results from simulation experiments involving 558 human subjects and a discussion of the insights these findings offer towards understanding human-robot trust repair.

2 Related Work

Researchers generally agree that trust-based decisions are characterized by situation in which the trustor is vulnerable and/or at risk and the actions of another individual can relieve or mitigate that risk [6, 8]. For humans interacting with robots or automated systems, human-like features such as politeness, facial features, and the system's speech, have been shown to increase trust [10, 12]. Humans also show a tendency to initially trust automated systems [2, 3, 7], even when they have no experience with the system. With experience, a person's trust in a system may be based on performance [7]. Handcock et al. [4] found that robot's performance had the strongest effect on trust. Yet it has also been shown that people will quickly come to overtrust automated systems and robots [11].

Most of these results have utilized relatively low-risk experimental paradigms such as economic games [5] or use of automated avatars for automated decision-making [13]. In contrast, our research focuses on human-robot trust in physically risky situations such as during search and rescue scenarios. Comparatively few studies have explored trust and the use of robots in emergency scenarios. Atkinson and Clark looked at different methodologies of studying human-robot interaction in a dangerous situation and found that human behavior carries forward to virtual environments and virtual simulations can be an effective method to study human-robot interactions [1].

Our own work has examined a variety of aspects related to robot led emergency evacuation. We have explored robot appearance [16], communication techniques [17], overtrust on a physical robot [14], and trust repair [15]. The research presented here builds upon our previous work on trust repair during emergency evacuations which shows that mistakes by a robot result in a sharp decrease in trust after the mistake, yet it was also shown that trust can be repaired if the robot apologizes or promises to do better. *Most importantly, this work demonstrated that the effectiveness of a trust repair statement strongly depends on the timing of the statement's delivery.* This paper attempts to dissect the reasons why the timing of a trust repair message by a robot impacts a person's trust in the system.

3 Trust Repair Timing

In our prior simulation research, a robot offered to lead a human subject to a meeting room, but made mistakes enroute to the room, eventually arriving at the location. In one condition, the robot apologized or promised immediately after the mistake. An emergency then occurred while the subject was in the meeting room and the subject was informed that they needed to quickly find an exit or their character would perish. The same robot offered to lead the subject to an exit. In a second, different condition, the robot apologized just prior to the subject deciding whether or not to follow the robot during the emergency. Figure 1 depicts the timing of the study's stages.

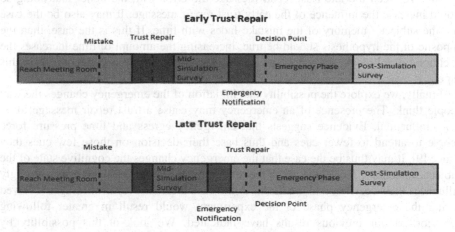

Fig. 1. A timeline of events in the experiment is depicted. The key difference is when the mistake, trust repair and decision point occurred. (Color figure online)

This research showed that only 40% of subjects followed the robot when it apologized or promised just after a mistake yet, 79% choose to follow the robot if it made the same apology or promise during the emergency [15]. Non-repair messages such as greetings or otherwise innocuous statements, on the other hand, do not repair trust. The study also revealed that trust does break when the robot makes a mistake and that the emergency strongly motivates people to find an exit quickly. But it was unclear why the timing of the trust repair statement (apology or promise) had such a large effect on people's decision whether or not to follow the robot.

The research presented here investigates several different hypotheses as to why the timing of trust repair statement might impact a person's decision to trust. Our previous experiments suggest several potential factors that might influence the importance of timing of trust repair messages. Our first step was to reproduce our prior results. Next, we examined if it is possible that the trust repair does not need to be read and internalized in order to influence the person. It might be possible that simply presenting a message will subconsciously influence the person. If this is the case, then we predict that reducing the display time of the message would result in the same tendency to follow the robot for the late trust repair message. We test this idea by varying the amount of time that the message is displayed. A manipulation check at the conclusion of the study asked subjects which trust repair statement was presented to them. Subjects that failed the manipulation check were excluded from the data.

We then consider the possibility that the trust repair message changes the subject's impression of the robot but that this change of impression is short-lived. If this is the case then the influence of the early repair statement may have faded by the time of the emergency, generating the results seen experimentally. We hypothesize that by reducing the amount of time between the early trust repair statement and the decision to follow the robot during the emergency, early repair statements will be more effective. To test this hypothesis we changed the length of the Mid-Simulation Survey reducing the time between the late trust repair message the error with the belief that doing so would increase the influence of the early trust repair message. It may also be the case that the subject's memory of the mistake fades with time. If this is the case, than the opposite of the hypothesis should be true, increasing the amount of time increases the likelihood of following the robot. We *do not* investigate this second hypothesis in this paper.

Finally, we explore the possibility that initiation of the emergency changes the way people think. The presence of an emergency may cause a trust repair message to be more influential. Evidence suggests that emergency egress and time pressure force people to attend to fewer cues and thus base their decision on those few cues they notice [9]. It may thus be the case that the emergency changes the cognitive state of the subject, influencing them to focus on the robot's repair statement which in turn strongly influences their decision-making. If this is the case then trust repair messages received during the emergency phase of the experiment would result in greater following behavior, as our previous results have indicated. We look at this possibility by removing the emergency, hypothesizing that a lack of emergency would result in a lack of subject motivation to exit resulting in approximately random subject decisions to follow.

4 Simulation Setup

The experiment is based on an online simulation environment created in Unity3D and a self-report survey embedded into the simulation. In addition to the survey data, participant's performance data is collected which includes their motion data, the time taken, exit route etc. The experiment starts with an on screen welcome and introduction, participants were offered a practice session without a robot in a different environment to familiarize themselves with their character and moving through the simulation. Once comfortable, they then proceed to the *Initial Navigation Phase* of the experiment (Fig. 1 blue). In this phase, participants are placed outside an office environment and their objective is to navigate to reach an internal meeting room. They are offered a guidance robot to lead them to the meeting room. The robot, however, makes mistakes leading them in a circuitous, inefficient route to the meeting room. In prior experiments we asked the participants to rate the robot's performance after taking the circuitous route and found that a vast majority of the subjects rated its performance as a guide as bad. After reaching the meeting room the participants move to the center of the room where they are able to see the robot. The robot then thanks the participant for following it to the room. Next, depending on the experimental condition, the robot either presents a trust repair message (Fig. 1 green) or the subject is presented with a mid-simulation survey which consists of Yes/No questions regarding the robot's performance and an opportunity for them to explain their answer (Fig. 1 orange). The final screen informs the participants about an emergency and asks the participants to leave the building (Fig. 1 red). Upon clicking next, the participants are again free to navigate the building (Fig. 1 purple). The robot waits outside the room and in conditions with late trust repair, will present the participant with a trust repair message. This is the decision point where the participant may choose to either use the robot for guidance to the exit or find their own way out from memory, following exit signs, or exploring. An on-screen timer informs the participants of the time they have left to exit the building. The simulation stops when the time runs out and the participants are presented with the post simulation survey screen (Fig. 1 light blue). The post-simulation survey consists of a manipulation check to ensure that participants were paying attention to the robot's trust repair message and other questions regarding the participant's decisions in the simulation. The questions are designed as binary Yes/No questions along with a paragraph response space to allow them to provide reasons for their responses. Figure 1 depicts a timeline of the major events in the experiment. The top timeline describes a condition in which trust is repaired early in the experiment. The second timeline describes a condition with late trust repair.

5 Experiments

Previous studies have examined the basic cases of early and late trust repair with varying messages types such as different kinds of apology and promises, attributing the poor performance to external or internal factors etc. [15]. Our objective here is to investigate whether it is possible to tease apart the factors that cause a delayed trust repair statement to be more successful. To that end, we ran multiple simulations with varying the experimental conditions as part of an exploratory study. For each condition, we enlisted 60 participants in a between-subject study with different conditions being the independent variable. Out of the 60 participants, we removed the participants that had failed the manipulation check as described previously, which resulted in an average sample of 35 participants in each of the conditions.

We examined four different independent variables. The *first independent variable* we examined was the timing of the trust repair message (early versus late). Examination of this independent variable was meant to replicate our previous study. In the early trust repair condition, as with our previous studies, the participant is presented with a trust repair after reaching the meeting room (see Fig. 1 top for timeline see Fig. 2 for example). In the late trust repair message condition, the trust repair message is presented during the emergency phase. For this condition, as the participant moves out of the room the robot can be seen with a speech bubble displaying a trust repair message. This message is displayed for the remaining portion of the emergency phase as long as the robot remains in the field of view of the participant.

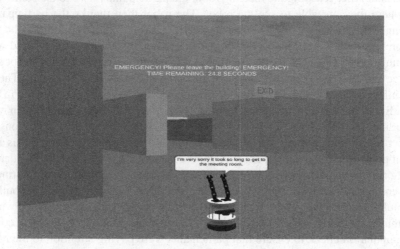

Fig. 2. Late trust repair message Screen. The emergency notice and timer are also depicted above the robot. This is the point at which the person must decide whether to follow the robot to the left, the emergency exit sign to the right, or go straight forward which is the way they came.

The *second independent* variable that we examined was the amount of time that the late repair message was displayed. After examining the initial results, it seemed that the length of time that the message displayed could have served as a confounding variable. Moreover, we hypothesized that the message needed to be internalized in order to be effective. We reasoned that brief messages would be less impactful because they are less likely to be considered by the participant. This condition differed only in the duration for which the late trust repair message bubble was displayed by the robot. We looked at 3 s and 5 s message display times.

A *third variable* that could impact the effect of trust repair messages is the length of time between the early and late messages. We hypothesized that the impact of the trust repair statement might be short lived. To investigate how length of time influences trust repair we varied the amount of time between the early repair message and the decision point in the emergency phase (see Fig. 1). To do this the mid-simulation survey was shortened to the Yes-No question only. This condition was otherwise identical to the prior conditions. Both the early and late cases were run for this category. The late case was the untimed version.

A *final variable examined* was whether or not framing the simulation as an emergency motivated subjects. To vary this variable, the emergency message screen was compared to simply asking the participants to leave the building. In this no emergency condition, the timer was also removed from the screen, though it was still running in the background. When the timer ran out, a message was displayed on screen informing the participants that they were unable to leave from the building in time. Both early and late (untimed) cases were run for this category.

The experiments were hosted on Amazon Mechanical Turk (AMT). The 'master' category qualification was used to select workers. Subjects were only allowed to participate once. Participants who failed the manipulation check were excluded from the analysis. The metric used to measure trust is the probability of following the robot to an exit versus not following the robot.

6 Results

A total of 558 participants were a part of the study, out of which, 35 submissions were considered invalid due to bad surveys, repeated attempts, etc. 234 participants failed the embedded manipulation check in the experiment and hence were excluded from the results. The results obtained from the experiments are presented in the Fig. 3. The difference in the percentage of participants following the robot to the exit in the Early and Late repair case can be clearly observed. These results are consistent with those of [15] where this phenomenon was first examined. We used chi-squared test for significance.

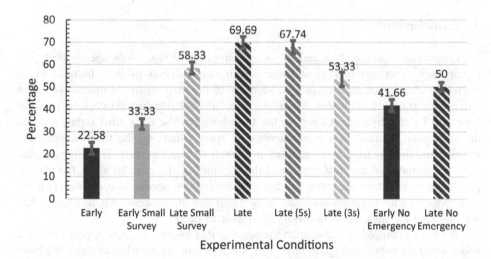

Fig. 3. Results of all cases of the experiment. The change in trust in each case is clearly visible. Early conditions are in solid color and Late conditions are in downward diagonals. (Color figure online)

Results for the first independent variable, *early versus late repair messages*, are depicted in blue in Fig. 3 and reproduce our prior results [15] with $(\chi^2(1, 64) = 14.24, p < 0.001)$. The results for the second independent variable, *the length of time the late repair message was displayed*, is depicted in orange diagonals for 5 s and yellow diagonals for 3 s in Fig. 3. The percentage of subjects that follow the robot after a late repair message that was untimed, limited to 5 s, limited to 3 s, or early message was found to change from 69.69% to 67.74% to 53.33% to 22.58%. Comparing early with late 5 s yields $(\chi^2(1, 62) = 12.76, p < 0.001)$. Comparing early with late 3 s gives $(\chi^2(1, 61) = 6.13, p = 0.013)$. These results indicate although message timing does impact the decision to follow, it is not the only factor. The results are evidence that the messages need to be internalized. The third independent variable considered was *the amount of time between the mistake and decision* and is depicted in green in Fig. 3, by comparing the results labeled "early" to "early small survey" $(\chi^2(1, 70) = 0.978, p = 0.322)$ and "late" to "late small survey." $(\chi^2(1, 69) = 0.962, p = 0.326)$, The data shows a 10.75% increase in likelihood of following the robot when the trust repair message is presented early and the time between the mistake and the decision to follow is reduced. Moreover, the data shows a 11.36% decrease when the trust repair message is presented late and the time between the mistake and the decision to follow is reduced. This data serves as evidence that memory of the mistake may influence the person's decision making in this situation and appears to be short-lived. Finally, the conditions depicted in red in Fig. 3 presents the results related to framing the situation as an emergency $(\chi^2(1, 86) = 0.584, p = 0.444)$. The data shows that when the situation is not framed as an emergency participants appear to randomly choose between following or not following the robot.

7 Conclusions

This paper has examined how and why the timing of trust repair messages impact trust repair itself. The results suggest some fundamental aspects of how humans make decisions when an emergency occurs. Memory of the trust repair (or mistake) and the emergency state act as factors that might affect the relationship between trust repair time and its effectiveness. Changing the time between the early trust repair and the decision point resulted in a small increase in trust. Changing the time between the mistake and the late trust repair resulted in a small decrease in trust. This suggests that both the memory of the trust repair and the memory of the mistake affect the participant's decision to trust the robot. Further experiments are needed to conclusively tease apart which factor becomes dominant in decision making process. We also found that internalizing the message is necessary for repair to occur.

We have attempted to tease apart the reasons that human subjects appear to trust a robot when the robot apologizes or promises just before the decision to trust. We have shown in our prior work and replicated in this work that the timing of these trust repair statement influences trust [15]. Our results serve as evidence that (1) a simulated emergency does motivate people to exit quickly and generate a sense of risk; (2) people need to read and internalize a trust repair message for it to be effective; (3) memory of the robot's mistake(s) may play a role in the decision to trust; and (4) these effects are replicable.

While the results presented here provide some insight into reason behind why timing of trust repair matters, there might be other factors that also play a role. It is important that we understand how the timing of a robot's message to a person impacts the person's decision making. The fact that message timing matters at all suggests an extra dimension of consideration. While it may be challenging to disentangle the factors that influence trust repair, it is necessary that we understand how a robot's interactions influence a person's trust. We believe that the insights gained from these experiments will add to our understanding of human-robot trust and trust itself.

Acknowledgement. Support for this research was provided by Air Force Office of Sponsored Research contract FA9550-17-1-0017.

References

1. Atkinson, D.J., Clark, M.H.: Methodology for study of human-robot social interaction in dangerous situations. In: Proceedings of the Second International Conference on Human-Agent Interaction. ACM, pp. 371–376 (2014)
2. Biros, D.P., Daly, M., Gunsch, G.: The influence of task load and automation trust on deception detection. Group Decis. Negot. **13**, 173–189 (2004)
3. Dzindolet, M.T., Peterson, S.A., Pomranky, R.A., Pierce, L.G., Beck, H.P.: The role of trust in automation reliance. Int. J. Hum.-Comput. Stud. **58**, 697–718 (2003)
4. Hancock, P.A., Billings, D.R., Schaefer, K.E., Chen, J.Y.C., de Visser, E.J., Parasuraman, R.: A meta-analysis of factors affecting trust in human-robot interactions. Hum. Factors **53** (5), 517–527 (2011)
5. King-Casas, B., Tomlin, D., Anen, C., Camerer, C.F., Quartz, S.R., Montague, P.R.: Getting to know you: reputation and trust in two-person economic exchange. Science **308**, 78–83 (2005)
6. Lee, J.D., See, K.A.: Trust in automation: designing for appropriate reliance. Hum. Factors **46**, 50–80 (2004)
7. Madhavan, P., Wiegmann, D.A.: Similarities and differences between human-human and human-automation trust: an integrative review. Theor. Issues Ergon. Sci. **8**(4), 277–301 (2007)
8. Mayer, R.C., Davis, J.H., Schoorman, F.D.: An integrative model of organizational trust. Acad. Manag. Rev. **20**(3), 709–734 (1995)
9. Ozel, F.: Time pressure and stress as a factor during emergency egress. Saf. Sci. **38**, 95–107 (2001)
10. Pak, R., Fink, N., Price, M., Bass, B., Sturre, L.: Decision support aids with anthropomorphic characteristics influence trust and performance in younger and older adults. Ergonomics **55**, 1059–1072 (2012)
11. Parasuraman, R., Riley, V.: Humans and automation: use, misuse, disuse, abuse. Hum. Factors **39**, 230–253 (1997)
12. Parasuraman, R., Miller, C.: Trust and etiquette in high-criticality automated systems. Hum.-Comput. Etiquette Commun. ACM **47**(4), 51–55 (2004)
13. Quinn, D.B., Pak, R., de Visser, E.J.: Testing the efficacy of human-human trust repair strategies with machines. In: Proceedings of the Human Factors and Ergonomics Society Annual Meeting. vol. 61, no. 1, pp. 1794–1798 (2017)
14. Robinette, P., Li, W., Allen, R., Howard, A.M., Wagner, A.R.: Overtrust of robots in emergency evacuation scenarios. In: Proceedings of ACM/IEEE International Conference on Human-Robot Interaction. Christchurch, New Zealand, pp. 101–108 (2016)

15. Robinette, P., Howard, A.M., Wagner, A.R.: Timing is key for robot trust repair. Social Robotics. LNCS (LNAI), vol. 9388, pp. 574–583. Springer, Cham (2015). https://doi.org/10.1007/978-3-319-25554-5_57
16. Robinette, P., Howard, A.: Emergency evacuation robot design. In: Thirteenth Robotics and Remote Systems for Hazardous Environments (2011)
17. Robinette, P., Wagner, A.R., Howard, A.: Assessment of robot guidance modalities conveying instructions to humans in emergency situations. In: RO-MAN. IEEE (2014)
18. Shell, D., Mataric, M.: Insight toward robot-assisted evacuation. Adv. Robot. **19**(8), 797–818 (2005)
19. Tang, B., Jiang, C., He, H., Guo, Y.: Human mobility modeling for robot-assisted evacuation in complex indoor environments. IEEE Trans. Hum.-Mach. Syst. **46**(5), 694–707 (2016)

"Let There Be Intelligence!"- A Novel Cognitive Architecture for Teaching Assistant Social Robots

Seyed Ramezan Hosseini[1], Alireza Taheri[1(✉)], Ali Meghdari[1], and Minoo Alemi[1,2]

[1] Social and Cognitive Robotics Laboratory, Sharif University of Technology, Tehran, Iran
taheri@mech.sharif.edu
[2] Department of Humanities, Islamic Azad University-West Tehran Branch, Tehran, Iran

Abstract. This paper endeavors to propose a novel cognitive architecture specialized for Teaching Assistant (TA) social robotic platforms. Designing such architectures could lead to a more systematic approach in using TA robots. The proposed architecture consists of four main blocks: Perception, Memory, Logic and Action Units. The designed cognitive architecture would help robots to perform a variety of visual, acoustic, and spatial sub-tasks based on cognitive theories and modern educational methods. It also provides a way to enable an operator to control the robot with defined plans and teaching scenarios. The proposed architecture is modular, minimalistic, extendable, and ROS compatible. This architecture can help teaching-assistant robots to be involved in common/expected educational scenarios, systematically. Our preliminary exploratory study was a case study that adopted the proposed architecture for RASA, a social robotic platform aimed at teaching Persian Sign Language (PSL) to hearing-impaired children. The last step is the evaluation. We observed that the architecture's capabilities adequately matched RASA's needs for its applications in teaching sign language.

Keywords: Cognitive architecture · Teaching-assistant robotic platform Social robots · Perception · Memory

1 Introduction

1.1 Cognitive Architecture

Defining cognitive architecture is hard as it is a multi-disciplinary term. Aggregating several accepted definitions [1–6] led us to the following definition: A cognitive architecture is a fixed structure that enables the system (a human or an artificially intelligent agent) to develop its understanding of the environment and processes by receiving new information and knowledge. Many well-known robots use widely accepted architectures or have their own architectures; e.g. the iCub robot [7, 8] has a customized architecture enabling it to behave like an infant.

© Springer Nature Switzerland AG 2018
S. S. Ge et al. (Eds.): ICSR 2018, LNAI 11357, pp. 275–285, 2018.
https://doi.org/10.1007/978-3-030-05204-1_27

Some state of the art cognitive architectures are described in the following. ACT-R [9, 10] is a successor of many cognitive architectures (HAM, ACT, and ACT*) developed by John R. Anderson at CMU. It is seeking a theory to describe human cognition and is based on the Unified Theory of Cognition. ACT-R is commonly used in theoretical experiments. The architecture consists of seven separate modules. The central module, ACT-R Buffers, provides access to all other modules. CLARION [3, 11] is a modular cognitive architecture developed by Sun at Rensselaer Polytechnic Institute. It has four mutually connected subsystems: Action-centered, Non-action-centered, Motivational, and Meta-cognitive subsystems. Its main characteristic is "the dichotomy of implicit and explicit cognition" [3]. Soar [6, 12, 13] was started in 1983 at CMU by Laird, Newell, and Rosenbloom. Their ultimate goal was providing "the foundation for a system capable of general intelligent behavior" [12]. Unified Theory of Cognition, Physical Symbol System, and Problem Space Theory are the basis of Soar. Soar has a wide range of applications, especially in Artificial Intelligence (AI) systems and robotics.

1.2 Teaching Assistant (TA) Social Robots

Social robots are widely used in the education and treatment of children. In the teaching process of children, social robots can play different roles:

- Robots who have more knowledge than their users in a specific content. They can act as teachers or teachers' assistants [14]. They can help teachers by improving the performance of the education process.
- Robots who have knowledge at the same level as their users. These robots can act as companions or playmates [15]. In this role, robots can model appropriate behavior patterns for children.
- Robots who have (or pretend to have) less knowledge than the individuals. They are ready to learn new things and concepts from the others and environments [16]. Robots give the users the opportunities to elicit novel social behaviors. Meanwhile, robots can show them appropriate feedback.

There is an increasing trend in using robotics technology in education. So far, the most common applications of social robots in educating children are: teaching a second language to typically-developing children and children with special needs [17, 18], cognitive rehabilitation of individuals with autism [19, 20], teaching the fundamentals of music [14], teaching physics and math [21], and educating children with cancer to reduce their distress [15].

1.3 Objective and Motivations

While there are some widely recognized architectures for robotic platforms, they are general purpose architectures heavily based on cognitive theories. To the best of our knowledge and as a gap in the literature, there is no known specialized cognitive architecture for TA robots. It is highly recommended to propose/develop comprehensive cognitive architectures for TA robots that will lead to a more systematic approach in a wide range of robotic-assisted platforms in education.

To this end, this paper introduces a novel cognitive architecture for teaching-assistant robotic platforms. While there is not enough room to describe all modules, we have tried our best to illustrate the modular implementable cognitive architecture in Sect. 2 of the paper. Finally, in a preliminary exploratory study, we have a case study and evaluation of our proposed cognitive architecture on a specific robot called RASA, which is used to educate individuals with hearing impairments through sign language.

2 Design of the Cognitive Architecture

2.1 Design Concepts

This section covers some concepts we have considered in designing the architecture.

- Minimalism: The architecture's main concern is TA robots. Thus, there is no need for general purpose architectures.
- Modularity: A modular design will lead to specialized parts and decrease the chance of interference between them.
- Extendibility: It must be extensible in order to handle unpredictable conditions or future optimization.
- The Robot Operating System (ROS) Compatibility: To ease the implementation process, it should be in coordination with ROS's distributed, peer to peer structure.

2.2 Overview of the Proposed Cognitive Architecture

An overview of the proposed cognitive architecture is shown in Fig. 1. It consists of four main parts: Logic, Memory, Perception, and Action Units. It should be noted that the elements of our architecture are designed based on what we learned in our survey and experience with TA robots' working conditions and needs in previous studies, in addition, we also considered cognitive theories and modern educational methods. Between the described state of the art architectures, Soar [6] is the most similar and CLARION [11] is the most dissimilar to the proposed architecture.

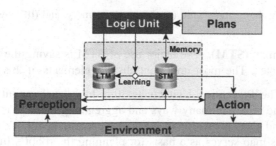

Fig. 1. Overview of the proposed cognitive architecture for TA robotic platforms.

According to Fig. 1, there are two channels for the interaction of the robot with users and the environment. One is through the Perception Unit's input and the other from the Action Unit's output. There are no direct connections between the Perception, Action, and Logic Units. The only way for their interactions is through the Memory Unit. Moreover, the robot operator can communicate only with the Logic Unit. Thus, all the main units have specialized tasks.

More details of the architecture's units- are presented in the following subsections.

2.3   Memory Unit

The Memory Unit in this architecture has the same rules as the Buffers Module in ACT-R, which serves as the central gateway to other modules and simultaneously represents the ACT-R's state at a given instant [9, 10, 22]. In the proposed architecture, the Memory Unit is the bridge connecting the rest of the units. It is a structure for saving and recalling structured and object-oriented data/metadata. It should also provide a place for information aggregation. The Memory Unit is divided into two sub-units: Short-Term Memory (STM) and Long-Term Memory (LTM). Their difference is in the durability and recall rate of the data. Part of the data which has a high recalling rate or short usage period is stored in the STM. The rest of the data is accumulated in the LTM. Both memory sub-units consist of two parts. This division helps to keep/handle Low Level and Abstract (High Level) data, separately (Fig. 2).

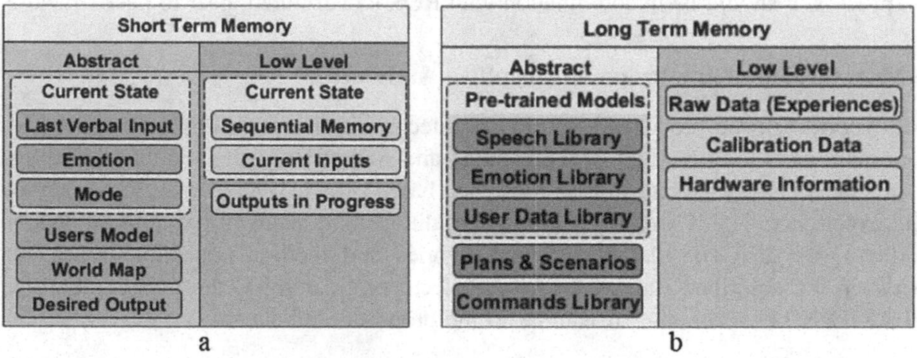

Fig. 2. Details of the memory unit: (a) short-term memory, and (b) long-term memory.

Short-Term Memory (STM). The major use of STM is saving the input/output data of the "Current State". The most important abstract elements of this memory are:

- World Map: The Perception Unit creates this high-level output after processing almost all of the inputs in many ways and aggregating them. It is a 3D map of the environment and elements within it. It can also contain the robot's own position and pose state. This map serves as a basis for planning the robot's future movements.
- Users' Status: All available users' data is stored in this memory. Population, personalities, emotions and actions' history are some examples of users' data. The mentioned list can be expanded further depending on the robot's abilities/ expectations.

- Current State: This box includes a pack of data which describes the current situation of the robot; e.g., its working mode, emotion, last commands, etc.
- Desired Output: The Logic Unit decides which outputs to produce. These desired outputs are different types such as verbal outputs, motions, etc. The Action Unit is in charge of producing these desired outputs. Hence, the Logic Unit stores them in this memory division and the Action Unit reads them.

The low-level elements of the STM are raw I/O of the robot which includes:

- Current State: It consists of inputs in two forms: One part is the flash memory which stores the "current moment's" inputs. The other is the sequential memory. Some perceptional modules (such as speech recognition,) need the time history of the inputs. Therefore, the sequential memory is the right place to store such data as time series.
- Outputs in Progress: Similar to inputs, some outputs (e.g. talking with users) cannot be performed instantly without knowing their time series. The mentioned series are stored in the "Outputs in Progress" sub-unit.

Long-Term Memory (LTM). The main duty of the LTM is storing the robot's experiences, knowledge, and governing rules. Similar to the STM, this memory stores the data in Low-Level and Abstract level.

The robot stores plans, scenarios, behavioral rules and predefined command at the abstract level. However, the most important data in this level are the trained models. These models are used in recognizing speech, face, object, emotion, etc.

Long-term low-level data consists of two essential parts:

- The first part is the robot's experiences; i.e. the data for training the models. Over time, useful resources from the STM will transfer to this part. This will lead to increase the robot's experience by improving the models' performance.
- The other part consists of fixed data for operating the robot; e.g. calibration data, hardware data, inverse and forward kinematics and dynamics of the robot, etc.

2.4 Perception Unit

The Perception Unit is the robot's connection port to its environment. It receives inputs, processes them into high-level abstract data, and stores them in the STM. Figure 3 shows a detailed view of this unit. According to Fig. 3, the data is converted to richer conceptual forms while it flows from the bottom to the top of the Perception Unit. In the first level, inputs are simple raw sensory data while the final outputs (at the top) are meaningful and complex.

In the first level, the robot receives low-level inputs from the environment and users from its sensors. In almost all social robots, these inputs are in the following three forms: acoustic, visual and spatial. However, extra spaces for more types of inputs are definitely foreseen in the proposed cognitive architecture.

The robot also can use its own feedback information (such as encoders' values) as the input. This input will help the robot understand its own situation in the environment (see "self-awareness" box in Fig. 3).

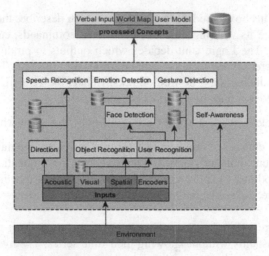

Fig. 3. Details of the perception unit.

Robots can process acoustic inputs in two levels: first, by detecting their direction and distance robot can localize audio sources. This is a low-level analysis. Second, by using speech recognition techniques the data can be transformed into verbal data.

Combining visual and spatial inputs is an appropriate solution to use the inputs for multi-modal environment exploration. Some common usages for these inputs in TA robots are collision detection, recognizing specific tools necessary for performing tasks, detecting human users in the environment (low-level detection for safety issues), face recognition, emotion analysis, and gesture recognition.

Finally, all processed data stores in the STM for later analysis in the Logic Unit.

2.5 Logic Unit

The Logic Unit's main concern is decision making and planning for outputs. There are two possible ways for this unit to get inputs. One way is using the data stored in the STM. The other way is commands and plans from the operator side. They can affect the robot's planning and decision-making method. The results of the Logic Unit's decisions and plans are stored in the STM.

The Logic Unit's other role of is controlling and supervising the learning process. If it finds some valuable inputs for learning, it transfers them to the LTM's low-level section. At a proper time, when the robot is idle, the training process inside LTM is triggered. Such a relationship between the LTM and the STM can also be seen in Soar [6].

2.6 Action Unit

The Action Unit must execute the Logic Unit's desired outputs, which have been stored in the STM (Fig. 4). Additionally, this unit must perform reflex actions, i.e. actions that do not need "thinking" or planning. Actions such as maintaining a safe distance from the users or smiling back at the audience in idle mode are examples of the reflex actions.

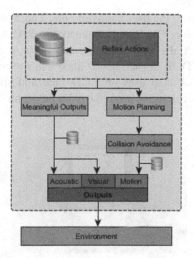

Fig. 4. Details of the action unit.

Planned outputs are in two categories: Some are motions; which need motion planning by considering and then preventing possible collisions. The rest, such as expressing emotions or performing a speech, are other types of meaningful actions. The robot can present them with images, voices, etc.

3 Evaluation

The study's main concern was to check whether the proposed architecture is potentially appropriate for different TA robots. While it is impossible to check all possible scenarios for TA robots in one paper, we are hopeful to address this question in later studies, upon implementing and testing the architecture in real situations. In this paper, we have discussed the adaptation of the architecture on a specific TA robot in complicated and difficult conditions of interacting through sign language. In the next subsections, after introducing the robot and its special needs and working conditions, we have studied whether the proposed architecture is a good choice for the case robot.

3.1 Case Study: The RASA Robot

RASA [23, 24] is a social robotic platform, which has been designed and manufactured in the Social Robotics Lab., Sharif University of Technology, Iran. RASA has 32 degrees of freedom (DOF). The RASA robot is shown in Fig. 5. RASA performs as a sign language teaching assistant for hearing-impaired children. Hence, it has a lot of special requirements. Some of these requirements are concerned with its hardware design which is not relevant to this article. We presume that it meets all these hardware requirements. RASA needs to consider what other typical teaching assistant robots need for performing their tasks. Besides that, it must have a greater focus on gesture and sign language recognition. Therefore, we have used a Kinect sensor [25] and a

Data Glove [26] for capturing the user's movements. These two extra sensors will help in Sign Language recognition. Other typical sensors in RASA are an RGB camera and a microphone array. RASA also has an additional option to communicate: Having 13 DOF in each arm (with 7 DOF in each hand) makes this robot able to perform a wide range of PSL signs. RASA also uses an LCD face and speakers as other tools of communication. The robot can move around on flat environments using its two wheels.

Fig. 5. The RASA robot.

Considering all the points above, the implementation of the designed cognitive architecture on RASA is shown in Fig. 6.

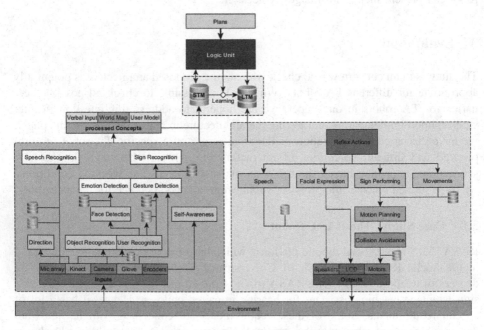

Fig. 6. Details of the adopted architecture for the RASA robot.

3.2 Working Conditions and Needs of RASA

Similar to the majority of teaching assistant robots, RASA can serve in various scenarios. Here are some probable/expected scenarios for RASA: Robot-Teacher-Interaction, Playing the role of a student, Robot-Child-Interaction, and Learning from Mentor.

RASA can interact with the child and respond to his/her actions. Performing such scenarios are complex due to unpredictable situations and children's behaviors. Moreover, these scenarios should guarantee the safety of the child during this interaction. RASA also learns new signs/words and movements from a mentor. Imitation learning is the basis of this scenario. This process is a way to improve the robot's knowledge level.

In summary, some of the expected high-level tasks of the robot are as follows: communication via language (sign or verbal), imitation learning, face detection and tracking, facial expressions detection and responding via appropriate facial gestures, movement, and sign language analysis of children/teacher.

3.3 Evaluation's Discussion

Indeed, using the proposed architecture makes simple tasks executable. Simple tasks are actions like recognizing or reproducing speech, signs, and facial expressions. If a robot is capable of doing all simple tasks, then with appropriate logic, it should be able to perform complex scenarios (i.e. a combination of simple ones) as well.

The only condition for performing these simple tasks is having properly trained models. One way for training models is using the 4th scenario described. This method simply needs implemented learning from demonstration methods in the Logic Unit. Hence, with suitable programming, the robot can train models by observing a few demonstrations. It can also reproduce/imitate them by using proper regenerative models (like HMMs for sign recognition). In a second training method, the operator can also directly import trained models to the LTM.

Currently, we are unable to conclude whether the current findings can be generalized to all TA robots' working conditions. However, based on our experiences and studies, we have tried our best to consider common scenarios of TA robots in the evaluation.

4 Conclusion

Regarding the increasing trend of using social robots in education, there is a serious need to have more systematic approaches to using TA robots. Designing comprehensive cognitive architectures which consider the different needs of TA robots could be a solution. This paper proposed a minimalistic, modular, extendable, and ROS compatible cognitive architecture to address the TA robot's special needs. Then, the architecture was specialized and evaluated for the case of a specific TA robot and its special needs. The preliminary assessments showed the appropriateness of the proposed cognitive architecture for the robot's four major working/expected scenarios.

Acknowledgment. This research was partially funded by the "Iran Telecommunication Research Center (ITRC)" and "National Elites Foundation" of Iran. We also appreciate the consultations received from our friend and colleague Mr. Mohammad Zakipour.

References

1. Ritter, F.E., Young, R.M.: Embodied models as simulated users: introduction to this special issue on using cognitive models to improve interface design. Int. J. Hum.-Comput. Stud. **55** (1), 1–14 (2001)
2. Vernon, D.: Artificial Cognitive Systems: A Primer. MIT Press (2014)
3. Sun, R.: The importance of cognitive architectures: an analysis based on CLARION. J. Exp. Theor. Artif. Intell. **19**(2), 159–193 (2007)
4. Braisby, N., Gellatly, A. (eds.): Cognitive Psychology. Oxford University Press (2012)
5. Friedenberg, J., Silverman, G.: Cognitive Science: An Introduction to the Study of Mind. Sage (2011)
6. Laird, J.E.: The Soar Cognitive Architecture. MIT press (2012)
7. Vernon, D., Metta, G., Sandini, G.: The icub cognitive architecture: interactive development in a humanoid robot. In: IEEE 6th International Conference on Development and Learning, 2007, ICDL 2007, pp. 122–127. IEEE, July 2007
8. Vernon, D., Von Hofsten, C., Fadiga, L.: A Roadmap for Cognitive Development in Humanoid Robots, vol. 11. Springer, Heidelberg (2011)
9. Anderson, J.R., Matessa, M., Lebiere, C.: ACT-R: a theory of higher level cognition and its relation to visual attention. Hum.-Comput. Interact. **12**(4), 439–462 (1997)
10. Anderson, J.R.: How Can the Human Mind Occur in the Physical Universe? Oxford University Press (2009)
11. Sun, R.: The CLARION cognitive architecture: extending cognitive modeling to social simulation. Cogn. Multi-Agent Interact. 79–99 (2006). https://doi.org/10.1017/CBO9780511 610721.005
12. Laird, J.E., Newell, A., Rosenbloom, P.S.: Soar: an architecture for general intelligence. Artif. Intell. **33**(1), 1–64 (1987)
13. Laird, J.E., Newell, A.: A universal weak method: summary of results. In: Proceedings of the Eighth International Joint Conference on Artificial Intelligence-Volume 2, pp. 771–773. Morgan Kaufmann Publishers Inc. August 1983
14. Taheri, A., Meghdari, A., Alemi, M., Pouretemad, H., Poorgoldooz, P., Roohbakhsh, M.: Social robots and teaching music to autistic children: myth or reality? In: Agah, A., Cabibihan, J.-J., Howard, A.M., Salichs, M.A., He, H. (eds.) ICSR 2016. LNCS (LNAI), vol. 9979, pp. 541–550. Springer, Cham (2016). https://doi.org/10.1007/978-3-319-47437-3_53
15. Alemi, M., Ghanbarzadeh, A., Meghdari, A., Moghadam, L.J.: Clinical application of a humanoid robot in pediatric cancer interventions. Int. J. Soc. Robot. **8**(5), 743–759 (2016)
16. Taheri, A., Alemi, M., Meghdari, A., Pouretemad, H., Basiri, N.M., Poorgoldooz, P.: Impact of humanoid social robots on treatment of a pair of iranian autistic twins. Social Robotics. LNCS (LNAI), vol. 9388, pp. 623–632. Springer, Cham (2015). https://doi.org/10.1007/978-3-319-25554-5_62
17. Alemi, M., Meghdari, A., Ghazisaedy, M.: The impact of social robotics on L2 learners' anxiety and attitude in English vocabulary acquisition. Int. J. Soc. Robot. **7**(4), 523–535 (2015)

18. Alemi, M., Meghdari, A., Basiri, N.M., Taheri, A.: The effect of applying humanoid robots as teacher assistants to help Iranian autistic pupils learn English as a foreign language. In: Tapus, A., André, E., Martin, J.C., Ferland, F., Ammi, M. (eds.) International Conference on Social Robotics, pp. 1–10. Springer, Cham (2015). https://doi.org/10.1007/978-3-319-25554-5_62

19. Taheri, A.R., Meghdari, A., Alemi, M., Pouretemad, H.R.: Clinical interventions of social humanoid robots in the treatment of a pair of high- and low- functioning autistic Iranian twins. Sci. Iran. Trans. B: Mech. Eng. **25**(3), 1197–1214 (2018)

20. Taheri, A., Meghdari, A., Alemi, M., Pouretemad, H.: Teaching music to children with autism: a social robotics challenge. Int. J. Sci. Iran Trans. G Socio Cognit. Eng. https://doi.org/10.24200/SCI

21. Mubin, O., Stevens, C.J., Shahid, S., Al Mahmud, A., Dong, J.J.: A review of the applicability of robots in education. J. Technol. Educ. Learn. **1**(209–0015), 13 (2013)

22. ACT-R's Official About Page, July 2018. http://act-r.psy.cmu.edu/about

23. Meghdari, A., Alemi, M., Zakipour, M., Kashanian, S.A.: Design and realization of a sign language educational humanoid robot. J. Intell. Robot. Syst. 1–15 (2018). https://doi.org/10.1007/s10846-018-0860-2

24. Zakipour, M., Meghdari, A., Alemi, M.: RASA: a low-cost upper-torso social robot acting as a sign language teaching assistant. In: Agah, A., Cabibihan, J.J., Howard, A., Salichs, M., He, H. (eds.) Social Robotics, pp. 630–639. Springer, Cham (2016). https://doi.org/10.1007/978-3-319-47437-3_62

25. Microsoft Kinect Home Page, July 2018. https://developer.microsoft.com/en-us/windows/kinect

26. Perception Neuron Motion Capture Home Page, July 2018. https://neuronmocap.com

Virtual Social Toys: A Novel Concept to Bring Inanimate Dolls to Life

Alireza Taheri[1], Mojtaba Shahab[1], Ali Meghdari[1(✉)],
Minoo Alemi[1,2], Ali Amoozandeh Nobaveh[1], Zeynab Rokhi[1],
and Ali Ghorbandaei Pour[1]

[1] Social and Cognitive Robotics Laboratory, Sharif University of Technology,
Tehran, Iran
meghdari@sharif.edu
[2] Department of Humanities, Islamic Azad University-West Tehran Branch,
Tehran, Iran

Abstract. Different social robotics studies are carried out to give robotic gadgets an interactive retrofit. In this research, we tried to present a new perspective on using interactive animated toys in a virtual environment. Such social toys would be able to interact with children in the same way as social robots. To this end, a 3D scanner setup and interface was designed/fabricated and implemented to extract the 3D model of an inanimate toy to be used in a virtual reality game. The children were asked to participate in a fifteen-minute game scenario and play with the interactive virtual social toy. Then the Believability, Acceptance/Attractiveness, and Vibrancy/Interaction of the virtual social toy were assessed quantitatively through a questionnaire. Our preliminary findings showed high scores in all three criteria by the children. However, 2-sample T-tests indicated a significant difference between the children and parents' viewpoints regarding the effectiveness of this generation of new toys.

Keywords: Social toys · Virtual reality · 3D scanner · Interactive games

1 Introduction

Since ancient times, toys have played an important role during childhood and even into the teenage years. Dolls and stuffed animals are considered a main category of toys. As a point in case, most children choose names for their dolls and play turn-taking games with them. In many cases, an emotional bond grows between the children and this type of toy. Here, the common state is that children like to interact with their dolls and action figures in the same way that they interact with another child using verbal communications, body gestures and facial expressions [1, 2]. Considering the importance of toys, over the last decade, different toy-based games have been invented, developed, and even specialized for education purposes [2, 3]. In this regard, possession of a controllable and interactive version of a child's favorite doll or figurine is quite valuable.

Propagation of studies on social robotics and the advent of commercial social robots in recent years, have brought the dream of humanlike interaction with toys

© Springer Nature Switzerland AG 2018
S. S. Ge et al. (Eds.): ICSR 2018, LNAI 11357, pp. 286–296, 2018.
https://doi.org/10.1007/978-3-030-05204-1_28

closer to reality. By improving the abilities of social robotic toys, they now have the capability to enhance different interaction scenarios [4–8], but they are still expensive, hard to handle and limited in the variety of character, shape and size compared to other available dolls and action figures. As mentioned in previous social robotics studies, the appearance of the robot is an issue [8, 9]. In [9], some of the participants were either afraid of the robot or simply not interested in the appearance of the robot. Considering the difficulties in implementing personal exterior details on robotic toys, it is currently impossible to personalize the robot's appearance for each child, but it is possible for children to have a custom stuffed dolls produced from their drawings or books illustrations [10]. Due to the limitations of the available social robots, some researchers have been interested in the development of virtual reality games for both education and treatment in an entertaining environment [11].

Combining the idea of using a fully controllable toy in an interactive game with the importance of the toy acceptability brought us to the novel concept of a virtual social toy. Our goal is to accurately develop dolls in a virtual environment that will be able to play the role of a social robotic toy in the game scenarios. This paper presents an initial attempt to introduce a platform for implementing the concept of virtual social toys. This platform consists of a 3D scanning setup for dolls and stuffed animals integrated with a framework assigning a skeleton to them, and a virtual environment coupled with a Microsoft Kinect sensor to control the movements of the virtual social toy. The desired work is a step forward for using children's own dolls inside an interactive game in a virtual environment instead of using actual social robotic toys. In this regard, the Believability, Acceptance and Attractiveness, and Vibrancy and Interaction quality of this concept were assessed during a pilot study.

2 Hardware and Software Requirements

2.1 Design and Fabricating a 3D Scanner

Any 3D scanner setup needs a camera and a depth sensor or a combination of multiple cameras [12–14]. In order to scan a 3D object, different mechanisms have been developed to hold or move the scanning camera depending on their application. In [12], a handheld setup is presented which has the ability to scan objects independent of their size, but non-uniform hand movements can affect scanner results. In another study, multiple cameras at different heights and angels were used to scan objects [13]. Although the quality of the 3D model is high, this kind of methods is both computationally and monetarily expensive. In [14], a swivel structure and three Kinects were used to capture the 3D model.

In this study, we have used a Microsoft Kinect sensor as the scanner camera since it is equipped with depth sensing technology, a built-in color camera, and an infrared emitter that can sense the location of objects. In order to increase the quality of the output model, a uniform and continuous motion of the Kinect is important. As the other two important parameters are easy fabrication and low manufacture cost, we used a fixed base to place the dolls and stuffed animals and a mechanism to rotate the Kinect around the object from top to bottom. The final designed mechanism has two active degrees of freedom. The overall structure is shown in Fig. 1. It spins around the base with a radius of 110 cm, so the maximum width and length of the subject can be up to 60 cm and the acceptable height is up to 1 m making it suitable for scanning large plushy bodies. The scanning process takes about two minutes.

Fig. 1. The designed 3D scanning mechanism.

The rotational movement is provided by a three wheeled mechanism. The Kinect is placed on a plate connected to a linear translation mechanism consisting of a ball screw in the middle of the plate and three guide bars on the corners. To connect the spinning structure to the base, a parallel linkage is fitted with hinges to the base.

2.2 3D Model Software Interface

In this step, blender [15] (an open 3D creation software) and Unity Personal [16] (a game engine) were used to complete the process and finalize the animated 3D model of the social toy. The outputs of the Kinect scanner are both a colored texture and a 3D model (in obj format). The 3D model was imported to the blender and a T position humanoid skeleton was assigned to the model for proper set up in the next step. Figure 2a shows the joints of the standard humanoid skeleton attached to the prepared model in a Unity environment. Thus, by rotating each part of the skeleton system, the respective part of the body would consequently rotate in the same way.

In the next step, the animated model was imported to Unity and the model's animation type was set to the humanoid state in the rig setting. The configured humanoid skeleton of the imported model in T position is illustrated in Fig. 2b.

Since the model was configured as humanoid, default animations could be used for the model. Furthermore, different desired animations could be easily recorded individually by using a Kinect sensor. Body movements of a human mediator standing in front of the Kinect would be recorded to be used for robot animations. In addition, the setup has the ability to animate the virtual model by using the Kinect sensor data and imitating the human mediator simultaneously. This real-time interaction allowed the modeled doll to response more naturally with more humanlike movements, which leads to a more attractive game environment for the children.

To sum up, the 3D output model of the scanner was imported in blender and the animated social toys became available in the Unity environment. They can now be used to design interactive game scenarios in which children are able to play with the animated version of their dolls, action figures or stuffed animals inside a virtual reality environment.

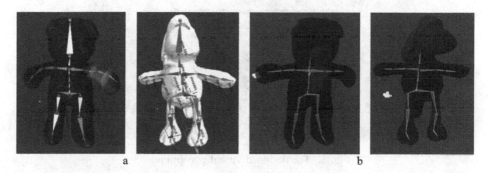

a   b

Fig. 2. (a) A humanoid skeleton attached to model in blender and (b) the configured humanoid model of the doll in Unity.

3 Methodology

3.1 Participants

Twenty one Iranian children including 13 boys and 8 girls between the age of 5-12 (mean age: 8.7, standard deviation: 2.0 years old) participated in this study with their parents, out of which four parents were absent.

3.2 Design of the Game

In this study, the designed game environment is a virtual playground in which children can interact with their animated social toy in different scenarios. We used a head-mounted virtual reality setup (HTC VIVE [17] headset), Kinect sensor and Unity personal game engine to establish the virtual environment. The virtual playground consists of the virtual social toy (we named it Pashmaloo which means plushy in Persian), a football goal and a number of balls with trees around them (Fig. 3).

In this game, each participant was asked to individually attend the virtual environment for one session in a Wizard of Oz control style study. In addition to the child, one of the parents, the game operator and human mediator were also present in the room. Although the movements of Pashmaloo were controlled by the human mediator performing in front of the Kinect, the children did not know this fact and thought that Pashmaloo was a self-controlled doll. The toy's character, movements and voice were chosen to match a famous bear character in an Iranian TV cartoon "Khers-e-Mehraboon".

Pashmaloo performed the following items during the gameplay: (1) a warmup greeting with the child, (2) singing and dancing with a sweet prerecorded song, (3) playing a simple football game with the child, and (4) a final farewell.

Fig. 3. The designed virtual playground.

The game started with a couple of warmup lines from Pashmaloo, introducing himself and asking the child to introduce him/herself. After the greetings part, the game operator played a prerecorded song as Pashmaloo danced to it. In the next step, Pashmaloo begins to play football (kicking a penalty) with the child. During the football game, the child was asked to pick a ball using a virtual reality hand controller and throw it toward the goal. Pashmaloo, as the goalkeeper, made funny moves and tried to dive and catch the ball. If a child missed the goal, Pashmaloo would encourage the child to aim at the goal again and try shooting more balls. Also, when a child scores Pashmaloo started to dance while verbally encouraging them. After playing football and to conclude the playing, Pashmaloo asked the children whether they prefer him to come back or not. Finally, he said goodbye and wished to see them again soon. This game scenario took about fifteen minutes on average. Figure 4 shows some snapshots of the game.

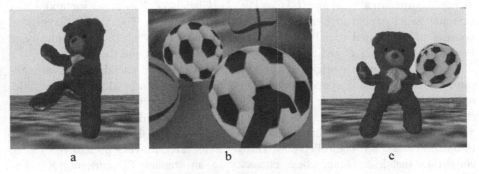

a   b   c

Fig. 4. Snapshots of the designed game.

3.3 Assessment Tool

A questionnaire was completed by the children and their parents after the game session in order to investigate the potential roles of virtual social toys in children's lives as well as the difference between the children and parents' viewpoints about the social toys. The 10 questions on the questionnaire were scored by the subjects qualitatively or discretely. Three main criteria including (1) Believability, (2) Acceptance and Attractiveness, and (3) Vibrancy and Interaction of the virtual social toy were scored/extracted from the questionnaires and are described in the results section. Table 1 shows the questionnaire used in this paper.

Table 1. The questionnaire used in this study to assess the Believability, Acceptance and Attractiveness, and Vibrancy and Interaction criteria.

Main criteria	Questions	Possible answers
Believability	Q1: Could the child match the virtual avatar with the real toy in the room?	No; Yes, with a hint; Yes, independently
	Q2: How similar was the virtual bear to the real toy?	0%; 25%; 50%; 75%; 100%
	Q3: How natural was the movements of the virtual toy?	0%; 25%; 50%; 75%; 100%
	Q4: How much can social toys show appropriate emotions?	0%; 25%; 50%; 75%; 100%
Acceptance and attractiveness	Q5: How attractive was the social toy?	0%; 25%; 50%; 75%; 100%
	Q6: Which one do you prefer? The real inanimate toy or the virtual animated one?	Real; Both; Virtual
	Q7: How good of a playmate are a virtual social toy?	0%; 25%; 50%; 75%; 100%
	Q8: Do you like having your toys animated?	No; Not Important; Yes
Vibrancy and interaction	Q9: Which game did you prefer? The toy's dancing or the football game?	Dance; Both; Football
	Q10: What games do you prefer to play with the virtual social toys?	The answers are categorized in the following three groups: Low, Medium, and High Active games

4 Results and Discussion

During the game sessions, each child attended the class with his/her parent. The child wore the headset and the parent could see the game via a monitor. There were also three real toys in the room one of which was Pashmaloo. As mentioned in the Methodology section, the virtual toy performed one "less-interactive" game (i.e. dancing) and one "interactive turn-taking" game (i.e. involving the child in kicking/throwing balls). After the session, the child and parent were asked to fill out the questionnaire. Figure 5 shows snapshots of our game sessions.

Regarding question 1, 62% of the children instantly recognized that the playmate character in the game is the virtual version of the real bear toy, Pashmaloo; 24% recognized it with a hint and 14% of the children did not understand the relationship between the physical toy and the virtual animal.

a   b

Fig. 5. Snapshots of the game sessions: (a) playing the designed VR-based game, and (b) recognizing the real toy.

Both the children and parents believed that the similarity of the virtual bear and real toy was high which confirms the applicability of the proposed animating process. Nevertheless, contrary to the children's answers, the parents did not believe that virtual social toys can show appropriate emotions during the child-toy-interaction (Fig. 6). We believe that this issue can be solved by improving the artificial intelligence, quality of actions, and verbal reactions of virtual social toys during the games (e.g. giving a microphone to the human-mediator for online verbal communication).

In our study, 85% of the children preferred the virtual social bear as their animated playmate, while 57% of the parents claimed that they prefer to play with the real inanimate bear toy if they were in their child's situation. However, 76% of the children and 65% of the parents wished that they could see at least one of their real toys being animated, talking and moving in the virtual reality environment.

In summary, according to the questionnaires' results (Fig. 7), both the Believability and Acceptance/Attractiveness mean scores of the social toy with regard to the children's viewpoints are higher than 70%. However, based on the parents' answers, a new generation of social toys could only be "medium" attractive and believable playmates for children. High acceptance rate of the virtual agent by the children in this study is in line with the considerable social robot's acceptability in [6, 9].

We would also like to investigate the preferred social toys-based games regarding the level of interaction/vibrancy. In our sessions, 67% of the children and 59% of the parents chose the dyadic/turn-taking "interactive" kicking ball game as their preference (in comparison to the less dyadic interactive dance). However, based on question 10, while 81% of the children claimed that they have a desire to play with the virtual toys

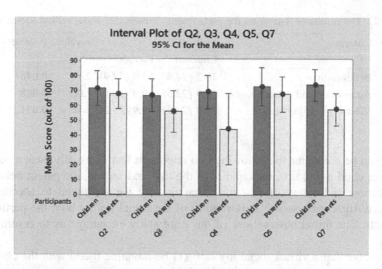

Fig. 6. Interval plot for the quantitative questions of the assessment tool.

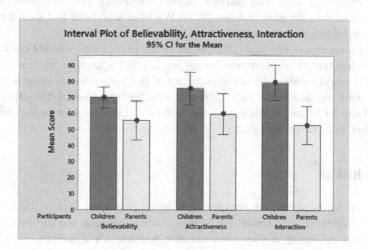

Fig. 7. Interval plot for the Believability, Acceptance/Attractiveness, and Vibrancy/Interaction.

which are "high active tasks", 40% of the parents preferred social toys-based games with "medium mobility" and 40% suggested "low active" (e.g. "thinking") games.

Previous findings led us to induce the difference between children and parents' preferences. Therefore, to investigate whether there is a significant difference between the children and parents' viewpoints regarding the three criteria of our study, 2-sample T-tests were performed on the scores and the results are presented in Table 2. In all of the mentioned criteria, the p-values are less than 0.05; hence, there are significant differences in the children and parents' viewpoints toward the social toys. According to our participants, we observed that the children would eagerly communicate with social toys as a new generation of toys; while about half of the parents showed doubt toward such toys or did not show any tendency to have animated toys during their childhood.

Table 2. The results of T-tests on the participants' viewpoints about virtual social toys.

#	Criteria	Mean (SD)		T-value	P-value
		Children	Parents		
1	Believability	70.2 *(14.6)*	55.9 *(23.9)*	2.17	**0.040**
2	Acceptance and Attractiveness	75.9 *(22.3)*	59.9 *(24.9)*	2.06	**0.048**
3	Vibrancy and Interaction	79.8 *(24.5)*	52.9 *(23.2)*	3.46	**0.001**

It should be noted that the following two important factors usually push a parent to buy his/her child a toy; first, the child likes the toy, and second, the parent believes in the usefulness and safety of that toy. That is why we attempted to ascertain the Acceptance/Attractiveness and Believability of the social toy by both the participants and parents. The initial observations of our pilot study encourage us to continue this idea.

We believe that a virtual social toy can: (1) be a unique friend with the children's desired shape, (2) even grow up with the child in time, (3) motivate its owner to do necessary childhood tasks and increase his/her obedience [18, 19], and (4) be an appropriate tool for educating children [5, 7]. We have high hope that such a new idea could make childhood more enjoyable.

As the limitations of this study, the gender of the participants was not considered as an independent variable. Moreover, using each child's favorite toy in the virtual environment could increase the acceptance rate of that virtual social agent for him/her. Having a small number of the participant was another limitation of this paper. Due to the lack of similar studies in this area in the literature, it was hard for us to compare our observations with the others' works.

5   Conclusion

In this paper, we presented the concept of bringing inanimate toys to life in a virtual environment referred to as virtual social toys. Using this idea, we can bring to life a child's dream of seeing his/her own favorite toy/doll alive, talking, moving, and eliciting emotions similar to social robots. To perform this proposed idea, we designed and fabricated a mechanism to provide 3D models of real toys in a virtual environment. Then, a software interface was developed to animate the toys. Currently, the process of scanning a desired toy and inserting it in our game takes about 3 h. This is quite fast to make an inanimate toy come alive in the virtual environment. Through a pilot study, 21 children and 17 parents were involved in a virtual-based game in which the children became the playmate of a virtual bear toy. We observed that the Believability and Acceptance rate of social toys are high for children and they prefer to be involved in dyadic interactive and active tasks with the animated toys. However, there was significant difference between the viewpoints of the children and their parents regarding the use of social toys. We hope that the main contribution of the paper will shed light to make children's worlds more appealing and positively affect their educations.

Acknowledgement. This research was funded by the "Cognitive Sciences and Technology Council (CSTC)" of Iran and "National Elites Foundation" of Iran. We also appreciate our lab members Mr. Behrad Mozaffari and Mr. Alireza Esfandbod for their cooperation.

References

1. Williams, R., Machado, C.V., Druga, S., Breazeal, C., Maes, P.: My doll says it's ok: a study of children's conformity to a talking doll. In: Proceedings of the 17th ACM Conference on Interaction Design and Children, pp. 625–631. ACM, June 2018
2. Trawick-Smith, J., Wolff, J., Koschel, M., Vallarelli, J.: Effects of toys on the play quality of preschool children: Influence of gender, ethnicity, and socioeconomic status. Early Childhood Educ. J. **43**(4), 249–256 (2015)
3. Shahab, M., et al.: Social Virtual reality robot (V2R): a novel concept for education and rehabilitation of children with autism. In: 5th IEEE RSI International Conference on Robotics and Mechatronics (ICRoM), pp. 82–87. IEEE, October 2017
4. Taheri, A.R., Meghdari, A., Alemi, M., Pouretemad, H.R.: Clinical interventions of social humanoid robots in the treatment of a set of high-and low-functioning autistic Iranian twins. Sci. Iran.-Trans. B: Mech. Eng. **25**(3), 1197–1214 (2018)
5. Taheri, A., Meghdari, A., Alemi, M., Pouretemad, H., Poorgoldooz, P., Roohbakhsh, M.: Social robots and teaching music to autistic children: myth or reality? In: Agah, A., Cabibihan, J.-J., Howard, A.M., Salichs, M.A., He, H. (eds.) ICSR 2016. LNCS (LNAI), vol. 9979, pp. 541–550. Springer, Cham (2016). https://doi.org/10.1007/978-3-319-47437-3_53
6. Meghdari, A., et al.: Arash: a social robot buddy to support children with cancer in a hospital environment. Proc. Inst. Mech. Eng. Part H: J. Eng. Med. **232**(6), 605–618 (2018)
7. Cabibihan, J.J., Javed, H., Ang, M., Aljunied, S.M.: Why robots? A survey on the roles and benefits of social robots in the therapy of children with autism. Int. J. Soc. Robot. **5**(4), 593–618 (2013)
8. Alemi, M., et al.: RoMa: a hi-tech robotic mannequin for the fashion industry. In: Kheddar, A., et al. (eds.) ICSR 2017, vol. 10652, pp. 209–219. Springer, Cham (2017). https://doi.org/10.1007/978-3-319-70022-9_21
9. Pour, A.G., Taheri, A., Alemi, M., Meghdari, A.: Human-robot facial expression reciprocal interaction platform: case studies on children with autism. Int. J. Soc. Robot. **10**(2), 179–198 (2018)
10. https://www.budsies.com/kids-drawings-stuffed-animals/. Accessed July 2018
11. Virvou, M., Katsionis, G.: On the usability and likeability of virtual reality games for education: the case of VR-ENGAGE. Comput. Educ. **50**(1), 154–178 (2008)
12. Munkelt, C., Kleiner, B., Torhallsson, T., Kühmstedt, P., Notni, G.: Handheld 3D scanning with automatic multi-view registration based on optical and inertial pose estimation. In: Osten, W. (ed.) Fringe 2013, pp. 809–814. Springer, Heidelberg (2014). https://doi.org/10.1007/978-3-642-36359-7_147
13. Dou, M., Fuchs, H., Frahm, J.M.: Scanning and tracking dynamic objects with commodity depth cameras. In: 2013 IEEE International Symposium on Mixed and Augmented Reality (ISMAR), pp. 99–106. IEEE, October 2013
14. Tong, J., Zhou, J., Liu, L., Pan, Z., Yan, H.: Scanning 3D full human bodies using kinects. IEEE Trans. Visual Comput. Graphics **18**(4), 643–650 (2012)
15. https://www.blender.org/. Accessed July 2018
16. https://unity3d.com/. Accessed July 2018

17. https://www.vive.com/us/. Accessed July 2018
18. Taheri, A., Meghdari, A., Alemi, M., Pouretemad, H.: Human-robot interaction in autism treatment: a case study on three pairs of autistic children as twins, siblings, and classmates. Int. J. Soc. Robot. **10**(1), 93–113 (2018)
19. Taheri, A., Meghdari, A., Alemi, M., Pouretemad, H.: Teaching music to children with autism: a social robotics challenge. Int. J. Sci. Iran. Trans. G: Socio-Cognitive Eng. (2018). https://doi.org/10.24200/SCI

Modular Robotic System for Nuclear Decommissioning

Yuanyuan Li[1(⊠)], Shuzhi Sam Ge[1], Qingping Wei[2], Dong Zhou[2],
and Yuanqiang Chen[2]

[1] Center for Robotics, University of Electronic Science and Technology
of China, No. 2006, Xiyuan Avenue, Chengdu, Sichuan, China
colin0221@163.com
[2] R&D Center, Dongfang Electric Company, No.18, Xixin Road, Chengdu,
Sichuan, China

Abstract. Because of the radioactivity, the nuclear environment operation requires robot system to complete. In this paper, a modular robot system for nuclear environment operation is developed, which is easy to maintain, reconfigurable and reliable. Besides, this paper proposes a vision-based method for robot tool changing with the base coordinates of robot inaccurate. The prototype test proves the feasibility of the robot system and the validity of the vision-based tool changing method.

Keywords: Nuclear decommissioning · Modular robot system
Vision-based tool changing

1 Introduction

With the development of nuclear industry, the related operations such as the maintenance of nuclear facilities, the disposal of radioactive waste and the decommissioning of nuclear facilities become more and more urgent. These operations has the following characteristics: 1. The environment has high temperature, high humidity and high radioactivity, and will cause great harm to human health; 2. These operations usually have large workload, and it's hard for human to undertake. For the above reasons, the works in the nuclear environments are not suitable for manual operation, and need to be assisted by robot or other automatic equipment.

The robotic system is very fragile in the nuclear environment. The robot working in Chernobyl nuclear disaster is damaged after only 7 min because of the electronic component failure [1]. Subsequently, RedZone company developed the Pioneer robotic system for the Chernobyl nuclear power plant [2]. Pioneer robot includes a tracked chassis and a 6-DOF manipulator with a load capacity of 45 kg. After the JCO nuclear accident in Japan in 1999, a number of Japanese companies developed various emergency rescue robot systems [3–5]. In the Fukushima nuclear accident, the Quince robot developed by Chiba Institute of Technology in Japan participated in the rescue work and was mainly used to measure the radioactivity level of the Fukushima nuclear power plant [6, 7]. For nuclear power plant maintenance, a visual servo-based steam generator blocking robot is invented for nuclear reactor [8].

© Springer Nature Switzerland AG 2018
S. S. Ge et al. (Eds.): ICSR 2018, LNAI 11357, pp. 297–307, 2018.
https://doi.org/10.1007/978-3-030-05204-1_29

Generally speaking, the robots for nuclear environment is simple in function, and difficult to maintain, thus it's difficult to adapt to the complex nuclear automation operation requirements.

2 Design and Analysis of Mechanism System

2.1 Work Environment and Requirement Analysis

The workspace of operations in nuclear environment is usually a large-scale closed room. Typical workspaces include reactor containment to be decommissioned, solid radioactive waste cutting and sorting plant, radioactive waste vitrification plant and waste storage tank to be cleaned. Reactor containment (Fig. 1a) is a cylinder structure with steel or concrete material, which has the diameter up to 20–50 m, and contains pressure vessels and intricate pipelines inside. Solid radioactive waste disposal plant (Fig. 1b) is the plant to sort and cut large pieces of solid radioactive waste into small pieces and package them to box to reduce volume, which is a rectangular space with length more than 10 m and width and height all more than 6 m. Figure 1c and d also shows the structure of radioactive waste vitrification plant and waste storage tank.

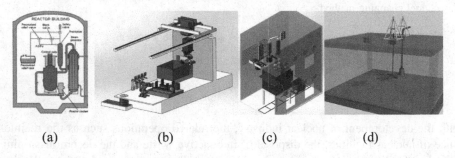

| (a) | (b) | (c) | (d) |

Fig. 1. Typical workspaces in nuclear environment: (a) reactor containment, (b) solid radioactive waste disposal plant, (c) radioactive waste vitrification plant, (d) radioactive waste storage tank.

2.2 Design of Mechanism

The workspace above requires robot to have large range of movement, dexterous moving ability, high motion accuracy and multiplicate end-of-arm tool system. To fulfill the above requirements, the robot system consists of three parts: modular mechanical arm, large-scale mobile platform and end-of-arm tool system (Fig. 2).

Fig. 2. Composition the robot system

2.2.1 Modular Mechanical Arm

The modular mechanical arm consists of three basic joint modules: swing joint, revolute joint and wrist joint. All joint modules have a uniform mechanical and electrical interface, thus each joint can connect any other joint quickly. According to above design, any joint module damaged can be replaced easily, and the mechanical arm can be reconfigured to various types to adapt different working conditions.

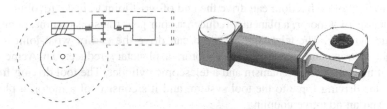

Fig. 3. Schematic diagram and model of swing joint

The schematic diagram of the swing joint is shown in Fig. 3. The swing joint consists of a motor, a planetary reducer, a worm-gear mechanism, structures, and auxiliary system (lubrication system, sealing system and so on). Due to self-locking property of worm-gear transmission system, the swing joint can maintain the current posture even in case of power failure in accident.

The schematic diagram of the revolute joint is shown in Fig. 4. The revolute joint consists of a motor, a planetary reducer, a spur gear transmission mechanism, a cycloidal pinwheel reducer, structures, and auxiliary system (lubrication system, sealing system and so on). The output flange of revolute joint is connected to the output of cycloidal pinwheel reducer, and performs a revolute motion under the action of the motor driving and the reducer transmission.

The schematic diagram of the wrist joint is shown in Fig. 5. The wrist joint module contains 3 degrees of freedom, in turn, tool revolute freedom, telescopic freedom and tool driving freedom.

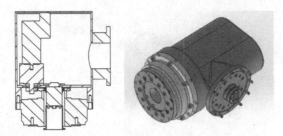

Fig. 4. Schematic diagram and model of revolute joint

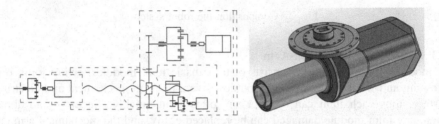

Fig. 5. Schematic diagram and model of wrist joint

The tool revolute freedom can drive the end of wrist joint to make revolute motion, and it consists of a motor, a planetary reducer, a spur gear transmission mechanism and a revolute cylinder. The telescopic freedom can drive the end of wrist joint to make telescopic motion, and it consists of a motor, a planetary reducer, an Acme thread screw-nut transmission mechanism and a telescopic cylinder. The tool driving freedom provides the driving force to the tool system, and it's consists of a motor, a planetary reducer, and an adaptive coupling.

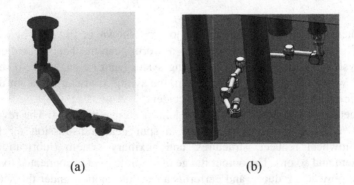

(a)   (b)

Fig. 6. Two configurations of manipulator

Here list two typical robot configurations.

Configuration 1 (Fig. 6a) consists of 3 swing joints, 2 revolute joint and 1 wrist joint. The sequence of these joints is as follows: revolute joint, swing joint, swing joint, revolute joint, swing joint and wrist joint. With this configuration, the manipulator has 7 degrees of freedom, which adds a telescopic freedom based on a traditional 6-degree-of freedom manipulator. This configuration allows the manipulator to reach arbitrary poses, and the telescopic freedom allows the end of manipulator to extend to narrow space.

Configuration 2 (Fig. 6b) consists of 1 revolute joint, 1 wrist joint and several swing joints. The swing joints are connected to the revolute joint, and the wrist joint is connected to the last swing joint. The number of swing joints according to the environment robot works. With this configuration, the manipulator can avoid obstacles including intricate pipes during work.

These two configurations adapt different working conditions. Configuration 1 can adapt dexterous works in most environments. But for the multi-obstacle environment, such as complex pipeline system, configuration 2 is the best choice because of the obstacles-avoid ability based on the muti-joints. These two configurations can easily reconstructed to each other based on the modular design.

2.2.2 Large-Scale Mobile Platform

The large-scale mobile platform (Fig. 7) consists of X-direction mobile platform, Y-direction mobile platform, Z-direction revolute and telescopic platform.

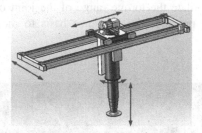

Fig. 7. Large-scale mobile platform

The X-direction mobile platform and the Y-direction mobile platform can move in two orthogonal directions (X-direction and Y-direction) in the horizontal plane, and they move through wheeled travel mechanism. The Z-direction revolute and telescopic platform (Fig. 7) can take the telescopic movement along the vertical axis (Z-direction) and the rotary motion around it.

2.2.3 End-of-Arm Tool System

The end-of-arm tool system can be divided into two parts: internal tools and external tools.

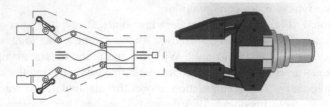

Fig. 8. Schematic diagram and model of gripping tool

The internal tools include various of gripping tools (Fig. 8) which are suitable for different operation objects. The internal tools can be connected to the end of wrist through a uniform quick connector. and driven by the tool motor installed inside the wrist. The internal tools has no driving component, and driven by the tool motor installed inside the wrist. The design motor hidden in the wrist saves the number of motors used, and the motor can be protected well by the wrist joint structure.

The external tools include other special tools such as disc saw, hydraulic shear, electric drill, screwdriver and so on, and mainly do high-power professional operations,. These tools have their own independent power and drive system, and can be clamped by clamps installed in the end of wrist to operate.

2.3 Mechanical Analysis and Simulation

Based on the dynamics simulation software ADAMS, a typical extreme condition (Fig. 9) is selected to simulate the torque range of the joint of the manipulator. The result showed in Fig. 10 provides the reference basis to motor selection and finite element simulation.

Fig. 9. Dynamics simulation for manipulator

According to the dynamical simulation results, we selected the typical structural components for finite element analysis, and optimized the structure according to the results (Fig. 11) to ensure the strength and weight of the structure.

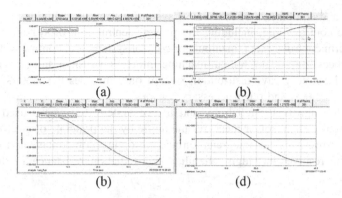

Fig. 10. Torque curve of main joints. (a) 1st swing joint, (b) 2nd swing joint, (c) 3rd swing joint, (d) 2nd revolute joint

Fig. 11. Finite element simulation analysis of main structures.

3 Design of Control System

The control system is divided into two parts: hot laboratory cave distribution system and control room distribution system (Fig. 12). Hot laboratory cave is the closed room for radioactive operation, and its high radioactivity can cause damage to human body and electronic equipment. In order to reduce the influence of radiation environment, the

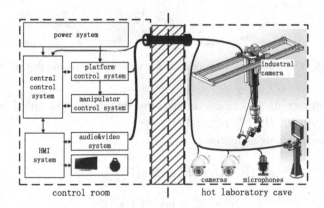

Fig. 12. Distribution of control system

core devices and equipments of the control system with weak radiation resistance are placed in the control room, including the power, central control system, large-scale mobile platform control system, manipulator control system, tool control system, audio and video processing system, human-machine interaction system and display system, etc. The hot laboratory cave distribution system only includes the motors, encoders, microphones, cameras and other necessary sensors.

In order to improve the reliability and life of system, resolver is used to be the encoder of motor. The resolver measures the angle by the principle of electromagnetic induction. Because it has no integrated circuit, no optical components and no precise alignment, the resolver has high reliability and radiation resistance in the nuclear environment.

4 Design of Automatic Tool Changing System Based on Vision

The conventional control method of robot tool quick changing is to provide a fixed path program for the robot by teach-in manner. Because the large range of motion, the repetitive positioning accuracy of the robot system is low and can't finish the tool quick changing operation by tool quick changing. In this system, a vision-based positioning method is proposed to complete the relative position recognition and tool change of the robot arm and tool (Fig. 13).

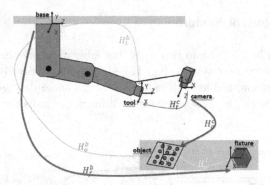

Fig. 13. The relative position relation for vision-based positioning method

This method mounts the camera on the wrist and defines the coordinate transformation matrix H_t^b, H_t^c, H_o^c, H_o^b, H_f^b, and H_o^f.

They has the relations as follows:

$$H_f^b = H_o^b * \text{inv}(H_f^o) \tag{1}$$

$$H_o^b = H_t^b * \text{inv}(H_t^c) * H_o^c \tag{2}$$

$$H_f^b = H_t^b * inv(H_t^c) * H_o^c * inv(H_f^o) \tag{3}$$

Among them, H_o^c can be measured by the camera to calibrate the relative position between camera and target. Once we get the relative position of the base coordinate system and the fixture coordinate system H_f^b, we can easily control the robot system to make the tool changing operation.

5 Prototype Manufacturing and Testing

A prototype for the configuration 1 of the manipulator has been designed and manufactured. A building block experiment (Fig. 14) has been done as a functional test, and the result shows that the manipulator arm operated stably and has high positioning accuracy. More experiments will be done to test the positioning accuracy, the dynamics performance and the load capacity.

Fig. 14. The function and accuracy test of based on building blocks experiment

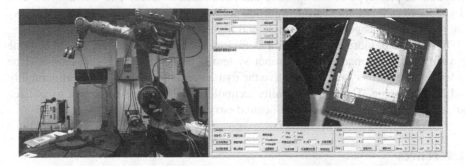

Fig. 15. Calibration experiment for vision-based positioning system

To verify the performance of the vision-based positioning method, a calibration experiment (Fig. 15) is done using a camera, a target plate, and the KUKA robot system (The prototype has not been finished before calibration experiment). The target plate is manually adjusted to different poses to test the calibration performance of the system. The results show that the system can well identify the position and angle coordinates of the target plate and has high precision. The average error of calibration is 0.00337671 pixels. Using multiple measurements, the final positioning accuracy of the shell is less than 1 mm (Fig. 16).

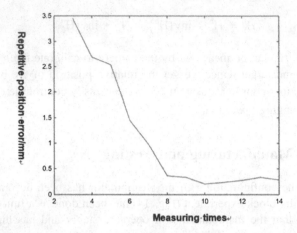

Fig. 16. Repetitive position error variation curve with measure times

6 Conclusion and Further Research

This paper presents a robot system for nuclear environment operation.

With the modular design concept, this robot system can be easily repaired or reconfigured to various types to adapt different working conditions. To implement tool changing automatically in the case of base coordinates of robot inaccurate, a vision-based method for robot tool changing is proposed. Dynamical simulation and finite element analysis has been done to check structure strength and assist drive component selection. A prototype of manipulator has been manufactured. The function test and vision-based calibration experiment for the prototype have been done, and result shows that this system has good performance and high tool-changing accuracy.

For next step, more function test and environmental adaptation test should be done to verify the performance of this robot system. The neural network system will be added to the control system to adaptive the dynamical changes due to reconfigurability and load changing. The Virtual Reality technology will also be combined to assisted human to control remotely for unstructured environment operation.

References

1. Abouaf, J.: Trial by fire: teleoperated robot targets chernobyl. IEEE Comput. Graph. Appl. **18**, 10–14 (1998)
2. Maimone, M., Matthies, L., Osborn, J.: A photo-realistic 3-D mapping system for extreme nuclear environments chernobyl. In: Conference on Intelligent Robots and Systems (1998)
3. Oka, K., Shibanuma, K.: Development of a radiation-proof robot. Adv. Robot. **16**, 493–496 (2002)
4. Mano, T., Hamada, S.: Development of a robot system for nuclear emergency preparedness. Adv. Robot. **16**, 477–479 (2002)
5. Hosoda, Y., Yamamoto, H., Hattori, M.: A robot for nuclear disaster prevention support. Adv. Robot. **16**, 485–488 (2002)

6. Rohmer, E., Ohno, K., Yoshida, T.: Integration of a sub-crawlers' autonomous control in quince highly mobile rescue robot. In: IEEE/SICE International Symposium on System Integration (2010)
7. Rohmer, E., Yoshida, T., Ohno, K.: Quince: a collaborative mobile robotic platform for rescue robots research for development. In: Proceeding of International Conference on Advanced Mechatronics (2010)
8. Duan, X.G., Yang, Y.: Control system for blocking plate manipulation robot based on visual servo. In: 13th International Conference on ICIA. IEEE (2013)

A New Model to Enhance Robot-Patient Communication: Applying Insights from the Medical World

Elizabeth Broadbent[1]() (iD), Deborah Johanson[1], and Julie Shah[2] (iD)

[1] The University of Auckland, Auckland 1142, New Zealand
e.broadbent@auckland.ac.nz
[2] Massachusetts Institute of Technology, Cambridge 02139, USA

Abstract. Socially assistive robots need to be able to communicate effectively with patients in healthcare applications. This paper outlines research on doctor-patient communication and applies the principles to robot-patient communication. Effective communication skills for physicians include information sharing, relationship building, and shared decision making. Little research to date has systematically investigated the components of physician communication skills as applied to robots in healthcare domains. We propose a new model of robot-patient communication and put forward a research agenda for advancing knowledge of how robots can communicate effectively with patients to influence health outcomes.

Keywords: Physician empathy · Healthcare robot · Communication

1 Introduction

Socially assistive robots are starting to be used in many healthcare applications. Animal-type robots, such as the seal robot Paro, are used to reduce the symptoms of dementia, including depressed mood, loneliness, and agitation [4, 25, 37]. Service-type robots interact with patients to collect medical data, provide companionship, telemedicine, and health education [8, 13, 21]. Robots are also used in people's homes to help patients manage long term conditions, for example, measuring vital signs and providing reminders to take medication and perform exercises [14]. There are questions around how socially assistive robots can best communicate with users to maximize their potential in healthcare [12].

Service type robots are typically programmed to communicate with patients through the use of touch screens and/or speech recognition. As technology advances, speech enabled healthcare devices will become more common. For example, Pillo is a start-up home health robot designed to answer health-related questions [33]. Conversational agents have rapidly developed over the past 3 years; Amazon is estimated to have sold 5 million Alexa-enabled devices (a wireless speaker that you can ask about the news, weather, search the web, control smart-home products and even chat with) between November 2016 and May 2017 [29].

© Springer Nature Switzerland AG 2018
S. S. Ge et al. (Eds.): ICSR 2018, LNAI 11357, pp. 308–317, 2018.
https://doi.org/10.1007/978-3-030-05204-1_30

In healthcare applications, it is important that people engage with robots and feel comfortable talking about their concerns. It is equally important that robots understand and provide accurate advice regarding these concerns, and that patients follow any information and advice given. This issue is very salient in traditional medical settings, where doctor-patient communication is critical. In this paper, we argue that we may be able to apply the findings from this literature to build better relationships between patients and robots in health domains.

This paper first provides an overview of doctor-patient communication, and how it influences health outcomes. This framework is then applied to healthcare robots, and related work is reviewed. Finally, a model and research agenda is created for building robots with good communication skills for interacting with patients in healthcare.

2 Learning from Doctor-Patient Communication

Good communication is at the heart of the medical consultation. Communication tasks in the consultation include relationship building, gathering information, providing information, reaching agreement, and shared decision making [35]. A doctor must be able to understand a patient's symptoms, feelings and perspectives, be able to communicate their understanding back to the patient, check the accuracy of their understanding, and then act on this in a therapeutic way. These skills can be said to comprise physician empathy [17], and have been found to be positively associated with both patient satisfaction levels and patient evaluations of medical treatment [41, 43].

Both verbal and non-verbal communication are involved in medical consultations. Verbal behaviors typically focus on information exchange and include asking questions, giving information, talking about a disease, tests, and treatment. This type of information exchange can be described as instrumental (cognitive) communication and it typically takes up most of the conversation time [31]. Non-verbal communication includes body position, eye gaze, voice tone, facial expressions, touch, and physical distance. Non-verbal behaviors often communicate affect (or emotion), including empathy, concern, and reassurance [31].

To allow patients to express their concerns, feel listened to, and be involved in treatment decisions it is important that physicians do not take control over the consultations by interrupting or asking questions too quickly. Paternalistic consultations describe situations where the doctor has the most control, whereas patient centered communication allows a patient to express all their concerns, symptoms, thoughts, feelings and expectations. Research has shown that physicians frequently interrupt patients before they have finished speaking [34], in which circumstances patients feel they should have talked more in the consultation.

Similarly, it is important to consider patients' preferences for treatment. In paternalistic decision making, the doctor makes the treatment decision and the patient is passive. In shared decision making, the doctor shares information about treatment options, make recommendations based on his/her knowledge, and engages in discussion with the patient about these options. Patients discuss the information and state their preferences, and then together doctor and patient can make a decision regarding treatment. Shared decision making has been linked to better outcomes, especially in chronic illness where patients have more involvement in long-term disease management [24].

Doctors also need to consider their use of language when talking with patients. The use of medical jargon can reduce patient participation in medical consultations due to patients' limited understanding of medical terminology [26, 32]. Therefore, clinicians need to use plain language and check patients' understanding of terms used throughout the consultation. Signs that a patient may not understand medical information include asking the doctor to repeat information, not using medical terms themselves, and not requesting additional services [26]. Doctors need to be alert to these and other signs of limited understanding.

Knowing when to apply certain verbal and non-verbal behaviors is critical in a medical context to ensure patients' informational, psychological, social, and physical privacy is respected. For example, while asking intimate questions and touching patients may be unavoidable in medical contexts, there are ways to do this that align with social norms, such as not watching a patient undress [31].

Several reviews have been conducted into the effects of doctor-patient communication on patient outcomes. Both qualitative and quantitative studies have been performed on a number of communication aspects, including randomized controlled trials. The most recent review found that training physicians about shared decision making increased patients' ratings of the relationship; training doctors in empathy increased patients' ratings of the doctors' empathy; and training doctors to detect patient distress reduced patient anxiety [35]. Furthermore, better information provision and patient education resulted in higher patient satisfaction, higher patient feelings of control over complex diseases and feelings of independence, higher patient compliance, better quality of life, and better health outcomes. Better communication skills were linked with higher patient quality of life, lower unnecessary use of antibiotics, and better patient emotional health, with open communication rated the most important factor by patients [35]. Meta-analysis has shown that patients are more than twice as likely to be adherent to treatment if their physician is a good communicator; and patients are 1.6 times more likely to be adherent if their medical provider has undergone communication skills training [44]. Evidence therefore clearly suggests that relationship building, information exchange, and shared decision-making skills are critical to health outcomes.

The Toronto Consensus Agreement recommends that the most important strategies to improve clinical communication are: to encourage patients to discuss their main concerns without interruption or premature closure; to use active listening and empathy – including the use of open ended questions, frequent summaries and clarification, and negotiation; to give clear explanations, check patient understanding, negotiate a treatment plan, and check compliance; and to avoid closed-ended questions, premature advice and premature reassurance [38].

3 How Can These Strategies Be Applied to Robots in Healthcare?

In theory, the recommendations from the Toronto Consensus could be applied to healthcare service robots, and making a robot that can perform all these activities represents a long-term goal. To break this into more achievable smaller goals, research is needed to improve robots' ability to perform each of these aspects. Some tasks will be easier than others.

First, research will have to investigate how robots can encourage patients to discuss their concerns, perhaps trying strategies already shown to work in medical contexts. For example, physicians can encourage patients to ask questions via questionnaire prompt lists [19]. This intervention to improve communication involves training both patients and physicians (separately) in communication strategies and it is likely that some form of patient training could improve robot-patient communication as well.

There are some very good guides for physicians on how to conduct a good consultation [22]. Advice includes strategies that could be easily applied to robots, such as using a patient's name, making good eye contact and using verbal prompts such as "go on" or head nodding. To teach a robot not to interrupt or prematurely close a conversation, the robot will have to sense when a patient is merely pausing, and when they have finished speaking. There are already multiple methods to do this via speech analysis, including pauses, and prosody [20], although their use in this context needs to be tested.

Second, researchers will have to program robots to use active listening and make empathetic statements. Active listening may mean robots will have to understand what patients are saying in context, which they currently struggle to do. While robots can easily be programmed to ask open opened questions, one of the most difficult challenges will be for them to understand patients' responses. At present, AI can pick up keywords and this can be done in a medical consultation if a robot is programmed with a medical dictionary. Making summaries and checking that these are correct is another area for future development. Gask and Usherwood [22] recommend repeating things back to the patient to check correct understanding, and this is possible for AI, however it is likely a more sophisticated integration of information into a summary would be a useful skill. Work on summarization of medical documents has been performed, however this has not included summarization of patients' concerns [2]. To express empathy, a robot could make statements to legitimize patient feelings such as "I think most people would feel the same way", as recommended for physicians [22]. Knowing when to correctly apply these may require the use of deep learning techniques as well as emotion detection software, using techniques including facial expression and voice analysis.

Third, giving clear information about diseases, treatments and tests could be fairly easy for a robot if it is connected to a valid, accurate, and up-to-date database of medical information. Negotiation of a treatment plan may be a challenge, but simple ways of offering alternatives, making recommendations with explanations, and asking if a treatment is acceptable could be a starting point. However, giving wrong information or making the wrong diagnosis could be very dangerous. It may be that robots should not be used be for such processes unless a human physician has been consulted. Once a human doctor has made a clinical diagnosis and checked the information that the robot is providing, then a robot could be a useful source of health information in people's homes and in clinical settings.

Other behaviors, not mentioned in the Toronto Consensus but part of the Hippocratic oath, such as confidentiality and doing no harm, need to be considered. Patients will have to be sure that robot will not inappropriately share their health information, but at the same time robots will act on any critical information by passing it on to human medical professionals in a timely manner. Social rules for appropriate behavior in a medical context, such as turning away when a patient gets undressed, will also have to be clearly defined and programmed.

While the principles of good doctor-patient communication are known, not all physicians apply them well. An advantage of healthcare robots is that they can be programmed to regularly apply these rules.

4 Which Aspects of Doctor-Patient Communication Have Been Researched in Healthcare Robotics?

Research on technology and health communication to date has mainly focused on patients' use of the web for health-related internet searches, patient portals for electronic health records, and online support groups [23]. Almost half of the research to date has focused on how people use technology and a quarter has focused on the impact of such technologies. The use of technology to improve health literacy is underresearched, and there is little research on the use of communication techniques within technologies.

There has been some research into the use of virtual agents for explaining informed consent in a health context, finding that a computer agent was well received [6]. The use of virtual agents for health behavior change has been studied, and the benefits of adding a combination of affective communication strategies has been demonstrated in one study [5]. The strategies included social dialogue, empathy statements (E.g. "I am sorry to hear you are not feeling well. It can be frustrating…"), humor, use of first name, and non-verbal immediacy behaviors (closer face proximity and more frequent facial animation, gesture, head nods and gaze) [5]. The addition of all these behaviors (together) to an agent designed to increase exercise behavior improved the bond formed between the user and the agent (includes items about liking and trust) [5]. The effects of each individual behavior were not examined separately. An expansion of this work used eclectic interventions to encourage both diet and exercise change [7]. The agent used in these studies used text based forced choice responses to fixed questions rather than open ended questions and responses.

Research in robotics into the effects of different communication behaviors in medical contexts is more limited. The robot's level of politeness has been investigated using a Nao robot, based on gesture and verbal requests in a Korean study about stress [28]. More polite gestures (head bowed and arms together) and less polite verbal requests (more direct) were associated with higher perceived benefits of compliance and higher intentions to comply than less polite gestures (pointing and an open stance) and more polite requests (less direct).

Eye gaze has been investigated in many robot studies [1]. For example, the role of vocal and non–vocal cues (including eye gaze and gestures) was investigated in a robot trying to persuade people to rank various items in a survival task [16]. Eye gaze behavior has been programmed into robots for children with autism to try to increase their social behaviors [39]. Robot eye gaze has also been found to facilitate human comprehension of robot speech [40]. However, to our knowledge, no studies have specifically investigated the role of robot eye gaze in improving robot-patient communication.

Similarly, studies have investigated whether robot head nodding can build rapport, but not directly in the area of patient communication. For example, one study investigated the effects of robot head movements on rapport with a chimpanzee robot in a non–medical setting [36]. In a more medical context, the effect of an android bystander on ratings of the doctor in an orthopedic clinic was improved when the robot nodded and smiled in synchrony with the patient [42]. However, in this case the robot was a bystander rather than having a direct medical provider role.

Some robots have been programmed with specific behaviors to create closer relationships in medical settings. For example, a Nao robot was designed to make statements about self-disclosure, empathy, and concern in a diary study with children with diabetes [18]. The robot was rated highly by the children, however it was not compared to a robot without these behaviors, so the role of these behaviors in creating a better relationship could not be determined.

The role of facial expressions in a medical context is yet to be determined. It has been recognized in HRI that there are different kinds of smiles, including embarrassed, trustful, relieved, surprised, anxious, superior and inferior smiles, and these can be modelled in an avatar with varying degrees of success [10]. Research has shown that people perceive a smiling robot as happiest when the smile is biggest and the robot as most appealing when the smile transition is slow rather than sudden [9]. Modelling a trustful smile would be the most appropriate in healthcare during some parts of the consultation.

To our knowledge, no research has specifically investigated the effects of a robot interrupting a person during a health conversation. Research into conversations between humans and robots in general indicates that although at first a robot may mistakenly interrupt a person, the person can learn to adapt their own speech and to read a robot's conversational cues, such as eye gaze and head tilt, to help conversation turn taking [11]. One study in a household setting, suggested that people get annoyed if a robot interrupts them many times while they are watching television [27].

Research into requirements for animal type companion robots includes recommendations that they should be warm, have fur, and be controlled by speech and hand movements, and make sounds that humans can understand [30]. Work into shared care networks has recommended ways in which technology may support the coordination of care for complex patients based on computational teamwork theory [3]. However, theory-based recommendations are lacking regarding healthcare service robots' communication skills for interactions with patients.

5 A New Model of Robot-Patient Communication

Adding to the literature to date on factors that enhance robot-patient communication, we propose an approach to systematically test the same factors that enhance doctor-patient communication. That is, one by one, we develop and test the effectiveness of each kind of behavior. To do this it is useful to apply a theory based on doctor-patient communication and adapt it to robots. One such model proposes that background variables (including characteristics of both the doctor and the patient), influence the content of the conversation (including instrumental and affective communication), which in turn affects patients' outcomes (including satisfaction, understanding, compliance and health). In Fig. 1, we present an adapted and expanded model for healthcare robots. A previous review has shown the importance of various human and robot factors on the acceptance of healthcare robots [15], and these findings can be integrated into the first part of the model (see Fig. 1). This model can serve as a testable theory for expanding our knowledge about HRI in medical contexts.

Background variables:
- Patient age, gender, culture, education, disease, personality, experience, needs , cognitive abilities
- Robot appearance, voice, gender, personality, adaptability

Communication:
- Affective and instrumental
- Verbal and non-verbal
- Relationship building
- Information exchange
- Shared decision making
- Confidentiality
- Social rules for appropriate medical behaviour

Patient outcomes:
- Satisfaction
- Understanding
- Engagement
- Self-management
- Compliance
- Health status

Fig. 1. A new model of robot-patient communication based on doctor-patient research.

Research into this model of robot-patient communication may serve two purposes. First, it may improve robot-patient communication, which may lead to greater patient satisfaction, better adherence, and better health outcomes with robots. Second, it may enable research into the factors that enhance doctor-patient communication. It has been recommended, for example, that future research investigate which specific aspects of communication are the most important for patient adherence [44]. Research with robots may be one way that this can be systematically investigated by manipulating each behavior independently, such as eye gaze, gesture, and head tilt; it would be almost impossible to individually manipulate these behaviors in a human doctor.

To maximize research efficiency, behaviors could be first tested in computer-based agents, building on previous studies with conversational agents [5]. In the second phase, the behaviors could be tested with robots in laboratory situations. This could allow us to establish whether communication behaviors have the same effects whether the communicator is a human, a virtual agent, or a robot. And in the third phase, robots programmed with these behaviors could be tested against robots without these behaviors with patients in healthcare settings.

6 Conclusion

In this paper, we proposed a new model to guide researchers in improving robot-patient communication. The key principles of doctor-patient communication were presented and discussed in relation to healthcare robots. Previous work has applied a limited selection of these principles with virtual agents, and few studies have investigated these principles in healthcare robots. The application of this model can shed light on strategies to improve human-robot interaction in healthcare and improve patient outcomes, and these strategies need to be evaluated in systematic experimental research.

References

1. Admoni, H., Scassellati, B.: Social eye gaze in human-robot interaction: a review. J. Hum.-Robot Interact. 6(1), 25–63 (2017)
2. Afantenos, S., Karkaletsis, V., Stamatopoulos, P.: Summarization from medical documents: a survey. Artif. Intell. Med. 33(2), 157–177 (2005)
3. Amir, O., Grosz, B.J., Gajos, K.Z., Swenson, S.M., Sanders, L.M.: From care plans to care coordination: opportunities for computer support of teamwork in complex healthcare. In: Proceedings of the 33rd Annual ACM Conference on Human Factors in Computing Systems, pp. 1419–1428. ACM (2015)
4. Bemelmans, R., Gelderblom, G.J., Jonker, P., de Witte, L.: Effectiveness of Robot Paro in intramural psychogeriatric care: a multicenter quasi-experimental study. J. Am. Med. Dir. Assoc. 16(11), 946–950 (2015)
5. Bickmore, T., Gruber, A., Picard, R.: Establishing the computer–patient working alliance in automated health behavior change interventions. Patient Educ. Couns. 59(1), 21–30 (2005)
6. Bickmore, T.W., Pfeifer, L.M., Paasche-Orlow, M.K.: Using computer agents to explain medical documents to patients with low health literacy. Patient Educ. Couns. 75(3), 315–320 (2009)
7. Bickmore, T.W., Schulman, D., Sidner, C.: Automated interventions for multiple health behaviors using conversational agents. Patient Educ. Couns. 92(2), 142–148 (2013)
8. Henkemans, O.A.B., et al.: Using a robot to personalise health education for children with diabetes type 1: a pilot study. Patient Educ. Couns. 92(2), 174–181 (2013)
9. Blow, M., Dautenhahn, K., Appleby, A., Nehaniv, C.L., Lee, D.C.: Perception of robot smiles and dimensions for human-robot interaction design. In: 2006 The 15th IEEE International Symposium on Robot and Human Interactive Communication, ROMAN 2006, pp. 469–474. IEEE (2006)
10. Borutta, I., Sosnowski, S., Zehetleitner, M., Bischof, N., Kuhnlenz, K.: Generating artificial smile variations based on a psychological system-theoretic approach. In: RO-MAN 2009 - The 18th IEEE International Symposium on Robot and Human Interactive Communication, pp. 245–250 (2009)
11. Breazeal, C.: Toward sociable robots. Robot. Auton. Syst. 42(3), 167–175 (2003)
12. Breazeal, C.: Social robots for health applications. In: 2011 Annual International Conference of the IEEE Engineering in Medicine and Biology Society, pp. 5368–5371 (2011)
13. Broadbent, E., Orejana, J.R., Ahn, H.S., Xie, J., Rouse, P., MacDonald, B.A.: The cost-effectiveness of a robot measuring vital signs in a rural medical practice. In: 2015 24th IEEE International Symposium on Robot and Human Interactive Communication (RO-MAN), pp. 577–581 (2015)

14. Broadbent, E., et al.: Robots in older people's homes to improve medication adherence and quality of life: a randomised cross-over trial. In: Beetz, M., Johnston, B., Williams, M.-A. (eds.) ICSR 2014. LNCS (LNAI), vol. 8755, pp. 64–73. Springer, Cham (2014). https://doi.org/10.1007/978-3-319-11973-1_7
15. Broadbent, E., Stafford, R., MacDonald, B.: Acceptance of healthcare robots for the older population: review and future directions. Int. J. Soc. Robot. 1(4), 319 (2009)
16. Chidambaram, V., Chiang, Y.-H., Mutlu, B.: Designing persuasive robots: how robots might persuade people using vocal and nonverbal cues. In: Proceedings of the Seventh Annual ACM/IEEE International Conference on Human-Robot Interaction, pp. 293–300. ACM (2012)
17. Derksen, F., Bensing, J., Lagro-Janssen, A.: Effectiveness of empathy in general practice: a systematic review. Br. J. Gen. Pract. 63, 606 (2013)
18. Van Der Drift, E.J.G., Beun, R.-J., Looije, R., Henkemans, O.A.B., Neerincx, M.A.: A remote social robot to motivate and support diabetic children in keeping a diary. In: Proceedings of the Proceedings of the 2014 ACM/IEEE International Conference on Human-robot Interaction, Bielefeld, Germany, pp. 463–470. ACM (2014). https://www.doi.org/10.1145/2559636.2559664
19. Epstein, R.M., Duberstein, P.R., Fenton, J.J., et al.: Effect of a patient-centered communication intervention on oncologist-patient communication, quality of life, and health care utilization in advanced cancer: the voice randomized clinical trial. JAMA Oncol. 3(1), 92–100 (2017)
20. Ferrer, L., Shriberg, E., Stolcke, A.: A prosody-based approach to end-of-utterance detection that does not require speech recognition. In: Proceedings of 2003 IEEE International Conference on Acoustics, Speech, and Signal Processing (ICASSP 2003), p. 1. IEEE (2003)
21. Gandsas, A., Parekh, M., Bleech, M.M., Tong, D.A.: Robotic telepresence: profit analysis in reducing length of stay after laparoscopic gastric bypass. J. Am. Coll. Surg. 205(1), 72–77 (2007)
22. Gask, L., Usherwood, T.: The consultation. Br. Med. J. 324(7353), 1567–1569 (2002)
23. Hu, Y.: Health communication research in the digital age: a systematic review. J. Commun. Healthc. 8(4), 260–288 (2015)
24. Joosten, E.A.G., DeFuentes-Merillas, L., de Weert, G.H., Sensky, T., van der Staak, C.P.F., de Jong, C.A.J.: Systematic review of the effects of shared decision-making on patient satisfaction, treatment adherence and health status. Psychother. Psychosom. 77(4), 219–226 (2008)
25. Jøranson, N., Pedersen, I., Rokstad, A.M.M., Ihlebæk, C.: Effects on symptoms of agitation and depression in persons with dementia participating in robot-assisted activity: a cluster-randomized controlled trial. J. Am. Med. Dir. Assoc. 16(10), 867–873 (2015)
26. Katz, M.G., Jacobson, T.A., Veledar, E., Kripalani, S.: Patient literacy and question-asking behavior during the medical encounter: a mixed-methods analysis. J. Gen. Intern. Med. 22(6), 782–786 (2007)
27. Koay, K.L., Syrdal, D.S., Walters, M.L., Dautenhahn, K.: Five weeks in the robot house – exploratory human-robot interaction trials in a domestic setting. In: 2009 Second International Conferences on Advances in Computer-Human Interactions, pp. 219–226 (2009)
28. Lee, N., Kim, J., Kim, E., Kwon, O.: The influence of politeness behavior on user compliance with social robots in a healthcare service setting. Int. J. Soc. Robot. 9, 1–17 (2017)
29. Levy, N.: Amazon passes 10 M Alexa-powered devices sold, survey says, with more models on the way. In: GeekWire (2017)

30. Ohkubo, E., Negishi, T., Oyamada, Y., Kimura, R., Naganuma, M.: Studies on necessary condition of companion robot in the RAA application. In: Proceedings 2003 IEEE International Symposium on Computational Intelligence in Robotics and Automation, vol. 101, pp. 102–106 (2003). (Cat. No.03EX694)
31. Ong, L.M.L., de Haes, J.C.J.M., Hoos, A.M., Lammes, F.B.: Doctor-patient communication: a review of the literature. Soc. Sci. Med. 40(7), 903–918 (1995)
32. Pieterse, A.H., Jager, N.A., Smets, E.M.A., Henselmans, I.: Lay understanding of common medical terminology in oncology. Psycho-Oncology 22(5), 1186–1191 (2013)
33. Pillohealth: Pillo: Your Personal Home Health Robot Indiegogo (2017)
34. Rhoades, D.R., McFarland, K.F., Finch, W.H., Johnson, A.O.: Speaking and interruptions during primary care office visits. Fam. Med. 33(7), 528–532 (2001)
35. Riedl, D., Schüßler, G.: The influence of doctor-patient communication on health outcomes: a systematic review. Z. Für Psychosom. Med. Psychother. 63(2), 131–150 (2017)
36. Riek, L.D., Paul, P.C., Robinson, P.: When my robot smiles at me: enabling human-robot rapport via real-time head gesture mimicry. J. Multimodal User Interfaces 3(1), 99–108 (2010)
37. Robinson, H., Macdonald, B., Kerse, N., Broadbent, E.: The psychosocial effects of a companion robot: a randomized controlled trial. J. Am. Med. Dir. Assoc. 14(9), 661–667 (2013)
38. Simpson, M., Buckman, R., Stewart, M., Maguire, P., Lipkin, M., Novack, D., Till, J.: Doctor-patient communication: the Toronto consensus statement. Br. Med. J. 303(6814), 1385–1387 (1991)
39. Simut, R., Costescu, C.A., Vanderfaeillie, J., Van de Perre, G., Vanderborght, B., Lefeber, D.: Can you cure me? Children with autism spectrum disorders playing a doctor game with a social robot. Int. J. Sch. Health 3(3), e60224 (2016)
40. Staudte, M., Crocker, M.W.: Investigating joint attention mechanisms through spoken human–robot interaction. Cognition 120(2), 268–291 (2011)
41. Steinhausen, S., et al.: Physician empathy and subjective evaluation of medical treatment outcome in trauma surgery patients. Patient Educ. Couns. 95(1), 53–60 (2014)
42. Takano, E., Matsumoto, Y., Nakamura, Y., Ishiguro, H., Sugamoto, K.: Psychological effects of an android bystander on human-human communication. In: 2008 8th IEEE-RAS International Conference on Humanoid Robots, pp. 635–639. IEEE (2008)
43. Zachariae, R., Pedersen, C.G., Jensen, A.B., Ehrnrooth, E., Rossen, P.B., von der Maase, H.: Association of perceived physician communication style with patient satisfaction, distress, cancer-related self-efficacy, and perceived control over the disease. Br. J. Cancer 88(5), 658 (2003)
44. Zolnierek, K.B., Dimatteo, M.R.: Physician communication and patient adherence to treatment: a meta-analysis. Med. Care 47(8), 826–834 (2009)

Towards Crossmodal Learning for Smooth Multimodal Attention Orientation

Frederik Haarslev[1], David Docherty[2], Stefan-Daniel Suvei[1],
William Kristian Juel[1], Leon Bodenhagen[1(✉)], Danish Shaikh[2],
Norbert Krüger[1], and Poramate Manoonpong[2,3]

[1] SDU Robotics, Maersk Mc-Kinney Moller Institute,
University of Southern Denmark, Odense, Denmark
{fh,stdasu,wkj,lebo,norbert}@mmmi.sdu.dk

[2] SDU Embodied Systems for Robotics and Learning,
Maersk Mc-Kinney Moller Institute, University of Southern Denmark,
Odense, Denmark
{dado,danish,poma}@mmmi.sdu.dk

[3] Bio-inspired Robotics and Neural Engineering Laboratory,
School of Information Science and Technology,
Vidyasirimedhi Institute of Science and Technology, Wangchan, Thailand

Abstract. Orienting attention towards another person of interest is a fundamental social behaviour prevalent in human-human interaction and crucial in human-robot interaction. This orientation behaviour is often governed by the received audio-visual stimuli. We present an adaptive neural circuit for multisensory attention orientation that combines auditory and visual directional cues. The circuit learns to integrate sound direction cues, extracted via a model of the peripheral auditory system of lizards, with visual directional cues via deep learning based object detection. We implement the neural circuit on a robot and demonstrate that integrating multisensory information via the circuit generates appropriate motor velocity commands that control the robot's orientation movements. We experimentally validate the adaptive neural circuit for co-located human target and a loudspeaker emitting a fixed tone.

Keywords: Sensor fusion · Neural control · Human robot interaction

1 Introduction

Orienting spatial attention [15] towards relevant events is a fundamental behaviour in humans. Spatial attention is governed by both top-down, endogenous as well as bottom-up, exogenous mechanisms. Endogenous orientation of spatial attention is driven by the purposeful assignment of neural resources to a relevant and expected spatial target. It is determined by the observer's intent and is a process requiring significant computational resources [13]. For example, when conversing with another person, our mental resources are engaged and our

© Springer Nature Switzerland AG 2018
S. S. Ge et al. (Eds.): ICSR 2018, LNAI 11357, pp. 318–328, 2018.
https://doi.org/10.1007/978-3-030-05204-1_31

spatial attention is directed towards that person. Exogenous orientation of spatial attention is driven by the sudden appearance of unexpected stimuli in the peripheral sensory space. It is determined by the properties of the stimuli alone and is manifested as an automatic reflexive saccade requiring significantly less computational resources [13]. For example, a loud noise or flash of light in our sensory periphery directs our attention via orientation of the eyes and/or head towards the spatial location of the event. This occurs even if our attention is focused elsewhere in space, for example when conversing intently with a person. In this article we focus on exogenous spatial attention orientation.

Spatial orientation behaviour is typically driven by the two dominant senses, vision and sound, providing the necessary sensory cues. Orienting towards an audio-visual target outside the visual field must initially engage auditory attention mechanisms. The resultant initial saccade towards the target may be inaccurate since auditory spatial perception is relatively inferior to its visual counterpart. Any error in orientation may then be compensated for by engaging the visual attention mechanisms that bring the target in the centre of the visual field and maintain it there. However, such sequential processing of auditory and visual spatial cues may result in unnecessary saccadic oscillations in more complex tasks. For example, orienting towards an unknown person that unexpectedly calls out our name from a location outside of the visual field. Although audio still initiates the orientation response, both auditory and visual spatial cues (that are also spatially congruent) are needed to generate an optimal orientation response. Processing of such multimodal cues results in smooth and efficient orientation behavior that minimises saccadic oscillations. Audio-visual multisensory cue integration has been studied from the perspective of Bayesian inference [7]. However, Bayesian cue integration implies that *a priori* auditory and visual estimates of spatial location as well as of their relative reliabilities are available. For a robot interacting with a human in a natural setting, the aforementioned *a priori* information cannot always be foreseen and integrated into the robot's programming.

We present an adaptive neural circuit for smooth exogenous spatial orientation. It fuses auditory and visual directional cues via weighted cue integration computed by a single multisensory neuron. The neural circuit adapts sensory cue weights, initially learned offline in simulation, online using bi-directional cross-modal learning via the Input Correlation (ICO) learning algorithm [14]. The proposed cue integration differs from true Bayesian cue integration in that no *a priori* knowledge of sensory cue reliabilities is required to determine the sensory cue weights. The neural circuit is embodied as a high-level adaptive controller for a mobile robot that must localise an audio-visual target by orienting smoothly towards it. We experimentally demonstrate that online adaptation of the sensory cue weights, initially learned offline for a given target location, reduces saccadic oscillations and improves the orientation response for a new target location.

2   Related Work

A comprehensive review of multimodal fusion techniques through a number of classifications based on the fusion methodology as well as the level of fusion can be found in [3]. There are a number of techniques reported in the literature that perform audio-visual fusion in the context of speaker tracking. Conventional approaches rely on particle filtering [12,16] as well as Kalman filtering and its extensions such as decentralized Kalman filters [6] and extended Kalman filters [8]. Other techniques reported in the literature include location-based weighted fusion [11], audio-visual localisation cue association based on Euclidean distance [20], Gaussian mixture models [18] and Bayesian estimation [10]. The goal of the present work is not to improve upon the numerous existing approaches to audio-visual spatial localisation. The majority of these systems either focus only on passive localisation or decouple the computations required for generating the subsequent motor behaviour from the computations performed for localisation. Spatial localisation in humans on the other hand utilises multimodal cues and is tightly coupled to the inevitable action that is subsequently performed, i.e. smoothly orienting towards the target. In human-robot interaction this natural and seemingly ordinary behaviour influences the trustworthiness of the robot [4] and hence the applicability of such a robot to real-world tasks. [2] have experimentally investigated user localisation and spatial orientation via multi-modal cues during human-robot interaction. However, they process auditory and visual sensor information sequentially to perform localisation. Furthermore, they decouple localisation from spatial orientation. We, on the other hand, present a neural learning architecture for crossmodal integration that tightly couples audio-visual localisation with smooth exogenous spatial orientation.

3   Materials and Methods

In the following, an overview of the robotic platform, the processing of audio and visual signals and the framework for fusing both signals is provided, as well as the experimental setup.

The Robot Platform. The Care-O-Bot (see Fig. 1) [9] is a research platform, developed to function as a mobile robot assistant that actively supports humans, e.g. in activities of daily living. It is equipped with various sensors and has a modular hardware setup, which makes it applicable for a large variety of tasks. The main components of the robot are: the omni-directional base, an actuated torso, the head containing a Carmine 3D Sensor and a high resolution stereo camera, as well as three laser scanners used for safety and navigation.

Auditory Processing. The auditory directional cue is extracted by a model of the peripheral auditory system of a lizard [5]. The model maps the minuscule phase differences between the input sound signals into relatively larger differences in the amplitudes of the output signals. Since the phase difference corresponds to the sound direction, the direction can be be formulated as a function of the sound amplitudes:

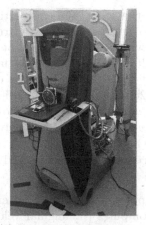

<table>
<tr><td>(a) Front view of the robot.</td><td>(b) Back view of the robot.</td></tr>
</table>

Fig. 1. The Care-O-Bot platform with key components highlighted: microphone array (1), cameras (2, 3), AR marker (4), and loudspeaker (5).

$$\left|\frac{i_\mathrm{I}}{i_\mathrm{C}}\right| = 20\left(\log|i_\mathrm{I}| - \log|i_\mathrm{C}|\right)\mathrm{dB}. \tag{1}$$

where $|i_\mathrm{I}|$ and $|i_\mathrm{C}|$ model the vibration amplitudes of the ipsilateral and contralateral eardrums. The sound direction information in (1) is subsequently normalised to lie within ± 1. Therefore, the auditory directional cue can now be formulated as

$$x_\mathrm{a} = \frac{\left|\frac{i_\mathrm{I}}{i_\mathrm{C}}\right|}{\displaystyle\max_{-\frac{\pi}{2}\geq\theta\leq+\frac{\pi}{2}}\left|\frac{i_\mathrm{I}}{i_\mathrm{C}}\right|}. \tag{2}$$

where θ is the sound direction. The model is implemented as a 4th-order digital bandpass IIR filter. The auditory direction cue as given by (1) is used as the auditory input x_a to the adaptive neural circuit. The peripheral auditory system, its equivalent circuit model and response characteristics, have been reported earlier in detail [19]. The model's frequency response is dependent on the phase differences between the input sound signals, which in turn is dependent on the physical separation between the microphones used to capture the sound signals.

An off-the-shelf multi-microphone array (Matrix Creator[1]) was used to capture the raw sound signals. The microphones were 40 mm apart, resulting in the model's frequency response lying within the range 400–700 Hz. This range is within the bounds of human speech fundamentals and harmonics (100 Hz to 17 kHz) whilst avoiding the background noise of the robot (approx. 258 Hz) and experimental arena (approx. 20 kHz).

---

[1]   www.matrix.one/products/creator.

Visual Processing. For the visual perception of the robot, the convolutional neural network YOLOv2 [17] was applied on 2D images taken with a Carmine sensor. YOLO is an object detection network showing state of the art performance on various object detection benchmarks. It is also significantly faster than other object detection architectures released since 2016. Since the computations are performed on a NVIDIA Jetson TX2[2], the YOLO-tiny variant is used resulting in a framerate of 5 Hz. The network outputs a bounding box for each detection, containing the centre of the box (u,v) and its size. Since only the relative direction of the person is required, only the horizontal position v is used. This is normalised with the image width to produce a number between ±1.

Crossmodal Learning. Figure 2 depicts the adaptive neural circuit for crossmodal integration. A single multisensory neuron computes the angular velocity ω of the robot as the weighted sum of auditory and visual directional cues x_a and x_v respectively. Audio-visual cue integration is therefore modelled as

$$\omega = w_v x_v(t) + w_a x_a(t) \tag{3}$$

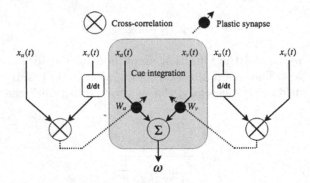

Fig. 2. The adaptive neural circuit. $x_a(t)$ and $x_v(t)$ are respectively the auditory and visual directional cues extracted by the robot that are fused to compute the robot's angular velocity ω. Synaptic weights, w_v and w_a, respectively scale the directional cues.

In (3) w_v and w_a are the synaptic weights that respectively scale the visual and the auditory directional cues. For updating the weights, two learning rules that reflect bi-directional crossmodal integration are defined:

$$\frac{\delta w_v(t)}{\delta t} = \mu x_v(t)\frac{\delta x_a(t)}{\delta t} \qquad \frac{\delta w_a(t)}{\delta t} = \mu x_a(t)\frac{\delta x_v(t)}{\delta t} \tag{4}$$

Both the learning rules employ the same learning rate μ. In either learning rule, the directional cue from one modality is multiplied with the time derivative

---

[2] www.nvidia.com/en-us/autonomous-machines/embedded-systems-dev-kits-modules/?section=jetsonDevkits.

of the directional cue from the other modality. Therefore, (4) represent cross-correlations between one directional cue and the rate of change of the other.

There are no vision weight updates when either the visual cue becomes zero and/or the auditory cue becomes constant or zero. This mechanism ensures that the weight updates progressively get relatively smaller the closer the target moves to the centre of the FoV and the slower it moves. This allows the weights to stabilise when the robot is pointing directly towards the target. A similar argument can be made for the auditory weight updates. Such bi-directional crossmodal learning allows both the visual and auditory cue weights to stabilise by compensating for errors in the directional cues extracted from either modality.

When the target is outside the FoV the visual cue x_v is zero. Therefore, the visual and auditory cue weights w_v and w_a are not updated and remain fixed at their initial values. The robot's turning behaviour initially depends only on the magnitude of the auditory cue. As the robot keeps turning, the human subject eventually appears within the FoV. Both visual and auditory cues x_v and x_a then become non-zero. As the robot continues to turn towards the human-loudspeaker target, it comes closer to the centre of the robot's auditory and FoV. Consequently, both the visual and auditory directional cues gradually decrease towards 0. The angular velocity ω, computed by (3), will also gradually decrease as a result. The robot should stop turning when it is aligned with the target.

Experimental Setup. The task of the robot in the experimental arena (Fig. 3), is to align towards an audio-visual target represented by a human subject (P) co-located with a loudspeaker (S). The angular position of the target relative to the robot's initial orientation is defined as left for $-45°$ and right for $45°$. The initial orientation of the robot in all trials is facing forward, defined as $0°$. The robot must adaptively fuse visual and auditory directional cues to generate appropriate motor velocity commands to orient towards the target. The adaptation comes from learning appropriate sensory cue weights w_v and w_a, respectively for the visual and auditory signals. The weights are initially learned offline in simulation and then adapted online to smoothen the orientation movements of the robot for targets not encountered previously.

Simulation Trials: The sensory cue weights of the neural circuit are first learned offline in simulation, using an instance of the neural circuit. In the simulation the target is placed on the right, meaning that the the weights learned offline represent optimised values for the target located to the right.

The weights w_a and w_v are randomly initialised to values between 0.01 and 0.05. At each simulation time step in a single trial, two simulated 600 Hz sinusoids, phase-shifted according to sound source location and microphone separation, are input to the ear model. These sinusoids model a loudspeaker emitting a 600 Hz tone from the target position. The normalised output x_a of the ear model maps to angular positions $\pm 90°$ relative to the initial orientation. The neural circuit computes the angular velocity using (3) and this orients the robot towards the target. As the target enters the FoV, the normalised visual directional cue

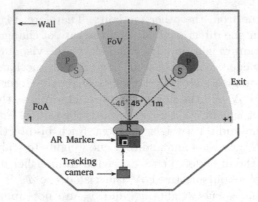

Fig. 3. Experimental setup where a loudspeaker (S) is placed 1m away from robot (R) at an offset from the centre by $\pm45°$ and with a person (P) standing just behind it. The field of view (FoV) is approx. $\pm29°$ and the field of audio (FoA) is approx. $\pm\,90°$.

x_v, between ±1 is generated. This maps to a FoV of approx. $\pm\,29°$ relative to the initial orientation. The weights w_a and w_v are subsequently updated via the ICO learning rules given by (4).

We quantify the orientation performance in terms of the orientation error. The orientation error is defined as the difference between the robot's orientation after any oscillations have died out and the target's angular position. We determine the average orientation error over a set of 10 trials with randomly initialised, but identical sensory cue weights. We perform this step 30 times to get 30 values for the average orientation error. We then perform an additional trial using, as the initial weights, the initial weights for the set with the lowest average orientation error. The weights learned at the end of this trial ($w_a = 0.027744$, $w_v = 0.034845$) are deemed as the optimised, offline-learned weights.

Real World Trials: The target is a human subject co-located with a loudspeaker emitting a 600 Hz tone. The real-world trials use another instance of the neural circuit that can adapt the offline-learned weights further, to generate smooth orientation movements. We perform two sets of trials, one where the target is located to the right and another where the target is located to the left. We perform 20 trials for each target location, where 10 trials are without online learning and 10 trials are with online learning. Therefore, 40 trials are performed in total. In all trials, the neural circuit is initialised with the offline-learned, optimised values for w_a and w_v.

A PrimeSense 3D sensor in conjunction with the ALVAR [1] software library tracks an AR marker attached to the robot (Fig. 1b). The tracking data is used to determine rotation angle of the robot relative to its initial orientation. The goal configuration, i.e. the robot facing the target and the person being in the center of the FoV, is identified manually and used as ground truth. We quantify the orientation performance of the robot in terms of the orientation error and time taken for any oscillations in the robot's movement to settle. The orientation error is defined as the difference between the robot's orientation after any oscillations have died out and the goal configuration. We define the time taken for the oscillations in the robot's movements to settle as the oscillation period. It is determined as the time from the first overshoot to when the standard deviation in orientation error reduces to below 0.3°.

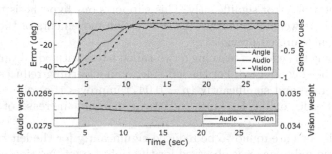

Fig. 4. Recordings from a single trial, with the target located on the left. Top: Auditory (solid black line) and visual (dotted lines) cues; the red line shows the orientation of the robot relative to the target. Bottom: weights for auditory (solid line) and visual (dotted line) cue. Shaded regions indicate the period in which audio-visual fusion occurs. (Color figure online)

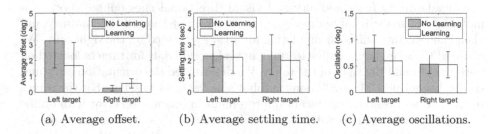

(a) Average offset.   (b) Average settling time.   (c) Average oscillations.

Fig. 5. Average results for the turning behaviour with and without learning with error bars indicating the standard deviation.

4   Results

In this section we present the results from the real-world trials. Figure 4 shows experimental data from a single trial where the development of the sensory cues, the corresponding weights and the orientation error is visible. It is evident that the orientation error initially decreases relatively slowly, when only the auditory cue is available. Once the visual cue becomes available (i.e. non-zero) the neural circuit fuses the two together to adaptively orient the robot towards the target.

The average performance of the turning behaviour it shown on Fig. 5 for both target configurations with and without learning. Since the offline weights are optimised for a target on the right side, significant improvement cannot be expected on that side. Using the offline weights for orienting to the left without fine-tuning them online results in greater orientation error in general. In this case, using online learning to further fine-tune the weights proves beneficial as it reduces orientation error significantly. This supports our hypothesis that online fine-tuning of the weights smoothes the orientation movements of the robot for a target not encountered previously.

For assessing the effect of learning a two-tailed t-test with equal variances not assumed has been conducted. For the left side, online learning reduces the offset by $49°$ in average and significantly ($p = 0.041$) improves the robot behaviour. For the right side, online learning leads to a marginal increase of the offset ($p = 0.020$).

The oscillations are found to be reduced significantly for the left target ($p = 0.043$) while no difference was observed for the right target. No significant effect has been found for the settling time although the trend for this measure was slightly positive for both targets.

5   Conclusion and Future Work

We have presented an adaptive neural circuit for multimodal and smooth exogenous spatial attention orientation, in a human-robot interaction scenario. The circuit adaptively fuses auditory and visual directional cues online to orient a mobile robot towards an audio-visual target. We first learned the auditory and visual cue weights offline in simulation for a target located on the right only. We adapted the weights via online learning in real world trials for targets located on both the left and the right of the robot. We determined the orientation error and time taken for possible oscillations in robot's movements to settle. For the target to the left, we observed significant improvement in orientation error with online learning as compared to without online learning. This supports our hypothesis that fine-tuning of the weights via online learning smoothes the orientation movements of the robot for a target not encountered previously.

The smooth spatial orientation behaviour can be subsequently extended to smoothly approach a human subject. Smooth approach can be achieved by extending the adaptive neural circuit to include the depth information. The sound localisation used here can be extended to localise natural human speech by combining multiple ear models with varying sound frequency responses.

Acknowledgement. This research was part of the SMOOTH project (project number 6158-00009B) by Innovation Fund Denmark.

References

1. Alvar 2.0. http://docs.ros.org/api/ar_track_alvar/html/
2. Alonso-Martín, F., Gorostiza, J.F., Malfaz, M., Salichs, M.A.: User localization during human-robot interaction. Sensors **12**(7), 9913–9935 (2012)
3. Atrey, P.K., Hossain, M.A., El Saddik, A., Kankanhalli, M.S.: Multimodal fusion for multimedia analysis: a survey. Multimedia Syst. **16**(6), 345–379 (2010)
4. van den Brule, R., Dotsch, R., Bijlstra, G., Wigboldus, D.H.J., Haselager, P.: Do robot performance and behavioral style affect human trust? Int. J. Soc. Robot. **6**(4), 519–531 (2014)
5. Christensen-Dalsgaard, J., Manley, G.: Directionality of the lizard ear. J. Exp. Biol. **208**(6), 1209–1217 (2005)
6. D'Arca, E., Robertson, N.M., Hopgood, J.: Person tracking via audio and video fusion. In: 9th IET Data Fusion Target Tracking Conference: Algorithms Applications, pp. 1–6 (2012)
7. David, B., David, A.: Combining visual and auditory information. In: Martinez-Conde, S., Macknik, S., Martinez, L., Alonso, J.M., Tse, P. (eds.) Visual Perception-Fundamentals of Awareness: Multi-Sensory Integration and High-Order Perception, Progress in Brain Research, Part B, vol. 155, pp. 243–258. Elsevier (2006)
8. Gehrig, T., Nickel, K., Ekenel, H.K., Klee, U., McDonough, J.: Kalman filters for audio-video source localization. In: IEEE Workshop on Applications of Signal Processing to Audio and Acoustics, pp. 118–121 (2005)
9. Graf, B., Reiser, U., Hägele, M., Mauz, K., Klein, P.: Robotic home assistant Care-O-bot 3 - product vision and innovation platform. In: IEEE Workshop on Advanced Robotics and its Social Impacts (2009)
10. Hoseinnezhad, R., Vo, B.N., Vo, B.T., Suter, D.: Bayesian integration of audio and visual information for multi-target tracking using a CB-member filter. In: IEEE International Conference on Acoustics, Speech and Signal Processing, pp. 2300–2303 (2011)
11. Kheradiya, J., Reddy, S., Hegde, R.: Active Speaker Detection using audio-visual sensor array. In: IEEE International Symposium on Signal Processing and Information Technology, pp. 480–484 (2014)
12. Kiliç, V., Barnard, M., Wang, W., Kittler, J.: Audio assisted robust visual tracking with adaptive particle filtering. IEEE Trans. Multimedia **17**(2), 186–200 (2015)
13. Mayer, A.R., Dorflinger, J.M., Rao, S.M., Seidenberg, M.: Neural networks underlying endogenous and exogenous visual-spatial orienting. Neuroimage **23**(2), 534–541 (2004)
14. Porr, B., Wörgötter, F.: Strongly improved stability and faster convergence of temporal sequence learning by utilising input correlations only. Neural Comput. **18**(6), 1380–1412 (2006)
15. Posner, M.I.: Orienting of attention. Q. J. Exp. Psychol. **32**(1), 3–25 (1980)
16. Qian, X., Brutti, A., Omologo, M., Cavallaro, A.: 3D audio-visual speaker tracking with an adaptive particle filter. In: IEEE International Conference on Acoustics, Speech and Signal Processing, pp. 2896–2900 (2017)
17. Redmon, J., Farhadi, A.: Yolo9000: Better, faster, stronger. arXiv preprint arXiv:1612.08242 (2016)
18. Sanchez-Riera, J., et al.: Online multimodal speaker detection for humanoid robots. In: 12th IEEE-RAS International Conference on Humanoid Robots, pp. 126–133 (2012)

19. Shaikh, D., Hallam, J., Christensen-Dalsgaard, J.: From "ear" to there: a review of biorobotic models of auditory processing in lizards. Biol. Cybern. **110**(4), 303–317 (2016)
20. Talantzis, F., Pnevmatikakis, A., Constantinides, A.G.: Audio-visual active speaker tracking in cluttered indoors environments. IEEE Trans. Syst. Man Cybern. Part B (Cybern.) **39**(1), 7–15 (2009)

A Two-Step Framework for Novelty Detection in Activities of Daily Living

Silvia Rossi$^{(\boxtimes)}$, Luigi Bove, Sergio Di Martino, and Giovanni Ercolano

University of Naples Federico II, Naples, Italy
{silvia.rossi,sergio.dimartino,giovanni.ercolano}@unina.it

Abstract. The ability to recognize and model human Activities of Daily Living (ADL) and to detect possible deviations from regular patterns, or anomalies, constitutes an enabling technology for developing effective Socially Assistive Robots. Traditional approaches aim at recognizing an anomaly behavior by means of machine-learning techniques trained on anomalies' dataset, like subject's falls. The main problem with these approaches lies in the difficulty to generate these dataset. In this work, we present a two-step framework implementing a new strategy for the detection of ADL anomalies. Indeed, rather than detecting anomaly behaviors, we aim at identifying those that are divergent from normal ones. This is achieved by a first step, where a deep learning technique determine the most probable ADL class related to the action performed by the subject. In a second step, a Gaussian Mixture Model is used to compute the likelihood that the action is normal or not, within that class. We performed an experimental validation of the proposed framework on a public dataset. Results are very close to the best traditional approaches, while at the same time offering the significant advantage that it is much easier to create dataset of normal ADL.

Keywords: Assistive Robots · Activities of Daily Living
Multi-class anomaly detection

1 Introduction

Dementia and age-related cognitive disorders are reaching epidemic proportions given the significant increase in the aging population. Symptoms of mental disorders are primarily manifested through changes in patients' behaviour while doing their daily activities. One of the main goals of the UPA4SAR project[1] (User-centred Profiling and Adaptation for Socially Assistive Robotics) is to detect such changes by means of reliable mechanisms able to dynamically recognize and model the user state and daily actions [4]. This is in order to correlate them to physiological states depending on the particular cognitive impairment (depression, apathy, hyperactivity, disorientation). To do so, a socially assistive

---

[1] This work has been partially supported by MIUR within the PRIN2015 research project UPA4SAR.

S. S. Ge et al. (Eds.): ICSR 2018, LNAI 11357, pp. 329–339, 2018.
https://doi.org/10.1007/978-3-030-05204-1_32

robot requires the ability to recognize and model human activities and their possible deviations, or anomalies [17], such as the robot can anticipate human needs and help him/her in a proactive way [8].

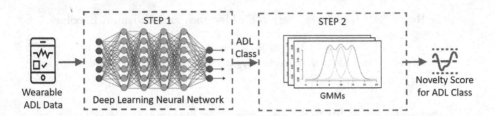

Fig. 1. The two step framework for novelty detection

In the literature, the most of the behavioral anomaly detection techniques are designed to recognize anomalies of a specific activity class (e.g., subject's falls while walking), by means of supervised learning approaches trained on fully labeled data about such activity and its anomaly examples [1,14]. In these cases, approaches, acting as two-class classifiers, achieve good results in the detection of specific behavioral anomalies, as falls. On the other hand, when dealing with anomalies due to age-related cognitive disorders, supervised classification methods cannot generally be used for three main reasons: (i) there is a number of different activities, each one with many potentially different anomalies; (ii) datasets of real-world anomalies are not available, and (iii) such anomalies are usually rare and unexpected, hence resulting in having an insufficient training data [11,13]. To make things more challenging, ethical issues regarding the collection of personal data from people suffering from cognitive impairment would require to rely, if possible, only on data collected when the ability to express a free and informed consent is still intact.

To address these issues, *novelty detection* methods might be employed since they involve the construction of a model of the normal class only, and so they do not require labelled anomalies in the training set. This makes them more suitable for the identification of real anomalies in an older and vulnerable population [7]. However, also novelty detection mechanisms are typically deployed as one-class classification approaches [3].

In this work, we address the problem of a general purpose detector able to discriminate whether an instance of the subject behavior could be an anomaly of a specific Activity of Daily Living (ADL) class (for example, walking or sitting watching tv) selected in a set of possible activities, to be employed within an Assistive Robot. Hence, a multi-class approach is a desideratum. The main idea is that the novelty detection problem can be addressed by a combination of a classification process and a density estimation learning mechanism. More in details, since we require to train models of different ADL classes, we employed deep neural networks both as features extractors, that provide the input to a density modeling mechanism, but also as an ADL classifier in order to identify the proper activity class and so its density model among the trained ones. The proposed system is composed of a Long Short-Term Memory architecture (LSTM) [6] that is used as a time-series feature extractor and to classify activities, and of a Gaussian Mixture Model (GMM) approach to model each ADL class and so to identify novel instances [15] (see Fig. 1).

The proposed framework has been preliminary evaluated using a public dataset of ADL. The results show that the approach is promising as it achieves a recall of 0.86 on anomalies. Thus, the proposed method performs as well as state-of-the-art methods for ADL classification, while at the same time offering the significant advantage that it is by far much easier to create dataset of normal ADL. Finally, it represents the first attempt using a multi-class classifier for novelty detection.

2   Related Work

In literature, different approaches are presented for dealing with novel detection in different domains (for an exhaustive review please refer to [16]). In this context, unconditionally probability density functions and Gaussian Mixture Models are typically directly deployed on the data to model its temporal pattern and as classifier mechanisms. For example, Bishop [2] used probability density functions to model the raw data that was also used to train a neural network. The aim of the density function was to measure the degree of novelty of the new input vector and so to validate the classification performance of the neural network. In our approach, GMM are used in combination with the neural network in a cascade process.

In the literature, some other approaches addresses the novelty detection problem by using a combination of neural networks and some modelling mechanisms, but always as one-class classifier (a review can be found in [10]). For example, in [9], an LSTM has been used for predicting the future trend of the input data in the case of ECG, space shuttle, power demand, and multi-sensor engine dataset. The probability distribution of the errors made while predicting on the normal data is used to obtain the likelihood of the normal behavior on the test data. The error vectors are modeled to fit a single multivariate Gaussian distribution and using the Maximum Likelihood Estimation with a threshold. In [18], fully convolutional neural networks are developed for detection and localization of anomalies in videos and Gaussian models, trained with respect to the output of different convolutional layers, are defined and used as a one-class classifier for the descriptions of normal regions.

In the domain of ADL, a novelty-based method for fall detection was used in [7]. As a supervised method for classification, the authors deployed a Convolutional Neural Network (CNN) with a one-class Support Vector Machine. In their approach, the feature space in which the detector should look for novelties is obtained by a CNN, which hierarchically extracts features that are, however, trained on a mixture of both ADL and fall examples. Then, only the normal data is fed through the CNN to train a novelty detector, which uses as input the features previously discovered by the CNN. In [12], the authors experimented the use of a novelty detection machine learning technique based on a one-class classifier that has only been trained on a single ADL in the domain of fall detection. In a more recent paper [11], the authors presented the combination of different novelty detectors, where each novelty detector takes into account a different feature extracted from acceleration time series. Finally, in [14], the authors compared different approaches for multi-class classification of ADL and falls. The dataset presented in [14] is the same public dataset used here.

3   The Proposed Two-Step Framework for Novelty Detection

In the project, we envision a behavioral monitoring strategy based on wearable sensors and robots. In particular, low-level activity recognition is performed by leveraging data from smartphones or wearable devices. This choice is motivated by the diffusion of smartphones as widely used personal devices. Then, a mobile robot is used as an active sensor whose perceptual abilities (the use of the camera) are activated to monitor the user only in the case of the detection of a possible anomaly [19].

To this aim, we address the problem of detecting a novel instance from wearable data, with respect to the different activities the user may be involved in. In this section, we introduce the proposed framework for novelty detection, whose main components are depicted in Fig. 1. In detail, the detection of the novelty of an ADL input, collected from a wearable device, is performed through two successive steps:

1. The input instance is classified as belonging to a particular ADL class i by using a combination of an LSTM-based network with a fully-connected layer.
2. The input instance is identified as a novel activity by means of a GMM that models the data representing the ADL class i.

Since the two modules exploit data-driven techniques, in the following sections, we describe how the training of this framework works in terms of a *Learning Phase* and a *Modeling Phase*.

3.1   System Training: Learning Phase

Wearable data of ADL are time-series, so one of the most widely used approaches for time-related data learning relies on Recurrent Neural Networks (RNNs) and consequently LSTM. The LSTM can be seen as a block with an internal recurrence, called self-loop, in addition to the outer recurrence of the RNN. With respect to an RNN, an LSTM cell has a greater number of parameters that are identified by a set of gating units. The input of an LSTM is the *hidden state* h^{t-1}, the *input vector* x^t, and also the LSTM self-loop that is represented by the *state unit* s^{t-1}. This state acts as a memory of the current history, and it has the ability to add or forget data by means of the *forget gate unit* f^t, the *external input gate unit* g^t, the *output gate unit* o^t [5]. The weight matrices and bias vectors are network parameters that are trained with the Back-Propagation Through Time (BPTT) algorithm.

The developed LSTM-based module consists of two LSTMs layers, each one including m LSTM-units, and a final fully-connected layer (see Fig. 2 (left)). The input of the first LSTM layer is a time series $X = \{x^1, x^2, \ldots, x^n\}$, with $x^i \in \Re^d$, where each x^i is a vector that is composed of d features $x^i = \{x_1^i, x_2^i, \ldots, x_d^i\}$. The LSTM units of the second layer are linked to a fully-connected layer for the classification of the ADL data, which has $m \times c$ nodes (where c represents the number of considered ADL classes). As previously discussed, the LSTM-based architecture will be trained on a dataset containing samples only of the considered normal c ADL classes.

3.2 System Training: Modeling Phase

After completing the deep model training, the second step requires training c GMMs, one for each ADL class.

A GMM model can be seen as a Gaussian mixture $P(z) = \sum_{k=1}^{K} \pi_k N(z|\mu_k, \Sigma_k)$ where, K represents the number of components of the Gaussian model, $\pi_k = p(k)$ is the probability of the k-th component, μ_k represents the average and Σ_k the co-variance of the k-th component.

Each GMM is trained using the output of the second LSTM layer once that the examples of a single ADL class are provided. Hence, each GMM is used to model the feature distribution of a single ADL class as computed by the LSTM (see Fig. 2 (right)). In details, the GMM train data is a $n \times m$ matrix where n is the number of data instances for a single ADL class, and m is the number of LSTM-units. The output gate values h^t of the LSTM are the input for the GMM ($h^t = \tanh(s^t)o^t$). Hence, the GMM training data are $Z = \{z^1, z^2, \ldots, z^n\}$, where $z^i = \{h_1^i, h_2^i, \ldots, h_m^i\}$.

3.3 Novelty Detection

Once a test instance is presented to the system, such instance is firstly classified by the LSTM module, then the result of the classification process is used to select a correspondent GMM to be used to decide on the novelty of the input data with respect to such ADL class (see Fig. 1).

To evaluate if a particular instance belongs to the class modeled by the GMM, we consider the log-likelihood value given by:

$$\ln p(z|\pi, \mu, \Sigma) = \ln \left\{ \sum_{k=1}^{K} \pi_k N(z|\mu_k, \Sigma_k) \right\}.$$

If such value is ≥ 0 then the instance is recognized as an element of the ADL class, otherwise, it will be considered as a novel instance of that class.

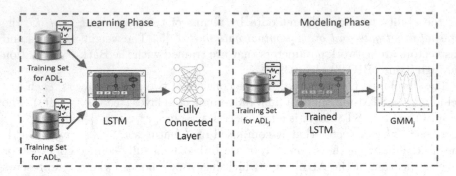

Fig. 2. The system training: learning (left) and modeling (right) phases

4   Experimental Evaluation

The proposed approach was empirically evaluated on a public dataset of sensor data about Human Activities, namely the *UniMiB SHAR (Smartphone-based Human Activity Recognition)* [14]. To get a deeper insight on the performance of the approach, we first evaluated the classification capabilities of the first module, and then the detection performances of the entire solution. In the following, we describe the experimental set-up and the obtained results.

The *UniMiB SHAR* contains 11,771 labeled records of human activities, intended as data sequences of 1 s consisting of acceleration data along the three Cartesian axes, collected by smartphones at 50 Hz. 30 persons were recruited (24 women and 6 men, age 18–60). Each record belongs to one of the 17 classes considered in the dataset: 9 are ADL (see Table 1), with 7,759 samples, and 8 are falls (e.g.: forward, backward, etc.) with 4,192 samples. The authors of the dataset used it to evaluate their approach, using a 5-fold cross-validation strategy in their experiments, and made available these 5 splits. We used these splits for our evaluation.

4.1   ADL Classification Results

For the evaluation of the LSTM-based classification module, we used only data of the 9 ADL classes. The parameters of the deep network were configured with a grid search algorithm, resulting in $m = 24$ LSTM units and 2 LSTM layers.

The performance of the classifier, averaged over the 5-folds, are reported in Table 1. As expected, we can notice that the LSTM module performance are proportional with the number of training examples, obtaining lower results for the classes with fewer instances, namely *Standing Up*, *Getting Up*, *Lying Down* and *Sitting Down*. Moreover, we noticed that, with those classes having few instances, misclassification mainly happens with respect to a corresponding dual class. For example, the class *Standing Up* is sometimes confused with *Sitting Down*, and *Getting Up* with *Lying Down*.

The dataset we employed was used also by its authors in [14] to evaluate the performances of four ADL classification techniques, namely K-Nearest Neighbor,

Table 1. 5-fold average values of LSTM classification

Class	Precision	Recall	F1-score	N. instances
1 Standing Up	0.73	0.84	0.78	30
2 Getting Up	0.74	0.55	0.63	43
3 Walking	0.93	0.97	0.92	347
4 Running	0.97	0.97	0.97	397
5 Going Up	0.90	0.89	0.89	184
6 Jumping	0.97	0.96	0.96	149
7 Going Down	0.91	0.90	0.90	264
8 Lying Down	0.75	0.70	0.72	59
9 Sitting Down	0.77	0.81	0.79	40
Avg/Total	**0.85**	**0.84**	**0.84**	**1513**

Support Vector Machines, three-layers feed forward network and Random Forest. In that paper, authors report results only in terms of Macro Average Accuracy (MAA), as it mediates the accuracy of each class with respect to the number of instances within that class. The four classification techniques used in [14] obtained MAA scores from 0.72 to 0.88. The MAA score of our proposal is 0.84. Note that, this evaluation metric gives a greater weight to the classes with a smaller number of instances, that, in our case substantially decreases the global performance.

4.2   Novelty Detection Results

Since there are 9 ADL classes in the employed dataset, after training the LSTM network, we trained 9 different GMMs. Each GMM has as input a matrix of dimension $n \times 24$, where n is the number of data instances belonging to the class c and 24 is the number of LSTM units in the second layer. For each GMM, the number of components was chosen using the Bayesian Information Criterion (BIC) approach. Gaussian parameters were trained using the Expectation Maximization (EM) algorithm. The number of Gaussian components with respect to each of the 9 ADL classes is as follows: *Standing Up* = 1; *Getting Up* = 5; *Walking* = 3; *Running* = 3; *Going Up* = 3; *Jumping* = 1; *Going Down* = 3; *Lying Down* = 2; *Sitting Down* = 1. It is worth noticing that the model with the highest number of components (i.e., 5) corresponds to the ADL class with the worse results in the classification step (*Getting Up*).

For the evaluation of the novelty detection capabilities of the entire system, we used again the 5-fold dataset, now enriched by the instances of the 8 falls classes. To measure the performances of the novelty detection, we considered as anomalies all the falls. Thus, we defined as a True Positive an instance of a falls class, which is detected as an Anomaly by the proposed framework. A False Positive is an instance of an ADL class miss-classified by the system as

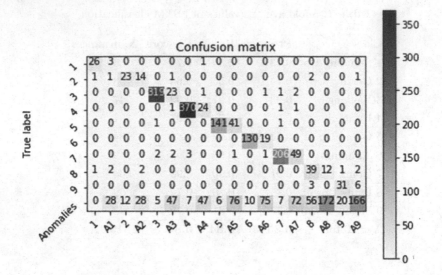

Fig. 3. A confusion matrix for the anomaly detection results for one fold

Table 2. 5-fold average values of classification/novelty detection results

Class	Precision	Recall	F1-Score	N. instances
1 Standing Up	0.87	0.76	0.81	30
2 Getting Up	0.64	0.47	0.54	43
3 Walking	0.97	0.92	0.94	347
4 Running	0.98	0.94	0.96	397
5 Going Up	0.95	0.73	0.83	184
6 Jumping	0.91	0.82	0.86	149
7 Going Down	0.94	0.81	0.87	264
8 Lying Down	0.41	0.61	0.49	59
9 Sitting Down	0.61	0.76	0.68	40
10 Anomalies	**0.77**	**0.86**	**0.81**	**834**
Avg/Tot	0.81	0.77	0.86	2347

an Anomaly. Consequently, for evaluation purposes, we are considering just one generic Anomaly class, even if the output of the system is the identification of an anomaly with respect to a specific ADL class. This is due to the fact that in the employed dataset, there are no ADL-related anomalies. Indeed they are only labeled with respect to falls classes (e.g. falling right, hitting obstacles...).

The results are summarized in Table 2, while in Fig. 3, a confusion matrix of the classification results of one fold is shown. Labels $A1 \ldots A9$ are used to identify anomaly instances belonging respectively to the classes $1 \ldots 9$. Note that most of the anomalies are labelled as anomalies of the classes *Lying Down* ($A8$) and

Sitting Down (*A*9) that are, indeed, the ADL classes that are "more related" with respect to the falls.

On the anomaly class, we obtained Precision = 0.77, Recall = 0.86, and F-1 Score = 0.81. The performance values are lower than the ones obtained during the classification phase, since the system is not trained and modeled on falls data, but only on ADL instances, so a slightly decrease of performance is a natural consequence. Moreover, let us recall that the data used as anomalies are not properly related to the considered ADL.

Moreover, as shown in Fig. 3, some instances of the ADL are correctly classified by the LSTM as belonging to the right class, but then are detected as anomalies by the GMM of that class. This could mean that the log-likelihood threshold used to discriminate whether an instance is an anomaly or not should be further investigated.

Contrary to the LSTM classification results, in this case, it is not possible to compare our performance with [14], since in that paper the goal was to recognize anomaly data as falls, so the authors used the system as a two-class classifier to evaluate whether an instance belongs to the global ADL class or the fall class.

5   Conclusions and Future Work

In this work, we presented a framework for multi-class novelty detection of Activities of Daily Living, which combines an LSTM-based deep learning architecture and Gaussian Mixture Models. With respect to the state of the art on anomaly detection, our approach does not rely on the availability of anomaly instances in the dataset, so the system is trained only on normal activities. The idea of training the classifiers only on ADL classes and not on anomalies makes the frameworks more flexible with respect to the novel data, that, when dealing with people with cognitive impairments, is difficult to obtain.

Moreover, in the presented work, we are not only interested in recognizing the input data as an anomaly, but also in identifying the ADL class corresponding to the anomaly. This kind of results could be useful for the safety of the elder person, but also for diagnostic reasons and for the improvement of the human-robot interaction itself. Hence, for these reasons, a multi-class classifier is used within the framework to provide the class information. Up to our knowledge, this is the first attempt to develop a multi-class classifier for novelty detection.

The proposed framework was tested on a public dataset, but since the considered dataset is unbalanced, lower results occurred in the case of classes with fewer instances. Nevertheless, the proposed method achieves performance comparable with state-of-the-art methods for ADL classification. As expected, the LSTM architecture achieves better results in cases of a large number of training instances. Moreover, we noticed that a miss-classification of instances in the case of classes with similar temporal pattern, such as the class Standing Up class is confused with the Sitting Down one, and Getting Up with Lying Down.

Since it is already known in the literature that LSTM provide interesting results on ADL time series data [4], but they require a significant amount of training data, as future work, we plan to evaluate the proposed solutions on bigger datasets to understand the achievable improvements.

References

1. Albert, M.V., Kording, K., Herrmann, M., Jayaraman, A.: Fall classification by machine learning using mobile phones. PLOS ONE **7**(5), 1–6 (2012)
2. Bishop, C.M.: Novelty detection and neural network validation. In: Gielen, S., Kappen, B. (eds.) ICANN 1993, pp. 789–794. Springer, London (1993). https://doi.org/10.1007/978-1-4471-2063-6_225
3. Clifton, L., Clifton, D.A., Watkinson, P.J., Tarassenko, L.: Identification of patient deterioration in vital-sign data using one-class support vector machines. In: FedCSIS, pp. 125–131 (2011)
4. Ercolano, G., Rossi, S.: Two deep approaches for ADL recognition: a multi-scale LSTM and a CNN-LSTM with a 3D matrix skeleton representation. In: 26th IEEE International Symposium on Robot and Human Interactive Communication (RO-MAN), pp. 877–882 (2017)
5. Goodfellow, I., Bengio, Y., Courville, A.: Deep Learning. MIT Press, Cambridge (2016)
6. Hochreiter, S., Schmidhuber, J.: Long short-term memory. Neural Comput. **9**(8), 1735–1780 (1997)
7. Lisowska, A., Wheeler, G., Inza, V.C., Poole, I.: An evaluation of supervised, novelty-based and hybrid approaches to fall detection using silmee accelerometer data. In: IEEE ICCVW, pp. 402–408, December 2015
8. Magnanimo, V., Saveriano, M., Rossi, S., Lee, D.: A Bayesian approach for task recognition and future human activity prediction. In: Robot and Human Interactive Communication, RO-MAN, pp. 726–731, August 2014
9. Malhotra, P., Vig, L., Shroff, G., Agarwal, P.: Long short term memory networks for anomaly detection in time series. In: Proceedings of ESANN, pp. 89–94. Presses universitaires de Louvain (2015)
10. Markou, M., Singh, S.: Novelty detection: a review's - part 2: neural network based approaches. Signal Process. **83**(12), 2499–2521 (2003)
11. Medrano, C., Igual, R., García-Magariño, I., Plaza, I., Azuara, G.: Combining novelty detectors to improve accelerometer-based fall detection. Med. Biol. Eng. Comput. **55**, 1849–1858 (2017)
12. Medrano, C., Igual, R., Plaza, I., Castro, M.: Detecting falls as novelties in acceleration patterns acquired with smartphones. PLOS ONE **9**(4), 1–9 (2014)
13. Meng, L., Miao, C., Leung, C.: Towards online and personalized daily activity recognition, habit modeling, and anomaly detection for the solitary elderly through unobtrusive sensing. Multimed. Tools Appl. **76**, 1–21 (2016)
14. Micucci, D., Mobilio, M., Napoletano, P.: UniMiB SHAR: a dataset for human activity recognition using acceleration data from smartphones. Appl. Sci. **7**(10), 1101 (2017)
15. Miljković, D.: Review of novelty detection methods. In: Mipro, 2010 Proceedings of the 33rd International Convention, pp. 593–598. IEEE (2010)
16. Pimentel, M.A., Clifton, D.A., Clifton, L., Tarassenko, L.: A review of novelty detection. Signal Process. **99**, 215–249 (2014)
17. Rossi, S., Ferland, F., Tapus, A.: User profiling and behavioral adaptation for HRI: a survey. Pattern Recognit. Lett. **99**(Supplement C), 3–12 (2017)

18. Sabokrou, M., Fayyaz, M., Fathy, M., Klette, R.: Deep-cascade: cascading 3D deep neural networks for fast anomaly detection and localization in crowded scenes. IEEE Trans. Image Process. **26**(4), 1992–2004 (2017)
19. Staffa, M., Gregorio, M.D., Giordano, M., Rossi, S.: Can you follow that guy? In: 22th European Symposium on Artificial Neural Networks, ESANN, pp. 511–516 (2014)

Design of Robotic System for the Mannequin-Based Disinfection Training

Mao Xu[1](✉), Shuzhi Sam Ge[1,2](✉), and Hongkun Zhou[3](✉)

[1] School of Automation and Institute for Future, Qingdao University,
Qingdao 266000, China
xumao820@gmail.com
[2] Department of Electrical and Computer Engineering,
National University of Singapore, Singapore 117576, Singapore
samge@nus.edu.sg
[3] 750 Test Site, China Shipbuilding Industry Corporation, Kunming 650051, China
zhouhongkun95@163.com

Abstract. The purpose of skills training is making trainers master skills correctly and utilize them efficiently in their work and life. As one of the most important skills training of nurses, the disinfection training is often trained on the medical mannequin. The effect of the mannequin-based disinfection training is often not ideal because of the lack of the feedback information generated by the disinfection training of novice nurses. To solve this problem, we design a new robotic system for the mannequin-based disinfection training by transforming the medical mannequin. The robotic system is made up of the force processing module, the location processing module and the data fusion module. The force processing module handles the vertical downward force applied by the forceps with sterilized cotton ball on the medical mannequin, and transmits the force filtered by the moving average filter to the data fusion module. The location processing module transmits the plane position information applied by the forceps to the data fusion module. The data fusion module integrates the location information and the force information to generate the pressure and the three-dimensional coordinate information of the forceps exerted on the medical mannequins. After the test of the West China Medical School, the output data of the newly designed robotic system meets the requirements of the sensing sensitivity and working range for the mannequin-based disinfection training. The new robotic system could also be utilized in other medical training fields, e.g. the massage training, the acupuncture training and so on.

Keywords: Robotic system · Disinfection training
Medical mannequin · Moving average filter · Data fusion

1 Introduction

The purpose of skills training is making trainers master and recover skills effectively, and improving their work and life. Robots are employed in some skills

© Springer Nature Switzerland AG 2018
S. S. Ge et al. (Eds.): ICSR 2018, LNAI 11357, pp. 340–348, 2018.
https://doi.org/10.1007/978-3-030-05204-1_33

training, especially in medicine, in order to improve training effects [1–6]. Yun et al. [1] designed a robotic system that trained social skills for children with autism spectrum disorder. Moorthy et al. [2] taught psychomotor skills to autistic children by employing a robotic training kit. Wang et al. [6] proposed the robotic training system for the catheter operation which combined a virtual-reality simulator and force sensation.

Medical simulation models are some simulation devices utilized in medical education [7–9]. They include an overall simulated human body, a simulated human body part, some medical instruments involved in medical treatment and so on [8]. Medical simulation models can be divided into the anatomical model, the partial task trainer, the computer interaction simulation system, and the physical driven simulator from different application scenes and different technical levels [9]. Anatomical models are mainly utilized to study the relationship of various organs and tissues of the human body, and help student to intuitively establish a knowledge framework of human anatomy [10]. Partial task trainers help students to intuitively comprehend the anatomy and physiology of a certain part of the human body or a certain system of the human body, as well as the occurrence and development of diseases [11]. Computer interaction simulation systems teach students normal and abnormal physiology and pharmacological responses [12]. Physical driven simulators simulate an autonomous and comprehensive physiological response when some operations are performed on simulators [13].

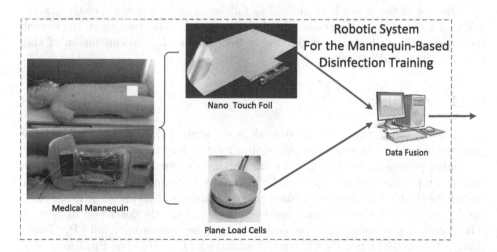

Fig. 1. The composition of the robotic system for the mannequin-based disinfection training

Medical mannequins are common medical training devices in medical simulation models [14]. They are utilized in the first aid skills training, the nursing skills training, the diagnostic skills training and so on [15]. As one of the most important skills training of nurses, the disinfection training is also often trained on the medical mannequin. The medical mannequin of the disinfection training consists of the body shape which is made of plaster or resin, and silicone case which represents the skin set on the body shape. Nurses use the forceps to train on the medical mannequin, and the forceps pick up sterilized cotton ball for imitating disinfection. The effect of the mannequin-based disinfection training is often not ideal because of the lack of the training data generated by the disinfection training of novice nurses.

In order to solve the lack of the feedback information, we design a new robotic system for the feedback information of the mannequin-based disinfection training. As shown in Fig. 1, the robotic system is composed of the nano touch foil, plane load cells and the modified medical mannequin. The foil is wrapped on the body shape, and provides the plane position information. Plane load cells are installed on the back of the medical mannequin, and capture the vertical downward force applied by the forceps on the medical mannequin. The new robotic system abstracts the abdominal region of the mannequin with a regular geometric model, and integrates the above information to generate the pressure and the three-dimensional coordinate information of the forceps exerted on the medical mannequin. After the test of the West China Medical School, the output data of the newly designed robotic system meets the requirements of the sensing sensitivity and working range for the mannequin-based disinfection training. At the same time, the new robotic system could also be utilized in other medical training fields, e.g. the massage training, the acupuncture training and so on.

The rest of the paper is organized as follows. The introduction of the framework of the new robotic system is given in Sect. 2. The two most important modules of the system are introduced in Sects. 3 and 4. The conclusion of this paper is presented in Sect. 5.

2   Framework

As shown in Fig. 2, the entire framework is made up of three parts, i.e. the force processing module, the location processing module and the data fusion module. The force processing module handles the vertical downward force applied by the forceps on the abdominal region of the medical mannequin. At the same time, it transmits the filtered force to the data fusion module in real time. The design and implementation of the force processing module are clearly described in Sect. 3. The location processing module makes use of the nano touch foil (ProTouch iFoil) which is developed by UC Nano Technologies Co. [16]. The ProTouch iFoil can directly transmit the plane position information to the data fusion module through the usb serial port. Due to the installation requirement of the ProTouch iFoil, a slight modification is made to the medical mannequin. The abdomen of the body sharp of the medical mannequin is wrapped in the regular shape element printed by 3D printer, in order to fit the installation requirement that ProTouch iFoil must be laid flat on a flat surface. The silicone case is set on the body sharp which is wrapped in the nano touch foil. According to the location information provided by the location processing module, the data fusion module integrates the location information and the force information to generate the pressure and the three-dimensional coordinate information of the forceps exerted on the medical mannequin. The fusion algorithm is clearly introduced in Sect. 4.

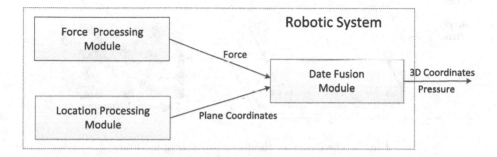

Fig. 2. The framework of the robotic system for the mannequin-based disinfection training

3 Force Processing Module

3.1 Design

The module consists of four high sensitivity plane load cells and the single-chip microcomputer (see Fig. 3). The microcomputer collects the vertical downward forces from four plane load cells, and transmits the change values of forces processed to the data fusion module in real time through the usb serial port. The data processing algorithm is introduced in Sect. 3.2. At the same time, an installation method of four plane load cells is designed in order to precisely capture vertical downward forces. Firstly, the buttons of the four load cells are installed on an acrylic plate which supports the whole equipment. Secondly, other acrylic plate is installed on the sensing surfaces of the four plane load cells due to the rugged bearing surface of the medical mannequin. At last, the medical mannequin is fixed on the above acrylic plate.

3.2 Data Processing

Due to the noise of the data collected by the plane load cell and the performance of the single-chip microcomputer, the moving average filter [17] is adopted to filter the data captured by every plane load cell. The moving average filter [17] can be described by

$$f_{i,k} = \frac{\sum_{j=k-N+1}^{k} g_{i,j}}{N} \tag{1}$$

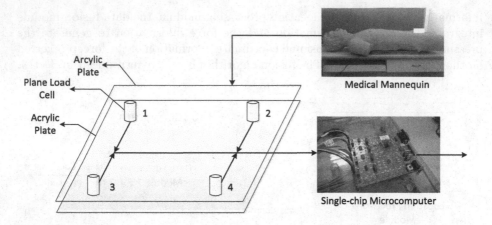

Fig. 3. The design of the force processing module

where $g_{i,j}$ is the jth force sampled by the ith plane load cell, N is the number of sliding windows, and $f_{i,k}$ expresses the kth filtered force of the ith sensor.

When there is nothing operating on the medical mannequin, the ith average pressure value of M filtered forces is the weight of the mannequin acquired by the ith sensor. The operation can be described by

$$f_i^s = \frac{\sum_{j=k}^{k+M} f_{i,j}}{M} \tag{2}$$

where f_i^s is the weight of the mannequin acquired by the ith sensor, $f_{i,j}$ is the kth filtered value of the ith sensor, and M expresses the number of time windows. At last, the force sent to the data fusion module can be expressed as

$$f_k = \sum_{i=1}^{4} (f_{i,k} - f_i^s) \tag{3}$$

where f_k is the kth vertical downward force exerted on the medical mannequin, f_i^s is the weight of the mannequin captured by the ith sensor, and $f_{i,j}$ is the kth filtered value of the ith sensor.

4   Data Fusion Module

In order to obtain the force and position information exerted by the forceps on the medical mannequin, the effective area of the mannequin, that is wrapped by the nano touch foil, is abstract as the regular shape (see Fig. 4).

According to the abstract model, the data fusion process are divided into three parts, i.e. the left semicircular area, the plane area and the right semicir-

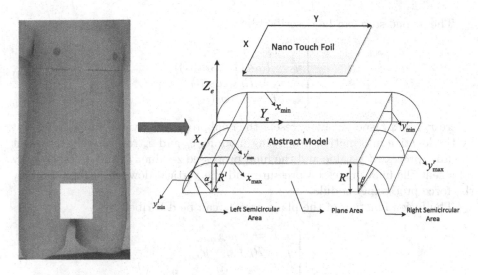

Fig. 4. The abstract model of the data fusion module

cular area. As the fusion processes of the three parts are different, the corresponding fusion method is selected by the Eq. 4.

$$
t = \begin{cases} t_l \ y_{min}^l \leq y < y_{max}^l, x_{min} \leq x \leq x_{max} \\ t_p \ y_{max}^l \leq y \leq y_{min}^r, x_{min} \leq x < x_{max} \\ t_r \ y_{min}^r < y \leq y_{max}^r, x_{min} \leq x < x_{max} \end{cases}
\tag{4}
$$

Where t is the selected fusion method according to x-value and y-value transmitted by the location processing module, t_l is the fusion method of the left semicircular area, t_p is the fusion method of the plane area, t_r is the fusion method of the right semicircular area. y_{min}^l expresses the y-value of the touch foil which is the minimum value on the left semicircular area, y_{max}^l is the y-value of the touch foil which is the maximum value on the left semicircular area, y_{min}^r also expresses the y-value of the touch foil which is the minimum value on the right semicircular area, y_{max}^r is also the y-value of the touch foil which is the maximum value on the right semicircular area. x_{min} and x_{max} express the minimum and maximum x-values of the touch foil on the abdomen of the medical mannequin. When x-value and y-value are beyond the above interval, the fusion module directly outputs an error that go beyond the boundaries.

The left fusion method t_l has two steps. The first step can be described by

$$
\alpha = \frac{y_{max}^l - y}{R_l}
\tag{5}
$$

where α is the rotation angle in the left semicircular area (see Fig. 4), y is the y-value sent by the location information processing module, R_l is the radius of the left semicircle, y_{max}^l expresses the maximum y-value of the left semicircular area.

The second step can be described by

$$
\begin{cases}
x_e = x - x_{min} \\
y_e = R_l * (1 - sin(\alpha)) \\
z_e = R_l * cos(\alpha) \\
f_e = f/cos(\alpha)
\end{cases}
\tag{6}
$$

where x_e and x respectively represent the final processed x-value and x-value sent by the location information processing module, y_e and z_e respectively represent the final processed y-value and the final processed z-value, f_e and f respectively represent the final processed pressure and the vertical downward force sent by the force processing module.

The fusion function of the plane area t_p can be described by

$$
\begin{cases}
x_e = x - x_{min} \\
y_e = R_l + y - y_{max}^l \\
z_e = R_l \\
f_e = f
\end{cases}
\tag{7}
$$

where y is the y-value which is transmitted by the location processing module, and R_l is the radius of the left semicircle.

The right fusion function t_r also has two steps. The first step can be described by

$$
\beta = \frac{y - y_{min}^r}{R_r}
\tag{8}
$$

where β is the rotation angle in the right semicircular area. The second step can be described by

$$
\begin{cases}
x_e = x - x_{min} \\
x_e = y_{min}^r - y_{max}^l + R_r * sin(\beta) \\
z_e = R_r * cos(\beta) \\
f_e = f/cos(\beta)
\end{cases}
\tag{9}
$$

The fusion information finally transfers the data structure of x_e, y_e, z_e and f_e. In the actual experiment, y_{min}^l is set to 178, y_{max}^l is set to 530, y_{min}^r is set to 896, y_{max}^r is set to 1265, both R_l and R_r are set to 229.5 ($(y_{max}^l + y_{max}^r - y_{min}^l - y_{min}^r)/\pi$), x_{min} is set to 212, and x_{max} is set to 1123. When the forceps sterilizes from left to right in the abdomen of the medical mannequin, the output of the new robotic system sees Fig. 5.

5   Conclusion

In this paper, a new robotic system has been designed to solve the lack of the feedback information for the mannequin-based disinfection training. The new system is divided into the force processing module, the location processing module and the data fusion module. After the test of the West China Medical School, the output of the robotic system meets the requirements of the sensing sensitivity and working range for the mannequin-based disinfection training.

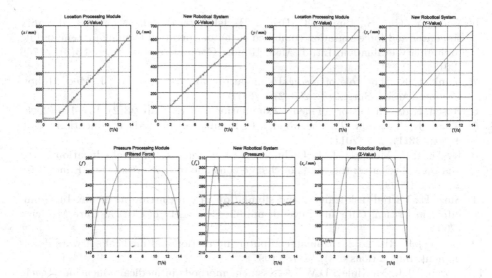

Fig. 5. The output of the robotic system for the mannequin-based disinfection training

With the newly designed robotic system for the mannequin-based disinfection training, the future plan are divided into two parts. The first part work will further optimize the abstract model of the mannequin to make the feedback data more accurate. Based on the new robotic system, the second part work will design and develop the new training system for the mannequin-based disinfection training to make the disinfection training more human and intelligent.

References

1. Yun, S.S., Choi, J., Park, S.K., Bong, G.Y., Yoo, H.: Social skills training for children with autism spectrum disorder using a robotic behavioral intervention system. Autism Res. **10**(7), 1306–1323 (2017)
2. Moorthy, R.S., Pugazhenthi, S.: Teaching psychomotor skills to autistic children by employing a robotic training kit: a pilot study. Int. J. Soc. Robot. **9**(1), 97–108 (2017)
3. Prasad, S.M., Maniar, H.S., Soper, N.J., Damiano Jr., R.J., Klingensmith, M.E.: The effect of robotic assistance on learning curves for basic laparoscopic skills. Am. J. Surg. **183**(6), 702–707 (2002)
4. Chang, L., Satava, R., Pellegrini, C., Sinanan, M.: Robotic surgery: identifying the learning curve through objective measurement of skill. Surg. Endosc. Other Interv. Tech. **17**(11), 1744–1748 (2003)
5. Gomez, P.P., Willis, R.E., Van Sickle, K.R.: Development of a virtual reality robotic surgical curriculum using the da Vinci Si surgical system. Surg. Endosc. **29**(8), 2171–2179 (2015)

6. Wang, Y., Guo, S., Tamiya, T., Hirata, H., Ishihara, H., Yin, X.: A virtual-reality simulator and force sensation combined catheter operation training system and its preliminary evaluation. Int. J. Med. Robot. Comput. Assist. Surg. **13**(3), e1769 (2017)
7. Kunkler, K.: The role of medical simulation: an overview. Int. J. Med. Robot. Comput. Assist. Surg. **2**(3), 203–210 (2006)
8. Rosen, K.R.: The history of medical simulation. J. Crit. Care **23**(2), 157–166 (2008)
9. Khan, K., Pattison, T., Sherwood, M.: Simulation in medical education. Med. Teach. **33**(1), 1–3 (2011)
10. Drake, R.L., McBride, J.M., Lachman, N., Pawlina, W.: Medical education in the anatomical sciences: the winds of change continue to blow. Anat. Sci. Educ. **2**(6), 253–259 (2009)
11. Sinz, E.: Partial-task-trainers and simulation in critical care medicine. In: Simulators in Critical Care and Beyond, pp. 33–41. Society of Critical Care Medicine (2004)
12. Gosbee, J., Ritchie, E.: Human-computer interaction and medical software development. Interactions **4**(4), 13–18 (1997)
13. Norcini, J.J., McKinley, D.W.: Assessment methods in medical education. Teach. Teach. Educ. **23**(3), 239–250 (2007)
14. Glisson, W.B., Andel, T., McDonald, T., Jacobs, M., Campbell, M., Mayr, J.: Compromising a medical mannequin. arXiv preprint arXiv:1509.00065 (2015)
15. Cooper, J., Taqueti, V.: A brief history of the development of mannequin simulators for clinical education and training. BMJ Qual. Saf. **13**(suppl 1), i11–i18 (2004)
16. Nano Touch Foil. http://www.ucnano.com/en/html/hxjs/nmckm/cptdjyy/. Accessed 22 Aug 2018
17. Reyes, P., Reviriego, P., Maestro, J., Ruano, O.: New protection techniques against seus for moving average filters in a radiation environment. IEEE Trans. Nucl. Sci. **54**(4), 957–964 (2007)

Learning to Win Games in a Few Examples: Using Game-Theory and Demonstrations to Learn the Win Conditions of a Connect Four Game

Ali Ayub[✉] and Alan R. Wagner

The Pennsylvania State University, State College, PA 16802, USA
{aja5755,alan.r.wagner}@psu.edu

Abstract. Teaching robots new skills using minimal time and effort has long been a goal of artificial intelligence. This paper investigates the use of game theoretic representations to represent interactive games and learn their win conditions by interacting with a person. Game theory provides the formal underpinnings needed to represent the structure of a game including the goal conditions. Learning by demonstration, has long sought to leverage a robot's interactions with a person to foster learning. This paper combines these two approaches allowing a robot to learn a game-theoretic representation by demonstration. This paper demonstrates how a robot can be taught the win conditions for the game Connect Four using a single demonstration and a few trial examples with a question and answer session led by the robot. Our results demonstrate that the robot can learn any win condition for the standard rules of the Connect Four game, after demonstration by a human, irrespective of the color or size of the board and the chips. Moreover, if the human demonstrates a variation of the win conditions, we show that the robot can learn the respective changed win condition.

Keywords: Game theory · Social learning · Interactive games
Active learning · Human-robot interaction

1 Introduction

In recent years, researchers have used interaction and demonstration to teach robots new activities [1–3]. Learning from demonstration (LfD) may offer a fast, intuitive, and relatively effort-free method for teaching a robot. Game theory provides the formal underpinnings needed to represent the structure of a social interaction. This paper combines these two approaches with the goal of allowing to a robot to learn a game-theoretic representation from demonstration with little prior knowledge.

Our research uses interactive games such as Connect Four to explore human-robot interaction. Games such as these are useful social paradigms that, we believe, could play an important role toward developing social robots. Interactive games are structured, both behaviorally and temporally, simplifying the task of organizing the robot's

© Springer Nature Switzerland AG 2018
S. S. Ge et al. (Eds.): ICSR 2018, LNAI 11357, pp. 349–358, 2018.
https://doi.org/10.1007/978-3-030-05204-1_34

behavior. Moreover, the structure of the interactions in these types of games are agreed upon before the game is played and typically followed by both parties.

This paper attempts to develop a computational process allowing a robot to learn the win conditions for the game Connect Four using a single demonstration and a few robot generated examples with a question and answer session led by the robot. Learning a game's win conditions is typically one of the first steps to learning a new game. A person will often explicitly ask and receive instruction about how to win a game and learn to play by watching just a few examples and some associated instructions. Towards the development of such a computational process, this paper seeks to investigate the following questions: How can a robot be equipped with a similar ability to learn the win conditions of an interactive game by watching a few examples shown by a naïve human? How can the system learn various derivative win conditions from one specific win condition shown by a human?

The overreaching objective of this research is to develop a process that allows most non-experts to teach a robot the interactive game of their choice. We thus aim to create a general process that will eventually be used to teach a robot to play a variety of games including card games, board games, and Improv games. In this paper, we develop an approach to learn the win conditions of the Connect Four game but we believe that our approach can be applied to learn the win conditions of other interactive games. The remainder of the paper begins with a brief discussion of the related work, followed by a discussion of our approach, experiments and results.

2 Related Work

The field of artificial intelligence has made significant progress in developing systems capable of mastering games such as Chess, poker, and even Go [4, 5]. Deep reinforcement learning has recently been used to train autonomous agents to play a variety of Atari and other games [6, 7]. Although the robot does learn how to play the game with a considerable accuracy, the process requires large amounts of data, time, and accurate perception.

Learning from demonstration (LfD) offers a way to reduce time and effort to teach robot new skills. LfD has been used to learn a variety of tasks like table tennis [1], pick and place various objects [3], and drawer opening [8] but there has been less work focused on using LfD to teach interactive games. Others have investigated the potential of learning by watching just a few examples. For example, [3] presented a one-shot learning mechanism for picking up an object by watching just a single video but the process required a huge amount of preliminary data and time to train the robot on very similar types of tasks. Other researchers have employed active learning in which a robot uses a question-answer session with a human to learn about a new activity [9–12]. Although using question and answer reduces the data and time required to learn a skill, it nevertheless is highly context dependent and may not be generalizable across different tasks. Some researchers have focused on the use of cognitive architectures like ACT-R and Soar to learn different goal directed actions [13, 14]. These approaches provide a formal method to reason about the actions taken to achieve a goal but there is a need to computationally represent those actions to be able to reason about them effectively. One objective of our research is to represent interactive games computationally in a way that makes knowledge transfer between known games and unknown games easy. This paper takes a step towards that objective.

Interactive two-player games can be formally represented using Game theory as stochastics games [15]. A game formally represents a strategic interaction among a set of players and a solution to a game is the set of strategies that can be used to best play the game. Previously, limited research has been done to investigate the application of game theory to control the interactive behavior of a robot with humans. Researchers in [16], attempted to formulate an abstracted link from game theory to control the interactive behavior of a social robot. In our previous work [17], we formulated the game-theoretic underpinnings needed to represent the interactive games and showed some preliminary results using simulations on how game theory can be used to learn different games by interaction with humans.

3   Representing Connect Four Using Game Theory

This paper focuses on the use of the techniques, mentioned in the previous section, on the game Connect Four. Connect Four requires player to place game chips in a 7×6 vertical matrix. Players win by creating a row, column, or diagonal of four continuous chips. The game is computationally simplistic which benefits our research because a broad age range of people can be easily taught to play the game.

Connect Four can be represented computationally as an extensive-form game (Fig. 1). It is a perfect information extensive-form game because at each stage both players have complete information about the state of the game, actions taken by the other player and the actions available to the other player in the next stage. At each turn, a player selects a column to place their respective colored chips, hence at each stage a player has a maximum of seven actions available. Figure 1 shows one stage of the extensive-form representation of the game.

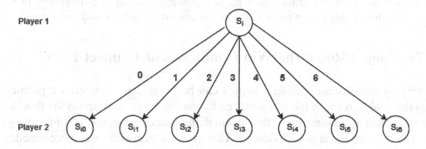

Fig. 1. Extensive-form game representation for one stage of the connect four game is depicted above. The lower nodes represent the game state after one of the seven actions (0–6) is chosen by player 2, the upper node depicts the current game state when player 1 chooses an action.

Images of the Connect Four game (Fig. 2 left) can be directly translated into an intermediate matrix format (Fig. 2 middle) indicating which player has pieces occupying specific positions in the matrix. This matrix can then be used to generate possible extensive-form games (Fig. 2 right) that can be checked against the game's win conditions. More importantly, the extensive-form game can be translated back into matrices and used to predict what different game states should look like or, as described later, presented to a person as potential win conditions for verification.

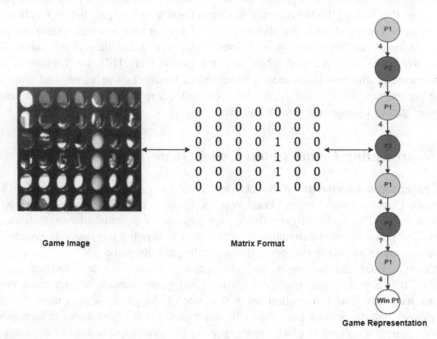

Game Image   Matrix Format

Game Representation

Fig. 2. A column win condition for the connect four game seen from the robot's perspective is shown above (left). The associated extensive-form representation is shown on the right, only the actions taken by the robot are depicted without representing all actions available at each stage. The numbers along with the arrows show the action number chosen by both players (4 by the human and ? by the robot since robot's actions are unknown). Best viewed in color.

4   Teaching a Robot the Win Conditions of Connect Four

Learning by demonstration from a human can be considered an inference problem in which the goal is to watch the actions taken by the human to accomplish the task. In the context of playing Connect Four, the person demonstrates a win condition for the game to the robot. Using the approach described above, the win condition is represented as an extensive-form game and we attempt to surmise what the rule underlying the win condition is by presenting the person with internally generated example board states and asking them whether the board depicts a winning game. Intuitively, the robot's behavior resembles the action of a person trying to learn a new game by generating fictional situations and asking whether these situations would result in a win.

To create the extended-form game structure, the robot asks a series of questions, beginning with basic questions. The robot first asks two questions: "How many players can play this game?" And "Is this a type of game in which players take alternative turns?" Once these questions are answered by the person, the robot knows how the player's actions will iterate and a largely empty extended-form game structure can be created. Next, the robot needs to match the preprogrammed basic components of the game such as what the board looks like, what are chips and their associated colors, how to physically perform the actions related to the game to the game itself. It does that by asking the person the name of the game. We used online code for the Connect Four game which includes tools for creating the requisite robot behavior and identifying the Connect Four game pieces [18]. In the future we hope to have the robot learn these items as well.

Next the robot learns the game's win conditions. First, the robot asks the human for a demonstration of a win condition (e.g. Fig. 2 left). Robot waits for the person to state, "I am done" to know that the person has demonstrated the win condition on the board. The robot converts the visual information obtained (image of the static board) into an extended-form game (Fig. 2 right). Figure 2 depicts the process of a column win. Clearly there are many other arrangements of the game pieces that will lead to other columns wins. Even though the robot does not have access to all of the game situations it can leverage the human to generate rules for winning. The robot asks the person about potential win conditions by creating different extended-form games and then converting these games to images representing the game situation that are presented to the person. The construction and use of images representing different possible game situations fosters *common ground* between the robot and the person [19]. Common ground describes the shared context that allows two individuals to fluidly communicate about a common topic. The image of the board obtained from the camera on the robot is altered to reflect possible extended-form games representing example game situations. Along with the image of the game situation a simple yes/no question is asked to confirm if that game situation will be a win condition or not. Figure 3 depicts all the stages in learning the win condition of the Connect Four game.

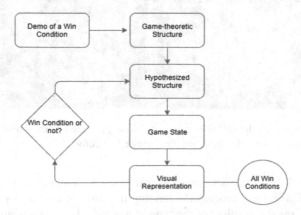

Fig. 3. A block diagram of our approach to learn the win conditions of the connect four game

Our process uses the extensive-form representation to generate potential game situations. To create these game situations, the robot first attempts to evaluate the unknowns (depicted as ? in Fig. 2). To do this, the robot generates a random action that differs from the robot's action for each of the unknowns in the demonstrated win condition and presents the situation to the person. Next the robot generates game situations in which the person takes the same action as the robot (resulting in mixed column situations). Next, the robot considers moves made prior, after, or in between the column action moves. The robot then tests if the total number of actions must be equal to the number of actions shown for the winning player, and can these actions be different than the one showed in the demonstration. An aspect of our approach is that the extensive-form formulation restricts the possible game situations that need to be asked about. Once a couple of samples of different types of extensive-form game situations are characterized by the person as containing win conditions or not, we generalize across related extensive-form games. Hence, we leverage the extensive-form game not only to create game situations for presentation to the person, but also as a means for creating subcategories of win-conditions that, collectively, describe a win rule.

As an example of how these predicted question answer sessions are performed, we show two different predicted questions related to the game-theoretic structure shown in Fig. 2. Given the game depicted in the figure, the robot first recognizes that player 2's actions are not shown, total number of actions shown by the human are four and there is only one type of action shown for player 1, and player 1 won the game. The robot generates two game situations related to the actions not shown for player 2, one focusing on whether or not the robot can take actions other than the ones shown by player 1 (moves to column 4) (Fig. 4 Left) and another examining if the robot can take actions that are the same as the one shown by player 1 (moves to column 4) (Fig. 4 Right). For a column win, the answer to the later situation is no.

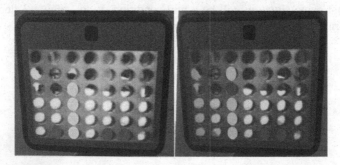

Fig. 4. Two examples of the different game situations presented to the human on the robot's monitor (located where a head would be). Best viewed in color.

We have used this process to generate win rules for column wins, row wins, and diagonal wins. The general process for creating the game situations for presentation to the person is the same regardless of the type of win rule. For some win rules, however, additional game situations need to be presented to the person. For example, diagonal wins require a specific pattern of moves by the other player. The robot therefore uses the diagonal win example to generate situations that break this pattern in different ways. The number of game situations required to learn a game rule depends on the rule. For a column win, seven game situations are generated. For a row win, eight game situations are created. And for a diagonal win, 12 different situations must be presented to the human.

5 Experiments

To evaluate this system, we used the Baxter robot manufactured by Rethink robotics. Google's text-to-speech API was used to communicate the questions in natural language to the person. The person answered the questions by typing inputs into a computer to avoid errors induced by the speech-to-text conversion process. The experimenter served as the robot's interactive partner for all the experiments. To evaluate our approach, we performed several experiments.

We hypothesized that the process described above would allow the robot to learn the three Connect Four win rules (four games pieces in a row, column, or diagonal). We tested the process by providing the robot with a single correct demonstration of one type of win rule (e.g. a column win) and a human then correctly answered the robot's questions about the self-generated game situations ("Is this a win for yellow?"). We repeated this process for the other types of win rules (row and diagonal).

Next, we tested the robot's ability to use the win rules to play a real game against a human opponent. We verified that the robot could correctly use the rules it had learned by playing ten games against the experimenter. Figure 5 (Left) shows an example of robot playing the game after learning the win conditions. For all these games the robot correctly applied the rules and demonstrated its ability to correctly identify if it or the person had won the game. Figure 5 (Right) depicts a screen the robot displays when it recognizes a winner. These experiments demonstrated that the robot could learn the win rules from a single demonstration and by using question and answer to present the person with different game situations, ultimately arriving at a set of extensive-form games constituting a win.

To further check the ability of our approach to learn different win rules we created variants of the Connect Four game for testing. The first variant which we called Connect Five, is the same as Connect Four but requires the players to create patterns of five in a row. Applying the same process, the robot was able to correctly learn the win rules for the Connect Five game and play the game against an opponent. We then created a Connect Three game. Once again, applying the same process, the robot was able to correctly learn the win rules for the Connect Three game and play the game against an opponent.

These experiments tested the robot's ability to learn the same win conditions under different circumstances. We varied the characteristics of the demonstration, the type of win conditions (row, column, diagonal), and the nature of the win conditions (connect 3, 4, and 5). The robot learned all the win conditions in all of these experiments. We considered conducting formal human subject experiments, but pilot testing indicated that the robot's performance was likely to remain perfect so long as the person

Fig. 5. An example of robot playing the connect four game after learning the rules (Left) and the message shown by the robot after the human wins the game (Right).

accurately answered the questions. We are currently also testing this approach on variants (different board colors, sizes, textures) of the same game. Here again we expect that the robot will learn all the conditions because method is independent of variations in the game board or pieces. Given that the natural source of variance in this paradigm is primarily the human subject and/or the game, future work will focus on testing this approach on games with a variety of rule versions (such as card games).

6   Conclusion

This paper has illustrated the use of game-theoretic representations of interactive games as a means of learning the win conditions of these games by interacting with a human. Our experiments show that a single demonstration accompanied with a few directed examples can be used to learn the win conditions of for the Connect Four game. The extended-form game is used represent the game state, to create realistic images for communication with the person, and to devise potential win conditions. Our experiments demonstrate the generality of the approach across win conditions, demonstrations, and game variants.

This paper makes several contributions. First, a method that connects the robot's perception of the game state to a computational and generally applicable representation is developed. These connections allow to the robot to generate visual predictions of future game states for grounded communication with the human. Second, our approach leverages the extended-form representation to make predictions about different game states. This limits the space of games states to a manageable number that the robot can ask the person about. Finally, we present a method that, we believe, will be generally applicable to a variety of different games (and possibly other HRI environments). Although we have yet to show it, we see no reason that prevents this method from generalizing across a wide variety of games and contexts. Ultimately, we hope that this avenue of research will not only offer a means for a robot to structure its interactions with a person, but also allow the robot to bootstrap an interactive exchange by using similar experiences represented in extended-form as a model for an upcoming interaction.

Naturally this research is not without limitations. We assume that the person demonstrates a valid win condition and that they correctly answer the questions about the other game situations. Moreover, this work does not address how the robot learns about the game's actions or the game components (board, tokens). Still, we strive to make as few assumptions as possible about the nature or structure of the game. Our hope is that the system will allow the robot to learn the structure of complete games.

The next step of our research will be to examine how the rules learned in this game can be transferred to less similar games. Considering, for example, card games one might use the process to look at different variants of poker or other games. Here learning by demonstration could perhaps be used to bootstrap the learning of new games from previously learned ones. Ultimately, we believe that these techniques take us one step closer to robots that can learn to interact across a wide variety of situations.

Acknowledgement. Support for this research was provided by Penn State's Teaching and Learning with Technology (TLT) Fellowship.

References

1. Mülling, K., Kober, J., Kroemer, O., Peters, J.: Learning to select and generalize striking movements in robot table tennis. Int. J. Robot. Res. (IJRR) **32**, 263–279 (2013)
2. Pastor, P., Hoffmann, H., Asfour, T., Schaal, S.: Learning and generalization of motor skills by learning from demonstration. In: International Conference on Robotics and Automation (ICRA) (2009)
3. Yu, T., et al.: One-shot imitation from observing humans via domain-adaptive meta-learning. In: Robotics: Science and Systems (RSS), Pittsburgh, PA, USA, June 2018
4. Silver, D., et al.: Mastering chess and shogi by self-play with a general reinforcement learning algorithm. arXiv Reprint arXiv:1712.01815 (2017)
5. Silver, D., et al.: Mastering the game of Go with deep neural networks and tree search. Nature **529**, 484–489 (2016)
6. Kamei, K., Kakizoe, Y.: An approach to the development of a game agent based on SOM and reinforcement learning. In: 5th IIAI International Congress on Advanced Applied Informatics (IIAI-AAI), Kumamoto, Japan (2016)
7. Dobrovsky, A., Borghoff, U.M., Hofmann, M.: An approach to interactive deep reinforcement learning for serious games. In: 7th IEEE International Conference on Cognitive Infocommunications (CogInfoCom), Wroclaw, Poland (2016)
8. Rana, M.A., Mukadam, M., Ahmadzadeh, S.R., Chernova, S., Boots, B.: Towards robust skill generalization: unifying learning from demonstration and motion planning. In: 2017 Conference on Robot Learning (CoRL) (2017)
9. Whitney, D., Rosen, E., MacGlashan, J., Wong, L.L., Tellex, S.: Reducing errors in object-fetching interactions through social feedback. In: IEEE International Conference on Robotics and Automation (ICRA), Singapore (2017)

10. Racca, M., Kyrki, V.: Active robot learning for temporal task models. In: Proceedings of the 2018 ACM/IEEE International Conference on Human-Robot Interaction, Chicago, IL, USA (2018)

11. Cakmak, M., Thomaz, A.L.: Designing robot learners that ask good questions. In: Proceedings of the Seventh Annual ACM/IEEE International Conference on Human-Robot Interaction, Boston, MA, USA (2012)

12. Hinrichs, T.R., Forbus, K.D.: Goes first: teaching simple games through multimodal interaction. Adv. Cogn. Syst. **3**, 31–46 (2014)

13. Stearns, B., Laird, J.E.: Modeling instruction fetch in procedural learning. In: 16th International Conference on Cognitive Modelling (ICCM), Madison, WI (2018)

14. Oh, J.H., et al.: Toward mobile robots reasoning like humans. In: Twenty-Ninth AAAI Conference on Artificial Intelligence (AAAI), January 2015

15. Osborne, M.J., Rubinstein, A.: A Course in Game Theory. MIT Press, Cambridge (1994)

16. Lee, K.W., Hwang, J.-H.: Human-robot interaction as a cooperative game. In: Castillo, O., Xu, L., Ao, S.I. (eds.) Trends in Intelligent Systems and Computer Engineering (IMECS 2007). LNCS, vol. 6, pp. 91–103. Springer, Boston (2008). https://doi.org/10.1007/978-0-387-74935-8_6

17. Wagner, A.: Using games to learn games: game-theory representations as a source for guided social learning. In: Agah, A., Cabibihan, J.-J., Howard, A.M., Salichs, M.A., He, H. (eds.) ICSR 2016. LNCS (LNAI), vol. 9979, pp. 42–51. Springer, Cham (2016). https://doi.org/10.1007/978-3-319-47437-3_5

18. Connect Four Demo: Rethink Robotics. http://sdk.rethinkrobotics.com/wiki/Connect_Four_Demo

19. Clark, H.H., Brennan, S.E.: Grounding in communication. Perspect. Socially Shar. Cogn. **13**, 127–149 (1991)

Semantics Comprehension of Entities in Dictionary Corpora for Robot Scene Understanding

Fujian Yan[1], Yinlong Zhang[2], and Hongsheng He[1]($\boxtimes$)

[1] Wichita State University, Wichita, KS 67260, USA
hongsheng.he@wichita.edu
[2] The Key Laboratory of Networked Control Systems,
Shenyang Institute of Automation, Shenyang 110016, China

Abstract. This paper proposes a method to help robots understand object semantics. The method presented in this paper can enhance robot's performance and efficiency while working with ambiguous instructions to interact with unfamiliar objects. Specifically, the proposed method can reduce the complexity of assigning the functions, properties or other characteristics for each object which robot may interact within a social environment. The method assists the robot to comprehend the scene based on semantics analysis of the dictionary definition. The proposed semantics comprehension method includes the comprehension of dictionary definitions, the formulation of logic representation, and the generation of natural-language descriptions. The applicability of the approach has been demonstrated. The model performance has been evaluated based on precision, recall, and f-score. Both logic representation formulation results and natural language representation results have been displayed.

Keywords: Reasoning · Robotic planning · Autonomous robots
Natural language process

1 Introduction

The relation between human beings and robots will be ubiquitous, like the relation that humans have with cell phones nowadays [2]. Social robots are expected to help humankind in medical assistance and labor shortages [3,9]. With the boosting trend of the robot interactions, the need for robots to understand and reason objects automatically within complicated social environment is urgent.

Consider the scenario where there is a robot and a cup in an environment and the robot is given an order to fill the cup with water. It is an easy instruction for human to comprehend. Humans have knowledge about cups and their functions. On the other hand, it is quite difficult for a robot to understand the purpose of an object without being given explicit instructions. In the previous

© Springer Nature Switzerland AG 2018
S. S. Ge et al. (Eds.): ICSR 2018, LNAI 11357, pp. 359–368, 2018.
https://doi.org/10.1007/978-3-030-05204-1_35

example, filling water would be an ambiguous instruction for the robot. Both subjects and objects of the commands are bypassed. To fulfill the task, some additional constrains have to be added to help improve the robot's understanding. In traditional robotic understanding, the object's constraints are provided each time to execute every task. For robotics applications in social environments, it is inefficient. It will be a great help if the robot can understand the semantics of the instruction and gather an understanding of the environment by itself. By combining the semantic understanding and the reasoning, robots can perform better, the illustration is shown as Fig. 1.

Fig. 1. Apply recognition on objects placed on table, the definition of them are gotten. The important elements are extracted from the dictionary definition. Logic tuples are formed based on these extractions. These logic tuples can be utilized in assisting robot in semantic comprehension and logic reasoning.

In this paper, a semantics comprehension method based on the dictionary definition is proposed. When humans encounter unfamiliar objects, they look up various resources such as Internet and dictionary definitions. This same method can be imposed into robot reasoning if the dictionary definitions can be translated into machine-readable data. With the improved understanding of the environments by the robot, the complexities in interaction between the human being and the robot is decreased. Using dictionary definitions, an object's knowledge can be ascertained. The proposed method is expected to assist robots to interact with objects which they have not encountered before. The neural network model is used to train the semantics comprehension model.

The main contribution for this work is to assist social robot to reason unfamiliar objects in social environments with the help of comprehension on dictionary corpora. Comprehension on dictionary corpora can be achieved by extracting the object's function, the category which the object belongs to, properties of object, and the architecture, configurations, and composition of the object.

2   Semantics Comprehension of Dictionary Definitions

The method claimed in this paper aims to divide the sentence into parts and use this small fragments to train a model to understand the dictionary definition. The fragment is based on four essential parts of the definition. Inspired from the concept of ontology [4,5,8], in English, some special words or phrases are existed which is capable to indicate the behavior of other words. These special words or phrases are landmarks in the sentence. By finding these landmarks, several behaviors such as the function of the object can be comprehended without knowing the meaning of the word which represented the function of the object. The definition is from the Oxford English dictionary and the WordNet dictionary corpora.

Inspired by [10], a neural network model is used to train the model to semantic analysis on dictionary definitions. To feed the labeled texts into the neural network model. Numeral transformed is applied to the labeled token data

$$V(T_1 \cdots T_n) = \nu_1 \cdots \nu_n \tag{1}$$

where V denotes vectorization on the labeled token data $T_1 \cdots T_n$, the results $\nu_1 \cdots \nu_n$ which is the vector of each tokenized data. These vectors are fed into the rest layers of neural network to resolve a model.

Figure 2 illustrates the strategy of the neural network model. The network contains four layers. Vectorization is needed to embed word tokens of dictionary definitions into one hundred and twenty eight dimensions vectors. After each word token is convert to the vector, a dictionary definition can be represented as a m × n matrix. Each row in this matrix represents a word token of the dictionary dictionary. To feed the input dictionary definition into a predict model, an attend process is needed. The trained model is aiming to perform the semantics comprehension tasks on dictionary definitions with paraphrasing the category, the function, the property, and the composition of the object.

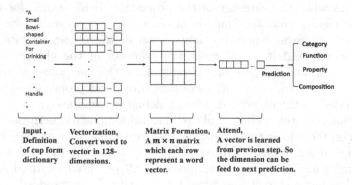

Fig. 2. Network model

3   Logic Representation

These semantic analysis results can be used by robots to infer and reason the surrounding environment. Robot can reason the environment with the assistance of four important elements. This process is similar to the human being in understanding the object according to the previously learned knowledge.

The structure and the word order of the natural language are complicated for robotic applications. On the other hand, the logic representation is meaningful and organized. It is convenient and comprehensive for robotic application. These logic representations can generate natural language descriptions with the help of the regression method.

Although the object recognition can help robots to find the location of the target object, the characteristics of the target object cannot be comprehended. The scene understanding proposed in this paper can help robots to comprehend the object based off object's category, property, function, and composition. The general form of the scene understanding is $\lambda\Omega.\Gamma(\omega,\gamma_1\cdots\gamma_n)$, where Ω is a variable which denotes the name of the expression, $\Gamma(\omega,\gamma_1\cdots\gamma_n)$ denotes the expression itself.

Assume that the object is recognizable in its environment space. The dictionary definition of the object is received. The model purposed in this paper can extract the meaningful elements from its dictionary definition. According to these elements, the following logic tuples in (2) can be derived

$$
\begin{aligned}
&\lambda Object.Cat(object, c_1 \cdots c_n)\\
&\lambda Object.Fun(object, f_1 \cdots f_n)\\
&\lambda Object.Pro(object, p_1 \cdots p_n)\\
&\lambda Object.Com(object, com_1 \cdots com_n)
\end{aligned}
\tag{2}
$$

where the Object is the name of this expression. The second object denotes the variable which is the recognized objects. "Cat" stands for the category, and it means what the category of the object is. "Fun" stands for the function, and it means what the function of object is. "Com" stands for the composition, and it means what the composition of the object is. "Pro" stands for the property, and it means what the property of the object is. $c_1\cdots c_n$, $f_1\cdots f_n$, $p_1\cdots p_n$, and $com_1\cdots com_n$ represent for the categories of the object, functions of the object, compositions of the object, and properties of the object in details based on the object's dictionary definition separately.

The robot comprehensible regulated natural language description is generated based on these logic tuples. For the category expression, the regulated natural language description is "Object is $c_1\cdots c_n$.". For the function expression, the regulated natural language description is "Object used for/used as/used to $f_1\cdots f_n$.". The method to choose "used for", "used to", or "used as" is based on the extracted functions from its dictionary definitions. Under the syntactic regulation, the word phrase "used for" is suitable for the extracted function which has "VERB" as the POS tagger and the extracted function is in the present continuous tense. The word phrase "used to" is suitable for the extracted function which has "VERB" as the POS tagger and the extracted function is in the present tense. The word phrase "used as" is suitable for the extracted function which has "NOUN" as POS tagger. For property expression, the regulated natural language description is "Object is $p_1\cdots p_n$.". For composition expression, the regulated natural language description is "Object consist of $com_1\cdots com_n$.".

There are ambiguous natural language instructions such as "Cutting the apple.". These instructions are ambiguous. It is difficult for the robot to build the connection between the action and the knife. The extracted elements from dictionary definitions of the object can help robots to reason the environment to reduce uncertainties.

4 Experiments

4.1 Experiment Setup

The definition of testing objects are from both the WordNet Dictionary [6] and the Oxford Online English Dictionary [7]. Both dictionaries have clearly structured definitions. The definition covers wide fields. The model is trained on Intel Core i7-5930 processors and a TITAN X GPU. A Sawyer robotic arm with seven degrees of freedom and an AR-10 humanoid hand is used, it has total ten degrees of freedom. The object recognition applied the tensorflow object recognition method. [1] A library of two hundred and forty daily used object's dictionary definitions are collected form the Oxford English Dictionary. Additionally, there are two groups of object's dictionary definitions. One is formed by another twenty four object's dictionary definitions collected from the Oxford English Dictionary as validation sets. The other one is twenty four object's dictionary definitions from the WordNet dictionary as validation set.

4.2 Dictionary Comprehension

The training dataset of dictionary definitions are annotated manually with four labels. These labels are category, function, property, and composition. The function which describes the functionality of the object, such as "cut, draw, and turn". The category which describes the upper level of the ontology of the object, such as "tool, instrument, and implement". The property describes the color of the object, the texture of the object, the taste of the object, and etc., such as "red, sweet, and crisp". The composition describes the composition elements of the object, such as "metal, handle, and neck".

The model is trained based on the collected dataset of dictionary definitions from the Oxford English Dictionary. Totally, there are two hundred and forty three definitions of daily used objects are collected. There are two groups of data collected additionally. Each group contains twenty definitions. One group of validation dataset is collected based on the WordNet Dictionary and the other one is collected based on the Oxford Dictionary. These two sets of validation groups are based on the same objects. The fscore of the model evaluated on the dataset of the WordNet Dictionary is 71.05%. The fscore of the model evaluated on the dataset of the Oxford English Dictionary is 80.51%. The reason for the difference between these two validations is due to structures of definitions are different. The definition structure of WordNet is more similar with word phrases instead of completed sentences. Compare with that, the structure of Oxford

Table 1. Performance results of evaluation on different groups of objects

Group	Precision	Recall	Fscore
Cutlery	88.00%	88.00%	88.00%
Fruit	82.19%	81.33%	85.31%
Tool	90.24%	85.71%	87.06%
Electronics	90.57%	85.71%	96.00%
Transport	80.00%	70.59%	75.00%

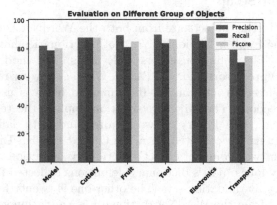

Fig. 3. Performance of precision, recall, and Fscore on different group of objects

dictionary definition is more complete and it is more similar with entire sentence structure. The evaluation accuracy should be improved if more data has been fed into the model training. However, the annotation and the data collection is time-costly.

There is a comparison experiment on the difference of the model performance on different group of objects. There are five different groups of objects. They are cutlery, fruit, tool, electronics, and transport. Each group includes ten objects. The definition of each object is from the Oxford online dictionary. The first group of the object is the cutlery which includes spoon, knife, fork, chopstick, tongs, toothpick, skillet, pepper mill, ladle, and slotted spoon. The second group of the object is the fruit which includes apple, pear, banana, mango, watermelon, melon, peach, papaya, pineapple, and grapefruit. The third group of the object which includes hammer, tape, shovel, screwdriver, rake, spanner, pliers, pincer, seal, and saw. The forth group of the object which includes oven, keyboard, mouse, computer, television, microwave, lamp, heater, monitor, and radio. The last group of the object which includes car, train, airplane, jeep, truck, boat, ship, rocket, motorcycle, and bicycle. The definitions for the tool, the cutlery and the electronics are mainly focused on the functions of objects. The definition for fruit is mainly focused on the property. The definition of transport is mainly focused on the composition. The evaluation results of each group's precision,

Table 2. Some results of dictionary semantic analysis

Object	Definition from Oxford [7]	Language description
Pool	An artificial pool for swimming in	A pool is a pool It is used for swimming It is artificial
Screwdriver	A tool with a flattened or cross-shaped tip that fits into the head of a screw to turn it	A screwdriver is a tool It is used to turn It is cross-shaped It consists of tip
Tray	A flat, shallow container with a raised rim, typically used for carrying the food and drink, or for holding small items or loose material	A tray is container It is used for carrying, holding It is flat, shallow, and raised
Skillet	A small metal cooking pot with a long handle, typically having legs	A skillet is a pot It is used for cooking It is small, long It consists of metal
Washer	A person or device that washes something	A washer is a device It is used to wash
Toothbrush	A small brush with a long handle, used for cleaning the teeth	A toothbrush is a brush It is used to clean
Basketball	The inflated ball used in basketball	A basketball is a ball It is inflated
Keyboard	A panel of keys that operate a computer or typewriter	A keyboard is a panel It is used to operate
Pen	An instrument for writing or drawing with ink, typically consisting of a metal nib or ball, or a nylon tip, fitted into metal or plastic holder	A pen is an instrument It is used for writing, drawing It consists of metal nib, nylon tip, and plastic holder
Cup	A small bowl-shaped container for drinking from, typically having a handle	A cup is a container It is used for drinking It is small, bowl-shaped It consists of handle
Scissors	An instrument used for cutting cloth, paper, and other material, consisting of two blades laid one on top of the other and fastened in the middle so as to allow them to be opened and closed by thumb and finger inserted through rings on the end of their handles	A scissors is an implement It is used for cutting

recall, and Fscore is demonstrated in Table 1. The Fig. 3 shows the evaluation on performance of the model on different groups of objects. The performance is better than model evaluation due to the definitions of the first group, the second group and the fourth group are mainly focused on functionality description. The frequency of indicating word phrases such as "used for", "used as" and "used to" are high. To understand the target object's function is an important aspect of robot semantic comprehension for its environment. The performance of the second group is better than overall evaluation. The property is also an

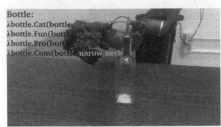
Bottle:
λbottle.Cat(bottle, container)
λbottle.Fun(bottle, storing)
λbottle.Pro(bottle, plastic)
λbottle.Com(bottle, narow neck)

A bottle is a container. It is used for storing. It is plastic.It consists of narrow neck.

Cup:
λcup.Cat(cup, container)
λcup.Fun(cup, drinking)
λcup.Pro(cup, small, bowl-shaped)
λcup.Com(cup, handle)

A cup is container. It is used for drinking. It is small,bowl-shaped. It consists of handle.

Knife:
λknife.Cat(knfie, instrument)
λknife.Fun(knfie, cutting, weapon)
λknife.Com(knfie, blade)

A knife is an instrument. It is used for cutting, weapon. It consists of blade.

Fork:
λfork.Cat(fork, instrument)
λfork.Fun(fork, lifting, holding)
λfork.Com(fork, prongs)

A fork is an instrument. It is used for lifting, holding. It consists of prongs.

Screwdriver:
λscrewdriver.Cat(screwdriver, tool)
λscrewdriver.Fun(screwdriver, turn)
λscrewdriver.Com(screwdriver, tip, cross − shaped)

A screwdriver is a tool. It is used to turn. It is cross-shaped. It consists of tip.

Scissors:
λscissors.Cat(scissors, implement)
λscissors.Fun(scissors, cutting)
λscissors.Com(scissors, blade)

A scissors is an instrument. It is used for cutting. It consists of blade.

Fig. 4. Experiment results of logic tuple and robot comprehensible sentences (Color figure online)

important aspect for robot to understand its environment. The performance of the fifth group is lower than the overall evaluation. The reason for that is the structure of transport's definition is unorganized which means that the frequency of indicating word phrase such as "with", "consist of", "belong to" is low. To increase the performance more data is needed. Table 2 are samples of object's dictionary definition results. These samples are selected from daily used objects. The first column is the object. The second column is the definition of the object. The third column is the logic language result.

4.3 Robotic Experiment

Objects are recognized based on TensorFlow object recognition method [1]. The object recognition processed on the workstation. The first Oxford dictionary definition of the object as a noun is fed into the trained semantics comprehended model. The following group of experiment results are shown in Fig. 4, both logic tuples and robot comprehensible regulated natural language commands are illustrated in these results. For logic tuples, the category of the object is displayed in red. The function of the object is displayed in green. The property of the object is displayed in blue. The composition of the object is displayed in yellow. There are six samples presented which are the bottle, the cup, the knife, the fork, the screwdriver, and the scissors. The definition of these six objects are from the Oxford English dictionary.

5   Conclusion

In this paper, both the robot semantics comprehension on dictionary definitions and the robot reasoning are discussed. Four important elements which are the category, the property, the composition, and the function are extracted based on object's dictionary definition. The neural network model is applied to train the model to automatically recognize and extract target entities. For social robot applications, social robots can help customers to prepare a meal based on the draft recipe such as sweet fruit salad. The robot will select objects in fruit category, and according to fruit's property to choose ones which are sweet. Another example is that robot can help in industry more independently, such that, the robot will know how to manipulate tools according to the tool's functions based on dictionary definitions.

References

1. Abadi, M., et al.: TensorFlow: a system for large-scale machine learning. In: Proceedings of the 12th USENIX Conference on Operating Systems Design and Implementation. OSDI 2016, pp. 265–283. USENIX Association, Berkeley (2016). http://dl.acm.org/citation.cfm?id=3026877.3026899
2. Breazeal, C.: Role of expressive behaviour for robots that learn from people. Philos. Trans. R. Soc. Lond. B: Biol. Sci. **364**(1535), 3527–3538 (2009)
3. Kamei, K., Zanlungo, F., Kanda, T., Horikawa, Y., Miyashita, T., Hagita, N.: Cloud networked robotics for social robotic services extending robotic functional service standards to support autonomous mobility system in social environments. In: 2017 14th International Conference on Ubiquitous Robots and Ambient Intelligence (URAI), pp. 897–902. IEEE (2017)
4. Maedche, A., Staab, S.: Ontology learning for the semantic web. IEEE Intell. Syst. **16**(2), 72–79 (2001)
5. McGuinness, D.L., Van Harmelen, F., et al.: Owl web ontology language overview. W3C Recomm. **10**(10), 5–6 (2004)
6. Miller, G.A.: WordNet: a lexical database for English. Commun. ACM **38**(11), 39–41 (1995)
7. Oxford University Press: Oxford Dictionary of English. Oxford University Press, Oxford (2010)

8. Ramanathan, V., et al.: Learning semantic relationships for better action retrieval in images. In: Proceedings of the IEEE Conference on Computer Vision and Pattern Recognition, pp. 1100–1109 (2015)
9. Scassellati, B., Admoni, H., Matarić, M.: Robots for use in autism research. Annu. Rev. Biomed. Eng. **14**, 275–294 (2012)
10. Yang, Z., Yang, D., Dyer, C., He, X., Smola, A., Hovy, E.: Hierarchical attention networks for document classification. In: Proceedings of the 2016 Conference of the North American Chapter of the Association for Computational Linguistics: Human Language Technologies, pp. 1480–1489 (2016)

The CPS Triangle: A Suggested Framework for Evaluating Robots in Everyday Life

Susanne Frennert(✉) 📵

Department of Technology in Health Care,
Royal Institute of Technology School, Stockholm, Sweden
susafren@kth.se

Abstract. This paper introduces a conceptual framework: the CPS triangle, which has evolved over four years of research on 'older people meet robots'. It is a synthesis of domestication theory, modern social practice theory and empirical data. Case studies on the domestication of one current technology, the robotic vacuum cleaner, and two emergent technologies, the eHealth system and the service robot, provide empirical evidence. Considering 'older people meet robots' within the framework of the proposed CPS triangle can help us to understand older people's domestication or rejection of robots. In the CPS triangle, C represents the cognitive dimension; P, the practical dimension; and S, the symbolic dimension. The CPS triangle is meant to serve as a tool rather than a rule. It is recommended that the CPS triangle be tested more widely in a range of contexts. It will require adaptation and customisation for the context of use.

Keywords: Framework · Robots · Older people · In 'the wild'

1 Introduction

Why is it important to understand the relationship between older people and robots? The awareness of demographic ageing and increased care costs, as well as the recognition of robots as a solution for independent living and ageing in place, the preferences of the society and most older people, has led to increased investments in and the development of technologies for older people [1]. As a result, older people are becoming a target group for political and economic interests. The development of robots for older people has been generally characterized by a lack of recognition of age differentiation. In particular, there is a spillover of the values of society at large. This means that developers' decisions about robots for older people carry the stamp of society's values that stress frailty, illness and vulnerability [2, 3]. Too often, ageing is regarded as problematic, and older people are understood as needing motivation and assistance. Under the guise of good intentions, this is actually false charity because it encourages passivity and alienation, thereby embodying and sustaining oppression. Old age often connotes negative changes, such as cognitive and physical limitations [4].

Research on older people and technology suggests that technology adoption by older users cannot be generalized. It cannot be assumed that all old people are technophobes [5]. It has been suggested that the attitude towards a specific technology has to be analysed within the context of social practice [6]. Joyce and Loe [7] reported

© Springer Nature Switzerland AG 2018
S. S. Ge et al. (Eds.): ICSR 2018, LNAI 11357, pp. 369–379, 2018.
https://doi.org/10.1007/978-3-030-05204-1_36

that older people actively identify, adapt and reject a range of technologies. The stereotypical portrayal of older people as technophobes might stem from Western cultural values. For example, young people are often portrayed as being interested in the latest technologies and eager to learn how to use them. In contrast, older people are depicted as being uninterested in technological change, experiencing difficulties in learning new technologies and having low physical and cognitive abilities [8, 9]. The reasons for older people's not using certain technologies targeted to them might lie in the technologies' implicit values. These can be an 'age script' or mid-life values, such as productivity, effectiveness and independence [10].

According to Akrich's terminology, designers develop a 'script', such as that for an actor in a movie, to guide the user's practices and actions when interacting with a specific artefact [11]. In his PhD thesis, Neven provided evidence for older users' being rendered passive and being categorised according to age in the design of new and emerging telehealth care technologies [4]. Neven used the notion of 'age scripts' to illustrate this phenomenon, which has influenced the approach to designing scripts for telehealth care environments [4]. Greenhalg *et al.* used ethnographical methods to assess the requirements for assisted living [12].

The insights provided by these approaches highlight the need to shift the focus 'from product (assistive technologies) to performance (supporting technologies-in-use)' [12]. The main challenge is to design technology that is appropriate for the socio-cultural and personalised context of the user. A complication is the heterogeneity of older people. In theory, there is no agreed-upon definition of 'older people' [13, p. 6] because the group is heterogeneous. Older people vary considerably in individual abilities, skills and experiences [14]. Age is likely to increase the differentiation within this 'group' more than within most other 'groups' because of life experiences and physical health status. Furthermore, older people have a lifetime of experiences, and their reasoned actions and behaviours differ from those of younger users because of societal norms, values, friends and family [15].

Given the rapid growth of the older population and the increasing digitisation of society, there is a need to expand and to further develop the technologies for older people in order to complement their personal care and assistance and to facilitate their participation in society [1]. In this context, the proposed CPS (cognitive, practical and symbolic dimensions) triangle will provide a conceptual tool for expanding our understanding and interpretations of the relationship between older people and robots. The objective of the framework is to provide a tool for evaluating and/or developing robots for older people.

This study will first elaborate on the synthesis of domestication theory and practice theory. Next, three case descriptions on older people meeting robots will be presented within the synthesised framework. The CPS triangle will be elucidated as a framework for examining the relationship between older people and robots. The proposed CPS triangle outlines some of the key issues and contradictions surrounding older people meeting robots. It has the power to increase our understanding of the relationship between older people and robots. It is hoped that the proposed CPS triangle will promote new ways of developing and evaluating robots targeted to older people. It has previously been argued that in 'the wild', the actual commitment is longer than in an experimental laboratory study. Thus, the motivational effect of participating in the development of new technologies might fade if the specific technology to be not what users want or need [16]. In 'the wild', actual use is harder to fake because it can be monitored; therefore, the actual use of an innovation can be understood. Conducting this research revealed the lack of a framework for studying robots in 'the wild' and determining the extent to which they complete older people's everyday practices within the context of the home.

This study proposes a framework that can increase our understanding of older people in relation to their use or rejection of robots. It is hoped that it can provide new ways of developing and evaluating robots targeted to older people. The study is not perfect; flaws will be found. The framework provides recommendations for studying the complex reality of Human-robot interaction in 'the wild' to generate practical and generalisable results that can be compared and validated.

2 The CPS Triangle

This research began as an exploration of the question: 'What do older people do with robots after they have been installed in their homes?' The research prompted an interest in theories about the social shaping of technology and domestication and their focus on technology in everyday practices, as well as the process of familiarisation with and the integration of new technologies into everyday practices. The goal of the research became the understanding of older people's experiences of 'domestication' robots. The assumption was that an increased understanding of older people and the process of adopting a robot could be gained only through uncovering their experiences and the meanings that they give to them.

Domestication theory and modern social practice theory are closely related to everyday practices and the use of technology. The theories describe a process and humanistic set of principles that can be associated with technology adoption, or rejection, and change. The domestication theory framework originates from the disciplines of anthropology and consumption research: specifically, studies regarding the role and meaning of television in domestic life [17]. A key question is: 'How and why do technologies emerge in a specific form?' [18].

Silverstone explored the processes of the shaping and adoption technologies and linked them to the concept of the domestication of animals [17]. The key stages in the domestication process were identified as appropriation, objectification, incorporation and conversion [18]. The appropriation stage describes the considerations and negotiations prior to and upon the entry of a specific technology into the home of the user. Objectification is the symbolic and spatial location given to the technology in the home by the users. Incorporation is the fit of the technologies with the routines and schedules. Conversion is the incorporation of the technology into the user's identity and the portrayal of the technology to others [17–20]. The domestication of technology has been found to be affected by both micro- and macro-level variables [21]. For example, the economy and the individual's status in the household (micro level) and cultural habits, attitudes and expectations (macro level) affect the decision about the integration of a technology into everyday life. In addition, members of a household can integrate the same technology differently into their own lives. Silverstone *et al.* defined this phenomenon as the 'moral economies of the household' [17]. The concept highlights the negotiation of the meaning of a specific technology within a household and between the household and the cultural context in which it exists.

Modern social practice theory is more a research approach than a coherent theory. It has been used in studies, such as those by Schatzki (2010), Shove *et al.* (2012), Reckwitz (2002) and Warde (2005), which drew heavily upon Bourdieu's praxeology, Gidden's structuration, late Foucault and Garfinkel [22]. Similar to domestication theory [17], modern practice theory [23, 24] consists of ecological models (see [22, 25–27]) that focus on linking action, individuality and social order through everyday practices [22]. Methods such as ethnography and observation are used in an attempt to focus on people's actions and habits. The models increase our understanding of the individual and collective aspects of the domestication of technology by considering the reasons for the integration of technology into people's everyday lives and the manner in which it is done; thus, social practices emerge and evolve [22, 23, 28, 29].

Practice theory focuses on the relationship between agency and structure [30]. Agency is the individual's capacity to act individually and independently to make choices. Structure is the social forces such as gender, age, class and context, that determine an individual's choices. An individual's intentional actions and interactions are understood to produce and to alter the social system and practices [31]. In practice theory, the social system is seen as consisting of a number of elements that are continually re-arranged [32]. Practice and actions create and reproduce the social system in which the actions are embedded [30]. It could be argued that there are similarities in the approaches of practice theory and domestication theory to technology adoption, adaptation and rejection. Both sets of theories highlight the importance of the practical, symbolic and cognitive dimensions in the domestication and integration of technology into everyday practices. The vocabulary from practice theory and domestication theory can be useful for deepening our understanding of the adoption, adaptation and rejection of robots.

Figure 1 illustrates the incorporation of the concepts of social practice theory, such as those by Shove, Schatzki and Gram-Hanssen [23, 26], into the domestication framework [29].

A. *The Cognitive Dimension*

The cognitive dimension includes the competence and skills for using the robot. The users need to know how to use a robot in order to create a new practice, i.e. to adopt the robot. Schatzki described this as 'knowing how to X, knowing how to identify X-ings, and knowing how to prompt as well as respond to X-ings' [26]. The user needs to be able to use her/his existing knowledge and to transfer that knowledge through interactions with the robot to achieve her/his goals for the interaction. In some cases, the user needs to learn new skills or to change prior understandings to be able to use the robot.

B. *The Practical Dimension*

The practical dimension of the domestication of a robot is affected by the context of use as well as the rules and procedures that prohibit or guide the user into certain patterns of use. For example, a driver should drive a car on the right side of the road,

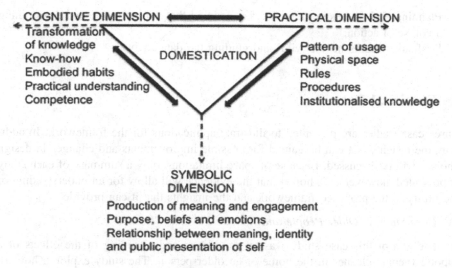

Fig. 1. A model of the dimensions in the CPS triangle

stop at red lights and stop if pedestrians would like to cross the street on zebra crossings (at least in Sweden) or else the driver might be penalised by the traffic police or other drivers. Similarly, users' actions might be inscribed in the artefact by 'scripts' [11], such as the beeping sound that would be heard if the driver does not put on the seatbelt or exceeds 300 km per hour (controlled by the fuel supply to the engine).

C: *The Symbolic Dimension*

The symbolic dimension includes both the individual aspects and the social structures. The individual's ability, needs and desires are affected by the norms and values of the social system. For example, having a car enables getting from A to B. Any car can do this; however, there are many brands and sizes of cars from which to choose. The purchase of a car is influenced by factors such as affordability, purpose (e.g. family or individual use), family needs, image (the car as a representation of identity) and the cars owned by friends and neighbours.

D. *Framework Objectives*

These three dimensions (cognitive, practical and symbolic) of the domestication of a robot are interrelated. Studying robots in everyday life is likely to require the careful examination of a range of challenges. The basic model of the CPS framework (Fig. 1) can facilitate the framing of a robot within a specific context. The domestication of a robot is made with the full consideration of the older individual's circumstances, such as the cognitive, practical and symbolic dimensions. Furthermore, the process of older peoples' domestication of robots is dynamic. There is constant movement and interaction among the cognitive, practical and symbolical dimensions. The framework can be useful for:

- Planning HRI studies in 'the wild', i.e. defining the problem space and determining a course of action.
- Evaluating robots in 'the wild' and guiding the data analysis.

3 Empirical Data

Three case studies are presented to illustrate applications for the framework. In addition, the insights that can be gained for possible improvements and changes in design choices will be discussed. Because of space limitations, only a summary of each study is presented; however, it is hoped that the evidence will allow for an understanding of the utility of the proposed framework and the insights that it can provide.

A. *Case Study 1: Older People and Robotic Vacuum Cleaners*

The aim of this case study was to provide an understanding of the effects of a robotic vacuum cleaner in the home of an older person. The study explored how 10 older people who participated in a 24-month study (autumn 2013 to late summer 2015) domesticated or rejected robotic vacuum cleaners [33]. A descriptive multi-case study design was applied. The data collection involved structured interviews, participant observation and in-depth interviews.

The purpose of the participant observation was to collect data on the participants' cleaning practices with and without the robotic vacuum cleaner. The participant observations were conducted before and several times after the robotic vacuum cleaner was 'moved' into the older participants' homes. The observations included walk-through tours of the older people's homes. The tours were modelled after the technology biography ethnography method [34]. The older people were asked to guide the researcher around the home and to show all the technology they used (personal technology history). Field notes were taken during the observations. Interviews were also conducted. Each participant was interviewed and observed four to five times: before the robotic vacuum cleaner was installed; one week after the vacuum cleaner was installed; and six, 13 and 24 months after the vacuum cleaner was installed. Each interview lasted approximately 45–90 min. The interviews, which were audio recorded, were conducted in the participants' homes. The objective was to explore the reasons why older people use, or do not use, robotic vacuum cleaners.

The key findings from the study were that the robotic vacuum cleaners were domesticated by nine out of 10 users [33]. The results indicate that the domestication process was imbued with the symbolic, practical and cognitive dimensions. In the context of older people meeting robotic vacuum cleaners, the practical dimension included the more frequent use of the robotic vacuum cleaner than the traditional vacuum cleaner by a majority of the participants. They took it to their second home if they had one. They carried the robotic vacuum cleaner from room to room to ensure that each room was properly cleaned before it started to clean another room. They created obstacles to prevent the robotic vacuum cleaner from entering certain areas because of concerns about damage to carpets or furniture.

A disadvantage was the older participants' perceptions of cleaning the brushes (an activity that needed to be performed frequently) and moving furniture around to provide clear spaces for the robot as difficult. The meaning, the symbolic dimension, of the robotic vacuum cleaner was the improvement to the quality of everyday life. While the robotic vacuum cleaner was cleaning the floors, the older participants could engage in more meaningful activities, such as hobbies or socialising. Some of the participants also found the robotic vacuum cleaners entertaining. The cognitive dimension of the robotic vacuum cleaner included the perception of ease of use and similarity to the utility of the traditional vacuum cleaner.

B. *Case Study 2: Older People and an eHealth System in the Making*

The aim of this case study was to understand older people's domestication or rejection of a possible eHealth system and to gain insights into the most important points for future development. The fieldwork was conducted between June 2013 and November 2014. The research was undertaken in a European Union (EU)-funded project on eHealth technologies for older people in their homes (www.giraffplus.eu). The study was conducted in the municipality of Örebro, Sweden.

The fieldwork on which this study was based consisted of interviews with 20 people, including the older participants in the home trials, their relatives and healthcare professionals; and participant-observations through home visits, including walk-trough tours in the older participants' domestic environments. The research drew on empirical data collected at three stages: before the eHealth system was installed, during the period the system was installed and used at the participants' homes, and after the system had been uninstalled [35]. The eHealth system collected daily behaviour and physiological data from sensors. It performed context recognition and, in particular, long-term trend analyses. The system consisted of a network of non-invasive wireless home sensors and a semi-autonomous telepresence robot. The sensors measured blood pressure and bed/chair occupancy. They could also detect a fall. At the centre of the system was a unique telepresence robot: the Giraff (for more detailed information, see [36]).

The results indicate that the eHealth system did not provide enough features to engage users. The design and utility of the robot and the system prevented active use because the robot was designed for the older user, who could call just one predetermined receiver, to be contacted only. In addition, the user could not access the data collected by the sensors, i.e. the practical dimension. The practical dimension also included the eHealth system's being limited to indoor use even though most of the participants spent a considerable amount of time outside their homes (e.g. doing errands, shopping, visiting friends, having lunch in the canteen or visiting outpatient rehabilitation). The relatives and healthcare professionals did not become engaged because the system did not support the technology cluster, such as smartphones and tablets, of which they were a part. The components of the cluster were the normal means of maintaining contact with the older individuals. Another reason for the unsuccessful appropriation was the potential older users' inability to control and to use the system (the cognitive dimension).

It is interesting and unfortunate that the design of the system reflected a stereotype of older people as passive receivers of care; however, the older participants wanted to have an active role in directing and controlling, i.e. mastering, the technology. Many of the older participants did not see themselves reflected in the wider representation of vulnerable older people for whom they thought the system had been designed. In addition, they felt that they were not in need of such an eHealth system at that time (the symbolic dimension). However, changing health circumstances were mentioned as the most likely reason for having such a system.

C. *Case Study 3: Older People and an Assistive Robot in the Making*

The aim of the study was to understand older people's domestication or rejection of an assistive robot. The fieldwork was conducted within the EU-funded project HOB-BIT (www.hobbit-project.eu). A robotic system was developed to assist older people and to enable them to continue living in their own homes longer. The robot had a mobile platform, multiple sensors, a multimodal user interface and an arm with a gripper. It also had features such as human detection, tracking, gesture recognition, gripping and learning (for more detailed information, see [37]).

A descriptive multi-case study was conducted. The data collection included interviews, diaries, robot walk-throughs, observations and robot use shadowing. Two robot prototypes were installed at seven older peoples' (average age 81) homes. Each trial lasted three weeks. The author participated in the installation of the robots. The author was involved in setting up the robot (localization, head calibration, arm references, etc.), introducing it to the older people and observing their use of it. Working on the installation of the robot allowed for the incorporation of interviews and observations. Thus, the author observed the evolution of the use of the robot. The participants were observed while learning about, interacting with and using the robot on several occasions. They were also interviewed individually in their homes on three occasions. The older participants were asked to use cameras and diaries to document their use of the robot.

The key findings indicate that the robot was perceived as easy to use despite the support and learning assistance that had to be provided repeatedly (the cognitive dimension). It became apparent that only a few tasks or functionalities could be introduced at any specific time and that repetition was necessary for the older participants' learning and mastery of the functionalities of the robot. Written and illustrated user guides were provided. They were highly appreciated by the participants. It became clear that learning the gestures for interaction with the robot was almost impossible because of the participants' unfamiliarity with this mode of operation. Touch screens and speech input were preferred. The practical dimension included the appreciation by a majority of the participants of the convenience of having the computer, radio, telephone, audio book and game functions in one place, the robot. However, most of the participants were set in their ways with respect to using the regular telephone instead of the robot for making calls.

A perceived disadvantage was the need to retrofit the home to accommodate the robot. For example, carpets, threshold ramps, full-length mirrors and glass tables had to be removed. The pattern of use was also restricted by the robot's inability to navigate narrow passages and high thresholds. Another disadvantage was the size. The robot was perceived as being too large, resulting in poor manoeuvrability in the average apartment. Many older people's apartments tend to be cluttered with inherited, purchased and cherished furniture. During the study, it became clear that most of the participants felt lonely at times. The robot became a companion (symbolic dimension), and in its presence, they felt less lonely. One of the older persons said: 'I feel less lonely since I have to think about the robot ... it keeps me occupied, and I got less time to think about myself and death.' Trying out the robot and participating in the research created an identity of its own and attracted attention, thus providing a topic of discussion with friends and family.

4 Conclusion

These three case studies illustrate the importance of understanding the dynamics of older people meeting robots and the domestication or rejection of robots. The focus cannot be on just the older individual or a specific robot. The context of the unique moments of the robot's completion of the everyday practices of the older individual must also be considered. This paper proposed a framework for studying the relationship between older people and robots in 'the wild'. The CPS framework can increase our understanding of older people with regard to robots and provide new ways of developing and evaluating robots that are targeted to older people.

References

1. Peine, A., Rollwagen, I., Neven, L.: The rise of the 'innosumer'—rethinking older technology users. Technol. Forecast. Soc. Change **82**, 199–214 (2014)
2. Neven, L.: 'But obviously not for me': robots, laboratories and the defiant identity of elder test users. Sociol. Health Illn. **32**(2), 335–347 (2010)
3. Frennert, S., Östlund, B.: Seven matters of concern of social robots and older people. Int. J. Soc. Robot. **6**(2), 299–310 (2014)
4. Neven, L.B.M.: Representations of the Old and Ageing in the Design of the New and Emerging: Assessing the Design of Ambient Intelligence Technologies for Older People. University of Twente (2011)
5. Essén, A., Östlund, B.: Laggards as innovators? Old users as designers of new services & service systems. Int. J. Des. **5**(3), 89–98 (2011)
6. Joyce, K., Loe, M.: A sociological approach to ageing, technology and health. Sociol. Health Ill. **32**(2), 171–180 (2010)
7. Joyce, K., Loe, M.: Technogenarians: Studying Health and Illness Through an Ageing, Science, and Technology Lens, vol. 11. Wiley, Hoboken (2011)
8. McMillan, S.J., Avery, E.J., Macias, W.: From havenots to watch dogs: understanding internet health communication behaviors of online senior citizens. Inf. Commun. Soc. **11**(5), 675–697 (2008)
9. Belk, R.: Possessions and self. J. Consum. Res. **15**(2), 139–168 (1988)
10. Neven, L.: Representations of the Old and Ageing in the Design of the New and Emerging. Assessing the Design of Ambient Intelligence Technologies for Older People (2011)
11. Akrich, M.: The description of technical objects. In: Bijker, W.E., Law, J. (eds.) Shaping Technology, Building Society: Studies in Sociotechnical Change, pp. 205–224. MIT Press, Cambridge (1992)

12. Greenhalgh, T., et al.: What is quality in assisted living technology? The ARCHIE framework for effective telehealth and telecare services. BMC Med. **13**(1), 91 (2015)
13. Victor, C.R.: The Social Context of Ageing, London. Routledge, Abingdon (2005)
14. Czaja, S., Lee, C.: The impact of aging on access to technology. Universal Access Inf. **5**(4), 341–349 (2007)
15. Ajzen, I.: The theory of planned behavior. Organ. Behav. Hum. **50**(2), 179–211 (1991)
16. Frennert, S.: Older People and the Adoption of Innovations (2014)
17. Silverstone, R., Hirsch, E.: Consuming Technologies: Media and Information in Domestic Spaces. Psychology Press, Hove (1992)
18. Haddon, L.: Domestication analysis, objects of study, and the centrality of technologies in everyday life. Can. J. Commun. **36**(2), 311–323 (2011)
19. Haddon, L.: Roger silverstone's legacies: domestication. New Media Soc. **9**(1), 25–32 (2007)
20. Livingstone, S.: On the material and the symbolic: Silverstone's double articulation of research traditions in new media studies. New Media Soc. **9**(1), 16–24 (2007)
21. Lie, M., Sørensen, K.H.: Making Technology Our Own?: Domesticating Technology into Everyday Life. Scandinavian University Press North America (1996)
22. Reckwitz, A.: Toward a theory of social practices: a development in culturalist theorizing. EJST **5**(2), 243–263 (2002)
23. Shove, E., Pantzar, M., Watson, M.: The Dynamics of Social Practice: Everyday Life and How It Changes. Sage, Thousand Oaks (2012)
24. Gram-Hanssen, K.: Understanding change and continuity in residential energy consumption. J. Consum. Cult. **11**(1), 61–78 (2011)
25. Schatzki, T.R., Knorr-Cetina, K., von Savigny, E.: The Practice Turn in Contemporary Theory. Psychology Press, Hove (2001)
26. Schatzki, T.R.: Site of the Social: A Philosophical Account of the Constitution of Social Life and Change. Penn State Press, University Park (2010)
27. Warde, A.: Consumption and theories of practice. J. Consum. Cult. **5**(2), 131–153 (2005)
28. Silverstone, R., Haddon, L.: Design and the domestication of ICTs: technical change and everyday life. In: Silverstone, R.A.M. (ed.) Communication by Design. The Politics of Information and Communication Technologies, pp. 44–74. Oxford University Press, Oxford (1996)
29. Sørensen, K.H., Aune, M., Hatling, M.: Against linearity on the cultural appropriation of science and technology. In: Between Understanding and Trust: The Public, Science and Technology, p. 165 (2000)
30. Gherardi, S.: How To Conduct a Practice-Based Study: Problems and Methods. Edward Elgar Publishing, Cheltenham (2012)
31. Cetina, K.K., Schatzki, T.R., von Savigny, E.: The Practice Turn in Contemporary Theory. Routledge, Abingdon (2005)
32. Shove, E.: Comfort, Cleanliness and Convenience: The Social Organization of Normality. Berg, Oxford (2003)
33. Frennert, S., Östlund, B.: The domestication of robotic vacuum cleaners among seniors. Gerontechnology **12**(3), 159–168 (2014)
34. Blythe, M., Monk, A., Park, J.: Technology Biographies: Field Study Techniques for Home Use Product Development. ACM (2002)
35. Frennert, S., Östlund, B.: What happens when seniors participate in new eHealth schemes? Disabil. Rehabil. Assist. Technol. **11**, 1–9 (2015)

36. Coradeschi, S., et al.: GiraffPlus: a system for monitoring activities and physiological parameters and promoting social interaction for elderly. In: Hippe, Z.S., Kulikowski, J.L., Mroczek, T., Wtorek, J. (eds.) Human-Computer Systems Interaction: Backgrounds and Applications 3. AISC, vol. 300, pp. 261–271. Springer, Cham (2014). https://doi.org/10.1007/978-3-319-08491-6_22
37. Fischinger, D., et al.: Hobbit—the mutual care robot. In: Workshop on Assistance and Service Robotics in a Human Environment Workshop in Conjunction with IEEE/RSJ International Conference on Intelligent Robots and Systems (2013)

Feature-Based Monocular Dynamic 3D Object Reconstruction

Shaokun Jin[2,3] and Yongsheng Ou[1,2,4(✉)]

[1] Guangdong Provincial Key Laboratory of Robotics and Intelligent System,
Shenzhen Institutes of Advanced Technology, Chinese Academy of Sciences,
Shenzhen 518055, China
ys.ou@siat.ac.cn
[2] Shenzhen Institutes of Advanced Technology, Chinese Academy of Sciences,
Shenzhen 518055, China
[3] Shenzhen College of Advanced Technology,
University of Chinese Academy of Sciences, Shenzhen, China
[4] The CAS Key Laboratory of Human-Machine-Intelligence Synergic Systems,
Shenzhen Institutes of Advanced Technology, Chinese Academy of Sciences,
Shenzhen 518055, China

Abstract. Dynamic 3D object reconstruction becomes increasingly crucial to various intelligent applications. Most existing algorithms, in spite of the accurate performances, have the problems of high cost and complex computations. In this paper, we propose a novel framework for dynamic 3D object reconstruction with a single camera in an attempt to address this problem. The gist of the proposed approach is to reduce the reconstruction problem to a pose estimation problem. We reconstruct the whole object by estimating the poses of its topological segmentations. Experiments are undertaken to validate the effectiveness of the proposed method in comparison with several state-of-art methods.

Keywords: Dynamic 3D object reconstruction
Topological segmentation · Pose estimation · Monocular

1 Introduction

3D object reconstruction has been a substantial technology required in industry [1]. It facilitates the visual understanding of dynamic social environment for the robots, therefore constituting one of the necessary techniques related to social robotics. 3D object reconstruction can be found in various intelligent applications incorporating real-time 3D visualization [2], integral imaging [3], the face detection technology [4], 3D object retrieval [5] and tomographic phase microscopy [6]. Though 3D static object reconstruction has reached its high level

This work was jointly supported by National Natural Science Foundation of China (Grant No. U1613210) and Shenzhen Fundamental Research Programs (JCYJ20170413165528221, JCYJ2016428154842603).

© Springer Nature Switzerland AG 2018
S. S. Ge et al. (Eds.): ICSR 2018, LNAI 11357, pp. 380–389, 2018.
https://doi.org/10.1007/978-3-030-05204-1_37

of maturity, there still maintain various challenges in the direction of 3D dynamic object reconstruction due to uncertain latent factors implicated by the dynamic scene. Thus, the necessity of effective and efficient approaches constitutes the motivations of researches in this direction.

In this paper, we mainly focus on the object reconstruction, which aims at recovering the overall 3-dimensional information. Algorithms for object reconstruction mainly exists in the form of multi-camera methods on account of a basic fact that the 3D object reconstruction requires images captured from multiple perspectives. A series of algorithms adopts the scheme of jointly executing the segmentation and reconstruction of a dynamic scene from various views [7]. Co-segmentation of images captured from distinct perspectives [8] and temporal coherence in reconstruction [9] are also applied as means to refine the accuracy of reconstruction results. Also, monocular ways for 3D object reconstruction are investigated such as the methods in [10]. They generally depends on appearance-based pixel categories and the stereo cues as input information and CRF as the model. The output results are the dense reconstruction of a dynamic scene and its segmentations.

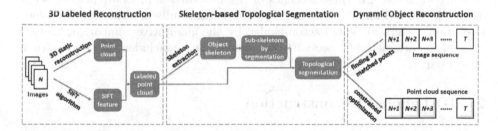

Fig. 1. In the first phase (the dashed box named 3D Labeled Reconstruction), images captured by a moving camera are applied to reconstruct the 3-dimensional information of an object in its stationary status and are utilized to extract SIFT features. The SIFT features are attached to the reconstructed 3d point cloud to label the corresponding points in R^3 (Specifically introduced in Sect. 2); in the second phase, there are two modules respectively named Skeleton-based Topological Segmentation (the second dashed box) and Dynamic Object Reconstruction (the third dashed box). The former module provides the labeled point cloud an appropriate topological segmentation (Specifically introduced in Sect. 3). The latter module compute the approximate pose and position of each topological part in respect with the camera based on the image captured at present and the labeled object point cloud. The reconstruction result can be subsequently acquired through re-organizing the topological parts at their new poses and positions (Specifically introduced in Sect. 4).

The work in this paper is to utilize a single camera to resolve the dynamic 3D object reconstruction. The problem addressed can be stated in a formulaic way: given the images $\left\{m_i^j\right\}_{\substack{i=1...N \\ j=1...M}}$ captured within time (the pose and position alters at each time $i \leq N$ in order that static 3D reconstruction of the object can be satisfactorily achieved) and images captured at time $i > N$, the expected result is the dense reconstruction of the object $\left\{P_i^j\right\}_{\substack{i>N \\ j=1...M}}$ at the same time $i > N$. In this sense, conventional surface reconstruction methods fail to recover 3-dimensional information from all perspectives. While existing object reconstruction approaches have the common problems of large computation consuming, considerable space requirement for restoration as well as high equipment (cameras) cost.

Accordingly, we consider to fully utilize the 3D information acquired from the foregoing frames and then reduce the dynamic object reconstruction problem to a re-organizing problem. The pipeline of the proposed approach is illustrated in Fig. 1. As shown in the flowchart, We first provides a stable way to segment an object point cloud topologically based on the segmentation of its skeleton. Then, the positions and poses of all topological parts are computed by solving an optimization problem at each frame. The object reconstruction result is finally obtained through a simple re-organization of the topological parts at their predicted positions and poses.

The remainder of this paper is structured as follows. Sections 2, 3 and 4 individually introduce the three modules of the proposed approach (enclosed with dashed boxes in Fig. 1) specifically. Experimental results are provided on a low resolution camera in Sect. 5 accompanied by the qualitative comparison to two state-of-the-art methods. Section 6 summarizes and concludes the contribution of this paper.

2 3D Labeled Reconstruction

In this paper, the equipment utilized is a single camera. Thus, we denote P_i^j as the coordinate of jth 3-dimensional point at i^{th} time and denote m_i^j as the corresponding image coordinate of P_i^j observed by the unique camera at i^{th} time. During the time $i \leq N$, $\{P_j\}$ maintain invariant. Meanwhile, the camera keeps changing its position and pose as well as capturing images $\left\{m_i^j\right\}_{\substack{i=1...N \\ j=1...M}}$ in order to realize 3d reconstruction $\left\{P_j^*\right\}_{j=1...M}$. In this paper, $\left\{d_j^i\right\}_{\substack{i=1...N \\ j=1...M}}$ is acquired through a similar computing or from a direct measurement. At any time $i > N$, the position and pose of the camera is fixed whilst $\{P_j\}$ keeps altering stochastically. $\forall x$, let $y = R_i x$, considering that R_i is a rigid transformation, we have

$$\|y\| = \|x\| \Rightarrow y^T y = x^T x \Rightarrow x R_i^T R_i x = x^T x$$
$$\Rightarrow x^T \left(R_i^T R_i - I\right) x = 0 \Rightarrow R_i^T = R_i^{-1} \tag{1}$$

Thus, we have

$$P_j = R_i^T \begin{bmatrix} \frac{d_j^i}{f^i} I_{2\times2} & O_{2\times1} \\ O_{1\times2} & d_j^i \end{bmatrix} \begin{bmatrix} m_j^i \\ 1 \end{bmatrix} - R_i^T t_i \tag{2}$$

For the image captured by the camera at i^{th} time ($i < N$), the keypoints and their corresponding descriptor vectors can be easily attained through SIFT algorithm as $\{(m_s^i, l_s^i)\}_{s=1...S}$. Then through Eq. (2), we can acquire $\{(P_s^i, l_s^i)\}_{s=1...S}$. For denotation simpleness, we define that any P_j that is occluded from the view of ith camera or whose corresponding m_j is not a keypoint still has a descriptor vector $l_j = 0$, which means we get $\{(P_j^i, l_j^i)\}_{\substack{i=1...N \\ j=1...M}}$ after N^{th} time. The consequent 3d labeled reconstruction is as the form of:

$$\{(P_j^*, l_j^*)\}_{j=1...M} = \left\{\left(P_j^*, \frac{\sum_i^N l_j^i}{\sum_i^N \mathrm{sgn}\left(\|l_j^i\|\right)}\right)\right\}_{j=1...M} \tag{3}$$

3   Skeleton-Based Topological Segmentation

We denote the skeleton of Ω as $S(\Omega)$ and the dilation of $S(\Omega)$ by B after T iterations as $B_T(S(\Omega))$. Suppose $C(\Omega) \subset S(\Omega)$, an equivalence relation $\sim_C$ implicated by $C(\Omega)$ is defined as $\forall p_1, p_2 \in S(\Omega)$, $p_1 \sim_{C_1} p_2$ if and only if p_1, p_2 are on a curve segment whose ends are two points in $C(\Omega)$ and no other points in $C(\Omega)$ are on the same curve segment.

Thus, the curve segments determined by $C(\Omega)$ are the equivalence classes $S_C(\Omega)$ defined as

$$S_C(\Omega) = S(\Omega)/\sim_C = \{\{p \in S(\Omega) : p \sim_C q\} : q \in S(\Omega)\} \tag{4}$$

It is simple to see that $\forall S_1, S_2 \in S_C$, the following two conditions cannot hold together:

$$S_1 = S_2 \tag{5}$$

$$(S_1 \cap S_2) \backslash C(\Omega) = \emptyset \tag{6}$$

In this paper, we propose two categories of points respectively denoted as $C_1(\Omega)$ and $C_2(\Omega)$ in order that $C(\Omega) = C_1(\Omega) \cup C_2(\Omega)$ determines $\sim_C$ in Eq. (4)

The First Category $C_1(\Omega)$. Assign indexes to each element in $S(\Omega)$, namely let $S(\Omega)$, where K is the total number of elements in $S(\Omega)$. Considering $\{p_k\}_{k=1...K}$ as the vertices of a graph and regarding the connection $\{e_{mn}\}_{\substack{0<m\leq K \\ 0<n\leq K}}$ between $\forall p_m, p_n \in \{p_k\}_{k=1...K}$ as the edges of the graph, an adjacency matrix $M(\Omega)$ can be acquired in the following form:

$$M(\Omega) = M(\Omega)^T = \begin{array}{c} \\ p_1 \\ p_2 \\ \vdots \\ p_K \end{array} \begin{array}{c} p_1\ p_2\ \cdots\ p_K \\ \left[\begin{array}{cccc} e_{11} & e_{12} & \cdots & e_{1K} \\ e_{21} & e_{22} & \cdots & e_{2K} \\ \vdots & \vdots & \ddots & \vdots \\ e_{K1} & e_{K2} & \cdots & e_{KK} \end{array}\right] \end{array} \tag{7}$$

where $e_{mn} = 1$ if p_m and p_n are adjacent to each other. Otherwise, $e_{mn} = 0$. Thus, the elements in $diag\,(M\,(\Omega))$ are all 0. Then the first category of points $C_1\,(\Omega)$ is defined as

$$C_1\,(\Omega) = \left\{ p_m \in \{p_k\}_{k=1...K} \,\middle|\, \sum_n^K e_{mn} > 2 \ or \ \sum_n^K e_{mn} = 1 \right\} \tag{8}$$

The Second Category $C_2\,(\Omega)$. Similar to $S_C\,(\Omega)$ (Eq. (4)), $S\,(\Omega)$ segmented by $C_1\,(\Omega)$ is

$$S_{C_1}\,(\Omega) = S\,(\Omega)\,/\sim_{C_1} \tag{9}$$

We define the function of the cth curve segment (suppose C curve segments totally) in $S_{C_1}\,(\Omega)$ as $r_c\,(u_c)$, where u_c is the arc length parameter of the function r_c and $u_c \in (0, L_c)$ (L_c is the length of the cth curve segment). Then the Frenet formulas of the cth curve is

$$\frac{d}{du_c} \begin{bmatrix} r_c \\ \alpha_c \\ \beta_c \\ \gamma_c \end{bmatrix} = \begin{bmatrix} 1 & 0 & 0 \\ 0 & \kappa_c & 0 \\ -\kappa_c & 0 & \tau_c \\ 0 & -\tau_c & 0 \end{bmatrix} \begin{bmatrix} \alpha_c \\ \beta_c \\ \gamma_c \end{bmatrix} \tag{10}$$

where α_c, β_c and γ_c are individually the unit vector tangent, normal unit vector and binormal unit vector of r_c; κ_c and τ_c are the curvature and torsion. We construct a quantum δ_c satisfying that $\delta_c \propto \kappa_c$ and $\delta_c \propto \tau_c$ as well as a threshold v. Then the second category of points $C_2\,(\Omega)$ is defined as

$$C_2\,(\Omega) = \{p = r_c\,(u_c)\,|\,\delta_c \geq v\}_{c=1...C} \tag{11}$$

Skeleton Dilation Under Constraints. Finally, we dilate each sub-skeleton in $S_C\,(\Omega)$, thus acquiring a topological segmentation of Ω in the proposed way. In each iteration $t \in \{1...T\}$, we remove the points that violate the following two constraints:

$$B_t\,(S_{c_1}\,(\Omega)) \cap B_t\,(S_{c_2}\,(\Omega)) = \emptyset \tag{12}$$

$$B_t\,(S_{c_1}\,(\Omega)) \cap \bar{\Omega} = \emptyset \tag{13}$$

where $S_{c_1}\,(\Omega)$ and $S_{c_2}\,(\Omega)$ represent two distinct sub-skeletons in $S_C\,(\Omega)$, $\bar{\Omega}$ is the external space of Ω.

Moreover, for the dilation of each sub-skeleton $S_{c_1}\,(\Omega)$ under constraints Eqs. (12) and (13), the corresponding total iteration times T satisfy that

$$B_{T+1}\,(\Omega) = B_T\,(\Omega),\ \ B_T\,(\Omega) - B_{T-1}\,(\Omega) \neq \emptyset \tag{14}$$

Then the dilation of sub-skeletons in $S_C\,(\Omega)$ under constraints in the form of Eqs. (12), (13) and (14) forms a equivalence relation for topological segmentations $(\Omega, \mathcal{T})$.

4   3D Reconstruction at i^{th} Time

Suppose the image captured at i^{th} time $(i > N)$ as $\left\{m_i^j\right\}_{j=1...M}$. Through SIFT algorithm, we can simply obtain the two-tuple set $\left\{\left(m_i^j, l_i^j\right)\right\}_{j=1...M}$. Compared to $\left\{\left(P_j^*, l_j^*\right)\right\}_{j=1...M}$, we can acquire a new two-tuple set $\left\{\left(m_i^{f_i}, P_{f_i}^*\right)\right\}_{f_i=j_1...j_F}$ as

$$\left\{\left(m_i^{f_i}, P_{f_i}^*\right)\right\}_{f_i=j_1...j_F} = \left\{\left(m_i^j, P_j^*\right) \middle| l_i^j \sim_{SIFT} l_j^*\right\} \tag{15}$$

where $l_i^j \notin \emptyset$, $l_j^* \notin \emptyset$, $\sim_{SIFT}$ indicates that two descriptor vectors are matched to each other under the similarity computing method of SIFT algorithm, and F is the total number of matched descriptor vector pairs. It is obvious that

$$\left\{m_i^{f_i}\right\}_{f_i=j_1...j_F} \subset \left\{m_i^j\right\}_{j=1...M} \tag{16}$$

$$\left\{P_{f_i}^*\right\}_{f_i=j_1...j_F} \subset \left\{P_{f_i}^*\right\}_{j=1...M} \tag{17}$$

In addition, $\left\{\left(m_i^{f_i}, P_{f_i}^*\right)\right\}_{f_i=j_1...j_F}$ implicates a bijective map φ_i : $\left\{m_i^{f_i}\right\}_{f_i=j_1...j_F} \rightarrow \left\{P_{f_i}^*\right\}_{f_i=j_1...j_F}$, which satisfy that

$$P_{f_i}^* = \varphi_i\left(m_i^{f_i}\right) \tag{18}$$

$$m_i^{f_i} = \varphi_i^{-1}\left(P_{f_i}^*\right) \tag{19}$$

Suppose $\mathcal{T} = \{[p] : p \in \Omega\} = \{\{q \in \Omega : q \sim p\} : p \in \Omega\}$ as the basis for the topology of space $\Omega = \left\{P_j^*\right\}_{j=1...M}$. We can get the basis for topology (denoted as $\mathcal{T}_i$) of the subset $\left\{P_{f_i}^*\right\}_{f_i=j_1...j_F} \subset \left\{P_{f_i}^*\right\}_{j=1...M}$ by

$$\mathcal{T}_i = \left\{T_c \cap \left\{P_{f_i}^*\right\}_{f_i=j_1...j_F} \middle| T_c \in \mathcal{T}\right\} \tag{20}$$

On account of Eq. (19), we can further acquire the basis for the topology (denoted as $\mathcal{T}_{m_i}$) of the set $\left\{m_i^{f_i}\right\}_{f_i=j_1...j_F}$ by

$$\mathcal{T}_{m_i} = \left\{\varphi_i^{-1}\left(T_{m_i}\right) \middle| T_{m_i} \in \mathcal{T}_i\right\} \tag{21}$$

Based on the proposed design, each element in $\mathcal{T}$ is a rigid component of Ω. Thus, when the object represented by Ω moves stochastically, the elements in $T_c \in \mathcal{T}$ have the same rigid transformation, namely, there exists a single pair (R_i^c, t_i^c) for T_c^i such that

$$T_c^i = R_i^c T_c + t_c^i \tag{22}$$

where R_i^c is a 3-dimensional rotation matrix, t_i^c is a 3-dimensional translation vector and $R_i^c T_c^i + t_c^i$ is defined as

$$R_i^c T_c^i + t_c^i = \left\{ R_i^c p + t_c^i \,\middle|\, p \in T_c^i, T_c^i \in \mathcal{T} \right\} \tag{23}$$

where p is denoted in the form of a column vector.

Define $T_{c_i} = T_c \cap \left\{ P_{f_i}^* \right\}_{f_i = j_1 \dots j_F}$, since $T_{c_i} \subset T_c$, based on Eq. (22), we can get the actual coordinates of $T_{c_i}^i$ at i^{th} time as

$$T_{c_i}^i = R_i^c T_{c_i} + t_c^i \tag{24}$$

Then, we can get another expression of $\varphi^{-1}(T_{c_i})$ as

$$\varphi^{-1}(T_{c_i}) = \left\{ m_i(p) \,\middle|\, p \in T_{c_i}^i \right\} \tag{25}$$

where $m_i(\cdot)$ is an operator to transform a 3-dimensional point to 2-dimensional coordinate related to the camera at i^{th} time, which is defined as

$$\forall p \in R^3, \quad m_i(p) = \frac{f^i}{[O_{1\times2}\ 1]\,p} \left[I_{2\times2}\ O_{2\times1} \right] p \tag{26}$$

Thus, we can compute a (R_i^c, t_i^c) for T_c^i by solving the following optimization problem:

$$(R_i^c, t_i^c) = \arg \min_{(R_i^c, t_i^c)} \sum_{p \in T_{c_i}} \left[\varphi^{-1}(p) - m_i(R_i^c p + t_i^c) \right]^2 \tag{27}$$

Finally, the raw result of the 3d reconstruction $\left\{ \tilde{P}_i^j \right\}_{\substack{i > N \\ j = 1 \dots M}}$ based on $\left\{ m_i^{f_i} \right\}_{f_i = j_1 \dots j_F}$ at i^{th} time is

$$\left\{ \tilde{P}_i^j \right\}_{i > N\ j = 1 \dots M} = \bigcup_{T_c \in \mathcal{T}} (R_i^c T_c + t_i^c) \tag{28}$$

5   Experiments and Discussions

We select the initial frame and four other nonconsecutive frames to display the experiment result in real environments (Fig. 2). For the image captured by a single fixed camera corresponded to each frame, we demonstrate four perspectives of the 3d object reconstruction.

Computation Efficiency. The proposed method is mainly divided into three parts (Fig. 1). The first part utilizes conventional methods for static 3d object reconstruction, which is actually efficient. The skeleton extraction and skeleton dilation in the second part are both one-off procedures, thus not consuming much time throughout the whole algorithm. The pose estimation in the third part is actually solving a simple constrained nonlinear optimization problem and can therefore guarantee being executed in real-time. Conventional algorithms [11,12] for dynamic 3d object reconstruction need to compare the information in multiple views to acquire a final result. The work in [11] provides a joint estimation

Images   Projections of reconstructed clouds under
                                    different views

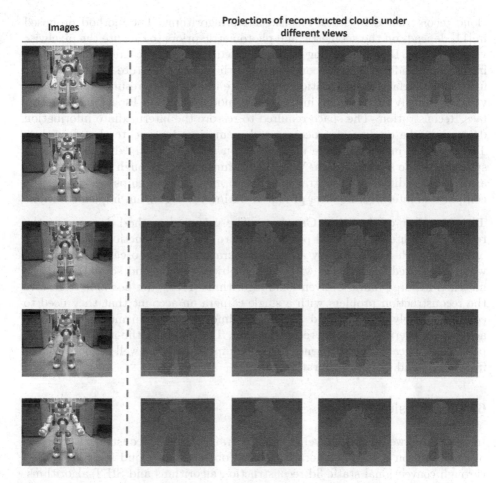

Fig. 2. Randomly selected frames to demonstrate the reconstruction result of the proposed approach. For each frame, we find projections under four appropriate views to display as many features of the cloud morphology as possible such that the overall 3-dimensional information of the results can be illustrated.

of depth and normal information based on the observation from distinct views. Moreover, a multi-view geometric consistency computing is undertaken for the image-based depth and normal fusion as well as the simultaneous refinement. Geometric errors as well as shading errors are analyzed depending on the local image gradient and computes a depth map for each perspective with respect to its neighbor views in [12]. Then it can be known qualitatively that traditional approaches are more complicated than the proposed algorithm because of the computation complexity executed on each of the multiple cameras.

Space Consuming. The proposed method reconstructs a dynamic object by estimating the pose and position of each topological part related to the camera. Thus, the space required is merely the counterpart to restore the object point cloud reconstructed by static reconstruction algorithms. The method proposed in [11] depends on the geometric and photometric priors to execute the pixelwise view selection. Dense modeling is also resulted from unstructured images. Both implicate considerable space consuming. Authors in [12] restore bicubic patches for smooth surface representation and restore intermediate results from distinct views for finally fusing them into a global model based on Floating Scale Surface Reconstrution. The space required to restore the intermediate information determines the quality of processor and memorizer to execute the algorithm. The proposed method can be undertaken on a low-cost chip due to the small space needed to store the data. While algorithms [11,12], though not introduced, are relatively difficult to be transplanted to any low-cost chips because of the complicated intermediate data produced during the algorithm implementation.

The Number of Applied Cameras. The proposed method depends on the re-organization of topological parts to acquire the reconstruction of a dynamic object. At each frame, merely a single camera is required to capture an image which is utilized to compare with labeled object point cloud so as to find the matched feature points. Conventional algorithms [11,12] are not able to resolve the reconstruction problem with a single camera on account that they need to comprehensively compute and analyze the information from multiple views to acquire the overall 3d object reconstruction. This impedes the algorithms from practical applications in the sense of high equipment cost as well as inconvenient installation and camera calibration.

6   Conclusion

In this paper, we devise a novel monocular framework to reconstruct a dynamic object based on a single camera. A labeled object point cloud is first acquired through conventional static 3d reconstruction algorithms and SIFT algorithms. Then we combine the skeleton extraction and dilation algorithms with the proposed method to segment skeletons so as to provide the object point cloud an appropriate topological segmentation. Finally, the dynamic 3d object reconstruction is resolved by estimating the poses and positions of all the topological parts of the object. Experiments are undertaken to demonstrate and evaluate the characteristics of the proposed approach, which compares relatively favorably to the-state-of-art methods in the sense of computation efficiencies, space consuming and the equipment cost.

References

1. Kahn, S., Bockholt, U., Kuijper, A., Fellner, D.W.: Towards precise real-time 3D difference detection for industrial applications. Comput. Ind. **64**, 1115–1128 (2013)
2. Chiew, W.M., Lin, F., Qian, K., Seah, H.S.: A heterogeneous computing system for coupling 3D endomicroscopy with volume rendering in real-time image visualization. Comput. Ind. **65**, 367–381 (2014)

3. Lee, J.J., Lee, B.G., Yoo, H.: Depth extraction of three-dimensional objects using block matching for slice images in synthetic aperture integral imaging. Appl. Opt. **50**, 5624–5629 (2011)
4. Saracchini, R.F.V., Stolfi, J., Leitao, H.C.G., Atkinson, G.A., Smith, M.L.: Robust 3D face capture using example-based photometric stereo. Comput. Ind. **64**, 1399–1410 (2013)
5. Wang, M., Hong, R., Yuan, X.T., Yan, S., Chua, T.S.: Movie2Comics: towards a lively video content presentation. IEEE Trans. Multimedia **14**, 858–870 (2012)
6. Choi, W., Fang, Y.C., Badizadegan, K., Dasari, R.R., Feld, M.S.: Extended depth of focus in tomographic phase microscopy using a propagation algorithm. Opt. Lett. **33**, 171–173 (2008)
7. Guillemaut, J.Y., Hilton, A.: Joint multi-layer segmentation and reconstruction for free-viewpoint video applications. Int. J. Comput. Vis. (IJCV) **93**, 73–100 (2010)
8. Chiu, W.C., Fritz, M.: Multi-class video co-segmentation with a generative multi-video model. In: The IEEE Conference on Computer Vision and Pattern Recognition (CVPR) (2013)
9. Goldluecke, B., Magnor, M.: Space-time isosurface evolution for temporally coherent 3D reconstruction. In: The IEEE Conference on Computer Vision and Pattern Recognition (CVPR), pp. 350–355 (2004)
10. Vineet, V., et al.: Incremental dense semantic stereo fusion for large-scale semantic scene reconstruction. In: IEEE International Conference on Robotics and Automation (ICRA) (2015)
11. Schönberger, J.L., Zheng, E., Frahm, J.-M., Pollefeys, M.: Pixelwise view selection for unstructured multi-view stereo. In: Leibe, B., Matas, J., Sebe, N., Welling, M. (eds.) ECCV 2016. LNCS, vol. 9907, pp. 501–518. Springer, Cham (2016). https://doi.org/10.1007/978-3-319-46487-9_31
12. Langguth, F., Sunkavalli, K., Hadap, S., Goesele, M.: Shading-aware multi-view stereo. In: Leibe, B., Matas, J., Sebe, N., Welling, M. (eds.) ECCV 2016. LNCS, vol. 9907, pp. 469–485. Springer, Cham (2016). https://doi.org/10.1007/978-3-319-46487-9_29

Adaptive Control of Human-Interacted Mobile Robots with Velocity Constraint

Qing Xu[1](✉) and Shuzhi Sam Ge[2]

[1] The School of Automation Science and Electrical Engineering,
Beihang University, Beijing 100191, China
xuq0909@buaa.edu.cn
[2] The Department of Electrical and Computer Engineering, and the Social Robotics
Lab, Interactive and Digital Media Institute (IDMI),
National University of Singapore, Singapore 117576, Singapore
samge@nus.edu.sg

Abstract. In this paper, we present an adaptive control for mobile robots moving in human environments with velocity constraints. The mobile robot is commanded to track the desired trajectory while at the same time guarantee the satisfaction of the velocity constraints. Neural networks are constructed to deal with unstructured and unmodeled dynamic nonlinearities. Lyapunov function is employed during the course of control design to implement the validness of the proposed approach. The effectiveness of the proposed framework is verified through simulation studies.

Keywords: Robot-human interaction · Motion constraints
Neural network control

1 Introduction

The incursion of social and service robots in less controlled human environments such as private homes opens a wide range of opportunities for different kinds of mobile robot applications [3]. Robots will navigate sharing the same physical space with humans and thus social competencies will be necessarily considered for control design to achieve social acceptance from the human side. As such, the research on safe control of mobile robots in close proximity with humans is gaining more attention. For the successful introduction of mobile robots in human environments, the robots velocities (heading and angular) must also be constrained.

In previous studies, there are many works focusing on reliability and safety control of mobile robots when moving in complex and dynamic environments, which is assured by preventing robots from approaching the humans and avoiding accidental collision. In [4,6], humans are considered as moving obstacles and collision-free motion is assured with the existence of such moving obstacles. Based on a minimal cost principle through a potential field defined on the basis of

S. S. Ge et al. (Eds.): ICSR 2018, LNAI 11357, pp. 390–399, 2018.
https://doi.org/10.1007/978-3-030-05204-1_38

the humans' perceived motion, in [7], novel approaches are proposed for a robot navigating in the environment with humans' participating. According to the prediction of future motions of humans and the probability of motion collision, [5] provides an approach to make robots to plan and evaluate paths with handling pedestrian disruption.

However, even though the above works can be adopted to generate different safe and collision-free reference trajectories, the motion constraints may still be violated due to the instantaneous control behavior or imperfect trajectory tracking performance which may result in hazards or damage. As a consequence, the efforts of this paper are focused on the planning trajectory tracking control of mobile robots with guaranteeing the velocity constraints not being violated.

Moreover, to cope with this kind of unstructured and unmodeled dynamic nonlinear system, Radial Basis Function Neural Networks (RBFNNs) in [2] are constructed in the process of controller design to approximate of the uncertain parameters of the robot dynamic model. And Barrier Lyapunov Functions (BLFs) are incorporated to realize trajectory tracking while guaranteeing constraint satisfaction. Different from previous works, the proposed BLFs-based adaptive control renders the tracking control and velocity constraints satisfied under one common control framework in spite of the perturbation caused during the adaptation process.

The rest of the paper is organized as follows. In Sect. 2, system description is presented and control framework as well as objective are discussed. In Sect. 3, combined adaptive kinematic/dynamic control is developed and it is rigorously proved that the robot is able to follow the desire trajectory, subject to the defined position and velocity constraints. In Sect. 4, simulation and experimental studies are presented to verify the effectiveness of the proposed method. Concluding remarks are given in Sect. 5.

2   Problem Formulation

In this paper, a general scenario is investigated where a two-wheel mobile robot is moving in a human-related environment. Two driving wheels are mounted on the base along the same axis with a free wheel in front of them. A vector $q = [x \ y \ \theta]^T$ is introduced to describe the position of the robot, with x and y being the coordinates of the center of mass of the robot, and θ being the orientation of the robot.

2.1   System Kinematics

The system kinematics of the mobile robot with respect to the linear velocity v and angular velocity ω is given as

$$\dot{x} = v\cos(\theta), \quad \dot{y} = v\sin(\theta), \quad \dot{\theta} = \omega \tag{1}$$

which can be further represented as

$$\dot{q} = H(q)z \tag{2}$$

with $z = [v\ \omega]^T$ denoting its internal state and

$$H(q) = \begin{bmatrix} \cos(\theta) & 0 \\ \sin(\theta) & 0 \\ 0 & 1 \end{bmatrix} \tag{3}$$

Differentiating (2) results in

$$\ddot{q} = H(q)\dot{z} + \dot{H}(q)z \tag{4}$$

The velocity constraint is defined as

$$|z_i| \leq k_{a,i} \tag{5}$$

where $k_{a,i}$ is the known upper bound of the actual velocity z_i with $i = 1, 2$.

2.2 System Dynamics

For the system dynamics of the mobile robot, they can be described by

$$M(q)\ddot{q} + C(q,\dot{q})\dot{q} + G(q) + F(\dot{q}) = B(q)u(t) + J^T(q)\lambda \tag{6}$$

where $M(q) \in R^{3\times 3}$ denotes the inertia matrix, $C(q,\dot{q}) \in R^3$ denotes the Coriolis and centrifugal forces, $G(q) \in R^3$ is the gravitational force, $B(q) \in R^{3\times 2}$ is input transformation matrix, which is known, $F(\dot{q}) \in R^3$ denotes the generalized friction, $u(t)$ is the control input, $J(q) \in R^{1\times 3}$ is the kinematic constraint matrix and λ is the Lagrangian multiplier in terms of the nonholonomic constraint.

Substituting the $\dot{q}$ and $\ddot{q}$ in (2) and (4) into (6) and left-multiplying $H^T(q)$, we have

$$M_1(q)\dot{z} + C_1(p, H(q)z)z + G_1(q) + F_1(q,\dot{q}) = \tau \tag{7}$$

2.3 Control Objectives

In our previous work [8], a constrained control velocity z_c has already been designed based on social force model for mobile robots operating in human environments to avoid position constraints. The control objective of this paper is thus to propose a control law to make the robot dynamics (7) to realize $z \to z_c$ as $t \to \infty$ without violating the actual velocity constraints (5), such that the mobile robot can track the desired trajectory while respecting the velocity constraints simultaneously.

3 Control Design

Denote the velocity tracking error as $e_z = [e_{z,1}, e_{z,2}]^T = z - z_c$ for system (7), the following asymmetric barrier Lyapunov function is selected

$$V_2 = \frac{1}{2} \sum_{i=1}^{2} \left(s(e_{z,i}) \log \frac{k_{1,i}^2(t)}{k_{1,i}^2(t) - e_{z,i}^2} + (1 - s(e_{z,i})) \log \frac{k_{2,i}^2(t)}{k_{2,i}^2(t) - e_{z,i}^2} \right) \tag{8}$$

where

$$k_{1,i}(t) = k_{a,i} - z_{c,i}, \quad k_{2,i}(t) = k_{a,i} + z_{c,i}, \quad s(\cdot) = \begin{cases} 1, & \text{if } \cdot > 0 \\ 0, & \text{if } \cdot \leq 0 \end{cases} \tag{9}$$

There exist positive constants $\underline{k}_{1,i}$, $\overline{k}_{1,i}$, $\underline{k}_{2,i}$ and $\overline{k}_{2,i}$ such that

$$0 < \underline{k}_{1,i} \leq k_{1,i}(t) \leq \overline{k}_{1,i}, \; \forall t \geq 0, \quad 0 < \underline{k}_{2,i} \leq k_{2,i}(t) \leq \overline{k}_{2,i}, \; \forall t \geq 0 \tag{10}$$

By a change of error coordinates, we have

$$\mu_{1,i} = \frac{e_{z,i}}{k_{1,i}}, \quad \mu_{2,i} = \frac{e_{z,i}}{k_{2,i}}, \quad \mu_i = \begin{cases} \mu_{1,i}, & e_{z,i} > 0 \\ \mu_{2,i}, & e_{z,i} \leq 0 \end{cases} \tag{11}$$

Then, (8) can be rewritten as

$$V_2 = \frac{1}{2} \sum_{i=1}^{2} \log \frac{1}{1 - \mu_i^2} \tag{12}$$

The derivative of V_2 is given by

$$\begin{aligned} \dot{V}_2 &= \sum_{i=1}^{2} [\frac{s(e_{z,i})\mu_{1,i}}{k_{1,i}(1 - \mu_{1,i}^2)}(\dot{e}_{z,i} - e_{z,i}\frac{\dot{k}_{1,i}}{k_{1,i}}) + \frac{(1 - s(e_{z,i}))\mu_{2,j}}{k_{2,i}(1 - \mu_{2,i}^2)}(\dot{e}_{z,i} - e_{z,i}\frac{\dot{k}_{2,i}}{k_{2,i}})] \\ &= B_1(e_z)\dot{e}_z + B_2(e_z) \end{aligned} \tag{13}$$

where

$$B_1(e_z) = \begin{bmatrix} \frac{s(e_{z,1})\mu_{1,1}}{k_{1,1}(1-\mu_{1,1}^2)} + \frac{(1-s(e_{z,1}))\mu_{2,1}}{k_{2,1}(1-\mu_{2,1}^2)} \\ \frac{s(e_{z,2})\mu_{1,2}}{k_{1,2}(1-\mu_{1,2}^2)} + \frac{(1-s(e_{z,2}))\mu_{2,2}}{k_{2,2}(1-\mu_{2,2}^2)} \end{bmatrix}^T$$

$$\begin{aligned} B_2(e_z) &= \sum_{i=1}^{2} [\frac{s(e_{z,i})\mu_{1,i}}{k_{1,i}(1 - \mu_{1,i}^2)}(-e_{z,i}\frac{\dot{k}_{1,i}}{k_{1,i}}) \\ &\quad + \frac{(1 - s(e_{z,i}))\mu_{2,i}}{k_{2,i}(1 - \mu_{2,i}^2)}(-e_{z,i}\frac{\dot{k}_{2,i}}{k_{2,i}})] \end{aligned} \tag{14}$$

Considering (7) and (13) can be rewritten as

$$\begin{aligned} \dot{V}_2 &= B_1(e_z)(M_1^{-1}(q)\tau - M_1^{-1}(q)(C_1(q, H(q)z)z \\ &\quad + G_1(q) + F_1(q, \dot{q})) - \dot{z}_c) + B_2(e_z) \\ &= B_1(e_z)(U(q) + P(q, \dot{q}, z) - \dot{z}_c) + B_2(e_z) \end{aligned} \tag{15}$$

where $U(q) = M_1^{-1}(q)\tau \in \mathbb{R}^2$ denotes the nominal control input and $P(q, \dot{q}, z) = -M_1^{-1}(q)(C_1(q, H(q)z)z + G_1(q) + F_1(q, \dot{q})) \in \mathbb{R}^2$.

Note that both $U(q)$ and $P(q, \dot{q}, z)$ incorporate unknown components, i.e., $M_1^{-1}(q)$, $C_1(q, H(q)z)$, $G_1(q)$ and $F_1(q, \dot{q})$. In the following, RBFNNs and GL operator in [2] are applied to approximate $M_1^{-1}(q)$ and $P(q, \dot{q}, z)$ as below

$$\begin{aligned} M_1^{-1}(q) &= \{W_M^*\}^T \bullet \{\Phi_M(q)\} + E_M \\ P(q, \dot{q}, z) &= \{W_P^*\}^T \bullet \{\Phi_P(q, \dot{q}, z)\} + E_P \end{aligned} \tag{16}$$

where $\{W_M^*\}$, $\{W_P^*\}$, $\{\Phi_M(q)\}$ and $\{\Phi_P(q, \dot{q}, z)\}$ are the GL matrices formed by optimal neural network weight vectors $W_{Mij}^* \in \mathbb{R}^{n_{WM}}$ and $W_{Pi}^* \in \mathbb{R}^{n_{WP}}$, and basis function vectors $\phi_{Mij} \in \mathbb{R}^{n_{WM}}$ and $\phi_{Pi} \in \mathbb{R}^{n_{WM}}$, respectively. $E_M \in \mathbb{R}^{2 \times 2}$ and $E_P \in \mathbb{R}^2$ are composed of NN approximation errors ε_{Mij} and ε_{Pi}, respectively. The matrices $M_1^{-1}(q)$ and $P(q, zq, \dot{q}, z)$ are then approximated as

$$\hat{M}_1^{-1}(q) = \{\hat{W}_M\}^T \bullet \{\Phi_M(q)\} - \delta_M$$
$$\hat{P}(q, \dot{q}, z) = \{\hat{W}_P\}^T \bullet \{\Phi_P(q, \dot{q}, z)\} - \delta_P \qquad (17)$$

where δ_M and δ_P will be used later to deal with the approximation error.

Following (17), the estimated $U(q)$ is written as

$$\hat{U}(q) = (\{\hat{W}_M\}^T \bullet \{\Phi_M(q)\} - \delta_M)\tau \qquad (18)$$

Subtracting $U(q)$, we have

$$U(q) - \hat{U}(q) = -\{\tilde{W}_M\}^T \bullet \{\Phi_M(q)\}\tau + (E_M\tau + \delta_M\tau) \qquad (19)$$

where $\{\tilde{W}_M\} = \{\hat{W}_M\} - \{W_M^*\}$

By adding and subtracting $\hat{U}(q)$ in (8), we have

$$\dot{V}_2 = B_1(e_z)(\hat{U}(q) + U(q) - \hat{U}(q) + P(q, \dot{q}, z) - \dot{z}_c) + B_2(e_z) \qquad (20)$$

An auxiliary matrix $H(e_z)$ is defined for the following control design as

$$H(e_z) = -\text{diag}\{L_{e_z,1}, L_{e_z,2}\}e_z - \text{diag}\{c_1, c_2\}e_z \qquad (21)$$

where $c_i = \sqrt{(\frac{\dot{k}_{i,1}}{k_{i,1}})^2 + (\frac{\dot{k}_{i,2}}{k_{i,2}})^2 + c}$, with $L_{e_z,i}$ and $c > 0$ being positive constant, for $i = 1, 2$.

Then, we have

$$B_1(e_z)H(e_z) + B_2(e_z)$$
$$= \sum_{i=1}^{2}[\frac{s(e_{z,i})\mu_{1,i}}{k_{1,i}(1 - \mu_{1,i}^2)}((-\sqrt{(\frac{\dot{k}_{1,i}}{k_{1,i}})^2 + (\frac{\dot{k}_{2,i}}{k_{2,i}})^2 + c}$$
$$-\frac{\dot{k}_{1,i}}{k_{1,i}})e_{z,i} - L_{e_z,i}e_{z,i}) + \frac{(1 - s(e_{z,i}))\mu_{2,i}}{k_{2,i}(1 - \mu_{2,i}^2)}$$
$$\times((-\sqrt{(\frac{\dot{k}_{1,i}}{k_{1,i}})^2 + (\frac{\dot{k}_{2,i}}{k_{2,i}})^2 + c} - \frac{\dot{k}_{2,i}}{k_{2,i}})e_{z,i}$$
$$-L_{e_z,i}e_{z,i})] \qquad (22)$$

Using the fact that

$$\sqrt{(\frac{\dot{k}_{1,i}}{k_{1,i}})^2 + (\frac{\dot{k}_{2,i}}{k_{2,i}})^2 + c} + s(e_{z,i})\frac{\dot{k}_{1,i}}{k_{1,i}} + (1 - s(e_{z,i}))\frac{\dot{k}_{2,i}}{k_{2,i}} \geq 0 \qquad (23)$$

The following inequality can be obtained

$$B_1(e_z)H(e_z) + B_2(e_z) \leq -\sum_{i=1}^{2} L_{e_z,i}\left(\frac{s(e_{z,i})\mu_{1,i}^2}{1-\mu_{1,i}^2} + \frac{(1-s(e_{z,i}))\mu_{2,i}^2}{1-\mu_{2,i}^2}\right) \quad (24)$$

Considering (22), the estimated nominal input can be designed as

$$\hat{U}(q) = H(e_z) + \dot{z}_c - \{\hat{W}_P\}^T \bullet \{\varPhi_P(q, \dot{q}, z)\} + \delta_P \quad (25)$$

and the control input τ can be calculated according to (18).

Remark 1. The singular issue related to the pseudo inverse can be handled using the SVD. For the special circumstances where $\hat{M}_1^{-1}(q)$ in (17) equals 0, it is replaced with the one of the last iteration to get the proper form of the control input.

Considering (16), (19) and (25), we have

$$\dot{V}_2 = B_1(e_z)(H(e_z) - \{\tilde{W}_P\}^T \bullet \{\varPhi_P(q, \dot{q}, z)\} - \{\tilde{W}_M\}^T \bullet \{\varPhi_M(q)\}\tau$$
$$+ (E_M\tau + \delta_M\tau) + (\delta_P + E_P)) + B_2(e_z) \quad (26)$$

Consider the additive term $B_1(e_z)(E_M\tau + \delta_M\tau)$ and $B_1(e_z)(E_P + \delta_P)$, if δ_M is chosen as $\delta_{M,ij} = -\text{sign}(B_{1,i}\tau_j)s_{M,ij}$ and δ_P is chosen as $\delta_{P,i} = -\text{sign}(B_{1,i})s_{P,i}$, $s_{M,ij}$ and $s_{P,i}$ are gain constants that satisfy $s_{M,ij} \geq \bar{\varepsilon}_{M,ij}$ and $s_{P,i} \geq \bar{\varepsilon}_{P,i}$, with $\bar{\varepsilon}_{M,ij}$ and $\bar{\varepsilon}_{P,i}$ being the corresponding upper bounds of $\varepsilon_{M,ij}$ and $\varepsilon_{P,i}$.

Hence, the following inequality can be derived

$$B_1(e_z)(E_M\tau + \delta_M\tau) \leq \sum_{i=1}^{2}\sum_{j=1}^{2} |B_{1i}\tau_j|(\bar{\varepsilon}_{M,ij} - s_{M,ij}) \leq 0$$

$$B_1(e_z)(E_P + \delta_P) \leq \sum_{i=1}^{2} |B_{1i}|(\bar{\varepsilon}_{P,i} - s_{P,i}) \leq 0 \quad (27)$$

By the aforementioned mathematical derivation, it can be obtained that

$$\dot{V}_2 \leq B_1(e_z)(H(e_z) - \{\tilde{W}_P\}^T \bullet \{\varPhi_P(q, \dot{q}, z)\}$$
$$- \{\tilde{W}_M\}^T \bullet \{\varPhi_M(q)\}\tau) + B_2(e_z) \quad (28)$$

where $\{\tilde{W}_P\} = \{\hat{W}_P\} - \{W_P^*\}$.

To analyze the boundedness of $\{\tilde{W}_P\}$ and $\{\tilde{W}_M\}$, an augmented Lyapnov function is proposed

$$V_3 = V_2 + \frac{1}{2}\sum_{i=1}^{2}\tilde{W}_{Pi}^T \Lambda_i^{-1}\tilde{W}_{Pi} + \frac{1}{2}\sum_{i=1}^{2}\sum_{j=1}^{2}\tilde{W}_{Mij}^T \varGamma_{ij}^{-1}\tilde{W}_{Mij} \quad (29)$$

where $\Lambda_i \in \mathbb{R}^{n_{W_P} \times n_{W_P}}$, $\Lambda_i = \Lambda_i^T > 0$ and $\varGamma_{ij} \in \mathbb{R}^{n_{W_M} \times n_{W_M}}$, $\varGamma_{ij} = \varGamma_{ij}^T > 0$.

Consider (28) and the following adaptation law for vectors $\hat{W}_{Mij}$ and $\hat{W}_{Pi}$ with $\beta_i, \gamma_{ij} > 0$

$$\dot{\hat{W}}_{Pi} = \Lambda_i(\phi_{Pi}(q, \dot{q}, z)B_{1i} - \beta_i\hat{W}_{Pi})$$
$$\dot{\hat{W}}_{Mij} = \Gamma_{ij}(\phi_{Mij}(q)\tau_j B_{1i} - \gamma_{ij}\hat{W}_{Mij}) \tag{30}$$

the following inequality can be obtained

$$\dot{V}_3 \leq B_1(e_z)H(e_z) + B_2(e_z) - \sum_{i=1}^{2}\beta_i\tilde{W}_{Pi}^T\hat{W}_{Pi} - \sum_{i=1}^{2}\sum_{j=1}^{2}\gamma_{ij}\tilde{W}_{Mij}^T\hat{W}_{Mij} \tag{31}$$

Based on the fact that

$$\tilde{W}_{Pi}^T\hat{W}_{Pi} \geq \frac{1}{2}\|\tilde{W}_{Pi}\|^2 - \frac{1}{2}\|W_{Pi}^*\|^2$$
$$\tilde{W}_{Mij}^T\hat{W}_{Mij} \geq \frac{1}{2}\|\tilde{W}_{Mij}\|^2 - \frac{1}{2}\|W_{Mij}^*\|^2 \tag{32}$$

we have

$$\dot{V}_3 \leq -\sum_{i=1}^{2}k_{e_z,i}\left(\frac{s(e_{z,i})\mu_{1,i}^2}{1 - \mu_{1,i}^2} + \frac{(1 - s(e_{z,i}))\mu_{2,i}^2}{1 - \mu_{2,i}^2}\right)$$
$$-\sum_{i=1}^{2}\frac{\beta_i}{2}\|\tilde{W}_{Pi}\|^2 - \sum_{i=1}^{2}\sum_{j=1}^{2}\frac{\gamma_{ij}}{2}\|\tilde{W}_{Mij}\|^2$$
$$+\sum_{i=1}^{2}\frac{\beta_i}{2}\|W_{Pi}^*\|^2 + \sum_{i=1}^{2}\sum_{j=1}^{2}\frac{\gamma_{ij}}{2}\|W_{Mij}^*\|^2 \tag{33}$$

Lemma 1. *For any $|\mu| < 1$, the following inequality holds*

$$\log\frac{1}{1 - \mu^2} < \frac{\mu^2}{1 - \mu^2} \tag{34}$$

Using Lemma 1, the following inequality can be obtained

$$\dot{V}_3 \leq -\rho_2 V_3 + \varsigma_2 \tag{35}$$

where

$$\rho_2 = \min\left(2L_{e_z,1}, 2L_{e_z,2}, \frac{\beta_i}{\lambda_{\max}(\Lambda_i^{-1})}, \frac{\gamma_{ij}}{\lambda_{\max}(\Gamma_{ij}^{-1})}\right) \tag{36}$$

$$\varsigma_2 = \sum_{i=1}^{2}\sum_{j=1}^{2}\frac{\gamma_{ij}}{2}\|W_{Mij}^*\|^2 + \sum_{i=1}^{2}\frac{\beta_i}{2}\|W_{Pi}^*\|^2 \tag{37}$$

Theorem 1. *Consider the mobile robot dynamics in (7), with the nominal control input (25), weight update laws (30) the constrained command velocity in [8]. If the initial velocities lie in the constraints, i.e.*

$$| z_i(0) | \leq k_{ai}, \ i = 1, 2 \tag{38}$$

the following conclusions can be obtained

(i) *The closed loop system signals e_z, $\{\tilde{W}_M\}$ and $\{\tilde{W}_P\}$ are semiglobally uniformly ultimately bounded.*

(ii) *The tracking error e_z asymptotically converges to the compact set $\{e_z| - \underline{D}_i(t) \leq e_{z,i} \leq \overline{D}_i(t)\}$, $i = 1, 2 \ \forall t > 0$ where*

$$\underline{D}_i(t) = k_{2i}(t)(1 - e^{-2(V_3(0)+\frac{\varsigma_2}{\rho_2})})$$
$$\overline{D}_i(t) = k_{1i}(t)(1 - e^{-2(V_3(0)+\frac{\varsigma_2}{\rho_2})}) \tag{39}$$

(iii) *The mobile robot's velocity z satisfies $| z_i | \leq k_{ai}, i = 1, 2, \ \forall t > 0$, i.e. the constraint is never violated.*

Proof. See Appendix A.

4 Simulation

In the following simulation studies, the effectiveness of the above proposed controller is verified. The mobile robot dynamic model in [1] is adopted in this paper. The velocity constraints in (5) are selected as $\| \omega \| \leq 0.25$ rad/s and $\| v \| \leq 0.15$ m/s. The initial posture of the mobile robot is set as $[-0.2 \ 1 \ \frac{\pi}{3}]^T$ and the reference trajectory is a sinusoidal trajectory which is described as $x_r(t) = 0.03t$, $y_r(t) = \cos(x_r(t))$.

The simulation results are illustrated in Fig. 1, where the position constraint, the linear velocity constraints and the angular velocity constraints are denoted by the blue solid circle, the green solid line and the green dashed line, respectively. It is shown that, with our proposed control framework, the actual trajectory can precisely track the desired one with quite small tracking errors while at the same time not violating the velocity constraints.

In order to make the result more convinced, one more contrast simulation experiment is conducted, where the controller in [1] is utilized without imposing the velocity and position constraints. The result is shown in Fig. 2, which can be seen that the mobile robot can successfully tracks the desired trajectory as well. However, since no motion and position constraints are taken into account, the velocities grow to an unacceptable higher level as to track the desired trajectory and the position constraint is violated during the transient process.

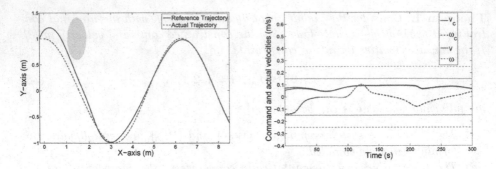

Fig. 1. Simulation results under the proposed controller in this paper.

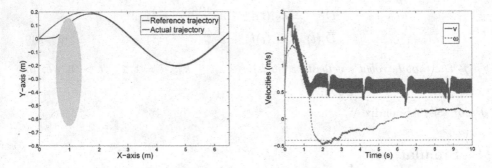

Fig. 2. The contrast simulation experiment results.

5   Conclusion

In this paper, an adaptive control strategy has been presented to cope with the motion constraints of mobile robots. An adaptive dynamic control to guarantee velocity constraints satisfaction has been applied to make the robot follow a desired trajectory. The validness of the addressed approach has been confirmed through simulation studies.

A   Appendix

A.1   Proof of Theorem 1

(i) Multiplying (35) by $e^{\rho_2 t}$ yields

$$\frac{d}{dt}(V_3(t)e^{\rho_2 t}) \leq \varsigma_2 e^{\rho_2 t} \tag{40}$$

Integrating (40) over $[0, t]$ yields

$$0 \leq V_3(t) \leq (V_3(0) - \frac{\varsigma_2}{\rho_2})e^{-\rho_2 t} + \frac{\varsigma_2}{\rho_2} \tag{41}$$

Further, it is easily found that

$$0 \leq V_3(t) \leq (V_3(0) - \frac{\varsigma_2}{\rho_2})e^{-\rho_2 t} + \frac{\varsigma_2}{\rho_2} \leq V_3(0) + \frac{\varsigma_2}{\rho_2} \tag{42}$$

Then, we can conclude that e_z, $\{\tilde{W}_M\}$ and $\{\tilde{W}_P\}$ are all bounded.

(ii) From (42), we have

$$V_3(0) + \frac{\varsigma_2}{\rho_2} \geq \begin{cases} \frac{1}{2}\log\frac{k_{1,i}^2(t)}{k_{1,i}^2(t)-e_{z,i}^2}, & 0 < e_{z,i} < k_{1,i} \\ \frac{1}{2}\log\frac{k_{2,i}^2(t)}{k_{2,i}^2(t)-e_{z,i}^2}, & -k_{2,i} < e_{z,i} \leq 0 \end{cases}$$

Taking exponentials on both sides of the above inequality, it can be easily obtained that

$$e_{z,i}^2 \leq \begin{cases} k_{1,i}^2(1 - e^{-2(V_3(0)+\frac{\varsigma_2}{\rho_2})}), & 0 < e_{z,i} < k_{1,i} \\ k_{2,i}^2(1 - e^{-2(V_3(0)+\frac{\varsigma_2}{\rho_2})}), & -k_{2,i} < e_{z,i} \leq 0 \end{cases}$$

Taking square root of both sides of the above inequality will lead to

$$\underline{D}_i(t) \leq e_{z,i} \leq \overline{D}_i(t) \ \forall t > 0, \ i = 1,2 \tag{43}$$

(iii) Since $z_i = e_{z,i} + z_{c,i}$ and $-k_{1,i}(t) \leq e_{z,i} \leq k_{2,i}(t)$, for $i = 1,2$, we infer that

$$-k_{2,i}(t) + z_{c,i} \leq z_i \leq k_{1,i}(t) + z_{c,i} \tag{44}$$

for all $t > 0$. From the definition of k_1 and k_2 in (9), we conclude that $\mid z_i \mid \leq k_{ai}$, $i = 1,2$, $\forall t > 0$.

References

1. Fierro, R., Lewis, F.L.: Control of a nonholonomic mobile robot using neural networks. IEEE Trans. Neural Netw. **9**(4), 589–600 (1998)
2. Ge, S.S., Hang, C.C., Lee, T.H., Zhang, T.: Stable Adaptive Neural Network Control. Springer, Boston (2013). https://doi.org/10.1007/978-1-4757-6577-9
3. He, W., Dong, Y.: Adaptive fuzzy neural network control for a constrained robot using impedance learning. IEEE Trans. Neural Netw. Learn. Syst. **29**(4), 1174–1186 (2017)
4. Lee, D., Liu, C., Liao, Y.W., Hedrick, J.K.: Parallel interacting multiple model-based human motion prediction for motion planning of companion robots. IEEE Trans. Autom. Sci. Eng. **14**(1), 52–61 (2016)
5. Shiomi, M., Zanlungo, F., Hayashi, K., Kanda, T.: Towards a socially acceptable collision avoidance for a mobile robot navigating among pedestrians using a pedestrian model. Int. J. Soc. Robot. **6**(3), 443–455 (2014)
6. Teatro, T.A.V., Eklund, J.M., Milman, R.: Nonlinear model predictive control for omnidirectional robot motion planning and tracking with avoidance of moving obstacles. Can. J. Electr. Comput. Eng. **37**(3), 151–156 (2014)
7. Ton, C., Kan, Z., Mehta, S.S.: Obstacle avoidance control of a human-in-the-loop mobile robot system using harmonic potential fields. Robotica **36**(4), 463–483 (2017)
8. Wang, C., Li, Y., Ge, S.S., Tong, H.L.: Adaptive control for robot navigation in human environments based on social force model. In: IEEE International Conference on Robotics and Automation, pp. 5690–5695 (2016)

Attributing Human-Likeness to an Avatar: The Role of Time and Space in the Perception of Biological Motion

Davide Ghiglino[1,2(✉)] ⓘ, Davide De Tommaso[1] ⓘ,
and Agnieszka Wykowska[1] ⓘ

[1] Istituto Italiano di Tecnologia, Via Morego, 30, 16163 Genoa, Italy
davide.ghiglino@iit.it
[2] DIBRIS, Università degli Studi di Genova,
Via Opera Pia 13, 16145 Genoa, Italy

Abstract. Despite well-developed cognitive control mechanisms in most adult healthy humans, attention can still be captured by irrelevant distracting stimuli occurring in the environment. However, when it comes to artificial agents, such as humanoid robots, one might assume that its attention is "programmed" to follow a task, thus, being distracted by attention-capturing stimuli would not be expected. We were interested in whether a behavior that reflects attentional capture in a humanoid robot would increase its perception as human-like. We implemented human behaviors in a virtual version of iCub robot. Twenty participants' head movements were recorded, through an inertial sensor, during a solitaire card game, while a series of distracting videos were presented on a screen in their peripheral field of view. Eight participants were selected, and their behavioral reactions (i.e. inertial sensor coordinates, etc.) were extracted and implemented in the simulator. In Experiment 2, twenty-four new participants were asked to rate the human-likeness of the avatar movements. We examined whether movement parameters (i.e. angle amplitude, overall time spent on a distractor) influenced participants' ratings of human-likeness, and if there was any correlation with sociodemographic factors (i.e. gender, age). Results showed a gender effect on human-likeness ratings. Thus, we computed a GLM analysis including gender as a covariate. A main effect of the time of movement was found. We conclude that humans rely more on temporal then on spatial information when evaluating properties (specifically, human-likeness) of biological motion of humanoid-shaped avatars.

Keywords: Human-likeness of robot behavior · Biological motion
Humanoid robots

1 Introduction

In designing artificial agents that are to appear human-like in order to increase perceived naturalness and facilitate social attunement, many researchers address the issue of creating human-like behavior. Several characteristics have been identified, and one crucial characteristic is variability [1]: behavioral observations demonstrate that

© Springer Nature Switzerland AG 2018
S. S. Ge et al. (Eds.): ICSR 2018, LNAI 11357, pp. 400–409, 2018.
https://doi.org/10.1007/978-3-030-05204-1_39

humans never display exactly the same behavior twice. For example, several studies demonstrated that subjects tend to adopt unique patterns of kinematic strategies to attend the very same target [2–5]. The recent advent of complex humanoid systems, allow researchers to implement fragmentized human behaviors in artificial agents, in order to study in more detail on what type of information humans rely most when evaluating biological motion. Furthermore, a deeper understanding of human perception of synthetic motion will facilitate, in the future, human-robot interaction [6]. This stems in part from the fact that humans, when interacting with other mammals [7], easily understand goals, motivation and beliefs behind human-like behaviors [8], also relying on motion clarity. It is not clear whether artificial motion patterns of a robot would be as easily understood and predicted. Therefore, it is of high importance to examine what parameters of robot behavior make it well-understood by the human users. Evidence from literature pointed out that motion cues might influence social attunement with artificial agents, enhancing even empathetic and mentalizing processes [9–11]. Starting with observing and recording human motion, several techniques can be used to transfer movement parameters to artificial agents [12, 13]. However, given the huge variability of humans' motion, it is still unclear which components of observed behaviors affect most the perception of human-likeness. The projection of human motion in simulation environment might be a suitable method to systematically study these factors.

1.1 Aim of Study

The goal of the present study was to investigate how human participants perceive biological movement displayed by an artificial agent, in terms of human-likeness. We selected an attention-capture scenario, because attention capture seems to be a very human-like phenomenon. Humans (and several other animal species) have developed mechanisms to attend relevant events in the environment. The "decision" of the brain to attend to a given event in the environment is made through a combination of bottom-up characteristics of the stimulus (e.g., the salience of the stimulus) and internal top-down factors of the agent (e.g., bias towards emotional stimuli, or towards a particular sound of, for example, one's own child's voice). However, in many cases, the brain attends stimuli that "capture" attention through their salience, although this disrupts a given task. Think, for example, of driving. The driver should be focused on the road ahead of him/her, and on keeping the car in the assumed lane. However, if there is a very loud distracting sound or bright light flashing in the peripheral vision, the driver might be distracted by this event, and in consequence, lose focus on the task, potentially causing an accident. Therefore, although evolutionarily adaptive, the attentional capture phenomenon can be disruptive for a task. In this context, one might think that artificial intelligence should be better adapted to successful completion of a given task, and not allow being distracted by peripheral events that might result in sub-optimal performance in a task. We reasoned, that "being distracted" – especially with variable ways of reacting to the distracting stimuli might be perceived as an essentially human-like feature. We therefore set out to test if equipping a humanoid robot with behaviors reflecting attentional capture would make it perceived as human-like, and which particular aspects of the behavior would be crucial for attributions of human-likeness. To this aim, we recorded human head- and eye movements during an attentional capture paradigm. The recorded behaviors were filtered, and eight different movement profiles were implemented on an iCub [14] simulator. Then, a group of participants was asked to rate the human-likeness of the movements of the simulator.

2   Materials and Methods

2.1   Attentional Capture with Humans

Selection of Distracting Stimuli. Sixty HD quality video were selected from You-Tube according to the following criteria: (1) presence of a single salient sound in the whole sequence (i.e. a phone ring, a woman laugh, a door slam, etc.); (2) absence of inappropriate contents (i.e. politic, racism, sexism, etc.); (3) more than 100 M views. Selected videos were edited using Apple Final Cut Pro [15], in order to make all of them last for the same amount of time (twenty seconds). Fifty-five anonymous Italian participants were asked to rate the emotional content of the videos through an online platform (soscisurvey.de, [16]), using a ten-point Likert scale (0 = not emotional at all; 10 = strongly emotional). One subgroup (n = 26) was asked to rate only the audio tracks of the videos. The other subgroup (n = 30) was asked to rate both the audio and the visual component of the videos. After collecting the data, ratings of the two groups were compared. Four of the sixty initial stimuli were excluded because of the inconsistency between ratings of the two groups. The remaining fifty-six videos were categorized into "Affective" and "Non-Affective" stimuli, using the median score of the raters as cutoff value between the two categories. Eighteen videos were then extracted, according to the following criteria: the nine with the lowest score ("Non-Affective" videos) and the nine with the highest score ("Affective" videos). By using Apple Final Cut Pro, audio tracks of the final eighteen videos were manipulated, in order to increase the salience of one single sound per video (i.e. the phone ring, the woman laugh, the door slam). Furthermore, we edited the videos in order to ensure that the physical properties of the sounds (i.e. volume and sampling rate, 44.1 kHz) were consistent. For each video, the volume of the single salient sound was increased, while all the other sounds were reduced. The final pool of videos was implemented in an attentional capture paradigm as distracting stimuli.

2.2   Experiment 1

Participants. Twenty-two healthy young adults (9 females; 19–34 years of age) were recruited. All participants were native Italian language speakers with no history of psychiatric or neurological diagnosis, substance abuse or psychoactive medication. All participants had normal or corrected-to-normal vision and reported no history of hearing impairment. Experimental protocols followed the ethical standards laid down in the Declaration of Helsinki and the local Ethics Committee (Comitato Etico Regione Liguria) approved procedures. Each participant provided written informed consent to participation in the experiment. Participants were not informed regarding the purpose of the study before the experiment, but were debriefed upon completion.

Experimental Design. Participants were seated in a sound attenuated experimental booth with dimmed light, in front of a notebook screen (HP Stream 14-ax011nl, 1366 × 768) (Fig. 1).

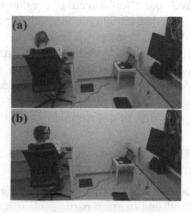

Fig. 1. Experimental setup: (a) participant is engaged in a solitaire game on the laptop; (b) participant reacts to a distracting stimulus.

Participants were instructed to perform a solitaire card game (spider one-suit) on the notebook, and to pay attention to the game. While participants were engaged in the card game, distracting stimuli were presented in the far periphery of their field of view (100° on the right, 227 cm of distance), on a second computer screen (DELL S2716DG, 2560 × 1440 pixels), interleaved by soft ambient sounds lasting for five second each (i.e. gentle rain). We exposed all participants to the same randomized sequence of distractors. The audio tracks of the distracting stimuli were played through loud-speakers (Logitech LGT-Z130), located under the second screen. The experiment was programmed and run on OpenSesame [17]. Participants' eye movements were recorded throughout the entire duration of the experiment with a mobile eye-tracking device [18]. Head movements were recorded using an inertial sensor (Bosch Sensortec BNO055 Intelligent 9-Axis Absolute Orientation Sensor, [19]) mounted on the eye-tracker and integrated in the OpenSesame experiment. We implemented a periodic task, running at 50 Hz, that requests every 20 ms the Euler angles to the inertial sensor. The absolute values of these angles, together with the sample timestamp (Timestamp, Yaw, Pitch and Roll) were saved in a .csv file, one for each distractor stimulus. Specifically, the periodic task was synchronized with the video stimuli, so that the duration of each inertial measure was aligned with the duration of the video. For each experiment, we collected 18 sessions for each participant, in total 360 .csv files.

Data Analyses. Participants' data were extracted from the eye-tracker and from the inertial sensor through Tobii Pro Lab and OpenSesame, respectively. Two participants were excluded due to noisy data. Participants' reactions to distracting stimuli were defined as head rotations of at least 30° the on the yaw axis (horizontal plane) of the inertial sensor. Reactions of participants were treated and analyzed as a count variable. For each subject, three final parameters were extracted: (1) total amount of distractions during the whole experiment, (2) total amount of distractions occurring during "Affective" stimuli, and (3) total amount of distractions occurring during "Non-Affective" stimuli. A Wilcoxon matched pairs test was used to verify a potential difference between "Affective" and "Non-Affective" conditions. Furthermore, in order to explore gender differences in distractibility among participants, a Fisher Exact Test was used to compare males and females, separately for "Affective" and "Non-Affective" conditions. In order to apply the Fisher Exact Test, the number of reactions was converted into a relative percentage estimated for each single subject. Finally, a binomial test (n = 20, p = 50%, 1 − α = .95) was used to identify the most distracting stimuli of our pool. Two sounds (a gunshot and a woman's orgasm) survived the .95 threshold, meaning that at least 70% of our sample reacted to that sound).

2.3   Implementation of Humans' Behaviors in an ICub Simulator

Selection of Behaviors. During the attentional capture paradigm, fifteen participants reacted to the sound "gun shot" and fourteen participants reacted to the sound "woman orgasm". Thus, we took into consideration the resulting twenty-nine reactions. For each reaction, we extracted two main parameters: (1) amplitude (°) of the movement; (2) time (s) spent on the distractor. The first parameter represented the angle of rotation of the head toward the distracting screen, and was calculated as the difference between the average position assumed by the head of the participant during the whole video and the maximum distance reached on the horizontal plane (yaw axis of the inertial sensor) during the same temporal window. The time spent on the distractor was estimated as the time spent by the subject on a point of the horizontal plane exceeding two standard deviations from the average position of the head. Setting this high threshold allowed us to extract thirteen reactions from the initial pool. Then, the median value of the amplitude (Mdn = 51.108°) and the median value of the time spent on distractor (Mdn = 1.664 s) were calculated and used as cutoff to classify the reactions. Specifically, reactions were divided in four categories, accordingly to the combination of the amplitude of the movement and the time spent on the distractor, namely:
(1) Amplitude and time above the median; (2) Amplitude above the median and time below the median; (3) Amplitude and time below the median; (4) Amplitude below the median and time below the median.

For each condition, the two most representative reactions were extracted (one for the "gun shot" and one for the "woman orgasm"). Eight reactions from eight different participants were selected as the final pool.

Reproduction of the Head Movements on iCub Simulator. The iCub simulator (Fig. 2) has been designed to reproduce the physics and the dynamics of the robot [20].

It has been implemented collecting data directly from the robot design specifications in order to achieve a replication as accurate as possible. Moreover, the software architecture is the same used to control the physical robot. Specifically, we decided to

Fig. 2. Example of the iCub simulator behaviour.

use the Direct Position Control algorithm [21] for sending the joint positions to the iCub head. According to the specifications in [22], the head joints are the ones with indexes 0, 1 and 2, respectively the neck Pitch, Roll and Yaw. At first, we needed to normalize the Euler angles recorded with the inertial sensor to get relative angles with respect to the initial head pose at the onset of the stimulus. In such a way, we transferred on the robot the relative rotation due to the distractor, assuming that the head had always the same starting pose. The experiment was designed to guarantee, with good approximation, this assumption. In fact, the participants were always looking straight at the screen whenever a video stimulus occurred. We excluded all the other recordings not satisfying this condition. This preprocessing of the data was enough to reproduce on the iCub simulator the head movements using the Direct Position Control algorithm. This control technique is used whenever joint positions are sent at a high frequency, because no trajectory generation in between is needed.

2.4   Experiment 2

Participants. Twenty-four participants (13 females; 26–60 years of age) completed an online survey evaluating the human-likeness of iCub simulator. Data collection was conducted in accordance with the ethical standards laid down in the Code of Ethics of the World Medical Association (Declaration of Helsinki), procedures were approved by the regional ethical committee (Comitato Etico Regione Liguria).

Experimental Design. Eight videos of six seconds each were recorded from the simulator. Videos were then uploaded on an online platform (soscisurvey.de) and associated with the following question: "In a scale from 1 (extremely mechanistic) to 10 (extremely human-like), how would you rate iCub behaviors in terms of human-likeness?". Each video and the associated question was presented ten times during the survey, mixed with the other items in a random order. Participants rated the human-likeness of the simulations, relying only on motion information. They were not informed that the behaviors were all based on previous recordings of humans' motions, but they were debriefed after the survey. In order to investigate whether the ratings were influenced by subjective factors, participants were also asked to complete the Empathy Quotient (EQ) questionnaire [23] after the survey.

Data Analyses. A two-sample T-Test was used to assess gender differences in our sample's ratings. Pearson's correlations were applied in order to evaluate possible correlations between participants' global ratings and subjective measures (i.e. EQ). In order to explore how the components of biological motion (amplitude of the movement and time spent on the distractor) affect ratings of human-likeness, statistical analyses were applied. Amplitude of the movement and time spent on the distractor were entered as two-level within-categorical predictors in the context of the General Linear Model (GLM). Gender of our participants was included in the model as nuisance covariate. Post hoc effects were estimated by calculating Bonferroni test.

3 Results

3.1 Experiment 1. Attentional Capture with Humans

Statistical analyses performed on the average number of reactions across participants revealed a significant difference between Non-Affective and Affective stimuli.

Specifically, Wilcoxon Matched Pairs Test detected a significant difference (N = 20, T = 3.5, Z = 3.789, p < .001) between average number of reactions occurred during Non-Affective stimuli (M = 2.30, SD = 2.00) and Affective stimuli (M = 5.60, SD = 2.46).

For both Non-Affective and Affective conditions, Fisher Exact Test revealed no significant effect of the gender (p > .05) on the distractibility during the experiment (Fig. 3).

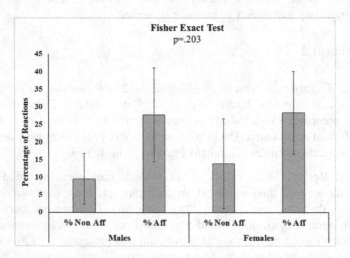

Fig. 3. Differences between males and females on the percentage of reaction displayed during Non-Affective (Non-Aff) and Affective (Aff) stimuli; vertical bars denote standard deviation of the data.

3.2   Experiment 2. Human-Likeness Survey

The two-sample T-Test revealed a significant difference ($t(23) = 2.425$, $p < .05$) of gender on the human-likeness ratings, pointing out that females ($M = 6.39$, $SD = 1.38$) usually rate higher human-likeness than males ($M = 4.90$, $SD = 1.64$). No correlation was found between ratings and subjects' Empathy Quotient scores.

The analyses modeled in the General Linear Model revealed no significant interaction between the amplitude of the movement and time spent on the distractor (F $(1,22) = 0.48$, $p = .50$). Furthermore, no main effect was found for the amplitude (F $(1,22) = 0.18$, $p = .68$), although results showed significant main effect of the time spent on the distractor ($F(1,22) = 9.18$, $p < .01$) (Fig. 4) surviving Bonferroni correction ($p < .01$). Specifically, results suggest that longer time spent on the distractor might determine higher human-likeness ratings.

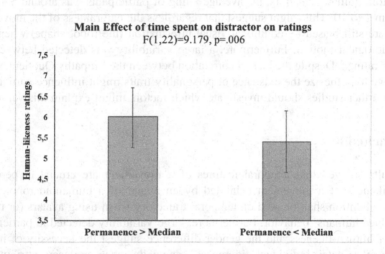

Fig. 4. Main effect of the "Time spent on distractor" on human-likeness ratings; vertical bars denote confidence intervals; Cousineau procedure was applied for correcting bars for within-participants comparisons.

4   General Discussion

The aim of our study was to examine parameters of biological motion implemented on a humanoid robot avatar that determine perceived human-likeness of the motion. In Experiment 1 we focused on the recording of human behaviors. We recorded participants' head and eye movements during an attentional paradigm. Before implementing the recorded data on an iCub simulator, a preliminary check of the data was required. Thus, we investigated whether differences between participants (males vs. females) or between conditions (Non-Affective vs. Affective) affected our results. No difference was found between males and females, suggesting that we could use all participants' recordings, regardless their gender, for subsequent implementation. At the same time, we found a difference between our experimental conditions. Specifically, results showed that Affective stimuli (i.e. a laugh, a cry, a scream, etc.) elicited more frequent reactions compared to Non-Affective ones (i.e. a phone ring, a metal drop, a door closing, etc.). We combined this result within the binomial test, in order to extract the most representative behaviors recorded during the attentional capture paradigm.

Then, eight behaviors of different participants were selected, extracted and, subsequently, implemented on an iCub simulator. An independent sample of participants was asked to rate the human likeness of the robot in the simulator, relying only on motion information. Our results showed that females' ratings of human-likeness were generally higher than males' ratings. This might suggest that females might be more prone to attribute human likeness than males to a robot simulator, regardless the physical properties of the movement displayed. In line with previous research [24] we also confirmed that humans, when asked to judge biological motion, rely more on temporal, than on spatial information. Interestingly, although all movement were copied from human behaviors, the average rating of participants was around 5.48 on a scale from 1 to 10. This might suggest that regardless the naturalness of the movement, humans are still biased by additional visual information (the robot shape) when evaluating biological motion. Furthermore, a large variability was detected between participants' ratings. Despite the lack of correlation between the Empathy Quotient and the ratings, we hypothesize the existence of personality traits might influence participants' ratings. Further studies should investigate which factors might explain this variability.

5   Conclusion

Our results showed that temporal features of a movement are crucial in perceived human-likeness of a movement exhibited by an avatar of a humanoid robot. Thus, particular attention shall be paid on temporal trajectory when using avatars (or robots) to reproduce humans' behavior. Furthermore, large variability detected in participants' ratings of human-likeness and the gender difference suggest the necessity of investigating in more detail individual differences, especially when exploring attribution of human-likeness to an artificial agent.

Acknowledgements. This project has received funding from the European Research Council (ERC) under the European Union's Horizon 2020 research and innovation programme (grant awarded to A. Wykowska, titled "InStance: Intentional Stance for Social Attunement. Grant agreement No: 715058).

References

1. Gielniak, M.J., Liu, C.K., Thomaz, A.L.: Generating human-like motion for robots. Int. J. Robot. Res. **32**(11), 1275–1301 (2013)
2. Freedman, E.G., Sparks, D.L.: Coordination of the eyes and head: movement kinematics. Exp. Brain Res. **131**(1), 22–32 (2000)
3. Stergiou, N., Decker, L.M.: Human movement variability, nonlinear dynamics, and pathology: is there a connection? Hum. Mov. Sci. **30**(5), 869–888 (2011)

4. Desmurget, M., Rossetti, Y., Prablanc, C., Jeannerod, M., Stelmach, G.E.: Representation of hand position prior to movement and motor variability. Can. J. Physiol. Pharmacol. **73**(2), 262–272 (1995)
5. Sorostinean, M., Ferland, F., Dang, T.-H., Tapus, A.: Motion-oriented attention for a social gaze robot behavior. In: Beetz, M., Johnston, B., Williams, M.-A. (eds.) ICSR 2014. LNCS (LNAI), vol. 8755, pp. 310–319. Springer, Cham (2014). https://doi.org/10.1007/978-3-319-11973-1_32
6. Wykowska, A., Chellali, R., Al-Amin, M., Müller, H.J.: Implications of robot actions for human perception. How do we represent actions of the observed robots? Int. J. Soc. Robot. **6** (3), 357–366 (2014)
7. Blakemore, S.J., Decety, J.: From the perception of action to the understanding of intention. Nat. Rev. Neurosci. **2**(8), 561 (2001)
8. Miller, L.E., Saygin, A.P.: Individual differences in the perception of biological motion: links to social cognition and motor imagery. Cognition **128**(2), 140–148 (2013)
9. Heider, F., Simmel, M.: An experimental study of apparent behavior. Am. J. Psychol. **57**(2), 243–259 (1944)
10. Frith, C.D., Frith, U.: Interacting minds–a biological basis. Science **286**(5445), 1692–1695 (1999)
11. Pollard, N.S., Hodgins, J.K., Riley, M.J., Atkeson, C.G.: Adapting human motion for the control of a humanoid robot. In: IEEE International Conference on Robotics and Automation, Proceedings, ICRA 2002, vol. 2, pp. 1390–1397. IEEE (2002)
12. Lee, J., Lee, K.H.: Precomputing avatar behavior from human motion data. Graph. Models **68**(2), 158–174 (2006)
13. Aggarwal, J.K., Cai, Q.: Human motion analysis: a review. Comput. Vis. Image Underst. **73** (3), 428–440 (1999)
14. Metta, G., Sandini, G., Vernon, D., Natale, L., Nori, F.: The iCub humanoid robot: an open platform for research in embodied cognition. In: Proceedings of the 8th Workshop on Performance Metrics for Intelligent Systems, pp. 50–56. ACM, August 2008
15. Apple Final Cut Pro X license and download [electronic resource]
16. Leiner, D.J.: SoSci Survey (Version 2.5.00-i1142) [Computer software] (2018). http://www.soscisurvey.com
17. Mathôt, S., Schreij, D., Theeuwes, J.: OpenSesame: an open-source, graphical experiment builder for the social sciences. Behav. Res. Methods **44**(2), 314–324 (2012)
18. TobiiAB, Stockholm (2015) 'Tobii Pro Glasses 2 Product Description'
19. Sensortec, B.: Intelligent 9-axis absolute orientation sensor. BNO055 datasheet, November 2014
20. http://wiki.icub.org/wiki/Simulator_README
21. http://wiki.icub.org/images/c/cf/ICub_Control_Modes_1_1.pdf
22. http://wiki.icub.org/wiki/ICub_joints#Head_2.0
23. Baron-Cohen, S., Wheelwright, S.: The empathy quotient: an investigation of adults with Asperger syndrome or high functioning autism, and normal sex differences. J. Autism Dev. Disord. **34**(2), 163–175 (2004)
24. Bisio, A., et al.: Motor contagion during human-human and human-robot interaction. PLoS ONE **9**(8), e106172 (2014)

Dancing Droids: An Expressive Layer for Mobile Robots Developed Within Choreographic Practice

Ishaan Pakrasi[✉], Novoneel Chakraborty, Catie Cuan, Erin Berl, Wali Rizvi, and Amy LaViers

Mechanical Science and Engineering Department,
University of Illinois Urbana-Champaign, Urbana, IL 61801, USA
{pakrasi2,alaviers}@illinois.edu

Abstract. In viewing and interacting with robots in social settings, users attribute character traits to the system. This attribution often occurs by coincidence as a result of past experiences, and not by intentional design. This paper presents a flexible, expressive prototype that augments an existing mobile robot platform in order to create intentional attribution through a previously developed design methodology, resulting in an altered perception of the non-anthropomorphic robotic system. The prototype allows customization through five modalities: customizable eyes, a simulated breath motion, movement, color, and form. Initial results with human subject audience members show that, while participants found the robot likable, they did not consider it anthropomorphic. Moreover, individual viewers saw shifts in perception according to performer interactions. Future work will leverage this prototype to modulate the reactions viewers might have to a mobile robot in a variety of environments.

Keywords: Human robot interaction · Robot characters
Household robots · Robot performance

1 Introduction

As robotic systems are becoming increasingly present in human-facing, social scenarios, they hold the potential to help in assistive tasks in the household. Particularly inside the growing market of older adults, robotic systems can be useful in both functional and affective tasks [4,5]. In a 2017 report [16] on automation, employment and productivity, social acceptance is described as one of the five key factors in the adoption of automated technologies. This acceptance is owed to multiple factors such as utility, ease of interaction, and hedonic value [27]. Another key factor comes from the concept of psychological attribution, whereby a user's opinion on technology is altered by their perception of a piece of technology, that is influenced by both the physical design characteristics as well as the story around the technology.

© Springer Nature Switzerland AG 2018
S. S. Ge et al. (Eds.): ICSR 2018, LNAI 11357, pp. 410–420, 2018.
https://doi.org/10.1007/978-3-030-05204-1_40

Further work suggests that there is a strong link between a user's perception of a robot's characteristics and subsequent user behavior [13, 28]. For instance, work in [24] outlines people's tendencies to interpret human behavior in terms of intentional causal mental states, such as beliefs, desires and intentions, suggesting that this interpretation is an automatic and immediate process that is hardwired into the brain's function. In [25], the authors find that the observation of intentional harm committed to an inanimate entity such as a robotic arm prompts an attribution of mind to the entity. [10] claims that the grouping of a robot in social organization based on gender, age or ethnic identity leads to increased anthropomorphic attribution of the robot, thereby leading to an increased sense of intentionality in its actions.

Users tend to create narratives that explain the animations of robotic devices. For example, consider the plethora of videos on the internet of cats on top of Roombas, and other attributions that range from hilarity to sadness, for this functional, relatively blank, yet prevalent, robotic device [3, 19]. In [12] we see instances where people name their Roomba robot, giving it a social identity. The achievement of social assimilation prompts the user to associate decisions made by the robot to its personality traits, as opposed to the functional algorithm that determines its movements. Prior work [2, 13, 14, 28] tell us that it is natural for humans to try and extract information from robotic actions, subsequently attributing intentionality to robot movement characteristics. In [12], for instance, user study participants describe the movements of a robot vacuum cleaning system, the Roomba as "cute" or "pathetic", even though such a correlation may not have been intentional aspects of the design.

Priming is a tool that can be used to tap into perception through an intentionally designed rhetoric that can be attached to different forms of technology. In [8], Darling et al. explore the relationship between emphatic concern and the effect of priming through stories on human-robot interaction. Results of the study show that people are less likely to strike the insects with a backstory and a name. Along with other prior work [9, 20, 23], this makes a case for the exploration of building characters around household robotic systems that can provide the user with a set of beliefs along with an associated predictability of behavior based on assumptions made from character traits of the system.

Inherently, performance art is an area that aims to suspend an audience's perception of reality through storytelling [11, 21, 26]. Thus, performance serves as a suitable medium to build characters around robots that prime the audience to induce a greater sense of attribution in subsequent interactions with the system. However, flexible platforms on which to build characters that can exhibit distinct character traits in a performance setting are needed in this setting. It is crucial that such a platform have distinguishable, customizable features that allow for the resolution of multiple, separable modes. To this effect, this paper uses the design methodology outlined in [18] and in-studio work with a dance choreographer to produce a customizable prototype suitable for theatrical settings and feasible for near term in-home integration.

The rest of this paper discusses this prototype, its development, and an initial characterization with human viewers. In Sect. 2, we review a previous design methodology employed here, along with an artistic exploration with an artist-in-residence. In Sect. 3, we discuss how this prototype was developed through artistic exploration with an artist-in-residence in a robotics lab, and the resulting design of our so-called Dancing Droid (DD). Section 4 outlines a user study and discusses its results. Concluding remarks are made in Sect. 5.

2 Implementing Desired Attribution Through Choreographic Practice

In prior work we developed a robot design methodology to project character archetypes onto robotic systems of different form factors [18]. This work uses the Kansei Engineering iterative design approach [17], in conjunction with the Product Channel Consumer paradigm [6] and Laban Movement Analysis [22]. This methodology focuses on the information transfer between the robotic system and user [15]. The methodology is outlined in [18], where we used it to abstract known, archetypal characters onto virtual robots. In that work, we learned that in developing backstories based on well-known fictional cartoons, user interactions with these robots come with a lifetime of biases as a result of repeated exposure and memories of the character traits. Thus, in this work, we wanted to explore more subtle, customizable characters with less exaggerated personality types, with the goal of increasing the predictability and familiarity of the hardware without inciting a lifetime of bias. Thus, an artist-in-residence was recruited to work in tandem with a hardware platform development [7].

Inside this residency, we have learned what kinds of features this artist would want in an on stage agent. Moreover, we have an opportunity in which to test perceptions of the robot in a highly flexible contextual embedding (live performance in a theater). Thus, the two efforts have become synergistic and create a unique opportunity to develop a prototype that will helps us learn how to create intentional priming experiences for users of future robot designs. In this collaboration, it became evident that a customizable, cheap robotic layer was needed to augment existing robotic platforms in order to fulfill the expectations of the artist. Through this artistic collaboration, we collaboratively accrued observations that informed our design goals. These observations are:

- The motion of the hardware is limiting; particularly sharp changes in velocity, which characterize a *flick* or *punch* require large force/torque profiles that real hardware struggles to create.
- The hard, plastic moldings of many robots restrict much of the texture of the onstage system. Moreover, several designs, such as on the Aldebaran NAO, tend to imply masculine gender through defined bicep muscles, broad shoulders, and fixed, industrial colorways.
- Many systems incite science fiction comparisons *immediately*, which can be hard to battle. This is especially true of humanoid systems.

- Touching, say a cheek, to these platforms does not create the kind of relationship that even, say, touching a peach to a cheek.
- Having the same robot portray different characters is challenging, specifically in non-humanoid form factors.
- Choreographing movement is an arduous process that involves a lengthy compile time and necessitates the presence of a programmer.

3   Hardware Development

As a result of the findings in the prior section, prototype features should include:

- Customizability in modalities such as color, shape, and texture.
- Expressivity through dynamically unconstrained degrees of freedom like lights.
- Bilateral symmetry established through eyes and movement orientation.
- Accessibility through the use of cheap and readily available parts.

The design in Fig. 1 was used to develop a prototype through the implementation choices described here. We use the iRobot Create 2.0 mobile platform as the form factor for the Dancing Droid (DD) prototype. This unit is cost effective, easy to work with, and shares the base design as one of the most popular and prevalent in-home robots, the iRobot Roomba. The DD is comprised of four modular components, easing the process of assembly. These four components, the shell, the core, the eyes, and the expressive lights, are delineated below with explanations of the fabrication and assembly process.

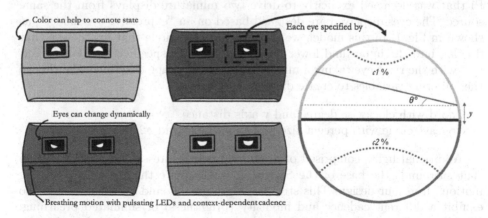

Fig. 1. Left: Different characters layered on the same base platform. Here, we see different versions of dynamically expressive eyes, different colors that can help to connote character traits. The center line represents an LED strip that pulsates to mimic breathing motion. Right: Expressive eye model (Color figure online)

Shell. The shell encloses the electronic components and gives the DD its intended shape. In order to keep the mass as low as possible, the shell is created by stacking sheets of Expanded PolyStyrene Foam (EPS). The EPS foam is obtained in sheets 1" thick and cut to size in order for it to fit in a laser cutter. The laser cutter is configured with the appropriate settings and the shapes to be cut are input as files generated by the Creo Parametric software package. Once cut, these pieces of EPS foam are glued together to form the base of the DD. The hemispherical top is made of EPS, and is obtained off the shelf. In order to have customizable color, both base and top are covered in colored lycra material.

Internal Control Architecture. This core is the center of computing and power distribution of the DD, as shown in Fig. 4a. The components are housed in a custom-designed and 3D printed shell that efficiently packs all the electronic components into a compact area, enabling it to fit inside of the shell described in Sect. 3. The components housed in the core are a Raspberry Pi 3 with Raspberry Pi Hat, an Arduino Uno with power distribution circuit, a 20100 mAh battery pack and a 3xAA (4.5 V) battery pack.

Dynamically Unconstrained Degrees of Freedom. Two 1.4" TFT LCD screens are positioned between the dome and the base to create expressive "eyes". As mentioned previously, these screens establish bilateral symmetry and provide an element that can change without less significant velocity constraints than the motion of the vehicle (the dynamic constraints of the LED screens are below the resolution of human perception). They are controlled the Raspberry Pi 3 by means of an Adafruit Snake Eyes Bonnet, an accessory for the Raspberry Pi that was designed explicitly to drive two miniature displays from the same source. The eyes displayed are designed based on an "expressive eye model", as shown in Fig. 1. In this model, we start with a base circle that for the eye that divided into the upper and lower halves. We provide specifications for the left eye, with the right eye taking a mirror image of the shape described. We change the following variables to create different eye shapes:

- Chord with clockwise degree and y-axis distance
- Concave circle with percent size $c1$ (upper half) and $c2$ (lower half).

Additional lights comprised of an individually addressable RGD LED strip that surrounds the base of the Styrofoam shell create the desired "breathing motion" from our design. This strip is programmable and can thus be used to exhibit a different cadence and intensity (brightness) of simulated breathing. Initially, we designed a smooth pulsating simulation of breathing, but this element can be modulated to show changing internal state to a human viewer in an intuitive manner – parallel to other tasks the robot may be fulfilling.

Assembly. This construction resulted in an expressive shell that is layered on top of a iRobot Create 2. By changing the programming logic in the Raspberry

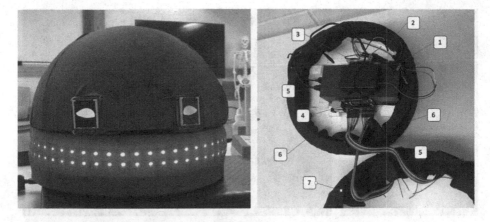

Fig. 2. The finished prototype is shown in the figure on the left, and the internal wiring is shown in the figure on the right. The numbered components are: (1) Power connection between expressive lights and three-cell battery. (2) Data connection between Arduino and expressive lights. (3) Arduino Uno with custom hat. (4) Raspberry Pi with Snake Eyes hat. (5) Ribbon Cables connected to TFT screens. (6) Bottom Shell. (7) Top Shell.

Pi 3 and the Arduino Uno, we can specify custom expressive eyes, breathing cadence and movement profiles. The finished product is shown in Fig. 2. This was used in a user study as is described in the following section.

4   Initial Characterization

The DD prototype was characterized in an showing of an artistic performance piece, entitled *Time to Compile*, at Brown University as part of a residency through the Conference on Research on Choreographic Interfaces (CRCI). The performance was attended by 40–50 individuals. Audience members, from a pool of 36 formal RSVPs, were optionally invited to participate in our user study. These audience members filled out a presurvey before the performance, a post-performance survey, and a post-interactive installation survey. The responses for the DD specific questions are gathered here. Complications with event logistics and audience appetite for participation results in a limited set of user responses. Audience members were asked to fill out multiple surveys on their phones over the course of the night, which was, in the end, not a convenient method for data collection. Future performance-as-research explorations will improve how the surveys are incorporated in a more controlled way into the actions requested of the audience (Fig. 2).

There were 7 participants who filled out the DD specific questionnaire. Of these, 3 were male, 3 were female, and 1 did not identify gender. The age range was 28–62 years old. During the performance, these participants were divided into two groups. Both groups saw the robot inside the larger context of *Time*

Fig. 3. Left: positive relationship (high valence, high power) during performance; Right: negative relationship (low valence, low power) during performance.

to Compile which takes place in the setting of an abstract robotics lab and uses four total performers to represent the process of programming on a team.

Group 1 participants saw the interaction with the DD during the second half of the performance, witnessing a positive relationship between human performer and robot (left of Fig. 3). The performer stood, redirected the DD's movement by tapping it with a foot or kicking it playfully, and smiled, demonstrating that it was a fun and positive interaction. If the DD went out of the boundaries of the performance space, the performer treated this momentary escape as a little joke, before containing the robot by redirecting its movement once more. The performer used calm, deliberate movements, displaying a positive relationship with the DD.

Group 2 participants saw the performer's interaction with the DD during the first half of the performance, witnessing a negative relationship between human performer and robot (right of Fig. 3). The performer struggled with the robot while on the ground, redirected the DD's movement by anxiously hitting it with a hand or foot, and appeared stressed and upset by the robot. If the DD went out of the boundaries of the performance space, the performer would realize it was far away then frantically try to catch it, back away or recoil if it was coming closer or made contact unexpectedly, displaying a negative relationship with the DD. Each of these vignettes were created by variable movement profiles of a human performer.

4.1   Results and Analysis

We aim to explore perceptions of the DD after viewing a positive or negative human interaction relationship as well as gain a baseline characterization of the robot through an established query method. We use an adaptation of the God-speed questionnaire, a measurement tool often used in human robot interaction

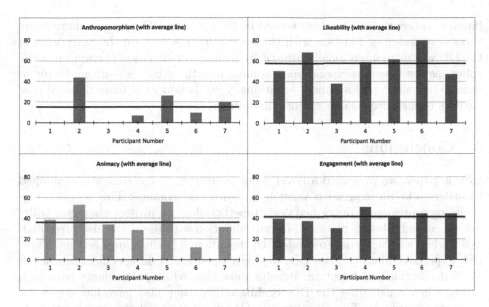

Fig. 4. Individual participants' ratings on the four Godspeed scales of Anthropomorphism, Likeability, Animacy, and Engagement. These results show that the lowest ratings were for Anthropomorphism (average of 15.2) and the highest were for Likeability (average of 57.8).

research, to evaluate the participants' attitude towards robots using semantic differential scales [1]. These questions condense to the three qualities of Anthropomorphism, Animacy, and Likeability. Additional questions also measure the participants' attitude about the robots' intelligence, outlook, and movement profile, leading a fourth combined quality of Engagement.

In Fig. 4, we see what each participant rated the DD on the four Godspeed scales of Anthropomorphism, Likeability, Animacy, and Engagement. The most negative scores were for Anthropomorphism, with an average score of 15.2. Even so, the most positive scores were for Likeability, with an average score of 57.8. Animacy and Engagement were similar, with an Animacy average score of 36.3 and an Engagement average score of 41.0. It is important to note that the Engagement scores may not be fully representative as the participants never interacted themselves with the DD, but only witnessed a human performer in different interaction modes. Future investigation of the perception of the DD could include a time for participant interaction with the robot, in order to examine how that personal engagement may alter their ratings of the robot.

For example, Participant 4 rated the DD very negatively, but also identified that past experience with robots included a lot of time with a different robot in the performance known as Baxter. This participant reported after the performance that the Baxter was "desirable", while the DD was "annoying" and "childish". It may be possible that this participant's past experience with Baxter influenced their perception even of other robots. They may use Baxter as a baseline concept of what robots should be like, but the DD does not share many aspects of design or function with Baxter. Future research on the perception of the DD will more intentionally investigate people's predisposed perception of the robot, as the bias participants have coming into the study is a strong factor to change in a short performance. Additionally, we hope to use more detailed user surveys to measure smaller changes in opinion.

5   Conclusions

In this paper, we presented a novel robot prototype design that was developed in order to be an expressive agent in a dance performance. This was done by applying a previously developed design methodology to project character traits onto a ground robotics platform. Initial validation with users was also presented. We worked with an artist to validate the results in a performance setting. Thus, this expressive platform, the DD, was developed based on specifications developed inside this collaboration. Results show that while participants gave high scores when considering the DD for Likeability, they also gave low scores for Anthropomorphism. The differences in Godspeed ratings between performance groups were not consistently strong enough to conclude that performance group defined the participants' perception of the DD.

In future work, we hope to conduct more user studies in theatrical settings and on more form factors. Theatrical settings, which are natively social environments as many people attend shows with friends and family, allow us to change individual knobs of our system such as priming and context elements on larger participant groups to get a clearer picture of the variety of impressions on human viewers that we can create using this platform.

Acknowledgement. This work was conducted under IRB #17427 and supported by a National Science Foundation (NSF) grant #1528036. The Conference on Research for Choreographic Interfaces (CRCI) provided support for *Time to Compile*, created by Catie Cuan in collaboration with the RAD Lab.

References

1. Bartneck, C., Kulić, D., Croft, E., Zoghbi, S.: Measurement instruments for the anthropomorphism, animacy, likeability, perceived intelligence, and perceived safety of robots. Int. J. Soc. Robot. **1**(1), 71–81 (2009)
2. Bianchini, S., Levillain, F., Menicacci, A., Quinz, E., Zibetti, E.: Towards behavioral objects: a twofold approach for a system of notation to design and implement behaviors in non-anthropomorphic robotic artifacts. In: Laumond, J.-P., Abe, N. (eds.) Dance Notations and Robot Motion. STAR, vol. 111, pp. 1–24. Springer, Cham (2016). https://doi.org/10.1007/978-3-319-25739-6_1
3. iRobotRoomba Brand Publishing, BuzzFeed News: Every pet on a roomba you ever need to see (2013). https://www.buzzfeed.com/irobotroomba
4. Breazeal, C.: Emotion and sociable humanoid robots. Int. J. Hum.-Comput. Stud. **59**(1), 119–155 (2003)

5. Broekens, J., Heerink, M., Rosendal, H., et al.: Assistive social robots in elderly care: a review. Gerontechnology **8**(2), 94–103 (2009)
6. Crilly, N., Moultrie, J., Clarkson, P.J.: Seeing things: consumer response to the visual domain in product design. Des. Stud. **25**(6), 547–577 (2004)
7. Cuan, C., Pakrasi, I., LaViers, A.: Time to compile: an interactive art installation. In: 16th Biennial Symposium on Arts & Technology, vol. 51, p. 19 (2018)
8. Darling, K., Nandy, P., Breazeal, C.: Empathic concern and the effect of stories in human-robot interaction. In: 2015 24th IEEE International Symposium on Robot and Human Interactive Communication (RO-MAN), pp. 770–775. IEEE (2015)
9. Dautenhahn, K.: The art of designing socially intelligent agents: Science, fiction, and the human in the loop. Appl. Artif. Intell. **12**(7–8), 573–617 (1998)
10. Eyssel, F., Kuchenbrandt, D.: Social categorization of social robots: anthropomorphism as a function of robot group membership. Br. J. Soc. Psychol. **51**(4), 724–731 (2012)
11. Fischer-Lichte, E.: The transformative power of performance. In: The Transformative Power of Performance, pp. 19–31. Routledge (2008)
12. Forlizzi, J., DiSalvo, C.: Service robots in the domestic environment: a study of the roomba vacuum in the home. In: Proceedings of the 1st ACM SIGCHI/SIGART Conference on Human-robot Interaction, pp. 258–265. ACM (2006)
13. Hendriks, B., Meerbeek, B., Boess, S., Pauws, S., Sonneveld, M.: Robot vacuum cleaner personality and behavior. Int. J. Soc. Robot. **3**(2), 187–195 (2011)
14. Knight, H., Simmons, R.: Expressive motion with x, y and theta: Laban effort features for mobile robots. In: The 23rd IEEE International Symposium on Robot and Human Interactive Communication, RO-MAN 2014, pp. 267–273. IEEE (2014)
15. LaViers, A.: An information theoretic measure for robot expressivity. arXiv preprint arXiv:1707.05365 (2017)
16. Manyika, J., et al.: A future that works: automation, employment, and productivity. Technical report, San Francisco, CA (2017)
17. Nagamachi, M.: Kansei engineering: a new ergonomic consumer-oriented technology for product development. Int. J. Ind. Ergon. **15**(1), 3–11 (1995)
18. Pakrasi, I., LaViers, A., Chakraborty, N.: A design methodology for abstracting character archetypes onto robotic systems. In: Paper Present at the 5th International Conference on Movement and Computing (MOCO), June, Genoa, Italy, pp. 28–30 (2018)
19. Rachel Zarrell, B.N.: This cat dressed as a shark riding a roomba with a shark-baby is the Zen you need today (2014). https://www.buzzfeed.com/rachelzarrell
20. Simmons, R., et al.: Believable robot characters. AI Mag. **32**(4), 39–52 (2011)
21. Stevens, C.J., et al.: Cognition and the temporal arts: investigating audience response to dance using pdas that record continuous data during live performance. Int. J. Hum.-Comput. Stud. **67**(9), 800–813 (2009)
22. Studd, K., Cox, L.: Everybody is a Body. Dog Ear Publishing, Indianapolis (2013)
23. Swift-Spong, K., Wen, C.K.F., Spruijt-Metz, D., Matarić, M.J.: Comparing backstories of a socially assistive robot exercise buddy for adolescent youth. In: 2016 25th IEEE International Symposium on Robot and Human Interactive Communication (RO-MAN), pp. 1013–1018. IEEE (2016)
24. Terada, K., Shamoto, T., Ito, A., Mei, H.: Reactive movements of non-humanoid robots cause intention attribution in humans. In: 2007 IEEE/RSJ International Conference on Intelligent Robots and Systems, IROS 2007, pp. 3715–3720. IEEE (2007)

25. Ward, A.F., Olsen, A.S., Wegner, D.M.: The harm-made mind: observing victimization augments attribution of minds to vegetative patients, robots, and the dead. Psychol. Sci. **24**(8), 1437–1445 (2013)
26. Ward, F.: No Innocent Bystanders: Performance Art and Audience. UPNE, Lebanon (2012)
27. Young, J.E., Hawkins, R., Sharlin, E., Igarashi, T.: Toward acceptable domestic robots: applying insights from social psychology. Int. J. Soc. Robot. **1**(1), 95–108 (2009)
28. Young, J.E., et al.: Evaluating human-robot interaction. Int. J. Soc. Robot. **3**(1), 53–67 (2011)

Semantic-Based Interaction for Teaching Robot Behavior Compositions Using Spoken Language

Victor Paléologue[1,2]([✉]) [ID], Jocelyn Martin[1], Amit Kumar Pandey[1], and Mohamed Chetouani[2]

[1] SoftBank Robotics Europe, 43 rue du colonel Pierre Avia, 75015 Paris, France
victor.paleologue@softbankrobotics.com
[2] Institut des Systemes Intelligents et de Robotiques (ISIR) UMR 7222, Sorbonne Université, 75005 Paris, France

Abstract. By enabling users to teach behaviors to robots, social robots become more adaptable, and therefore more acceptable. We improved an application for teaching behaviors to support conditions closer to the real-world: it supports spoken instructions, and remain compatible the robot's other purposes. We introduce a novel architecture to enable 5 distinct algorithms to compete with each other, and a novel teaching algorithm that remain robust with these constraints: using linguistics and semantics, it can recognize when the dialogue context is adequate. We carry out an adaptation of a previous experiment, so that to produce comparable results, demonstrate that all participants managed to teach new behaviors, and partially verify our hypotheses about how users naturally break down the teaching instructions.

Keywords: Teaching robots · Natural language interaction Interactive task learning

1 Introduction

Today's social robots must be adapted to each use case to be acceptable. Letting users teach behaviors using spoken language could be adequate to adapt them.

A previous work [13] demonstrated an application enabling PEPPER robots to support such teaching, given perfect speech transcription and this model:

- A task (t) is a function that can be executed by the robot.
- A behavior is a task made of a k-arrangement ($t_1, ..., t_k$) of tasks.
- An action is a unitary task, that cannot be decomposed.
- A task is declared by a statement in the infinitive form.

Behaviors made of other behaviors are called "composite behaviors".

When a user says "to greet is to raise the right arm and to say hello", the application decomposes grammatically the utterance, and recognizes "to greet"

© Springer Nature Switzerland AG 2018
S. S. Ge et al. (Eds.): ICSR 2018, LNAI 11357, pp. 421–430, 2018.
https://doi.org/10.1007/978-3-030-05204-1_41

as a new task declaration to associate with enumeration of task declarations "to raise the right arm" and "to say hello", hence matching the teaching pattern. It saves a new behavior labeled "to greet" as a sequence of the tasks labeled "to raise the right arm" and "to say hello". With this composition mechanism and a set of pre-defined tasks, users were able to produce new behaviors through natural language interaction.

This paper demonstrates improvement in the application, enabling PEPPER robots to support teachings using their default automatic speech recognition (ASR) engine to perform the transcription: the extension of the behavior composition algorithm to support realistic teaching utterances, and a novel architecture to make it cohabit with competing interaction algorithms.

In details, the following hypotheses were made:

1. PEPPER's default ASR provides exploitable results for our teaching algorithm based on natural language processing (NLP) and semantic analysis.
2. Users are all able to perform a teaching, given a short set of instructions.
3. Users may naturally attempt to teach behaviors in several sentences, and will cut their sentences before or after "is to" and between steps of enumerations.
4. Users may naturally attempt to describe behaviors first, and then label them, e.g.: "to raise the right arm and to say hello is to greet".
5. Robotic algorithms written independently can be run in competition without conflict if: they can recognize the context they are relevant with, they suggest reactions of the robot instead of executing them, an algorithm selects the most appropriate reaction.

Next section reports the current state of the art in the teaching of behaviors using natural language, and details why this study differs. Section 3 recalls the model implemented, explains the new architecture and the algorithm of the teaching interaction. Section 4 recalls the experiment and discloses its results. Section 5 discusses the results and check these hypotheses.

2   Related Work

Research on teaching behaviors takes root in programming using spoken language, such as [10]. It was then applied to robots, and allowed the composition of behaviors [14], or the definition of custom trigger conditions [21]. Thanks to recent progress, the domain of interactive machine learning reached the realm of robotics [3,9], creating new research trends.

Nyga [12] and Tenorth [18] investigated new ways to understand instructions provided in natural language, like found on WIKIHOW[1], and perform them on a robot. Sorce and Lallée researched how to teach tasks that can be cooperative [5,17] and introspectable. Other researchers achieved the inclusion of parameters in the task plans [8], or to learn jointly primitive behaviors [11].

---

[1] http://www.wikihow.com.

Recently, a work from Scheutz [16] managed to put together most of these features, and added object learning to it, making it the most complete teaching of behaviors so far.

In our research, we try to achieve this teaching of behaviors in a way to be more flexible, more robust to naive users, i.e. that are not trained for this teaching. We target a safer and more affordable robot, PEPPER, so that to get it as close as possible to real-world conditions. Because real-world conditions suppose a variety of applications installed on the robot, we try to put as few constraints as possible in our software architecture, unlike HRI-specific ones [7,15,19], and try to apply use standards, like in CRAM [2].

Doing so forces applications to consider what the pragmatics of the interaction [20] are, and focus more on user's expectations [1]. We expect that this approach will allow us to support a larger variety of behaviors in a companion robot at home [4], and a deeper control of the interaction.

3 Model

3.1 Semantic Agent

The robot's behavior is driven by an agent, named SEMANTIC AGENT. It takes NAOQI[2] events as input, and uses NAOQI functions to perform actions in return. Figure 1 details the architecture of the SEMANTIC AGENT.

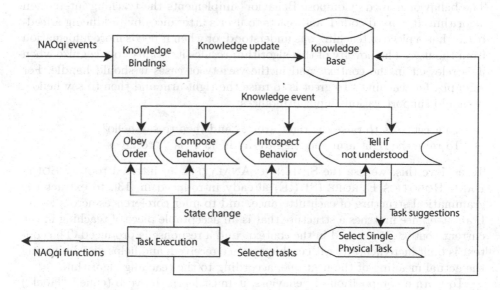

Fig. 1. Overview of the SEMANTIC AGENT. Square boxes are fixed components of the software. Sheared boxes are amovible behaviors.

---

[2] NAOQI is the software running by default on PEPPER and NAO robots.

All events, including ASR results, are translated into an uniform knowledge data structure that can be stored in a triple base. Behaviors are amovible software components that can react to changes in the knowledge base and produce tasks in response. In order to prevent conflicts or to circumvent irrelevant behaviors, tasks are not executed directly. Instead, they are only suggested, and another component selects them.

In Fig. 1, "Obey Order", "Compose Behavior", "Introspect Behavior" and "Tell if not understood" are behaviors and will suggest tasks in reaction to the user's speech. Data and code paths can be shared arbitrarily between behaviors, but they remain designed independently, and need to build their own form of context, and figure out by themselves if the context is appropriate for a response. See Subsect. 3.2 for an example of context.

The behavior "Select Single Physical Task" implements a selection algorithm to prevent conflicts between tasks. It does not produce tasks *per se*, but reason on and manipulate them.

The selected tasks are then executed, potentially impacting the environment, and updating the state of their source behavior. The actual execution of the task happens in the source behavior's process, granting a lot of freedom in the development: there is no constraint about how a task is implemented, other than the use of LIBQI[3] and how it communicates with its source behavior.

3.2   Behavior Composition

The behavior named "Compose Behavior" implements the teaching interaction algorithm. It is hard-coded, and reacts to user's utterances by producing a feedback when a piece of teaching was understood, or when it needs more information from the user. The novelty of this algorithm resides its ability to recognize when it is relevant in the context, and in the variety of cases it should handle. For example, for teaching "To greet is to raise the right arm and then to say hello", it should support various input utterances:

- "To greet", "is to raise the right arm", "and then to say hello".
- "To raise the right arm and then to say hello", "is", "to greet".

To achieve this, we use the SEMANTIC ANALYZER, an internal tool by SOFT-BANK ROBOTICS EUROPE (SBRE) already introduced in [13], to extract the grammatical structure of each utterance, and to infer coreferences across them. If an utterance matches a structure that is an acceptable piece of teaching in the current context, it is saved in the context, and a response is produced. The context is built incrementally with each utterance received, and helps discriminating the actual meaning of the next one, according to the teaching algorithm.

To learn a composition of behaviors, it must learn the verb (called "label") used to label the new behavior, and the sequence of tasks (called "recipe") it will correspond to. The label and every tasks are verbs in the infinitive form, with potential complements (called "task declaration"). The recipe is therefore

---

[3] LIBQI provides NAOQI's RPC mechanisms: https://github.com/aldebaran/libqi.

an enumeration of task declarations. The label and the recipe will be associated using the verb "be" at the present form.

When an utterance is input, the algorithm discriminates whether it consist in a task declaration (or an enumeration of them), an association, an agreement or a disagreement, or a combination of such, thanks to the SEMANTIC ANALYZER. If it is a task declaration, the context is used to check whether it is being associated (an association statement preceded the utterance), whether it may be part of an ongoing enumeration, or whether it stands alone. This kind of reasoning on the context therefore tries to find a match of a pragmatic frame [6]. The same kind of reasoning is applied to all forms of accepted utterances, for as many permutations of context possible.

When a teaching seems complete enough, the algorithm tries to check whether it is finished. But since there is no indication about the end of the sentence by the ASR, the algorithm pro-actively suggests a reaction of the robot saying "is that all?", and hopes for an answer from the user. In this specific context, agreements and disagreements have a meaning regarding whether the teaching has ended or not. Whereas in the context of the enumeration of tasks, a disagreement usually means that the latest utterance was wrong, and the user is about to correct it.

3.3   Telling It Was Not Understood

When the robot has no response to an utterance, it would inform the user by replying "sorry, I don't understand", as a fallback. This is a separate behavior that should be designed as independently as possible to be compatible with other behaviors should not know about. Therefore, we cannot directly use the fact that no other behavior suggested a response to trigger the fallback.

Instead, we rely on the state of the interaction and on a pragmatic rule: when a user says something to the robot, the robot should respond to maintain the engagement. If the robot does not say or do anything back within tenths of second, the behavior will suggest a task for saying "sorry, I don't understand".

To do so, the behavior does not need to depend to other behaviors, but instead tracks knowledge events describing what the robot or the user say.

4   Experiment

4.1   Protocol

Our experiment is equivalent to a previous one [13], so that to produce comparable results. The same PEPPER robot was used, but running a preview of NAOQI OS 2.9, the new version of the SEMANTIC AGENT and using PEPPER's default ASR instead of the mock-up used previously. The same ANDROID application on the tablet was used, for a comparable user experience.

9 volunteers from SBRE were selected to interact with the robot, one by one, in a room with the experimenter. They receive a sheet of instructions describing

Known Behaviors	Known Behaviors	Known Behaviors
Say *	Say *	Say *
<Raise, Lower> your <arms, left arm, right arm, head>	<Raise, Lower> your <arms, left arm, right arm, head>	<Raise, Lower> your <arms, left arm, right arm, head>
Move <forward, back>	Move <forward, back>	Move <forward, back>
Turn <left, right, away>	Turn <left, right, away>	Turn <left, right, away>
Look <left, right, forward>	Look <left, right, forward>	Look <left, right, forward>
To teach a behavior	**To teach a behavior**	**To teach a behavior**
In one sentence, using an *existing* verb : to + <verb> is to + <verbal group>, ...	In one sentence, using an *existing* verb : to + <verb> is to + <verbal group>, ...	In one sentence, using an *existing* verb : to + <verb> is to + <verbal group>, ...
Examples : To greet is to raise the right arm and say hello To welcome is to move forward and greet	Examples : To help is to raise the left arm and ask how you can help To care is to move forward and help	Examples : To promote is to look forward and say that acme has great products To solicit is to move forward and promote

Fig. 2. Sheets of instructions, respectively themed for home, care and business.

the behaviors already known by the robot, the rule for composing behaviors, and two examples themed according a domain of application among *home*, *care* and *business*. They are identical to those of the first experiment, see Fig. 2. Each domain was represented equally and randomly (3 participants for each domain).

Each participant is given 10 min to compose as many behaviors as possible, observed by the experimenter taking notes. Then, the experimenter asks the robot what it learned, using the formula "what is <task declaration>", as in: "what is to welcome?". The robot responds by reformulating the behavior from his perspective. Finally, the logs of the SEMANTIC AGENT containing the transcriptions and the notes are collected.

4.2 Evaluation

The collected transcripts are then analyzed, to produce same measures as in [13]:

- The number of utterances (or instructions) provided by the users (*IC*).
- The average rate of instructions misrecognized *(Mis%)*.
- The average time in seconds needed to teach a behavior, including the time lost with misrecognized instructions or any other error (*AT w Err*).
- The average normalized edit distance (*MED*) between the decomposition in natural language done by the robot and the expected one.
- The percentage of behaviors that were successfully taught, among the total number of behaviors attempted to be taught (*TS%*).
- The percentage of users who managed to teach behaviors (*UTS%*).
- The percentage of users who managed to teach composite behaviors (*UTSC%*).

The users were asked after the experiment (from 1 to 5) how:

- successful the teaching felt. It is the Experienced Teaching Success (*ETS*).
- easy the interaction felt. It is the Experienced Interaction Ease (*EIE*).

We add to that the number of successfully taught behaviors (BS).

The results are shown in the Table 1, highlighting the domain the users were asked to focus themselves on. In brief, the results show that 100% of users managed to teach behaviors to the robot ($UTS\%$) but only 11.11% managed to teach composite behaviors ($UTSC\%$). We will discuss this in Subsect. 5.2.

Table 2 compares these results (N) with the previous ones ($N-1$). The data from the previous experiment was re-analyzed to ensure the results are comparable, and therefore different from published previously. In addition, the data was annotated with the causes of misrecognition, and compute distinct misrecognition rates: $MisA\%$ for errors due to the ASR, $MisS\%$ for errors due to our algorithms, $MisU\%$ for utterances that the system is not designed to support.

Table 1. Measurements on the transcripts, per domain.

Domain	IC	Mis%	At w Err	MED	TS%	UTS%	UTSC%	ETS	EIE
Home	181	59%	180 s	0.86	26%	100%	0%	2.3/5	2.3/5
Care	149	53%	94 s	0.85	55%	100%	33%	1.7/5	2.0/5
Business	150	54%	105 s	0.40	52%	100%	0%	2.3/5	2.3/5
All	480	55%	111 s	0.68	46%	100%	11%	2.1/5	2.2/5

Table 2. Comparison with the results of the previous experiment.

Experiment	MisA%	MisS%	MisU%	Mis%	At w Err	MED	ETS	EIE
N-1	0%	30%	9%	39%	84 s	0.52	3/5	3/5
N	34%	11%	10%	55%	112 s	0.68	2/5	2.2/5

5 Discussion

5.1 Hypotheses Validation

Table 2 shows a decrease by 19 points of $MisS\%$ since the previous experiment, proving the progress of the semantic analyis and of the teaching algorithm.

But overall, $Mis\%$ increased by 16 points, mostly because of the introduction of the ASR ($MisA\%$ of 34%). Consequently, $At\ w\ Err$ increased from 84s to 112s, the MED from 0.52 to 0.68, and the feeling of success ($ETS\ \&\ EIE$) decreased. Despite this, the teaching remained successful for 100% of users, and this validates our hypotheses 1 and 2. When a task declaration could not be understood by the ASR, the participants naturally switched to another one, rooted with another verb, and it usually worked.

As for hypothesis 3, a further analysis of the transcriptions shows that the 77,78% of users tried a step-by-step teaching. Among them, 100% of them cut before "is to" and between enumerations. 57,14% cut after "is to". The hypothesis is therefore validated. In addition, there were a lot of cuts after the words "to say", probably due to the complexity of the statement that followed it.

Hypothesis 4, however, was not verified: users did not tell the recipe before the label. It may be due to the instruction sheets which showed only one way of teaching, and biased the participants.

Finally, the teaching was proven possible despite the competing objectives of the behaviors "Obey orders", "Compose Behaviors" and "Tell if not understood". Hypothesis 5 is verified in this contrained scenario, and can now be tested with a larger range of behaviors.

5.2   Observational Analysis

Teaching is possible regardless the domain of application. But given the small size of the sample, we cannot conclude on a strong domain independance.

The low rate of users able to teach composite behaviors ($UTSC\%$: 11%) is problematic. It is difficult to explain why users did not manage to compose deeper behaviors, but it probably has a correlation with $Mis\%$. Some participants abandoned teaching composite behaviors after several errors, and switched to other behaviors, starting back from the first depth of behaviors. Others did not realize it was possible. Our main hypothesis is that it is a usability issue, that could be tackled given that we can reduce the rate misunderstanding ($Mis\%$), which is mainly due to the ASR.

$MisA\%$ (34%) is probably not only due to ASR limitations, but also to the participants' accent (often French). If we performed the experiment in the native language of the participants, $MisA\%$ would decrease.

After errors, participants usually tried to repair the teaching, but the teaching algorithm did not support this. Instead, it considered most utterances as part of the taught behaviors: the context was misunderstood. Repairing the teaching consisted in repeating an utterance, commenting the situation, or asking to restart the teaching.

Participants got sometimes lost in the teaching, and expected more accurate feedback from the robot. "Ok" did not feel good enough, and was even misleading in some cases. Until participants managed to teach a behavior, they could not tell what the robot actually understood, despite a textual feedback of the last utterance on the tablet.

Introduction to self, and polite formulations were still not supported, as reported in the previous experiment. The lack of support for parameters in the behavior composition was seen by participants as a handicap to produce realistic behaviors.

Some participants tried to explain the behavior using substantives, indicative forms and imperative forms, as variations of the teaching formula. They sometimes expressed a closure of the teaching by themselves with a "that's all" or a "ok", but it was not caught by the agent.

Finally, the MED measure hardly expresses the accuracy of the teaching of behaviors, because it depends on how the behavior is reformulated, whereas we aim at allowing a variety of ways to teach. A better measure should be found to express a rate of equivalence between behaviors.

6   Conclusion and Future Work

We produced a stand-alone application to make a standard PEPPER teachable, given instructions. Most of our hypotheses about how the users would provide spoken instructions were verified. With this and the data gathered by our experiment, it could support even more realistic interactions.

We proposed a software architecture that allows each behavior to be written as separate components, letting them perform their own part of the decision-making while avoiding conflicts with each other. It can be tested further by experiments "in the wild".

Acknowledgments. This work was partially supported by the European Union's Horizon 2020 project Culture Aware Robots and Environmental Sensor Systems for Elderly Support (http://www.caressesrobot.org) under grant 737858; by the Ministry of Internal Affairs and Communication of Japan; and by the European Union's Horizon 2020 project MultiModal Mall Entertainment Robot (http://www.mummer-project. eu) research and innovation program under grant 688147.

References

1. Amershi, S., Cakmak, M., Knox, W.B., Kulesza, T.: Power to the people: the role of humans in interactive machine learning. AI Mag. **35**(4), 105–120 (2014)
2. Beetz, M., Mösenlechner, L., Tenorth, M.: CRAM - a cognitive robot abstract machine for everyday manipulation in human environments. In: 2010 IEEE/RSJ International Conference on Intelligent Robots and Systems (IROS), pp. 1012–1017. IEEE, October 2010. https://doi.org/10.1109/IROS.2010.5650146
3. Chernova, S., Thomaz, A.L.: Robot Learning from Human Teachers. Morgan & Claypool, San Rafael (2014)
4. Dominey, P.F., Paléologue, V., Pandey, A.K., Ventre-Dominey, J.: Improving quality of life with a narrative companion. In: 2017 26th IEEE International Symposium on Robot and Human Interactive Communication (RO-MAN), Lisbon, Portugal, September 2017
5. Dominey, P.F., et al.: Cooperative human robot interaction with the Nao humanoid: technical description paper for the "radical dudes". RoboCup@ Home Technical Description Papers: Germany-Singapore (2010)
6. Fillmore, C.J.: Frames and the semantics of understanding. Quaderni di Semantica **6**(2), 222–254 (1985)
7. Fischer, T., et al.: iCub-HRI: a software framework for complex human-robot interaction scenarios on the iCub humanoid robot. Front. Robot. AI **5** (2018). https://doi.org/10.3389/frobt.2018.00022

8. Gemignani, G., Bastianelli, E., Nardi, D.: Teaching robots parametrized executable plans through spoken interaction. In: Proceedings of the 2015 International Conference on Autonomous Agents and Multiagent Systems, pp. 851–859. International Foundation for Autonomous Agents and Multiagent Systems (2015)

9. Laird, J.E., et al.: Interactive task learning. IEEE Intell. Syst. **32**(4), 6–21 (2017). https://doi.org/10.1109/MIS.2017.3121552

10. Lauria, S., Bugmann, G., Kyriacou, T., Bos, J., Klein, E.: Personal robot training via natural-language instructions. IEEE Intell. Syst. **16**, 38–45 (2001)

11. Liu, C., et al.: Jointly learning grounded task structures from language instruction and visual demonstration, pp. 1482–1492. Association for Computational Linguistics (2016). https://doi.org/10.18653/v1/D16-1155

12. Nyga, D.: Interpretation of natural-language robot instructions. Ph.D. thesis, University of Bremen - Institute of Artificial Intelligence, Bremen, April 2017

13. Paléologue, V., Martin, J., Pandey, A.K., Coninx, A., Chetouani, M.: Semantic-based interaction for teaching robot behavior compositions. In: 2017 26th IEEE International Symposium on Robot and Human Interactive Communication (RO-MAN), Lisbon, Portugal, September 2017

14. Rybski, P.E., Yoon, K., Stolarz, J., Veloso, M.M.: Interactive robot tasktraining through dialog and demonstration. In: Proceedings of the ACM/IEEE International Conference on Human-Robot Interaction, pp. 49–56. ACM (2007). https://doi.org/10.1145/1228716.1228724

15. Schermerhorn, P., Kramer, J., Brick, T., Anderson, D., Dingler, A., Scheutz, M.: DIARC: A Testbed for Natural Human-Robot Interaction, p. 8 (2006)

16. Scheutz, M., Krause, E., Oosterveld, B.: Spoken Instruction-Based One-Shot Object and Action Learning in a Cognitive Robotic Architecture, p. 9 (2018)

17. Sorce, M., Pointeau, G., Petit, M., Mealier, A.L., Gibert, G., Dominey, P.F.: Proof of concept for a user-centered system for sharing cooperative plan knowledge over extended periods and crew changes in space-flight operations. In: The 24th IEEE International Symposium on Robot and Human Interactive Communication (RO-MAN), Kobe, Japan, pp. 776–783. IEEE, August 2015. https://doi.org/10.1109/ROMAN.2015.7333565

18. Tenorth, M., Nyga, D., Beetz, M.: Understanding and executing instructions for everyday manipulation tasks from the world wide web. In: 2010 IEEE International Conference on Robotics and Automation (ICRA), pp. 1486–1491. IEEE (2010)

19. Trafton, G., Hiatt, L., Harrison, A., Tamborello, F., Khemlani, S., Schultz, A.: ACT-R/E: an embodied cognitive architecture for human-robot interaction. J. Hum.-Robot Interact. **2**(1), 30–55 (2013)

20. Vollmer, A.L., Wrede, B., Rohlfing, K.J., Oudeyer, P.Y.: Pragmatic frames for teaching and learning in human-robot interaction: review and challenges. Front. Neurorobotics **10**, 1–20 (2016). https://doi.org/10.3389/fnbot.2016.00010

21. Weitzenfeld, A., Dominey, P.F.: Cognitive robotics: command, interrogation and teaching in robot coaching. In: Lakemeyer, G., Sklar, E., Sorrenti, D.G., Takahashi, T. (eds.) RoboCup 2006. LNCS (LNAI), vol. 4434, pp. 379–386. Springer, Heidelberg (2007). https://doi.org/10.1007/978-3-540-74024-7_36

Comfortable Passing Distances for Robots

Margot M. E. Neggers[✉], Raymond H. Cuijpers, and Peter A.M. Ruijten

Eindhoven University of Technology, Eindhoven, The Netherlands
{m.m.e.neggers,r.h.cuijpers,p.a.m.ruijten}@tue.nl

Abstract. If autonomous robots are expected to operate in close proximity with people, they should be able to deal with human proxemics and social rules. Earlier research has shown that robots should respect personal space when approaching people, although the quantitative details vary with robot model and direction of approach. It would seem that similar considerations apply when a robot is only passing by, but direct measurement of the comfort of the passing distance is still missing. Therefore the current study measured the perceived comfort of varying passing distances of the robot on each side of a person in a corridor. It was expected that comfort would increase with distance until an optimum was reached, and that people would prefer a left passage over a right passage. Results showed that the level of comfort did increase with distance up to about 80 cm, but after that it remained constant. There was no optimal distance. Surprisingly, the side of passage had no effect on perceived comfort. These findings show that robot proxemics for passing by differ from approaching a person. The implications for modelling human-aware navigation and personal space models are discussed.

Keywords: Proxemics · Passing distance · Passing side · Pepper

1 Introduction

In recent years, more and more autonomous service robots are being developed that need to operate in environments with people, e.g. museum tour guides [10] or automated cleaning systems [4]. Moreover, much research focuses on robots with a dedicated social task like elderly care [1] or the rehabilitation of autistic children [18]. A recent focus is on socially-assistive robots (SARs) which are robots that can help humans solely through social interaction [5].

With these developments, many different groups of people will encounter robots in public spaces, both engineers and novice users. In these encounters it is important that people feel comfortable in the proximity of a robot and that they accept it in their environment. Therefore, robots should adhere to a set of social rules and show socially acceptable behaviour. As a minimum, a robot should be able to navigate in a human- and robot-friendly way [13], thereby respecting social distances.

© Springer Nature Switzerland AG 2018
S. S. Ge et al. (Eds.): ICSR 2018, LNAI 11357, pp. 431–440, 2018.
https://doi.org/10.1007/978-3-030-05204-1_42

1.1   Human Proxemics

We can use knowledge on human proxemics to understand how humans deal with social distances and thereby be able to create natural navigational models with robots. Hall [7] introduced personal space around a person and divided it into four different zones: the intimate zone ($\leq$45 cm), the personal zone (45 cm–120 cm), the social zone (120 cm–350 cm) and the public zone (>350 cm).

Whereas Hall divided personal space into concentric circles, personal space can also be egg-shaped, with distances being slightly bigger in front of a person than behind [8], or ellipse-shaped with higher distances in the direction of motion [9]. The latter shape is also obtained in the so-called "social force model", where actors are assumed to influence each other's motion through repulsive forces. Personal space may also be asymmetrical, with smaller distances at the person's dominant side [6]. This effect may be related to cultural conventions: depending on which side the traffic drives, people seem to have a preferred side when passing another person [2].

1.2   Robot Proxemics and Human-Aware Navigation

Several studies have investigated the relation between personal space and perceived comfort in robot approach behaviour with differing results [17]. Some studies show comfortable stopping distances ranging from the intimate zone (less than 45 cm) to the personal zone (more than 120 cm) [24,25], while others find distances ranging from 160 to 180 cm [20,23], which is larger than the distance we allow other humans to approach us. These studies differed on the type of robot and the robot's behaviour, showing that comfortable approach distances depend on robot appearance, behaviour and skills [14], context [12], and activity and personality of the user [19].

The above studies all investigated preferred stopping distances, but they did not focus on the perceived comfort when passing a person. Several navigational models that take passing behaviour into account have been developed. Examples of this are models that plan socially acceptable paths and directions [3,15,16], those that take social acceptability into account [21,22], or those that use the social force model for a mobile robot or wheelchair to navigate safely through a crowd [26]. All these models are able to find socially acceptable paths, but they do not quantify the perceived comfort of the passing distances and sides and/or did not measure the preferred passing distances at the moment of passage.

1.3   The Current Study

The aim of the current study is to experimentally find the most comfortable passing distance and side of passage for a robot that passes a human in a corridor. Based on [15], we expected people to feel more comfortable with increasing passing distances, up to a point where distances would become 'unnaturally' large. Given the fact that the study was conducted in the Netherlands, where traffic drives at the right side of the road, we also expected people to feel more comfortable with a robot passing at their left side [2]. These expectations were tested in a controlled environment in which a robot passed people at different distances and sides, after which people indicated their feelings of comfort.

2   Method

2.1   Participants and Design

Thirty-two participants (17 males and 15 females, $M_{age} = 32.0, SD_{age} = 16.3$, range $= 19$ to 81) participated in an experiment with a 9 (Passing Distance: 50–130 cm) $\times$ 2 (Passing Side: Left vs. Right) $\times$ 2 (Sequence: Descending vs. Ascending) within-subjects design. Passing Distance varied between 50 cm and 130 cm, with steps of 10 cm. Passing Side alternated between every two consecutive trials, and Sequence changed after half of the trials. A fixed order of all 36 trials was used for all participants. Due to some technical issues with the robot, 72 out of the 1152 trials could not be used (6.25%). The experiment lasted 30 min for which participants were paid €5, or €7 for non-students.

2.2   Materials and Procedure

The experiment was conducted with the Pepper robot (Softbank Robotics) in a room in which a corridor was created between one of the walls and a wall of poster boards. Figure 1a shows the corridor with the robot at one of its starting positions. On the floor two lines of tape (one red, one blue) indicate where the participant should walk. Figure 1b shows the experimental configuration schematically. The red and blue lines indicate the walking trajectory of the participant and the dots indicate the starting positions of the robot.

Upon arrival in the lab, participants read and signed an informed consent form that informed them about the aim and the procedure of the experiment. They also completed a few demographic questions and indicated their familiarity with interacting with robots. The experiment started by informing the participant via a computer screen on which line (either the red or the blue one, see Fig. 1) and in which direction (towards the back wall or away from it) they were expected to walk. Participants were instructed to walk over the line at a normal walking speed, and the robot would start at the opposite side of the room and pass them while moving at a constant speed. After each trial, participants had to indicate their level of comfort with two items. The first one measured the extent to which they felt comfortable passing the robot, and the second one measured the extent to which the robot passed them at a comfortable distance, both on 7-point scales ranging from 'not at all' to 'completely'. Meanwhile the experimenter placed the robot at its new starting position. This procedure was repeated for all 36 trials, after which participants were thanked, debriefed and paid for their participation.

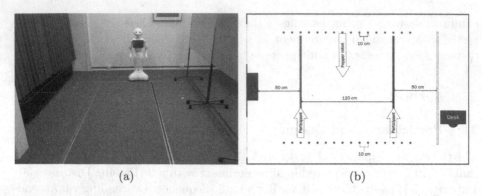

(a)   (b)

Fig. 1. Overview of the experimental setup, with (a) a picture of the room, with the temporary walls, the robot, and the red and blue lines for the participant to walk on, and (b) a schematic overview of the walking lines and distances, and all starting points of the robot, indicated by the dots. (Color figure online)

3   Results

For our analyses, we used the average value of the two comfort questions as the dependent variable, as they were highly correlated with $r(30) = 0.86$, and $p < 0.001$). Figure 2 shows the average comfort ratings as a function of passing distance for both left and right passages of the robot. As can been seen in this figure, the comfort ratings increase with distance and saturate to a maximum value at about 100 cm. There is practically no difference between passages on the right and left side of the participants.

To test the hypothesis that people would feel more comfortable with increasing passing distances, and that they would feel more comfortable with a robot passing at their left side, data on perceived comfort were submitted to a Linear Mixed model with Passing Distance, Passing Side, and Sequence as independent variables. Results showed a main effect of Passing Distance ($F(8, 218.00) = 52.54, p < 0.001, r^2 = 0.63$), as perceived comfort appeared to increase with increasing Passing Distances. More specifically, perceived comfort was lowest for a passing distance of 50 cm ($M = 4.13, SD = 1.62$), and highest for a passing distance of 110 cm ($M = 6.68, SD = 0.59$). Results also showed a main effect of Sequence ($F(1, 659.75) = 65.09, p < 0.001, r^2 = 0.21$). Perceived comfort was smaller for the decreasing sequence ($M = 5.66, SD = 1.01$) than for the increasing sequence ($M = 6.20, SD = 0.82$). Finally, results showed a significant interaction between Passing Distance and Sequence ($F(8, 221.76) = 6.74, p < 0.001, r^2 = 0.12$). In Fig. 3 the average comfort rating is shown as a function of passing distance for both an increasing and a decreasing sequence.

3.1   Evaluation of Passing Side and Direction of Increase

To quantify the effects of passing side and direction of increase, we fitted a non-linear model to take the increase with distance into account. We first used

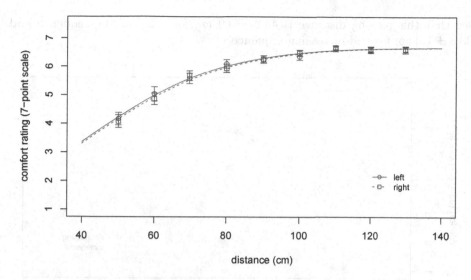

Fig. 2. Visualization of the average comfort level per passing distance for the robot passing on the left (solid red line) and right (dashed blue line) of the participant. The lines indicate the best fitting inverted Gaussian (see text for details). The error bars represent SE. (Color figure online)

a second-order polynomial to fit the data, but this has two drawbacks: (1) a second-order polynomial has a maximum, whereas our data seem to saturate at a maximum level of comfort, and (2) extrapolating beyond the measured range leads to insensible results, i.e. negative ratings. We also tried to fit a model of the form $a + b \exp(-cx)$. This also produced a good fit, but only if the intercept is unrealistically small (about $a = -15$). A straightforward expression that does not suffer from these drawbacks is the inverted Gaussian. An additional advantage is that, as it turns out, a good fit can be obtained with one parameter less than using the second order polynomial or the exponential function. The fitted equation is shown below:

$$c = 1 + a_0(1 - \exp(-\frac{d^2}{2(\sigma + a_1\,\varepsilon + a_2\,\eta)^2})), \tag{1}$$

where ε is a dummy variable which has the value 1 if the robot passed on the right and 0 if it passed on the left. Similarly, η is a dummy variable which is 1 if the distance is increasing over trials and 0 if it was decreasing. The variable d represents passing distance, σ is the width of the inverted Gaussian and c represents the perceived level of comfort. The fit results are shown in Table 1. As before the effect of side of passage is not significant ($a_1 = 0.5, p = 0.617$). Setting it to zero slightly changes the other parameter values (see Table 2). The effective width of the inverted Gaussian is $\sigma + a_2\eta$, which reflects the passing distance for a comfort rating of $1 + a_0(1 - \exp(-\frac{1}{2})) \approx 4.5$. From Table 2 we see that this passing distance is 44.2 ± 0.9 cm for a decreasing sequence and 33.8 ± 1.0 cm for and increasing sequence.

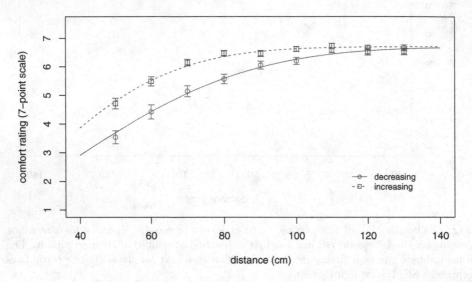

Fig. 3. Visualization of the average comfort level per increasing passing distance (dashed blue line) and decreasing passing distance (solid red line). The lines indicated the best fitting inverted Gaussian. The error bars represent SE. (Color figure online)

Table 1. Fitted parameter values and summary statistics of Eq. 1.

Parameter	Estimate	SE	t value	p	
σ	43.9	1.0	42.27	<2e−16	***
a_0	5.708	0.056	101.14	<2e−16	***
a_1	0.5	1.0	0.50	0.617	
a_2	−10.3	1.0	−10.19	<2e−16	***

***Significant difference of less than $p < 0.001$

The effective width of the inverted Gaussian captures the effect of an increasing/decreasing distance sequence nicely, but it does not tell us which comfort level is considered acceptable. If we knew, we could simply set a bar value for the level of comfort, e.g. 6. We then find a value for $d = 90.5$ cm for decreasing distance and a value of $d = 69$ cm for increasing distance. The average of these two values is $d = 79.75$ cm.

Table 2. Fitted parameter values and summary statistics of Eq. 1 with effect of side of passage set to zero ($a_1 = 0$).

Parameter	Estimate	SE	t value	p	
σ	44.2	0.9	49.06	<2e−16	***
a_0	5.707	0.056	101.17	<2e−16	***
a_2	−10.4	1.0	−10.20	<2e−16	***

***Significant difference of less than $p < 0.001$

4   Discussion

In this paper we experimentally determined an acceptable passing distance and passing side in a corridor scenario. Participants were asked to walk a corridor, and were passed by a Pepper robot at different distances and different sides in a total of 36 trials.

We expected the level of comfort to increase with distance, which was confirmed by our results. Contrary to previous findings [15], the level of comfort did not decrease for very large distances. It could be that our created hallway was not broad enough, and that the used distances were too small to observe this effect. It is also possible that the level of comfort does not decrease at all and a passing robot is not perceived as less comfortable when it is far away.

In previous findings [15] preferred clearance was 40 cm. In our study there is no optimal passing distance, but if we set the bar at a comfort level of 6, we obtain a distance of about 80 cm. This may seem very large, but the passing distance includes the size of the robot and the participant. The base of the Pepper robot measures 48 cm, which means that it extended 24 cm towards the person. Similarly, the average shoulder width of humans is about 40 cm, which means that the person also extends about 20 cm towards the robot. The effective clearance is therefore about 36 cm, which corresponds with previous findings. The latter value was obtained by setting an arbitrary criterion above which the comfort level is considered acceptable. This criterion is clearly subjective and may vary across participants.

We measured no effect of passing side on level of comfort, contrary to our hypothesis. A possible explanation of this finding is mentioned by Kirby et al. [11]. They state that although passing a person on the right side of the corridor may be social convention, it may have less priority than the task constraints e.g. if you need to reach an office at the left side of a corridor. In other words, if the task constraint supercedes the social convention, it is not perceived as strange or uncomfortable. So for our scenario, it is not necessary to take a preferred passing side into account, but it is unclear whether the same applies to other interaction scenarios. It does show that models of human-aware navigation need to be verified in a given context.

Another interesting finding of this study is that we found a significant difference in level of comfort between a sequence of trials with increasing distances vs. trials with decreasing distances. Apparently, a decreasing distance over trials creates a feeling of uneasiness or danger that is not present when distance increases over trials. This finding may be explained by an artefact of a fixed scale where participants respond relative to previous judgements.

4.1 Limitations and Future Work

The current study was conducted with only one type of robot. Previous studies on robot proxemics point out differences between different robots [20, 24]. Furthermore, we used a fixed environment, with e.g. a fixed width of the hallway, no presence of other people and a single activity of the person. Context is also known to have an important effect on robot proxemics [12]. The robot in our study also did not signal while passing, which has shown to be an important aspect [15]. Future research and more data is needed to quantify these effects and build context awareness in our models.

In our design the robot followed a straight trajectory when passing the participant. However, despite the precise positioning of the robot, there could be a small deviation in its path. Therefore, the actual distance between robot and participant could deviate somewhat from the intended distance. Although we think that this influence is minor, this problem could be solved with location trackers. Additionally, the order of the trials were fixed for convenience. Some participants indicated that they anticipated the next trial beforehand, which explains the observed hysteresis. Future work should take this effect into account or prevent it by randomising the experimental trials.

4.2 Conclusion

We measured comfortable passing distances and sides of a robot in a hallway scenario. We found that passing distances from 80 cm (from the middle of the person to the middle of the robot) are deemed acceptable and that passing side has no effect on comfort. Robots should respect these rules on proxemics, to create more natural and comfortable interactions in human environments.

References

1. Bemelmans, R., Gelderblom, G.J., Jonker, P., De Witte, L.: Socially assistive robots in elderly care: a systematic review into effects and effectiveness. J. Am. Med. Directors Assoc. **13**(2), 114–120 (2012)
2. Bitgood, S., Dukes, S.: Not another step! Economy of movement and pedestrian choice point behavior in shopping malls. Environ. Behav. **38**(3), 394–405 (2006)
3. Charalampous, K., Kostavelis, I., Gasteratos, A.: Robot navigation in large-scale social maps: an action recognition approach. Expert Syst. Appl. **66**, 261–273 (2016)
4. Elkmann, N., Hortig, J., Fritzsche, M.: Cleaning automation. In: Nof, S. (ed.) Springer Handbook of Automation, pp. 1253–1264. Springer, Heidelberg (2009)
5. Feil-Seifer, D., Mataric, M.J.: Defining socially assistive robotics. In: 9th International Conference on Rehabilitation Robotics, ICORR 2005, pp. 465–468. IEEE (2005)

6. Gérin-Lajoie, M., Richards, C.L., Fung, J., McFadyen, B.J.: Characteristics of personal space during obstacle circumvention in physical and virtual environments. Gait Posture **27**(2), 239–247 (2008)
7. Hall, E.T.: The Hidden Dimension. Anchor Books, New York (1966)
8. Hayduk, L.A.: The shape of personal space: an experimental investigation. Can. J. Behav. Sci./Revue Canadienne des sciences du comportement **13**(1), 87 (1981)
9. Helbing, D., Molnar, P.: Social force model for pedestrian dynamics. Phys. Rev. **51**(5), 4282–4286 (1995)
10. Kanda, A., Arai, M., Suzuki, R., Kobayashi, Y., Kuno, Y.: Recognizing groups of visitors for a robot museum guide tour. In: 2014 7th International Conference on Human System Interactions (IISI), pp. 123–128. IEEE (2014)
11. Kirby, R., Simmons, R., Forlizzi, J.: Companion: a constraint-optimizing method for person-acceptable navigation. In: Robot and Human Interactive Communication, RO-MAN 2009, pp. 607–612. IEEE (2009)
12. Koay, K.L., Syrdal, D., Bormann, R., Saunders, J., Walters, M.L., Dautenhahn, K.: Initial design, implementation and technical evaluation of a context-aware proxemics planner for a social robot. In: Kheddar, A., et al. (eds.) ICSR 2017. LNCS, vol. 10652, pp. 12–22. Springer, Cham (2017). https://doi.org/10.1007/978-3-319-70022-9_2
13. Lam, C.P., Chou, C.T., Chiang, K.H., Fu, L.C.: Human-centered robot navigation: towards a harmoniously human-robot coexisting environment. IEEE Trans. Robot. **27**(1), 99–112 (2011)
14. Mead, R., Matarić, M.J.: Robots have needs too: how and why people adapt their proxemic behavior to improve robot social signal understanding. J. Hum.-Robot Interact. **5**(2), 48–68 (2016)
15. Pacchierotti, E., Christensen, H.I., Jensfelt, P.: Evaluation of passing distance for social robots. In: The 15th IEEE International Symposium on Robot and Human Interactive Communication, ROMAN 2006, pp. 315–320. IEEE (2006)
16. Papadakis, P., Rives, P., Spalanzani, A.: Adaptive spacing in human-robot interactions. In: 2014 IEEE/RSJ International Conference on Intelligent Robots and Systems (IROS 2014), pp. 2627–2632. IEEE (2014)
17. Rios-Martinez, J., Spalanzani, A., Laugier, C.: From proxemics theory to socially-aware navigation: a survey. Int. J. Soc. Robot. **7**(2), 137–153 (2015)
18. Robins, B., Dautenhahn, K., Te Boekhorst, R., Billard, A.: Robotic assistants in therapy and education of children with autism: can a small humanoid robot help encourage social interaction skills? Univ. Access Inf. Soc. **4**(2), 105–120 (2005)
19. Rossi, S., Staffa, M., Bove, L., Capasso, R., Ercolano, G.: User's personality and activity influence on HRI comfortable distances. In: Kheddar, A., et al. (eds.) ICSR 2017. LNCS, vol. 10652, pp. 167–177. Springer, Cham (2017). https://doi.org/10.1007/978-3-319-70022-9_17
20. Ruijten, P.A.M., Cuijpers, R.H.: Stopping distance for a robot approaching two conversating persons. In: 2017 26th IEEE International Symposium on Robot and Human Interactive Communication (RO-MAN), pp. 224–229. IEEE (2017)
21. Sisbot, E.A., Alami, R., Siméon, T., Dautenhahn, K., Walters, M., Woods, S.: Navigation in the presence of humans. In: 2005 5th IEEE-RAS International Conference on Humanoid Robots, pp. 181–188. IEEE (2005)
22. Sisbot, E.A., Marin-Urias, L.F., Alami, R., Simeon, T.: A human aware mobile robot motion planner. IEEE Trans. Robot. **23**(5), 874–883 (2007)
23. Torta, E., Cuijpers, R.H., Juola, J.F.: Design of a parametric model of personal space for robotic social navigation. Int. J. Soc. Robot. **5**(3), 357–365 (2013)

24. Walters, M.L., et al.: The influence of subjects' personality traits on personal spatial zones in a human-robot interaction experiment. In: IEEE International Workshop on Robot and Human Interactive Communication, ROMAN 2005, pp. 347–352. IEEE (2005)
25. Walters, M.L., Dautenhahn, K., Te Boekhorst, R., Koay, K.L., Syrdal, D.S., Nehaniv, C.L.: An empirical framework for human-robot proxemics. In: Proceedings of New Frontiers in Human-Robot Interaction (2009)
26. Zanlungo, F., Yücel, Z., Ferreri, F., Even, J., Saiki, L.Y.M., Kanda, T.: Social group motion in robots. In: Kheddar, A., et al. (eds.) ICSR 2017. LNCS, vol. 10652, pp. 474–484. Springer, Cham (2017). https://doi.org/10.1007/978-3-319-70022-9_47

Reduced Sense of Agency in Human-Robot Interaction

Francesca Ciardo[1(✉)], Davide De Tommaso[1], Frederike Beyer[2],
and Agnieszka Wykowska[1]

[1] Italian Institute of Technology, Genoa, Italy
francesca.ciardo@iit.it
[2] Queen Mary University, London, UK

Abstract. In the presence of others, sense of agency (SoA), i.e. the perceived relationship between our own actions and external events, is reduced. This effect is thought to contribute to diffusion of responsibility. The present study aimed at examining humans' SoA when interacting with an artificial embodied agent. Young adults participated in a task alongside the Cozmo robot (Anki Robotics). Participants were asked to perform costly actions (i.e. losing various amounts of points) to stop an inflating balloon from exploding. In 50% of trials, only the participant could stop the inflation of the balloon (Individual condition). In the remaining trials, both Cozmo and the participant were in charge of preventing the balloon from bursting (Joint condition). The longer the players waited before pressing the "stop" key, the smaller amount of points that was subtracted. However, in case the balloon burst, participants would lose the largest amount of points. In the joint condition, no points were lost if Cozmo stopped the balloon. At the end of each trial, participants rated how much control they perceived over the outcome of the trial. Results showed that when participants successfully stopped the balloon, they rated their SoA lower in the Joint than in the Individual condition, independently of the amount of lost points. This suggests that interacting with robots affects SoA, similarly to interacting with other humans.

Keywords: Sense of agency · Human-robot interaction
Diffusion of responsibility

1 Introduction

Artificial agents are already present in our everyday life. We interact with a voice assistant of our smartphone, with a GPS navigation system, and with the Google assistant. All of these artificial agents are not physically embodied, thus they cannot physically act in order to produce a change in our physical environment. However, in the near future, also robots will be present in our houses, at work, and in social spaces, like airports or train stations [1]. Through their embodiment, robots will be able not only to support our work passively, by giving us information, but they will be able to act in our environment and change it. Thus, they will be involved in various tasks, including, for instance, providing assistance in emergency situations. In this scenario, it appears crucial to investigate how embodied artificial agents may affect decision-making and

© Springer Nature Switzerland AG 2018
S. S. Ge et al. (Eds.): ICSR 2018, LNAI 11357, pp. 441–450, 2018.
https://doi.org/10.1007/978-3-030-05204-1_43

social cognition in humans. This would be advantageous for both social robotics and psychology. On the one hand, by examining social cognition in HRI, we can design and develop robots that are well tailored to the humans' needs and expectations [2]. On the other hand, psychology can benefit from a systematic examination of various mechanisms involved in social interaction [3, 4] through a method with a high degree of ecological validity (interactive protocols with embodied robots), and excellent experimental control at the same time. Following this approach, we focused on a well-known phenomenon in social contexts, i.e. diffusion of responsibility.

Diffusion of responsibility is a common phenomenon that reflects humans' tendency to decrease the likelihood of performing an action in the presence of others. This phenomenon is thought to underlie decision-making bias in group behavior. For instance, the likelihood that someone will intervene in an emergency situation decreases in a crowd [5, 6]. Also effort invested in a project is decreased in the presence of a large group [7]. Evidence from experimental psychology also shows that groups tend to make riskier choices [8, 9] and are more aggressive than individuals [10, 11]. Taken together, evidence shows that in the presence of others humans tend to feel less responsible for the consequences of their actions, especially when those consequences are negative [12]. Decreased level of sense of agency (SoA) [13, 14] has been postulated to play a critical role in this type of diffusion of responsibility. SoA refers to the feeling that one can control external events through one's own actions [15].

Given the above considerations, it appears crucial to investigate how the presence of not only other humans, but also artificial embodied agents may change the experience of humans' own action, i.e. SoA. Previous research in HRI mainly focused on task agency and moral responsibility attribution to the robot [16]. For example, in Kim and Hinds's work [17] a robot autonomously moving during a cooperative game was considered more responsible for task accuracy than a robot moving according to users' instructions. However, these studies did not address the question of how the presence of the artificial agent, robotic or computerized, affects SoA in humans.

SoA in humans has been traditionally investigated through implicit and explicit measures. Implicit measure of SoA is obtained through measuring changes in perceived temporal duration between an action and a sensory effect associated with it [see 18 for a review]. The typical result is known as "intentional binding" - the tendency of individuals to perceive the action-effect intervals shorter when they themselves have performed the action, as compared to when an action-effect event has been produced by others. Explicit measure of SoA is assessed by asking participants to rate on a scale whether, and to what extent, they were in control of a certain action effect [e.g. 13, 14]. Obhi and Hall [19] used intentional binding to compare SoA in human-human interaction (HHI) and in HCI. Results showed intentional binding effect only for the HHI, but not when participants were playing against a computer. In two recent studies, Beyer and colleagues [13, 14] showed that an explicit measure of SoA is affected by "presence" of others when participants believe they are playing with another human, even if they were actually playing with the computer. This effect has been reported also at the electrophysiological level [13] with a reduction of the feedback-related negativity amplitude evoked by outcome monitoring. In a subsequent neuroimaging study, Beyer and colleagues [14] found increased activity in areas associated with mentalizing processes, such as the bilateral Temporo-Parietal Junction (TPJ) and precuneus, during the social, compared to individual, task condition. Taken together, evidence suggests, that in the presence of others, we are likely to feel less responsible for the action outcomes, as we take into consideration other agents potentially performing the task. This results in the decrease of sense of agency at the individual level.

Aim

To date, it is not known whether in direct interactions, humans perceive robots as intentional agents, or 'embodied computers'. In the case of the former, one would expect similar diffusion of responsibility (and decreased SoA) as in the presence of other humans. In the latter, SoA should be comparable to a situation when we act alone. The present study aimed at addressing this question. To this end, we asked participants to perform a game with the Cozmo robot (Anki Robotics). Participants were asked to perform costly actions (i.e. losing various amounts of points) to stop an inflating balloon from bursting in individual vs. joint contexts.

2   Materials and Methods

2.1   Participants

Eighteen healthy adults (mean age = 24.3 ± 4.2; 11 Males; 3 left-handed) took part in the study. The study was approved by the local ethical committee (Comitato Etico Regione Liguria). Participants gave a written consent prior to their participation. All had normal or corrected-to normal vision, received an honorarium for their participation, and were debriefed about the purpose of the study at the end of the experiment.

2.2   Apparatus and Stimuli

The Cozmo Robot

The Cozmo robot (Anki robotics, see Fig. 1, Left panel) is a commercial platform designed for educational tasks. It is a tiny wheeled robot that can move, lift objects and recognize people' faces. It is equipped with several sensors and actuators, i.e. a proximity sensor for obstacle detection and avoidance, a camera for detecting visual features in the environment, a display for showing facial expressions and a lift for interacting with objects. A set of three interactive cubes are part of the platform. Cozmo is able to detect and distinguish them, but also to move or lift them from one place to another. The cubes can be used as bidirectional interfaces. In fact they can light up in different colors and detect vibrations. Cozmo is controllable via a mobile application compatible with iOS and Android. Moreover a Python based SDK allowing access to the basic functionalities of the robot and cubes. We integrated the Cozmo robot with Opensesame through the Cozmo SDK available for Python 3.6. It is necessary to install the Cozmo SDK for Windows, as described in [20], and import the module in an Opensesame script as a normal Python package. The implementation of the task is based on the 'Quick Tap' example application provided in the Cozmo SDK [21]. Such application provides the developer an example of interaction between Cozmo robot and cubes and to familiarize with asynchronous events. The flow of the application is driven by the events and not by a sequence of steps. We used the same approach for implementing our task within Opensesame. Specifically, we pre-assigned a cube for the participant and the other one for Cozmo. Cozmo was programmed to wake up or go to sleep mode depending on the experimental condition. During the Joint condition Cozmo was programmed to tap its assigned cube in the 60% of the joint trials. For detecting the cubes' events, we implemented a callback routine that is executed every time a cube is tapped. Since we could access the cube ID inside this callback, we knew which player tapped that cube. Therefore we could record the responses of the two players depending of the onset of the stimuli. The experiment was carried out in a fully lit room. The experimental setup consisted of: (1) a mobile Android device in which the standard Cozmo application with 'SDK enabled option' was running, (2) a laptop connected with Cozmo through the Android Debug Bridge (adb) as described in [22], (3) the Cozmo robot together with two Cozmo Cubes (4.5 × 4.5 × 4.5 cm), on which responses were performed, (4) a 21' in. screen (1920 × 1080) to display the task. A participant was seated facing Cozmo. The screen laid horizontally on the table between the participant and Cozmo. One Cozmo Cube was located on each side of the screen (see Fig. 1, Right panel). Stimuli consisted of pictures of a pin and a red balloon (113 × 135 pixels). Responses during the game were executed by tapping with the full hand the respective cube. SoA ratings were collected using a Wi-Fi mouse. Stimulus presentation, response timing, and data collection were controlled by Opensesame software [23] version 3.2.4 for Windows, which is compatible with Python 3.6.

Fig. 1. Left panel: a picture of Cozmo robot taken in the S4HRI lab at IIT. Right panel: experimental setup during Joint condition.

2.3 Procedure

The task was designed based on the diffusion of responsibility (DOR) task used in Beyer et al. [13, 14]. Participants were instructed to perform a game where they had to stop the inflation of a balloon before it would reach a pin and burst (see Fig. 2). Participants were instructed that, at the beginning of the game, they and Cozmo would receive 2500 points each, and in each trial, they and Cozmo could lose up to 100 of these points. Participants were instructed to try and maximize their individual game score. The task consisted of 12 blocks of 10 trials each. Blocks were randomly assigned to either the 'Individual' or the 'Joint' condition. At the beginning of 'Individual' blocks, Cozmo stepped away from its cube and entered into the sleep mode. Participants were instructed that in the Individual trials they were the only ones in charge of preventing the balloon from bursting. If they would not act the balloon would burst and they would lose the maximum amount of points. At the beginning of 'Joint' blocks, Cozmo woke up and took up its position close to the respective cube. Participants were instructed that, in these trials, both they, and Cozmo, would be playing, and they could use their respective cube to stop the inflation of the balloon. If neither the participant nor Cozmo acted, the balloon would burst and both would lose the same amount of points. If Cozmo stopped the inflation of the balloon, the participant would not lose any points. If the participant stopped the balloon, they would lose a number of points according to the size at which they stopped it, and Cozmo would not lose any points. Cozmo was programmed to act only in the 60% of the Joint trials (i.e. 36 out of 60 Joint trials). In the Joint condition, Cozmo's tap was triggered when the 90% of the inflating sequence was completed and no action was executed by the participant. At the beginning of each trial a frame indicating the condition of the game (Individual or Joint) was presented for 1000 ms, followed by a wait frame (1500 ms) indicating that a new trial was starting. Then a fixation point was displayed for a random 800–1000 ms time. Next, the balloon at its starting size was presented. After 500 ms, the balloon started inflating towards the pin. At any point, participants could tap their cube to stop the inflation of the balloon. If they did so, the balloon stopped at its current size for 1000 ms. If participants did not react in time, the balloon reached the pin and it burst as indicated by the sign "Pop" presented for 1000 ms. Subsequently, a fixation dot was presented for a time random between 800 and 1000 ms. Afterwards, a feedback frame indicating how many points participants lost was displayed for 2000 ms. Then, an 8-point Likert scale with the question 'How much control did you feel over the outcome?' (in Italian) was presented. The endpoints of the scale labels were 1 = 'No control' and 8 = 'Complete control' (in Italian). Participants were instructed that the later they stopped the balloon, the fewer points they would lose. However, they were told that if the balloon burst, they would lose the maximum amount of points. As a result, the action (i.e. stopping the balloon) resulted to be costly, but less costly than not acting. In order to make it difficult to always stop the balloon close to the pin, the speed with which the balloon inflated varied within and across trials.

2.4 Data Analysis

To fully characterize the risk-taking behavior in the task, we counted the number of trials for each participant, in which the balloon was stopped by the participant (Valid trials), the balloon burst (Missed trials), and in which Cozmo acted (Cozmo trials). Frequencies of Valid, Missed, and Cozmo trials were compared through paired sample t-tests. For SoA ratings, we analyzed only Valid trials, i.e. when the participant acted and successfully stopped the balloon. As dependent variables, we used (for each participant) agency ratings. Data were analyzed using linear mixed-effects models. Agency ratings were modeled using Condition (Individual, Joint) and the number of lost points in each trial, plus their interactions. The outcome of the trial (i.e. the amount of lost points) was standardized for each participant. Fixed effects were modeled as participant random effects (random intercepts and slopes). Analyses were conducted using the

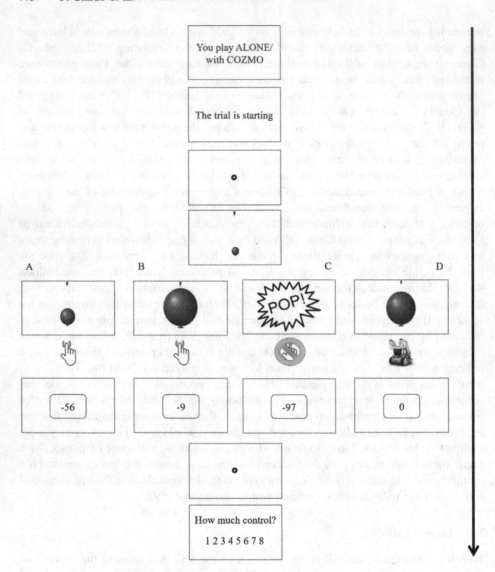

Fig. 2. DOR task. Outline of a low-risk valid trial (A), a high-risk valid trial (B), a missed trial (C), and a Cozmo trial (D).

lme4 package [24] in R. Parameter estimates (β) and their associated t-tests (t, p-value), calculated using the Satterthwaite approximation for degrees of freedom [25] are presented to show the magnitude of the effects, with bootstrapped 95% confidence intervals [26].

3 Results

The balloon burst significantly more frequently when participants performed the task alone than when playing with Cozmo, as indicated by higher percentage of Missed trials in the Individual (M = 19.5%, SE = 1.9) than in the Joint condition (M = 13.1%, SE = 1.1, see Fig. 3) [t_{17} = 4.27, p < 0.001]. In the Joint condition, Cozmo acted more often than the balloon burst, as Missed trials were less frequent than Cozmo trials (M = 29.7%, SE = 1.5) [t_{17} = 11.02, p < 0.001].

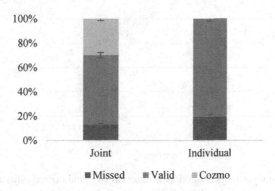

Fig. 3. Frequencies of responses plotted as a function of Missed (red), Valid (blue), and Cozmo trials (yellow) across Joint and Individual condition (left and right bar, respectively). (Color figure online)

Sense of Agency
Results showed a significant reduction in agency ratings in the Joint (M = 6.21, SE = .07) compared to the Individual (M = 6.47, SE = .06) condition [β = −0.27 $t_{15.97}$ = −2.53, p = .022, 95% CI = (−0.49, −0.06)]. Agency ratings were also predicted by the amount of lost points (Outcome) [β = −0.38, $t1_{8.08}$ = −5.46, p < .001, 95% CI = (−0.52, −0.25)], with smaller losses being associated with higher SoA ratings, see Fig. 4. There were no significant interactions.

Discussion
The present study aimed at examining whether the phenomenon of reduced SoA previously found in HHI would also be observed during HRI. To this end, we asked participants to rate their SoA during a game with the Cozmo robot where they were asked to perform costly actions (i.e. losing various amounts of points). Comparing task performance between a Joint and an Individual condition, results showed a lower percentage of missed trials in the former. Moreover, in the Joint condition the percentage of trials in which Cozmo stopped the balloon was higher than the percentage of bursting trials. These results indicate that participants adopted different strategies across conditions and adapted their behavior to the presence of Cozmo. When participants successfully stopped the balloon, they rated their SoA lower in the Joint than in the Individual condition, independently of the amount of lost points. This result suggests that interacting with robots reduces SoA, similarly to the case of HHI. Moreover, in

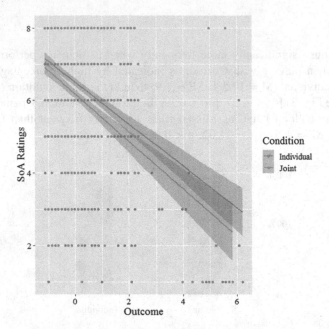

Fig. 4. Sense of agency ratings plotted as a function of standardized outcome (i.e. z-scores of the number of lost points in each trial) across Individual (red dots) and Joint (blue dots) conditions. (Color figure online)

accordance with previous studies using explicit measures of agency [13, 14], results indicate that SoA is reduced for more negative outcomes. This result confirms that participants followed the instructions and rated their perceived control over the outcome, rather than over the success of the trial (i.e. independent of whether the balloon burst or not). In contrast with previous studies showing that SoA is not affected in HCI [e.g. 19], our findings indicate that in HRI, the embodied presence of an artificial agent reduces SoA in humans. According to the model of Beyer and colleagues [13, 14], our results suggest that participants might have attributed mental states to Cozmo in a similar way as they would do towards a human co-agent. This is an important phenomenon in the context of future scenarios where robots will be present in our social environments. Similarly to the presence of other humans, they might evoke diffusion of responsibility. Therefore, in emergency situations, it would be best if robots are able to efficiently detect an emergency signal and act upon it, as the human counterparts may not be efficient and fast enough.

4   Conclusions

In social presence of others, humans perceive lower agency over their own actions, which might be a result of diffusion of responsibility. The results of the present study showed that also in the presence of a robot, humans tend to reduce the perceived sense of agency related to their actions. We propose that the design of robots' behavior in social contexts should consider the impact of the presence of an embodied artificial agent on humans' decision-making.

Acknowledgments. This project has received funding from the European Research Council (ERC) under the European Union's Horizon 2020 research and innovation programme (grant awarded to A. Wykowska, titled "InStance: Intentional Stance for Social Attunement. Grant agreement No: 715058).

References

1. Murphy, R.R., Nomura, T., Billard, A., Burke, J.L.: Human-robot interaction. IEEE Robot. Autom. Mag. **17**(2), 85–89 (2010). https://doi.org/10.1109/MRA.2010.936953
2. Wiese, E., Metta, G., Wykowska, A.: Robots as intentional agents: using neuroscientific methods to make robots appear more social. Front. Psychol. **8**, 1663 (2017)
3. Kompatsiari, K., Tikhanoff, V., Ciardo, F., Metta, G., Wykowska, A.: The importance of mutual gaze in human-robot interaction. In: Kheddar, A., et al. (eds.) ICSR 2017. LNCS, vol. 10652, pp. 443–452. Springer, Cham (2017). https://doi.org/10.1007/978-3-319-70022-9_44
4. Wykowska, A., Chaminade, T., Cheng, G.: Embodied artificial agents for understanding human social cognition. Phil. Trans. R. Soc. B **371**(1693), 20150375 (2016)
5. Darley, J.M., Latane, B.: Bystander intervention in emergencies: diffusion of responsibility. J. Pers. Soc. Psychol. **8**(4p1), 377–383 (1968)
6. Chekroun, P., Brauer, M.: The bystander effect and social control behavior: the effect of the presence of others on people's reactions to norm violations. Eur. J. Soc. Psychol. **32**(6), 853–867 (2002)
7. Karau, S.J., Williams, K.D.: Social loafing: a meta-analytic review and theoretical integration. J. Pers. Soc. Psychol. **65**(4), 681–706 (1993)
8. Wallach, M.A., Kogan, N., Bem, D.J.: Diffusion of responsibility and level of risk taking in groups. J. Abnorm. Soc. Psychol. **68**(3), 263–274 (1964)
9. Bradley, G.L.: Group influences upon preferences for personal protection: a simulation study. J. Saf. Res. **26**(2), 99–105 (1995)
10. Bandura, A., Underwood, B., Fromson, M.E.: Disinhibition of aggression through diffusion of responsibility and dehumanization of victims. J. Res. Pers. **9**(4), 253–269 (1975)
11. Meier, B.P., Hinsz, V.B.: A comparison of human aggression committed by groups and individuals: an interindividual–intergroup discontinuity. J. Exp. Soc. Psychol. **40**(4), 551–559 (2004)
12. Bandura, A.: Social cognitive theory of self-regulation. Organ. Behav. Hum. Decis. Process. **50**(2), 248–287 (1991)
13. Beyer, F., Sidarus, N., Bonicalzi, S., Haggard, P.: Beyond self-serving bias: diffusion of responsibility reduces sense of agency and outcome monitoring. Soc. Cogn. Affect. Neurosci. **12**(1), 138–145 (2017)
14. Beyer, F., Sidarus, N., Fleming, S., Haggard, P.: Losing control in social situations: how the presence of others affects neural processes related to sense of agency. eNeuro **5**(1) (2018). https://doi.org/10.1523/ENEURO.0336-17.2018. ENEURO-0336
15. Frith, C.D.: Action, agency and responsibility. Neuropsychologia **55**, 137–142 (2014)
16. van der Woerdt, S., Haselager, P.: When robots appear to have a mind: the human perception of machine agency and responsibility. New Ideas Psychol. (2017). https://doi.org/10.1016/j.newideapsych.2017.11.001

17. Kim, T., Hinds, P.: Who should I blame? Effects of autonomy and transparency on attributions in human-robot interaction. In: IEEE International Symposium on Robot and Human Interactive Communication 2006 (ROMAN 2006). IEEE Publishing, Hatfield/New York (2006)
18. Pfister, R., Obhi, S.S., Rieger, M., Wenke, D.: Action and perception in social contexts: intentional binding for social action effects. Front. Hum. Neurosci. **8**, 667 (2014)
19. Obhi, S.S., Hall, P.: Sense of agency and intentional binding in joint action. Exp. Brain Res. **211**(3–4), 655–662 (2011)
20. Cozmo SDK installation for Windows. https://cozmosdk.anki.com/docs/install-windows.html
21. Cozmo Quick Tap. https://github.com/anki/cozmo-pythonsdk/blob/master/examples/apps/quick_tap.py
22. Android Debug Bridge. cozmosdk.anki.com/docs/adb.html
23. Mathôt, S., Schreij, D., Theeuwes, J.: OpenSesame: an open-source, graphical experiment builder for the social sciences. Behav. Res. Methods **44**(2), 314–324 (2012)
24. Bates, D., Maechler, M., Bolker, B., et al.: lme4: linear mixed-effects models using Eigen and S4 (Version 1.1-7) (2014). http://cran.r-project.org/web/packages/lme4/index.html
25. Kuznetsova, A., Brockhoff, P.B., Christensen, R.H.B.: lmerTest: tests in Linear Mixed Effects Models (Version 2.029) (2015). https://cran.r-project.org/web/packages/lmerTest/index.html
26. Efron, B., Tibshirani, R.J.: An Introduction to the Bootstrap. CRC Press, Boca Raton (1994)

Comparing the Effects of Social Robots and Virtual Agents on Exercising Motivation

Sebastian Schneider$^{(\boxtimes)}$ and Franz Kummert$^{(\boxtimes)}$

Applied Informatics, CITEC, Bielefeld University, 33616 Bielefeld, Germany
{sebschne,franz}@techfak.uni-bielefeld.de

Abstract. Preventing diseases of affluence is one of the major challenges for our future society. Researchers introduced robots as a tool to support people on dieting or rehabilitation tasks. However, deploying robots as exercising companions is cost-intensive. Therefore, in our current work, we are investigating how the embodiment of an exercising partner influences the exercising motivation to persist on an abdominal plank exercise. We analyzed and compared data from previous experiments on exercising with robots and virtual agents. The results show that the participants had longer exercising times when paired with a robot companion compared to virtual agents, but not compared to a human partner. However, participants perceived the robots partner as more likable than a human partner. This results have implications for SAR practitioners and are important for the usage of SAR to promote physical activity.

Keywords: Socially Assistive Robots · Exercising · Embodiment

1 Introduction

The World Health Organization (WHO) states in their key facts[1] about physical activity (PA) that insufficient PA is not only one of the leading risk factors for death worldwide but also a key risk factor for Noncommunicable Diseases (NCDs) such as cardiovascular diseases, cancer, and diabetes. However, getting people motivated to increase their PA is a challenging problem [3]. A variety of factors influence people to start an exercise regimen [3] and having social support is one of the most positively associated factors for adults [16]. However, appropriate assistance from peers, coaches or physicians, which could facilitate starting and sticking to a workout, is not available for everybody. It includes finding and scheduling with the associates and often to commute to other places.

Supported by grants from the Cluster of Excellence Cognitive Interaction Technology 'CITEC' (EXC 277), Bielefeld University.

[1] All of these facts are on the WHO website:http://www.who.int/en/news-room/fact-sheets/detail/physical-activity, retrieved 08/14/2018.

© Springer Nature Switzerland AG 2018
S. S. Ge et al. (Eds.): ICSR 2018, LNAI 11357, pp. 451–461, 2018.
https://doi.org/10.1007/978-3-030-05204-1_44

Hence Socially Assistive Robots (SARs) [6] have been introduced as a suitable tool to facilitate motivation because people are likely to anthropomorphize non-biological artifacts [4] and treat media and technology human-like [12]. In our previous work, we have presented the effects of exercising together with a robot as a partner [14]. However, today's technologies allow for changing the representation of the partner easily. Smartphone applications, exercising videos on online platforms or exercising with human partners via internet video calls are possible variations. Those technologies could be used to emulate the feeling of working out together with a partner. Compared to those technology, it raises the question whether Embodied Robot (ER) are necessary in a task where no physical interaction is needed? Deploying ERs comes with issues regarding their physical ability and their maintenance. Thus, Virtual Agents (VAs) have a substantial advantage over robots, because they are easily deployable, do not have physical limitations, are cheaper and need less care than robots. However, do ERs and VAs elicit the same social and motivational effects? Li [11] tried to answer this question with a recent research survey which shows that in most cases robots are in favor of VAs[2]. However, there are also works that are showing contradicting results [9,13]. While other works investigated the embodiment effects of SAR for rehabilitative tasks [5], we are interested in measuring quantifiable motivational impacts of an embodied SAR during an abdominal exercising task. Our previous studies showed the motivational effects of working out co-actively with a SAR or receiving encouraging feedback from a SAR [14,15]. In the present work, we want to look at whether co-actively exercising robots are enhancing people's motivation to exercise compared to virtual partners.

This work is organized as follows: The next section reviews previous and related works. Section 4 introduces the study design and data acquisition. Section 5 presents the results and Sect. 6 discusses the results. The final section concludes the results and gives an outlook.

2   Related Work

Previous works investigated the effects of a robot's embodiment in different tasks. These works include studies on SAR supporting on cognitive tasks [10], which showed that an embodied robot increases a learning gain. A study on authority and personal space in a book moving task showed that people are more willing to obey orders from an embodied agent and give them more personal space [1]. However, studies on language learning and teaching showed no differences in terms of learning gains between agent embodiment [9,13].

A recent meta-review on the benefits of being physically present investigated not only the impact of embodiment but also on co-presence [11]. Their results show that a physically present robot compared to a telepresent robot had stronger effects regarding the participant's response, are more persuasive and increase response time. Compared to virtual agents, co-present robots are

---

[2] They distinguished different levels of an agent's presence (i.e., embodied remote-located vs. virtually represented), but here we are referring to both as VAs).

more convincing, increase user's attention and response speed, are favored, and users show more positive attitudes towards co-present robots. Regarding the differences between a telepresent and virtual represented robot they did not find any differences. The authors conclude that co-present robots have a benefit compared to virtual agents or telepresent robots, but subsequent studies showed contradicting results [9,13]. Thus, it remains an ongoing question what the actual benefits of being physically present are and in which tasks they have an impact.

Regarding the embodiment effects of SAR specially designed for exercising or rehabilitation tasks, there is only one work investigating the impact of robot embodiment in a long-term study [5]. They compared a physical robot with its virtual counterpart in a longitudinal study with five 20-min exercising sessions over a period of two-weeks. Their results provide evidence that users perceive a physically embodied robot as more enjoyable, valuable, helpful and socially attractive compared to the virtual robot. However, these are subjective evaluations from the participants that do not show whether embodied SAR have a quantifiable and observable motivational effect compared to virtual agents.

3   Hypothesis

The present research contributes to the ongoing efforts in understanding the effects of embodiment and tries to close the research gap by showing that embodied robots not only are perceived as more sociable, enjoyable and helpful but also increase exercising time. Based on the previous research from [11] and [5] we have the following hypothesis:

A robot companion enhances a human's motivation to persist on an exercise compared to a virtual partner (**H1**).

To test this hypothesis, we combine the data of the two previously done experiments on abdominal plank exercises with virtual agent partners and robot partners. We analyze the data to investigate whether there is a motivational effect in persisting on the task due to the different partner embodiments.

4   Planned Data Analysis

To investigate whether embodied robots show an advantage in terms of exercising motivation compared to VAs, we analyze the data of the previous studies from [14] and [15] and from [7]. Feltz et al. [7] conducted a study to compare the motivational effects of exercising with a humanoid virtual partner with a hardly human-like appearance (Hardly Human Partner (HHP)), a nearly human-like appearance (Nearly Human Partner (NHP)) and with a human partner (Human Partner (HP)) (see Fig. 2) compared to a condition in which the subject is always exercising alone (Individual Condition (IC)). Their result shows that even though it is a small effect, exercising with a VA is more motivating than having no partner at all, which we have also investigated for having robot partners. In the previous works we replicated the study of [7] and replaced the HP and VA with the humanoid robot platform Nao (see Fig. 1). However, we included some changes in the study design due to the usage of a robotic agent. We changed the exercises from forearm planks to full planks due to the robot's limited Degree of Freedom (DoF). Additionally, due to the physical limitation in exercising abilities of current humanoid robot platforms, we are interested in whether a robot that is exercising co-actively with the user is required. Thus, we previously included a condition where we tested the effects of just having a robot instructor (Robot Instructor (RI)).

We showed that a co-actively exercising robot companion (Robot Companion (RC)) leads to higher motivation to persist the exercises than exercising alone, but not for the robot that is just instructing the user (RI). Adding encouraging feedback leads to greater exercising performance when the robot is instructing (Robot Instructor with Feedback (RIF)) but did not lead to higher performance in the companion condition (Robot Companion with Feedback (RCF)). We have attributed this results to ceiling effects due to the difficulty of the exercises[3]. Now, we have the opportunity to compare the persistence data from the studies with robots and compare our results with the results from exercising with virtual companions and humans. For the reader's comprehension, we summarize in the following subsections the planned data analysis and used measurements.

4.1   Conditions and Experimental Design

Participants in both studies were assigned to one of nine conditions, which we will explain now.

HP. In [7] the Human Partner (HP) was a college-aged partner whose video was prerecorded.

NHP. In [7] the Nearly Human Partner (NHP) was the same video as the HP, but with a computerized effect applied to the video.

HHP. In [7] the Hardly Human Partner (HHP) were a three-dimensional graphical characters. The character was animated to perform the plank exercises.

RC. In [14] the Robot Companion (RC) partner was the humanoid robot platform Nao. Nao's motion were animated using Choregraphe to perform the plank exercises together with the human.

RI. In [14] the Robot Instructor (RI) partner was the same humanoid robot platform. However, instead of exercising co-actively with the human, it simply structures the exercise session.

RCF. In [15] the Robot Companion with Feedback (RCF) had the same behavior as in the RC. However, the robots also gave encouraging feedback while exercising (see [15] for detailed information).

---

[3] Participants reported in post-study interviews that they would have liked to exercise longer but that they had too much pain in the wrist due to the exercises.

RIF. In [15] the Robot Instructor with Feedback (RIF) had the same behavior as in the RI. However, the robot also gave encouraging feedback while exercising.

IC and IC_2. Are the baseline conditions were participants exercised a second time individually. IC is the isolated condition from [7] and IC_2 is the isolated condition from [14].

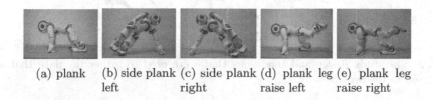

(a) plank   (b) side plank   (c) side plank   (d) plank leg   (e) plank leg
                 left   right   raise left   raise right

Fig. 1. The five different abdominal plank exercises used in this study.

In the robot condition studies, participants (n = 95) were randomly assigned to three conditions (IC_2, RC, RI, RIF, RCF). Participants were mostly students (51 male, 44 female; mean age $[M]$ = 25.4 years; standard deviation $[SD]$ = 5.6) from Bielefeld university acquired by flyers distributed on the campus. They received seven Euros as monetary compensation. Three participants from the IC were excluded. One was an outlier already persisting much less during the first part of the session when the participants were exercising by themselves compared to all other participants. Two other persons were excluded because they were doing the exercises wrong. One participant in the RI condition had to be excluded from the survey evaluation because the data were missing. In all other cases, no outliers have been removed.

Feltz et al. [7] randomly assigned participants (n = 120) to four exercise conditions (IC, NHP, HHP, HP) with 30 participants in each condition. Participants were undergraduate students (60 females, 60 males; mean age $[M]$ = 19.41 years; standard deviation $[SD]$ = 1.52) recruited from a large Midwestern university who completed the experiment for course credit.

4.2   Procedure

The procedure to obtain the data for this analysis is depicted in Fig. 2 and was the same for both studies (see [14] or [7]). Each participant arrived at the lab and was instructed to do five abdominal plank exercises as long as they can (no experimenter was in the same room). Afterward, participants were told that they have to do the five exercises again. They rested for ten minutes and were told their average exercising time during Block 1. Then, the manipulation and the participants were assigned to one of the conditions. In the partner conditions, participants were told that the time of the partner who quits first will count and that the partner can exercise on average 40% longer. This creates an unfavorable comparison which is vital for the Köhler effect and proofed to

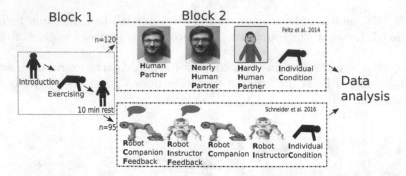

Fig. 2. The study design and conditions that were used to gather the data that are analysed in the present work.

elicit the highest motivational gain. Each participant exercised with the partner, answered a survey after the experiment, and was debriefed. This is just a brief explanation of the procedure. Due to the paper limitation, we cannot give a full detailed overview of the procedure and would like to ask the reader to look at the referenced papers describing the study procedure in more detail.

5   Results

In both studies several different measures have been collected. However, we will not use all of them for the evaluation, because we are mainly interested in the perception of the partner and the persistence on the exercises. Thus, the persistence, Godspeed questionnaire [2], and Physical Activity Enjoyment Scale (PAES) [8] were used.

We tested the data for homogeneity of variance using a Levene's Test and for normality using a Shapiro-Wilk test. Since most of the data is not normally distributed, we used non-parametric tests (e.g. Kruskal-Wallis Rank Sum Test (KW-Test) and Wilcoxon rank sum test (WC-Test)).

5.1   Persistence

As a primary dependent variable we used the average difference persistence time in seconds between the two blocks (Block 2 - Block 1). This approach controls for individual differences in strength and fitness and shows possible changes in persistence. At first, we compare the exercising times on Block 1 between the two studies from Feltz et al. ($M = 57.7, SD = 23.94$) and Schneider and Kummert ($M = 65.45, SD = 22.02$) to assure that the baseline exercising times are equivalent. The exercising time is significantly affected by the studies, $W = 3933, p < .01, r = -.19$. This difference is possibly due to the changes in the exercise from forearm planks to full planks, which makes the exercises harder to persist but likely more challenging for the user and thus more interesting to persist them longer. Hence, we decided to adjust the Block 1 measures to compensate for the difference in the exercises. We used the average of participants' exercising time on Block 1 between the two studies as an adjustment value. Participants in study [7] exercised on average 7.78 s less in Block 1 than in the studies from [14,15]. We used this value and added it to the exercising time of Block 1 for the NHP, HHP, and HP conditions. Figure 3 shows the adjusted results obtained for the average block scores of Block 2 subtracted with the average block score of Block 1. This figure shows the significant difference between the conditions against a base-mean. A 8 (conditions) x 1 (persistence) KW-Test on the adjusted persistence scores showed a significant main effect for the conditions, $H(8) = 67.93, p < .001$. Persistence time in the HP, RC, RCF and RIF conditions is significantly higher against the base-mean. The IC, IC_2 and HHP conditions are significantly lower than the base-mean. Due to the limitations of the paper, we cannot report the post-hoc analysis after the KW-Test for the persistence time comparing the significant differences between the conditions. A KW-Test for difference between the conditions on the perceived PAES showed no significant differences, $H(7) = 4.99, p = .66$.

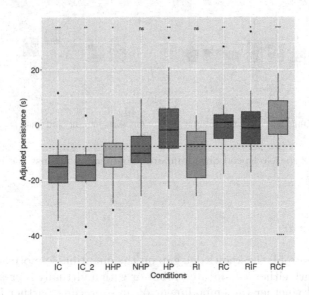

Fig. 3. Average adjusted persistence difference (s) between Block 2 and Block 1 for the different conditions. Comparison against the mean baseline of all conditions.

5.2 Perception of Partner

We tested the perception of the partner using the four sub-scales of the Godspeed questionnaire (animacy, likability, anthropomorphism and intelligence) using KW-Tests. The scores on the Godspeed questionnaire are shown in Fig. 4. We found significant main effects for the perceived animacy of the agents ($H(6) = 17.24, p < .01$), anthropomorphism ($H(6) = 21.83, p < .01$) and likability ($H(6) = 30.13, p < .001$) but not for intelligence ($H(6) = 7.03, p = .31$).

The HP and RC are both significantly rated as more animated than then HHP (we cannot report all the critical differences from the pairwise KW-Test due to the limitation of this paper). The HHP was rated as significantly less anthopomorphic than the HP and the RI was rated as significantly less anthropomorphic than the NHP. The RC and RCF were perceived as significantly more likable than the HP and NHP. Additionally, the RCF was rated as significantly more likable than the NHP.

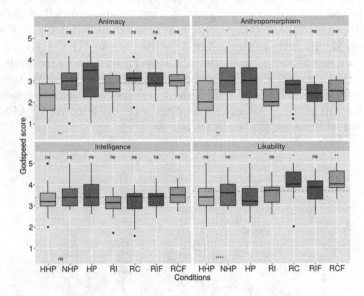

Fig. 4. Scores of the Godspeed questionnaire. Comparison against the mean baseline of all conditions.

6   Discussion

This work aims to fill the knowledge gap on the quantifiable motivational effects of exercising with either a co-located robot or with a virtually represented agent. We questioned whether the embodiment of an exercising partner increases the motivation to persist during a conjunctive task. The analysis of the available data support our hypothesis **H1**. Participants in the conditions with a robot companion (RC and RCF) exercised significantly longer than with a virtual partner (NHP and HHP). These results show that the human participants paired with a co-located RC are more motivated to exercise longer than with a telepresent or virtual representation of the partner. Moreover, the HP does not elicit a stronger motivational effect compared to a robot. It shows that a robot exercising partner could be at least as motivational as a HP, but more evaluation is needed to assure this. Thus, the studies need to be replicated due to three differences between them.

First, the data have been acquired by two different research groups in different countries. The found effect can be due to cultural differences or subtle difference in the study conduction. Even though we tried to replicate the study as close as possible, we can not guarantee that everything went exactly the same.

Second, we changed the exercises a little bit. Due to the limited DoF of the robot platform, we needed to implement slightly different exercises. The change from forearm plank exercises to full plank exercises results in different exercising times on Block 1. It is likely that the forearm plank exercises were not challenging enough for the participants and thus they instead stopped the exercising due to boredness and not fatigue. This change makes it difficult to compare the data of the two experiments. Our solution was to adjust the exercising time on Block 1 of data from [7] by adding the average difference on this block between the two studies. This approach is reasonable and helps to get an initial view on the motivational effects due to the partner's embodiment, but it still needs to be verified with the same exercises across all conditions.

Third, the virtual representation of the partner was not the same as the used robot. To be sure that the differences are not due to the representation, the study needs replication with a virtual representation of the same robotic platform. At last, the HP condition was not a co-located partner as in the robot conditions. This difference in co-location could be an explanation why the persistence in the HP conditions was not significantly higher than in the robot conditions. A TV displayed the HP, and the experimenters told the participants that the HP is in a different room connected via a webcam. This difference in the embodiment between the human and robot conditions might also influence the results and shows that future research should target this issue. However, it seems to be almost impossible to conduct such an experiment with a co-located human, since the partner has to be always more capable than the participants to implement the Köhler effect. The need for a more trained exercising partner is a hard requirement that seems to be challenging to fulfill. The results of the Godspeed questionnaire showd that participants rated the animacy and anthropomorphism of the robot differently between the robot conditions and the NHP and HP condition.

Furthermore, the results show a difference in likability between the conditions. Participants rated that they liked the robot companion conditions (RC and RCF) not only more than the NHP and HHP condition but also more than in the HP. This difference in perceived likability is an intriguing quantifiable backup for the feedback from participants during post-study interviews. Many participants said that they would prefer to exercise with a robot partner than a HP. They argued that the robot is not evaluating or judging them while exercising and thus feel more comfortable with a robotic partner than a HP. This participant feedback supports a future application of SAR as a rehabilitation and exercising tool for people with social anxieties, which might prevent them from exercising in groups. Thus robots could facilitate the motivational effects of exercising in groups for such a user population.

7   Conclusion

The question of an agent's embodiment is crucial to ask regarding maintenance, cost-benefit ratio, and deployability. Using robots for socially assistive tasks will only be beneficial if they prove to have an advantage compared to other agent representations. Regarding the usage of SAR as exercising partners, we wanted to fill the research gap and provide evidence that a SAR will not only affect the user's perception of the robot but will also enhance the user's motivation to exercise and thus potentially increase the PA. However, the presented evidence needs further approval with long-term interaction studies and unified benchmarks. Therefore, the research community needs to standardize tasks, robots and virtual agents to measure the motivational effects of having SAR.

Acknowledgments. We would like to thank Feltz et al. for providing their dataset and discussing their work which was supported by grant 1R21HL111916-01A1 from the National Heart, Lung, and Blood Institute.

References

1. Bainbridge, W.A., et al.: The benefits of interactions with physically present robots over video-displayed agents. Int. J. Soc. Robot. **3**(1), 41–52 (2011)
2. Bartneck, C., et al.: Measurement instruments for the anthropomorphism, animacy, likeability, perceived intelligence, and perceived safety of robots. Int. J. Soc. Robot. **1**(1), 71–81 (2009)
3. Bauman, A.E., et al.: Toward a better understanding of the influences on physical activity: the role of determinants, correlates, causal variables, mediators, moderators, and confounders. Am. J. Prev. Med. **23**(2), 5–14 (2002)
4. Epley, N., et al.: On seeing human: a three-factor theory of anthropomorphism. Psychol. Rev. **114**(4), 864 (2007)
5. Fasola, J., et al.: A socially assistive robot exercise coach for the elderly. J. Hum.-Robot Interact. **2**(2), 3–32 (2013)
6. Feil-Seifer, D., et al.: Defining socially assistive robotics. In: Proceedings of the IEEE International Conference on Rehabilitation Robotics (ICORR 2005), pp. 465–468 (2005)
7. Feltz, D.L., et al.: Cyber buddy is better than no buddy: a test of the Köhler Motivation Effect in exergames. Games Health: Res. Dev. Clin. Appl. **3**(2), 98–105 (2014)
8. Kendzierski, D., et al.: Physical activity enjoyment scale: two validation studies. J. Sport Exerc. Psychol. (1991)
9. Kennedy, J., et al.: Comparing robot embodiments in a guided discovery learning interaction with children. Int. J. Soc. Robot. **7**(2), 293–308 (2015)
10. Leyzberg, D., et al.: The physical presence of a robot tutor increases cognitive learning gains. In: Proceedings of the 34th Annual Conference of the Cognitive Science Society. Cognitive Science Society, Austin (2012)
11. Li, J.: The benefit of being physically present: a survey of experimental works comparing copresent robots, telepresent robots and virtual agents. Int. J. Hum.-Comput. Stud. **77**, 23–37 (2015)

12. Reeves, B., et al.: The media equation: how people treat computers, television and new media like real people. Comput. Math. Appl. **5**(33), 128 (1997)
13. Rosenthal-von der Pütten, A.M., Straßmann, C., Krämer, N.C.: Robots or agents – neither helps you more or less during second language acquisition. In: Traum, D., Swartout, W., Khooshabeh, P., Kopp, S., Scherer, S., Leuski, A. (eds.) IVA 2016. LNCS (LNAI), vol. 10011, pp. 256–268. Springer, Cham (2016). https://doi.org/10.1007/978-3-319-47665-0_23
14. Schneider, S., et al.: Exercising with a humanoid companion is more effective than exercising alone. In: 2016 IEEE-RAS 16th International Conference on Humanoid Robots (Humanoids), pp. 495–501. IEEE (2016)
15. Schneider, S., Kummert, F.: Motivational effects of acknowledging feedback from a socially assistive robot. In: Agah, A., Cabibihan, J.-J., Howard, A.M., Salichs, M.A., He, H. (eds.) ICSR 2016. LNCS (LNAI), vol. 9979, pp. 870–879. Springer, Cham (2016). https://doi.org/10.1007/978-3-319-47437-3_85
16. Trost, S.G., et al.: Correlates of adults' participation in physical activity: review and update. Med. Sci. Sports Exerc. **34**(12), 1996–2001 (2002)

The Relevance of Social Cues in Assistive Training with a Social Robot

Neziha Akalin[✉], Andrey Kiselev, Annica Kristoffersson, and Amy Loutfi

Örebro University, 701 82 Örebro, Sweden
neziha.akalin@oru.se
http://mpi.aass.oru.se

Abstract. This paper examines whether social cues, such as facial expressions, can be used to adapt and tailor a robot-assisted training in order to maximize performance and comfort. Specifically, this paper serves as a basis in determining whether key facial signals, including emotions and facial actions, are common among participants during a physical and cognitive training scenario. In the experiment, participants performed basic arm exercises with a social robot as a guide. We extracted facial features from video recordings of participants and applied a recursive feature elimination algorithm to select a subset of discriminating facial features. These features are correlated with the performance of the user and the level of difficulty of the exercises. The long-term aim of this work, building upon the work presented here, is to develop an algorithm that can eventually be used in robot-assisted training to allow a robot to tailor a training program based on the physical capabilities as well as the social cues of the users.

Keywords: Social cues · Facial signals · Robot-assisted training

1 Introduction

For a social robot that shares a space with humans, being able to communicate appropriately and adapting its behavior based on the users' needs, as well as understanding social context are important skills. Social robots have the potential to provide both companionship and physical exercise therapy.

Social signals are communicative or informative signals that provide information, directly or indirectly, about social interactions [17]. One of the main advantages of social signals is that they are continuous and can be all gathered throughout the interaction. Thus, they may be used as part of an adaptation process for considering the user's point of view and preferences. Despite the fact that there are studies [11,18] using social signals as part of adaptation of robot behaviors, these studies did not consider the understanding of key social signals in a particular scenario such as robot-assisted training. In this paper, we address the understanding of key facial signals including emotions and facial actions (FA) during a physical and cognitive training with a social robot. In the

S. S. Ge et al. (Eds.): ICSR 2018, LNAI 11357, pp. 462–471, 2018.
https://doi.org/10.1007/978-3-030-05204-1_45

experiment, participants performed basic arm exercises with the social robot. We obtained facial features by using Affdex SDK [15] and applied a recursive feature elimination (RFE) algorithm to select a subset of discriminative facial features.

The contributions of this paper include: (i) identifying the relevant facial features during a physical and cognitive training with a social robot; (ii) discovering small subset of common facial features as *valence, lip corner depressor, lip pucker*, and *eye closure*; (iii) leaving an open possibility to use the identified features in the adaptation of the robot training program. In the remainder of this paper, an overview of related studies is given in Sect. 2. The method, experimental design and procedure are described in Sect. 3. The detailed explanation of data analysis is given in Sect. 4. Experimental results are presented in Sect. 5, and the paper is concluded in Sect. 6.

2   Related Work

2.1   Robot-Assisted Training

Research on robot-assisted training is vast and covers applications for cognitive and physical assistance such as post-stroke rehabilitation, cognitive assistance for dementia, therapy for Autism Spectrum Disorders, tutoring systems for deaf children and for language learning.

There are studies that employ robots as exercise coaches or exercise assistants [8–10,12]. In [10], authors investigated the role of embodiment in exercise coaches by comparing physically and virtually embodied coaches. Their results showed that elderly participants preferred the physically embodied robot coach over the virtual coach regarding its enjoyableness, helpfulness, and social attraction. Authors also assessed the motivational aspects of the scenario [9]. The robot provided feedback based on the task success which helped to keep participants more engaged. Similarly, in [12], the Nao humanoid robot was a training coach with a positive or corrective feedback mechanism for elderly people. In [8], authors presented an engagement-based robotic coach system with one-on-one and multi-user interactions. Their experimental results showed that the robotic coach was positively accepted by older adults either with or without cognitive impairment.

As these studies emphasize, a more engaging training robot could increase the enthusiasm of elderly people to exercise more and to sustain long-term interaction. We claim that factoring in social signals in training robots is just as important as the feedback mechanism.

2.2   Facial Features

The human face affords various inferences at a glance such as gender, ethnicity, health and emotions. Moreover, it is one of the richest and most powerful tools in social communication. Facial expressions analysis has been used in a variety of applications for understanding users and enhancing their experience. Affective facial expressions can facilitate robot learning when incorporated within a reward signal in reinforcement learning (RL) [2]. These features, which are capable of boosting the robot learning in a particular scenario, need further investigation.

The Facial Action Unit Coding System (FACS) is a taxonomy that is geared towards standardizing facial expression measurement by describing and encoding movements of the human face and FAs [6].

The human-in-the-loop approaches provide human assistance explicitly or implicitly to the learning agent. The two facial affective expressions of smile as positive and fear as negative reward were incorporated with the environment reward to enhance the agent learning in continuous grid-world mazes [2]. In [11], the authors presented a tutoring scenario. The facial affective states of the student were combined into a reward signal in order to provide personalized tutoring. Another study, [18], used social signals as a reward by considering body and head positions to obtain engagement of the user and adapt the robot's personality accordingly to keep the user engaged in the interaction.

3   Method

Our methodology consists in a physical memory game with three difficulty levels: easy, medium and hard. By using different levels of difficulty, we expected to elicit different facial expressions in the participants. The participants' interactions served the purpose of collecting data via video recordings and questionnaires. We recorded all of the interactions using a video camera focused at the users' faces.

3.1   The Experiment

Each session began with informing the participant about the experiment and the robot. Before starting, the participant read and filled out the consent form. Thereafter, the robot welcomed the participant and provided information about the training program. The participant started with a warm-up session to familiarize them with the experimental procedure. Participants tended to start the exercise during the demonstration and it took them some time to understand that they were supposed to wait before repeating until it was over. Therefore warm-up was helpful. Further information is given in Sect. 3.2.

Before conducting experiments, we had pre-experiments with two participants. The early experiments helped to adapt different experimental parameters such as the length of the warm-up session, number of exercises, the required time for each level and the questionnaires, the participants' proximity to the robot and the positioning of the video camera. Thirteen participants (6 male, 7 female) took part in the experiments ($\mu_{age} = 32.28, \sigma_{age} = 6.08$). An illustration of the experiment is shown in Fig. 1.

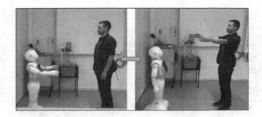

Fig. 1. A participant exercising with the Pepper robot.

3.2 Procedure

The following procedure was used for each participant:

1. The researcher instructed the participant about the experiment and robot.
2. The participant read and signed the consent form. The participant was also informed that there are three levels and between each level, they would fill out a questionnaire.
3. The robot introduced itself and explained the experimental procedure.
4. The participant started with a warm-up session (~3 min).
5. Thereafter, the easy level including 10 exercises started, 5 of them had one (e.g. arms up, arms side, etc.) and 5 of them had two successive arm exercises (e.g. arms up and arms to the side, arms in front and arms up, etc.). At the beginning of each exercise, there was a beep sound indicating that a new exercise was about to start.
6. At the end of the easy level, the participants filled out the following Likert scale questionnaire in which each question had options ranging from 'Strongly disagree'(1) to 'Strongly agree'(5):
   - The exercises were easy to execute (in terms of physical effort)
   - The exercises were easy to remember
   - I would like to exercise with the robot again
7. The experiment continued with the medium and hard level consecutively. The medium level comprised three (e.g. arms up and arms in front and arms to the side, etc.) and four successive arm exercises whereas hard level comprised five and six successive arm exercises. The participant filled out the same questionnaire after each level. At the end, they also provided demographic information (age, gender).

The sequence of exercises is a random combination of basic arm exercises, three example arm exercises are given in Fig. 2. Our aim is both physical and cognitive training. Since participants need to remember the sequence of exercises during the scenario, the level of difficulty is based on the number of exercises. It starts with one exercise and increases up to six exercises based on the average human memory span, 7 ± 2 [16].

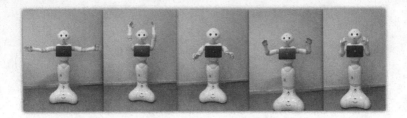

Fig. 2. Pepper robot: performing basic arm exercises.

4   Data Analysis

The facial features analysis was carried out over datasets created by participants exercising with the social robot. The facial features of the participants were obtained from their video recordings by using Affdex SDK [15], and manually annotated based on different criteria such as:

- determination (first exercise of the sequence: the participants is challenged or the last exercise of the sequence: the participant is unchallenged);
- performance of the participant (the participant performed the exercise correctly or not);
- the difficulty level of the exercise (easy, medium and hard).

Determination Dataset: Motivation is an important factor for sustained exercising. The motivation of participants was not the same in the first and the last exercises of the sequence. Self-determination theory (SDT) examines the effects of different types of motivation that is a basis of behavior [5]. Optimally challenging activities are intrinsically motivating [4]. We also observed that the motivation of participants decreased towards the last sequence of the exercise. We isolated the first (challenged) and the last (unchallenged) sequence of exercises to constitute the determination dataset.

Performance Dataset: To constitute the performance dataset, an annotator watched and annotated the video recordings based on the sequence of exercise correctness of the participants.

Difficulty Dataset: The difficulty dataset includes the beginning and ending of each level (e.g. beginning time of easy level and ending time of easy level, etc.)

We segmented each participant's data by correlating the time stamps in the features file and the annotation file. We applied moving average (window size 10) and random sampling. All participants' data were combined to form the resulting dataset. Based on the different criteria mentioned above, the datasets described in Table 1 were created. An example line from the raw data is given in Fig. 3.

The set of features in the datasets include:

- emotions: anger, contempt, disgust, fear, joy, sadness, and surprise
- engagement: facial expressiveness of the participant
- valence: the pleasantness of the participant
- FAs: brow furrow, brow raise, cheek raise, chin raise, dimpler, eye closure, eye widen, inner brow raise, jaw drop, lid tighten, lip corner depressor, lip press, lip pucker, lip stretch, lip suck, mouth open, nose wrinkle, smile, smirk, and upper lip raise
- head orientation: pitch, yaw, and roll
- label: the corresponding criteria

Table 1. Summary of datasets.

Dataset	Features	Examples	Classes
Determination	33	18382	Challenged, unchallenged
Performance	33	39984	Correct, wrong
Difficulty	33	198420	Easy, medium, hard

TimeStamp	pitch	yaw	roll	joy	fear	disgust	sadness	anger	surprise	contempt	valence
13.4	-20.4097	-4.9017	1.67	0.002	0.0018	0.3955	0.0829	0.002	0.1952	0.1881	-27.423
engagement	**smile**	**innerBrowRaise**	**browRaise**	**browFurrow**	**noseWrinkle**	**upperLipRaise**	**lipCornerDepressor**	**chinRaise**	**lipPucker**	**lipPress**
3.3273	0.6481	0.0002	0.0002	0.0904	0.0006	0	52.741	0.264	0.0019	0.1669
lipSuck	**mouthOpen**	**smirk**	**eyeClosure**	**attention**	**eyeWiden**	**cheekRaise**	**lidTighten**	**dimpler**	**lipStretch**	**jawDrop**
0.9608	0.7347	0.2151	0.0004	96.8313	0	0.0069	0.5775	0.5248	0.0085	0.0116

Fig. 3. An example line from raw data.

4.1 Feature Selection Method

Feature selection is widely used to select a subset of the original inputs by eliminating irrelevant inputs. RFE is an iterative procedure based on the idea of training a classifier, computing the ranking criterion, and removing the feature that has the smallest ranking criterion [13]. The most common version of RFE uses a linear Support Vector Machine (SVM-RFE) as classifier [13]. An alternative method is using Random Forest (RF) [1] instead of SVM as a classifier in the RFE. RF [1] is an effective prediction tool used in classification and regression. It consists of a combination of decision tree predictors such that each tree depends on the randomly sampled examples.

The RFE with RF was applied to all three datasets. The top five features were selected based on the feature importance. The selected features in each dataset are given in Table 2.

One of the variable importance measures in RF is mean decrease accuracy (MDA). The index MDA is used for quantifying the variable importance that is measured by change in prediction accuracy in exclusion of a single variable [3]. The variables that generate a large mean decrease in accuracy are more important for classification. MDA for each dataset is given in Fig. 4.

Table 2. Selected features.

Dataset	Determination	Difficulty	Performance
Features	Valence	Lip corner depressor	Valence
	Cheek raise	Lip pucker	Lip pucker
	Lip corner depressor	Inner brow raise	Lip corner depressor
	Eye closure	Lid tighten	Cheek raise
	Lip pucker	Cheek raise	Eye closure

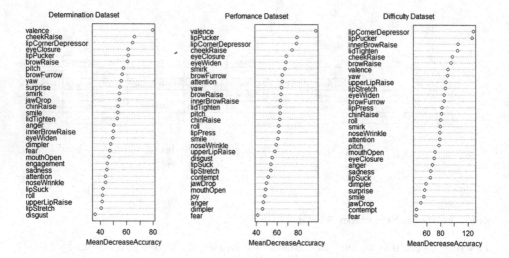

Fig. 4. Mean decrease accuracy of features in each dataset.

The four selected features of *valence*, *lip corner depressor*, *lip pucker* and *eye closure* are common in each dataset. A figure depicting the selected features on a time scale is given in Fig. 5. RF-RFE was experimentally found to be the best option for our approach. Due to the size of the difficulty dataset, applying another feature selection algorithm such as SVM-RFE and genetic algorithm was challenging.

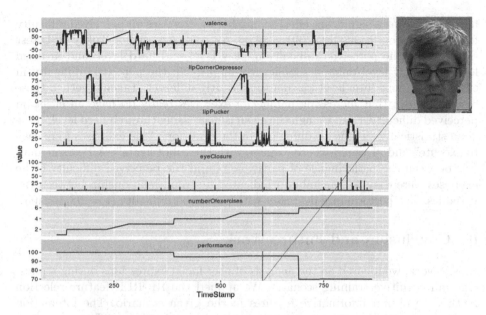

Fig. 5. Selected features on a time scale (on the side a frame from the video at the given moment).

5   Results and Discussion

This study sets out to understand the facial signals during a physical and cognitive training scenario. It is important to understand the facial signals that may help in the adaptation process of the robot behaviors. Using social signals in the adaptation process is beneficial as discussed in Sect. 2.2. The discriminative features were found to be *valence, lip corner depressor, lip pucker* and *eye closure.* Four selected features out of five are common in datasets. *Lip corner depressor* has been shown to be related to lack of focus [19] and *eye closure* is related to boredom [14]. *Lip pucker* is associated to thinking [7]. It means that the participants lost their attention and got bored throughout the interaction. The robot may catch these signals to re-engage the participant to the interaction. This is the first step towards the adaptation process of robot behaviors. In [11], authors used facial valence and engagement as a part of the reward signal, they found that engagement did not change in response to the robot's behaviors. We believe that investigating the social signals in a particular scenario is important for understanding the informative features that can improve the adaptation process.

The purpose of employing the questionnaire was to validate that the level of difficulty was increased from easy level to hard level. The results have statistically significance in the question "the exercises were easy to remember". A one-way between subjects analysis of variance (ANOVA) was conducted to compare the effect of number of exercises on perceived difficulty; easy, medium and hard. There was a significant effect of number of exercises on perceived difficulty for the three conditions [$F(2, 30) = 14.06$, $p < .05$]. A post hoc Tukey HSD test showed that the perceived difficulty in easy level and hard level; and medium level and hard level differed significantly at $p < .05$; the perceived difficulty in easy level and medium level was not significantly different. Taken together, these results suggest that increasing number of exercises really do have an effect on perceived difficulty. Even though the mean is decreasing through hard level, there is no statistically significant difference in the questions "the exercises were easy to execute" and "I would like to exercise with the robot again". A Pearson analysis between the performance of participants and the perceived difficulty ("the exercises were easy to remember") indicated a strong relationship between the variables. The performance decreases with perceived difficulty ($r = .98,,p < .05$).

6   Conclusion and Future Work

In this work, we focused on the analysis of user facial expressions during a physical and cognitive training scenario. We applied the RF-RFE feature selection method to obtain informative features in the given scenario. The interaction videos of the participants were annotated and created three different datasets to study facial expressions under different conditions. This study is a first step towards understanding the social signals that will enable us to incorporate appropriate facial signals in the adaptation process and formulating the problem as reinforcement learning. The most common discriminative features are: *valence*, *lip corner depressor*, *lip pucker* and *eye closure*. The features, other than *valence*, are related to negative feelings so they can be used as a punishment in the adaptation of the robot behavior. The contribution of the present work lies in providing a basis for the choice of different facial features in different conditions during a training scenario. In our future work, we will perform closed-loop experiments involving implicit human-robot interaction based on multi-modal social cues including the facial features obtained in this study. We will formulate the problem as reinforcement learning and alter the robot's behavior in order to address human needs.

Acknowledgement. This work has received funding from the European Union's Horizon 2020 research and innovation programme under the Marie Skłodowska-Curie grant agreement No. 721619 for the SOCRATES project.

References

1. Breiman, L.: Random forests. Mach. Learn. **45**(1), 5–32 (2001)
2. Broekens, J.: Emotion and reinforcement: affective facial expressions facilitate robot learning. In: Huang, T.S., Nijholt, A., Pantic, M., Pentland, A. (eds.) Artificial Intelligence for Human Computing. LNCS (LNAI), vol. 4451, pp. 113–132. Springer, Heidelberg (2007). https://doi.org/10.1007/978-3-540-72348-6_6
3. Calle, M.L., Urrea, V.: Letter to the editor: stability of random forest importance measures. Brief. Bioinform. **12**(1), 86–89 (2010)

4. Danner, F.W., Lonky, E.: A cognitive-developmental approach to the effects of rewards on intrinsic motivation. Child Dev. **52**, 1043–1052 (1981)
5. Deci, E.L., Ryan, R.M.: The "what" and "why" of goal pursuits: human needs and the self-determination of behavior. Psychol. Inq. **11**(4), 227–268 (2000)
6. Ekman, P., Rosenberg, E.L.: What The Face Reveals: Basic and Applied Studies of Spontaneous Expression Using the Facial Action Coding System (FACS). Oxford University Press, Oxford (1997)
7. El Kaliouby, R., Robinson, P.: Real-time inference of complex mental states from facial expressions and head gestures. In: Kisačanin, B., Pavlović, V., Huang, T.S. (eds.) Real-Time Vision for Human-Computer Interaction, pp. 181–200. Springer, Boston (2005). https://doi.org/10.1007/0-387-27890-7_11
8. Fan, J., et al.: A robotic coach architecture for elder care (ROCARE) based on multi-user engagement models. IEEE Trans. Neural Syst. Rehabil. Eng. **25**(8), 1153–1163 (2017)
9. Fasola, J., Mataric, M.J.: Using socially assistive human-robot interaction to motivate physical exercise for older adults. Proc. IEEE **100**(8), 2512–2526 (2012)
10. Fasola, J., Matarić, M.J.: A socially assistive robot exercise coach for the elderly. J. Hum.-Robot Interact. **2**(2), 3–32 (2013)
11. Gordon, G., et al.: Affective personalization of a social robot tutor for children's second language skills. In: AAAI, pp. 3951–3957 (2016)
12. Görer, B., Salah, A.A., Levent Akın, H.: An autonomous robotic exercise tutor for elderly people. Auton. Robots **41**(3), 657–678 (2017)
13. Guyon, I., Weston, J., Barnhill, S., Vapnik, V.: Gene selection for cancer classification using support vector machines. Mach. Learn. **46**(1–3), 389–422 (2002)
14. McDaniel, B., D'Mello, S., King, B., Chipman, P., Tapp, K., Graesser, A.: Facial features for affective state detection in learning environments. In: Proceedings of the Annual Meeting of the Cognitive Science Society, vol. 29 (2007)
15. McDuff, D., Mahmoud, A., Mavadati, M., Amr, M., Turcot, J., el Kaliouby, R.: AFFDEX SDK: a cross-platform real-time multi-face expression recognition toolkit. In: Proceedings of the 2016 CHI Conference Extended Abstracts on Human Factors in Computing Systems, pp. 3723–3726. ACM (2016)
16. Miller, G.A.: The magical number seven, plus or minus two: Some limits on our capacity for processing information. Psychol. Rev. **63**(2), 81 (1956)
17. Poggi, I., D'Errico, F.: Social signals: a psychological perspective. In: Salah, A., Gevers, T. (eds.) Computer Analysis of Human Behavior, pp. 185–225. Springer, London (2011). https://doi.org/10.1007/978-0-85729-994-9_8
18. Ritschel, H., Baur, T., André, E.: Adapting a robot's linguistic style based on socially-aware reinforcement learning. In: 2017 26th IEEE International Symposium on Robot and Human Interactive Communication (RO-MAN), pp. 378–384. IEEE (2017)
19. Vail, A.K., Grafsgaard, J.F., Boyer, K.E., Wiebe, E.N., Lester, J.C.: Predicting learning from student affective response to tutor questions. In: Micarelli, A., Stamper, J., Panourgia, K. (eds.) ITS 2016. LNCS, vol. 9684, pp. 154–164. Springer, Cham (2016). https://doi.org/10.1007/978-3-319-39583-8_15

Attitudes of Heads of Education and Directors of Research Towards the Need for Social Robotics Education in Universities

Kimmo J. Vänni[1]([⊠]), John-John Cabibihan[2], and Sirpa E. Salin[1]

[1] Tampere University of Applied Sciences, Kuntokatu 3,
33520 Tampere, Finland
{kimmo.vanni, sirpa.salin}@tamk.fi
[2] Qatar University, Doha 2713, Qatar
john.cabibihan@qu.edu.qa

Abstract. We explored the attitudes of the Heads of Education and the Directors of Research towards the need for Social Robotics Courses in Finland. The methods consisted of a cross-sectional survey (n = 21) and data was analyzed with descriptive methods and Pearson correlation tests. The results showed that the attitudes of respondents towards social robots were positive and they stated that robotics courses would be essential for universities. The respondents reported that the social service and healthcare sector will use social robots in the near future, but more training sessions are needed. So far, universities have offered only few applied robotics courses for healthcare students. This study also found that the surveyed universities have not yet taken into account the development of service and social robotics in the healthcare sector.

Keywords: Social robots · Robots in education, healthcare · Attitude
Training

1 Introduction

Social robots have been defined about twenty years ago [1–4]. Social robots were classified in two main categories: (1) non-social assistive and (2) social assistive (companion and service) [5].

Societies have focused on developing the use of services from robots. Earlier studies report that robots as co-workers is an emerging research topic [6–11]. The use of social and service robots in healthcare services has recently been one focus area especially in Finland [12]. There has been a pressure to use robots in services due to the increasing healthcare costs in Europe [13] and a poor dependency ratio [14]. The trend shows that there is a lack of labor force in the service sector and one solution is to deploy robots. The requirements for advancing the use of new technology such as robots is included in top-level strategic reports (e.g. The Strategic Research Agenda for Robotics in Europe, SRA2020 [15] and a future trend in Europe [16]).

The use of robots in services pre-suppose that the users and customers are familiar with robots and their capabilities. From the users' point of view, the familiarization to a

S. S. Ge et al. (Eds.): ICSR 2018, LNAI 11357, pp. 472–482, 2018.
https://doi.org/10.1007/978-3-030-05204-1_46

robot's services should be done step by step [17, 18]. That is also the case regarding the implementation of a robot as a co-worker [9]. Societies are looking for a better use of social and service robots but there is a lack of professionals who are familiar with robots and those who are able to use robots as a tool in the service sector. For example, some workers in the healthcare sector do not know what kind of robots are available and what services robots may offer [9].

The ecosystem for the use of social and service robots is still fragmented as compared to industrial robotics. There are robot designers and engineers, manufacturers, and traders but social robot education is not yet a common subject in the curricula of social and healthcare studies in European universities. Universities offer technical robotics courses for engineering and computer science students, but courses for social service and healthcare students, which focus on implementation, usage, and development of social robotics from the employees' and the end users' point of views are scarce. There are some examples of social robotics courses that are available from Australia [19], Germany [20], Netherlands [21] and Russia [22]. According to MastersPortal.com [23] there are 126 master level courses in robotics that are available worldwide but majority of those focus on industrial robotics such as factory automation. Some of the courses focus on artificial intelligence, and some are dedicated to mechatronics. Only a few universities such as the University of Pisa (UNIPI) and the Scuola Superiore Sant'Anna (SSSA) from Italy offer bionics courses which relate to the use of robots in healthcare. In addition, Aalborg University from Denmark offers a course in interaction, which focuses on physical interaction design. Taken together, there are available robotics courses for engineering and computer science students but the selection of the applied social robotics courses focused on social service and healthcare students is limited.

Figure 1 presents the core knowledge and application areas of the ecosystem of social robotics, which are possible topics in social robot training at universities. There are three focus areas: robots, ICT systems (servers, IoT) and services (e.g. healthcare). In addition, virtual agents and computer games may offer new applications, which can be used in parallel with the robots. Each focus area relates to its core application areas, but to widen a perspective and to focus on the intersection of the focus areas may offer new business options. We emphasize that current robot development and education have focused on the technical issues and on software. However, from the point of view of the social robotics ecosystem, the implementation and use cases of robots should be taken into account. We state that the Finnish Universities of Applied Sciences (FUASs) do not offer robotics courses for social service and healthcare students even if the Heads of Education and Directors of Research perceive that there should be applied robotics courses available. We assume that an increase in productivity [9, 17] in the social and healthcare sector entails that graduate students are familiar with social robots and application areas. In sum, the need for social and service robots is evident [9, 12, 24]. In addition, some of the healthcare professionals may need vocational courses for implementing and using social and service robots at work [9, 25].

The aim of the current study was to explore the attitudes and perceptions of the Heads of Education and Directors of Research towards a need for social robotics education in FUASs. The objectives were to assess the present state of robotics courses

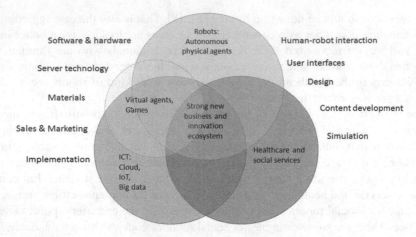

Fig. 1. Ecosystem of social robotics with the core knowledge and application areas.

for healthcare students, the future needs, and the attitudes of the key decision makers to steer education and research towards the use of robotics.

2   Methods

There are 23 FUASs in Finland. This study was based on an explorative cross-sectional survey questionnaire conducted in 2016 among Heads of Education and Directors of Research of FUASs. The number of respondents was 21 (14 women and 7 men) and they represented 16 FUASs. All the participants gave their consent to the survey. The respondents represented administration (n = 12) and research (n = 6) departments. Three respondents represented faculties. Participants were categorized by age into six groups and they represented those groups as follows: (<25, 25–34, 35–44, 45–54, 55–64, 65+). The respondents participated in a two-hour workshop where the basic information regarding social robots were presented.

2.1   Survey Data

Data on attitudes, perceptions, and future need for social robots was based on multiple questions. We asked the respondents to assess the readiness level of the social and healthcare sector in using robots with three questions. We asked for example "How mature is the social and healthcare sector now for using social robots?" We also asked them to assess a timescale when the social robots would be needed and finally, we asked them to assess the need for robotics education and its significance for social service and healthcare students with six separate questions. We asked, for example, "Does your university offer robotics courses for social and healthcare students?", "How important would it be that your university may offer robotics courses for social and healthcare students?" Regarding the ordinal variables, the response options were on a five-point Likert scale (1 = poor/minor/not at all, 5 = excellent/major/a lot). We also asked the respondents to assess which topics would be important. The options were: (1) programming, (2) implementation, (3) user interfaces, (4) robot fusion to other systems, (5) robot usage in real cases, (6) robot and information system. The quantitative survey data was analyzed with SPSS 25 software (Statistical Package for the Social Sciences).

2.2 Variable Design and Statistical Analyses

Because the study was explorative and descriptive, the dependent and independent variables were not designed. The survey questions and variables were reported as such and the interventions between variables except correlations were not assessed.

Due to the explorative nature of the study and the limited number of respondents, the study emphasized descriptive statistics and Pearson Correlation test. Additionally, the $\chi 2$–test and Wilcoxon rank test were used.

3 Results

Table 1 presents the respondents' earlier knowledge on social robots and their attitudes towards using robots in social and healthcare work. The responses were re-classified and dichotomized into two categories "Yes" (Likert options from 3 'some extent' to 5 'a lot') and "No" (Likert options from 1 'not at all' to 2 'a little').

Table 1 shows that majority of the respondents did not have earlier knowledge and experience on social robots. Only a few women knew something about social robots and those that were in use in the healthcare sector. A fear that robots would take over the work places was not addressed, even if women were more worried about that issue as compared to men. Overall, the respondents stated that social robots would be useful and those would be needed quite soon. They perceived that robots would increase productivity. All respondents perceived that the social and healthcare sector would be mature for using social robots at some level. However, the respondents stated that robots are not able to replace humans even if robots will be common in the social and healthcare sector in the near future. The respondents' opinions regarding the need for a long-term robot training at work were diverse. About half of the respondents stated that a long-term training would be needed, whereas the other half stated that medium-term training would be adequate. The respondents found that the ethical issues were a significant concern in using the robots. However, we did not ask them to define the ethical issues in detail.

Table 2 presents the current state and the need for robot education for social and healthcare students. 'Yes' and 'No' options were dichotomized in a similar way than in the Table 1. The respondents perceived that it would be important that universities are able to offer social robotics courses for social and healthcare students. They stated that robotics education should be a regular part of the curriculum in healthcare studies. The respondents assumed that robotics training during their studies may familiarize students to use robots at work and may educate students to face real patients better at work. Even if the robotics education was found to be essential, only a few universities offer robotics courses for social and healthcare students. The most relevant topics for

Table 1. Respondents' perception on social robots and their attitudes towards robots

	Men (n = 7)		Women (n = 14)		Total (n = 21)		Statistics*	
	n	%	n	%	n	%	χ2	P
Do you have earlier knowledge on social robots?								
Yes	4	57	2	14	6	29	15.9	.003
No	3	43	12	86	15	71		
Will robots take over the work places?								
Yes	1	14	5	36	6	29	24.0	.000
No	6	86	9	64	15	71		
Will robots be needed as soon as possible?								
Yes	5	71	11	79	16	76	15.4	.004
No	2	29	3	21	5	24		
Would robots be useful in healthcare work?								
Yes	7	100	12	86	19	89	24.9	.000
No	0	0	2	14	2	11		
Would robots increase productivity?								
Yes	7	100	12	86	19	89	13.5	.009
No	0	0	2	14	2	11		
Is the social and healthcare sector now mature for using social robots?								
Yes	7	100	14	100	21	100	65.4	.000
No	0	0	0	0	0	0		
Are there relevant ethical issues to use robots in the healthcare sector?								
Yes	5	71	14	100	19	89	18.7	.001
No	2	29	0	0	2	11		
Could a robot replace a worker?								
Yes	4	57	3	21	7	33	28.2	.000
No	3	43	11	79	14	67		
Do the implementation of robots require a long-term training at work?								
Yes	4	57	8	57	12	57	32.5	.000
No	3	43	6	43	9	43		
Do you think robots will be used in the healthcare sector in the near future?								
Yes	7	100	13	93	20	95	19.2	.001
No	0	0	1	7	1	5		

*χ2 and P–values based on 5-point Likert scale.

education purposes were the implementation and usage of robots in the real environment. The importance of robot fusion to other systems was found to be moderate, but the courses regarding programming were found to be poor. The results showed that the Heads of Education and Directors of Research emphasized the need for some technical training which will prepare the students to use robots at work.

Table 3 presents the means and standard deviations of the used variables. It shows that the earlier knowledge of social robots among respondents was quite poor. The table also shows that the respondents were not worried about the robots that would be taking over their workplaces. The results presented that robots would be useful in the healthcare sector and those may increase productivity. The respondents were unanimous in stating that social robots are needed in the healthcare sector and robotics education would be essential for social and healthcare studies. The respondents also

Table 2. The current state and the need for robotics training in FUASs (n = 21)

	Men (n = 7)		Women (n = 14)		Total (n = 21)		Statistics*	
	n	%	n	%	n	%	χ2	P
Is it important that universities may offer robot courses for healthcare students?								
Yes	7	100	13	7	20	95	14.0	.007
No	0	0	1	93	1	5		
Will a robotics education prepare the students to face real patients?								
Yes	5	71	13	93	18	86	15.9	.003
No	2	29	1	7	3	14		
Should robotics courses be part of the curriculum in social and healthcare studies?								
Yes	6	86	13	93	19	90	21.1	.000
No	1	14	1	7	2	10		
Does your university offer robotics courses for healthcare students?								
Yes	1	14	5	36	6	29	14.5	.006
No	6	86	9	64	15	71		
Should the healthcare studies familiarize students to use robots at work?								
Yes	7	100	13	93	20	95	22.6	.000
No	0	0	1	7	1	5		
Which robotics topics would be important in the curriculum?								
Programming	0	0	2	14	2	10		
Implementation	3	43	8	57	11	52		
User interfaces	1	14	3	21	4	19		
Robot fusion	2	29	7	50	9	43		
Robot usage	7	100	10	71	17	81		
Information systems	3	43	1	7	4	19		

* χ2 and P–values based on 5-point Likert scale.

Table 3. The means and standard deviations of the used variables. The range was from 1 (poor, disagree) to 5 (excellent, agree) n = 21.

	Mn	SD
Earlier knowledge of robotics	2.24	.94
Robots will take over workplaces	1.86	.65
Need for robots in the healthcare sector	*4.20*	.93
Robots would be useful in the healthcare sector	*3.71*	.78
Readiness of the healthcare sector to use robots	2.14	.48
A robot as a team member	3.43	.93
A robot as a work mate	3.43	.87
A robot as a substitute	2.33	.66
A robot may increase productivity	*3.52*	.93
There are ethical issues regarding the use of robots	2.76	.77
The length of robot training session in health care sector	2.43	.51
Robots will be common in the near future	3.52	.75
Robotics education is essential for universities	*4.05*	.86
Robotics training may educate students to face real patients	*3.24*	.89
The present state of robotics training for health care students	1.95	.80
The level of familiarizing students to face robots at work	*3.52*	.68
Robotics training as a part of the curriculum of studies	3.33	.80

claimed that the training with social robots may help students face real patients at work and prepare them to use social robots at work.

We compared the *need for robots in the healthcare sector* with some of the related variables with Wilcoxon rank test and found e.g. that the *need for robots* was ranked higher than *readiness to use robots* ($Z = -3.9$, $P < 0.001$). It was also higher compared to *knowledge of robotics* ($Z = -3.6$, $P < 0.001$), *robot training currently* ($Z = -3.9$, $P < 0.001$), *robot training may educate to face patients* ($Z = -3.1$, $P < 0.01$) and *robot may increase productivity* ($Z = -2.4$, $P < 0.05$).

Table 4 shows some correlation coefficients between the selected variables. We tested all the variables but reported only those, which have correlation between. Variables such as *Robots will take over workplaces*, *Need for robots in healthcare sector*, *Readiness of healthcare sector to use robots* and *Ethical issues* did not have significant correlation between any variable. Correlations showed two clusters. One relates to usage of robots and their usefulness at work. For example, respondents who perceived that robots are useful, also stated that robot may increase productivity ($r = 0.628$, $P < 0.01$), *robots will be common in the near future* ($r = 0.608$, $P < 0.01$) and *studies should familiarize students to face robots at work* ($r = 0.577$, $P < 0.01$). Another cluster relates to social robotics education. The importance of robotics training correlate with the importance to have *robotics training as a part of curriculum* ($r = 0.702$, $P < 0.01$). Familiarizing students during studies to face social robots at work correlate with an *increase of productivity* ($r = 0.494$, $P < 0.05$), *usefulness of robots* ($r = 0.577$, $P < 0.01$) and all the variables, which concerns robotics education. Unfortunately, we are able to present only a limited table of correlations because the whole table would have been too large.

4   Discussion

We hypothesized that the FUASs do not offer the targeted and applied social robotics courses for social and healthcare students, even if the Strategic Research Agenda for Robotics in Europe, SRA2020 [15] and policies of European governments favor to advance ICT and robotics in healthcare. We assumed that Heads of Education and Directors of Research of the FUASs are aware of robots and are willing to implement robotics courses as a part of the curriculum. Our hypothesis and predictions matched well with the results of the study. Even if there are a wide variety of robotics courses available in universities, those relate to industrial robotics such as manufacturing automation and industrial services. There are numerous courses of artificial intelligence, programming, robot design, and mechatronics that are available in Europe and worldwide. Those courses often target engineering and information science students. The respondents stated that there is a need for social robotics education for social and healthcare students but the topics relate to the usage and implementation of social robots. They assumed that social and healthcare students do not need programming skills or knowledge on how to develop user interfaces. Respondents' attitudes towards social robots were comparable to the results of earlier studies [9, 12], which reported that robots are useful, are able to increase productivity, and are needed soon or in the near future in social and healthcare sector. Results showed that robotics education

Table 4. Pearson correlation coefficients between some of the variables (n = 21)

		Knowledge of robots	Usefulness of robots	Robots will be common	Robot education is essential	Education prepare to face patients	State of robot education	Familiarizing students with robots	Robot education in curriculum
Robot increase productivity	R	.478*	.628**	.233	.217	.326	.370	.494*	.226
	Sig.	.028	.002	.310	.346	.149	.099	.023	.326
Robots will be common	R	.451*	.608**	1	.345	.329	.375	.710**	.363
	Sig.	.040	.003		.125	.146	.094	.000	.106
Robot education is essential	R	.353	.316	.345	1	.570**	.291	.551**	.702**
	Sig.	.116	.163	.125		.007	.201	.010	.000
Familiarizing students with robots	R	.575**	.577**	.710**	.551**	.528*	.688**	1	.678**
	Sig.	.006	.006	.000	.010	.014	.001		.001
Robot education in curriculum	R	.355	.240	.363	.702**	.589**	.494*	.678**	1
	Sig.	.114	.294	.106	.000	.005	.023	.001	

*Correlation is significant at the 0.05 level. **Correlation is significant at the 0.01 level.

during studies prepare graduates to face real patients, familiarize them to use robots at work, and may increase their productivity at work. Wilcoxon rank test showed that need for robots in the healthcare sector was ranked positively higher than other tested variables, which means that a current state of knowledge and training should be improved.

The current study showed that the development of social robotics ecosystem and widespread use of social robots at work entail that social and healthcare students and graduates are familiar with social robots. Robotics education during studies mitigate the fears of using social robots in real cases and follows theories of *the Technology Acceptance Model* (TAM) [26] and *the Unified Theory of Acceptance and Use of Technology* (UTAUT) [27]. We suggest that social and healthcare education programs should include multidisciplinary development projects experimenting with the use of robots in nursing care. The experience would make the use of robots familiar and enables the planning of courses with businesses such as hospitals. Innovative experiments must become part of modern nursing care.

The main contribution of this study was that it focused on the needed changes in the curriculum for social and healthcare sector, which was not previously explored. The study addressed that even if robotics education is common among engineering and ICT students, there is a lack of targeted courses for social and healthcare students. This study reinforced the ecosystem of social robotics and showed that a starting point of widespread use of social robots in the healthcare sector requires robotics courses also for social and healthcare students.

The limitation of this study was the relatively low number of respondents (i.e. 23 FUAS), which made it more challenging to use more specific statistical analysis methods. However, the respondents represented the FUASs well, because the total number of eligible respondents in Finland is about 50. We can argue that another research method such as the interview method would have been better. Another limitation was that the study concerned only FUASs. However, earlier discussions with our European university colleagues in workshops and seminars strengthen the results of this study that the need for robotics education for social and healthcare students is essential. Third limitation was that a survey was conducted in 2016. However, the results are still adequate and need for robotics education is still urgent.

As a conclusion, this study presented that social robot education for social and healthcare students is needed and it may strengthen usage of robots and the whole social robotics ecosystem. We recommend to develop new approaches and social robotics courses for non-engineering students, and collaboration between engineering, ICT and healthcare faculties.

References

1. Tapus, A., Mataric, M., Scassellati, B.: The grand challenges in socially assistive robotics. Robot. Autom. Mag. IEEE **14**(1), 35–42 (2007)
2. Duffy, B., Rooney, C., O'Hare, G., O'Donoghue, R.: What is a social robot? In: 10th Irish Conference on Artificial Intelligence and Cognitive Science, University College Cork, Ireland, 1–3 September 1999

3. Fong, T., Thorpe, C., Baur, C.: Collaboration, dialogue, and human-robot interaction. In: Jarvis, R.A., Zelinsky, A. (eds.) Robotics Research. Springer, Heidelberg (2001). https://doi.org/10.1007/3-540-36460-9_17

4. Li, H., Cabibihan, J.J., Tan, Y.K.: Towards an effective design of social robots. Int. J. Soc. Robot. 3(4), 333–335 (2011)

5. Heerink, M., Kröse, B., Evers, B., Wielinga, B.: Assessing acceptance of assistive social agent technology by older adults: the almere model. Int. J. Soc. Robot. 2(4), 361–375 (2010)

6. Haddadin, S., Suppa, M., Fuchs, S., Bodenmüller, T., Albu-Schäffer, A., Hirzinger, G.: Towards the robotic co-worker. In: Pradalier, C., Siegwart, R., Hirzinger, G. (eds.) Robotics Research. Springer Tracts in Advanced Robotics, pp. 261–282. Springer, Heidelberg (2011). https://doi.org/10.1007/978-3-642-19457-3_16

7. Sauppe, A., Mutlu, B.: The social impact of a robot co-worker in industrial settings (2015). http://pages.cs.wisc.cdu/~bilge/pubs/2015/CHI15-Sauppe.pdf

8. Vänni, K.J., Korpela, A.K.: Role of social robotics in supporting employees and advancing productivity. In: Tapus, A., André, E., Martin, J.-C., Ferland, F., Ammi, M. (eds.) ICSR 2015. LNCS (LNAI), vol. 9388, pp. 674–683. Springer, Cham (2015). https://doi.org/10.1007/978-3-319-25554-5_67

9. Vänni, K., Salin, S.: A need for service robots among health care professionals in hospitals and housing services. In: Kheddar, A., et al. (eds.) ICSR 2017. LNCS, vol. 10652, pp. 178–187. Springer, Cham (2017). https://doi.org/10.1007/978-3-319-70022-9_18

10. Diep, L., Cabibihan, J.-J., Wolbring, G.: Social robotics through an anticipatory governance lens. In: Beetz, M., Johnston, B., Williams, M.-A. (eds.) ICSR 2014. LNCS (LNAI), vol. 8755, pp. 115–124. Springer, Cham (2014). https://doi.org/10.1007/978-3-319-11973-1_12

11. Ge, S.S., et al.: Design and development of nancy, a social robot. In: 8th International Conference on Ubiquitous Robots and Ambient Intelligence (URAI), pp. 568–573 (2011)

12. Vänni, K.J., Korpela, A.K.: An effort to develop a web-based approach to assess the need for robots among the elderly. In: Agah, A., Cabibihan, J.-J., Howard, A.M., Salichs, M.A., He, H. (eds.) ICSR 2016. LNCS (LNAI), vol. 9979, pp. 712–722. Springer, Cham (2016). https://doi.org/10.1007/978-3-319-47437-3_70

13. Munton, T., Alison, M., Marrero, I., Llewellyn, A., Gibson, K., Gomersall, A.: Getting out of hospital? The evidence for shifting acute inpatient and day case services from hospitals into the community. The Health Foundation, London (2015). http://www.health.org.uk/publications/getting-out-of-hospital

14. Muszyńska, M., Rau, R.: The old-age healthy dependency ratio in Europe. J. Population Ageing 5(3), 151–162 (2012)

15. euRobotics AISBL: Strategic Research Agenda for Robotics in Europe 2014–2020, Applications: Societal Challenges, pp. 59–64 (2015). http://www.eu-robotics.net/cms/upload/PPP/SRA2020_SPARC.pdf

16. Saritas, O., Keenan, M.: Broken promises and/or techno dreams? The future of health and social services in Europe. Foresight 6(5), 281–291 (2004)

17. Vänni, K.: Robot applications in communication. In: Smart technology solutions support the elderly to continue living in their own homes. Reports of the Ministry of the Environment 7/2017, 44-51. Ministry of the Environment in Finland (2017)

18. Ge, S.S.: Social robotics: integrating advances in engineering and computer science. In Proceedings of Electrical Engineering/Electronics, Computer, Telecommunications and Information Technology International Conference, pp. 9–12 (2007)

19. Strachan, F.: UNSW offers first social robotics course in Australia (2016). https://newsroom.unsw.edu.au/news/art-architecture-design/unsw-offers-first-social-robotics-course-australia

20. University of Freiburg. Social Robotics Laboratory (2018). http://srl.informatik.uni-freiburg.de/teaching

21. Vrije Universitet Amsterdam (2018). https://www.vu.nl/en/study-guide/2017-2018/exchange/index.aspx?view=module&origin=50989971x50989856&id=51406920
22. Tomsk State University (2016). http://en.tsu.ru/news/tsu-is-launching-a-social-robotics-course-on-coursera
23. MastersPortal (2018). https://www.mastersportal.com/disciplines/255/robotics.html
24. Andrade, A., et al.: Bridging the gap between robotic technology and health care. Biomed. Signal Process. Control **10**, 65–78 (2014)
25. Diep, L., Cabibihan, J.J., Wolbring, G.: Social robots: views of special education teachers. In: Proceedings of the 3rd Workshop on ICTs for improving Patients Rehabilitation Research Techniques, pp. 160–163 (2015)
26. Davis, F.: Perceived usefulness, perceived ease of use, and user acceptance of information technology. MIS Q. **13**(3), 319–340 (1989)
27. Venkatesh, V., Morris, M., Davis, G., Davis, F.: User acceptance of information technology: toward a unified view. MIS Q. **27**(3), 425–478 (2003)

Coordinated and Cooperative Control of Heterogeneous Mobile Manipulators

María F. Molina[✉] and Jessica S. Ortiz[✉]

Universidad de las Fuerzas Armadas ESPE, Sangolquí, Ecuador
{mfmolina1,jsortiz4}@espe.edu.ec

Abstract. This paper proposes a multilayer scheme for the cooperative control of $n \geq 2$ heterogeneous mobile manipulators that allows to transport an object in common in a coordinated way; for which the kinematic modeling of each mobile manipulator robot is performed. Stability and robustness are demonstrated using the Lyapunov theory in order to obtain asymptotically stable control. Finally, the results are presented to evaluate the performance of the proposed control, which confirms the scope of the controller to solve different movement problems.

Keywords: Cooperative control · Kinematic modeling · Lyapunov method

1 Introduction

The robotics nowadays has reached a high level of importance, since robots perform common tasks that require locomotion and manipulation capabilities [1–3]. Traditionally, the robots are used in the automotive, electrical, metallurgical, chemical and food industries, as well as in tasks of daily life, such as sweeping, vacuuming or mowing grass [4, 5]. The tasks can be carried out individually or cooperatively in different areas, being of cooperative form more efficient in terms of manipulability, flexibility, accessibility and manoeuvrability, allowing greater efficiency in industrial processes [6].

The cooperative control of mobile autonomous robots is widely studied due to its importance in applications of sensor networks, mobile robots, flight of formation of spaceships and in other areas [7]. The multirobot systems have two approaches: centralized and decentralized. The first approach, the lead unit plans and controls, determining the behaviour of the other robots [8, 9]; while in the decentralised approach each robot makes its own decisions according to the local information available [10, 11]. The centralized approach facilitates optimal global solutions and is vulnerable to failures, while the decentralized approach has the advantage of fault tolerance, robustness and reliability, for this reason it is considered the most suitable for implementation in robotics [12, 13].

The study of the cooperation of heterogeneous robots has evolved due to the fundamental capacities of each robot in the equipment, such is the case of a heterogeneous multirobot system composed of several UGV and a single UAV, in which different control schemes are realized with various degrees of cooperation [14]. In [15], they proposes the construction of a map through multiple cooperative aerial and terrestrial robots with the implementation of hardware, firmware and software of the frame

© Springer Nature Switzerland AG 2018
S. S. Ge et al. (Eds.): ICSR 2018, LNAI 11357, pp. 483–492, 2018.
https://doi.org/10.1007/978-3-030-05204-1_47

of multirobot cooperation proposed. In [16], they proposes a method tolerant to aggression for the stabilization and navigation of compact formations of autonomous aerial and terrestrial robots that cooperate in surveillance scenarios. In [17], they presents a strategy of hybrid adaptive control and fixation to ensure that all heterogeneous robots in the cooperation-competition network follow a trajectory. In [18], they centres on the design, development and test of an Artificial Intelligence System that facilitates the cooperative behavior of teamwork of mobile heterogeneous robots.

In work [5] performs a cooperative control with up to two mobile robots unlike the present work that a multilayer scheme is developed for the cooperative control of $n \geq 2$ mobile heterogeneous manipulators that allow to transport an object in common in a coordinated way; for which it will have realize the kinematic modeling of each mobile manipulator robot. Unlike [19], the design of the controller is based on·a cascaded kinematic control, based on a virtual structure formed between the operating ends of the multiple mobile heterogeneous manipulator robots. The stability and robustness is demonstrated using the Lyapunov theory in order to obtain asymptotically stable control. Finally, the results are presented to evaluate the performance of the proposed control, which confirms the scope of the controller to solve different problems of movement.

2   Kinematic Model

2.1   Kinematic Model of Mobile Manipulator

The kinematic model of an mobile manipulator gives the location and orientation of the end-effector $\mathbf{h}(t)$ as a function of the robotic arm configuration and the mobile platform position, *i.e.,* $f : \mathcal{M}_p \times \mathcal{N}_{a1} \times \mathcal{N}_{a2} \times ... \mathcal{N}_{an} \rightarrow \mathcal{M}$, hence $(\mathbf{q}_p, \mathbf{q}_{a1}, \mathbf{q}_{a2}, ..., \mathbf{q}_{an})$ $\mapsto \mathbf{h}(t) = f(\mathbf{q}_p, \mathbf{q}_{a1}, \mathbf{q}_{a2}, ..., \mathbf{q}_{an})$, where, $\mathcal{N}_{a1}, \mathcal{N}_{a2} ... \mathcal{N}_{an}$ are the configuration space of the robotic arm, $\mathcal{M}_p$ is the operative space of the mobile platform and $\mathbf{h}(t)$ represents the position and orientation of the end effector of the mobile manipulator (see Fig. 1).

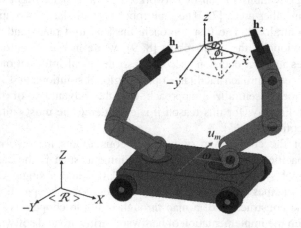

Fig. 1. Mobile manipulator robot with two robotic arms.

For a mobile platform with two robotic arms located in the upper base of the mobile platform, it is considered that the generalized coordinates $h_1(t)$, $h_2(t)$, correspond to the end-effector of each robotic arm (1).

$$\begin{cases} h_{xi} = x \pm aC_\Psi + l_{2i}C_{q2i}C_{q1i,\psi} + l_{3i}C_{q2i,q3i}C_{q1i,\psi} + l_{4i}C_{q2i,q3i,q4i}C_{q1i,\psi} \\ h_{yi} = y \pm aS_\Psi + l_{2i}C_{q2i}S_{q1i,\psi} + l_{3i}C_{q2i,q3i}S_{q1i,\psi} + l_{4i}C_{q2i,q3i,q4i}S_{q1i,\psi} \\ h_{zi} = h_{alt} + l_{1i} + l_{2i}S_{q2i} + l_{3i}S_{q2i,q3i} + l_{4i}S_{q2i,q3i,q4i} \end{cases} \quad (1)$$

where, $i = 1, 2$ represents each robotic arm mounted on the mobile platform; ψ is the orientation of the mobile platform. Derivate (1) with respect to the coordinates hx, hy, hz, the kinematic model of the mobile manipulator is obtained, defined as:

$$\dot{\mathbf{h}}_\mathbf{n}(t) = \mathbf{J}_i(\mathbf{q}_\mathbf{p}, \mathbf{q}_\mathbf{a1}, \mathbf{q}_\mathbf{a2})\mathbf{v}_\mathbf{n}(t) \quad (2)$$

where, $\dot{\mathbf{h}}_\mathbf{n}(t) = [\dot{h}_{i1} \quad \dot{h}_{i2}]^T$, is the velocity vector of the end-effectors of the double mobile manipulator, $\mathbf{v}_n = [\mathbf{v}_\mathbf{q}^T \quad \mathbf{v}_\mathbf{a1}^T \quad \mathbf{v}_\mathbf{a2}^T]^T$ is the control vector of mobility of the double mobile manipulator with dimension and $\mathbf{J}_n(\mathbf{q}_\mathbf{p}, \mathbf{q}_\mathbf{a1}, \mathbf{q}_\mathbf{a2})$ is the Jacobian matrix that establishes a linear mapping between the velocities vector of the final effectors and the velocities vector of the mobile manipulator.

2.2 Kinematic Transformation

The method the cooperative coordinated proposed control considers two or more mobile manipulators. In the first case, two mobile manipulators are considered, to determine the kinematic transformation, the virtual point is fixed in the X-Y-Z plane between the midpoint of each final effector of the robotic arms; the virtual point is defined by. $\mathbf{P}_F = \frac{1}{2}[(h_{x1} + h_{x2}) \quad (h_{y1} + h_{y2}) \quad (h_{z1} + h_{z2})] \in \mathcal{R}'$ that represents the position of its centroid on the inertial system $<\mathcal{R}>$ [6]; while, the vectorial structure of the virtual form is defined for, $\mathbf{S}_F =$

$$\left[\sqrt{(h_{x2} - h_{x1})^2 + (h_{y2} - h_{y1})^2 + (h_{z2} - h_{z1})^2} \quad \arctan\left(\frac{h_{y2}-h_{y1}}{h_{x2}-h_{x1}}\right) \quad \arctan\left(\frac{h_{y2}-h_{y1}}{h_{x2}-h_{x1}}\right)\right],$$

where d, is the distance between the position of the end-effector $\mathbf{h}_1$ and $\mathbf{h}_2$, θ_F and ϕ_F represents its orientation with respect to the Y-axis and the Z-axis, respectively in inertial frame $<\mathcal{R}>$. The point of interest of the system is denoted in a simplified way $\mathbf{r} = [\mathbf{P}_F \quad \mathbf{S}_F]$ [5].

Remark 1: $\mathbf{h}_i$ represent the position the end-effector of the n-th mobile manipulator. The positions forward and inverse, give the relationship between the virtual structure pose-orientation-shape and the end-effector positions of the mobile manipulators, *i.e.*, $\zeta(t) = f(\mathbf{x})$ and $\mathbf{x}(t) = f^{-1}(\zeta)$, where $\zeta(t) = [\mathbf{P}_F \quad \mathbf{S}_F]^\mathbf{T}$ and $\mathbf{x} = [\mathbf{h}_1^T \quad \mathbf{h}_2^T]^T$.

When making the derivative of direct and inverse kinematic transformations with respect to a time variation of $\mathbf{x}(\mathbf{t})$ and $\zeta(\mathbf{t})$, obtained by the Jacobian matrix $\mathbf{J}_F$, which is denote by

$$\dot{\zeta} = \mathbf{J}_F(\mathbf{x})\dot{\mathbf{x}} \tag{3}$$

and when you apply the inverse you get

$$\dot{\mathbf{x}} = \mathbf{J}_F^{-1}\dot{\zeta} \tag{4}$$

3   Scalability for the Cooperative Control

In this section the cooperation control of multiple heterogeneous mobile manipulators is described in a generalized way to the transport an object in common, using the kinematic transformation presented in Sect. 2. The Fig. 2, presents a multilayer scheme for cooperative control in order to execute tasks of navigation and manipulation between multiple mobile heterogeneous manipulators. Each layer functions as an independent module that deals with a specific part of the problem of coordinated cooperative control the multi-layer scheme is defined by the task planning layer, the formation control layer, the kinematic control layer, the robot layer and the environment layer.

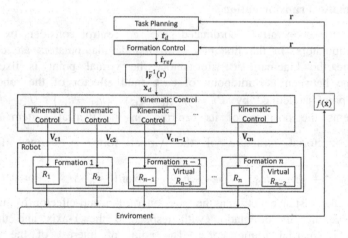

Fig. 2. Multi-layer control scheme.

To perform scalability, projections are made between the operating ends of a pair of robots, which form a virtual operator (see, Fig. 3). In this way, according to the analysis presented, the point of interest of the object transported by two mobile manipulators based on the training is $\zeta_1 = [\,h_{x1} \quad h_{y1} \quad h_{z1} \quad d_{F1} \quad \theta_{F1} \quad \phi_{F1}\,]^T \in \mathcal{R}^s$ which is a virtual robot that is located at the midpoint formed by the first end-effector $\mathbf{h}_1$ and the second end-effector $\mathbf{h}_2$. Adding another robot to perform the cooperation task defines another point of interest $\zeta_2 = [\,h_{x2} \quad h_{y2} \quad h_{z2} \quad d_{F2} \quad \theta_{F2} \quad \phi_{F2}\,]^T$, which

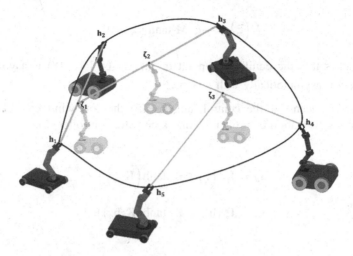

Fig. 3. Multiple heterogeneous mobile manipulators.

is formed by the virtual robot ζ_1 and the third end-effector $\mathbf{h_3}$. For $n \geq 2$ heterogeneous mobile robots, is formed by the virtual robot $n - 2$ with point of interest ζ_{n-2} and the n-th heterogeneous robot. They define the characteristics of the object transported by the position, distance and the desired angles that exist between the robots.

4 Control Strategy

In this section proposed a control algorithm based on inverse kinematics. By means of the derivation in time of the forward and inverse kinematic transformations, the relation between the time variations of $\mathbf{x(t)}$ and $\mathbf{r(t)}$, represented by the Jacobian matrix $\mathbf{J_F}$ and $\mathbf{J}$ is the Jacobian matrix that establishes a linear mapping between the velocities vector of the final effectors and the velocities vector of the mobile manipulator. The implementation of the control of multiple heterogeneous mobile manipulators, it is based on the formation of the control and kinematic control of mobile manipulators.

The structure of the formation controller is similar that kinematic controller, therefore the following control law is proposed (5).

$$v = \mu^{-1}\left(\dot{\xi}_d + \mathbf{M}\tanh\left(\tilde{\xi}\right)\right) \tag{5}$$

Where, μ^{-1} is the inverse μ matrix; $\dot{\xi}_d$ is the vector of desired velocities; $\mathbf{M}$ a definite positive matrix that weighs the control actions of the system; $\tilde{\xi}$ is the vector of control errors with $\tilde{\xi} = \xi_\mathbf{d} - \xi$.

Assuming the velocity is constant, then $\dot{\tilde{\xi}} = \dot{\xi}_\mathbf{d}$. For the stability analysis the following Lyapunov candidate function is considered $V\left(\tilde{\xi}\right) = \frac{1}{2}\tilde{\xi}^T\tilde{\xi} > 0$. Its time derivate on the trajectories of the system is

$$\dot{V}\left(\tilde{\xi}\right) = -\tilde{\xi}^T \mathbf{M} \tanh\left(\tilde{\xi}\right) < 0 \tag{6}$$

This implies that the equilibrium point of the closed loop (8) is asymptotically stable, $\tilde{\xi}(t) \to 0$ asymptotically with $t \to \infty$.

Remark 2: By means of the control analysis (5) the following control laws are obtained for the formation controller (7) and kinematic controller (8).

$$\dot{x}_d = \mathbf{J}_{\mathbf{F}}^{-1}\left(\dot{\zeta}_d + \mathbf{K}_1 \tanh\left(\mathbf{K}_2\tilde{\zeta}\right)\right) \tag{7}$$

$$\mathbf{v}_n = \mathbf{J}_n^{\#}\left(\mathbf{h}_{dn} + \mathbf{K}_n \tanh\left(\mathbf{K}_n\tilde{\mathbf{h}}_n\right)\right) \tag{8}$$

5   Results and Discussion

A 3D simulator was developed in Matlab to evaluate the performance of the proposed control scheme, in which the uniciclo, car-like and omnidirectional robots are considered, which are composed of a mobile platform and one or two robotic anthropomorphic. The Fig. 4 shows the stroboscopic movement in the *XYZ* space of the reference system $< \mathcal{R} >$, which makes it possible to check that the proposed controller is performing adequately when carrying out cooperation and coordination tasks when a common object is transported cooperatively between the mutiple heterogeneous mobile manipulators.

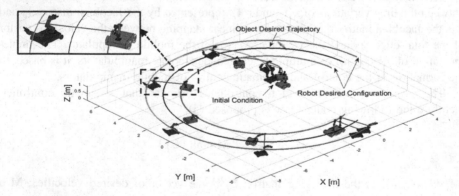

Fig. 4. Stroboscopic movement of the mobile manipulator.

The Fig. 5 indicates the control errors of the position between the ends of the robotic arms; the form and orientation errors, i.e. the distance between the operating ends and the angles that form the object with the arms on the planes XY and YZ with respect to the reference system, is presented in Fig. 6 illustrates; in the two graphs it can be seen that the control errors tend to zero asymptotically when $t \to \infty$.

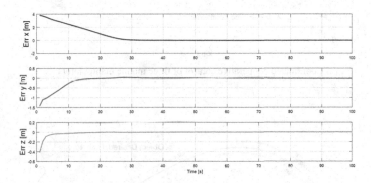

Fig. 5. Errors of position of the point of interest or midpoint of the operative ends.

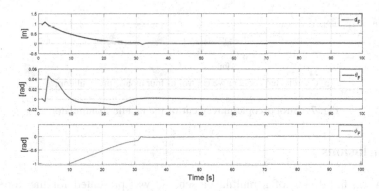

Fig. 6. Errors of shape of the object to be transported

Figure 7 shows the stroboscopics movements of $n \geq 2$ heterogeneous mobile robots, confirming that the implemented control is adequate as the robots followed the desired trajectory.

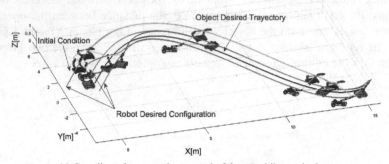

(a) Coordinated cooperative control of three mobile manipulators

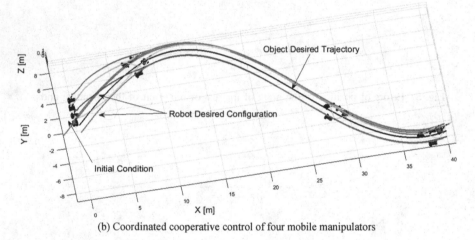

(b) Coordinated cooperative control of four mobile manipulators

Fig. 7. Stroboscopic movement of the mobile manipulator.

6   Conclusions

In this work, the design of a multilayer scheme was presented for the coordinated cooperative control of $n \geq 2$ heterogeneous mobile manipulators for trajectory tracking that allows to transport an object in common. In the controller design employs a kinematic cascading control implemented on a virtual structure formed between the operating extremes of multiple heterogeneous mobile manipulator robots. Stability and robustness are verified with the Lyapunov method. The simulation experiments using a virtual structure allow to determinate the performance of the proposed control scheme, validating the efficiency of the controller in solving different motion problems through a choice of control references.

Acknowledgments. The authors would like to thanks to the Corporación Ecuatoriana para el Desarrollo de la Investigación y Academia – CEDIA for the financing given to research, development, and innovation, through the CEPRA projects, especially the project CEPRA 2015; Tele-Operación Bilateral de Múltiples Manipuladores Móviles and to Grupo de Investigación en Automatización, Robótica y Sistemas Inteligentes, GI-ARSI, for the support to develop this paper.

References

1. Hentout, A., Messous, A., Bouzoula, B.: Multi-agent control approach for autonomous mobile manipulators: simulation results on RobuTER/ULM. In: 19th World Congress the International Federation of Automatic Control, pp. 8503–8508 (2014)
2. Andaluz, V., Roberti, F., Toibero, J., Carelli, R.: Passivity-based visual feedback control with dynamic compensation of mobile manipulators: stability and L2-gain performance analysis. Robot. Auton. Syst. **66**, 64–74 (2015)
3. Andaluz, V., Roberti, F., Toibero, J., Carelli, R.: Adaptive unified motion control of mobile manipulators. Control. Eng. Pract. **20**, 1337–1352 (2012)
4. Lopez, I.: Skill acquisition for industrial robots: from stand-alone to distributed learning. In: IEEE International Conference on Automatica (ICA-ACCA) (2016)
5. Ortiz, J.S., Aldás, J.V., Andaluz, V.H.: Mobile manipulators for cooperative transportation of objects in common. In: Gao, Y., Fallah, S., Jin, Y., Lekakou, C. (eds.) TAROS 2017. LNCS (LNAI), vol. 10454, pp. 651–660. Springer, Cham (2017). https://doi.org/10.1007/978-3-319-64107-2_53
6. Andaluz, V.H., Molina, M.F., Erazo, Y.P., Ortiz, J.S.: Numerical methods for cooperative control of double mobile manipulators. In: Huang, Y., Wu, H., Liu, H., Yin, Z. (eds.) ICIRA 2017. LNCS (LNAI), vol. 10463, pp. 889–898. Springer, Cham (2017). https://doi.org/10.1007/978-3-319-65292-4_77
7. Ortiz, J.S., Molina, M.F., Andaluz, V.H., Varela, J., Morales, V.: Coordinated control of a omnidirectional double mobile manipulator. In: Kim, Kuinam J., Kim, H., Baek, N. (eds.) ICITS 2017. LNEE, vol. 449, pp. 278–286. Springer, Singapore (2018). https://doi.org/10.1007/978-981-10-6451-7_33
8. Janssen, R., van de Molengraft, R., Bruyninckx, H., et al.: Cloud based centralized task control for human domain multi-robot operations. Intell. Serv. Robot. **9**, 63–77 (2016)
9. Ortiz, J.S., Zapata, C.F., Vega, A.D., Santana, G.A., Andaluz, V.H.: Heterogeneous cooperation for autonomous navigation between terrestrial and aerial robots. In: Kim, Kuinam J., Kim, H., Baek, N. (eds.) ICITS 2017. LNEE, vol. 449, pp. 287–296. Springer, Singapore (2018). https://doi.org/10.1007/978-981-10-6451-7_34
10. Sabattini, L., Secchi, C., Levratti, A., Fantuzzi, C.: Decentralized control of cooperative robotic systems for arbitrary setpoint tracking while avoiding collisions. IFAC **48**, 57–62 (2015)
11. Razak, R., Sukumar, S., Chung, H.: Decentralized adaptive coverage control of nonholonomic mobile robots. IFAC **49**, 410–415 (2016)
12. Zaerpoora, A., Ahmadabadia, M.N., Barunia, M.R., Wang, Z.D.: Distributed object transportation on a desired path based on constrain and move strategy. Robot. Auton. Syst. **50**, 115–128 (2005)
13. Hekmatfar, T., Masehian, E., Javad, S.: Cooperative object transportation by multiple mobile manipulators through a hierarchical planning architecture. In: International Conference on Robotics and Mechatronics, pp. 503–508 (2014)

14. Rosa, L., Cognetti, M., Nicastro, A., Alvarez, P., Oriolo, G.: Multi-task cooperative control in a heterogeneous ground-air robot team. IFAC **48**, 53–58 (2015)
15. Hu, H., Xuan, Q., Yu, W., Zhang, C.: Second-order consensus for heterogeneous multi-agent systems in the cooperation–competition network: a hybrid adaptive and pinning control approach. Nonlinear Anal.: Hybrid Syst. **20**, 21–36 (2016)
16. Nasir, A., Hsino, A., Hartmann, K., Chen, C., Roth, H.: Heterogeneous capability multi-robots cooperative framework. In: Proceedings of the 1st IFAC Conference on Embedded Systems, vol. 45, pp. 157–162 (2012)
17. Naidoo, N., Bright, G., Stopforth, R.: The cooperation of heterogeneous mobile robots in manufacturing environments using a robotic middleware platform. IFAC **49**(12), 984–989 (2016)
18. Saska, M., Krajník, T., Vonásek, V., et al.: Fault-tolerant formation driving mechanism designed for heterogeneous MAVs-UGVs groups. J. Intell. Robot. Syst. **73**, 603–622 (2014)
19. Andaluz, V., Rampinelli, V., Carrelli, R., Roberti, F.: Coordinated cooperative control of mobile manipulators. In: IEEE International Conference on Industrial Technology, pp. 300–305 (2011)

Robotic Healthcare Service System to Serve Multiple Patients with Multiple Robots

Ho Seok Ahn$^{(\boxtimes)}$, Sheng Zhang, Min Ho Lee, Jong Yoon Lim,
and Bruce A. MacDonald

CARES, University of Auckland, Auckland, New Zealand
{hs.ahn,jy.lim,b.macdonald}@auckland.ac.nz,
{zshe129,mlee242}@aucklanduni.ac.nz

Abstract. This paper presents a robot system for a healthcare environment, especially for a family doctor practice. The robot system includes a sensor manager and a robot system for a general doctor's practice, which enables multiple robots to serve multiple patients at one time, by sharing vital signs devices. A receptionist robot assigns one patient to one nurse assistant robot using a patient identification system. Our previous work included three sub-systems: a receptionist robot, a nurse assistant robot, and a medical server. However, this could only serve one patient and one vital signs device at any one time, which means we can use only one of vital signs devices prepared for patients and wastes their time waiting. In addition, patients should enter their identification data to robot by themselves, which takes another long time as well as can make errors on the data. We implemented the new system with multiple robots and new patient identification system using QR code, and did a pilot study to confirm the new system's functionalities. The results show the new system talks well with multiple robots to support multiple patients by identifying them using QR codes, and measures their vital signs well by sharing the devices.

Keywords: Healthcare robot system · Vital sign measuring system
Sensor manager system · Health condition management · General practice

1 Introduction

In recent years, the robotics industry is growing rapidly, and people have more access to robots. Robots can assist, guide and accompany people in daily life [1]. In hospitals, robots are not new anymore. Some robot systems help medical personnel with physical work. For example, a robot helps staff transport goods and samples for an orthopaedic department [2, 3]. Some help people with physical aspects of healthcare, i.e., RIMAN helps nurses or family members to lift patients safely [4]. Some robots are used for helping people manage chronic obstructive pulmonary disease at home [5], and some robots help provide some services of doctors or nurses in real environments [6, 7].

In our previous study, we found that robots can be acceptable to older people [8]. From 2010, we deployed robots in a real older care environment for several weeks to interact with staff and residents as a feasibility test [9, 10]. Based on our acceptability and feasibility tests, we carried out a range of experiments in private and public spaces

© Springer Nature Switzerland AG 2018
S. S. Ge et al. (Eds.): ICSR 2018, LNAI 11357, pp. 493–502, 2018.
https://doi.org/10.1007/978-3-030-05204-1_48

in a retirement village and hospital from 2011, and found that robots can help humans [11–14]. We showed a positive cost-effectiveness analysis of a robot measuring vital signs in a rural medical practice in 2014 [6, 7]. We asked young people to use our robots designed for older people to find whether it can be helpful to young people as well in 2014 [15–17]. We studied how healthcare robots might help patients who have specific problems, such as chronic obstructive pulmonary disease [18] and dementia [19].

During this research, we designed and developed a robot system for healthcare facility environments [1]. It consists of three main subsystems: a receptionist robot, a nurse assistant robot, and a medical server. The receptionist robot interacts with a patient and asks the nurse assistant robot to measure vital signs of the patient. The nurse assistant robot controls the vital signs devices, and updates the results to the medical server. It works well, but has a limitation that one robot manages all healthcare devices, but can control only one of them at once. This limits the throughput of the healthcare devices and wastes patients' time waiting. Also patients should enter their personal info through robot's touch screen by themselves for robot to identify patients, which takes time to enter the personal info, and sometimes makes difficult to identify patients due to typo. To address these limitations, we designed a second system that makes it possible to share the expensive healthcare devices among multiple robots that can serve multiple patients. We implemented this system with a new patient identification system using QR code and the Sensor Manager system [20].

The rest of this paper is organized as follows. In Sect. 2, we introduce the design of the new healthcare robot system focusing on the receptionist robot system and the nurse assistant robot system. We explain the new patient identification system with medical server and new sensor manager system in Sect. 3. We show our pilot study with the proposed system in Sect. 4, and conclude this paper in Sect. 5.

2 Healthcare Robot System Version 2

2.1 Overall System Architecture

Figure 1 shows the overview of the new healthcare robot system that has four components: a receptionist robot "ReceptionBot", a nurse assistant robot "CareBot", a sensor managing system version 2 "Sensor Manager 2", and a medical server "Robogen". ReceptionBot works at reception for a healthcare facility, especially a (General practice) GP office; it collects patients' information, generates personal QR codes, gives instructions depending on the purpose of the patients' visit, and assigns one CareBot to each patient. CareBot works in a GP room; it identifies its patient with the personal QR code, assists the patient to measure vital signs, and uploads the results to Robogen. Then, human doctors can check the recorded data through the Robogen user interface and give feedback to the patient. Sensor Manager 2 is responsible for managing multiple healthcare devices in the GP room. When CareBot asks Sensor Manager 2 which healthcare devices it can use, then Sensor Manager 2 assigns available healthcare devices to the CareBot. Sensor Manager 2 also receives commands from every CareBot and controls the healthcare devices according to the command.

Robogen communicates with ReceptionBots and CareBots in real-time, and manages all the data, such as patients' information, medical history and robot interaction log.

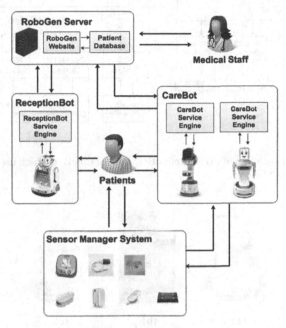

Fig. 1. System overview of the healthcare robot system Version 2, which consists of four subsystems: a receptionist robot system "ReceptionBot", a nurse assistant robot system "CareBot", a sensor manager system "Sensor Manager 2", and a medical server "RoboGen". We can use multiple CareBots in this system.

2.2 Receptionist Robot System: ReceptionBot

Figure 2(a) shows the architecture of ReceptionBot. We use the UoA Robotic Software Framework Manager, or Robot Manager (RM) for short, which helps integrate different programming frameworks easily, and minimizes the impact of framework differences and new versions [21]. With RM, we can easily design and change the system architecture. This is the reason why the system architectures of ReceptionBot and CareBot, shown in Fig. 2(b), are similar. ReceptionBot uses four components from three SW frameworks: speech recognition from ROS, face detection from OpenRTM, speech generation and sound direction detection from ROCOS.

These components use hardware resources of robot platforms, such as the camera, microphone, and speakers. As a robot platform of ReceptionBot, we use iRobiQ, a small cute robot manufactured by Yujin Robot, as shown in Fig. 3(a). This is the reason why we use Yujin voice engine and ROCOS, which are developed by the company [1]. It has two arms which are used mainly for getting attention, indicating emotions and gestures. It is also equipped with some touch sensors at different parts of its body. This enables the programming of realistic responses when users pat, tap, touch, or nudge the robot.

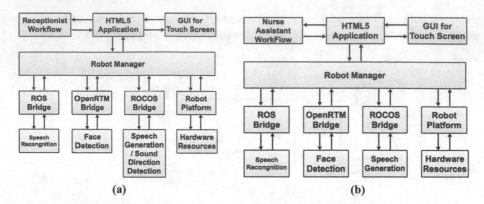

Fig. 2. A system architecture of (a) ReceptionBot, and (b) CareBot, which use the UoA Robotic Software Framework Manager.

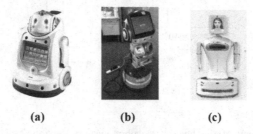

Fig. 3. Robot Platforms: (a) iRobiQ, (b) Cafero, (c) Silbot3.

ReceptionBot talks with the Robogen and the patient identification system, will be described in Sects. 3.1 and 3.2, respectively. Especially, ReceptionBot checks whether the patients are already registered to the RoboGen or not, and help them register to the RoboGen if they are not in the RoboGen. ReceptionBot issues the secured personal QR code to patients, then patients show it to their CareBots.

2.3   Nurse Assistant Robot System: CareBot

Figure 2(b) shows the system architecture of CareBot. We developed the CareBot application using HTML5 web technologies. CareBot uses two components from two SW frameworks; face detection from OpenRTM, and speech generation with Festival. These components use hardware resources of the robots, such as the camera and speakers. It is easy to add additional healthcare sensor devices on CareBot by using Sensor Manager 2. We use two different robot platforms as CareBots: Cafero and Silbot3.

Cafero, as shown in Fig. 3(b), is a kiosk type robot manufactured by Yujin Robot. It is about 1.2 m high, and it is capable of self-navigation to cruise in the rooms. The robot hardware consists of a differential drive mobile platform, two single board computers, sonar sensors, Hokuyo URG 04-LX laser scanner, microphone, speakers, touch screen mounted on an actuated head, camera, and USB ports. The robot runs Windows XP with a custom proprietary software platform to run the service. The touch helps interactions by showing message or pictures and accepts inputs through the touch screen.

SILBOT-3 is a general-purpose platform in the aspect of economy and function in the Intelligent Robot, as shown in Fig. 3(c). It is suitably designed for education & healthcare service. It is equipped a large touch screen on its head, which could express various expression. Except regular sonar sensors and 3-D camera for navigation system, it also provides interaction functions by using touch sensor on its body, arms and hands. The system development environment (SDK) as excellent researching aids for study in College.

These CareBots does not ask patients to enter their personal info directly to robots anymore. Instead of this procedure, CareBots ask patient to show their personal QR code issued by the ReceptionBot. When CareBots capture the patients' QR code with their cameras, CareBots talk with the Robogen to get patients' info. CareBots also talk with Sensor Manager 2 to check which vital signs devices they can use. When the Sensor Manager 2 assigns available vital signs device to each CareBot, CareBot measures patient's vital sign with the assigned device, and upload the result to the RoboGen.

3 Software for Healthcare Robot System Version 2

3.1 Medical Server: RoboGen

We have been using a medical server system "Robogen", which manages and stores all the medical data including patients' information, measurement data, interaction records, and robots' log for over 10 years. Robogen is built by the Microsoft ASP.NET and MVC framework and a Microsoft SQL server. ReceptionBots and CareBots connect to RoboGen through web-services, and they communicate asynchronously. The robot application drives the interaction with patients, whereas the web centric RoboGen infrastructure brings in other clinical roles to complete the loop in the healthcare workflow. Users and family members as well as specialists such as doctors, nurses, and psychologists can access the user data through the RoboGen website, if they have permission [1].

3.2 Patient Identification System

As shown in Fig. 4, we have developed a patient identification system. Patients could get their QR code from QR code generation software, and utilize the personal QR code in healthcare application to show their identity. In our healthcare system, ReceptionBot provides a unique QR code for each patient. Patients could use their QR codes to authenticate themselves instead of entering their private information on CareBots. Robogen not only stores patient information in database, but also generates a unique and random string for every patient. ReceptionBot can get this string by using patient's name or ID to request from Robogen. Many open source libraries could convert this string into a QR encoded image easily. On our CareBots, we integrated a QR decoding system into the healthcare application, which could use camera to capture the QR code image and then decode it back to string. Robogen provides finding patient by QR code string function, so CareBots could get patient information by using this function quickly.

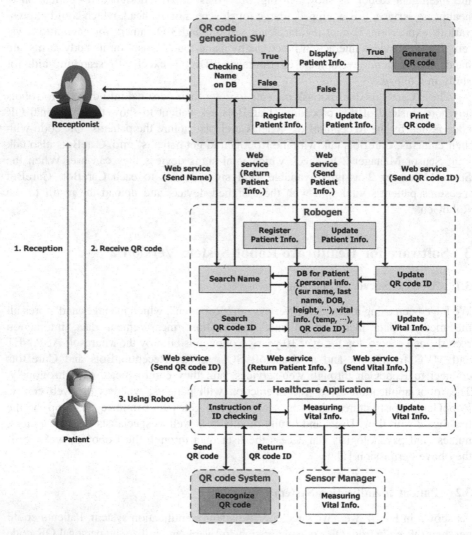

Fig. 4. A patient identification system, which use personal QR code. All the data are saved to RoboGen, which is a medical server, and ReceptionBots and CareBots recognize their patient using secured personal QR code.

The patient identification system has two significant advantages. One is to provide a user-friendly method for patients to be verified in healthcare system. They could print out the QR code or store the QR code in their smartphone and then scan it on CareBots. CareBots could finish all procedures and recognize the patient in a short time. The other is chosen to address the privacy issue for patients. None of the patient details are stored in the QR code which ensures some level security in the case it get stolen.

3.3 New Version of Sensor Manager System: Sensor Manager 2

There are usually many different types of healthcare devices in healthcare facilities, such as blood pressure monitor, blood oxygen meter, and blood glucose meter. These devices normally have different communication protocol, application programming interface and control system. It is hard for our robot applications to support all different kinds of devices directly.

To manage these complex conditions and utilizes healthcare devices effectively between CareBots, we designed a new sensor manager system [20]. It consists of three subsystems each of which function in a distributed system: a sensor manager server, robot clients and healthcare devices. In our system, CareBots play roles as robot clients. When a patient interacts with CareBot to measure vital signs using healthcare devices, CareBot sends requests to the sensor manager server using the predefined API, which is supported by the sensor manager system. Then, the sensor manager system checks available healthcare devices and assigns one of them to CareBot.

4 Pilot Study: A ReceptionBot and Two CareBots

4.1 Study Environment

ReceptionBot works at reception and is responsible for greeting and communication when patients come to the GP clinic room. It should work as a human receptionist, but it cannot do all jobs of a human receptionist, such as discussion illness conditions. In this design, the primary task of the robot receptionist is to help patients get their QR code which is an essential preparation for using nurse assistant robots. If a patient has never visited the GP clinic before, the robot receptionist talks with the patient to collect information and print a QR code. If the patient has been to the clinic before, the information has been stored in the database. The robot receptionist will help the patient retrieve the QR code from Robogen.

Two CareBots work in the GP room where they help patients measure their vital signs and upload the measurement result to Robogen for medical staff to review. Although they cannot do all the tasks of a human nurse, such as giving an injection and handling complex situations, they can measure vital signs independently and provide some simple feedback based on the result, which saves nurse's time. While obtaining the QR code, ReceptionBot assigns a CareBot for the patient. The patient follows the given instructions to find the CareBot. Sensor Manager 2 is managing healthcare devices for measuring blood pressure, blood oxygen level, pulse rate, blood glucose level and weight. The measured data is uploaded to Robogen so that medical staff can check it through Robogen.

4.2   Pilot Study

In our study, two researchers in our lab played the role of the patients. The purpose of this study is verifying the feasibility of the newly proposed system through pilot study. ReceptionBot is waiting for patients at the reception and detects the people near to the entrance. If people continue getting closer to the reception, it asks the visitor what the purpose of visiting is. The visitor answers to the question and communicates with the robot by pressing the buttons on robot's screen.

If ReceptionBot recognizes the visitor comes to meet doctor, it assumes the visitor as a patient, and checks whether the patient is registered to the RoboGen or not. If the patient is not registered to the RoboGen, the ReceptionBot do the registration procedure for the patient. Then, the ReceptionBot issues a QR code for the patient and assign the patient to one of CareBots. If the patient is already registered to the RoboGen, we skip the registration procedure. This registration procedure is one of the newly integrated functions on the new system. ReceptionBot assigns one CareBot to the patient, and the CareBot guides the patient to move to the assigned GP room.

If there is another patient to be served, the ReceptionBot does the same procedure for the patient, and other robot is assigned to the patient. For this, the ReceptionBot should check which CareBot is available to serve new patient. This multiple robot supporting system is another newly integrated function. In this study, we used two CareBots; one is Cafero, and the other one is Silbot3.

CareBots identify their patients with QR code issues by the ReceptionBot. Patients just shows their QR code to their CareBots, and CareBots get the patients' info from the RoboGen using the newly developed patient identification system. CareBot talks with Sensor Manager 2 to find available healthcare device for its patient, and helps the patient to measure their vital data. Sensor Manager 2 talks with all different healthcare devices and control them. When the patient finishes one task, CareBot retrieves the result data from Sensor Manager 2, and update it to Robogen. If CareBot needs to measure different vital sign, it repeats the same procedure.

4.3   Discussion

The ReceptionBot has three key functions to perform in this pilot study: (1) recognizing person, (2) registering patients, and (3) assigning CareBots to patients. The first function is same as the first version, but the other two functions are different, which we checked through the pilot study. We manage the patient list through the RoboGen, and we can recognize whether the patient is registered or not. Also we can register the new patient to our system. As the new system support multiple robots for multiple patients, it is important to know the status of all CareBots. Even we checked two CareBots in our pilot study, we can check their availability and assign them to different patients.

The CareBot has four key functions to perform in this pilot study: (1) guiding patient to GP room, (2) identifying patients, and (3) measuring vital signs, and (4) uploading the results. The first and fourth functions are same as the first version, so we focused on the second and third functions in our pilot study. CareBots ask patient to show their QR code instead of asking them to enter personal info through touch screen. It reduces the time for patients to enter all their personal info to robot using touch screen as well as reduces the errors on data from typo. As we should support multiple patients by sharing vital signs devices, talking with the Sensor Manager 2 and using exact healthcare device is important here. The processing latency of Sensor Manager 2 was less than 10 ms, and the latency of wireless communication was 10 ms to 60 ms, which depends on the wireless network environment. There was no significant delay on the communication between CareBots and Sensor Manager 2, as well as no confliction for sharing healthcare devices in our pilot study.

5 Conclusion

We designed a new version of robotic healthcare service system that supports multiple patients as well as sharing healthcare devices. We developed the patient identification system using QR code, and it reduced the patients' time to enter their personal info as well as reduced the errors on data. The new system assigns different CareBots to different patients, and the ReceptionBot can manage multiple CareBots safely. For supporting multiple patients, sharing vital signs devices with multiple CareBots is important, and we used the Sensor Manager 2 that manages different healthcare devices. From the pilot study, we confirmed that the new healthcare service system manages different robots and healthcare devices safely. As we just did small pilot study, we need more complex evaluation with reasonable number of robots and patients as a future work. Like our previous studies, we will do the next study in real environment, such as hospital.

References

1. Ahn, H.S., Lee, M.H., MacDonald, B.A.: Healthcare robot systems for a hospital environment: CareBot and ReceptionBot. In: IEEE International Symposium on Robot and Human Interactive Communication, pp. 571–576 (2015)
2. Ljungblad, S., Kotrbova, J., Jacobsson, M., Cramer, H., Niechwiadowicz, K.: Hospital robot at work: something alien or an intelligent colleague? In: ACM Conference on Computer Supported Cooperative Work, pp. 177–186 (2012)
3. Fernando, J.B., Tanigawa, T., Naito, E., Yamagami, K., Ozawa, J.: Collision avoidance path planning for hospital robot with consideration of disabled person's movement characteristic. In: 1st IEEE Global Conference on Consumer Electronics, pp. 392–396 (2012)
4. Mukai, T., Onishi, M., Odashima, T., Hirano, S., Luo, Z.: Development of the tactile sensor system of a human-interactive robot "RI-MAN". IEEE Trans. Robot. 24(2), 505–512 (2008)
5. Simonov, M.: A socially assistive robot for persons with chronic obstructive pulmonary disease (COPD). Gerontechnology 11(2), 353 (2012)
6. Broadbent, E., Orejana, J.R., Ahn, H.S., Xie, J., Rouse, P., MacDonald, B.: The cost-effectiveness of a robot measuring vital signs in a rural medical practice. In: IEEE International Symposium on Robot and Human Interactive Communication, pp. 577–581 (2015)
7. Orejana, J.R., MacDonald, B.A., Ahn, H.S., Peri, K., Broadbent, E.: Healthcare robots in homes of rural older adults. In: Tapus, A., André, E., Martin, J.C., Ferland, F., Ammi, M. (eds.) Social Robotics. LNCS (LNAI), vol. 9388, pp. 512–521. Springer, Cham (2015). https://doi.org/10.1007/978-3-319-25554-5_51

8. Kuo, I.H., et al.: Age and gender factors in user acceptance of healthcare robots. In: IEEE International Symposium on Robot and Human Interactive Communication, pp. 214–219 (2009)
9. Broadbent, E., Tamagawa, R., Kerse, N., Knock, B., Patience, A., MacDonald, B.: Retirement home staff and residents' preferences for healthcare robots. In: IEEE International Symposium on Robot and Human Interactive Communication, pp. 645–665 (2009)
10. Stafford, R.Q., et al.: Improved robot attitudes and emotions at a retirement home after meeting a robot. In: IEEE International Symposium on Robot and Human Interactive Communication, pp. 82–87 (2010)
11. Robinson, H., MacDonald, B.A., Kerse, N., Broadbent, E.: Suitability of healthcare robots for a dementia unit and suggested improvements. J. Am. Med. Dir. Assoc. **14**(1), 34–40 (2012)
12. Ahn, H.S., et al.: Design of a kiosk type healthcare robot system for older people in private and public places. In: Brugali, D., Broenink, Jan F., Kroeger, T., MacDonald, Bruce A. (eds.) SIMPAR 2014. LNCS (LNAI), vol. 8810, pp. 578–589. Springer, Cham (2014). https://doi.org/10.1007/978-3-319-11900-7_49
13. Jayawardena, C., Kuo, I.-H., Broadbent, E., MacDonald, B.A.: Socially assistive robot healthbot: design, implementation, and field trials. IEEE Syst. J. **10**, 1056–1067 (2016)
14. Ahn, H.S., et al.: Entertainment services of a healthcare robot system for older people in private and public spaces. In: International Conference on Automation, Robotics and Applications (2015)
15. Ahn, H.S., Lee, M.H., Broadbent, E., MacDonald, B.A.: Gathering healthcare service robot requirements from young people's perceptions of an older care robot. In: International Conference on Robotic Computing, pp. 22–27 (2017)
16. Ahn, H.S., Lee, M.H., Broadbent, E., MacDonald, B.A.: Is entertainment services of a healthcare service robot for older people useful to young people. In: International Conference on Robotic Computing, pp. 330–335 (2017)
17. Ahn, H.S., Santos, M.P.G., Wadhwa, C., MacDonald, B.: Development of brain training games for a healthcare service robot for older people. In: Beetz, M., Johnston, B., Williams, M.-A. (eds.) ICSR 2014. LNCS (LNAI), vol. 8755, pp. 1–10. Springer, Cham (2014). https://doi.org/10.1007/978-3-319-11973-1_1
18. Broadbent, E., et al.: Using robots at home to support patients with COPD: a pilot randomised trial. J. Med. Internet Res. (2017)
19. Darragh, M., et al.: Homecare robots to improve health and well-being in mild cognitive impairment and early stage dementia: results from a scoping study. J. Am. Med. Dir. Assoc. (2017)
20. Zhang, S., Ahn, H.S., Lim, J.Y., Lee, M.H., MacDonald, B.A.: Design and implementation of a device management system for healthcare assistive robots: sensor manager system version 2. In: Kheddar, A., et al. (eds.) ICSR 2017. LNCS, vol. 10652. Springer, Cham (2017). https://doi.org/10.1007/978-3-319-70022-9_53
21. Ahn, H.S., Lee, M.H., MacDonald, B.A.: Design of a robotic software manager for using heterogeneous components of different frameworks. J. Softw. Eng. Robot. **8**(1), 116–127 (2017)

Perception of Control in Artificial and Human Systems: A Study of Embodied Performance Interactions

Catie Cuan(✉), Ishaan Pakrasi, and Amy LaViers

Mechanical Science and Engineering Department,
University of Illinois Urbana-Champaign, Urbana, IL 61801, USA
crcuan@gmail.com, {pakrasi2,alaviers}@illinois.edu

Abstract. Robots in human facing environments will move alongside human beings. This movement has both functional and expressive meaning and plays a crucial role in human perception of robots. Secondarily, how the robot is controlled – through methods like movement or programming and drivers like oneself or an algorithm – factors into human perceptions. This paper outlines the use of an embodied movement installation, "The Loop", to understand perceptions generated between humans and various technological agents, including a NAO robot and a virtual avatar. Participants were questioned about their perceptions of control in the various agents. Initial results with human subjects demonstrate an increased likelihood to rate a robot and a robotic shadow as algorithmically controlled, versus a human performer and a human-shaped VR avatar which were more likely rated as human actor controlled or split between algorithm/human actor. Participants also showed a tendency to rate their own performance in the exercise as needing improvement. Qualitative data, collected in the form of text and drawings, was open-ended and abstract. Drawings of humans and geometric shapes frequently appeared, as did the words "mirror", "movement", and variations on the word "awareness".

Keywords: Human robot interaction · Robot performance
Embodied learning · Virtual reality

1 Introduction

As humans continuously welcome new forms of technology into their quotidian experience, the mysterious intricacies of how those technologies affect their lived, embodied experience, and resulting actions, is a question for researchers and artists. In many cases, perceptions of robots varied based on cultural context as well as previous exposures to robots in media [3,4]. As that media-based, disembodied experience is supplanted with daily life experience alongside robots, perceptions will change. Moreover, an understanding of how humans perceive robots requires multiple contexts of interaction, social influence from others, and knowledge of humans' own perception of self.

© Springer Nature Switzerland AG 2018
S. S. Ge et al. (Eds.): ICSR 2018, LNAI 11357, pp. 503–512, 2018.
https://doi.org/10.1007/978-3-030-05204-1_49

The SoftBank NAO, a widely-used humanoid [35], has numerous applications in education and socialization for children [12], including in autism research [36]. Further research has examined the effects of NAO's motion [14] and conversational capacity [19] on human interactions with the robot, showing that non-verbal cues enhance interaction with the NAO.

Previous researchers have used a Kinect in conjunction with a robot to track human movement in an interactive environment. This has occurred in research detecting elderly adults for elder care [26] as well as in robot teleoperation [11, 32]. Researchers have also employed virtual reality and mixed reality systems to teleoperate robots [34,42]. The overarching methodology in these teleoperation systems is to map ranges and poses of human movement onto robot actions, outlining rules of translation, limits, and parameters (such as speed).

There will be an estimated 82 million virtual reality (VR) headset users worldwide by 2020 [21]. In contrast, there will be an estimated 1.68 billion TV users by 2021 [37]. Therefore virtual reality remains a relatively novel technology for most people. Virtual reality has applications in stroke rehabilitation [23] and K-12 instruction [28] as well as entertainment and gaming. Many of these applications involve virtual characters, or facsimiles of humans in VR, that play pivotal roles in the content and scenarios of the simulation, thus defining the user experience. Earlier work towards building expressive virtual characters has remarked upon the importance of emotion, non-verbal communication, and personality in virtual characters, not only speech-based communication [41]. Trust of virtual characters may vary based on previous exposures to VR and other forms of virtual characters. Additionally, theory that people generally treat computers as social actors [33] supports the notion that VR users may themselves be emotionally affected by the VR environments they engage with [7].

Embodied interaction with various technologies like VR is also highlighted as a pedagogical strategy. Immersive simulations were used to teach students about science and understand their misconceptions about the field [25]. An immersive VR environment was used to teach physics - the sensation of presence and gesture control (increased embodiment in learning) led to better retention of certain types of knowledge when used during the encoding phase [16–18]. Several embodied learning studies show that the body plays a critical role in thinking, reasoning, and retention [1].

Embodied dyadic interactions which share similar behavior patterning have been shown to increase positive arousal and valence in different contexts, such as a mother and infant [38], structured argument pairings [22], childhood playgroups [5] and opposite-sex romantic dates [13]. Tendency towards similarity may be conscious or conscious as seen in [8]. Embodied dyadic interactions frequently appear in dance and dance therapy. In one study, posture sharing, or intentioned dyadic movement mirroring, was found to increase positive assessments of self-performance and pair performance [2,30]. The "mirror game" is a form of an improvised dyadic interaction between two movers, often dancers, without a leader. The two parties stand facing one another and attempt to remain synchronized in their motion. Mirror games between dancers, improvisers, and musicians without leaders have been shown to create more complex, novel motion than those with a clearly defined leader [31].

Humans have a demonstrated tendency towards behaving in a manner which increases or maintains positive self-evaluation [40]. Additional studies have shown that this effect increases when in proximity to others (social comparison) and when comparing one's own performance in one field or task towards another (dimensional comparison) [39].

In [24,27], we see that human interaction with technology can often lead to frustration. [6] outlines how this frustration develops based on prior experiences, psychological characteristics, and social systems, and often occurs when user expectation does not match interaction outcome. In the case of moving robots, an intentional design of movement that takes into consideration the end user's past characteristics could lead to an interactive experience that matches user expectation, and thus is less frustrating.

Many dance historians see the study of dance as a critical aspect of human anthropology [20]. Dance frequently appears in social interaction across cultures, as a method of signaling adulthood (for example, during quinceaneras - [9]), passing down folktales (a frequent practice for Native American tribes [29]), and selecting a romantic partner (in the case of high school students [15]. The socialness of dance is further evidenced by the common pairing of dance and live music, creating interactions between the dancers and the musicians (whether in performance or at recreational events).

An early version of "The Loop", an interactive, embodied installation, was outlined in [10]. The instantiation in this paper modifies and builds upon that earlier work towards the question on understanding how humans perceive robots and how moving tasks with robots versus computer-based tasks with robots alter human perceptions of the robots in question. Section 2 discusses the artistic themes and research questions explored; Sect. 3 explains the user study design; Sect. 4 presents the results; and Sect. 5 summarizes the work.

2 Artistic and Research Motivation

Artistic themes and research motivations were initially outlined in [10] and are extended for context below. "The Loop" is a subsection of "Time to Compile", a collaboration between an artist and a robotics lab. The three central themes of "Time to Compile" are the following:

- *Are humans becoming more robot-like?* Humans' rich subjectivity and susceptibility to change renders them more likely to alter their behaviors and interactions when working with machines. Machines are less dynamic in this capacity and therefore, less likely to change quickly.
- *The hidden human network.* While various novel technologies possess an inherent mysticism for the uninitiated user, all machines and technologies are built by human beings. Unmasking this network is central to the piece.
- *Time to Compile.* The vastly different compile times for a short dance versus a computer program reveal the human experience of working across disciplines

and bodies, as well as the frustration that may occur when relying on a tool, such as a machine, rather than one's own bodily functionality.

In addition to these three central themes, "The Loop" was designed for this instantiation with additional research questions in mind: How does a movement-based task with a robot differ than a programming-based task with a robot? What are the perceptions of control for each? Finally, how does self-evaluation change based on the degree to which a task is embodied? In posing these questions, the installation was a symbiotic research and artistic initiative, allowing each to inform the textures and experiences of the other.

The design elements of "Time to Compile" include live dance, text, music, projection, film, and props. "The Loop" experience shared similar elements and was designed to feel abstract, continuous, meditative, and welcoming. The music, ushers, lighting, and verbal instructions purposely supported these sentiments. For example, the usher noted "There is no right or wrong way to do this. Simply make choices when you are unsure of what to do".

3   Study Structure

The study structure was as follows: Study participants were told that an artistic installation and experiment was open for a fixed time block. They were invited to arrive at their leisure and participate. Once study participants arrived, they filled out a consent form and were instructed to wait in an area outside the installation. One by one, they were guided by an usher to five stations, where they were prompted to "Follow the motion of the agent you see in front of you." They interacted at each station for 50 s, prompted by the beginning and ending of an amplified musical track. In some cases, they could see the next stations, and in other cases, the station was hidden from view. A minimum of one and a maximum of five participants could be in the installation at one time. The agents at each station are listed below with the controlling element described in italics, Fig. 1 shows the structure.

- Station 1: A NAO robot. *The NAO robot performed a repeated loop of pre-programmed movements through the software program Choregraphe.*
- Station 2: A video projection of a NAO robot, at larger scale. The screen was roughly 7 ft high, making the projected shadow roughly six feet tall. *The video projection was a pre-recorded video of the same movement sequence from Station 1.*
- Station 3: An HTC VIVE headset broadcasting a virtual avatar in the shape of a person. *The VR avatar's movement was controlled by a Microsoft Kinect positioned to capture the Station 4 participant's movement.*
- Station 4: A moving human performer ("Performer 1"). *Performer 1 watched a live Skype feed from the moving participant at Station 2 and attempted to copy the Station 2 participant as closely as possible. Performer 1 occasionally improvised movement when the Skype connection was poor.*

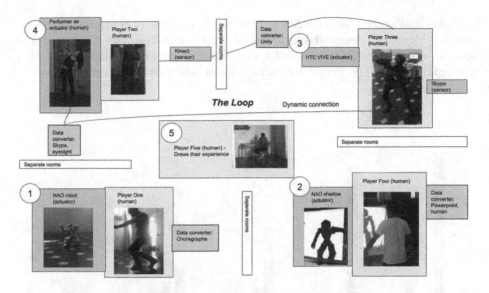

Fig. 1. "The Loop" station agents and their relevant software. The installation was spread across three rooms. In order, each station was separated by a wall, though Stations 1 and 3 were in the same room. The solid connecting line shows a dynamic, live connection between Stations 3 and 4.

Station 5 differed from the other stations: participants were invited to draw a picture of their experience. At the end of all five stations, participants then filled out a survey with the following question for each station: "At the (station number) station, what do you think was motivating the movement of the (agent in motion - for example, at Station 1 it would have been "robot")? (Select more than one if you would like.)"

4   Results

There were 19 total participants. The experience lasted roughly 10 min for each participant. Each participant completed a survey and a drawing; the survey and drawing were not paired together with the participant number. Over half the time, participants rated the NAO and shadow of the NAO at Stations 1 and 2 as being algorithmically controlled. Performer 1 was most frequently rated as being controlled by a human actor. The VR avatar was split between human and algorithm in terms of control.

It is noteworthy that at all of the stations, human actor and automated algorithm appeared in the highest and second highest positions. Additional work is necessary to understand if this distribution occurred because participants believe the human actor may be working in conjunction with or as the creator of the algorithm, or if participants were undecided or mystified between the two. Figure 2 shows the distribution of responses at each station. In actuality, the NAO and shadow of the NAO at Stations 1 and 2 were controlled by a pre-recorded algorithm designed and programmed by an artist. The VR avatar and human performer in Stations 3 and 4 were live elements controlled by the other participants as well as Performer 1's movement interpretation and influence.

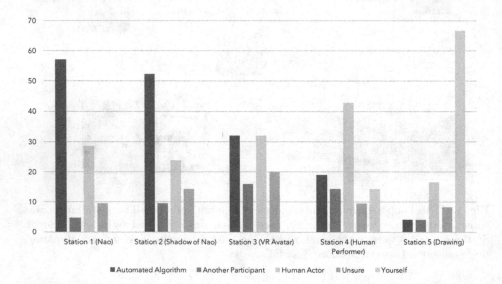

Fig. 2. Perceptions of control for the agents at each station. Each participant selected an average of 1.17 choices at each station. Station 3 (VR avatar) and Station 5 (drawing) each garnered 24 responses, all other stations garnered 21. The values shown in this graph are on a 100 point scale - computed by dividing the number of times a particular response appeared by the total number of checked responses for that station. These choices were discerned by participants who did not know the structure of the installation but could interpret based on what they were seeing at each station.

Samples of the drawings from Station 5 are highlighted in Fig. 3. The drawings provided a opportunity for creative, qualitative feedback that may provide further insight into the subconscious aspects of the participant's experience. Human shapes appeared in 16 of the 19 drawings. 3 of the 19 drawings featured arrows pointing between different human shapes, alluding to the connections between the different stations. An additional 3 drawings showed humans with smiling expressions, while 4 drawings featured humans with confused or frowning expressions. This may be linked to participants' feedback that the exercise was challenging, or that the "movements were sometimes hard to follow". Figure 4 highlights attributes of the drawings.

In written responses to the prompt "Write a few sentences about your experience", 11 of the 19 participants used words like "difficult" and "challenging". Many of them also compared the stations to one another or tried to rank them in terms of difficulty. This monitoring of self-performance was unexpected and

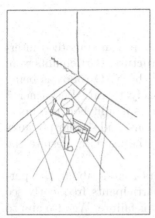  

Fig. 3. A sampling of participants' drawings from Station 5. On the left, a human figure is suspended in an grid of varying lines. In the center, pathways are drawn between moving humans and others. On the right, a human mover is shown with a disembodied shadow of themselves or another. As a group, they all illustrate recognition of connectedness and relationship the external world.

Feature in drawing	Number of occurrences
Humans	16
Arrows pointing between humans	3
Robots	3
Abstract, geometrical shapes (no humans in picture)	3
Circles enveloping human bodies	3
Windows or mirrors	3

Fig. 4. This table shows frequently illustrated features of the participants' drawings. Humans appeared most often, while elements like arrows and windows illustrate a desire to understand the underlying structure of the installation and connections between participants.

provokes additional questions about frustration when interacting with technology in general, whether through computer-based or movement-based exercises. The social aspects of the exercise – such as occasionally being able to see other participants moving, presence of ushers, and interaction with other participants as mediated through the loop-like structure – may have led to additional feelings of self-evaluation or wanting to appear skillful in front of others.

5   Conclusions

In this paper, we presented an instantiation of "The Loop", an embodied inter-active art installation, with a formalized experiment structure. Participants were more likely to rate the NAO robot and the shadow of the NAO robot as being controlled by algorithms, whereas they were more likely to rate Performer 1 being controlled by a human actor and the VR avatar as a split between both. Participants drew detailed pictures of humans, connections, and similar postures in their pictures. Self-assessment was frequent during the exercise, despite the open, non-competitive prompting.

In future work, we will conduct more experiments asking about the per-ceived difficulty of each station to understand why participants frequently see an abstract movement task through the lens of success or failure. We also aim to test whether other types of robots, with more or less humanoid features as the NAO, will result in similar perceptions of control. Further experiments will probe how embodied exercises with robots generate feelings of empowerment or belit-tlement for participants, as contrasted with a computer or programming-based task.

Acknowledgement. This work was conducted under IRB #17427 and supported by a National Science Foundation (NSF) grant #1528036. The authors would like to thank the organizing committee of the 5th Annual Conference on Movement and Computing, which was the site of this experiment and provided production support. Novoneel Chakraborty contributed to the creation of the installation. The authors wish to thank Alexandra Bacula, Roshni Kaushik, and Cameron Scoggins for their assistance in running the experiment on site.

References

1. Abrahamson, D., et al.: You're it! body, action, and object in STEM learning. In: Proceedings of the International Conference of the Learning Sciences: Future of learning (ICLS 2012), vol. 1, pp. 283–290 (2012)
2. Ashenfelter, K.T., Boker, S.M., Waddell, J.R., Vitanov, N.: Spatiotemporal sym-metry and multifractal structure of head movements during dyadic conversation. J. Exp. Psychol.: Hum. Percept. Perform. **35**(4), 1072 (2009)
3. Bartneck, C., Nomura, T., Kanda, T., Suzuki, T., Kato, K.: Cultural differences in attitudes towards robots. In: Proceedings of the Symposium on Robot Companions (SSAISB 2005 Convention), pp. 1–4 (2005)
4. Bartneck, C., Suzuki, T., Kanda, T., Nomura, T.: The influence of people's culture and prior experiences with Aibo on their attitude towards robots. Ai Soc. **21**(1–2), 217–230 (2007)
5. Benenson, J.F., Apostoleris, N.H., Parnass, J.: Age and sex differences in dyadic and group interaction. Dev. Psychol. **33**(3), 538 (1997)
6. Bessiere, K., Ceaparu, I., Lazar, J., Robinson, J., Shneiderman, B.: Social and psychological influences on computer user frustration. In: Media Access: Social and Psychological Dimensions of New Technology Use, pp. 169–192 (2004)
7. Bradley, M.M., Lang, P.J.: Emotion and motivation. In: Handbook of Psychophys-iology, 2nd edn, pp. 602–642 (2000)

8. Burgoon, J.K., Stern, L.A., Dillman, L.: Interpersonal Adaptation: Dyadic Interaction Patterns. Cambridge University Press, Cambridge (2007)
9. Cantú, N.E.: La quinceañera: towards an ethnographic analysis of a life-cycle ritual. South. Folk. **56**(1), 73 (1999)
10. Cuan, C., Pakrasi, I., LaViers, A.: Time to compile: an interactive art installation. In: 16th Biennial Symposium on Arts & Technology, vol. 51, p. 19 (2018)
11. Du, G., Zhang, P., Mai, J., Li, Z.: Markerless kinect-based hand tracking for robot teleoperation. Int. J. Adv. Robot. Syst. **9**(2), 36 (2012)
12. Gelin, R., et al.: Towards a storytelling humanoid robot. In: AAAI Fall Symposium: Dialog with Robots, Arlington (2010)
13. Grammer, K., Kruck, K.B., Magnusson, M.S.: The courtship dance: patterns of nonverbal synchronization in opposite-sex encounters. J. Nonverbal Behav. **22**(1), 3–29 (1998)
14. Han, J., Campbell, N., Jokinen, K., Wilcock, G.: Investigating the use of non-verbal cues in human-robot interaction with a Nao robot. In: 2012 IEEE 3rd International Conference on Cognitive Infocommunications (CogInfoCom), pp. 679–683. IEEE (2012)
15. Hansen, S.L.: Dating choices of high school students. Fam. Coord. **26**, 133–138 (1977)
16. Johnson-Glenberg, M.: Immersive VR and education: embodied design principles that include gesture and hand controls. Front. Robot. AI **5**, 81 (2018)
17. Johnson-Glenberg, M.C., Megowan-Romanowicz, C.: Embodied science and mixed reality: how gesture and motion capture affect physics education. Cogn. Res.: Princ. Implic. **2**(1), 24 (2017)
18. Johnson-Glenberg, M.C., Megowan-Romanowicz, C., Birchfield, D.A., Savio-Ramos, C.: Effects of embodied learning and digital platform on the retention of physics content: centripetal force. Front. Psychol. **7**, 1819 (2016)
19. Jokinen, K., Wilcock, G.: Multimodal open-domain conversations with the Nao robot. In: Mariani, J., Rosset, S., Garnier-Rizet, M., Devillers, L. (eds.) Natural Interaction with Robots, Knowbots and Smartphones, pp. 213–224. Springer, New York (2014). https://doi.org/10.1007/978-1-4614-8280-2_19
20. Kaeppler, A.L.: II. Dance ethnology and the anthropology of dance. Danc. Res. J. **32**(1), 116–125 (2000)
21. Kendal, R.: Infographic: virtual reality stats everyone should see. Technical report, BOSS Magazine, 01 August 2018. https://thebossmagazine.com/virtual-reality-statistics-infographic/
22. Kuhn, D., Shaw, V., Felton, M.: Effects of dyadic interaction on argumentive reasoning. Cogn. Instr. **15**(3), 287–315 (1997)
23. Laver, K.E., Lange, B., George, S., Deutsch, J.E., Saposnik, G., Crotty, M.: Virtual reality for stroke rehabilitation. Cochrane Database Syst Rev. (11), Art. No.: CD008349 (2017). https://doi.org/10.1002/14651858.CD008349.pub4
24. Lazar, J., Jones, A., Shneiderman, B.: Workplace user frustration with computers: an exploratory investigation of the causes and severity. Behav. Inf. Technol. **25**(03), 239–251 (2006)
25. Lindgren, R., Tscholl, M.: Enacted misconceptions: using embodied interactive simulations to examine emerging understandings of science concepts. International Society of the Learning Sciences, Boulder, CO (2014)
26. Machida, E., Cao, M., Murao, T., Hashimoto, H.: Human motion tracking of mobile robot with Kinect 3D sensor. In: 2012 Proceedings of SICE Annual Conference (SICE), pp. 2207–2211. IEEE (2012)

27. McCarthy, J., Wright, P.: Technology as experience. Interactions **11**(5), 42–43 (2004)
28. Merchant, Z., Goetz, E.T., Cifuentes, L., Keeney-Kennicutt, W., Davis, T.J.: Effectiveness of virtual reality-based instruction on students' learning outcomes in K-12 and higher education: a meta-analysis. Comput. Educ. **70**, 29–40 (2014)
29. Morris, R., Wander, P.: Native American rhetoric: dancing in the shadows of the ghost dance. Q. J. Speech **76**(2), 164–191 (1990)
30. Navarre, D.: Posture sharing in dyadic interaction. Am. J. Danc. Ther. **5**(1), 28–42 (1982)
31. Noy, L., Dekel, E., Alon, U.: The mirror game as a paradigm for studying the dynamics of two people improvising motion together. Proc. Natl. Acad. Sci. **108**(52), 20947–20952 (2011)
32. Qian, K., Niu, J., Yang, H.: Developing a gesture based remote human-robot interaction system using Kinect. Int. J. Smart Home **7**(4), 203–208 (2013)
33. Reeves, B., Nass, C.: The Media Equation: How People Treat Computers, Television, and New Media. Cambridge University Press, Cambridge (1997)
34. Rosen, E., et al.: Communicating robot arm motion intent through mixed reality head-mounted displays. arXiv preprint arXiv:1708.03655 (2017)
35. Shamsuddin, S., et al.: Humanoid robot NAO: review of control and motion exploration. In: 2011 IEEE International Conference on Control System, Computing and Engineering (ICCSCE), pp. 511–516. IEEE (2011)
36. Shamsuddin, S., et al.: Initial response of autistic children in human-robot interaction therapy with humanoid robot NAO. In: 2012 IEEE 8th International Colloquium on Signal Processing and its Applications (CSPA), pp. 188–193. IEEE (2012)
37. Statista: Number of TV households worldwide from 2010 to 2021. Technical report, Statista, 01 January 2018. https://www.statista.com/statistics/268695/number-of-tv-households-worldwide/
38. Stern, D.N.: Mother and infant at play: the dyadic interaction involving facial, vocal, and gaze behaviors (1974)
39. Strickhouser, J.E., Zell, E.: Self-evaluative effects of dimensional and social comparison. J. Exp. Soc. Psychol. **59**, 60–66 (2015)
40. Tesser, A.: Toward a self-evaluation maintenance model of social behavior. In: Advances in Experimental Social Psychology, vol. 21, pp. 181–227. Elsevier (1988)
41. Vinayagamoorthy, V., et al.: Building expression into virtual characters (2006)
42. Whitney, D., Rosen, E., Phillips, E., Konidaris, G., Tellex, S.: Comparing robot grasping teleoperation across desktop and virtual reality with ROS reality. In: Proceedings of the International Symposium on Robotics Research (2017)

A Robotic Brush with Surface Tracing Motion Applied to the Face

Yukiko Homma$^{(\boxtimes)}$ and Kenji Suzuki

Artificial Intelligence Laboratory, University of Tsukuba,
1-1-1 Tennodai, Tsukuba 305-8573, Japan
yukiko@ai.iit.tsukuba.ac.jp, kenji@ieee.org

Abstract. The purpose of this research is to develop an assistive robot for applying make-up. The developed robot consists of a frame for the human face and a robotic brush unit. The robotic brush consists of a cosmetic with two motors and a spring. The motors are used to control the direction of the brush on the face, while the spring controls the force of the brush on the face. The robot is designed to safely interact with the human face by reducing the complexity of its components and control method. We tested the robot on a mannequin head to verify its performance and safety. A pilot study with a single participant was also conducted to evaluate the human-robot interaction.

Keywords: Robot assisted make-up · Care robotics
Physical human-robot interaction

1 Introduction

Providing assistance in activities of daily living is one of the critical roles of assistive technology. This includes bathing and showering, personal hygiene, grooming, dressing, toilet hygiene, transferring, and self-feeding. Applying make-up is categorized as part of grooming, and this activity is important especially for women. Women often apply make-up to enhance their beauty and for manner even in the office [1]. Although most of women apply make-up every morning, some consider it inconvenient. One source of dissatisfaction is the amount of time spent applying make-up [1]. Therefore, there is a need to simplify and speed up this process.

The make-up application process can be divided into four steps: (1) skincare, (2) base make-up, (3) partial make-up, and (4) evaluation. The skincare step involves washing the face and applying basic cosmetics. The base make-up step involves applying the base and foundation. The partial make-up step includes applying lip color, cheek color, and eye make-up. The evaluation step involves evaluating the results after executing each of these three steps. Previous research looked into steps (2) and (3) to let the user know the "ideal" make-up [2]. In this research, they developed a system which simulates a predefined "ideal" make-up and informs the user of the difference. Electric face brushes are also used to

© Springer Nature Switzerland AG 2018
S. S. Ge et al. (Eds.): ICSR 2018, LNAI 11357, pp. 513–522, 2018.
https://doi.org/10.1007/978-3-030-05204-1_50

reduce the time taken to wash one's face [3]. As there are few studies dedicated to speeding up the process of applying make-up, we propose a robot-assisted method that can apply make-up quickly and efficiently.

Each face is covered by skin on an individual skull frame. The mechanical characteristics of the skin are softness and resilience [4]. In order to apply make-up and wash the face, assistive devices have to be able to trace the contour of the face without applying too much pressure on the skin based on the skin's mechanical characteristics. This presents some technical challenges because the robot has to be precise and safe for humans.

A related work on human skin contour tracing was proposed by [5] for medical applications. They used a robot with a parallel-link mechanism and six pneumatic actuators to trace the contours of the stomach. Their aim was to create a robot with ultrasonic probe that can move over the stomach without causing discomfort to the human. Contour tracing is achieved via a feedback control mechanism that adjusts the internal pressure of pneumatic actuators in response to the contact pressure. However, the high of degrees-of-freedom (DoF) in [5] made it costly and difficult for applications to an assistive robot for daily life.

Therefore, considering that this robot will be used in daily life, we propose a desktop-sized robot to assist the application of make-up. The robot must be safe for humans and be able to apply make-up quickly and proficiently. In this study, we focus on the application of foundation, which is the first layer of cosmetics applied to the skin in make-up terminology. This is because the foundation is known to have the highest frequency of use [6].

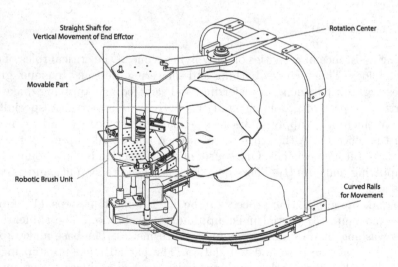

Fig. 1. Overview of the robot

2   Methodology

The robot-assisted make-up application can be roughly divided into two methods:

1. Surface Tracing (make-up is applied with a tool)
2. Spraying (make-up is sprayed from a nozzle)

Although there are the advances in automated spraying by robots [7], this is unsuitable for certain types of cosmetic products owing to the high viscosity and risk of users inhaling the sprayed product. In addition, spraying is different from washing the face. Thus, we focus on the surface tracing method. We propose a desktop-type robot for home use, which has a simple design and control mechanism.

Figure 1 depicts the design of the developed robot. The robot has an inverted U-shaped frame with actuators mounted on curved rails to allow movement around the face. Cosmetic tools, like the foundation brush, are attached to the end effector part.

2.1   Actuator Design

The robotic brush as the end effector is controlled in a cylindrical coordinate system. We used a few motors and an elastic body. This method simplifies the system and can assist in applying make-up. The end effector will be changed for each cosmetic product. A foundation brush was attached to the robot as the end effector for the experiment. In order to follow and track the skin surface, traditional robotic systems usually need to obtain the contact force and/or position feedback [8]. In this study, we utilized a constant spring to trace the skin surface without using any force and the proposed robot controls the position of the end effector by two motors and a constant force spring. The parameters are defined like in Figs. 2 and 3. The position of the end effector P is described by $P(R - r_E, \theta, h)$ in the cylindrical coordinates (r, θ, z). $R - r_E$ is determined by the size of system R and the deformation of the length of the spring and brush r_E. h is determined by the motor.

2.2   Tracing Motion with Constant Force Spring

The robotic brush has two axes of movement, one in the horizontal direction and the other in the vertical direction. The use of curved rails in the horizontal direction ensures that the face is always within reach of the end effector. Therefore, the robot can control its horizontal position and direction at the same time.

The coordinate on the semicircle axis is expressed as θ, the coordinate on the vertical axis is expressed as h. The movements of these coordinate are controlled by motors and the end effector is moved to any θ and h.

Figure 3 describes the mechanical configuration used by the robot. r_F represents the distance from the center of the inverted U-shaped frame to the surface

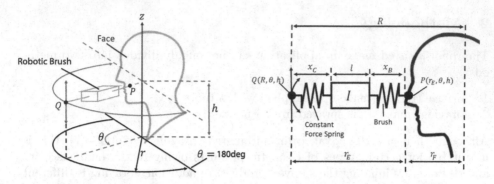

Fig. 2. Axes controlled by motors   **Fig. 3.** Model of the robotic brush

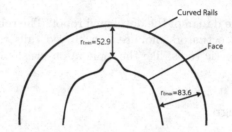

Fig. 4. Distance between face and curved axis

of the face. This variable changes according to the contours of the face, given as $r_F = s(\theta, h)$, where θ (Fig. 2) is the angle of the end effector and h (Fig. 2) is the height of the end effector. r_E represents the length of the end effector and the brush. This consist of the length of the constant force spring x_C, length of brush L, and the length of the brush hairs x_B. Given that R and the total length of r_E and r_F do not change, tracing motions can be performed by adjusting the length of the constant force spring x_C. Therefore, the length of the constant force spring at point $Q(\theta, h, R)$ is

$$x_C = R - (x_B + l) - s(\theta, h) \qquad (1)$$

When Q moves to $Q'(\theta + \Delta\theta, h + \Delta h, R)$ the amount of change of x_C, x_B is expressed as $\Delta x_C, \Delta x_B$, and we can obtain the expression below.

$$x_C + \Delta x_C = R\{(x_B + \Delta x_B) + l\} - s(\theta + \Delta\theta, h + \Delta h) \qquad (2)$$

As Fig. 4 shows, the maximum amount of change of $s(\theta, h)$ is approximately 30 mm. On the other hand, the maximum amount of change of brush hair $\Delta x(Bmax)$ is approximately 5 mm. Because the lengths of R and l are static and the variable range of x_B is too small to fit to $s(\theta, h)$, if we consider $x_B \cong x_B + \Delta x_B$, we obtain

$$\Delta x_C = s(\theta, h) - s(\theta + \Delta\theta, h + \Delta h) \qquad (3)$$

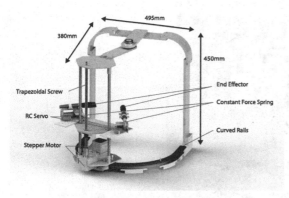

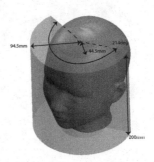

Fig. 5. Composition of system

Fig. 6. Range of motion

Thus, the amount of change of Δx_C have to be controlled depending on that of s.

On the other hand, the magnitude of change of the force from the brush to the face is expressed as $k\Delta x_C$ using an experimental constant variable k. The research proposes an assistive method for make-up application with constant pushing force of the brush onto the face of K_0. Thus, the spring constant k must be changed depending on the magnitude of change in the length of the spring Δx_C and satisfy the formula below.

$$k(x_C)x_C = K_0 \tag{4}$$

For these reasons, we propose a method that uses a constant force spring with sufficient stroke and constant force K.

3 System Design

This robot consists of a cosmetic brush as the end effector, a mechanism for moving the position of the brush, and control circuits. Figure 5 shows the locations of each part and the size of the system. Figure 6 illustrates the range of motion of the system. Figure 7 shows the picture of the actual system.

The mechanism for moving the end effector position has two motors. For vertical movement, we used a stepper motor (PKP244D23A2, ORIENTAL MOTOR Co., Ltd.) and trapezoidal thread (MTSTRW10-322-F15-V6-S10-Q6, MISUMI Group Inc.). For horizontal movement, we used a curved rail (RLGE25-180deg-175.5, Yamazaki Co., Ltd.) and a stepper motor. The curved rail has cleats around its circumference. The stepper motor utilizes a system of three gears to move along the curved rail. The gears were selected such that the distance between their teeth is similar to that between the grooves of the cleats. We used a constant force spring (output: 0.49 N) to control the force and position in the vertical direction to the face. The spring was installed as shown in Fig. 8. A RC servo (SG-90, Tower Pro Pte Ltd.) was installed on the root of the brush for switching between the contact/non-contact states.

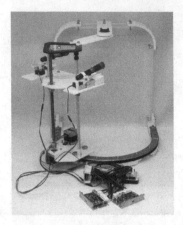

Fig. 7. Picture of actual system

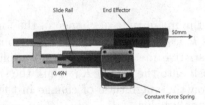

Fig. 8. Figure of robotic brush

We used a microcontroller (Arduino Mega 2560, Arduino Holdings) to control the three motors. Each stepper motor is connected to a motor driver circuit (CVD223FBR-K, Oriental Motor Inc.). The pulse-width modulation (PWM) signals to control the rotation speed and digital signal to control the direction of rotation are given to the motor drive circuit by the controller. To control the RC servo, the controller sends the PWM signal. Figure 1 shows the basic performance of the developed robotic system.

4   Experiment

4.1   Range of Movement

To examine the robot's range of movement, we tested the robot using half the face of a mannequin head. The end effector used for this experiment was a water painting brush. Blue colored water is in the brush. To clarify the range of movement, we make the difference image between bare-skinned mannequin and the result of this application. Figure 9 shows these three pictures.

4.2   Force Applied on the Face

We measured the force applied on the mannequin's face by the developed robotic system. We connected a linear spring (spring constant: 0.098 N/mm) and a con-

Table 1. Basic performance of system

Maximum velocity in vertical direction	25.0 mm/s
Maximum acceleration in vertical direction	370 mm/s^2
Maximum angular velocity in horizontal direction	236 deg/s
Maximum angular acceleration in horizontal direction	350 deg/s^2

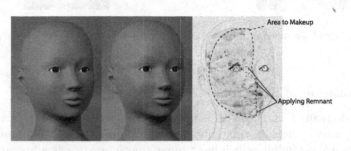

Fig. 9. Mannequin head with food coloring, bare skin (left), spread result (center), difference image (right) (Color figure online)

stant force spring in series. By observing the telescopic motion of the linear spring, we can estimate the output of the constant force spring. In this experiment, the robot traced the mannequin's face six times, from the center of the face ($\theta = 90°$) to the side ($\theta = 15°$) (Fig. 11). The experiment was conducted with two types of brushes, *Brush1* (foundation brush 131, Shiseido Company, Limited) and *Brush2* (liquid foundation brush, Daiso Industries Co., Ltd.). Figure 10 shows the average force and standard deviation. The results show that the output force depends on the characteristics of the brush. We observed a large difference between *Brush1* and *Brush2*. The force applied by Brush1 is almost constant throughout the tracing movements, while the force applied by *Brush2* fluctuates quite widely.

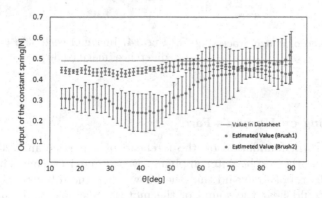

Fig. 10. Force applied to face

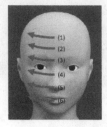

Fig. 11. Path of the tracing motion

Fig. 12. Area used for image processing

4.3 Evaluation of Skin Tone

We applied cream foundation to a mannequin head using the robot with one brush to evaluate the skin tone after make-up application. The mannequin we used is called Bioskindoll, which has similar characteristics as a human face. We applied cream foundation to the center line of the forehead in advance since the robot does not have the ability to supply cosmetic products. The robot spread the foundation in the horizontal direction. The method of the evaluation is by comparing the make-up done by the robot and a human. We used the area in Fig. 12 for image processing, and Fig. 13 shows the method of image processing. We evaluated the effect of application speed using two different operating speeds. Figure 14 shows the image of each skin and difference images. To make it clear, the difference image's contrast is emphasized.

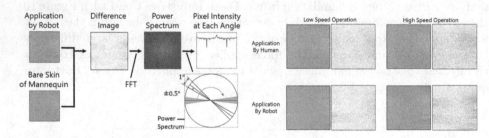

Fig. 13. Method of image processing

Fig. 14. Image of each skin (left) and difference image (right)

4.4 Applying on Human's Face

We applied cream foundation on the forehead of a participant (20 s, female). Figure 16 shows the result. After applying, we obtained the participant's feedback about the robot. She said that she knew when the robot touched her face because she could hear the sound of the motors. She also said that the force touching her face was constant and did not feel uncomfortable.

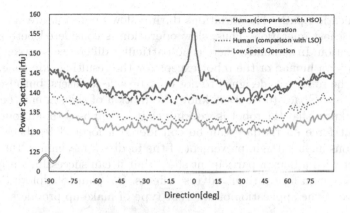

Fig. 15. Average of intensity of pixels per one degree

Fig. 16. Result of applying on human face

5   Discussion and Conclusions

We proposed a robotic brush system with two DoF to assist in make-up application. We provided a simple design that utilizes a cosmetic brush attached to an actuator to apply make-up to the human face. The robot successfully traced about 75% of the area upon which make-up will be applied by a human, which is represented by the dotted line as illustrated in Fig. 9. We calculated the traced area from the captured image. The remaining area will decrease if we increase the size of the end effector. The difference between the results of *Brush1* and *Brush2* is attributed to the difference in the characteristics of the brushes. The two brushes have different brush lengths and densities, which affect the amount of force exerted on the face. The standard deviation is large immediately after *Brush1* touches the face because of the change in the speed of the brush at the beginning of contact. Before the brush touches the face, the speed of the brush in the vertical direction toward the face accelerated owing to the reaction force of the spring. The speed, therefore, depends on the distance between the face and the root of the brush. Because of the difference in speed at the beginning of contact, the position at which the brush settles is different. The pixel intensity of robot application was high at approximately 0° as shown in Fig. 15. This means that the application result is similar to lateral stripes owing to the effect of the application path. The variations during slow operation are smaller than those during fast operation. Thus, slow operation is considered better for uniform application. In summary, there is no particular difference between make-up application by a human or the robot except for the resulting skin tone.

Lastly, the robot was designed to not only be safe for users, but also provide some form of feedback to let users know the motion of the system. This allows the user to know that the robot is working as it is supposed to, although applying constant force on the face can be considered a form of feedback. Further considerations include the improvement of the feedback mechanics. Pilot testing of the robot with a human participant show that it can successfully apply foundation to a human face without adverse effects. We plan to explore the design of assistance in the application of different type of make-up products.

References

1. Life Media: Research Bank Homepage. http://research.lifemedia.jp2010/09/784.html
2. Alashkar, T., Jiang, S., Fu, Y.: Rule-based facial makeup recommendation system. In: 2017 12th IEEE International Conference on Automatic Face & Gesture Recognition (FG 2017), pp. 325–330 (2017)
3. Panasonic: EH-SC65. http://panasonic.jp/face/cleansing/products/EH-SC65.html
4. Asano, A., Suzuki, T., Omata, S.: Mechanical properties of skin and its method of measurement. J. Jpn. Soc. Biorheol. 6(3), 109–117 (1992)
5. Ando, K., Saito, S., Aoki, Y., Ozawa, K., Masuda, K.: Development of probe scan mechanism for echography using pneumatic actuators and its estimation control in contact force on body surface. J. Robot. Soc. Jpn. 28(7), 792–801 (2010)
6. POLA Research Institute of Beauty&Culture. http://www.po-holdings.co.jp/csr/culture/bunken/report/pdf/20171120make2017.pdf
7. Asakawa, N., Takeuchi, Y.: Teachingless spray-painting of sculptured surface by an industrial robot. In: Proceedings of International Conference on Robotics and Automation, vol. 3, pp. 1875–1879 (1997)
8. Yoshikawa, T., Sudou, A.: Dynamic hybrid position/force control of robot manipulators: on-line estimation of unknown constraint. In: Proceedings of IEEE Conference on Robotics and Automation, pp. 1231–1236 (1990)

MagicHand: In-Hand Perception of Object Characteristics for Dexterous Manipulation

Hui Li, Yimesker Yihun, and Hongsheng He[✉]

Wichita State University, Wichita, KS 67260, USA
hongsheng.he@wichita.edu

Abstract. An important challenge in dexterous grasping and manipulation is to perceive the characteristics of an object such as fragility, rigidity, texture, mass and density etc. In this paper, a novel way is proposed to find these important characteristics that help in deciding grasping strategies. We collected Near-infrared (NIR) spectra of objects, classified the spectra to perceive their materials and then looked up the characteristics of the perceived material in a material-to-characteristics table. NIR spectra of six materials including ceramic, stainless steel, wood, cardboard, plastic and glass were collected using SCiO sensor. A Multi-Layer Perceptron (MLP) Neural Networks was implemented to classify the spectra. Also a material-to-characteristics table was established to map the perceived material to their characteristics. The experiment results achieve 99.96% accuracy on material recognition. In addition, a grasping experiment was performed, a robotic hand was trying to grasp two objects which shared similar shapes but made of different materials. The results showed that the robotic hand was able to improve grasping strategies based on characteristics perceived by our algorithm.

Keywords: Object characteristics identification · Dexterous grasping
NIR spectrum · Neural network

1 Introduction

Dexterous grasping is a required ability for many tasks that are expected to be performed by robots, ranging from the assembly of cars in an automobile factory to manipulation of cooking utensils in a kitchen. A successful dexterous grasping system is essential to apply sufficient contact forces to the object and maintain grasp stability which requires the fingertips are placed on the relevant point of an object. To achieve this, two sub-problems are addressed: grasp planning and grasp execution. Considerable progress has been made in development of algorithms for efficient grasp planning [2,3,6]. Algorithms have been implemented to generate grasps in structured or unstructured environments for known, partially known or unknown objects. Despite these achievements, proposing grasp planning algorithms based on characteristics of an object remains a challenge.

© Springer Nature Switzerland AG 2018
S. S. Ge et al. (Eds.): ICSR 2018, LNAI 11357, pp. 523–532, 2018.
https://doi.org/10.1007/978-3-030-05204-1_51

Nowadays most object recognition methods are based on images or videos of an object [5]. An object is first recognized, the shape of that object is determined and then the grasping strategy is selected based on the shape of the object. However, there are two problems with this approach. Firstly, from pictures or videos of an object, useful properties which would affect the grasping such as mass, density, hardness and fragility can be hardly perceived. Secondly, when working in natural environments, there could be situations where the lighting conditions are too dim and dark to get a good picture or video for the algorithms to identify the object.

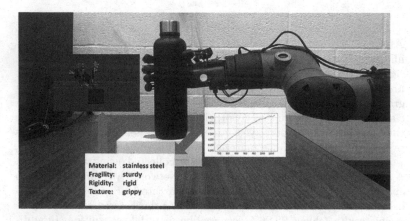

Fig. 1. Deciding grasping strategies based on characteristics of object: SCiO sensor takes NIR spectrum from object, then the material of the object are perceived based on the NIR spectrum and three characteristics are mapped to the perceived material. At last grasping strategies is decided based on characteristics of the object.

Near-infrared spectroscopy (NIR or NIRS) is a low-cost, simple, fast and nondestructive technique to analyze the spectrum of the material on molecular level. Recently, near infrared (NIR) spectroscopy, due to its fast analysis, good precision and accuracy for multi-parameters, is increasingly becoming one of the most efficient analytical tools [1,4,8]. In this paper, we propose a novel way to use NIR spectrum to recognize the properties of objects with specific intent of using the information for dexterous grasping. NIR can work functionally under dark environments and the characteristics of NIR allow to determime properties directly from an object. A multiplayer perceptron (MLP) neural network was implemented to fit the NIR data. A MLP is a class of feed forward artificial neural network which consists of at least three layers of nodes. Except for the input nodes, each node is a neuron that uses a nonlinear activation function. MLP neural network is very efficient for tabular dataset and classification prediction problems which fits the problem in this paper very well.

This technique could be helpful in many social aspects. For example, in manufacturing industry, one of the biggest issues in manufacturing and automation is safety. Knowing the characteristics of an object before hand, a robot hand is able to perfrom different grasp strategies on different objects. Much lower grasp force will apply to a human hand than a metal part. In this way many safety issues can be solved.

2 Characteristics Recognition

In this section, we describe the complete workflow of the proposed system step by step (Fig. 1). In Sect. 2.1, a spectral pre-processing method is described. A new Multilayer Perceptron (MLP) neutral network is implemented to classify the data by materials of the objects in Sect. 2.2. In Sect. 2.3, a material-to-characteristics table was established to map characteristics to perceived material.

2.1 Data Pre-processing

The goal of pre-processing is to remove extraneous signals such as background offsets and noise while enhancing spectral features. However, in this work, all the data that used for training and validating the algorithm are collected by hand with a light proof shade (Fig. 2a) in an ideal environment. The background offsets and noise could be neglected. In this case, the data set is standardized to fit the MLP neutral network. This step is to constrain all the data in the same scale to improve learning ability of an algorithm.

a) Experiment data acquisition   *b) Practical data acquisition*

Fig. 2. Spectrum acquisition of experiment spectrum (dataset A) and practical spectrum (dataset B)

2.2 Materials Classification

Multilayer Perceptron (MLP) neutral network is a classical and common type of artificial neutral network. This network is flexible, fast and especially efficient for tabular datasets and classification prediction problems. All these features fit the problem in this paper very well.

In this paper, a six layers MLP neutral network was developed specifically for the NIR datasets. Rectified Linear Units (ReLU) is used as activation function in the first five layers to train the network. In the first layer, instead of 331 neurons (number of features in data set), 2^{10} neurons was used so that more parameters can be generated to improve the accuracy. In the next four layers, for each layer, the number of neurons were decreased by half ($2^{10}, 2^9, 2^8, 2^5$) to further calibrate the model. In the last layer (the output layer) a Softmax function and six neurons are used to classify the data.

2.3   Characteristics Mapping

In this part, in order to map the characteristics of a material, a material-to-characteristics table was established base on Rao's object dataset (Table 1). Three characteristics including fragility, rigidity and texture were extracted and assigned to each corresponding materials. After the material of an object is perceived, Three characteristics (fragility, rigidity and texture) values are mapped to that material. These information will then feed into Rao's grasping algorithm to improve the grasping strategies.

Table 1. Characteristics of material mapping list

Materials	Fragility	Rigidity	Texture
Wood	Sturdy	Rigid	Rough
Glass	Medium	Rigid	Smooth
Plastic	Medium	Soft	Smooth
Ceramic	Sturdy	Rigid	Slippery
Cardboard	Medium	Rigid	Rough
Stainless steel	Sturdy	Rigid	Grippy

3   Experiment Evaluation

In this section, we investigated the accuracy of the material detection and properties mapping using the proposed method. The experiment uses two datasets to evaluate the developed algorithm in real world environment. The purpose of this experiment is to evaluate our algorithm in real world environment.

a. SCIO Sensor   b. AR 10 Robotic Hand   c. Sawyer Robotic Arm   d. Experiment Set

Fig. 3. Equipment set: (a) SCiO sensor: a small, hand-held near-infrared spectrometer which can detect signature on molecular level. (b) AR10 robotic hand: a lightweight, reliable, powerful, servo-actuated robotic hand with 10 degree of freedom (DOF). (c) Sawyer robotic arm: a high performance robot arm with 7 degree of freedom (DOF). (d) Experiment set: the AR10 hand is attached to Sawyer arm and the SCiO sensor is fixed to wrist of the arm.

3.1   Experiment Setup

In this experiment, a SCiO sensor (Fig. 3a), an AR10 robotic hand (Fig. 3b) and a Sawyer robotic arm (Fig. 3c) are assembled together as shown in Fig. 3d. An object holder was attached to a fixed point on the work desk. A DELL OPTIPLEX 9010 workstation was used to control the whole system. On the software side, Robot Operating System (ROS), Sawyer SDK, AR10 control package, python and SCiO Lab were used in this experiment.

3.2   Datasets

In this paper, two datasets were collected. Dataset A is collected manually in an ideal environment, this dataset is used to train the MLP neutral network. Dataset B is collected by robotic hand in a practical work environment. This dataset is used to evaluate the performance of the algorithm in real world environments. For both datasets, NIR spectra of six different materials including ceramic (label 0), stainless steel (label 1), wood (label 2), cardboard (label 3), plastic (label 4) and glass (label 5) were collected. Each spectrum includes 331 features which are reflectance intensities of the surface of the object from wavelength 740 nm to 1071 nm. Figures 4 and 5 show the spectrum of the two datasets.

Sample Fields. In dataset A, we collected ten objects each for ceramic, wood, plastic and cardboard, nine objects for stainless steel and five objects for glass. For each object, ten samples were selected for spectrum collection. For samples of large size such as plates, stainless steel pans and cardboard boxes, around 30 scans were collected on each sample. Fewer scans were taken on small samples such as spoons, forks and plastic cups. In total, 15936 spectra were collected and most of samples were objects of daily use.

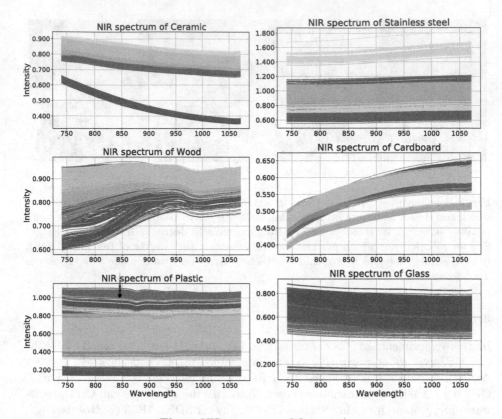

Fig. 4. NIR spectrum of dataset A

In dataset B, two objects for each material are selected. For each object two samples were chosen and five scans were taken from each sample. In total, there were twelve objects, twelve samples and 60 spectra in dataset B.

Sample Acquisition. The data collecting system for dataset A includes a SCiO sensor, a light proof shade and a calibration device. All data in dataset A is collected by hand in a lab environment (room temperature 75° F degrees). While acquisition, the sample was placed steadily on a table in the lab. The shade was attached to the sensor. While scanning, the sensor was kept as close to the surface of the sample as possible (Fig. 2a). The acquisition time was around two seconds for each scan. Each sample was scanned about 30 times in different locations. The senor was re-calibrated after scanning each sample.

Dataset B was acquired using the same data collection approach except that the SCiO sensor was attached to the wrist of Sawyer arm (Fig. 3d). An object holder was placed on a fixed point and the sample was placed on the object holder. The spectrum data of that sample was collected using the robot hand (Fig. 2b). Five different scans were taken from each sample and the sensor was calibrated each time it finished scanning a sample.

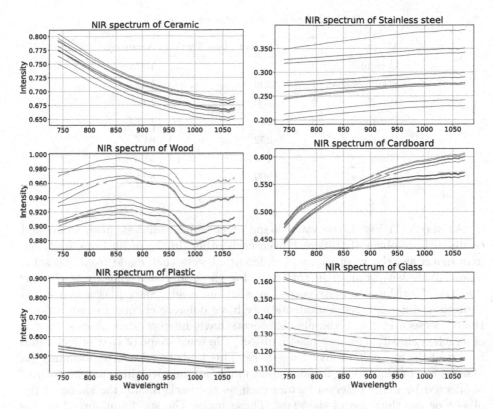

Fig. 5. NIR spectrum of dataset B

3.3   Results and Discussion

Evaluating the Classifier on Ideal Dataset. The algorithm was trained and evaluated using the spectra in an ideal dataset (dataset A) which was collected manually. First, we extract one object from each material in the dataset. This part of the data (1803 scans) was separated and used as the validation set to evaluate the final performance of the classifier. The rest of data in dataset A was divided into training and testing set. 70% of the data was selected randomly to train the network and the rest 30% of the data was used as the testing set. We tuned the hyper-parameters as follows: 64 batch size, 50 epochs and ADAM optimizer with 0.0001 learning rate. The algorithm achieved overall 99.96% accuracy.

To evaluate the performance of the network, the pre-extracted validation data (1803 scans), which was completely new for the algorithm, was fed into the network. A total 1609 correct predictions were achieved by the algorithm (Table 2). The algorithm made perfect predictions (100% accuracy) on ceramic, stainless steel, wood and cardboard and a good predictions on plastic (84% accuracy). However, predictions on glass (51.3% accuracy) were not satisfactory.

Table 2. Predicted results for dataset A

Material	Label	Correct classification	Accuracy
Ceramic	0	303	100%
Stainless steel	1	300	100%
Wood	2	300	100%
Cardboard	3	300	100%
Plastic	4	252	84%
Glass	5	154	51.3%
Total result		1609	89.2%

As shown in Fig. 4, the wave shape of ceramic, stainless steel, wood and cardboard are obviously different from each other. In the mean time, for those four materials, the wave shape of different objects that made from the same material are very similar. In this case, for these four materials, it is obvious that the algorithm can make correct predictions easily. Since plastic is a broad definition, different plastic products may have different chemical compositions. Hence, as seen in Fig. 4, the plastic objects have different wave shapes. In this case, when classifying a new plastic object, the wave shape of that object could be out of the algorithm's knowledge base. This leads to a lower performance on plastics recognition. Being a transparent material, the spectrum of a glass object is affected by many external factors such as the background, the shape of the object or the thickness of the glass. These makes the spectrum spread over a wider range which leads to mis-classification.

Table 3. Predicted results for dataset B

Material	Label	Correct classification	Accuracy
Ceramic	0	10	100%
Stainless steel	1	10	100%
Wood	2	10	100%
Cardboard	3	10	100%
Plastic	4	10	100%
Glass	5	10	100%
Total result		60	100%

Evaluating the Classifier on Practical Dataset. The proposed algorithm was evaluated on a practical dataset (dataset B). Using the data collected by robotic hand, the prediction result (Table 3) achieved a 100% (60/60) accuracy. There are two reasons that may lead to this perfect result. Firstly, the light proof shade greatly reduced external noises which is the largest difference between a practical and an ideal environment. Secondly, there were only sixty testing samples in this experiment, As the number of testing samples increase, the accuracy will be more practical. However, the current result is adequate to show that this algorithm is capable of working in a practical environment.

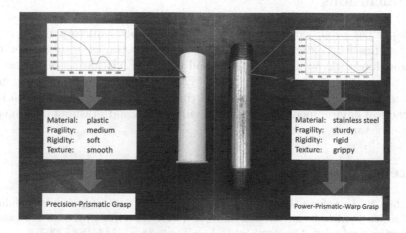

Fig. 6. Different grasping methods based on different characteristics

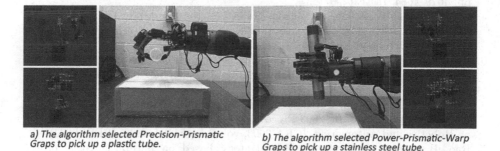

a) The algorithm selected Precision-Prismatic Graps to pick up a plastic tube.

b) The algorithm selected Power-Prismatic-Warp Graps to pick up a stainless steel tube.

Fig. 7. The algorithm selected Precision-Prismatic Grasp to pick up a plastic tube

Characteristics Mapping. In this part, a grasping experiment was performed on two objects, one plastic tube and one stainless steel tube. These two tubes have similar shapes but different characteristics (Fig. 6). From the characteristics we can infer that the two tubes may require different grasping methods. According to Rao's work [7], Precision-Prismatic Grasp (Fig. 7a) should be used to pick up the plastic tube and Power-Prismatic-Warp Grasp (Fig. 7b) should be applied to stainless steel tube. In the experiment, the spectra of the tubes were collected by the robot hand and fed into our system to perceive their materials.

Then characteristics were mapped to each material. Based on the characteristics, the robotic hand applied Precision-Prismatic Grasp on plastic tube and Power-Prismatic-Warp Grasp on stainless steel tube which matched our expectations.

4   Conclusions

This paper has proposed a novel way to use NIR spectrum to perceive object characteristics for dexterous manipulation. The experiment results show that our algorithm works well on both ideal and practical NIR datasets on material recognition and characteristics mapping. The proposed algorithm shows great performances on material recognition and characteristics mapping in both ideal and practical environments. Our method will greatly aid grasping decisions for dexterous grasping by robots.

References

1. Balabin, R.M., Safieva, R.Z., Lomakina, E.I.: Comparison of linear and nonlinear calibration models based on near infrared (NIR) spectroscopy data for gasoline properties prediction. Chemom. Intell. Lab. Syst. **88**(2), 183–188 (2007)
2. Brost, R.C.: Automatic grasp planning in the presence of uncertainty. Int. J. Robot. Res. **7**(1), 3–17 (1988)
3. Goldfeder, C., Allen, P.K., Lackner, C., Pelossof, R.: Grasp planning via decomposition trees. In: 2007 IEEE International Conference on Robotics and Automation, pp. 4679–4684. IEEE (2007)
4. Li, J., Huang, W., Zhao, C., Zhang, B.: A comparative study for the quantitative determination of soluble solids content, pH and firmness of pears by ViS/NIR spectroscopy. J. Food Eng. **116**(2), 324–332 (2013)
5. Lowe, D.G.: Object recognition from local scale-invariant features. In: 1999 the Proceedings of the Seventh IEEE International Conference on Computer Vision, vol. 2, pp. 1150–1157. IEEE (1999)
6. Miller, A.T., Knoop, S., Christensen, H.I., Allen, P.K.: Automatic grasp planning using shape primitives. In: 2003 Proceedings of the IEEE International Conference on Robotics and Automation, ICRA 2003, vol. 2, pp. 1824–1829. IEEE (2003)
7. Rao, B.: Learning robotic grasping strategy based on natural-language object descriptions (2018)
8. Wilson, B.K., Kaur, H., Allan, E.L., Lozama, A., Bell, D.: A new handheld device for the detection of falsified medicines: demonstration on falsified artemisinin-based therapies from the field. Am. J. Trop. Med. Hyg. **96**(5), 1117–1123 (2017)

Robots and Human Touch in Care: Desirable and Non-desirable Robot Assistance

Jaana Parviainen(✉) ⓘ, Tuuli Turja ⓘ, and Lina Van Aerschot ⓘ

Faculty of Social Sciences, University of Tampere, Tampere, Finland
{jaana.parviainen, tuuli.turja,
lina.van.aerschot}@uta.fi

Abstract. Care robots are often seen to introduce a risk to human, touch based care. In this study, we analyze care workers' opinions on robot assistance in elderly services and reflect them to the idea of embodied relationship between a caregiver, care receiver and technology. Our empirical data consists of a survey for professional care workers (n = 3800), including registered and practical nurses working in elderly care. The questionnaire consisted scenarios of robot assistance in care work and in elderly services and the respondents were asked to evaluate whether they see them as desirable. The care workers were significantly more approving of robot assistance in lifting heavy materials compared to moving patients. Generally, the care workers were reserved towards the idea of utilizing autonomous robots in tasks that typically involve human touch, such as assisting the elderly in the bathroom. Stressing the importance of presence and touch in human care, we apply the ideas of phenomenology of the body to understand the envisioned robot-human constellations in care work.

Keywords: Care robots · Elderly care · Human-robot interaction · Touch · Triadic care

1 Introduction

Some of the critical voices have brought up concerns of care technologies and suggested that they may create of risk of dehumanizing and depersonalizing care and objectifying the care receivers by jeopardizing their individuality and subjectivity. For example, Barnard and Sandelowski [1] have suggested that clinical and sterile environments characterized by standardization and strict regulation may fail to uphold and support human-centered care. In these kinds of environments with highly palpable and audible presence of equipment, people may sometimes become treated as extensions of the machinery. However, many care workers, nurses and caregivers welcome tools, techniques, equipment and robots that can assist them in work tasks, especially in physically demanding ones. Hence, there seems to be some tension between the ideals of 'touch-based' care and 'technology-driven' care, or 'humanistic' care and 'techno-logic frameworks' of care [2, 3].

We examine professional care workers' opinions on robot assistance in care work and specifically in elderly services. We introduce on one hand in which tasks robotic assistance is perceived as an acceptable idea and, on the other hand, care workers

© Springer Nature Switzerland AG 2018
S. S. Ge et al. (Eds.): ICSR 2018, LNAI 11357, pp. 533–540, 2018.
https://doi.org/10.1007/978-3-030-05204-1_52

evaluations of undesirable robotic assistance in elderly care. In this paper, we will analyze these findings with a phenomenological approach and discuss the triadic relationship between a caregiver, care receiver and technology. Drawing upon the phenomenology of the body and Latour's [4] concept of *ensemble,* we develop a new approach to robot care as an embodied practice, triadic care.

2 The Importance of Touching in Elderly Care

Touching in care work is inevitable, because clients are dependent on nurses for many activities in daily living: washing, feeding, lifting, dressing, and other similar type of care activities that are related to the wellbeing and medical treatment of older, disabled or sick people. Care workers may use different forms of touch depending on their work tasks and communication with clients. Touching can be functional, purposeful and instrumental when lifting or feeding the client but still carry affective intentions, such as, comforting, reassuring and encouraging. Whether nursing touch is comforting, i.e. helping the patient to cope with the illness and its related stressors, or protective, protecting the patient from physical harm, the nurse's touch is supposed to be "professional touch". From the ethical point of view, professional touch refers to a special professional and ethical attitude in which the client's body is cared for and attended mindfully and respectfully but not too personal, emotional or intimate manners. Touch is also sharply separated from violence such as sexual abuse and harassment [5]. This implies that certain type of touching is considered appropriate in some social contexts and with some body parts, but decidedly inappropriate in others.

Body work is an essential part of care profession for it involves direct, hands-on activities, handling, assessing and manipulating bodies [6]. Professional touch in human care can take different forms. Depending on work tasks and social contexts, we can talk about instrumental touch [7], therapeutic touch [8] and expressive touch [9]. All tactile communication is reciprocal in nature: when a nurse touches a client s/he also being touched by the client [10]. Touching a lived body, a care worker reflects usually internally how her/his touch is being felt by the other body.

Being touched by others or being seen by others is considered especially crucial to the wellbeing of babies but also elderly people [11]. However, according to Langland and Panicussi [12], the more unable to communicate elderly people are due to, for example, memory disorders or other cognitive impairments, the more touch deprived they become. Yet, people with communicative or social restrictions often interpret feelings and affects that touching mediates and experience pleasure or displeasure within physical care practices [13].

Not all touching in care work is pleasurable for care workers or clients. In problematic situations—when a patient is violent, sexually aroused or psychotic—a care worker may need to call for colleagues or safeguards to help. In nurse–client relationships, feelings of disgust, shame, guilt or embarrassment are also common. These negative feelings are not seen to fit into the idea of professional nurse behavior. Some tasks like removing feces and changing diapers include bodily co-presence [14]. These tasks can be felt disgusting but simultaneously raise feelings of empathy.

Touching becomes a more complex phenomenon when new technologies intervene in nurse–client relationships. Robotics for lifting patients out of their bed or into the bath, for example, do not necessarily mean that direct touching the patients has become more limited. New equipment may be used with a minimum of human effort but still require human presence to support, surveille or encourage the activity.

3 Desirable and Non-desirable Robot Assistance

Methods
To analyze the acceptance of robot assistance in care tasks we used a survey data collected from professional care givers (n = 3800). The data was collected during the fall 2016 and was based on a random sample of Finnish elderly care workers. The questionnaire included multiple choice questions about educational and occupational background, experiences with assistive tools in healthcare and attitudes toward robots presented in a variety of care work scenarios. Regarding the work scenarios we used a question from used in Eurobarometer studies including also the response scale from 1 to 10 (see appendix A for specific questions). Assessing these scenarios respondents scaled firstly the usability of robotic assistance in care work (α 0.93) and secondly robotic assistance in elderly services. The latter were further categorized into autonomous robot assistance scenarios (α 0.97) and tele-operated robot assistance scenarios (α 0.95). We present our preliminary and descriptive results in percentages, means (M) and differences between means (t). The statistical difference between single assessments of robot-assisted work scenarios are observed by confidence intervals of 95%.

Results
Most of the respondents were women (95%) working in public sector (78%). They were typically practical nurses (56%) or registered nurses (35%), the rest being for example head nurses or physiotherapists (9%). The age of the respondents varied from 17 to 70, the average being 46.5 years. Healthcare technology was fairly familiar to the respondents; safety phone to 71%, meal automaton to 11%, and Paro seal to 8%, to list few.

Care work consists a variety of tasks and physical labor is often a central part of the activities [15]. The questionnaire presented scenarios of care tasks performed or assisted by a robot. The variety of scenarios emphasized tasks that include body work. Firstly, respondents were to evaluate how comfortable they felt about the idea of robot assisting them in moving or lifting patients and heavy materials and also assisting them in threatening situations at work. Secondly, they were to evaluate how useful they perceive robot assistance in elderly care scenarios such as helping a physically impaired resident to move around in the home and in the bathroom.

The respondents were most comfortable with the idea of a robot helping them with physically straining work. Figure 1 shows that care workers were significantly more approving of robot assistance in lifting heavy materials compared to lifting patients. Regarding lifting or moving patients, the respondents were more comfortable with the idea of a separate robotic assistant compared to an exoskeleton for a worker to wear. However, moving patients using an autonomous stretcher was remarkably less welcomed compared to lifting patients with any robotic assistance. Summarizing these results, care workers see robots desirable primarily in other tasks than patient work. In addition, if robots are used in patient work, the care workers prefer situations where a care worker is present.

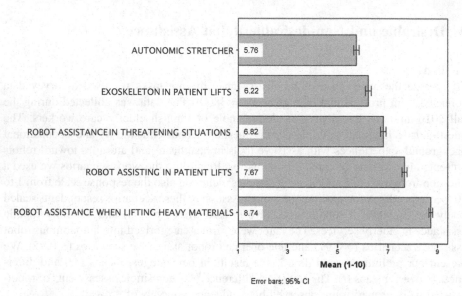

Fig. 1. Acceptance of robot assistance at work, means on a scale from 1 to 10

Care workers saw potential in robots assisting in threatening situations. This is not surprising as studies have shown that care workers have to endure and be prepared for aggression of patients and their close-ones [6, 16, 17]. In care scenarios touching is usually seen as something that is happening in care workers' terms. Here the respondents suggest that robotic applications could be also suitable in protective use where care workers are targets of unwanted contact.

When asked specifically about which elderly services could use robotic assistance, the respondents felt easier to see the benefits in tele-operated robots ($M = 5.45$) compared to autonomous robots ($M = 5.16$; $t = -6.13$; $p < .001$). Figure 2 presents the means for some of the scenarios. Out of these scenarios, care workers were mostly willing to see robots in situations where physical contact is not necessary, namely demonstrating light exercises to an elderly person. This kind of entertainment-like coaching by a robot was perceived more feasible than tele operated physiotherapy with a therapist. In addition, most of the respondents did not consider autonomous robots conducting physiotherapy suitable. The robotic assistance in bathing, dressing and in the toilet were met with a similar refusal. However, general support in moving around the residence was viewed more positively. Especially a robot which is remotely operated and monitored by care professionals could be used in the homes of older people as an assistants for moving, walking and getting up.

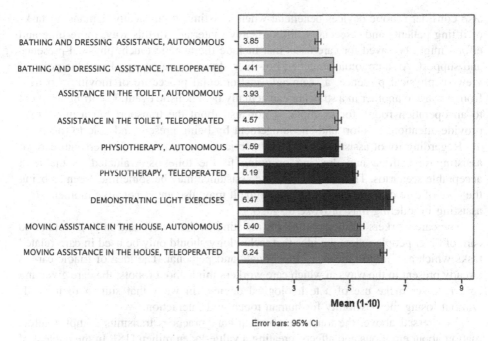

BATHING AND DRESSING ASSISTANCE, AUTONOMOUS — 3.85

BATHING AND DRESSING ASSISTANCE, TELEOPERATED — 4.41

ASSISTANCE IN THE TOILET, AUTONOMOUS — 3.93

ASSISTANCE IN THE TOILET, TELEOPERATED — 4.57

PHYSIOTHERAPY, AUTONOMOUS — 4.59

PHYSIOTHERAPY, TELEOPERATED — 5.19

DEMONSTRATING LIGHT EXERCISES — 6.47

MOVING ASSISTANCE IN THE HOUSE, AUTONOMOUS — 5.40

MOVING ASSISTANCE IN THE HOUSE, TELEOPERATED — 6.24

Mean (1-10)

Error bars: 95% CI

Fig. 2. Acceptance of robot assistance in elderly care, means on a scale from 1 to 10

4 Towards Triadic Care

Care ethics is closely connected to professional touching and the physical presence of care workers with clients. Medical technologies have often been considered extensions of the nurse's body, but in the context of assisting robotics, the robot can be seen as a technological medium between the care worker and the client. Turkle [18] and van Wynsberghe [19] claim that embodied practices in human care, even if technologically assisted, always require a reciprocal interaction between the care-receiver and care-giver. Instead of focusing merely on the nurse–patient relationship, we call our approach "triadic care", which captures an idea of human-robot-human interaction instead of human-robot interaction. The notion of triadic care identifies the different roles of the care worker, care receiver and robot in care praxis. In the middle of this care triangle there are professional touching and embodied practices such as lifting, bathing, feeding, moving the care receiver and delivering medications/food/sheets to the room including social and cultural context of care settings. Different devices, tools and technologies can be used to assist in these tasks or even to conduct them autonomously but the devices are always in relation to the persons taking part in care giving and receiving activities.

The nurses' opinions on useful and acceptable robot assistance may be seen to oppose the ideas of standardized, technologized care and endorse the ideas of human dignity and individuality. Using here the triadic approach to care, nurses see robotics useful to distance and protect themselves physically from aggressive patients. They also consider robotic devices beneficial when assisting in physically demanding tasks of lifting patients and, especially, lifting heavy materials. In this way, more time and efforts might be saved for care tasks that include therapeutic touch, physical presence and support. An autonomic stretcher, however, draws more doubts. From the point of view of physical presence, a seemingly instrumental procedure of moving a patient from a ward to another in a stretcher can actually be a holistic event. Escorting a patient to an operation room, for example, is not just about the transport but a nurse may provide attention, comfort and encouragement by being present and able to touch.

Regarding robot assistance in elderly services, using a robot for personal care of assisting in bathing and dressing or going to the toilet is evaluated as the least acceptable scenarios. This kind of intimate assistance may be sometimes seen as being the core of care even though at the same time it may also entail negative moments (i.e. assisting in toileting may provoke disgust).

The care workers opinions on robots assisting in their work and in tasks related to care of older people reflect the idea that technology should only be used in care-related tasks which are not too intimate, affectionate and personal. The idea of triadic care is already present in the ways in which care workers think about robots: the care giver and care receiver make use of a technological devices in ways that suit to their needs without losing the possibility for human touch and interaction.

As stressed above, the touch involved in care practices transmits complex information about emotions and affects, creating a value-laden milieu [18]. In the context of triadic care, robotics is characterized as an interpersonal intervention that can develop a partnership and reciprocity in the nurse–client relationship.

5 Discussion

Identifying the significance of touch associated with the use of robots in elderly care is a necessary first step toward ethical discussions that can address senior persons' intimacy, individuality, autonomy, and rights to touch and being touched. More research is needed to examine how robotics will change nurses' working conditions and capabilities of using their touch in human care and to what extent can human touch be replaced by a robot.

Taking seriously the idea that touching and presence are crucial for the wellbeing of elderly people, we do not see the development of robots should aim at replacing caregivers. We suggest, as many other researchers [20–22], that robots should be designed to improve the quality of care rather than just to save money in the health *care sector*. When a care robots becomes a part of the network the distribution of roles and responsibilities as well as the care processes will change [19, 23]. If robotics does automate some of the tasks in human care, it is necessary to consider how to arrange mediating interdependencies within care relationships. van Wynsberghe [19] suggests an approach of value sensitive design and taking the ethical considerations as the first priority in the design process of care robots. She states that technologies are products of our culture and built on societal values and norms. Yet, technologies also change our culture and have far reaching impact on our societies: "social norms, values and morals find their way into technologies both implicitly and explicitly and act to reinforce beliefs or to alter beliefs and practices" [19]. The use of independently functioning robots, even for some tasks, would fundamentally alter relations between caregivers and care receivers and nurses' care practices in elderly care.

Appendix A

In the last section of the questionnaire there are examples of care work tasks, which could, in principle, be done with robots or done with robot assistance. Please rate every scenario by how comfortable would you feel about robot assisting you with that specific task.

1 = very uncomfortable...........................10 = very comfortable

- Robotic and autonomous stretcher
- Robot moving heavy materials or large amount of goods
- Robot assisting in moving or lifting a patient
- Robo-power suit (exoskeleton) for a care worker to wear while moving or lifting a patient
- Robot assisting in threatening situations

In what kind of tasks would you consider robot assistance as useful in elderly services?

1 = not at all useful...............................10 = very useful

(a) Human-operated robots:

- Assisting the elderly move around the house (i.e. lifting)
- Escorting the elderly outside the home (i.e. going to a store)
- Assisting in bathing and dressing up
- Assisting in the toilet
- In physiotherapy

(b) Autonomous robots:

- Assisting the elderly move around the house (i.e. lifting)
- Escorting the elderly outside the home (i.e. going to a store)
- Assisting in bathing and dressing up
- Assisting in the toilet
- In physiotherapy

References

1. Barnard, A., Sandelowski, M.: The shaping of organizational routines and the distal patient in assisted reproductive technologies. Nurs. Inq. **16**(3), 241–250 (2001)
2. McConnell, E.A.: The coalescence of technology and humanism in nursing practice: it doesn't just happen and it doesn't come easily. Holist. Nurs. Pract. **12**, 23–30 (1998)

3. May, C., Fleming, C.: The professional imagination: narrative and the symbolic boundaries between medicine and nursing. J. Adv. Nurs. **25**, 1094–1100 (1997)
4. Latour, B.: We Have Never Been Modern. Harvard University Press, Cambridge (1993). (Trans. C. Porter)
5. Paterson, M.: The Senses of Touch: Haptics, Affects and Technologies. Berg, Oxford (2007)
6. Twigg, J., Wolkowitz, C., Cohen, R.L., Nettleton, S.: Conceptualising body work in health and social care. Sociol. Health Illn. **33**, 171–188 (2011)
7. Routsalo, P.: Physical touch in nursing studies: a literature review. J. Adv. Nurs. **30**(4), 843–850 (1999)
8. Bullough, V.L., Bullough, B.: Should nurses practice therapeutic touch? Should nursing schools teach therapeutic touch? J. Prof. Nurs. **14**(4), 254–257 (1998)
9. Belgrave, M.: The effect of expressive and instrumental touch on the behavior states of older adults with late-stage dementia of the Alzheimer's type and on music therapist's perceived rapport. J. Music Ther. **46**(2), 132–146 (2009)
10. Merleau-Ponty, M.: The Visible and the Invisible, Followed by Working Notes. Northwestern University Press, Evanston (1968). (Trans. A. Lingis)
11. Routasalo, P., Isola, A.: The right to touch and to be touched. Nurs. Ethics **3**, 73–84 (1996)
12. Langland, R.M., Panicucci, C.L.: Effects of touch on communication with elderly confused clients. J. Gerontol. Nurs. **8**(3), 152–155 (1982)
13. Bush, E.: The use of human touch to improve the well-being of older adults: a holistic nursing intervention. J. Holist. Nurs. **19**(3), 256–270 (2001)
14. Wolkowitz, C.: The social relations of body work. Work Employ Soc. **16**(3), 497–510 (2002)
15. Cohen, R.L.: Time, space and touch at work: body work and labour process (re)organisation. In: Twigg, J., Wolkowitz, C., Cohen, R.L., Nettleton, S. (eds.) Body Work in Health and Social Care: Critical Themes, New Agendas. Blackwell, Hoboken (2011)
16. Banerjee, A., Daly, T., Armstrong, P., Szebehely, M., Armstrong, H., Lafrance, S.: Structural violence in long-term, residential care for older people: comparing Canada and Scandinavia. Soc. Sci. Med. **74**(3), 390–398 (2012). https://doi.org/10.1016/j.socscimed. 2011.10.037
17. Hintikka, N., Saarela, K.L.: Accidents at work related to violence – analysis of Finnish national accident statistics database. Saf. Sci. **48**(4), 517–525 (2010)
18. Turkle, S.: Alone Together: Why We Expect More from Technology and Less from Each Other. Basic Books, New York (2012)
19. van Wynsberghe, A.: Designing robots for care: care centered value-sensitive design. Sci. Eng. Ethics **19**, 407–433 (2013)
20. Jenkins, J., Draper, H.: Care, monitoring, and companionship: views on care robots from older people and their carers. Int. J. Soc. Robot. **7**(5), 673–683 (2015)
21. Alaiad, A., Zhou, L.N.: The determinants of home healthcare robots adoption: an empirical investigation. Int. J. Med. Inf. **83**(11), 825–840 (2014)
22. Kristoffersson, A., Coradeschi, S., Loutfi, A., Severinson-Eklundh, K.: An exploratory study of health professionals' attitudes about robotic telepresence technology. J. Technol. Hum. Serv. **29**(4), 263–283 (2011)
23. Verbeek, P.: Morality in design; design ethics and the morality of technological artifacts. In: Vermaas, P., Kroes, P., Light, A., Moore, S. (eds.) Philosophy and Design: From Engineering to Architecture, pp. 91–102. Springer, Berlin (2008). https://doi.org/10.1007/978-1-4020-6591-0_7

The Effects of Driving Agent Gaze Following Behaviors on Human-Autonomous Car Interaction

Nihan Karatas[(⊠)], Shintaro Tamura, Momoko Fushiki, and Michio Okada

Interaction and Communication Design Lab, Toyohashi University of Technology,
Toyohashi, Aichi 441-8580, Japan
{karatas,tamura,fushiki17}@icd.cs.tut.ac.jp, okada@tut.jp
http://www.icd.cs.tut.ac.jp/

Abstract. Autonomous cars have been gaining attention as a future transportation option due to an envisioning of a reduction in human error and achieving a safer, more energy efficient and more comfortable mode of transportation. However, eliminating human involvement may impact the usage of autonomous cars negatively because of the impairment of perceived safety, and the enjoyment of driving. In order to achieve a reliable interaction between an autonomous car and a human operator, the car should evince intersubjectivity, implying that it possesses the same intentions as those of the human operator. One critical social cue for human to understand the intentions of others is eye gaze behaviour. This paper proposes an interaction method that utilizes the eye gazing behaviours of an in-car driving agent platform that reflects the intentions of a simulated autonomous car that holds the potential of enabling human operators to perceive the autonomous car as a social entity. We conducted a preliminary experiment to investigate whether an autonomous car will be perceived as possessing the same intentions as a human operator through gaze following behaviours of the driving agents as compared to the conditions of random gazing as well as when not using the driving agents at all. The results revealed that gaze-following behaviour of the driving agents induces an increase in the perception of intersubjectivity. Also, the proposed interaction method demonstrated that the autonomous system was perceived as safer and more enjoyable.

Keywords: Autonomous car · Driving agent · Gaze following
Intentional stance · Social presence · Safety

1 Introduction

Recently, a great deal of research has been conducted on highly autonomous vehicles which make their own driving decisions, minimizing human interventions, with the vision of decreasing human error and achieving a safer, more energy efficient and more comfortable mode of transportation [1]. However, eliminating

© Springer Nature Switzerland AG 2018
S. S. Ge et al. (Eds.): ICSR 2018, LNAI 11357, pp. 541–550, 2018.
https://doi.org/10.1007/978-3-030-05204-1_53

human involvement from driving might threaten the trust and perceived safety, and suppress a drivers' joy of driving which in turn lead to a refusal to use autonomous cars.

Researches have demonstrated that an increase in perceived anthropomorphism positively affects perceived trust of autonomous vehicles [2,3]. However, in these studies, the interaction between the system and the human is still not natural nor intuitive due to the system lacking the exhibition of continuous sociability. We believe that through building a reciprocal interaction between a human operator and an autonomous car, where the parties can perceive each other as social entities and understand each other's intentions, a reliable interaction can be established.

Fig. 1. A conceptual diagram of the NAMIDA platform. It consists of one base unit containing three movable heads with one degree of freedom each (*left*). The base unit of NAMIDA, which attaches to the dashboard of a car is within the peripheral vision of the driver (*right*).

Intentional stance is a strategy for understanding an entity's behaviour by treating it as a rational entity whose actions are governed by its beliefs and desires [4]. Intentional stance is closely related to social presence, which defines the degree of awareness of the other entity in an interaction and the sense of access to the other's mind [5]. Intersubjectivity emerges as humans feel that others feel or act on as if they have the same intentions [6]. This intersubjective sharing is critical, because it creates a shared space of common psychological ground that enables human-like cooperative communication through comprehending each other's intentions.

One social interaction for humans is to adopt the intentional stance of others using the ability to interpret the eye gazing of others and then interpret their actions [4]. Researchers in cognitive science and developmental psychology consider gaze following to be one of the essential components in social interaction and learning [7]. It also contributes to understanding of what others think, feel and intend to do [8,9].

A number of studies in Human-Robot Interaction and Human-Agent Interaction have shown that with eye gazing behaviours, robots can gain the ability to give information to their interlocutors [10,11]. In situated human-machine interaction, the robot's or agent's gaze could be used as a cue to facilitate the user's comprehension of the robot's instructions [12]. Expressive eye gaze is one behaviour that can make intentions and desires more explicit [13]. Even when users are unaware of the intended communication, robots can reveal their intentions implicitly through eye gazes and influence human behaviours [14]. Researches have demonstrated that robots can use gazes to establish joint attention in their attempts of learning from demonstrations, as well as in soliciting feedback when there is uncertainty [15]. People also rate a robot as more natural and competent when it builds joint attention while performing a task [16].

In this study, we employ a robotic, driving agent platform, NAMIDA (Fig. 1), to utilize eye gazing cues to reveal the intentions of the robots, correspondingly the social presence of an autonomous car. We analyzed whether the gaze following behaviours of the robots can facilitate interaction between a human operator and an autonomous car.

1.1 Perceived Agency

Using a robotic driving agent as an interface for an autonomous car might create ambiguity for the humans' perceptions. The interface can either be perceived as a companion for the driver that is independent from the autonomous system (e.g., passenger), or as an authority who is directly connected to the system and responsible for the autonomous driving. When humans feel an engagement with a social entity, they tend to feel safer in their interactions with that entity [17]. We expect that when the robots' intentions (e.g., watching the road and being aware of) synchronize with the autonomous car's actions (take an action according to the situations on the road), the human operator will infer the existence of dependency (authority) of the driving agents to the autonomous system, which we will define it as the "perceived agency" of the robots. We also expect that this perceived agency would lead to an increase in the perception of safety.

2 Method

2.1 System Design

The NAMIDA platform involves one base unit that attaches to the dashboard of a car, containing three movable heads with one degree of freedom each within the driver's peripheral vision. The round shaped head of each robot allows for the positioning of their eyes with full color LED light emission. The movement of the robots is enabled by three servomotors linked to the Arduino platform inside each head that is attached to the main board.

2.2 Gaze Following Behaviors of NAMIDA

Joint attention is an active bilateral process which involves attention manipulation, but it can only be fully realized when the parties are aware of each other's attention [18]. Even though response and feedback behaviours are necessary to realize a joint attention that makes robots more competent and socially interactive within a human-robot interaction, however, in this study, we only focused on the one aspect of the joint attention which is the gaze following behaviours that are the active unilateral process of simultaneous looking.

2.3   Conditions

We conducted an experiment by employing our NAMIDA platform with three conditions in an autonomous driving environment:

i No NAMIDA (NN): the robots were not used. They were covered with a black piece of cloth (Fig. 2 (*left*)).
ii NAMIDA with Random gaze Behaviors (NRB): The robots were placed on the dashboard and were set to watch the front side of the road (as passengers) with the head movement data set that was normally distributed within a range from −15 to +15 degrees (Fig. 2 (*middle*)).
iii NAMIDA with Following Behaviors (NFB): The robots were constantly following the eye gaze of the participants (Fig. 2 (*right*)).

Fig. 2. The NN (*left*), NRB (*middle*) and NFB (*right*) conditions are shown. The *red* circle represents the gaze point of the human operator. The *blue arrows* represent the gaze direction of the robots. (Color figure online)

2.4   Experimental Setup

We set up our experiment in a simulated autonomous driving environment that consists of three monitors placed on the dashboard, an adjustable driver seat and a steering wheel. We used UC-win Road Ver.13[1] as the simulation software. The experiment room was dimmed to enhance the reality of the driving task.

In the simulated road, we placed five situations (checkpoints) along the way where each one triggered an action for the autonomous system to take. Three of the checkpoints indicate turning actions (signaling, slowing down, changing lanes and turning right or left), one checkpoint to indicate an underground passageway (signaling, slowing down, changing lanes) and one to indicate an automobile accident in the underground passageway (signaling, slowing down and passing by the automobile accident carefully). The maximum speed of the car was set to 40 km/h. The robots were enabled to track the human operator's eye gaze using the Tobii Pro Glasses 2 tracker.

---

[1] http://www.forum8.co.jp/product/ucwin/road/ucwin-road-1.htm.

Table 1. Subjective assessment questionnaire consists of Perceived Agency (PA), Perceived Enjoyment (PE), Perceived Safety (PS), Social Presence (SP), Intentional Stance of NAMIDA (ISN).

Code	Questions
PA1	I felt that Namida and the car were connected
PA2	I felt that Namida was independent from the car
PA3	I felt that Namida reflected the car's mind
PE1	I think the driving was enjoyable
PE2	I think the driving was fascinating
PE3	I think the driving was boring
PS1	I think the driving was safe
PS2	I think the driving was relaxing
PS3	I think the driving was calm
PS4	I think the driving was surprising
SP1	I perceived that I was in the presence of the car
SP2	I felt that the car was watching me and was aware of my presence
SP3	The thought that the car is not a real person crosses my mind often
SP4	The car appeared to be sentient (conscious and alive) to me
SP5	I perceived the car as being only machine, not as living creature
ISN1	I felt that the robots could understand my intention
ISN2	I thought that the robots shared my feelings
ISN3	The robots seemed to care about me
ISN4	The robots were trying to get involved with me
ISN5	I thought the attention of the robots depended on my attention
ISN6	I felt a connection between me and the robots

2.5 Procedure

22 participants (3 female, 19 male) from 19 to 40 years old (M = 24.82, SD = 6.31)) took part in our experiment. We conducted a counterbalanced within-subject-study. All participants had a current driving license. Upon arrival, each participant was given an explanation about the experiment. Before starting the experiment, the participants were asked to fill out a demographic questionnaire. After each session, they were asked to fill out the subjective assessment questionnaire using a 5-point Likert scale, ranging from 1 (strongly disagree) to 5 (strongly agree) (Table 1). Except for PA, the questionnaire items were prepared based on the work in [19–21].

In the simulation, the participants were told that they had to go to a train station, and that the autonomous car would take them there using the best route, so their task was to carefully watch the environment and interact with the robots during the autonomous driving. Before starting the experiment, the participants undertook a trial session for a few minutes in order for them to adapt to the environment. After the trial, the real sessions started. Each session took approximately five minutes.

3   Results

Perceived Agency (PA) and Intentional Stance of NAMIDA (ISN) questions were given only after the NRB and NFB conditions. The validity of the questions were analyzed through conducting an internal reliability analysis. For the PA, the results showed that the Cronbach's alpha was greater than 0.68 under both NRB and NFB conditions ($\alpha = 0.855$ and $\alpha = 0.688$, respectively). A subsequent paired t-test revealed significant difference between two conditions $(t(21) = -1.734,\ {}^*p < 0.048)$. The NFB was rated significantly higher (M = 3.189, SD = 0.91) than the NRB condition (M = 2.295, SD = 1.032) (Fig. 3a, Table 2).

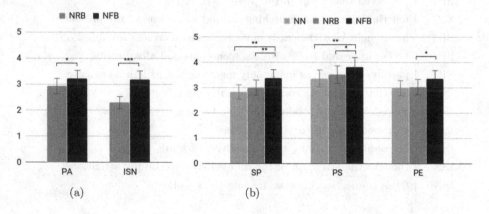

(a)   (b)

Fig. 3. The graphs indicate the mean values of each subjective factor and the conditions where the factors are significantly different (*p < 0.05, **p < 0.01, ***p < 0.001).

The results for the validity of the ISN questionnaire showed that the Cronbach's alpha was $\alpha = 0.937$, $\alpha = 0.907$ for the NRB and the NFB conditions, respectively. A paired t-test was conducted to investigate whether the gaze behaviours of the robots influenced their perceived intentional stance. The results showed that under the NFB (M = 3.114, SD = 0.915) condition the participants rated the related questions significantly higher than under the NRB condition (M = 2.205, SD = 0.999), $(t(21) = -4.252,\ {}^{***}p < 0.001)$ (Fig. 3a, Table 2(*left*)).

The results of the validity analysis of the Social Presence (SP) questions showed that the Cronbach's alpha was $\alpha = 0.658$, $\alpha = 0.785$, and $\alpha = 0.811$ for NN, NRB and NFB conditions, respectively. Then we conducted a one-way within subject ANOVA to investigate whether the gaze following behaviours of NAMIDA affect the perceived social presence. The results showed a significant

Table 2. The table on the *left* shows the t values for a paired t-test analysis (PA and ISN, F values for a one-way repeated ANOVA (PA, SP, ISN, PS and PE factors), and p values for the corresponding analysis for each factor. The table on the *right* shows the Pearson's correlation analysis. The values on the correlation table represents the r values ($*p < 0.05$, $**p < 0.01$, $***p < 0.001$).

		F/t value	p-value		PA	SP	ISN	PS	PE
t-test	PA	-1.734	<0.048*	PA	–				
	ISN	-4.252	<0.001***	SP	0.208	–			
ANOVA	SP	9.872	<0.001***	ISN	0.344*	0.569***	–		
	PS	6.408	0.004**	PS	0.488***	0.506***	0.423**	–	
	PE	4.27	0.021*	PE	0.218	0.066	0.270	0.168	–

difference among the conditions $(F(2,42) = 9.872, ***p < 0.001)$. The Bonferroni correction revealed that the main score for the NFB (M = 3.372, SD = 0.458) condition was significantly higher than the NN (M = 2.827, SD = 0.701) condition; $(t(21) = -3.552, **p = 0.006)$ and NRB (M = 3, SD = 0.436) condition; $(t(21) = -3.355, **p = 0.009)$ (Fig. 3b, Table 2(*left*)).

The Cronbach's alpha for the Perceived Safety questionnaire (SP) was under *0.68* in three conditions ($\alpha = 0.664$, $\alpha = 0.57$ and $\alpha = 0.667$ for NN, NRB and NFB conditions, respectively). However, when we excluded the PS4 question, the Cronbach's alpha for each condition became $\alpha = 0.774$, $\alpha = 0.693$ and $\alpha = 0.757$ for NN, NRB and NFB conditions, respectively. After excluding the PS4, we conducted a one-way within subject ANOVA to investigate whether the gazing behaviours of the robots affected perceived safety. The results showed a significant difference among the conditions $(F(2,42) = 6.408, **p = 0.004)$. The Bonferroni correction revealed that the main score for the NFB (M = 3.807, SD = 0.436) condition was significantly higher from the NN (M = 3.364, SD = 0.601) condition $(t(21) = -2.941, **p = 0.008)$, and NRB (M = 3.511, SD = 0.52) condition $(t(21) = -2.784, *p = 0.011)$ (Fig. 3b, Table 2(*left*)).

The validity test of the Perceived Enjoyment (PE) questionnaire showed that the Cronbach's alpha was $\alpha = 0.841$, $\alpha = 0.844$ and $\alpha = 0.811$ for NN, NRB and NFB conditions, respectively. We then conducted a one-way within subject ANOVA to investigate whether the gaze following behaviour of NAMIDA affected perceived enjoyment. The results showed a significant difference among the conditions $(F(2,42) = 4.27, *p = 0.021)$. The Bonferroni correction revealed that the main score for the NFB (M = 3.348, SD = 0.43) condition was significantly higher than the NRB (M = 3.03, SD = 0.435) condition $(t(21) = -2.672, *p = 0.043)$ (Fig. 3b and Table 2(*left*)). However, the NFB condition did not show a significant difference with the NRB condition on perceived enjoyability.

The Pearson correlation coefficients results among the five subjective assessment factors are shown in Table 2(*right*). The results showed that there was a moderate positive correlation between ISN and PA $(r = 0.344, *p = 0.022)$, PS and PA $(r = 0.488, ***p < 0.001)$, PS and ISN $(r = 0.423, **p = 0.002)$. On the other hand, there was a strong positive correlation between the ISN and SP $(r = 0.569, ***p < 0.001)$, SP and PS $(r = 0.506, p***p < 0.001)$.

4   Discussion

In this study, we investigated the effectiveness of gaze following behaviours of a robotic driving agent platform to enhance human-autonomous car interaction. The proposed interaction method was expected to increase the perceived agency and comprehend the intentional stance of the robots; and social presence of the autonomous car. In addition, we expected there to be an increase in perceived safety and enjoyability with the autonomous driving system.

The results verified that under the NFB condition, the participants attributed the robots a higher level of agency which means the gaze following behaviours were associated better with the actions of the simulated autonomous car by the participants. Consequently, the gaze following behaviours were an influence in the robots being perceived as the authority of the car rather than a passenger. We also found that under the NFB condition, the participants perceived the intentional stance of the robots significantly better than under the NRB condition which led us to infer that the gaze following behaviours of the robots hold the potential of building intersubjectivity with the human operator. Moreover, the results showed that under the NFB condition, the participants' sense of social presence of the autonomous system was better compared to the NN and NRB conditions. The strong correlation between the intentional stance of the robots and the social presence of the autonomous car indicated that realizing the intentions of robots contributed to perceiving the autonomous car as being a social entity more than under the other conditions.

Perceived safety was found significantly higher under the NFB condition compared to the NN and NRB conditions. It can be inferred that the robots gaze following behaviours persuaded the participants that the robots were paying attention to the environment as much as the human operators themselves. Perceived enjoyment was found significantly higher under the NFB condition compared to the NRB condition; however, it was not significantly higher compared to the NN condition. It can be said that, without the robots, the participants could also enjoy the autonomous driving by observing and reasoning the car's actions. However, in the case of employing the robots, it was significantly more enjoyable when the robots were responsive to gazing of the participants.

Lichtenthäler et al. [22] have shown that when a robot's behaviour was legible, perceived safety of humans increased. In this respect, we expected that the intentional stance of the robots will positively correlate with the perceived safety. We also expected a positive correlation between the social presence of the autonomous car and the perceived safety. The moderate correlations between PS and SP, PS and ISN pointed out our expectations above. Also, the moderate correlations between PS and PA, PS and SP indicated that perceiving the robots as an authority has a potential to ameliorate the perception of the system as a social entity that might affect the perceived safety.

4.1 Limitations

The recruitment of mostly male participants limited our results to make broader generalizations. Also, the factors that we measured in this study were highly depend on the participants' own understanding of the question items. Therefore, in our next study, we will consider to verify our findings with the support of both qualitative and quantitative assessments of the participants within a greater gender balance study.

5 Conclusion

In this study, we proposed an autonomous car-human operator interaction paradigm in order to achieve a reliable interaction with an autonomous car, such that the autonomous system and the human could sense each other's intentions and be aware of each other's presence. The results of this pilot study showed that perceiving an autonomous car as a social entity through the gaze following behaviours of a driving agent platform was possible and has the potential to improve the perceived safety and enjoyment of the autonomous driving system. Future studies will investigate methods to improve the relationship between an autonomous car and a human operator in terms of increasing the perceived safety, trust and pleasure of autonomous driving.

Acknowledgement. This research has been supported by Grant-in-Aid for scientific research of KIBAN-B (18HQ3322) from the Japan Society for the Promotion of Science (JSPS).

References

1. Poczter, S.L., Jankovic, L.M.: The google car: driving toward a better future? J. Bus. Case Stud. **10**(1), 7 (2014)
2. Waytz, A., Heafner, J., Epley, N.: The mind in the machine: anthropomorphism increases trust in an autonomous vehicle. J. Exp. Soc. Psychol. **52**, 113–117 (2014)
3. Hock, P., Kraus, J., Walch, M., Lang, N., Baumann, M.: Elaborating feedback strategies for maintaining automation in highly automated driving. In: Proceedings of the 8th International Conference on Automotive User Interfaces and Interactive Vehicular Applications, pp. 105–112. ACM (2016)
4. Dennett, D.C.: The Intentional Stance. MIT press, Cambridge (1989)
5. Sallnäs, E.L., Rassmus-Gröhn, K., Sjöström, C.: Supporting presence in collaborative environments by haptic force feedback. ACM Trans. Comput.-Hum. Interact. (TOCHI) **7**(4), 461–476 (2000)
6. Beebe, B., Knoblauch, S., Rustin, J., Sorter, D., Jacobs, T.J., Pally, R.: Forms of Intersubjectivity in Infant Research and Adult Treatment. Other Press, New York (2005)
7. Brooks, R., Meltzoff, A.N.: The development of gaze following and its relation to language. Dev. Sci. **8**(6), 535–543 (2005)
8. Tomasello, M., Carpenter, M.: Shared intentionality. Dev. Sci. **10**(1), 121–125 (2007)

9. Baron-Cohen, S.: The evolution of a theory of mind (1999)
10. Karatas, N., Yoshikawa, S., Tamura, S., Otaki, S., Funayama, R., Okada, M.: Sociable driving agents to maintain driver's attention in autonomous driving. In: 2017 26th IEEE International Symposium on Robot and Human Interactive Communication (RO-MAN), pp. 143–149. IEEE (2017)
11. Mutlu, B., Shiwa, T., Kanda, T., Ishiguro, H., Hagita, N.: Footing in human-robot conversations: how robots might shape participant roles using gaze cues. In: Proceedings of the 4th ACM/IEEE International Conference on Human Robot Interaction, pp. 61–68. ACM (2009)
12. Skantze, G., Hjalmarsson, A., Oertel, C.: Turn-taking, feedback and joint attention in situated human-robot interaction. Speech Commun. **65**, 50–66 (2014)
13. Takayama, L., Dooley, D., Ju, W.: Expressing thought: improving robot readability with animation principles. In: 2011 6th ACM/IEEE International Conference on Human-Robot Interaction (HRI), pp. 69–76. IEEE (2011)
14. Mutlu, B., Yamaoka, F., Kanda, T., Ishiguro, H., Hagita, N.: Nonverbal leakage in robots: communication of intentions through seemingly unintentional behavior. In: Proceedings of the 4th ACM/IEEE International Conference on Human Robot Interaction, pp. 69–76. ACM (2009)
15. Lockerd, A., Breazeal, C.: Tutelage and socially guided robot learning. In: Proceedings of the 2004 IEEE/RSJ International Conference on Intelligent Robots and Systems, (IROS 2004), vol. 4, pp. 3475–3480. IEEE (2004)
16. Huang, C.M., Thomaz, A.L.: Effects of responding to, initiating and ensuring joint attention in human-robot interaction. In: 2011 IEEE of RO-MAN, pp. 65–71. IEEE (2011)
17. Sauppé, A., Mutlu, B.: The social impact of a robot co-worker in industrial settings. In: Proceedings of the 33rd Annual ACM Conference on Human Factors in Computing Systems, pp. 3613–3622. ACM (2015)
18. Kaplan, F., Hafner, V.: The challenges of joint attention (2004)
19. Heerink, M., Kröse, B., Evers, V., Wielinga, B.: The influence of social presence on acceptance of a companion robot by older people (2008)
20. Bailenson, J.N., Blascovich, J., Beall, A.C., Loomis, J.M.: Equilibrium theory revisited: mutual gaze and personal space in virtual environments. Presence: Teleoperators Virtual Environ. **10**(6), 583–598 (2001)
21. Suzuki, N., Takeuchi, Y., Ishii, K., Okada, M.: Effects of echoic mimicry using hummed sounds on human-computer interaction. Speech Commun. **40**(4), 559–573 (2003)
22. Lichtenthäler, C., Lorenzy, T., Kirsch, A.: Influence of legibility on perceived safety in a virtual human-robot path crossing task. In: 2012 IEEE of RO-MAN, pp. 676–681. IEEE (2012)

Virtual Reality Social Robot Platform: A Case Study on Arash Social Robot

Azadeh Shariati[1(✉)], Mojtaba Shahab[1], Ali Meghdari[1(✉)],
Ali Amoozandeh Nobaveh[1], Raman Rafatnejad[2],
and Behrad Mozafari[1]

[1] Social and Cognitive Robotics Laboratory,
Sharif University of Technology, Tehran, Iran
azadeh.shariati@mail.kntu.ac.ir, meghdari@sharif.edu
[2] Faculty of Engineering, Islamic Azad University,
North Tehran Branch, Tehran, Iran

Abstract. The role of technology in education and clinical therapy cannot be disregarded. Employing robots and computer-based devices as competent and advanced learning tools for children indicates that there is a role for technology in overcoming certain weaknesses of common therapy and educational procedures. In this paper, we present a new platform for a virtual reality social robot (VR-social robot) which could be used as an auxiliary device or a replacement for real social robots. To support the idea, a VR-robot, based on the real social robot Arash, is designed and developed in the virtual reality environment. "Arash" is a social robot buddy particularly designed and realized to improve learning, educating, entertaining, and clinical therapy for children with chronic disease. The acceptance and eligibility of the actual robot among these children have been previously investigated. In the present study, we investigated the acceptability and eligibility of a virtual model of the Arash robot among twenty children. To have a fair comparison a similar experiment was also performed utilizing the real Arash robot. The experiments were conducted in the form of storytelling. The initial results are promising and suggest that the acceptance of a VR-robot is fairly compatible to the real robot since the performance of the VR-robot did not have significant differences with the performance of the real Arash robot. Thereby, this platform has the potential to be a substitute or an auxiliary solution for the real social robot.

Keywords: Acceptance · Arash social robot · Storytelling experiment
Virtual model · Virtual reality social robot (VR-Robot)

1 Introduction

Social robots and computer-based devices can influence children's lives, and recently have been widely utilized for entertainment, education, and therapeutic interventions for children with different disease and disabilities [1–5]. One of the problems with youngsters with chronic disease, especially cancer, is their education. They don't have enough time to go to school amid their treatment. Sometimes treatment is a protracted procedure which can last as long as half a year or more. Moreover, it has been

© Springer Nature Switzerland AG 2018
S. S. Ge et al. (Eds.): ICSR 2018, LNAI 11357, pp. 551–560, 2018.
https://doi.org/10.1007/978-3-030-05204-1_54

demonstrated that social robots can decrease children's level of depression, anxiety, and anger during the medical care process [6]. The Arash robot, which is the main instrument in this paper, is a mobile social robot developed and constructed for children in the hospital environment, in particular ones with cancer. Beside clinical intervention, the robot can entertain, motivate, and educate children. It can also help to suppress their depression, anger, and distress [7–9].

The introduction of head-mounted displays (HMDs) by Oculus Rift has helped Virtual Reality (VR) to enter a brand new generation, and it has since been used for educational purposes. Virtual reality has been helpful in developing cognitive skills that contain remembering and understanding as well as skills of controlling emotional responses in stressful situations [10]. An important factor in children's education is the learning environment. Virtual reality is one of the best choices for changing the visual environment at low cost. Another advantage of this console is it being user-friendly and easy to carry [11]. The Arash robot is not a fully autonomous device as it requires a professional operator to control it. Moreover, all hospitals may not be able to afford to buy the robot. These shortcomings encouraged the authors to introduce the concept of virtual reality robots (VR-robots) which have the potential to be substituted instead of real social robots. To support the idea of VR-social robots, a virtual model of Arash was designed and utilized in an experiment. The investigation was conducted to assess children's level of engagement and acceptance, and their feelings about the virtual robot in comparison with the real robot. The investigation was devised to be conducted in the form of storytelling. The results of this comparison will enhance the Arash robot virtualization for use as a robot complement and lead to a modification of the robot's simulation process as well as determining children's acceptance of the VR's replacement of the robot in the training. We defined four steps to achieve the research goal, including robot simulation in the VR environment, preparation of stories for the real robot and VR-robot, storytelling to children by the two devices, questioning children by an instructor and finally analyzing the results for acceptability. The obtained results confirm high engagement and interest of children with the VR-robot as well as the real robot.

2   Research Questions

(1) Can a real social robot be replaced by a VR-social robot?
(2) What are the children opinions about interaction with a VR-social robot vs. the real social robot?
(3) What are the anthropomorphism, likability, safety, animacy, and intelligent of the VR-robot in comparison with the real robot from a child's point of view?
(4) How well could the real social robot/VR-social robot convey the story to children as a storyteller?

3 Research Methodology

3.1 Participants

Participants were twenty healthy children ranging in age from 5 to 12 years old. All the children had seen the Arash robot before the test and used the VR device at least once before the experiment. However, none of them had interacted with a social robot before the session. The mean age of the participants was 8.5 years (M = 8.5) with a standard deviation of 1.86 (SD = 1.86). Males accounted for 60% (n = 12) of all participants, and females made up 40% of all participants. The participants were selected from healthy children. Most children with cancer have to undergo chemotherapy, which often has an associated risk of increasing infections. The HMD contacts directly with the children's face and must pass some hygiene standards, as our device does not yet pass, we preferred to perform the experiments with healthy children.

3.2 Instruments

The Arash Social Robot

The main instrument used in this article is the Arash robot. Its design features and specifications are presented in Table 1. The Arash robot is able to produce human-like body gestures in its upper body and can move on its wheeled mobile base. There are 12 degrees of freedom (DoFs) in the upper body and 3 DoFs in the lower body. The Arash robot is semi-autonomous [8–10]. It is able to speak, change its facial expression, and produce different body-gestures. The robot operating system is based on ROS (robotic operating system), the dialogues and gestures are loaded on the device before the session and the Wizard of Oz technique is used to manage the sessions, i.e. a human operator is in charge of sending commands to the robot. The schematic of the robot is presented in Fig. 1.

Table 1. Specifications of *Arash* robot.

Specifications	Value
Height, weight, max speed	130 cm, 24 kg, 0.8 m/s
Actuators	5 DC motors, 9 servomotors, 1 linear motor
Sensors	Microphones, gyro, ultrasonic sensors, Kinect, camera, touch sensor, encoders, accelerometer, LiDAR
Operating system	ROS on Ubuntu 14.04
Total DOFs	15-DOFs (waist: 2, arms: 8, neck: 2, based: 3-DOFs)

The VR-Social Robot

3D Modeling

In this section, our goal is to integrate the 3D model of the robot into an animated model in order to be intractable in the VR environment. The 3D model of the Arash robot (in Solidworks software) has a large volume due to its details. Although the

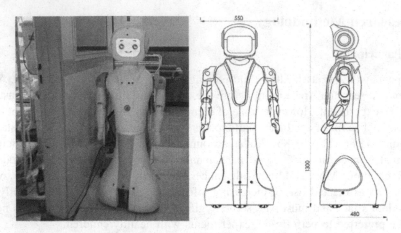

Fig. 1. The Arash social robot [7].

unnecessary parts of the model were omitted, the model size was still large. Therefore, MeshLab software was used to decrease the size of the model without affecting its efficiency. Furthermore, Arash needed to be placed in a solid T position to properly execute the corresponding skeleton model of the robot in the Unity software. Then, the final model was ready to be imported into the Blender software for the bone joining. The final model of the skeleton of the robot is shown in Fig. 2-a.

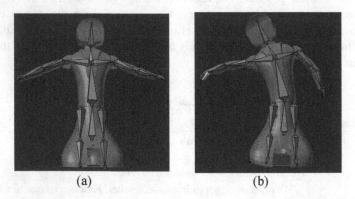

(a)   (b)

Fig. 2. (a) The humanoid standard skeleton for the Arash robot model. (b) The skeleton attached to the 3D model so they will rotate in the same way.

In the next step, the humanoid skeleton was attached to the 3D model and each part of the 3D model was carefully bound to the relevant bone. The skeleton system was constructed according to the standard humanoid skeleton model; as a result, all joints of the model were distinguished correctly and the model was fully defined in the Unity software (Fig. 2-b).

Since this model was considered a humanoid model different types of standard humanoid animations (running, walking, etc.) could be implemented for the Arash robot. In addition, by using a Kinect sensor, we have the ability to record any specifically desired animation by an individual standing in front of the Kinect and moving his body. The final model of the animated Arash robot is shown in Fig. 3.

Fig. 3. The final model of the animated Arash robot; components of the classroom: blackboard, tables, chairs, bookcases, computer, printer and projector.

Designing the Virtual Environment
We have designed a virtual environment for interaction of the Arash VR-robot with children. The Virtual Reality Setup used in this study is the VIVE by HTC [12] and the graphics of the environment are designed in UNITY 5 software. The virtual environment consists of a classroom. The components of this virtual classroom are the 3D animated virtual robot and the decoration which consists of a blackboard, tables, chairs, bookcases, computer, printer, and projector (see Fig. 3). In the virtual classroom, the interaction scenario is that the Arash VR-robot, as a virtual friend, tells two different stories to the children after a brief greeting. The animation of the virtual robot while telling the stories was recorded using a Kinect sensor. The procedure was very simple: An individual stands in front of the Kinect and moderately moves his body, especially his hands and legs, in the same manner as the body movements of the real robot during storytelling as the related animation was recorded. Figure 3 shows the Arash VR-robot while it is telling the story.

3.3 Experimental Setup

Several experiments were conducted to measure the Arash VR-robot's applicability, acceptance and attractiveness to children in comparison with the real robot. In these experiments the VR-robot was compared with the real robot. Storytelling can teach and convey different concepts to children; additionally, it can be utilized to ask precise queries. Accordingly, the storytelling method has been used to compare the VR-robot and real robot. In an author's previous paper, children's acceptance of the Arash robot as a storyteller was assessed, and the results were very promising [7]. In this study, the prospect of the Arash VR-robot as a storyteller will be compared with the real Arash robot. In fact, we wanted to assess the participant's opinion about and enjoyment with the VR-robot as a storyteller.

All the children listened to two stories which were selected by consulting with child psychologists. The stories had approximately the same level of complexity and difficulty. The first story was the story of the "Lion and the mouse", and the second story was the story of the "Pigeons and the hunter". The main moral of both stories is to explore the themes of kindness and cooperation. The time duration of each story was about 3 min. Both stories were narrated by a female voice actor. The tests are counterbalanced, which means that half of the participants (selected randomly) listened to the story of the "Pigeons and the hunter" by Arash VR-robot and then listened to the story of the "Lion and the mouse" by the real Arash robot and vice versa for the other half of the participants. Moreover, to have a fair comparison, each of two groups were further divided into two more groups with half of the children listening first to the real robot and the other half first listening to the VR-robot.

The experiment took place at the social and cognitive laboratory, Sharif University of Technology, Tehran, Iran. At the beginning of the experiment, the Arash robot (real/VR) introduces himself to children for a couple of minutes, then tells them that they are going to hear two stories and finally they will be asked some questions about the stories and about the amount of attractiveness of the robot in two environments. Next, after Arash concludes the story he asks the participants whether they would like him to come back or not, and lastly he says goodbye. This storytelling procedure takes about 3 min. The actual robot and the VR-robot as storytellers are presented in Fig. 4. The procedures followed were in accordance with the ethical standards of the responsible committee on human experimentation at Sharif University of Technology and with the Helsinki Declaration of 1975, as revised in 1983.

Fig. 4. Children listening to the Arash robot storyteller and the VR-robot storyteller.

3.4 Assessment Tools

Three questionnaires were utilized after each story to investigate the performance of the real social robot and the VR-social robot.

(a) The Godspeed questionnaire: assesses the likeability, perceived intelligence, animacy, anthropomorphism, and perceived safety of the VR-robot vs. real robot [13].
(b) The Self-Assessment Manikin (SAM): evaluates the perceived pleasure, arousal, and dominance created by the VR-robot or the real robot [14].

(c) The Transportation Scale-Short Form (TS-SF): examines the level of immersion in a story narrated by the VR-robot or the real robot [15, 16]. All questions were rated on a 5-point Likert-type smiley face scale [17].

4 Results and Discussion

In this experiment, we examined how well the children got involved with the story told by the real robot/the VR-robot. Twenty out of 20 participants (100%) were willing and accepted to listen to the robot storyteller and 20 participants (100%) were willing and accepted to listen to the VR-robot storyteller. After the storytelling by each of the two devices, the Bartneck, SAM, and TS-SF questionnaires were asked from the children. Figure 5 and Tables 2, 3, 4 demonstrate the performance of participants while listening to the real robot and the VR-robot. Mean score, standard deviation, and p-value of a t-test were calculated. The Godspeed test was performed to evaluate the Arash robot and the VR-robots' appearance and performance from the children's point of view. The questionnaire was asked from the children to evaluate the anthropomorphism, animacy, likeability, perceived intelligence, and perceived safety of the real robot/the VR-robot. As it is clear from Table 2, the mean score of the real robot storyteller in all items was higher than the VR-robot storyteller; however, the differences are not significant. The mean score of perceived safety and likability of two devices are approximately the same (4.84 vs. 4.81 for likability, and 4.63 vs. 4.54 for safety for the real and virtual robot, respectively). These scores are considered as high scores; this means that children liked both the real robot and the VR-robot very much and feel safe while interacting with them. The anthropomorphism mean score, which assess the human-like character of the robots, is 3.99 for the real robot vs. 3.82 for the VR-robot. These mean scores demonstrate that the real robot and the virtual one are not completely human-like; this is promising since their design avoids the uncanny valley phenomenon. The mean score of animacy is 4.42 for the real robot vs. 4.14 for the VR-robot. This is reasonable since Arash is a physical creature and may be more conducive to projecting animacy to children; however, by improving the VR environment\VR-robot we can increase that score. Moreover, high scores in intelligence for both items demonstrate that children perceived the real robot and the VR-robot as intelligent creatures (4.81 vs. 4.66, respectively). Over all, no significant difference is observed in any item, which insured that the children's perception of the real robot is very similar to the VR-robot. The second questionnaire was the TS-SF. the TS-SF test was used to measure the level of involvement with the story as told by a storyteller. Figure 5 and Table 3 demonstrate the performance of participants while listened to the real Arash robot and the Arash VR-robot storyteller. As it is clear from Table 3, the mean scores of cognition, emotional-affective, visual imaginary, and transportation for the real robot are higher than the VR-robot. But again, the differences are not significant (p-values < 0.05). The third questionnaire is the SAM, where the mean score of perceived valance of VR-robot was higher than the real robot (4.61 for the VR-robot vs. 4.47 for the real robot). This means that both sessions pleased the children; however, the VR session produced more pleasure. Also, the mean score of the dominance of VR-robot was higher than the real robot, which means that children were affected by the virtual robot more than the real robot. Another item in the SAM questionnaire is Arousal. Arousal is an item that shows the level of stimuli and excitement associated with a personal reaction. The mean score of arousal for the VR-robot is approximately the same as the real robot; however, the mean score of the real robot is a bit higher. This is reasonable since Arash has a physical body which could stimulate children more than the virtual robot. However, the mean scores being close to each other (4.32 vs. 4.27) is very encouraging and shows that the VR-robot can stimulate children approximately similar to the real robot. The obtained results are very promising; with all the scores being more than 3 (out of 5) and no significant difference being observed between the real robot and the VR-robot. Overall, the experimental results indicate that this platform has the potential to be an auxiliary substitute for the real social robot.

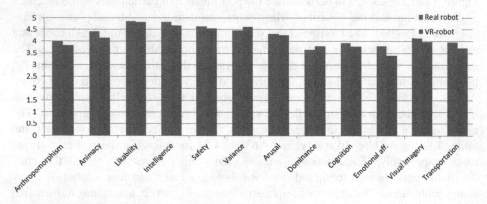

Fig. 5. Mean scores (VR-robot and real robot) of the anthropomorphism, animacy, likability, intelligence, and safety (Godspeed questionnaires; valence, arousal, and dominance (SAM test), cognition, emotion, imagination, transportation (TS-SF test).

Table 2. The mean score, standard deviation, and p-value of scores of the Godspeed test.

No.	Item	Score's mean[a] (SD[b])		P-value
		Real robot	VR-robot	
1	Anthropomorphism	3.99 (0.85)	3.82 (0.82)	0.26
2	Animacy	4.42 (0.73)	4.14 (0.77)	0.12
3	Likability	4.84 (0.34)	4.81 (0.32)	0.39
4	Intelligence	4.81 (0.39)	4.66 (0.51)	0.15
5	Safety	4.63 (0.58)	4.54 (0.67)	0.33

[a]Score's mean is over 5. [b]SD: standard deviation.

Table 3. The mean score, standard deviation, and p-value of scores of the SAM questionnaire.

No.	Item	Score's mean[a] (SD[b])		P-value
		Real robot	VR-robot	
1	Valence	4.47 (0.85)	4.61 (0.59)	0.29
2	Arousal	4.32 (1.23)	4.27 (0.88)	0.44
3	Dominance	3.65 (1.26)	3.80 (1.19)	0.35

[a]Score's mean is over 5. [b]SD: standard deviation.

Table 4. The mean score, standard deviation, and p-value of scores of the TS-SF test.

No.	Item	Score's mean[a] (SD[b])		P-value
		Real robot	VR-robot	
1	Cognition	3.93 (0.86)	3.78 (1.09)	0.31
2	Emotional-affective	3.8 (1.10)	3.39 (0.96)	0.11
3	Visual imagery	4.13 (0.66)	3.98 (0.69)	0.24
4	Transportation	3.95 (0.64)	3.72 (0.73)	0.11

[a]Score's mean is over 5. [b]SD: standard deviation.

5 Conclusion

In this study, a virtual reality social robot platform is introduced. To support the idea a virtual reality robot (VR-robot), based on a real social robot named Arash, was designed and developed in the VR environment. Arash is a social robot designed, constructed, and modified by the authors for children with chronic disease, in particular cancer. Children tend to interact with social robots; but, there are some problems associated with actual robots, such as difficulty in carrying and transporting, high cost, and the need for expert operators. Thereby, a new concept for a virtual reality robot (VR-robot) is introduced which has the potential to be a substitute and an auxiliary solution for real robots in some occasions. After completing the design of the VR-robot, several experiments were carried out to evaluate the favorability and desire of children to interact with the VR-robot compared to the real robot. The experiment was conducted using storytelling. In the experiment, each participant listened to two stories, one narrated by the VR-robot and another narrated by the real robot. After each storytelling, three questionnaires were asked from the children to evaluate some features of the robot. The Godspeed was used to measure the anthropomorphism, animacy, likeability, perceived intelligence, and perceived safety from a children's point of view. Their pleasure, arousal, and dominance while interacting with the VR-robot/real robot were measured by the TS-SF; and their imagination, emotion, cognition and transportation into the stories by the two storytellers were measured by the SAM. The obtained results are very promising; with all the scores being more than 3 (out of 5) and no significant difference observed between the real robot and the VR-robot. Overall, the experimental results indicate that this platform has the potential to be an auxiliary substitute for the real social robot.

Acknowledgements. This project is supported and funded by the Iranian National Science Foundation-INSF (http://en.insf.org/) and the Office of the Vice-President in Science and Technology. We also thank Mrs. S. L. Holderread for the English editing of the paper. Moreover, Mr. Alireza Esfandbod is appreciated for his effective collaboration in the virtual robot modeling.

References

1. Benitti, F.B.: Exploring the educational potential of robotics in schools: a systematic review. Comput. Educ. **58**(3), 978–988 (2012)
2. Elahi, M.T., et al.: "Xylotism": a tablet-based application to teach music to children with autism. In: Kheddar, A., et al. (eds.) Social Robotics. LNCS, vol. 10652, pp. 728–738. Springer, Cham (2017). https://doi.org/10.1007/978-3-319-70022-9_72
3. Taheri, A.R., Meghdari, A., Alemi, M., Pouretemad, H.R.: Clinical interventions of social humanoid robots in the treatment of a pair of high- and low-functioning autistic Iranian twins. Scientia Iranica, Trans. B: Mech. Eng. **25**(3), 1197–1214 (2018)
4. Taheri, A., Meghdari, A., Alemi, M., Pouretemad, H.: Teaching music to children with autism: a social robotics challenge. Int. J. Sci. Iran. Trans. G Soc. Cognit. Eng. (2018). https://doi.org/10.24200/SCI.2017.4608
5. Striepe, H., Lugrin, B.: There once was a robot storyteller: measuring the effects of emotion and non-verbal behaviour. In: Kheddar, A., et al. (eds.) Social Robotics. LNCS, vol. 10652, pp. 126–136. Springer, Cham (2017). https://doi.org/10.1007/978-3-319-70022-9_13
6. Alemi, M., Ghanbarzadeh, A., Meghdari, A., Moghadam, L.J.: Clinical application of a humanoid robot in pediatric cancer interventions. Int. J. Soc. Robot. **8**(5), 743–759 (2016)
7. Meghdari, A., et al.: Arash: a social robot buddy to support children with cancer in a hospital environment. Proc. Inst. Mech. Eng. Part H: J. Eng. Med. **232**(6), 605–618 (2018)
8. Meghdari, A., Shariati, A., Alemi, M., Amoozandeh, A., Khamooshi, M., Mozafari, B.: Design performance characteristics of a social robot companion "Arash" for pediatric hospitals. Int. J. Humanoid Robot. **15**, 1850019 (2018)
9. Meghdari, A., Alemi, M., Khamooshi, M., Amoozandeh, A., Shariati, A., Mozafari, B.: Conceptual design of a social robot for pediatric hospitals. In: 4th International Conference Robotics and Mechatronics (ICROM), pp. 566–571. IEEE (2016)
10. Jensen, L., Konradsen, F.: A review of the use of virtual reality head-mounted displays in education and training. Educ. Inf. Technol. **23**(4), 1515–1529 (2016)
11. Shahab, M., et al.: Social virtual reality robot (V2R): a novel concept for education and rehabilitation of children with autism. In: 2017 5th RSI International Conference on Robotics and Mechatronics (ICRoM), pp. 82–87. IEEE (2017)
12. https://www.vive.com/us/
13. Bartneck, C., Kulić, D., Croft, E., Zoghbi, S.: Measurement instruments for the anthropomorphism, animacy, likeability, perceived intelligence, and perceived safety of robots. Int. J. Soc. Robot. **1**(1), 71–81 (2009)
14. Bradley, M.M., Lang, P.J.: Measuring emotion: the self-assessment manikin and the semantic differential. J. Behav. Ther. Exp. Psychiatry **25**(1), 49–59 (1994)
15. Appel, M., Gnambs, T., Richter, T., et al.: The transportation scale—short form (TS-SF). Media Psychol. **18**(2), 243–266 (2015)
16. Green, M.C., Brock, T.C.: The role of transportation in the persuasiveness of public narratives. J. Pers. Soc. Psychol. **79**(5), 701 (2000)
17. Read, J.C., MacFarlane, S.J., Casey, C.: Endurability, engagement and expectations: measuring children's fun. In: Interaction Design and Children, vol. 2, pp. 1–23. Shaker Publishing, Eindhoven (2002)

Novel Siamese Robot Platform
for Multi-human Robot Interaction

Woo-Ri Ko[1]([⊠]) [iD] and Jong-Hwan Kim[2]

[1] Electronics and Telecommunications Research Institute (ETRI), 218 Gajeong-ro,
Yuseong-gu, Daejeon 34129, Republic of Korea
wrko@etri.re.kr
[2] Korea Advanced Institute of Science and Technology (KAIST), 291 Daehak-ro,
Yuseong-gu, Daejeon 34141, Republic of Korea
johkim@rit.kaist.ac.kr

Abstract. Service robots have been designed to support people in public places, i.e. schools, museums, shopping malls, etc. However, the existing one-headed robots have a limitation that they cannot interact with
a person behind them while interacting with another person in front
of them. To overcome the limitation, we propose a novel Siamese robot
platform motivated by "Siamese twins" in nature. The proposed Siamese
robot consists of two heads, two arms, and a body to cover all directions.
Two separate individuals share the arms and the body, and therefore
we also propose three coordination schemes to mediate the individuals.
Experiments were carried out with a physical Siamese robot, "Siambot"
in a real environment, and the results show that the proposed Siamese
robot is efficient and effective in multi-human robot interaction. A video
showing the strengths of the Siamese robot can be found at https://
youtu.be/99P4O35v4Ck.

Keywords: Social robot · Human-robot interaction · Intelligent agent

1 Introduction

To use in public places, service robots used should be able to attract and hold
attention of customers or passengers. For this multi-human robot interaction
(m-HRI), there has been a lot of research on developing robots with human-like
appearance [3,4,7,9]. However, the existing robots have a limitation in interaction with a crowd since they cannot recognize a person behind them while
interacting with another person in front of them. To overcome the limitation,
we propose a novel robot platform, i.e. Siamese robot, which consists of multi-
heads, multi-arms, and a body. As Siamese twins in nature, a Siamese robot is
efficient in m-HRI. Compared to a typical one-headed robot, it has a chance of
communing with more people since it has multi-heads to cover all directions.

Supported by the ICT R&D program of MSIP/IITP. [2017-0-00162, Development of
Human-care Robot Technology for Aging Society].

S. S. Ge et al. (Eds.): ICSR 2018, LNAI 11357, pp. 561–568, 2018.
https://doi.org/10.1007/978-3-030-05204-1_55

Besides, in comparison with two separate one-headed robots, it can save hardware resources and battery to control body while maintaining the performance of m-HRI. This is because the individuals of Siamese robot can share the limbs as needed.

In order to attract people's attention, Siamese robot should generate proper behaviors to its current situation. For each individual, this problem can be solved by using a behavior selection method proposed in [5]. Once selected, the remaining problem is to coordinate the decisions of the individuals, that is, to determine the 'authorship' to control shared limbs [8]. In this paper, we propose three coordination schemes in winner-take-all and cooperative ways.

2   A Novel Robot Platform, Siamese Robot

The term "Siamese twins" is often used as a synonym for conjoined twins which are identical twins joined in utero. The conjoined twins share some organs and/or limbs, as well as having areas of joint movement [8]. On the basis of conjoined site of body, they are classified into several types such as xiphopagus, parapagus, etc. [6]. A famous example of xiphopagus twins is Chang and Eng Bunker born in 1811 in Thailand, which is formerly known as Siam. They fused in the xiphoid cartilage so they have a single body with four arms and four legs [2]. Each twin control over the two arms and two legs on their side of the body. Parapagus twins is fused at abdomen and pelvis, but not thorax. A famous example is Abigail and Brittany Hensel born in 1990 and they have a single body with separate heads, a chest, two arms, and two legs [11]. Each twin controls her half of their body, operating one of the arms and one of the legs.

Motivated by parapagus type of Siamese twins, we propose a novel robot platform, i.e. Siamese robot, which has two heads, two arms, a single torso and a mobile base. Figure 1 shows a physical Siamese robot, "Siambot," developed in Robot Intelligence Technology Laboratory at the Korea Advanced Institute of Science and Technology (KAIST). The width, length, height, and weight are 62.0 cm, 62.0 cm, 140.0 cm, and 70.0 kg, respectively. The robot consists of three parts: (1) two heads; (2) upper body; and (3) lower body. Each head has 19 degrees of freedom (DOFs) and perceives external environment through a Xtion camera and a thermal imaging sensor. The upper body has 24 DOFs (11 DOFs for each arm and 2 DOFs for waist), a speaker, and Odroid XU3 controller. The lower body has three omni wheels for high-mobility.

3   Intelligence Operating Architecture (iOA)

A number of cognitive architectures were proposed to build an intelligent agent which recognizes the current situation, generates proper behaviors according to its own personality, and learns from experiences [10]. However, there have been no system that multiple agents share the same physical robot, i.e. Siamese robot. In this need, we propose an intelligence operating architecture (iOA), as shown in Fig. 2. The iOA consists of six modules for each individual and two modules for

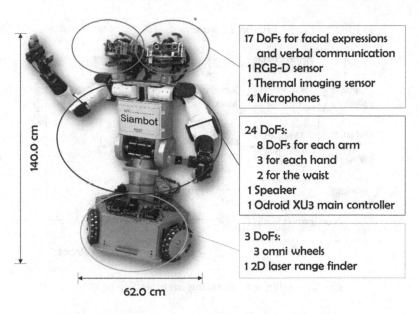

140.0 cm

Siambot

17 DoFs for facial expressions
and verbal communication
1 RGB-D sensor
1 Thermal imaging sensor
4 Microphones

24 DoFs:
8 DoFs for each arm
3 for each hand
2 for the waist
1 Speaker
1 Odroid XU3 main controller

3 DoFs:
3 omni wheels
1 2D laser range finder

62.0 cm

Fig. 1. Parapagus type of Siamese robot, "Siambot".

an arbiter. The context and internal modules deal with the strengths of context and internal state, respectively. In the problem solving module, the event most similar to the current situation is retrieved among the past experiences stored in the memory module. The memory module is pre-trained by the learning module using a number of simulated experiences generated in the simulation module. In the coordination module, a coordinated behavior between two individual is selected and it is generated through the actuator module. The detailed procedure for coordination will be described in the following.

4 Coordination Schemes

Individuals of a Siamese robot share some limbs and therefore they should clearly decide who will have the authority to control the joint limbs at a certain time (authorship of action) [8]. we propose three coordination schemes to distribute the authorship of each limb. The first and the second schemes are performed in a winner-take-all strategy where a dominant individual (DI) gains the authorship of every limb that it needs and the other individual takes the authorship of the rest of limbs. The third scheme finds the best combination of the first individual's behavior and the second individual's behavior, to make both of individuals somewhat satisfied.

In the first scheme, the DI, D, is decided at time t as

$$\Psi_J^D(t) = \max_{j,d}\{\Psi_j^d(t)\}, \quad d = 1, 2, \quad j = 1, 2, \ldots, m, \tag{1}$$

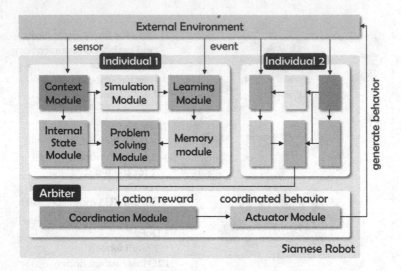

Fig. 2. Intelligence operating architecture (iOA).

where Ψ_j^d is the jth internal state strength of the dth individual and m is the number of internal states. Given an evaluation value of the kth behavior of the dth individual, $E(b_k^d)$, which can be calculated as in [5], the evaluation value of the non-dominant individual (NDI), N, is given as follows:

$$E(b_k^N) = \begin{cases} E(b_k^N) & \text{if } b_k^N \text{ and } b_k^D \text{ can be generated at the same time} \\ 0 & \text{otherwise} \end{cases} \tag{2}$$

Note that if b_k^N and b_k^D are facial expressions, all pairs can be generated at the same time. If they are gestures, the pairs that do not use the same arm, e.g. 'raising left arm' and 'putting left arm front' gestures, can be generated at the same time; The left arm of N is the right arm of D. If movements, the opposing pairs, e.g. 'moving forward' and 'moving backward,' can be generated together. Then, the winner behaviors $b_K^d, d = 1, 2$, with the highest evaluation values are indexed at K^d as follows:

$$E(b_K^d) = \max_k E(b_k^d), \quad d = 1, 2. \tag{3}$$

In the second scheme, the DI, D, is decided as

$$\Omega_J^D(t) = \max_{j,d}\{\Omega_j^d(t)\}, \quad d = 1, 2, \quad j = 1, 2, \ldots, n, \tag{4}$$

where Ω_j^d is the jth context strength of the dth individual and n is the number of contexts. Then, the actions of the DI and NDI are selected by Eqs. (2) and (3).

In the last scheme, the evaluation value $E(\{b_i^1, b_j^2\})$ of the combination of b_i^1 and b_j^2, is computed as

$$E(\{b_i^1, b_j^2\}) = \begin{cases} E(b_i^1) \cdot E(b_j^2) \\ \quad \text{if } b_i^1 \text{ and } b_j^2 \text{can be generated at the same time} \\ 0 \quad \text{otherwise} \end{cases} \tag{5}$$

Then, the winner behaviors b_I^1 and b_J^2 are indexed at I and J, respectively:

$$E(\{b_I^1, b_J^2\}) = \max_{i,j} E(\{b_i^1, b_j^2\}). \tag{6}$$

5 Experiments

The overall system for experiments is described in Fig. 3. A physical Siamese robot, "Siambot," perceives environment through Xtion cameras, and the perceived data is transmitted to Odroid XU3 board with an USB connection. To extract context information, it is again transmitted to a separate laptop with Intel Core i7-6700 2.6 GHz, GTX-980, and 8 GB RAM, via Wi-Fi. A coordinated behavior is selected in the ROS-based [1] behavior selection system and sent back to "Siambot" for generation.

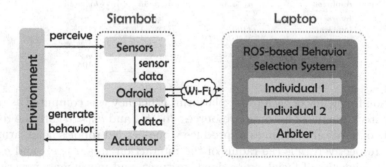

Fig. 3. Overall system for experiments.

To perform m-HRI, 10 criteria and 38 actions were defined for each individual, as shown in Tables 1 and 2. The criteria for selecting actions are the internal states of an individual that change instantaneously [5] and the contexts perceived by external sensors. The strength of each criterion is represented as a value between 0 and 1. According to the strengths of the criteria, the combination of a facial expression, a gesture, and a movement is selected and generated as a behavior.

In order to show the effectiveness on m-HRI, the proposed two-armed Siamese robot (parapagus type) is compared with a one-headed robot and a four-armed Siamese robot (xiphopagus type). Table 3 shows the interaction area and action

Table 1. Defined 10 criteria for behavior selection.

		Criterion
Internal state	Motivation	Power (need to attract attention), social contact (need for friends), curiosity (need to learn)
	Emotion	Arousal (how excited), valence (how favorable), stance (how approachable)
	Homeostasis	Rest (need to rest)
Context		Distance, number of people, loudness

Table 2. Defined 38 actions.

	Action
Facial expression	None, anger, disgust, fear, happiness, sadness, surprise, tiredness
Gesture	None, raise left/right/both arms, wave left/right/both arms strongly, wave left/right/both arms softly, fold hands, put left/right/both arms in front, block, put left/right/both arms on waist, cover face
Movement	None, move forward/backward, circle largely in left/right direction, circle in place in left/right direction, turn left/right, move left/right

Table 3. Interaction area and action generation frequency.

	One-headed robot	Four-armed Siamese robot	Two-armed Siamese robot
Hardware resources	$h_h + h_a + h_b \approx 3h$	$2h_h + 2h_a + h_b \approx 5h$	$2h_h + h_a + h_b \approx 4h$
Interaction area (efficiency)	$\pi r^2/2$ (100%)	πr^2 (120%)	πr^2 (150%)
Action generation frequency (efficiency)	$e_f + e_g + e_m \approx 3e$ (100%)	$2e_f + 2e_g + w_m e_m \approx 5.09e$ (102%)	$2e_f + w_g e_g + w_m e_m \approx 4.33e$ (108%)

generation frequency of each robot platform. Efficiency was computed as ratio to the required amount of hardware resources. h_h, h_a, and $h_b(\approx h)$ are the required amounts of hardware resources to produce a one-headed robot's head, arms, and a body, respectively. r is the radius of the interaction area. e_f, e_g, and $e_m(\approx e)$ are the frequencies of facial expressions, gestures, and movements generated by a one-headed robot, respectively. w_g and w_m are the weights calculated as

$$w_g = 1 + \{n_n n_g + n_l(n_n + n_l) + n_r(n_n + n_r) + n_b n_n\}/(n_g n_g),$$
$$w_m = 1 + (1/n_m), \tag{7}$$

where n_m and n_g are the numbers of movements and gestures, respectively, and n_n, n_l, n_r, and n_b are the numbers of gestures with no arm, left arm, right arm, and both arms, respectively.

To verify the feasibility of the coordination schemes, the behavior generation frequencies of DI and NDI were measured from 1,000 times of behavior generation (Fig. 4). Note that we only demonstrated the context-based winner-take-all scheme which is a more extreme strategy. The results show that both DI and

NDI generated all defined behaviors. However, due to the nature of the winner-take-all method, DI generated more active actions (e.g. moving forward (m_2)) and gestures with both arms (e.g. putting both arms front (g_{14})), than NDI.

	DI	NDI		DI	NDI		DI	NDI
f_1	7.5%	8.4%	g_1	4.9%	8.2%	m_1	7.9%	13.8%
f_2	25.5%	20.8%	g_2	2.7%	5.3%	m_2	20.4%	11.1%
f_3	9.6%	16.8%	g_3	2.0%	6.7%	m_3	7.0%	8.9%
f_4	12.0%	9.3%	g_4	3.7%	4.3%	m_4	4.4%	3.4%
f_5	10.6%	5.9%	g_5	1.4%	4.1%	m_5	3.8%	3.1%
f_6	16.3%	22.6%	g_6	1.7%	4.6%	m_6	9.1%	8.4%
f_7	9.9%	7.1%	g_7	0.8%	2.7%	m_7	9.4%	10.5%
f_8	8.6%	9.1%	g_8	5.9%	5.5%	m_8	11.2%	7.5%
			g_9	6.0%	7.5%	m_9	10.5%	8.2%
			g_{10}	5.5%	5.6%	m_{10}	8.0%	12.8%
			g_{11}	4.2%	4.5%	m_{11}	8.3%	12.3%
			g_{12}	3.2%	3.9%			
			g_{13}	4.8%	4.4%			
			g_{14}	9.8%	3.8%			
			g_{15}	8.2%	4.4%			
			g_{16}	8.7%	5.8%			
			g_{17}	9.6%	8.4%			
			g_{18}	8.8%	4.6%			
			g_{19}	8.1%	5.7%			

Fig. 4. Behavior generation frequencies of DI and NDI.

6 Conclusion

We proposed a novel Siamese robot platform for m-HRI and its three schemes to coordinate the robot's individuals. The experimental results showed that the Siamese robot is efficient in m-HRI since it has larger interaction area and generates behaviors more frequently considering the required amount of hardware resources. Moreover, the proposed coordination schemes successfully coordinated the conflicted behaviors and did not cause behavioral imbalance between individuals. For further work, experiments will be carried out in real environment to discuss the acceptability of the robot design.

References

1. http://www.ros.org/
2. Cywer, S., Bloch, C.E.: Conjoined twins: a review with a report of a case. S. Afr. Med. J. **38**, 817–821 (1964)

3. Hashimoto, T., Kobayashi, H., Kato, N.: Educational system with the android robot SAYA and field trial. In: 2011 IEEE International Conference on Fuzzy Systems (FUZZ), pp. 766–771. IEEE (2011)
4. Hung, I.C., Chao, K.J., Lee, L., Chen, N.S.: Designing a robot teaching assistant for enhancing and sustaining learning motivation. Interact. Learn. Environ. **21**(2), 156–171 (2013)
5. Ko, W.R., Kim, J.H.: Behavior selection of social robots using developmental episodic memory-based mechanism of thought. In: 3rd IEEE International Conference on Consumer Electronics-Asia (ICCE-Asia). IEEE (2018)
6. Kokcu, A., Cetinkaya, M.B., Aydin, O., Tosun, M.: Conjoined twins: historical perspective and report of a case. J. Matern.-Fetal Neonatal Med. **20**(4), 349–356 (2007)
7. Kondo, Y., Takemura, K., Takamatsu, J., Ogasawara, T.: A gesture-centric android system for multi-party human-robot interaction. J. Hum.-Robot Interact. **2**(1), 133–151 (2013)
8. Murray, C.D.: The experience of body boundaries by Siamese twins. New Ideas Psychol. **19**(2), 117–130 (2001)
9. Shiomi, M., Kanda, T., Ishiguro, H., Hagita, N.: Interactive humanoid robots for a science museum. In: Proceedings of the 1st ACM SIGCHI/SIGART Conference on Human-Robot Interaction, pp. 305–312. ACM (2006)
10. Vernon, D., Metta, G., Sandini, G.: A survey of artificial cognitive systems: implications for the autonomous development of mental capabilities in computational agents. IEEE Trans. Evol. Comput. **11**(2), 151–180 (2007)
11. Weathers, H.: Abigail and Brittany Hensel: an extraordinary bond. Mail Online (2006)

An Attention-Aware Model for Human Action Recognition on Tree-Based Skeleton Sequences

Runwei Ding[1], Chang Liu[1], and Hong Liu[1,2]($\boxtimes$)

[1] Shenzhen Graduate School Peking University, Shenzhen, China
dingrunwei@pku.edu.cn, changliu.pkuece@gmail.com
[2] Key Laboratory of Machine Perception, Peking University, Beijing, China
hongliu@pku.edu.cn

Abstract. Skeleton-based human action recognition (HAR) has attracted a lot of research attentions because of robustness to variations of locations and appearances. However, most existing methods treat the whole skeleton as a fixed pattern, in which the importance of different skeleton joints for action recognition is not considered. In this paper, a novel CNN-based attention-ware network is proposed. First, to describe the semantic meaning of skeletons and learn the discriminative joints over time, an attention generate network named Global Attention Network (GAN) is proposed to generate attention masks. Then, to encode the spatial structure of skeleton sequences, we design a tree based traversal (TTTM) rule, which can represent the skeleton structure, as a convolution unit of main network. Finally, the GAN and main network are cascaded as a whole network which is trained in an end-to-end manner. Experiments show that the TTTM and GAN are supplemented each other, and the whole network achieves an efficient improvement over the state-of-the-arts, e.g., the classification accuracy of this network was 83.6% and 89.5% on NTU-RGBD CV and CS dataset, which outperforms any other methods.

Keywords: Human action recognition · Skeleton · Attention-ware model
Tri-directional Tree Traversal Map (TTTM)

1 Introduction

Human action recognition has been applied in various fields, such as video surveillance, human-computer interaction. Earlier works have often focused on RGB videos [1, 2], which involve many complex illuminations and cluttered backgrounds. Recently, with the fast development of cost-effective depth camera sensors as the Microsoft Kinect [3], acquiring depth information can be a fast and affordable way to gather information. Different from RGB or depth data, skeletons [4] are invariant to viewpoint or appearance, which suffer less intra-class variances and convey significant high-level information. This is, why the skeleton-based discovery of pose-based features outperforms that of appearance features discovery [5].

Compared with the hand-crafted methods [6, 7], Recurrent Neural Network (RNN) with Long Short-Term Memory (LSTM) neurons has achieved a better

© Springer Nature Switzerland AG 2018
S. S. Ge et al. (Eds.): ICSR 2018, LNAI 11357, pp. 569–579, 2018.
https://doi.org/10.1007/978-3-030-05204-1_56

performance, due to its strong ability of modeling sequential data. However, traditional LSTM networks are incapable of memorizing the information of an entire sequence [8], and cannot efficiently learn the spatial relations between the joints. Many improved LSTM structures are proposed to model the spatial and temporal information of skeleton sequence. The authors of [9] proposed a model on top of a 3-part LSTM as follows: the spatial attention part has joint-selection gates; the temporal attention part has frame-selection gates and the backbone is included in the LSTM part. Each part is pre-trained separately for initialization and the entire network is trained end-to-end.

The high complexity of LSTM [10] drives many researchers to choose CNN-based methods. In fact, an essential ability [11] of Convolutional Neural Networks (CNN) has been proven as follows: CNN can learn representations effectively from 2D grids. Kim [12] designed a new CNN-based model, TCN. When fed into 3D skeletons, TCN can explicitly learn the spatiotemporal representations for action recognition. Therefore, TCN is much faster and more interpretable than LSTM-based RNN models.

Skeletons can be seen as a series of 3D data with natural order. Putting the raw skeleton sequence into a model may fail to match the structural properties of the skeleton, which is crucial for action recognition. Ding [13] introduces a technique that encodes skeleton sequences using a tensor-based linear dynamical system (tLDS). With the extracted joint points viewed via a depth camera, tLDS converts the skeletons from an n-order tensor into an (n−1)-order tensors that retains the original spatiotemporal information. Yan [14] designs a graph-based CNN model named ST-GCN, which first encodes dynamic skeletons using graph theory, and achieves superior performance compared to previous methods. However, not only ST-GCN but also many other methods treat the entire skeleton as a fixed pattern. For example, ST-GCN generates the same adjacency matrix of the skeleton graph for all samples.

It's unreasonable to consider that hand joints are of the same importance between two actions of 'brush teeth' and 'kicking other person'. To learn more informative joints in each kind of action, we design a CNN-based attention network named Global Attention Network (GAN) that describes semantic meaning by generating several attention masks. Future-more, we design a tree-based network which can not only represent the skeleton structure efficiently but also gain many benefits from GAN.

2   Global Attention Network (GAN)

For skeletons of a certain action, there are several 'key joints' that are particularly distinguishable from other joints. The imitation of the human attention mechanism and catching of key skeleton joints is a challenging task.

2.1   Structure of GAN

We propose a GAN, which can be seen as an attention branch of this model. The structure is shown in Fig. 1. It is a CNN-based model which takes a sequence of skeleton features as input. Inspired by well-known CNN models, we construct repeat convolution blocks followed by the nonlinear activation function, ELU.

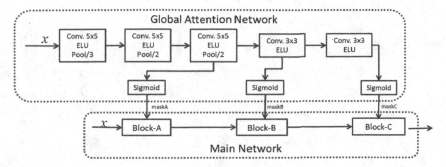

Fig. 1. Overall architecture of the proposed network.

The kernel size of the first three convolution blocks is 5, and it is set to 3 for the last two blocks. A pooling operation is performed in the first three blocks, whose stride is 3, 2, and 2. By the three-flow output mechanism, either of the 3rd or 4th convolution blocks delivers 2 outputs: O_i and F_i. F_i is both one output of $block_i$ and the input of $block_{i+1}$. The last block with single output also generates O_i. All output masks are normalized by the sigmoid function Sig,

$$mask_i = Sig(O_i), i \in \{A, B, C\} \tag{1}$$

whose values range from 0 to 1.

2.2 Interpret-Ability of GAN

The input to GAN is $X_t^i \in R^{T \times D} (t \in T, i \in D)$ with one single channel, where T is the number of frames in one skeleton sequence sample, and the dimension of feature map at frame t is D.

It is observed that human action is consistent and continuous along the temporal domain, whose motion mode may change in a natural continuous way but not in an uncertain sharp way. According to this conclusion, a new mapping function p: to reduce the dimension in temporal domain is obtained:

$$X_t^i \in R^{D \times D} = p(X_t^i \in R^{T \times D}) \tag{2}$$

It could simplify calculation and describe the motion mode with little information loss. p is the pooling layer of GAN. For example, $X_{t=t_0}^{i=i_0}$ in a certain mask has explicable meaning with left hand joint in the y-th channel, where t_0 is a time interval.

3 Tree-Based Structure Construction

3.1 Tree-Based Traversal

The skeleton joints are popularly represented as a tree-based pictorial structure [15]. Figure 2(a) shows the skeleton of the human body.

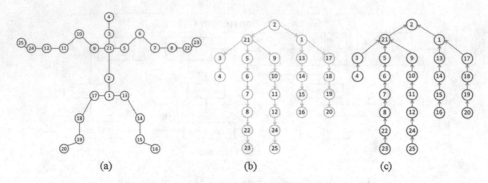

Fig. 2. (a) Configuration of body joints in the NTU-RGB+D dataset. (b) The visiting order of trees structure skeleton joints in a reverse traversal procedure. (c) The visiting order of tree structure skeleton joints in an inverse traversal procedure.

Simplest Chain. In the simplest joint chain model, the joint visiting order is [1, 2, 3, 4, 5, 6, 7, 8, 9, 10, 11, 12, 13, 14, 15, 16, 17, 18, 19, 20, 21, 22, 23, 24, 25].

Depth-First. Inspired by the depth-first traversal method [16], the tree structure can be unfolded to a chain as [2, 21, 3, 4, 3, 21, 5, 6, 7, 8, 22, 23, 22, 8, 7, 6, 5, 21, 9, 10, 11, 12, 24, 25, 24, 12, 11, 10, 9, 21, 2, 1, 13, 14, 15, 16, 15, 14, 13, 1, 17, 18, 19, 20, 19, 18, 17, 1, 2]. Each connection in the tree is met twice mechanically in this depth-first tree traversal scheme.

3.2   Tri-Directional Tree Traversal Map (TTTM)

To form a hierarchical representation of the skeleton sequence, we proposed a Tri-directional Tree Traversal Map (TTTM). As shown in the Fig. 3, the TTTM contains the following 3 parts: the root-leaf part, the leaf-root part and the node-node part. Each part is a 2-dimension feature map as a tensor of (N, N) dimensions, where N is the number of nodes in skeleton tree. Therefore, the shape of the TTT is $(3, N, N)$, which can discover strong long-term spatial dependency patterns in vector $R^{N \times N}$.

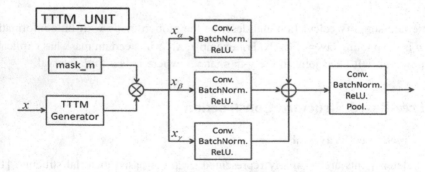

Fig. 3. Illustration of the main network unit with attention.

How to build TTTM? We first adapt the depth-first traversal principle and divide it into two procedures. We define the original tree on the skeleton sequence as $T = (V,V)$. In this tree, the node set $V = \{v_i | i = 1,2,\ldots,N\}$ includes all the joints. $\alpha = (v_{i,\ldots},v_j)$, and $\beta = (v_{m,\ldots},v_n)$ are two lists of distinct element of V. In the reverse traversal procedure, let α store all the nodes one by one in order. Similarly, let β store all the order nodes during backtracking. Then, considering the self-connection of skeleton joints, let $\gamma = (v_1,v_2,\ldots,v_N)$ to store all nodes in a 1-2-...-N order. Each α,β,γ contains V nodes.

In graph theory, a tree is an undirected graph [17], in which one path connects any two vertices. The three traversal lists preserved the spatial action pattern via square unsymmetrical matrices named the adjacency matrix, which can also capture directional information. Given an undirected tree $T = (V,A)$ of N nodes, where $V = (v_i)_{i=1}^N$ is the set of nodes, and A is an adjacency matrix $A \in R^{N \times N}$, and records the connections between nodes. The value of A is defined by the following formula:

$$A_{ij} = f(v_i, v_j) = \begin{cases} 0, v_i, v_j \notin m \\ 1, v_i, v_j \in m \end{cases} \tag{3}$$

where $m \in \{\alpha,\beta,\gamma\}$ is a node list, and v_j must be the nearest neighbor of v_i. Finally we stack the generated matrix A, exactly, on the axis 0. Therefore, we finally generate TTTM as:

$$TTTM = stack(A^\alpha, A^\beta, A^\gamma) \tag{4}$$

We define the tree Laplacian matrix L as $L = D - A$, where $D(D \in R^{N \times N})$ is the diagonal degree matrix, and $D_{ii} = \sum_j A_{ij}$. We normalize the original matrix A by a factor $= \frac{1}{\sqrt{D_{ii}D_{jj}}}$, and A is multiplied by F. Then we get the normalized Laplacian matrix:

$$L_n l = I - D^{\frac{1}{2}}AD^{\frac{1}{2}} = D^{-\frac{1}{2}}LD^{\frac{1}{2}} \tag{5}$$

where I is the identity matrix.

4 Main Network

4.1 Main Network Unit with Attention

As shown in the Fig. 3, the TTTM generator produces TTTM once to be fed into a sequence of skeleton features. The input x to this network is a three-dimensional tensor which can be treated as a 2D image. Therefore, we choose 2D convolution operation later according to the definition of CNNs in dealing with natural 2D images.

The outputs of GAG are several masks, flexible and adaptable to input sequence. In such a TTTM Network unit, each mask is a tensor with the size of (C,N,N), and the final masks are determined as follows:

$$masks = \sum_m mask_m, m \in \{A, B, C\} \tag{6}$$

After x goes through the TTTM generator, the split-flow system S gains new feature map to feed the remainder network. The definition of S is:

$$S(i) = x \otimes A_i \odot mask_m, i \in \{\alpha, \beta, \gamma\} \tag{7}$$

Where $\otimes$ denotes matrix multiplication, $\odot$ denotes element wise product between two matrices, and A_i is a term of formula (2) with normalization.

A TTTM_UNIT contains 4 convolution operators. The first three operators are the same as follows: a 2D convolution layer followed by a batch normalization layer with a ReLU none-linear activation function. They can be defined as f, and combine the outputs of 3 f branches as:

$$y = \sum_i f(S(i)) = \sum_i f(x \otimes A_i \odot mask_m) \tag{8}$$

The 4th operator f^+ has one more pooling layer and takes y as input.

$$f_{out} = f^+(y) = f^+\left(\sum_i f(x \otimes A_i \odot mask_m)\right) \tag{9}$$

where f_{out} is the final output of TTTM_UNIT.

4.2 Structure of the Main Network

We adopt ST-GCN as the baseline of the main network. TTTM_UNITs with residual connections replace the ST-GCN units in nine layer convolution operators parted into 3 blocks, and the kernel size of all convolution operators is 9. The output channel of block-A is 64, block-B is 128, block-C is 256. Before going through block-B or and block-C, there is a 2-stride pooling operation. To avoid overfitting, we use dropouts with $p = 0.5$ after each TTTM_UNIT. Global average pooling, that converts the output into a 256 dimension feature vector, is performed after block-C. Finally the softmax loss is chosen as the classifier (Fig. 4).

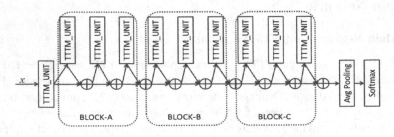

Fig. 4. The framework for the main network.

5   Experiments

5.1   Datasets

NTU RGB+D. The NTU RGB+D dataset [18] is currently the largest 3D skeleton action recognition dataset. This dataset contains 60 different action classes including daily, mutual and health-related actions. It has 56880 skeleton samples with 2 benchmarks: Cross-Subject (CS) and Cross-View (CV).

Kinetics-400 Dataset. The Kinetics-400 dataset [19] is a large-scale, high-quality RGB dataset. It consists of approximately 300000 video clips from YouTube website. There are over 400 human action classes, and at least 600 video clips for each action class. Here we use the public available OpenPose [20] to extract skeletons from RGB videos. It can estimate 18 human joint locations on 2D coordinates. We choose a subset of Kinetics-400 named Kinetics Motion to evaluate the proposed model, whose training set and validation set contains 240000 clips and 20000 clips, respectively.

5.2   Visualization of GAN

We choose two typical kinds of skeleton sequence clips from NTU RGB-D dataset. As shown in Fig. 5, the left is the 'pickup' action, and the right is the 'clapping' action. The two heat maps describe the joint importance evolution rule of 'pickup' and 'clapping' over time. The brighter these pixels, the more significant and informative this corresponding joint. As discussed in Sect. 2.2, each raw value denotes the importance of N joints at T_0 time interval, and each column denotes the response over time of the corresponding joint.

We find that GAN has a positive response to the waist joint, the left knee joint and the left hand joint while performing the 'pickup' action. By contrast, the two most significant joints of action 'clapping' are the right hand joint and the left hand joint. This phenomenon is consistent with our intuition, which strongly proves that GAN is able to explicate motion pattern.

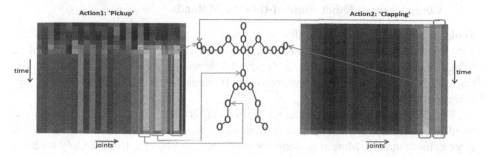

Fig. 5. Example of two typical first masks generated actions by GAN.

5.3   Effectiveness of TTTM and GAN

Effectiveness of TTTM: The simplest chain has the lowest accuracy on the NTU-RGB + D dataset, because it loses interdependency relations between skeleton joints. The bidirectional tree traversal scheme, which is a 1-dimension feature representation, also loses some spatial information of skeleton joints. Each node can only obtain the context information from certain neighbor nodes, its ancestors and descendants follow by the order of depth-first traversal structure. In previous works, ST-GCN outperforms any other hand-craft part assignment or traversal methods. The TTTM gains similar accuracy with the Spatial temporal graph, because the hierarchical nature of the TTTM leads to great expressive power.

Effectiveness of GAN: GAN can be an attention branch for other structured data network as graph-based, tree-based, etc. When different skeleton structure networks are combined with GAN, they all achieve significant accuracy improvement. As shown in Table 1, adding GAN to ST-GCN leads to 1.5% increase of CS and 0.6% increase of CV, while the combination of GAN and TTTM has 1.9% increase and 1.4% increase of CS and CV, respectively. It is noteworthy that the accuracies of a naked TTTM without attention are decreased or even lower than naked ST-GCN on CS or CV. We can reasonably infer that TTTM is more sensitive to GAN and the combination satisfies the mutual benefit of both.

Table 1. Methods without attention on the NTURGB+D dataset.

Methods	CS		CV	
	N/o	GAN	N/o	GAN
Simplest chain	77.1%	79.4%	84.1%	85.2%
BTT [16]	79.2%	80.6%	85.1%	85.1%
Spatial temporal graph [14]	81.5%	83.0%	88.3%	88.9%
TTTM	**81.7%**	**83.6%**	**88.1%**	**89.5%**

5.4   Comparison to Other State-of-the-Art Methods

Table 2 lists the accuracy of different methods on the NTU-RGB+D dataset, while Table 3 shows the results on the Kinetic Motion dataset, compared with the baseline ST-GCN, TTTM+GAN achieves 2.1% and 1.2% accuracy gains on CS and CV settings of NTU-RGB+D dataset, respectively. It outperforms ST-GCN as well as any other methods on this dataset.

For the Kinetics dataset, different from NTU-RGBD whose depth cameras are fixed, RGB videos are shot by hand-held devices. Kinetics suffers from view shift and large camera motion. Moreover, there are many human-object activities. Only skeleton data may lose much scene and object information which is key to action recognition. This explains why our method is inferior to RGB-based or Optical Flow-based methods (Table 3).

Table 2. Comparison on the NTU-RGB+D dataset with CS and CV settings.

Methods	CS	CV
Lie group [21]	50.1%	52.8%
H-RNN [22]	59.1%	64.0%
Deep LSTM [18]	60.7%	67.3%
PA-LSTM [18]	62.9%	70.3%
ST-LSTM+TS [23]	69.2%	77.7%
Temporal Conv [12]	74.3%	83.1%
C-CNN+MTLN [24]	79.6%	84.8%
ST-GCN [14]	81.5%	88.3%
TTTM+GAN	**83.6%**	**89.5%**

Table 3. Comparison on the Kinetics dataset.

Methods	Accuracy
RGB CNN [11]	57.0%
Optical [11] flow	49.5%
Feature Enc [9]	14.9%
Deep LSTM [1]	16.4%
ST-GCN [23]	30.7%
TTTM+GAN	**31.9%**

When compared with these methods using skeleton data only, the method proposed in this work achieves the highest accuracy 31.9% on the Kinetics dataset, which is better than ST-GCN with a 1.2% accuracy increase.

6 Conclusion

In this paper, we present a novel model for action recognition using skeleton data. Specifically, the global Attention Network (GAN) is designed to select discriminative joints automatically over time. A skeleton tree-based traversal method, TTTM, is also proposed to better represent the connections of skeleton joints. Experimental results proved the effectiveness of GAN and TTTM, and their combination achieves the best performance over other state-of-the-art methods on both the NTU-RGB+D dataset and the Kinetics dataset.

Acknowledgments. This work is supported by National Natural Science Foundation of China (NSFC, No. U1613209), Scientific Research Project of Shenzhen City (No. JCYJ20170306164 738129, CKCY2017050810242781).

References

1. Baxter, R.H., Robertson, N.M., Lane, D.M.: Human behavior recognition in data-scarce domains. Pattern Recognit. **48**(8), 2377–2393 (2015)
2. Chen, H., Wang, G., Xue, J., He, L.: A novel hierarchical framework for human action recognition. Pattern Recognit. **55**(C), 148–159 (2016)
3. Zhang, Z.: Microsoft Kinect sensor and its effect. IEEE Multimed. **19**(2), 4–10 (2012)
4. Ding, M., Fan, G.: Multilayer joint gait-pose manifolds for human gait motion modeling. IEEE Trans. Cybern. **45**(11), 1–8 (2015)
5. Yao, A., Gall, J., Fanelli, G., Gool, L.-V.: Does human action recognition benefit from pose estimation? In: British Machine Vision Conference, pp. 67.1–67.11. British Machine Vision Association (2011)
6. Vemulapalli, R., Arrate, F., Chellappa, R.: Human action recognition by representing 3D skeletons as points in a lie group. In: 2014 IEEE Conference on Computer Vision and Pattern Recognition (CVPR), pp. 588–595. IEEE, Columbus (2014)
7. Yang, X., Tian, Y.: Eigen joints-based action recognition using Naïve-Bayes-nearest-neighbor. In: 2012 IEEE Conference on Computer Vision and Pattern Recognition Workshops, pp. 14–19. IEEE, Providence (2012)
8. Ke, Q., Bennamoun, M., An, S., Sohel, F., Boussaid, F.: Learning clip representations for skeleton-based 3D action recognition. IEEE Trans. Image Process. **27**, 2842–2855 (2018)
9. Song, S., Lan, C., Xing, J., Zeng, W., Liu, J.: An end-to-end spatio-temporal attention model for human action recognition from skeleton data. In: AAAI Conference on Artificial Intelligence, pp. 4263–4270. AAAI, San Francisco (2017)
10. Pascanu, R., Gulcehre, C., Cho, K., Bengio, Y.: How to construct deep recurrent neural networks. In: The 30th International Conference on Machine Learning, Beijing, China (2014)
11. Tu, Z., et al.: Multi-stream CNN: learning representations based on human-related regions for action recognition. Pattern Recognit. **79**, 32–43 (2018)
12. Kim, T.-S., Reiter, A.: Interpretable 3D human action analysis with temporal convolutional networks. In: IEEE Conference on Computer Vision and Pattern Recognition Workshops, pp. 1623–1631. IEEE Computer Society, Honolulu (2017)
13. Ding, W., Liu, K., Belyaev, E., Cheng, F.: Tensor-based linear dynamical systems for action recognition from 3D skeletons. Pattern Recognit. **77**, 75–86 (2018)
14. Yan, S., Xiong, Y., Lin, D.: Spatial temporal graph convolutional networks for skeleton-based action recognition. arXiv preprint arXiv:1801.07455 (2018)
15. Yang, Y., Ramanan, D.: Articulated pose estimation with flexible mixtures-of-parts. In: 2011 IEEE Conference on Computer Vision and Pattern Recognition (CVPR), pp. 1385–1392. IEEE, Colorado Springs (2011)
16. Liu, J., Shahroudy, A., Xu, D., Chichung, A.-K., Wang, G.: Skeleton-based action recognition using spatio-temporal LSTM network with trust gates. IEEE Trans. Pattern Anal. Mach. Intell. **PP**(99), 1 (2017)
17. Cayley, A.: XXVIII. On the theory of the analytical forms called trees. Lond. Edinb. Dublin Philos. Mag. J. Sci. **13**(85), 172–176 (1857)
18. Shahroudy, A., Liu, J., Ng, T., Wang, G.: NTU RGB+ D: a large scale dataset for 3D human activity analysis. In: 2016 IEEE Conference on Computer Vision and Pattern Recognition (CVPR), pp. 1010–1019. IEEE, Las Vegas (2016)
19. Kay, W., et al.: The kinetics human action video dataset. arXiv preprint: arXiv:1705.06950 (2017)

20. Cao, Z., Simon, T., Wei, S., Sheikh, Y.: Realtime multi-person 2D pose estimation using part affinity fields. In: 2017 IEEE Conference on Computer Vision and Pattern Recognition (CVPR), pp. 1302–1310. IEEE, Honolulu (2017)
21. Veeriah, V., Zhuang, N., Qi, G.: Differential recurrent neural networks for action recognition. In: 2017 IEEE Conference on Computer Vision and Pattern Recognition (CVPR), pp. 4041–4049. IEEE, Honolulu (2017)
22. Du, Y., Wang, W., Wang, L.: Hierarchical recurrent neural network for skeleton based action recognition. In: 2017 IEEE Conference on Computer Vision and Pattern Recognition (CVPR), pp. 1110–1118. IEEE, Honolulu (2017)
23. Liu, J., Shahroudy, A., Xu, D., Wang, G.: Spatio-temporal LSTM with Trust gates for 3D human action recognition. In: Leibe, B., Matas, J., Sebe, N., Welling, M. (eds.) ECCV 2016. LNCS, vol. 9907, pp. 816–833. Springer, Cham (2016). https://doi.org/10.1007/978-3-319-46487-9_50
24. Ke, Q., Bennamoun, M., An, S., Sohel, F., Boussaid, F.: A new representation of skeleton sequences for 3D action recognition. In: 2017 IEEE Conference on Computer Vision and Pattern Recognition (CVPR), pp. 4570–4579. IEEE, Honolulu (2017)

Predicting the Target in Human-Robot Manipulation Tasks

Mahmoud Hamandi[1], Emre Hatay[1], and Pooyan Fazli[2(✉)]

[1] Electrical Engineering and Computer Science Department,
Cleveland State University, Cleveland, OH 44115, USA
{m.hamandi,e.hatay}@csuohio.edu
[2] Department of Computer Science, San Francisco State University,
San Francisco, CA 94132, USA
pooyan@sfsu.edu

Abstract. We present a novel approach for fast prediction of human reaching motion in the context of human-robot collaboration in manipulation tasks. The method trains a recurrent neural network to process the three-dimensional hand trajectory and predict the intended target along with its certainty about the position. The network then updates its estimate as it receives more observations while advantaging the positions it is more certain about. To assess the proposed algorithm, we build a library of human hand trajectories reaching targets on a fine grid. Our experiments show the advantage of our algorithm over the state of the art in terms of classification accuracy.

Keywords: Human-robot collaboration · Robot manipulation
Robot learning

1 Introduction

Automated systems have been increasingly used in factories for the past decade [1–3]. However, these machines are usually placed in isolation from any humans due to safety reasons [4] and their lack of understanding of human motion. Interest in human-robot coexistence is increasing in manufacturing environments [5]. Significant productivity can be achieved if humans and robots can share the same workspace and work in close proximity. Robots can reduce the task completion time by concurrently working with humans.

With the increased proximity between humans and robots, it becomes imperative for the robots to be aware of humans and plan their motions in such a way that avoids cluttering the shared workspace, blocking human path, or inflicting injuries. Inspired by these requirements, this work investigates the early classification of human arm motion, where the robot has to predict the target position the human is reaching for and plan its actions accordingly.

Early work presented by Jung and Park [6] learned the relation between the intended target of an operator and their pose through a neural network.

© Springer Nature Switzerland AG 2018
S. S. Ge et al. (Eds.): ICSR 2018, LNAI 11357, pp. 580–587, 2018.
https://doi.org/10.1007/978-3-030-05204-1_57

Their work connected the 3-dimensional target position with the pose of the human shoulder, elbow, and wrist, which they consider enough to understand the hand motion. Although their work is promising, it does not consider an online prediction phase, but rather understands the connection between the pose and the target positions to build an ergonomic product for the human operator.

Mainprice *et al.* [7] provided a solution for the problem, where they learn a Gaussian Mixture Model representation for each possible target location and classify the arm trajectories online as reaching to the most probable one. The target classification is followed by a voxel occupancy calculation to know the safe area for the robot to reach. While this approach provides promising results, it requires extensive data (25 trajectories) for each possible target location, rendering it difficult to generalize to continuous spaces.

Later, Perez and Shah [8] presented another method, where they learn a motion library consisting of a Gaussian distribution for each target location and classify each trajectory to the most probable target after adding task level priors. Then during runtime, they warp each path to match the learned one using Dynamic Time Warping (DTW) [9] and classify the trajectory as reaching to the highest Gaussian probability density function. This approach is able to learn target specific trajectories with less data than the former method, however, it is not certain to generalize to unseen targets.

Similar to the above methods, Macda *et al.* [10] presented a framework where they find the most likely sequence from the pool of sample trajectories stored in a lookup table and assume the human will follow a similar trajectory to the target. While these approaches can classify a small number of discrete targets accurately, it is desirable to learn a continuous space representation that allows targets to be placed anywhere in the workspace.

Mainprice *et al.* [11] presented an interesting approach, where they predict the trajectory of the human using STOMP algorithm [12]. Their approach learns the human motion cost function from demonstrations using path integral inverse optimal control [13] and then predict the target and human motion online after applying the cost functions into STOMP. While this approach is very promising, it requires an accurate capture of the pose of multiple joints of the human arm while reaching for the target in real-time.

In this paper, we propose a network architecture, which we refer to as Human-INtended Target (HINT) that predicts the target position the human is reaching for in continuous environments solemnly from the trajectory of the tip of his hand. In addition, the network is trained to output its confidence of the estimate and update its belief as it receives more observations.

Figure 1 shows the offline and online phases of our system. In the offline stage, we build a dataset of hand trajectories reaching for one of the targets placed on a table and train the network to match the collected hand positions and targets. Then, in the online stage, we predict the target position intended by the human each time we receive a new hand position. The target position will be used later to help the robot plan its trajectory in a safe manner. We compare the performance of HINT with other methods from the literature to show the advantage of the proposed algorithm over the state of the art.

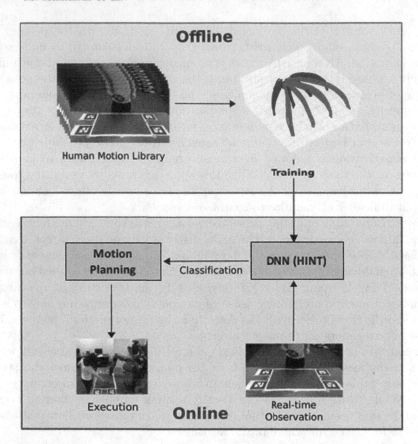

Fig. 1. In the offline phase, the network (HINT) is trained to match the collected hand trajectories and corresponding target positions. In the online phase, hand positions are detected in real time and corresponding target positions are predicted. Human intended target positions are used later to plan the robot motion in a safe manner.

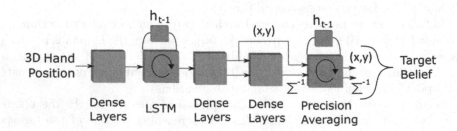

Fig. 2. HINT network architecture.

2   Technical Approach

In this paper, we design a recurrent neural network shown in Fig. 2 that predicts the reaching target and its confidence about the estimate for the given hand trajectory. The network reads the current hand position in the 3-dimensional space and processes the input with a series of four dense layers, each with 128 nodes followed by a *tanh* activation function. This first group of dense layers are followed by a recurrent *LSTM* layer with 128 hidden nodes. The recurrent layer is then followed by a group of three dense layers with 128, 64, and 2 nodes respectively, which output the (x, y) position of the target. The first two of these layers are equipped with a *tanh* activation function, while the last one has no activation function.

The output (x, y) position of the target is fed into another row of dense layers along with the output of the 64 node dense layer. This extra row of dense layers is used to predict the precision Σ^{-1} of the (x, y) estimate. As such, this row of dense layers is constructed out of three consecutive layers, with 32, 16, and 4 nodes respectively, where the first two have a *tanh* activation function, while the last has no activation function. The output 4 nodes represent the 2-dimensional precision matrix.

The output (x, y) and precision Σ^{-1} are then processed by a new recurrent layer, which we refer to as the the Precision Averaging layer, to provide the final target position and precision. This layer averages previously estimated positions based on their confidence and can be explained mathematically as:

$$(\mathbf{p}, \Sigma^{-1}) = (\frac{\Sigma_{new}^{-1} \mathbf{p}_{new} + \gamma \Sigma_{old}^{-1} \mathbf{p}_{old}}{\Sigma_{new}^{-1} + \gamma \Sigma_{old}^{-1}}, \Sigma_{new}^{-1} + \gamma \Sigma_{old}^{-1}), \tag{1}$$

where $\mathbf{p}_{old}$ and Σ_{old}^{-1} are the predicted target position (x, y) and precision for the previous step of the trajectory, $\mathbf{p}_{new}$ and Σ_{new}^{-1} are the predicted target position (x, y) and precision up to the Precision Averaging layer after seeing the last step of the trajectory, $(\mathbf{p}, \Sigma^{-1})$ are the resultant target prediction (x, y) and precision calculated by the layer, and γ is a discount factor chosen to balance between the effect of the old prediction and the new one.

The network is trained to minimize the squared error between the predicted and the actual target position. Since the predicted (x, y) position is a precision-weighted average of all previous predictions, the network learns to output a precision for each prediction relative to its certainty about the target position, so that the final estimate would be dominated by the values it is more certain about.

To use the network for classification, we choose the class with the minimum distance to the predicted target position. However, due to the network's ability to output (x, y) positions in a continuous space instead of choosing a class, it is able to generalize to locations that it has not seen during training, while if it was trained for classification it would have been restricted to the training classes.

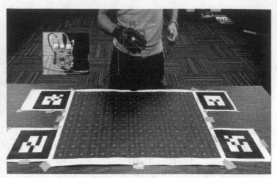
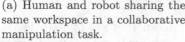

(a) Human and robot sharing the same workspace in a collaborative manipulation task.

(b) The setup from the robot's point of view. (A) shows the microcontroller processing the IMU data, and (B) shows the red LED detected by the depth camera.

Fig. 3. Human-robot collaboration setup.

3   Experiments

To assess the performance of our algorithm, we collected a dataset of hand trajectories reaching for one of the cells of the grid shown in Fig. 3. The targets were chosen randomly out of the 176 possible targets presented by the 16×11 grid fixed on the table, with each target being represented by a $5 \times 5\,cm^2$. The aim of the grid is to discretize the workspace for a human to visually find a randomly assigned target while being fine enough for the network to learn a continuous probability distribution of the target.

The human subject was instructed to start from the position where they feel most comfortable at and reach for the target being displayed on a screen in front of him. As the targets changed, the human was allowed to move freely and as such multiple start positions exist for each trajectory. As the human reached for the target, we collected the hand position using a depth camera as well as readings from a 6-DOF IMU fixed to the hand, RGB images from the camera, and the point cloud generated by the camera. In total, we collected 704 trajectories distributed equally over the 176 target positions, with the order being chosen at random to assure the independence between one trajectory and another. These trajectories were split equally between training and testing, with some target positions being represented in only one of the two sets. Each target is represented by zero to four trajectories in the training set, and the remaining of the four collected trajectories are placed in the test set. To detect and track the hand position in the image and the point cloud, we fixed a bright LED light on the tip of the hand as shown in Fig. 3, which we tracked in the image and point cloud to record the 3-dimensional position of the hand. In addition, the image and the point cloud allow the detection of the grid location inferred by the four AR markers placed near the grid edges.

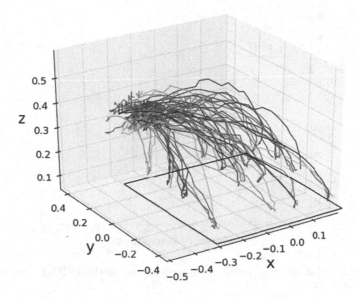

Fig. 4. Sample hand trajectories reaching 16 targets in the grid.

Figure 4 shows the collected trajectories for 16 targets in the grid, demonstrating that the trajectories are difficult to separate especially near the starting position.

4   Results

We compare our algorithm with one other method from the literature [8] where they suggest to build a motion library presenting a probability flow tube (PFT) [14] for each target position, i.e., the mean and variance of each position along the trajectory. During online classification, they warp the test trajectory using Dynamic Time Warping (DTW) [9] to match the trajectories with those in the motion library. Finally, they classify the target location as the one with the smallest Mahalanobis distance [15] based on the matched means and variances from the motion library. It should be noted that this algorithm is not real time for more than 3 target positions without multi-threading, while our dataset presents 176 target positions.

Figure 5 shows the average classification accuracy of our method and the benchmark algorithm. As the graph shows, our method has a higher accuracy throughout the trajectory. In addition, PFT has near zero accuracy in the beginning where the trajectories are non-separable, while our algorithm has near 30% accuracy. It is also observed that near the end of the trajectories HINT reaches a plateau of 80%, while PFT reaches only 30%. This can be related to two reasons: first, PFT is designed to be trained on roughly 20 demonstrations of each class to build an understanding of the shape of the trajectories and the possible variance of each, while the dataset presented here has zero to four examples of

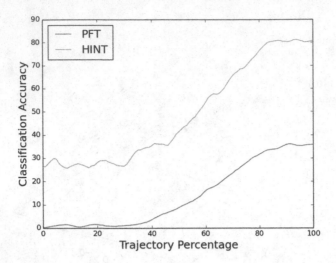

Fig. 5. Classification accuracy comparison between our method, HINT, and the benchmark method, PFT.

each in the training set. Second, since HINT learns to output an (x, y) position instead of a class, it is able to generalize to targets not shown in the training set.

5   Conclusion and Future Work

We presented HINT, a novel method for early prediction of human intended target. Our deep learning based method reads 3-dimensional hand positions and predicts the 2-dimensional target position and its confidence about the prediction. We built an extensive dataset of hand trajectories reaching for known targets on a table. Our dataset contains multiple trials for each target position, with each trial starting from a randomly chosen position. HINT outperformed the benchmark algorithm PFT by 50% in classification accuracy when trained and tested on the created dataset. In the future, we intend to collect our data with a motion capture system to reduce the noise in the recorded positions.

Acknowledgments. The authors would like to thank Nuo Zhou for her assistance in developing the software and collecting the data.

References

1. Lasota, P.A., Fong, T., Shah, J.A., et al.: A survey of methods for safe human-robot interaction. Found. Trends Robot. **5**(4), 261–349 (2017)
2. Broquere, X., Sidobre, D., Herrera-Aguilar, I.: Soft motion trajectory planner for service manipulator robot. In: IEEE/RSJ International Conference on Intelligent Robots and Systems, IROS, pp. 2808–2813 (2008)

3. Calinon, S., Sardellitti, I., Caldwell, D.G.: Learning-based control strategy for safe human-robot interaction exploiting task and robot redundancies. In: IEEE/RSJ International Conference on Intelligent Robots and Systems, IROS, pp. 249–254 (2010)
4. Dhillon, B., Fashandi, A., Liu, K.: Robot systems reliability and safety: a review. J. Qual. Maint. Eng. **8**(3), 170–212 (2002)
5. Shi, J., Jimmerson, G., Pearson, T., Menassa, R.: Levels of human and robot collaboration for automotive manufacturing. In: Proceedings of the Workshop on Performance Metrics for Intelligent Systems, PerMI, pp. 95–100 (2012)
6. Jung, E.S., Park, S.: Prediction of human reach posture using a neural network for ergonomic man models. Comput. Ind. Eng. **27**(1–4), 369–372 (1994)
7. Mainprice, J., Berenson, D.: Human-robot collaborative manipulation planning using early prediction of human motion. In: Proceedings of the IEEE/RSJ International Conference on Intelligent Robots and Systems, IROS, pp. 299–306 (2013)
8. Pérez-D'Arpino, C., Shah, J.A.: Fast target prediction of human reaching motion for cooperative human-robot manipulation tasks using time series classification. In: Proceedings of the International Conference on Robotics and Automation, ICRA, pp. 6175–6182 (2015)
9. Kruskal, J., Liberman, M.: The Symmetric Time-Warping Problem: From Continuous to Discrete. Addison-Wesley, Reading (1983)
10. Maeda, G., Maloo, A., Ewerton, M., Lioutikov, R., Peters, J.: Anticipative interaction primitives for human-robot collaboration. In: Proceedings of the AAAI Fall Symposium Series, pp. 325–330 (2016)
11. Mainprice, J., Hayne, R., Berenson, D.: Predicting human reaching motion in collaborative tasks using inverse optimal control and iterative re-planning. In: Proceedings of the IEEE International Conference on Robotics and Automation, ICRA, pp. 885–892 (2015)
12. Kalakrishnan, M., Chitta, S., Theodorou, E., Pastor, P., Schaal, S.: STOMP: stochastic trajectory optimization for motion planning. In: Proceedings of the IEEE International Conference on Robotics and Automation, ICRA, pp. 4569–4574 (2011)
13. Kalakrishnan, M., Pastor, P., Righetti, L., Schaal, S.: Learning objective functions for manipulation. In: Proceedings of the IEEE International Conference on Robotics and Automation, ICRA, pp. 1331–1336 (2013)
14. Dong, S., Williams, B.: Learning and recognition of hybrid manipulation motions in variable environments using probabilistic flow tubes. Int. J. Soc. Robot. **4**(4), 357–368 (2012)
15. De Maesschalck, R., Jouan-Rimbaud, D., Massart, D.L.: The mahalanobis distance. Chemom. Intell. Lab. Syst. **50**(1), 1–18 (2000)

Imitating Human Movement Using a Measure of Verticality to Animate Low Degree-of-Freedom Non-humanoid Virtual Characters

Roshni Kaushik[✉] and Amy LaViers

University of Illinois at Urbana-Champaign, Urbana, IL 61801, USA
{rkaushi2,alaviers}@illinois.edu

Abstract. Imitating human motion on robotic platforms is a task which requires ignoring some information about the original human mover as robots have fewer degrees of freedom than a human. In an effort to generate low degree of freedom motion profiles based on human movement, this paper utilizes verticality, computed from motion capture data, to animate virtual characters. After creating correspondences between the verticality metrics and the movement of three and four degree of freedom virtual characters, lay users were asked whether the imitation of the characters' movements was effective compared to pseudo-random motion profiles. The results showed a statistically significant preference for the verticality method for the higher DOF character and for the higher DOF character over the lower DOF character. Future work includes extending the verticality method to more virtual characters and developing other methodologies of motion generation for users to evaluate a more diverse set of motion profiles. This work can help create automated protocols for replicating human motion, and intent, on artificial systems.

Keywords: Virtual characters · Human motion · Robotics Anthropormorphism

1 Introduction

Human movement is a complex phenomenon involving a large number of degrees of freedom changing simultaneously in many contexts. These complexities raise many research questions including a correspondence problem: translating high degree of freedom human movement to lower degree of freedom characters. A solution to this problem may be important in immersing robots in social contexts. One approach to this problem involves the understanding and dissection of various properties of human movement using motion capture and other analysis techniques in order to apply those same properties to the generation of motion profiles for virtual characters.

Virtual characters have been animated using human motion capture data using a variety of mechanisms. A mapping between the human poses and the

© Springer Nature Switzerland AG 2018
S. S. Ge et al. (Eds.): ICSR 2018, LNAI 11357, pp. 588–598, 2018.
https://doi.org/10.1007/978-3-030-05204-1_58

character poses can be generated by using a few key human poses from a motion capture session of a human moving in the style of the character [15]. A dancing game was developed that generated a real-time animation of virtual dancers on a screen that corresponded to the motion capture movement of human dancers using a matching algorithm that recognized specific dance moves [13]. From a puppetry perspective, motion for animated non-human characters was generated using direct feature mapping before a human motion-capture movement was used to control the characters in real-time [11]. A methodology for creating correspondences between groups of body parts on different characters allowed for the generation of motions on different characters from the same source [1].

Many other methodologies have created correspondences between human motion capture markers and movements of non-human movers. A humanoid robot has been controlled by virtually connecting human motion capture markers with points on the robot with translational springs in order to find correspondences [9]. Additionally, a mapping between human and humanoid robot markers was investigated in order to emulate human behaviors during social interaction [8]. Head motion, specifically, during human conversation (nods, tilts, etc.) were recorded for robots to display more "natural" nonverbal cues during a human interaction [7], and head movements during dyadic conversations were analyzed with respect to the making and breaking of symmetry [3]. Dance performances have been synthesized by combining a musical analysis and a motion analysis using motion capture that utilized intensity and the key frames on the music beats [12]. Motion preferences of humans were calculated and analyzed by users comparing the movements of various amoebas to a motion capture bhangra dancer to determine which amoeba behaviors mimicked the dancer's movement best [6].

Motion capture is not the only tool used to model human movement to control a non-human mover. Coupled inverted pendulums can be used to model dancers performing the waltz so a human mover can move with a robot follower in basic steps [14]. On-board sensors were utilized to record aspects of tango dancers and compute several performance metrics [2]. An evolutionary dynamics approach using replicator-mutator dynamics has been used to model dominance in group dance performances [10]. An energy metric was developed by replicating human trajectories on wheeled robots that related to observers' assessment of the human performance in the context of salsa [4].

1.1   A Spectrum of Movers

We start with the premise of a spectrum of movers (Fig. 1) organized by degrees of freedom (DOF). Human movement has a large and unknown number of degrees of freedom, and the goal is to imitate that human movement with characters of finite and smaller DOF. The figure is organized with virtual or simulated characters in the top row and robots and hardware implementations in the second row. Recording human movement with motion capture already reduces the DOF to 111 and is an approximation of the actual motion. We will then generate

3 DOF (*Rollbot*) and 4 DOF (*Broombot*) virtual characters which represent an incremental progression in motion capabilities, i.e. adding one DOF.

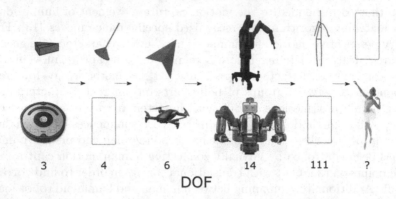

DOF

Fig. 1. A spectrum of "movers" with increasing degrees of freedom from left to right. The top row illustrates simulated robots, including the *Rollbot*, *Broombot* (used in this paper), and a motion capture skeleton. The bottom row illustrates actual robots/hardware implementations. Each column is labeled with number of degrees of freedom associated with the visual shape of the platform. An empty white box is used where no established correlate exists. Working in simulation provides a starting point for actual hardware implementation.

1.2 Verticality

In the effort to model the high-DOF of a motion capture skeleton with a low-DOF model to control simple robots, we utilized a modified version of a measure introduced in a previous work [5], which we have dubbed verticality. The verticality metric is simply a subset of a motion capture skeleton that emulates the leaning of the torso. As shown in previous work, analysis of a specific verticality metric (the vector from the pelvis to the neck) correlates with expert observations of interactive motion. To further evaluate the effectiveness of the verticality to characterize human motion, we will utilize it to create a correspondence between human motion capture and two low-DOF simulated robots.

We will explain the computation process for a specific verticality metric in Sect. 2 and the chosen correspondence between the verticality metric and two simulated robots from the spectrum discussed above in Sect. 3. Sections 4 and 5 introduce the development and results of a user study, respectively, while Sect. 6 summarizes the contribution of the paper and points to future directions of exploration.

2 Computing the Verticality Metric

We will first outline how the verticality metric is computed using data from an OptiTrack motion capture system. We recorded the global Cartesian trajectories

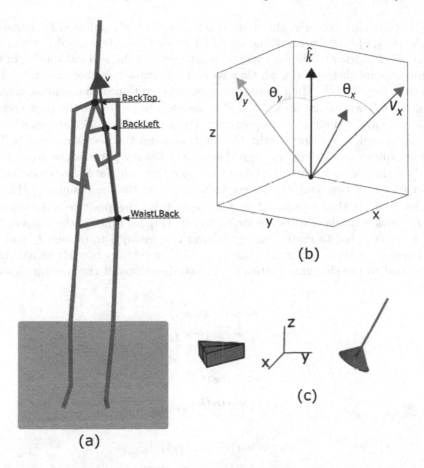

Fig. 2. This figure demonstrates the construction of virtual characters, simple enough to be implemented on robotic hardware, from motion capture data. (a) Position of the two markers used for the verticality vector (*WaistLBack* and *BackLeft*) and the marker used for translation (*BackTop*) on the motion capture skeleton. Verticality vector v is displayed in blue. (b) Illustration of the projections v_x and v_y and the verticality angles θ_x and θ_y for a verticality vector v at one time step. (c) Illustration of the 3 DOF simulated robot (*Rollbot*) with x-y translation and z-axis rotation and the 4 DOF simulated robot (*Broombot*) with x-y translation and rotation about the x and y axes. (Color figure online)

of 37 markers placed on a motion capture suit. This results in a $37 \times 3 = 111$ DOF, time-dependent system. To compute a low dimensional verticality signal, we focused on the trajectories of two points: *WaistLBack* and *BackLeft*. These two markers, along with the *BackTop* marker (used to represent horizontal translation) are shown in Fig. 2(a). Before performing further computations in the data, we reduced the noise in the signals mentioned above by smoothing over any points where the motion capture system lost the position of one of the markers and by re-sampling each signal to reduce computation time.

The verticality vector v, shown in blue in Fig. 2(a), is computed by subtracting the (x, y, z) coordinates of the *BackLeft* marker from the coordinates of the *WaistLBack* marker to obtain a vector that represents the vertical leaning of the motion capture skeleton at each time step. This vector v is then normalized at each time step to $\bar{v} = v/||v||$ to characterize the direction of the leaning torso.

In the following equations, $\hat{i}, \hat{j}$, and $\hat{k}$ are used to represent the unit vectors in the x, y, and z directions, respectively. From the 3 dimensional signal $\bar{v}$, we will obtain angles that characterize the rotation about the x-axis and y-axis. The motion capture data's axes are aligned such that the x-y plane is the ground. To calculate the angles in these two directions, we first calculate the projection of vector $\bar{v}$ at each time step on the y-z plane (v_x) and the x-z plane (v_y) (Eq. 1). The angle θ_x is then computed as the angle from the positive z-direction $\hat{k}$ and v_x, with a similar procedure for θ_y and v_y (Eq. 2). Finally, the signs of the angles are adjusted to match the right-hand rule in Eq. 3 to obtain $\bar{\theta}_x$ and $\bar{\theta}_y$. After repeating this process for each time-step, we obtain two 1D signals that correspond to the changing verticality in two directions of the motion capture skeleton.

$$
\begin{aligned}
v_x &= \hat{i} \times (\bar{v} \times \hat{i}) \\
v_y &= \hat{j} \times (\bar{v} \times \hat{j})
\end{aligned}
\tag{1}
$$

$$
\begin{aligned}
\theta_x &= \cos(\hat{k} \cdot v_x) \\
\theta_y &= \cos(\hat{k} \cdot v_y)
\end{aligned}
\tag{2}
$$

$$
\begin{aligned}
\bar{\theta}_x &= sign\{v_x \cdot (\hat{k} \cdot v_x)\}|\theta_x| \\
\bar{\theta}_y &= sign\{v_y \cdot (\hat{k} \cdot v_y)\}|\theta_y|
\end{aligned}
\tag{3}
$$

Figure 2(b) illustrates the projections and angles calculated from this geometric method. For each motion capture dataset, the data outputted from this analysis is the two dimensional rotation $\{\bar{\theta}_x(t), \bar{\theta}_y(t)\}$ (hereafter referred to as $\{\theta_x(t), \theta_y(t)\}$ for simplicity) as well as the two dimensional translation of the *WaistLBack* marker as $\{x(t), y(t)\}$.

3   Verticality-Driven Simulated Robots

Since we have four different DOF (two translation, two rotation) coming from the motion capture, we can construct simulated robots with up to four DOF. The lowest DOF simulated robot constructed was the 3 DOF robot *Rollbot* (Fig. 2(c) left), which can translate in the xy-plane and has one rotation about its own z-axis. The triangular shape and color scheme serve the purpose of making the rotations more visually apparent. The 4 DOF robot *Broombot* (Fig. 2(c) right) can translate in the xy-plane and rotate about its own x and y axes. Again, the dual colors attempt to make any rotation more visually apparent.

Table 1. Correspondence between verticality and simulated robot motion

	Rollbot	*Broombot*
x translation	$x(t)$ + offset	$x(t)$ + offset
y translation	$y(t)$ + offset	$y(t)$ + offset
x rotation	-	$\theta_x(t)$
y rotation	-	$\theta_y(t)$
z rotation	$\theta_x(t) + \theta_y(t)$	-

The correspondence between the verticality metrics and the robots' DOF is a design choice and can take a number of forms. We chose a simple correspondence, shown in Table 1. For the translation, the robots mimic the planar (x, y) position with the addition of a offset in the horizontal plane. This allows multiple movers (human and robot) to be animated simultaneously. For the *Rollbot*, the sum of the two motion capture rotation angles was taken as the one rotational degree of freedom, and for the *Broombot*, the x and y motion capture angles were taken directly as the x and y rotational degrees of freedom.

4   User Study Development Comparing *Rollbot - Broombot*

In this user study, we attempted to answer the question: Do users identify a verticality-based robot as imitating a human better than "random" robot? To generate a dataset on which to test, we needed to first determine a method for generating "random" signals to drive the two robots.

4.1   Random Periodic Motion

In this pseudo-random method, we only modified the rotation components of the robot motion. The translation components remained the same as the verticality method, mirroring that of the human in motion capture. For each of the other three angles (x and y rotation of the *Broombot* and z rotation for the *Rollbot*), a pseudo-random value was generated at each time-step. The frequency of the random oscillations was determined based on the re-sampling rate and a hand-tuned constant, shown in Eq. 4. This constant was chosen to match the speed of movement of the motion capture data since a robot changing orientation with much higher or lower speed than a human could bias users and not provide a proper comparison. T is the total number motion capture frames and $\tilde{T}$ is the number of frames after resampling. This frequency is constant for every time step, but random amplitudes A_r, A_{b_x}, A_{b_y} are generated at each time step in $\left[-\frac{\pi}{2}, \frac{\pi}{2}\right]$. Putting all these values together, the three angles at each time step are computed as shown in Eq. 5.

$$\omega_r = \frac{T}{400\tilde{T}}$$
$$\omega_b = \frac{T}{200\tilde{T}} \tag{4}$$

$$\theta_{z,Rollbot} = A_r \sin(\omega_r t)$$
$$\theta_{x,Broombot} = A_{b,x} \sin(\omega_b t) \tag{5}$$
$$\theta_{y,Broombot} = A_{b,y} \sin(\omega_b t)$$

4.2   User Study Questionnaire

We collected approximately 5 min of motion capture data, with the individual in the motion capture suit not given any specific instructions as to the type of movement, except to generate large variation. As the individual is trained in contemporary Western dance, the motions performed were roughly in that style. We then chose three different parts of the recorded movement to use for robot motion generation. For each of these three motion capture excerpts, we generated three different cases of robot motion, enumerated below. A still image from an animation is shown in Fig. 3.

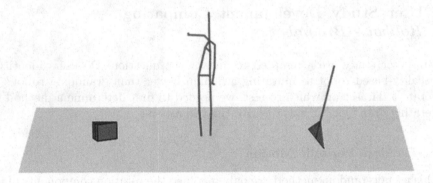

Fig. 3. Still image from an example animation for the *Rollbot - Broombot* user study with three movers (two simulated robots and one human motion capture skeleton). The robots were driven by either the verticality or the pseudo-random method, and users were asked which robot better imitated the human movement.

1. *Rollbot* Verticality vs. Random Periodic
2. *Brooombot* Verticality vs. Random Periodic
3. *Brooombot* Verticality vs. *Rollbot* Verticality

We generated 3 videos for Cases 1 and 2 and 2 videos for Case 3, but also created 8 mirrored videos that switched the positioning of the movers in each video. Each user was presented with a total of 8 questions in a random order. For each of the 8 questions, the user was randomly shown either the original or mirrored video and asked a question with two parts:

1. Which robot (left or right) imitates the human skeleton (center) best?
2. Please explain why you made the choice you did for the previous question.

This study was developed using SurveyMonkey and administered using Amazon Mechanical Turk (MTurk) to 20 online participants.

5   User Study Results and Discussion

We first compared the number of participants identifying the verticality-based motion as imitating the human skeleton movement better with the number preferring the random periodic motion (Fig. 4(a)). In the case of *Rollbot* motion (Case 1), the users had no preference between the verticality and random periodic robot motion. Some excerpts from their justifications include: "They are almost identical" and "I could not tell any difference in the way the robot moved." However, in the case of *Broombot* motion (Case 2), the users preferred the verticality motion 77% of the time, with one user commenting: "This broom seems to be moving exactly like the human skeleton."

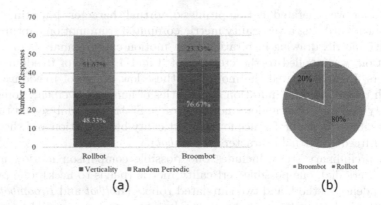

(a)   (b)

Fig. 4. (a) Number of responses identifying the verticality-based robot motion (blue) and random periodic robot motion (orange) as imitating the human skeleton movement best for the *Rollbot* and *Broombot* movements. (b) Percentage of participants identifying the *Rollbot* verticality-based motion (purple) and the *Broombot* verticality-based motion (green) as imitating the human skeleton best (total of 40 responses). (Color figure online)

We then compared the verticality based motion between the *Rollbot* and *Broombot* in Case 3 (Fig. 4(b)). The users preferred the *Broombot* 78% of the time, with users commenting: "overall movement is more active and copies movements better" and "it can emulate the leaning of the upper torso."

We then performed one-sample two-sided t-tests on all three datasets (Table 2), comparing the resulting percentages with a "random" choice of 50%. The degrees of freedom were $60 - 1 = 59$ for Cases 1 and 2 and $40 - 1 = 39$ for

Table 2. P-values for one sample t-tests on user study results ($p = 0.01$ significance)

	Two-sided t-test	One-sided t-test
Verticality *Rollbot*	0.799	0.601
Verticality *Broombot*	9.622e−6	4.811e−6
Verticality *Broombot* vs. *Rollbot*	3.379e−5	1.689e−5

Case 3. For Case 1, the two-sided t-test was not significant ($p > 0.01$), so the probability of choosing verticality over random periodic cannot be distinguished from 0.5 for the *Rollbot*. For Case 2, both the two-sided and one-sided t-tests were significant at the 0.01 level, showing that users preferred the verticality motion over the random periodic motion for the *Broombot*. For Case 3, both the two-sided and one-sided t-tests were also significant, illustrating the users' preference of the *Broombot* over the *Rollbot* when both were using verticality.

6 Conclusion and Future Work

In this paper, we generated motion profiles of virtual characters imitating human movement by utilizing a verticality metric computed from motion capture. This verticality metric, drawing inspiration from motion capture analysis of interactive motion, was applied to the creation of 3 and 4 degree of freedom virtual characters. Users evaluated the motion of these low degree of freedom characters with respect to their imitation capabilities of human movement, comparing verticality and a pseudo-random motion profile. Statistical analyses on the user responses illustrated a preference for the verticality-based motion and the higher degree of freedom virtual character (*Broombot*).

This preliminary study includes one possible comparison motion method (random periodic), one possible verticality metric (pelvis to neck), one possible correspondence method, and two simulated robots (*Rollbot* and *Broombot*) with specific physical structure and appearance. In future studies, we will be exploring more variety in each of those potential directions (i.e. adding more robots with different morphologies and degrees of freedom, using different "random" motion generation, generalizing the verticality vector used to many general vectors on the human motion capture skeleton, etc). This will allow users to compare the effectiveness at imitation and various other motion modes (i.e. mirroring, etc.) across more diversity of movement, including more characters from the spectrum of movers.

Implementing these motion profiles generated through verticality on actual hardware expands the range possible research questions we can explore. For example, the *Rollbot* motion can be transferred to the motion of a planar robot such as the iRobot Create (a Roomba). With hardware implementation, we open the potential for real-time translation of a human moving in a motion capture suit to a robot moving, using our verticality measure as the translator. While filling in more gaps in the spectrum, we can investigate more trends that emerge when increasing DOF and moving between simulated and hardware implementations.

An automated methodology to generate low degree of freedom movements based on the rich variety of possible human movements would provide a great diversity of robotic motion profiles that could interpret and emulate intent in human motion. Such a framework could facilitate meaningful interactions between a variety of robotic platforms in contexts like co-robots in factories, tele-operated robots in space, and empathetic systems in healthcare.

References

1. Abdul-Massih, M., Yoo, I., Benes, B.: Motion style retargeting to characters with different morphologies. In: Computer Graphics Forum, vol. 36, pp. 86–99. Wiley Online Library (2017)
2. Arvind, D., Valtazanos, A.: Speckled tango dancers: Real-time motion capture of two-body interactions using on-body wireless sensor networks. In: Sixth International Workshop on Wearable and Implantable Body Sensor Networks, BSN 2009, pp. 312–317. IEEE (2009)
3. Ashenfelter, K.T., Boker, S.M., Waddell, J.R., Vitanov, N.: Spatiotemporal symmetry and multifractal structure of head movements during dyadic conversation. J. Exp. Psychol.: Hum. Percept. Perform. **35**(4), 1072 (2009)
4. Baillieul, J., Özcimder, K.: The control theory of motion-based communication: problems in teaching robots to dance. In: American Control Conference (ACC), pp. 4319–4326. IEEE (2012)
5. Kaushik, R., Vidrin, I., LaViers, A.: Quantifying coordination in human dyads via a measure of verticality. In: Proceedings of the 5th International Conference on Movement and Computing, p. 19. ACM (2018)
6. Kingston, P., Egerstedt, M.: Motion preference learning. In: American Control Conference (ACC), pp. 3819–3824. IEEE (2011)
7. Liu, C., Ishi, C.T., Ishiguro, H., Hagita, N.: Generation of nodding, head tilting and eye gazing for human-robot dialogue interaction. In: 2012 7th ACM/IEEE International Conference on Human-Robot Interaction (HRI), pp. 285–292. IEEE (2012)
8. Minato, T., Ishiguro, H.: Generating natural posture in an android by mapping human posture in three-dimensional position space. In: IEEE/RSJ International Conference on Intelligent Robots and Systems, IROS 2007, pp. 609–616. IEEE (2007)
9. Ott, C., Lee, D., Nakamura, Y.: Motion capture based human motion recognition and imitation by direct marker control. In: 8th IEEE-RAS International Conference on Humanoid Robots, Humanoids 2008, pp. 399–405. IEEE (2008)
10. Özcimder, K., Dey, B., Lazier, R.J., Trueman, D., Leonard, N.E.: Investigating group behavior in dance: an evolutionary dynamics approach. In: American Control Conference (ACC), pp. 6465–6470. IEEE (2016)
11. Seol, Y., O'Sullivan, C., Lee, J.: Creature features: online motion puppetry for non-human characters. In: Proceedings of the 12th ACM SIGGRAPH/Eurographics Symposium on Computer Animation, pp. 213–221. ACM (2013)
12. Shiratori, T., Nakazawa, A., Ikeuchi, K.: Synthesizing dance performance using musical and motion features. In: Proceedings 2006 IEEE International Conference on Robotics and Automation, ICRA 2006, pp. 3654–3659. IEEE (2006)

13. Tang, J.K., Chan, J.C., Leung, H.: Interactive dancing game with real-time recognition of continuous dance moves from 3D human motion capture. In: Proceedings of the 5th International Conference on Ubiquitous Information Management and Communication, p. 50. ACM (2011)
14. Wang, H., Kosuge, K.: Control of a robot dancer for enhancing haptic human-robot interaction in waltz. IEEE Trans. Haptics **5**(3), 264–273 (2012)
15. Yamane, K., Ariki, Y., Hodgins, J.: Animating non-humanoid characters with human motion data. In: Proceedings of the 2010 ACM SIGGRAPH/Eurographics Symposium on Computer Animation, pp. 169–178. Eurographics Association (2010)

Adaptive Neural Control for Robotic Manipulators Under Constrained Task Space

Sainan Zhang[1](✉) and Zhongliang Tang[2]

[1] Center for Robotics, University of Electronic Science and Technology of China,
Chengdu 611731, People's Republic of China
zhangsainan_isit@163.com
[2] HuaWei Technologies Co., Ltd., Shanghai 31000, People's Republic of China

Abstract. A fundamental requirement in human-robot interaction is the capability for motion in the constrained task space. The control design for robotic manipulators is investigated in this paper, subject to uncertainties and constrained task space. The neural networks (NN) are employed to estimate the uncertainty of robotic dynamics, while the integral barrier Lyapunov Functional (iBLF) is used to handle the effect of constraint. With the proposed control strategy, the system output can converge to an adjustable constrained space without violating the predefined constrained region. Semi-globally uniformly ultimate boundedness of the closed-loop system is guaranteed via Lyapunov's stability theory. Simulation examples are provided to illustrate the performance of the proposed strategy.

Keywords: Constrained task space · Robots · Neural networks (NN)
Integral barrier Lyapunov functionals

1 Introduction

Due to the increasing demands on robots and humans to share the same workspace or task, research on the safe control for robotic manipulators, in interaction with humans, is gaining importance [4,6,7]. In recent years, similar research works have been developed to handle the safety issue for robotic tasks [1,14]. In particular, when the robotic applications are related to human-robot interaction, robots must be subject to certain motion constraints, which typically include constraints of position and velocity [33]. Therefore, it is essential for robotic manipulators to be able to perform safe control under constrained task space.

There is a remarkable increasing attention on robotic control [19], and it is a fact that there exist constraints in actual robotic systems, especially in the human-robot cooperation [18]. Great system performance degradation may

© Springer Nature Switzerland AG 2018
S. S. Ge et al. (Eds.): ICSR 2018, LNAI 11357, pp. 599–608, 2018.
https://doi.org/10.1007/978-3-030-05204-1_59

result from the violation of constraints. Therefore, it is significant and necessary to solve the effect of constraints in the control design for robot manipulators. In [12], Hongan introduces the impedance control strategy for robot-environment interactions. The impedance control is firstly proposed, that not to track the desired position, but rather to regulate the robot-environment interaction dynamics. During the decades, impedance control has been widely studied. In [20], a decentralized fuzzy control approach is applied to a practical robotic platform with impedance interaction, where two cooperating robotic manipulators are carrying out more complicated tasks which may not be accomplished by a single manipulator, and fuzzy logic systems are developed to tackle the uncertain robotic model. Impedance control design has been used to solve for robot control in [3,17,24,32].

Recently, the use of barrier Lyapunov Functional (BLF) for solving the control problem with constraint has been an active area [21]. A survey paper on model predictive control about constraint-handling methods is established in [23]. Then, the BLF control strategy have been extended to the control for nonlinear systems in [22,25,30,31] and the application in robot [8], flexible marine riser [10] and flexible crane system [11]. Next, the integral barrier Lyapunov functionals (iBLFs) are developed in [13,16,29]. The advantage of iBLFs-based control strategy is that the state constraint is directly mixed with the error terms. Although previous research works have addressed the constraint effect by using iBLFs, there is an urgent requirement to apply the iBLF technology to solve challenging problems, that is improving the safe human-robot interaction. Moreover, another important motivation of this paper is that, it is difficult to push the iBLFs technology to the robotic control due to the highly coupled nonlinear dynamics and great capability in performing complex and complicated tasks, especially some operational requirements under real-world working conditions. Therefore, the problem for robotic control with constraints needs to be further developed.

An adaptive neural network control technique is studied for robotic manipulators under constrained task space. The main contributions of the proposed approach are given as follows:

(i) Different from the conventional barrier Lyapunov functions, in this paper, integral barrier Lyapunov functions are developed to handle the motion control of robotic manipulators under constrained task space, without carrying out an additional mapping to the error space. The proposed control strategy generates the constrained output, and guarantees the stability of the whole system.

(ii) Unknown packaged functions are estimated by constructing appropriate neural networks, and adapting parameters are utilized to approximate the unknown bounds of NNs approximation error. All signals in the closed-loop system are bounded.

The outline of the paper is given as follows. Section 2 shows the problem formulation, followed by the control design and stability analysis in Sect. 3. Section 4 offers simulation examples. The last part contains the conclusion.

2   Preliminaries and Problem Formulation

Consider the following robotic in joint space [5,15]

$$M(q)\ddot{q} + C(q,\dot{q})\dot{q} + G(q) = \tau \tag{1}$$

where $q = [q_1, \cdots, q_n]^T \in \mathbb{R}^n$ is the position; $M(q) \in \mathbb{R}^{n \times n}$, $G(q) \in \mathbb{R}^n$, and $C(q,\dot{q}) \in \mathbb{R}^n$, is the inertia matrix, gravitational force, and Centripetal and Coriolis force, respectively; $\tau = [\tau_1, \cdots, \tau_n]^T \in \mathbb{R}^n$ is the control input. In this paper, $M(q)$, $C(q,\dot{q})$ and $G(q)$ are unknown.

Assume $x = [x_1, \cdots, x_n]^T \in \mathbb{R}^n$ is the position vector in task space, using the transformation between the joint space and task space: $\dot{x} = J(q)\dot{q}$, where $J(q) \in \mathbb{R}^n$ is the Jacobian matrix. The dynamics in task space is considered as

$$M_x(q)\ddot{x} + C_x(q,\dot{q})\dot{x} + G_x(q) = \tau_x \tag{2}$$

where $G_x(q) = J^{-T}(q)G(q)$, $M_x(q) = J^{-T}(q)M(q)J^{-1}(q)$, $\tau_x = J^{-T}(q)\tau$, and $C_x(q,\dot{q}) = J^{-T}(q)(C(q,\dot{q}) - M(q)J^{-1}(q)\dot{J}(q))J^{-1}(q)$. Several basic properties of above dynamics are listed as follows [2,26,27].

Property 1: $M_x(q)$ is bounded positive definite and symmetric.
Property 2: The matrix $\dot{M}_x(q) - 2C_x(q,\dot{q})$ is skew symmetric, such that $y^T(\dot{M}_x(q) - 2C_x(q,\dot{q}))y = 0, \forall y \in \mathbb{R}^n$.

The following result is recalled for stability analysis.

Lemma 1 [28]. *The following inequality holds for $\forall \delta > 0, \forall x_i \in \mathbb{R}$*

$$0 \leq |x_i| - x_i \tanh(\frac{x_i}{\delta}) \leq 0.2785\delta. \tag{3}$$

The control objective is to design an adaptive NN controller to ensure the constraint is not violated such that $|x_i| < k_{c_i}$, $t > 0$, where k_{c_i} is the bound of x_i, while the output y is driven to track the desired trajectory $x_d = [x_{d_1}, \cdots, x_{d_n}]^T \in \mathbb{R}^n$ to a bounded compact set.

3   Control Design and Stability Analysis

Under the condition that the system states x and $\dot{x}$ in system (2) are all available for feedback, the adaptive NN control is proposed in this section. Assume the error signals as

$$z = [z_1, \ldots, z_n]^T = x - x_d \tag{4}$$
$$\omega = [\omega_1, \ldots, \omega_n]^T = \dot{x} - \alpha \tag{5}$$

where $\alpha = [\alpha_1, \ldots, \alpha_n]^T$ is the virtual control. The iBLF is proposed as follows

$$V_{x_i}(z_i, x_{d_i}) = \int_0^{z_i} \frac{\sigma k_{c_i}^2}{k_{c_i}^2 - (\sigma + x_{d_i})^2} d\sigma \tag{6}$$

Let $\sigma = \theta z_i$, based on the analysis in [28], there is

$$\frac{z_i^2}{2} \leq V_{x_i} \leq z_i^2 \int_0^1 \frac{\theta k_{c_i}^2}{k_{c_i}^2 - (\theta z_i + x_{d_i})^2} d\theta. \tag{7}$$

The Lyapunov functional candidate is

$$V_1 = \sum_{i=1}^n V_{x_i} \tag{8}$$

The time derivative of (8) is

$$\dot{V}_1 = \sum_{i=1}^n \left(\frac{k_{c_i}^2 z_i}{k_{c_i}^2 - x_i^2}(\omega_i + \alpha_i - \dot{x}_{d_i}) + \frac{\partial V_{x_i}}{\partial x_{d_i}} \dot{x}_{d_i} \right) \tag{9}$$

where

$$\frac{\partial V_{x_i}}{\partial x_{d_i}} = z_i \left(\frac{k_{c_i}^2}{k_{c_i}^2 - x_i^2} - \rho_i(z_i, x_{d_i}) \right) \tag{10}$$

and

$$\rho_i(z_i, x_{d_i}) = \frac{k_{c_i}}{2z_i} \ln \frac{(k_{c_i} + z_i + x_{d_i})(k_{c_i} - x_{d_i})}{(k_{c_i} - z_i - x_{d_i})(k_{c_i} + x_{d_i})} \tag{11}$$

with

$$\lim_{z_i \to 0} \rho_i(z_i, x_{d_i}) = \frac{k_{c_i}^2}{k_{c_i}^2 - x_{d_i}^2} \tag{12}$$

The virtual control $\alpha = [\alpha_1, \ldots, \alpha_n]$ is designed as

$$\alpha_i = -\kappa_{z_i} z_i + \frac{(k_{c_i}^2 - x_i^2)\dot{x}_{d_i} \rho_i}{k_{c_i}^2}, \quad i = 1, \ldots, n \tag{13}$$

where $\kappa_{z_i} > 0$. Substituting (13) into (9), it yields

$$\dot{V}_1 = -\sum_{i=1}^n \frac{\kappa_i k_{c_i}^2 z_i^2}{k_{c_i}^2 - x_i^2} + \sum_{i=1}^n \frac{k_{c_i}^2 z_i \omega_i}{k_{c_i}^2 - x_i^2} \tag{14}$$

Then, the following Lyapunov candidate functional is chosen as

$$V_2 = V_1 + \frac{1}{2}\omega^T M_x \omega \tag{15}$$

The time derivative of V_2 is

$$\dot{V}_2 = -\sum_{i=1}^n \frac{\kappa_{z_i} k_{c_i}^2 z_i^2}{k_{c_i}^2 - x_i^2} + \sum_{i=1}^n \frac{k_{c_i}^2 z_i \omega_i}{k_{c_i}^2 - x_i^2} + \omega^T[\tau_x - C_x \dot{x} - G_x - \tau_x - M_x \dot{\alpha}] \tag{16}$$

The ideal control τ_x^* is designed as

$$\tau_x^* = -K_\omega \omega - \phi + C_x \dot{x} + G_x + M_x \dot{\alpha} \tag{17}$$

where $K_\omega = \text{diag}[\kappa_{\omega_1}, \ldots, \kappa_{\omega_n}] > 0$, and $\phi = [\phi_1, \ldots, \phi_n]^T$, with

$$\phi_i := \frac{k_{c_i}^2 z_i}{k_{c_i}^2 - x_i^2}. \tag{18}$$

However, due to the unknown robot dynamics, i.e., the terms M_x, C_x and G_x are all unknown, which results in the fact that τ_x^* is not available. Thus, the NN is used to estimate the uncertainty, and then the adaptive NN control τ is proposed as

$$\tau = J^T \tau_x$$
$$\tau_x = -K_\omega \omega - \phi + \hat{W}^T S(Z) - \hat{p} * \tanh(\frac{\omega}{\delta}) \tag{19}$$

where $\hat{W} = [\hat{W}_1, \ldots, \hat{W}_n]^T \in \mathbb{R}^{n \times l}$ are the NN estimation weights of ideal weight W^* with estimation errors $\tilde{W} = \hat{W} - W^*, \|\tilde{W}\| \leq s_w^*$, and input vector $Z = [x^T, \dot{x}^T, \alpha^T, \dot{\alpha}^T]$. $\hat{p} = [\hat{p}_1, \ldots, \hat{p}_n]^T \in \mathbb{R}^n$ are the estimation of unknown parameters $p^* = s^* s_w^* + \epsilon^*$ with $\delta > 0$. τ_{x_i} could represent as

$$\tau_{x_i} = -\kappa_{\omega_i} \omega_i - \phi_i + \hat{W}_i^T S_i(Z) - \hat{p}_i \tanh(\frac{\omega_i}{\delta_i}) \tag{20}$$

The term $W^{*T} S(Z)$ is used to estimate the uncertainty in τ_x^* as

$$C_x \dot{x} + G_x + M_x \dot{\alpha} = W^{*T} S(Z) + \epsilon \tag{21}$$

where $\| \epsilon \| \leq \| \epsilon^* \|$ is the estimation error. We design the adaptive law as

$$\dot{\hat{W}}_i = -\Gamma_i [S_i(Z) \omega_i + \sigma_i \hat{W}_i] \tag{22}$$
$$\dot{\hat{p}}_i = \omega_i \tanh(\frac{\omega_i}{\delta_i}) - \sigma_{p_i} \hat{p}_i \tag{23}$$

where $\hat{p}_i(0) > 0, \tilde{p}_i = \hat{p}_i - p_i^*$ is the estimation error; $\Gamma_i > 0$, $\delta_i > 0$; $\sigma_i > 0$ and $\sigma_{p_i} > 0$. The stability analysis of the system is given by the following theorem.

Theorem 1. *For robotic manipulators (2), under the proposed control (13) and (19) with the NN weights updated by (22) and adapting parameter updated by (23), provided that the initial conditions $x(0) \in \Omega_x$ and $\hat{W}_1(0)$, $\hat{p}_1(0)$ are bounded, all signals in the closed-loop system are semi-global uniformly ultimately bounded, the task space constraints are guaranteed and particularly the tracking error $z \in \mathbb{R}^n$ converge to a small neighborhood of origin as $\lim_{t \to \infty} \|z(t)\| \leq \sqrt{\frac{2C}{K}}$, with the constants $K \in \mathbb{R}^+$ and $C \in \mathbb{R}^+$ are defined in (31) and (32), respectively.*

Proof. Consider the following Lyapunov function as

$$V = V_2 + \frac{1}{2} \sum_{i=1}^{n} \tilde{W}_i^T \Gamma^{-1} \tilde{W}_i + \frac{1}{2} \sum_{i=1}^{n} \tilde{p}_i^2. \tag{24}$$

Taking the time derivative of V is

$$\dot{V} = -\sum_{i=1}^{n} \frac{\kappa_{z_i} k_{c_i}^2 z_i^2}{k_{c_i}^2 - x_i^2} + \omega^T (\tilde{W}^T S - \epsilon - \hat{p} * \tanh(\frac{\omega}{\delta})) - \omega^T K_\omega \omega$$

$$- \sum_{i=1}^{n} \tilde{W}_i^T [S_i \omega_i + \sigma_i \hat{W}_i] + \sum_{i=1}^{n} \tilde{p}_i [\omega_i \tanh(\frac{\omega_i}{\delta_i}) - \sigma_{p_i} \hat{p}_i]. \tag{25}$$

By using the Young Inequalities to obtain

$$-\tilde{W}_i^T \sigma_i \hat{W}_i \le \frac{\sigma_i}{2} (\| W_i^* \|^2 - \| \tilde{W}_i \|^2) \tag{26}$$

$$-\sigma_{p_i} \tilde{p}_i \hat{p} \le -\frac{\sigma_{p_i}}{2} \tilde{p}_i^2 + \frac{\sigma_{p_i}}{2} p_i^{*2} \tag{27}$$

Since $\| -\epsilon \| \le \| \epsilon^* \| \le \| p^* \|$ and utilizing Lemma 1, it yields

$$-\omega^T \epsilon - \omega^T [\hat{p} * \tanh(\frac{\omega}{\delta})] + \sum_{i=1}^{n} \omega_i \tilde{p}_i \tanh(\frac{\omega_i}{\delta_i})$$

$$\le p^* [\| \omega \| - \omega^T \tanh(\frac{\omega}{\delta})] \le \sum_{i=1}^{n} 0.2785 \delta_i p_i^* \tag{28}$$

Substituting (26)–(28) into (25), results in

$$\dot{V} \le -\sum_{i=1}^{n} \frac{\kappa_i k_{c_i}^2 z_i^2}{k_{c_i}^2 - x_i^2} - \omega^T K_\omega \omega + 0.2785 \sum_{i=1}^{n} \delta_i p_i^*$$

$$- \sum_{i=1}^{n} \frac{\sigma_i}{2} \| \tilde{W}_i \|^2 + \sum_{i=1}^{n} \frac{\sigma_i}{2} \| W_i^* \|^2 - \sum_{i=1}^{n} \frac{\sigma_{p_i}}{2} \tilde{p}_i^2 + \sum_{i=1}^{n} \frac{\sigma_{p_i}}{2} p_i^{*2}. \tag{29}$$

which implies

$$\dot{V} \le -KV + C \tag{30}$$

with the positive constants as

$$K = \min\left(2\lambda_{\min}(K_z), \min_{i=1,2,\cdots,n} (\sigma_{p_i}), \frac{2\lambda_{\min}(K_\omega)}{\lambda_{\max}(M_x)}, \min_{i=1,2,\cdots,n} \left(\frac{\sigma_i}{\lambda_{\max}(\Gamma_i^{-1})}\right)\right) \tag{31}$$

$$C = 0.2785 \sum_{i=1}^{n} \delta_i p_i^* + \sum_{i=1x}^{n} \frac{\sigma_{p_i}}{2} \| W_i^* \|^2 + \sum_{i=1}^{n} \frac{\sigma_{p_i}}{2} p_i^{*2} \tag{32}$$

Integrating the above inequality, it yields

$$V \leq (V(0) - \frac{C}{K})e^{-Kt} + \frac{C}{K} \leq V(0)e^{-Kt} + \frac{C}{K} \tag{33}$$

For any bounded initial conditions, when $t \to \infty$, V is bounded. Using $\frac{1}{2}\sum_{i=1}^{n} z_i^2 \leq V$, $\frac{1}{2}\sum_{i=1}^{n} \tilde{W}_i^T \Gamma^{-1} \tilde{W}_i \leq V$ and $\frac{1}{2}\sum_{i=1}^{n} \tilde{p}_i^2(t) \leq V$, the errors signals $z_i, \tilde{W}_i, \tilde{p}_i, i = 1, \ldots, n, \forall t \geq 0$, are uniformly bounded as

$$|z_i| \leq \sqrt{2(V(0) + \frac{C}{K})}, \quad |\tilde{p}_i| \leq \sqrt{2(V(0) + \frac{C}{K})} \tag{34}$$

which also means ultimately bounded as $\lim_{t\to\infty} |z_i(t)| \leq \sqrt{\frac{2C}{K}}$, $\lim_{t\to\infty} \| \tilde{W}_i \| \leq \sqrt{\frac{2C}{K}}$ and $\lim_{t\to\infty} |\tilde{p}_i(t)| \leq \sqrt{\frac{2C}{K}}$. Since V is bounded, there is $V \to \infty$, as $|x_i| \to k_{c_i}$, $i = 1, \ldots, n$, which implies the constrained region in task space is guaranteed. This completes the proof.

4 Simulation

In this section, we consider a robotic manipulator with two rotary degrees and one prismatic degree of freedom. The matrices $M_x(q)$, $C_x(q,\dot{q})$, $F_x(q,\dot{q})$, $G_x(q)$ and J, and the robotic parameters are defined in [9]. In simulation studies, the desired trajectory is defined as

$$x_d = [0.2, -\cos(\pi t), \sin(\pi t)]^T \tag{35}$$

The end-effector x_1, x_2 and x_3 are subject to the task space constraints simultaneously

$$-k_{c1} < x_1 < k_{c1}, \quad -k_{c2} < x_2 < k_{c2}, \quad -k_{c3} < x_3 < k_{c3}, \forall t \leq 0 \tag{36}$$

where $k_{c1} = 0.25$, $k_{c2} = 1.3$ and $k_{c3} = 1.3$. In order to be more practical, we consider the initial positions of the end-effector as $x = [0.21, 0.64, 0.84]^T$ and $x = [0, 0, 0]^T$.

In this simulation, the control parameters are set as $\kappa_{z1} = 5$, $\kappa_{z2} = 5$, $\kappa_{z3} = 5$ and $K_W = \text{diag}[100, 10, 10]$. A number of $2^9(512)$ nodes with centers $\mu_i = 0.0$ are used for each $S_i(Z)$. The parameters $\Gamma_1, \Gamma_2, \Gamma_3, \sigma_1, \sigma_2$ and σ_3 are chosen the same value as $\Gamma_1 = \Gamma_2 = \Gamma_3 = 100$, $\sigma_1 = 1$, $\sigma_2 = 1$ and $\sigma_3 = 1$. The variances of centers are both set as $\eta^2 = 25$. The initial weight $\hat{W}_{1,i} = \hat{W}_{2,i} = \hat{W}_{3,i} = 0$ ($i = 1, 2, \cdots, 512$).

Figure 1(a) illustrates the tracking performance of the closed-loop system for the end-effector x_1, x_2 and x_3. From the figure, we can clearly learn that the proposed control (19) can track the desired trajectory successfully and the end-effector are both bounded in $\pm k_{c1}$, $\pm k_{c2}$ and $\pm k_{c3}$, respectively. From Fig. 1(b), it can be observed that the tracking error will eventually converge to a small value near zero. Figure 1(c) represents the corresponding control signal. The norms of

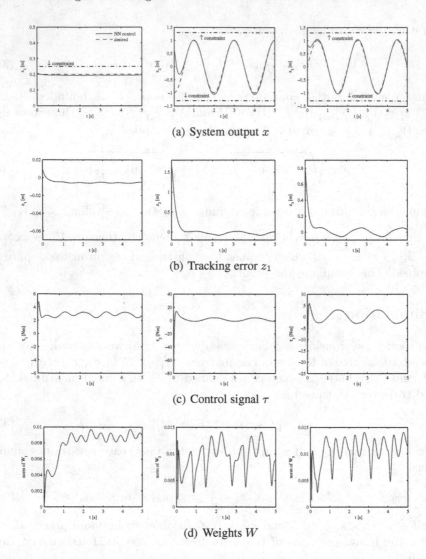

(a) System output x

(b) Tracking error z_1

(c) Control signal τ

(d) Weights W

Fig. 1. Simulation results

$\| \hat{W}_1 \|$, $\| \hat{W}_2 \|$ and $\| \hat{W}_3 \|$ are shown on Fig. 1(d). By the learning abilities of NNs, the proposed control can achieve control under the robot with unknown system dynamics. From Fig. 1(d), the boundedness of NN estimation weights are guaranteed. All in all, the proposed control can successful ensure the end-effector the desired trajectory while always remain in constrained task space.

5   Conclusions

Adaptive NN control for motion control of robotic manipulators with uncertainty in constrained task space has been proposed in this paper, where the iBLF is used to handle the constraint, and neural networks are employed to estimate the uncertainty. Through Lyapunov synthesis, task space vector of end-effector have been proved coverage to an adjustable small neighborhood around a desired trajectory, and all signals in the closed system are bounded. The performance and effectiveness of the proposed control have been illustrated through simulation.

References

1. Avanzini, G.B., Ceriani, N.M., Zanchettin, A.M., Rocco, P., Bascetta, L.: Safety control of industrial robots based on a distributed distance sensor. IEEE Trans. Control. Syst. Technol. **22**(6), 2127–2140 (2014)
2. Cheah, C., Liu, C., Slotine, J.J.E.: Adaptive Jacobian tracking control of robots with uncertainties in kinematic, dynamic and actuator models. IEEE Trans. Autom. Control **51**(6), 1024–1029 (2006)
3. Dong, Y., Ren, B.: UDE-based variable impedance control of uncertain robot systems. IEEE Trans. Syst., Man, Cybern.: Syst. (2017)
4. Fink, J.: Anthropomorphism and human likeness in the design of robots and human-robot interaction. In: Ge, S.S., Khatib, O., Cabibihan, J.-J., Simmons, R., Williams, M.-A. (eds.) ICSR 2012. LNCS (LNAI), vol. 7621, pp. 199–208. Springer, Heidelberg (2012). https://doi.org/10.1007/978-3-642-34103-8_20
5. Ge, S.S., Lee, T.H., Harris, C.J.: Adaptive Neural Network Control of Robotic Manipulators. World Scientific, River Edge (1998)
6. Goodrich, M.A., Schultz, A.C., et al.: Human-robot interaction: a survey. Found. Trends Hum.-Comput. Interact. **1**(3), 203–275 (2008)
7. Hancock, P.A., Billings, D.R., Schaefer, K.E., Chen, J.Y., De Visser, E.J., Parasuraman, R.: A meta-analysis of factors affecting trust in human-robot interaction. Hum. Factors **53**(5), 517–527 (2011)
8. He, W., Chen, Y., Yin, Z.: Adaptive neural network control of an uncertain robot with full-state constraints. IEEE Trans. Cybern. **46**(3), 620–629 (2016)
9. He, W., Dong, Y.: Adaptive fuzzy neural network control for a constrained robot using impedance learning. IEEE Trans. Neural Netw. Learn. Syst. **29**, 1174–1186 (2017)
10. He, W., Ge, S.S., How, B.V.E., Choo, Y.S., Hong, K.S.: Robust adaptive boundary control of a flexible marine riser with vessel dynamics. Automatica **47**(4), 722–732 (2011)
11. He, W., Zhang, S., Ge, S.S.: Adaptive control of a flexible crane system with the boundary output constraint. IEEE Trans. Ind. Electron. **61**(8), 4126–4133 (2014)
12. Hogan, N.: Impedance control - an approach to manipulation. I - Theory. II - Implementation. III - Applications. J. Dyn. Syst., Meas., Control **107**, 1–24 (1985)
13. Kim, B.S., Yoo, S.J.: Adaptive control of nonlinear pure-feedback systems with output constraints: integral barrier Lyapunov functional approach. Int. J. Control, Autom. Syst. **13**(1), 249–256 (2015)
14. Lacevic, B., Rocco, P., Zanchettin, A.M.: Safety assessment and control of robotic manipulators using danger field. IEEE Trans. Robot. **29**(5), 1257–1270 (2013)

15. Lewis, F., Jagannathan, S., Yesildirak, A.: Neural Network Control of Robot Manipulators and Non-Linear Systems. CRC Press, Boca Raton (1998)
16. Li, D.J., Li, J., Li, S.: Adaptive control of nonlinear systems with full state constraints using integral barrier Lyapunov functionals. Neurocomputing **186**, 90–96 (2016)
17. Li, Y., Ge, S.S.: Human-robot collaboration based on motion intention estimation. IEEE/ASME Trans. Mechatron. **19**(3), 1007–1014 (2014)
18. Li, Z., Huang, Z., He, W., Su, C.Y.: Adaptive impedance control for an upper limb robotic exoskeleton using biological signals. IEEE Trans. Ind. Electron. **64**(2), 1664–1674 (2017)
19. Li, Z., Su, C., Wang, L., Chen, Z., Chai, T.: Nonlinear disturbance observer based control design for a robotic exoskeleton incorporating fuzzy approximation. IEEE Trans. Ind. Electron. **62**(9), 5763–5775 (2015)
20. Li, Z., Yang, C., Su, C.Y., Deng, S., Sun, F., Zhang, W.: Decentralized fuzzy control of multiple cooperating robotic manipulators with impedance interaction. IEEE Trans. Fuzzy Syst. **23**(4), 1044–1056 (2014)
21. Liu, Y.J., Tong, S.C.: Barrier Lyapunov functions for Nussbaum gain adaptive control of full state constrained nonlinear systems. Automatica **76**(2), 143–152 (2017)
22. Liu, Y.J., Tong, S.: Barrier Lyapunov functions-based adaptive control for a class of nonlinear pure-feedback systems with full state constraints. Automatica **64**(C), 70–75 (2016)
23. Mayne, D.Q., Rawlings, J.B., Rao, C.V., Scokaert, P.O.: Constrained model predictive control: stability and optimality. Automatica **36**(6), 789–814 (2000)
24. Mehdi, H., Boubaker, O.: Stiffness and impedance control using Lyapunov theory for robot-aided rehabilitation. Int. J. Soc. Robot. **4**(1), 107–119 (2012)
25. Meng, W., Yang, Q., Sun, Y.: Adaptive neural control of nonlinear MIMO systems with time-varying output constraints. IEEE Trans. Neural Netw. Learn. Syst. **26**(5), 1074–1085 (2015)
26. Slotine, J.J.E., Li, W.: On the adaptive control of robot manipulators. Int. J. Robot. Res. **6**, 49–59 (1987)
27. Slotine, J.J.E., Li, W.: Applied Nonlinear Control. Prentice-Hall, Englewood Cliffs (1991)
28. Tang, Z.L., Ge, S.S., Tee, K.P., He, W.: Adaptive neural control for an uncertain robotic manipulator with joint space constraints. Int. J. Control **89**(7), 1428–1446 (2015)
29. Tee, K.P., Ge, S.S.: Control of state-constrained nonlinear systems using integral barrier Lyapunov functionals. In: 2012 IEEE 51st Annual Conference on Decision and Control (CDC), pp. 3239–3244. IEEE (2012)
30. Tee, K.P., Ge, S.S., Tay, E.H.: Barrier Lyapunov functions for the control of output-constrained nonlinear systems. Automatica **45**(4), 918–927 (2009)
31. Tee, K.P., Ren, B., Ge, S.S.: Control of nonlinear systems with time-varying output constraints. Automatica **47**(11), 2511–2516 (2011)
32. Yi, S.: Stable walking of qauadruped robot by impedance control for body motion. Int. J. Control Autom. **6**(2), 99–110 (2013)
33. Zhang, H., Luo, Y., Liu, D.: Neural-network-based near-optimal control for a class of discrete-time affine nonlinear systems with control constraints. IEEE Trans. Neural Netw. **20**(9), 1490–1503 (2009)

Multi-pose Face Registration Method for Social Robot

Ho-Sub Yoon[1,2(✉)], Jaeyoon Jang[1,2], and Jaehong Kim[1]

[1] ETRI, HMI Group, Daejeon, South Korea
{yoonhs, jangjy, jhkim504}@etri.rr.kr
[2] UST, School of ICT, Daejeon, South Korea

Abstract. This paper presents a multi-pose face registration method for social robot application. A social robot means that it is an autonomous robot to interact and communicate with humans. The first thing in communicating with people is to recognize who they are. To do this, the social robot should basically have a face recognition function. Although many face recognition algorithms have been developed in the past, the development of algorithms that are robust to real-time pose changes is underway. In this paper, we try to a multi-pose face registration method for pose invariant face recognition. To measure the robustness of the proposed method, comparisons were made between the registering of front face only versus the registering multiple pose faces based on their respective recognition similarity values. As a result, it was confirmed that the confidence value of similarity always keeps a high value when the proposed method is used compared to when not using it, despite the fact that the face was entered in various poses.

Keywords: Face-registration · Multi-pose · Social robot

1 Introduction

A social robot means that it is an autonomous robot to interact and communicate with humans or other autonomous physical agents to follow social behaviors and rules [1]. Social robot research focuses on the social relationship interaction between robots and humans. It is a multidisciplinary field with artificial intelligence, robotics, human-computer interaction, and social sciences. A lot of people want a social robot to play an essential role to solve practical problems and to be a part of human life by assisting with daily tasks. The first thing in communicating with people is to recognize who they are. To do this, the social robot should basically have a face recognition function. Although many face recognition algorithms have been developed in the past, the development of algorithms that are robust to real-time pose changes is underway. When we analyze the previous face recognition method which is strong in pose, we can divide it into two ways. The first way is a method of registering a plurality of pose faces by randomly selecting of specific side face images including front face. In this case, when the face to be recognized is input, it is recognized as a face having the highest value of similarity compared with all of the plural registered face images. The disadvantage of this method is that calculation time is long because it is necessary to

© Springer Nature Switzerland AG 2018
S. S. Ge et al. (Eds.): ICSR 2018, LNAI 11357, pp. 609–619, 2018.
https://doi.org/10.1007/978-3-030-05204-1_60

calculate the similarity score with a large number of registered face images, and it is difficult to register faces of all desired directions. That is, in order to input a desired pose, the system has to request a specific pose to user and manually capture the pose. Also, since all possible poses cannot be requested from the user, performance degradation occurs when an unregistered pose face enters the input. Because of the drawbacks of this first way, recent most studies attempt a second way: to make frontal face. For the face frontalization, first step is facial landmarks detection on a non-frontal face. Second step is a frontalization using several difference approaches. Hassner [2] proposed the viewing real-world faces in 3D using 3D face models, fitting a 3D morphable model [3], or creative [4]. If we create 3D morphable face model using difference views of same face, we can get the matching score between query image and 3D morphable face [5, 6]. Using this approach, recognition algorithm is get breakthrough results. Another approach is using statistical models. This approach infer a frontal view using statistical face frontalization [7]. Also, these methods have been explored for inferring frontal faces using deep learning [8]. Although a variety of methods have been studied in this way, Banerjee's [9] study should be considered as to frontalize or not to frontalize. From this study, they asserted:

1. "Frontalization is a computationally expensive pre-processing step, it need a lot of cost. When they decide to make frontalization face, the large number of failure frontalization modes are introduced, because of loss of data, i.e., lower yield, occlusions, and extreme poses. It means that the performance benefit of frontalization can be considered increasing computational resources."
2. "The usefulness of frontalization is depending on how the facial recognition system is used. If, a lot of faces with extreme poses, occlusions, and illumination was included training data sets using deep learning approach, it is possible that frontalization step may cause degrade recognition performance. Therefore, face frontalization is not a good choice for superior results always."

In order to solve this problem, we try to a new multi-pose registration method and GUI that enables the system to automatically register faces of various poses automatically. Our approach don't need to make a frontalization 3D face model, but it has similar effects using a multi-pose registration face images. Also, our approach is not depending on the face recognition method. It is possible to use pre-processing step even though any kinds of deep learning based recognition system.

The flowchart in Fig. 1 shows the processing order of the proposed method. The difference between the proposed method and the first way is that if the previous multiple pose registration process is performed manually, the proposed method proceeds automatically and the system GUI guides the user to register all necessary pose. The composition of this paper is as follows. Section 2 describes previous studies on multi-pose face registration. Section 3 describes how to measure pose from the image input described, and Sect. 4 describes how to register and recognize multiple pose. In Sect. 5, it describes experiment and results and finally, Sect. 6 describes conclusion and future works.

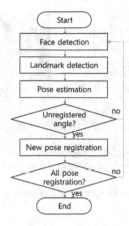

Fig. 1. The propose method for multi-pose registration

2 Related Work

A lot of researchers try to handle pose variations. In this chapter, we review several techniques to handle pose variation as well as multi-pose registration. In order to obtain a pose invariance under geometric transformations, consisting registration faces for pre-processing step is proposed [10, 11], In this case, face registration aims to find the transformation or the deformation which reduces the inconsistency between two or more faces. These transformations change the facial texture, geometry, motion while reducing variations in rotation, translation, and scale changes. Therefore, these registration method should be induced artifacts and they have a negative impact on the consistency of facial characteristics [12].

Recently, the focus about test DB for pose-invariance shifts from primarily in dealing with controlled datasets, such as Multi-PIE [13] to dealing with un-controlled datasets, such as LFW data set [14] and IJB-A [15] which was considered to be challenging competition under the real world environment. Figure 2 shows the sample images of Multi-PIE, LFW and IJB-A. Through this pictures, we can see that the test images gradually reflect more realistic world by containing various expressions, poses and illuminance changes.

As mentioned earlier in the introduction chapter, frontalization method in order to solve variations in pose have some problem such as complex pre-processing step, significant loss of data and so on.

Recently, the remarkable deep learning [16] methods such as convolutional neural networks (CNNs) has allowed face recognition performance on hard datasets to improve significantly. For example, because CNNs can get the ability to automatically learn complex representations of face data, Google FaceNet based on a CNN Method [17] reached over 99% verification accuracy on the LFW dataset.

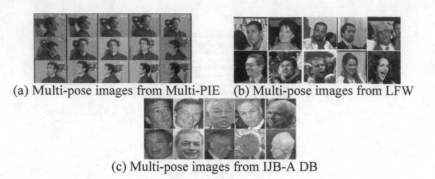

(a) Multi-pose images from Multi-PIE   (b) Multi-pose images from LFW

(c) Multi-pose images from IJB-A DB

Fig. 2. The sample of multi-pose image DB

To obtain pose-invariance CNN, one approach is to train a single CNN using a large enough pose dataset covering a diverse set of poses. FaceNet is an example of that, it is possible to learn faces trained on 260 million images with an end-to-end learning system. Also, DeepID [18] shows remarkable performance using a large ensemble of networks which is trained on different patches of the face based on Joint Bayesian metric learning.

3 Pose Estimation

To provide a proposed GUI that automatically registers various face poses, three types pose angles (yaw, pitch, rotate) from the input face should be calculated. To calculate the pose angles, we first detect the face, extract the 68 point landmark from the detected face, and map it to the 3D face as shown in the flowchart from Fig. 1. Figure 3 shows the face detection results using popular a popular face detector in Dlib [19]. This face detector was trained by the HOG (Histogram of Oriented Gradients) feature and a linear classifier.

(a) Detected face   (b) Detected landmark

Fig. 3. The results of face and land mark detector

Our facial landmark detection method is based on an ensemble of regression trees (ERT) [20]. When training each node of the ERT, a two-pixel difference is used by considering the exponential distance from an estimated landmark. Each regression cascade steps of the ERT is composed of gradient boosting trees.

Our landmark detection algorithm can find 68 point facial position. To estimate pose angle using these landmark point, we try to mapping 3D face model, because accuracy of pose angle is better when we use 3D depth information of landmark points also. To make the 3D face model including depth information, 68-point annotations in a 300-W database [21, 22] are reconstructed into 3D landmark annotations based on the motion structure. The 3D landmark annotations allow for the generation of a point distribution model (PDM):

$$X_{\{3n\times1\}} = M_{\{3n\times1\}} + \sum_{i=1}^{d} s_i B(:,i)_{\{3n\times d\}} = X(e) \tag{1}$$

Where M is the mean shape and B is the basis of the shape variation. The parameter vector s_i is an i_{th} shape vector that determines the specific shape. The results vector X contains 3D positions of n facial landmarks. Using under equation, we can obtain the projection on the PDM P from Eq. (2):

$$e_{\{d\times1\}} = P(L_{\{3n\times1\}}) = B^T_{\{d\times3n\}}(L - M)_{\{3n\times1\}} \tag{2}$$

Where P represents a projection on PDM in Eq. (2) and L is any facial landmark transformed by $T(Z)$ in (3).

$$\begin{aligned} where\, L &= T(Z), \\ T(Z) &= s_{\{1\times1\}}(I_{\{n\times n\}} \otimes R_{\{3\times3\}})Z_{\{3n\times1\}} + 1_{\{n\times1\}} \otimes t_{\{3\times1\}} \end{aligned} \tag{3}$$

Where s is scale, R is 3D rotation, and t are the 3D translation parameters, respectively. We have to minimize the value of the Euclidean distance between M and L for a similarity transformation T:

$$minimize\|L - M\|^2 \tag{4}$$

A 3D landmark shape is estimated through Eq. (1)–(4) and then transformed using AAM fitting through simulation [23]. The estimated 3D landmarks depths are adapted to a weak perspective transformed by the center of gravity. Figure 4 shows the result of calculated yaw, pitch and rotate angle from 3D model landmark points.

From these step, we should have to more complex calculation, but we get the 30% higher pose estimation values.

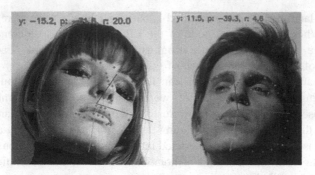

Fig. 4. The example of calculated yaw, pitch and rotate angles

4   Multi-pose Registration

As we mentioned before, multi-pose registration methods have good effect for face recognition. Recently, a representative example of multi-pose registration for face recognition is the iPhone X. In Fig. 5, iPhone X users register various poses of face while watching the smart phone screen [24]. The iPhone X uses 3D-imaging and infrared technology to create a depth map of your face during face registering.

Fig. 5. The GUI of iPhone X for face registration

To register face id at iPhone X, users should have to move left to right and up and down. The face registration GUI of iPhone X do not give users any information about registered faces excepting progressing bar. We can guess that they make 3D face model using these various 3D input faces. From this situation, some people move theirs head to fast and radically and some people move their head to slow and passively. These difference of attitude when they register to faces will make 3D face model of different quality. To solve this problem, we propose multi-pose registration method using the dot-matrix breaking GUI based on direction of gaze in Fig. 6.

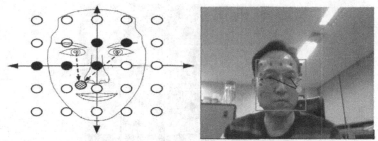

(a) The dot-matrix breaking GUI   (b) The example image of propose GUI

Fig. 6. The GUI of proposed method for face registration (Color figure online)

In this Fig. 6, a red dot represents the angle of yaw, pitch variation. It means that the center red dot represent (yaw = 0, pitch = 0) degree when we define the x, y coordination (yaw angle, pitch angle). Table 1 shows the 5 × 5 matrix angle value with the interval of angle variation $10°$ that matched each red dots.

Table 1. Yaw and pitch angles corresponding 5 × 5 red dots

(20, 20)	(10, 20)	(0, 20)	(−10, 20)	(−20, 20)
(20,10)	(10, 10)	(0, 10)	(−10, 10)	(−20, 10)
(20, 0)	(10, 0)	(0, 0)	(−10, 0)	(−20, 0)
(20, −10)	(10, −10)	(0, −10)	(−10, 10)	(−20, −10)
(20, −20)	(10, −20)	(0, −20)	(−10, 20)	(−20, −20)

At that time, current gaze angle is defined at green dot in Fig. 6, which will move to break the red dots. When the moving green dot overlapped the red dot points, red dots are deleted and a new face is registered that represent each yaw, pitch angle variation. Figure 7 shows the results of registered faces using by our proposed dot-matrix breaking GUI.

From this approach, if we want to register more faces or more angles, we can expand the 5 × 5 matrix to 3 × 3, 5 × 5, 7 × 7 and so on. Also, we can change the interval of angle variation from $5°$ to $22.5°$. For example, it is possible that we defines the 7 × 7 red dot matrix and the interval between dots interval defines $8°$. It means we can get 49 registered faces which represent from $24°$ to $−24°$ yaw and pitch variation. In general, the more registered face, the better recognition rate can be. But it takes a more time to register, which can be inconvenient for the user, and it can require more memory and calculations when recognizing. To consider the user's convenience and various factors, we have done a lot of experiments. From the final results, we use the 5 × 5 matric with 10° interval now.

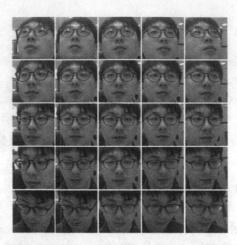

Fig. 7. The results of registered faces by proposed method

5 Experiment and Results

In order to emphasis the advantage of the proposed method, it is necessary to test whether the performance improves by actually applying the face recognition algorithm. The remarkable deep learning [16] methods such as convolutional neural networks (CNNs) has allowed face recognition performance on hard datasets to improve significantly. Because CNNs possess the ability to automatically learn complex representations of face data, they systematically outperform older methods based on hand-crafted features. For this study, we used the MFM [25] architecture which was used as an activation function as max-feature-map selection rather than ReLU [16]. This architecture consists of five convolution layers, one fully-connected layer, and one softmax layer based on CASIA-WebFace [26] for CNN training. The advantage of this architecture have not only lighter model than other CNN approaches [17, 27] but also good performance 99.3% on LFW DB.

Figure 8 show the similarity value table according to various pose input. In Fig. 8, we can find maximum similarity value at the most similar gaze direction between registered pose and input pose. Also, the minimum similarity values are fined around the long distance gaze angle such as (20, 20), (−20, 20), (20, −20) and (−20, −20). When we compare the similarity values in the Fig. 8(b) table, we can see that the difference between the minimum (52.58) and maximum (91.81) value is very large. That means, even though it is CNNs based recognition system which use a lot of training data sets including pose variation, it can be seen that the difference of the degree of similarity is very large depending on the pose variation. As same as in Fig. 8(c), (d), when the gaze direction of input face is (0, −20), the similarity value of registered pose direction (0, −20) has maximum value as 87.18. In Fig. 8(e), (f), when the gaze direction of input face is (−20, 0), the similarity value of registered pose direction (−20, 0) has maximum value as 89.62.

68.9	67.11	74.51	79.42	66.37	62.42	53.02	55.86	62.8	59.85	60.96	60.26	61.39	71.56	63.52
85.16	83.95	86.52	86.14	82.46	64.7	60.18	60.99	63	62.11	82.95	72.58	74.22	82.8	87.81
85.87	88.96	91.81	88.65	79.81	61.87	73.35	61.72	69.68	60.18	81.37	77.82	84.23	83.77	89.62
70.7	72.77	87.49	74.64	74.03	62.05	83.29	71.29	83.85	77.89	70.59	57.76	77.31	62.71	63.49
52.58	55.82	70.78	59.2	65.15	66.49	68.78	87.18	66.81	78.74	48.08	52.9	63.1	55.63	59.34
(b) Similarity values					(d) Similarity values					(f) Similarity values				

Fig. 8. The results of similarity value according to registered angle faces

If we register 25 faces with different poses for one person as shown in the example above, the registration storage becomes larger and the processing time may be delayed. However, in the proposed method, since only 256 feature values are stored at the time of registering per one face, even if registering 25 faces, there is no need for a lot of storage space. Also, when calculating the similarity value, it does not calculate 25 times, but calculates only one corresponding face with the same pose or four faces around it.

The proposed multi-pose registration method has the same effect on all other recognizers, not only on the MFM [25] face recognizer used in the experiment. To prove this, when we performed the same experiment using Google FaceNet [17] method as face recognizer, we got the very similar experimental results.

Generally, to prove the superiority of the proposed algorithm, it is necessary to compare with the results of similar studies about multi-pose registration. However, in the absence of similar studies which can compare our approach, only these experimental results can be shown.

6   Conclusion

A social robot is a robot in which a person and a robot can form a social relationship with each other. The beginning of a social relationship is to recognize each other, to do this social robots basically need face recognition. In the robot environment, recognizing faces entered in various poses is a difficult problem that has not been solved yet. In this paper, we propose a multi-pose face registration method using dot-matrix breaking GUI to solve this problem.

The proposed method has high recognition performance for pose change due to recognition with the existing face recognizer MFM and FaceNet. In addition, the recognition speed is the same as that of the case where only one is registered, or the difference is slightly increased. Future research will include more accurate ways to calculate the pose of the profile face and will test the proposed method for the previous face recognition method rather than the deep running approach.

Acknowledgment. This work was supported by the IT R&D program of MOTIE/KEIT [10077553], Development of Social Robot Intelligence for Social Human-Robot Interaction of Service Robots.

References

1. https://en.wikipedia.org/wiki/Social_robot
2. Hassner, T.: Viewing real-world faces in 3D. In: Proceedings of IEEE CVPR (2013)
3. Blanz, V., Vetter, T.: Face recognition based on fitting a 3D morphable model. IEEE TPAMI **25**(9), 1063–1074 (2003)
4. Hassner, T., Harel, S., Paz, E., Enbar, R.: Effective face frontalization in unconstrained images. In Proceedings of IEEE CVPR (2015)
5. Zhang, X., Gao, Y.: Face recognition across pose: a review. Pattern Recognit. **42**(11), 2876–2896 (2009)
6. Taigman, Y., Yang, M., Ranzato, M., Wolf, L.: Deepface: closing the gap to human-level performance in face verification. In: Proceedings of IEEE CVPR (2014)
7. Sagonas, C., Panagakis, Y., Zafeiriou, S., Pantic, M.: Robust statistical face frontalization. In: Proceedings of IEEE ICCV, pp. 3871–3879 (2015)
8. Yim, J., Jung, H., Yoo, B., Choi, C., Park, D., Kim, J.: Rotating your face using multi-task deep neural network. In: Proceedings of IEEE CVPR (2015)
9. Banerjee, S., Brogan, J., Križaj, J., Bharati, A., RichardWebster, B.: To frontalize or not to frontalize: a study of face pre-processing techniques and their impact on recognition. GroundAI, arXiv:1610.04823 (2016)
10. Liao, C., Chuang, H., Duan, C., Lai, S.: Learning spatial weighting via quadratic programming for facial expression analysis. In: Computer Vision and Pattern Recognition Workshops, CVPRW, pp. 86–93. IEEE (2010)
11. Sandbach, G., Zafeiriou, S., Pantic, M.: Markov random field structures for facial action unit intensity estimation. In: International Conference on Computer Vision Workshops, ICCVW, pp. 738–745 (2013)
12. Chew, S., et al.: In the pursuit of effective affective computing: the relationship between features and registration. IEEE Trans. Syst. Man Cybern. B **42**(4), 1006–1016 (2012)
13. Gross, R., Matthews, I., Cohn, J., Kanade, T., Baker, S.: Multi-PIE. Image Vis. Comput. (2010)
14. Huang, G.B., Ramesh, M., Berg, T., Learned-Miller, E.: Labeled faces in the wild: a database for studying face recognition in unconstrained environments. Technical report 07-49, University of Massachusetts, Amherst, October 2007
15. Klare, B.F., et al.: Pushing the frontiers of unconstrained face detection and recognition: IARPA Janus Benchmark-A. In: CVPR (2015)
16. LeCun, Y., Bengio, Y., Hinton, G.: Deep learning. Nature **521**(7553), 436–444 (2015)
17. Schroff, F., Kalenichenko, D., Philbin, J.: FaceNet: a unified embedding for face recognition and clustering. In: Proceedings of IEEE CVPR (2015)
18. Sun, Y., Wang, X., Tang, X.: Deeply learned face representations are sparse, selective, and robust. In CVPR (2015)
19. King, D.E.: Dlib-ml: a machine learning toolkit. J. Mach. Learn. Res. **10**, 1755–1758 (2009)
20. Kazemi, V., Sullivan, J.: One millisecond face alignment with an ensemble of regression trees. In: Proceedings of the IEEE Conference on Computer Vision and Pattern Recognition (2014)
21. Sagonas, C., et al.: 300 faces in-the-wild challenge: the first facial landmark localization challenge. In: Proceedings of the IEEE International Conference on Computer Vision Workshops (2013)
22. Sagonas, C., et al.: A semi-automatic methodology for facial landmark annotation. In: Proceedings of the IEEE Conference on Computer Vision and Pattern Recognition Workshops (2013)

23. Saragih, J., Göcke, R.: Learning AAM fitting through simulation. Pattern Recognit. **42**(11), 2628–2636 (2009)
24. https://mashable.com/2017/10/31/apple-iphone-x-one-face-for-face-id/#tgQTyO.KfOqs
25. Wu, X., et al.: A light CNN for deep face representation with noisy labels. arXiv preprint arXiv:1511.02683 (2015)
26. Yi, D., Lei, Z., Liao, S., Li, S.Z.: Learning face representation from scratch. arXiv:1411. 7923
27. Parkhi, O.M., Vedaldi, A., Zisserman, A.: Deep face recognition. In: Proceedings of BMVC (2015)

Author Index

Printed in the United States
By Bookmasters